Studies in Marxism and Social Theory

Making Sense of Marx

Studies in Marxism and Social Theory

Edited by G. A. COHEN, JON ELSTER AND JOHN ROEMER

The series is jointly published by the Cambridge University Press and the Editions de la Maison des Sciences de l'Homme, as part of the joint publishing agreement established in 1977 between the Fondation de la Maison des Sciences de l'Homme and the Syndics of the Cambridge University Press.

The books in the series are intended to exemplify a new paradigm in the study of Marxist social theory. They will not be dogmatic or purely exegetical in approach. Rather, they will examine and develop the theory pioneered by Marx, in the light of the intervening history, and with the tools of non-Marxist social science and philosophy. It is hoped that Marxist thought will thereby be freed from the increasingly discredited methods and presuppositions which are still widely regarded as essential to it, and that what is true and important in Marxism will be more firmly established.

Also in the series

ADAM PRZEWORSKI   *Capitalism and Social Democracy*

Making Sense of Marx

Jon Elster

Professor of Political Science,
University of Chicago
and Research Director,
Institute for Social Research, Oslo

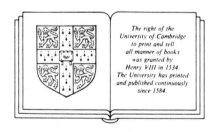

The right of the
University of Cambridge
to print and sell
all manner of books
was granted by
Henry VIII in 1534.
The University has printed
and published continuously
since 1584.

Cambridge University Press
Cambridge
London   New York   New Rochelle
Melbourne   Sydney

Editions de la Maison des Sciences de l'Homme
Paris

Published by the Press Syndicate of the University of Cambridge
The Pitt Building, Trumpington Street, Cambridge CB2 1RP
32 East 57th Street, New York, NY 10022, USA
10 Stamford Road, Oakleigh, Melbourne 3166, Australia
and Editions de la Maison des Sciences de l'Homme
54 Boulevard Raspail, 75270 Paris Cedex 06

First published 1985
Reprinted 1986

Printed in Great Britain at The Bath Press, Avon

Library of Congress catalogue card number: 84–17640

British Library Cataloguing in Publication Data

Elster, Jon
Making sense of Marx.—(Studies in Marxism
and social theory)
1. Marx, Karl, 1818–1883
I. Title   II. Series
335.4'092'4   HX39.5

ISBN 0 521 22896 4 hard covers
ISBN 0 521 29705 2 paperback

ISBN 2 7351 01142 hard covers (France only)
ISBN 2 7351 01150 paperback (France only)

PP

To Kristian, Martin and Jakob

In our day, everything seems pregnant with its contrary. Machinery gifted with the wonderful power of shortening and fructifying human labour, we behold starving and overworking it. The new-fangled sources of wealth, by some weird spell, are turned into sources of want. The victories of art seem bought by the loss of character. At the same pace that mankind masters nature, man seems to become enslaved to other men or to his own infamy. Even the pure light of science seems unable to shine but on the dark background of ignorance. All our invention and progress seem to result in endowing material forces with intellectual life, and in stultifying human life into a material force. This antagonism between modern industry and science on the one hand, modern misery and dissolution on the other hand; this antagonism between the productive powers and the social relations of our epoch is a fact, palpable, overwhelming, and not to be controverted.

(Karl Marx, Speech at the anniversary of *The People's Paper*, 1856)

Table of contents

Detailed table of contents

Preface and acknowledgments

This book has a long history. Some of it may be worthwhile recounting here. I began serious work on Marx in 1968, when I went to Paris to study with Jean Hyppolite, who had helped me earlier with my Master's thesis (on Hegel). He died a week before I was to meet him. At the time I was *pensionnaire étranger* at the Ecole Normale Supérieure; but I did not feel at home among the Althusserian Marxists who set the tone there. Instead, with Gaston Fessard as an intermediary, I turned to Raymond Aron who agreed to be my thesis supervisor. The three years I frequented his seminar were immensely stimulating. When I arrived, I did not know there existed such a discipline as historical sociology. Thanks to Aron and some of the other members of the seminar, notably Kostas Papaioannou, I learned to see Marx in a historical context and in the context of historical problems. At the same time I was discovering Marxist economic theory, in the wake of the "capital controversy". I was excited at these rigorous formulations of Marx's theory, and then depressed when it turned out that their main use was to prove rigorously that it was wrong.

I completed my thesis in 1971. For a while I looked for a publisher, but ceased looking when it occurred to me that there would probably not be any public for the kind of book I had written. As with the present book, the emphasis was on rational-choice theory, micro-foundations, and the philosophy of explanation. In France at the time, and to some extent still today, my methodological commitments automatically would lead readers to place me on the political right. Somehow methodological individualism and political individualism (or libertarianism) had become associated with one another. Hence I could not expect an interested Marxist readership. As for the non-Marxists, they would probably find the residual Marxism in my own views too much for them. So I left Marx and went on to other work, mostly but not wholly unrelated to what I had been doing. Over the following decade I completed five books that are cited extensively in the present work. *Leibniz et la Formation de l'Esprit Capitaliste* (1975) was a study in historical sociology, an attempt to understand the preoccupations of this polymath in the light of transformations that the European economy was undergoing at the time.

Logic and Society (1978) applied modal logic to sociological theories and problems. This helped me, among other things, to get a grip on the elusive notion of "social contradictions". *Ulysses and the Sirens* (1979) and *Sour Grapes* (1983) are studies in rationality and irrationality, with the main emphasis falling on preference formation and the scope and limits of character planning. *Explaining Technical Change* (1983) is an exposition of some themes in the philosophy of explanation, including a case study on the problem of innovation. When I finally returned to Marx, I found that I had been greatly helped by what I had been doing in the meantime. Whatever the merits and demerits of the present work, it has better foundations than the version I wrote thirteen years ago.

I returned to Marx because I became aware that the intellectual atmosphere was changing. Above all, the publication of G. A. Cohen's *Karl Marx's Theory of History* came as a revelation. Overnight it changed the standards of rigour and clarity that were required to write on Marx and Marxism. Also I discovered that other colleagues in various countries were engaged in similar work. A small group formed and met in 1979, and has later met annually. The discussions in this group, including extensive comments on successive drafts, have been decisive for the shaping of this book. In particular, the contributions of John Roemer (now stated in his path-breaking *A General Theory of Exploitation and Class*) turned out to be crucial. An interesting outcome of these discussions is that the sense in which we felt able to call ourselves Marxists has undergone a change over the years. I do not feel that I can speak for others than myself, except to say that there is probably not a single tenet of classical Marxism which has not been the object of insistent criticism at these meetings. Yet some kind of unstated consensus has emerged, even though I feel neither called upon nor competent to explain it here. Perhaps it will emerge implicitly from the other books to be published in the series in which this work appears.

I wish to thank many institutions and persons for their assistance. The Norwegian Research Council for the Humanities has supported my work on Marx on a generous scale, from 1968 to 1971, and then again from 1979 to 1982. The University of Oslo gave me a leave of absence at a crucial time in 1982, which I spent in the stimulating atmosphere of All Souls College, Oxford. The Maison des Sciences de l'Homme (Paris) has helped in many ways, notably by supporting the meetings of the research group mentioned above. Also I want to thank my students in the Political Science Department of the University of Chicago, to whom, on three occasions, I taught the material that turned into this book. Their incisive questioning forced me to rethink many issues. Cambridge University Press has proved consistently helpful, patient and encouraging. In an act of pure friendship, Stephen Holmes read the whole manuscript with great care to weed out infelicities of style.

G. A. Cohen read drafts of all chapters and made detailed comments that necessitated extensive revisions. I have also learned more from discussions with him than I am able to state, since I am sure there are many ideas that I believe to be my own and that actually originated with him. John Roemer has been equally involved, by his comments, by his own work and by his contributions in discussion. Their intellectual comradeship has been invaluable. Arthur Stinchcombe also read the whole manuscript, and provided a healthy dose of sociological scepticism. Individual chapters have been read by Pranab Bardhan, Robert Brenner, Bernard Chavance, Aanund Hylland, the late Leif Johansen, Serge Kolm, Margaret Levi, Claus Offe, Gunnar Opeide, Adam Przeworski, Rune Slagstad, Ian Steedman, Robert van der Veen, Philippe van Parijs, Michael Wallerstein and Erik Wright. The attention with which they read the work is attested by the fact that they all detected a mistake in an earlier version of chapter 4, when I made Wilt Chamberlain out to be a baseball player. Chamberlain, of course, played basketball. They also helped me to avoid a number of more consequential errors. I want to thank them all for their involvement in what almost amounts to a collective work. Almost, but not quite: although they bear some of the responsibility for some of the remaining mistakes, I must take most of them on myself.

Oslo, January 1984   J. E.

Introduction

1. Explanation and dialectics

One often meets the view that what remains valid in Marx today is his *method*, rather than any substantive theoretical propositions. As will be made clear in later chapters, I do not share this idea. Marx's views on technical change, exploitation, class struggle and belief formation retain an importance beyond the value they may have as instances of the Marxist method, if there is one. Yet I also believe that there is a specifically Marxist method for studying social phenomena – a method that can be and has been put to fertile use even by those who disagree with Marx's substantive views. In fact, this method is so widely applied today that few would think of referring to it as "the Marxist method". In historical perspective, however, Marx was a pioneer in the use of this methodology. Even today, not all of his insights have been exhausted. To put it briefly, he emphasized the unintended consequences of human action, arguing that they are to be understood in the causal-cum-intentional framework that has become the standard language of the social sciences. This idea is clearly related to earlier theories of history that saw it as "the result of human action, not of human design".[1] Yet Marx lent a specificity and a precision to this view that in fact transformed it completely, showing history to be intelligible rather than perversely opaque. True, Marx also professed and practised other methodological views, largely of Hegelian origin. I shall be arguing, however, that these are of little or no intrinsic interest.

In 1.1 I begin by stating and justifying the principle of methodological individualism, not infrequently violated by Marx, yet underlying much of his most important work. The converse of the principle is that of *methodological collectivism*, which is closely related to two other methods of Hegelian inspiration, namely *functional explanation* (1.4) and *dialectical deduction* (1.5.1). Although not logically entailed by one another, these methods often go together and reinforce one another in what has turned out to be a disastrous scientific practice. In my opinion the many failures of Marx and later Marxists derive largely from this misguided framework, hence much of the present work will be devoted to showing how it is possible to address the questions raised by Marx without having recourse to it.

More specifically, I shall argue that Marx himself offers an alternative framework that allows for a much more precise and fertile analysis. On this view, social science explanations are seen as three-tiered. First, there is a causal explanation of mental states, such as desires and beliefs (1.3.1). Next, there is intentional explanation of individual action in terms of the underlying beliefs and desires (1.2). Finally, there is causal explanation of aggregate phenomena in terms of the individual actions that go into them. The last form is the specifically Marxist contribution to the methodology of the social sciences. I discuss it first as a particular mode of causal analysis (1.3.2) and then again as a particular form of dialectical reasoning (1.5.3).

I shall return to these methodological tenets again and again in the present work. The task of this chapter is to set out the abstract logic of the argument, relatively uncluttered by examples. Later chapters will provide illustrations of both the defective and the sound methodological stances. It is quite extraordinary, in my view, how Marx could shift from near-nonsense to profound insight, often within the same work. In the *Grundrisse*, for instance, we have on the one hand the most striking statements of methodological collectivism and dialectical deduction, and, on the other hand, equally striking analyses of the way in which micro-motives are aggregated into macro-behaviour, to use T. C. Schelling's phrase. It is my

---

[1] For a historical survey, see Hayek's essay with this title, taken from the writings of Adam Ferguson.

firm belief – it is the basis, in fact, for the whole enterprise of writing this book – that the central insights of Marx are so valuable that we would do him and us a disservice were we to accept *en bloc* the methodology in which they were embedded.

1.1. Methodological individualism

By this I mean the doctrine that all social phenomena – their structure and their change – are in principle explicable in ways that only involve individuals – their properties, their goals, their beliefs and their actions. Methodological individualism thus conceived is a form of reductionism. To go from social institutions and aggregate patterns of behaviour to individuals is the same kind of operation as going from cells to molecules. The rationale for reductionism can briefly be stated as follows. If the goal of science is to *explain by means of laws*, there is a need to reduce the time-span between explanans and explanandum – between cause and effect – as much as possible, in order to avoid spurious explanations. The latter arise in two main ways: by the confusion of explanation and correlation and by the confusion of explanation and necessitation. The first occurs when there is a third variable that generates both the apparent cause and its apparent effect, the second when the effect is brought about by some other cause that preempts the operation of the cause cited in the law. Both of these risks are reduced when we approach the ideal of a continuous chain of cause and effect, that is when we reduce the time-lag between explanans and explanandum.[1] This, again, is closely associated with going from the aggregate to the less aggregate level of phenomena. In this perspective, reductionism is not an end in itself, only a concomitant of another desideratum. We should add, however, that a more detailed explanation is also an end in itself. It is not only our confidence in the explanation, but our understanding of it that is enhanced when we go from macro to micro, from longer to shorter time-lags. To explain is to provide a *mechanism*, to open up the black box and show the nuts and bolts, the cogs and wheels, the desires and beliefs that generate the aggregate outcomes. "Art and Science cannot exist but in minutely organized Particulars."[2]

Since the doctrine of methodological individualism is a highly contested one in the social sciences, much as it was formerly in biology, some

[1] Cp. Beauchamp and Rosenberg, *Hume and the Problem of Causation*, ch. 6; also my *Explaining Technical Change*, p. 29.
[2] William Blake, *Jerusalem*.

elucidation is in place. First, the doctrine does not presuppose selfishness, nor even rationality, at the level of individual action. As argued in 1.2.1, there is a presumption in favour of these features of individual behaviour, but it is grounded in purely methodological considerations, not in any substantive assumptions about human nature. Secondly, methodological individualism holds only in extensional contexts. When aggregate entities appear in intensional contexts, they are not reducible to lower-level entities. People often have beliefs about supra-individual entities that are not reducible to beliefs about individuals. "The capitalists fear the working class" cannot be reduced to statements about the feelings of capitalists about individual workers, while "The capitalist profit is threatened by the working class" can be reduced to a complex statement about the consequences of actions taken by individual workers. Thirdly, many properties of individuals, such as "powerful", are inherently relational, so that an accurate description of one individual may involve reference to others. This point is elaborated in 2.3.1. Lastly, the desirability of reduction should not blind us to the dangers of *premature reductionism*. Pascal criticized Descartes for yielding to that temptation in his mechanistic biology: "Il faut dire en gros: 'Cela se fait par figure et mouvement', car cela est vrai. Mais de dire quels, et composer la machine, cela est ridicule. Car cela est inutile, et incertain, et pénible."[1] Similarly there is a real danger that attempts to explain complex social phenomena in terms of individual motivations and beliefs may yield sterile and arbitrary explanations. In 6.2, I argue that this may be the case for the problem of finding micro-foundations for collective action. In such cases we are better off with a black-box explanation for the time being, although it is important to keep in mind that this is only *faute de mieux*. Methodological collectivism can never be a desideratum, only a temporary necessity.

Methodological collectivism – as an end in itself – assumes that there are supra-individual entities that are prior to individuals in the explanatory order. Explanation proceeds from the laws either of self-regulation or of development of these larger entities, while individual actions are derived from the aggregate pattern. This frequently takes the form of functional explanation, if one argues that objective benefits provide a sufficient explanation for the actions that, collectively, generate them. There is no logical connection, however, since the collectivist methodology may also be wedded to a causal mode of explanation. Conversely, functional explanation may be compatible with methodological

---

[1] *Pensées* 79.

individualism, if one insists on the necessary existence of some underlying mechanism.[1] In Marx, however, the two tend to go together, as will be amply shown throughout this work.

In Marx's philosophy of history (2.4), *humanity* appears as a collective subject whose inherent striving towards full realization shapes the course of history. Within the theory of capitalism, *capital* plays a similar role. The emphasis on the explanatory role of "capital in general" is especially striking in the *Grundrisse*,[2] as in the following argument against those who, like Ricardo, believe that the notion of competition is prior to that of capital. On the contrary, Marx asserts:

The predominance of capital is the presupposition of free competition, just as the despotism of the Roman Caesars was the presupposition of the free Roman 'private law'. As long as capital is weak, it still relies on the crutches of past modes of production, or of those which will pass with its rise. As soon as it feels strong, it throws away the crutches, and moves in accordance with its own laws. As soon as it begins to sense itself and become conscious of itself as a barrier to development, it seeks refuge in forms which, by restricting free competition, seem to make the rule of capital more perfect, but are at the same time the heralds of its dissolution and of the dissolution of the mode of production resting on it. Competition merely *expresses* as real, posits as an external necessity, that which lies within the nature of capital; competition is nothing more than the way in which the many capitals force the inherent determinants of capital upon one another and upon themselves.[3]

One could not wish for a more explicit denial of methodological individualism. It can be usefully contrasted with the approach advocated and practised by John Roemer, generating class relations and the capital relationship from exchanges between differently endowed individuals in a competitive setting. The details of his analysis are set out in chapters 4 and 6 below. The overwhelmingly strong argument for this procedure is that it allows one to demonstrate as theorems what would otherwise be unsubstantiated postulates.

On the other hand one should not forget that Marx also was committed to methodological individualism, at least intermittently. *The German Ideology*, in particular, rests on a strong individualist and anti-teleological approach to history, as is made clear in 2.4 below. Also, one may cite the phrase from the *Economic and Philosophical Manuscripts*: "Above all we must avoid postulating 'society' again as an abstraction *vis-à-vis* the

---

[1] This, for instance, is the view of G. A. Cohen in his various writings on functional explanation.
[2] Cp. Rosdolsky, *Zur Entstehungsgeschichte*, pp. 61–71.
[3] *Grundrisse*, p. 651.

individual."[1] In the context where it occurs, however, this phrase may also be seen as a commitment to *ethical* individualism, that is the view that the goal of communism is the development of men, not of Man.[2] Methodological individualism is a doctrine about how social phenomena are to be explained, not about how they should be evaluated.[3] Marx never wavered in his view that the main attraction of communism is that it will make possible the full and free realization of the individual (2.2.7); but he did not similarly and consistently place the individual at the centre of the explanation of the process leading up to the communist stage.

1.2. Intentional explanation

Among Marxists there is a widespread resistance to the use of rational-choice models and to intentional models more generally. Some of the reasons underlying this attitude are quite respectable, others are less so. Some are general, others more specific. They will become clearer as I proceed. I shall first sketch a general account of the nature of intentional explanations, and then go on to discuss their importance in Marx.

1.2.1. The nature of intentional explanation[4]
The explananda of intentional explanations are individual actions. When collective action is explained by its goal or purpose, this must either be understood distributively, in the sense that each actor in the group acts for the sake of that goal, or with reference to the goal or purpose of leaders who are able to induce or compel others to execute their policy. The crucial step in an intentional explanation is the specification of the goal – the future state of affairs for the sake of which the action is undertaken. The action may then be explained by the intended consequence, that is the realization of that state. The explanation is in no way invalidated if the consequence does not in fact come about, nor if it is logically incoherent so that it could not conceivably come about. With a few exceptions, however, I shall disregard the latter possibility and consider only *coherent* plans. This means that I shall consider only rational-choice explanations, as a subset of the wider category of intentional explanation.

---

[1] *Economic and Philosophical Manuscripts*, p. 299.
[2] For this distinction, see Cohen, "Marx's dialectic of labour", as well as 2.2 below.
[3] In *From Mandeville to Marx*, Louis Dumont does not distinguish between the ethical and the methodological sense of the individualism he finds in Marx. For a clear statement and discussion of the distinction, see Kolm, *Le Bonheur-liberté*, ch. 5.
[4] For fuller expositions, see ch. 3 of my *Explaining Technical Change* and ch. I of my *Sour Grapes*.

A rational-choice explanation of action involves showing that the action was rational and was performed because it was rational. That the action is rational means that given the beliefs of the agent, the action was the best way for him to realize his plans or desires. Hence rationality goes together with some form of maximizing behaviour. The maximand may, but need not be, some material reward accruing to the agent. Not all rational actions are selfish. The assumption that agents are selfishly motivated does, however, have a methodological privilege, for the following reason. For non-selfish behaviour, for example altruism, to be possible, some other agent or agents must be selfishly motivated, but not vice versa. Non-selfish behaviour is logically parasitic on selfishness, since there can be no pleasures of giving if there are no selfish pleasures of having. Or again, if I am concerned about your welfare, the latter cannot *solely* be made up of your concern for mine. (A similar relation of parasitism obtains between the second-order benefits that arise from participating in a political movement and the first-order benefits that constitute the goal of that movement.[1] In 6.2.3, I return to both of these issues.)

Choices take place within constraints that jointly determine the feasible set confronting the agent. In the standard account the preferences guiding the choice and the constraints defining the feasible set are given independently of one another. In the more general case, however, the two may be connected. The feasible set may be intentionally shaped according to one's preferences, as in the story of Ulysses and the Sirens.[2] Conversely, the preferences may be caused by the feasible set, as in the fable of the fox and the sour grapes.[3] Of these two non-standard phenomena, the first has only a marginal importance in the Marxist corpus. Marx did not believe that men – individually or collectively – had an incentive to bind themselves and precommit their future choices. I briefly return to this issue in 2.2.6 and 7.3.3. By contrast, the second – the issue of endogenous preference formation – is quite important, and is discussed in more detail in 1.3.1.

Given this framework, we can state some of the reasons why Marxists have been hesitant in embracing rational-choice explanations. First, it has been argued that constraints may not only shape preferences, but also preempt them – if their joint effect is to exclude all alternatives but one. If, say, there is only one consumption bundle that satisfies both the income constraint and the calorie constraint, then appeal to preferences

---

[1] Cp. *Sour Grapes*, ch. II.9.   [2] Cp. my *Ulysses and the Sirens*, ch. II.
[3] Cp. *Sour Grapes*, ch. III.

is redundant.[1] This objection may be valid in special cases, but there is no general reason to expect the constraints to narrow down the feasible set to exactly one alternative. In particular, were one to argue that the ruling class tries to manipulate the subjects by acting on their feasible set, this would imply that the ruling class itself has some scope for deliberate action and choice. Also, a rational ruling class would only reduce the feasible set so much that the alternative preferred within it by the subjects is also the one preferred within the unrestricted set by the class. Secondly, it has been objected that the singling out of one action within the feasible set can take place by some other mechanism than rational choice, for example by roles, norms or traditions. This objection is surely misguided. Tradition operates by influencing preferences, not by replacing them. Thirdly, one can argue that preferences cannot be the rock-bottom explanatory level. Rather, one has to look at the causal mechanisms by which preferences are shaped and changed. I postpone this issue to 1.3.1.

An important sub-variety of rational action is strategic behaviour, that is choices that take account of the conjectured or anticipated choices of other agents. The incorporation of the strategic aspect into rational-choice theory allows one to formulate three sets of interdependencies that pervade social life. (i) The reward of each depends on the rewards of all, by envy, altruism or solidarity.[2] (ii) The reward of each depends on the choices of all, by general social causality. (iii) The choice of each depends on the choices of all, by strategic reasoning. The third objection above can then be restated as follows: rational-choice theory is not able to take into account that (iv) the preferences of each depend on the actions of all.[3]

1.2.2. Purposive explanation in Marxist economics
The following discussion anticipates that of chapter 3, which provides a fuller exposition of the central notions of Marx's economic theory. Here I

[1] G. A. Cohen points out to me that this needs a qualification. Assume three constraints A, B and C jointly determining a unique feasible option x. An agent may be unaware of constraint A, and yet prefer x in the larger feasible set defined by B and C, in which case the selection of x, while *necessitated* by the constraints, is actually *explained* jointly by preferences and constraints.

[2] This is *not* inconsistent with the methodological privilege of selfish behaviour invoked above. The interdependency of rewards is necessarily hierarchical, in the sense that there must be some first-order rewards that do not depend on any other. The interdependency of choices may be hierarchical, if there are some agents that can make up their minds without anticipating what others will do, but it can also be perfectly reciprocal.

[3] The objection could be met if preferences are conceptualized as part of the *outcome* of behaviour, produced jointly with the primary goal. If so, rational agents might abstain from engaging in certain activities that, while individually desirable, could have unwanted preference change as a collective side-effect. If the situation is that of a Prisoner's Dilemma, some form of altruism would be needed to achieve this self-control.

only shall consider the behavioural assumptions of the theory and, in particular the role, if any, played by rational choice. Did Marx – like the modern neoclassical economist – explain consumer and producer behaviour in terms of maximization?

Consider first consumer behaviour, in particular working-class consumption. In a well-known passage in *Capital I* Marx comes close to suggesting that the consumption of the worker is uniquely determined by his need to reproduce his labour-power, with no residual left for choice:

The value of labour-power is determined, as in the case of every other commodity, by the labour-time necessary for the production, and consequently also the reproduction, of this special article . . . If the owner of labour-power works to-day, tomorrow he must again be able to repeat the same process in the same conditions as regards health and strength. His means of subsistence must therefore be sufficient to maintain him in his normal state as a labouring individual. His natural wants, such as food, clothing, fuel, and housing, vary according to the climatic and other physical conditions of his country. On the other hand, the number and extent of his so-called necessary wants, as also the modes of satisfying them, are themselves the product of historical development, and depend therefore to a great extent on the degree of civilization of a country, more particularly on the conditions under which, and consequently on the habits and degree of comfort in which, the class of free labourers has been formed. In contradistinction therefore to the case of other commodities, there enters into the determination of the value of labour-power a historical and moral element. Nevertheless, in a given country, at a given period, the average quantity of the means of subsistence necessary for the labourer is practically known.[1]

In the 1861–3 *Critique* some passages even suggest a von Neumann view of the production process, in which the labour inputs are notionally replaced by multiples of a unique consumption bundle. "Just as the coal and oil consumed by the machine enter into the labour process, so the means of subsistence which keep the worker going as a worker enter into the labour process too."[2] This, however, is a model of a slave economy, not of a capitalist one.[3] As is further argued in 3.2.2, Marx had strong theoretical reasons for wanting to keep workers' consumption fixed, since otherwise the labour value of goods might depend on preferences. Yet even assuming that the workers' needs are given, this does not imply that there is no scope for choice among alternative ways of fulfilling them. Even at the minimal subsistence level, needs can be satisfied in many different ways,[4]

---

[1] *Capital I*, pp. 170–1.   [2] *Zur Kritik (1861–63)*, p. 118.
[3] Cp. Morishima, *Theory of Economic Growth*, pp. 96–7.
[4] Sen, *Poverty and Famines*, pp. 24ff. Cp. also Seton and Morishima, "Aggregation in Leontief matrices and the labour theory of value", p. 206, note 8.

and a fortiori this must hold when needs rise above this level to incorporate a "historical and moral element".

At other times Marx shows himself fully aware of the importance of consumer choice under capitalism, as in the following passage from the *Grundrisse*:

> [The worker] is neither bound to particular objects, nor to a particular manner of satisfaction. The sphere of his consumption is not qualitatively restricted, only quantitatively. This distinguishes him from the slave, serf etc. Consumption certainly reacts on production itself, but this reaction concerns the worker in his exchange as little as it does any other seller of a commodity ... [The] relative restriction on the sphere of the workers' consumption (which is only quantitative, not qualitative, or rather, only qualitative as posited through the quantitative) gives them as consumers ... an entirely different importance as agents of production from that which they possessed e.g. in Antiquity or in the Middle Ages, or now possess in Asia.[1]

Here Marx captures nicely the aggregate economic impact of free consumer choice. Other passages, cited in 4.2 below, argue that the freedom of choice that belongs to the worker as a consumer also tends to transform him into an autonomous, responsible being. These views are quite incompatible with the assumption of "fixed coefficients of consumption" underlying the notion of the value of labour-power in *Capital*. In spite of the inherent implausibility of that assumption, it has with a few exceptions been retained by most later Marxist writers on the topic.[2] I would not deny that it may be a useful simplification in some cases, but then it must be defended as such, and not on the grounds of a methodological superiority that it does not possess.

Next, consider producer behaviour. Although the notion of profit as the engine of capitalist production is central in Marxism, the behavioural assumption of profit maximization is infrequently invoked. Yet many analyses only make sense if it is presupposed. In particular, Marx argued that the establishment of an economy-wide rate of profit takes place by capital moving from low-profit to high-profit sectors.[3] Also, the choice of technique – which, contrary to a widespread view, was not denied by Marx – must be guided by profit-maximizing considerations.

---

[1] *Grundrisse*, p. 283; cp. also p. 464.

[2] Exceptions are Johansen, "The labour theory of value and marginal utilities", and Roemer, *Analytical Foundations*, chs. 7 and 8.

[3] John Roemer points out to me that all that can be rigorously proved (cp. ch. 3 of his *Analytical Foundations*) is the existence of an equal-rate-of-profit equilibrium, a weaker statement than the dynamical assertion in the text. Yet Marx certainly believed that the equilibrium would be established by capital flowing from low-profit to high-profit sectors. For the present methodological purposes, it makes no difference whether we take the strong or the weak statement to represent his position.

More controversially, the process of technical change may be similarly directed, leading to a rational preference for some types of innovation over others (3.3.2). Capitalist entrepreneurs are *agents* in the genuinely active sense. They cannot be reduced to mere place-holders in the capitalist system of production.

This view goes against a widespread interpretation of Marx. It is often said that he attached little importance to intentional explanation in economics, since the basic units of his theory are "character masks"[1] rather than individuals. The capitalist, in particular, is only the "conscious support" of the capitalist process,[2] and only enacts the laws regulating it. Even capitalist consumption can be seen as "capital's expenses of reproduction".[3] This is well in line with the view that the worker is the passive embodiment of his consumption bundle, rather than an active human being capable, among other things, of waging a struggle for a larger bundle. The conclusion often drawn from this argument is that the capitalist does not "choose" his actions, but is "forced" by his need to survive in the competitive market.[4] I believe this way of stating the issue is misleading. "Choosing" only means comparing alternatives and picking the best of them. The choice may well be said to be forced if all alternatives but one are unacceptable (4.2.3), but it is no less of a choice for that. Rather, the relevant distinction is that between forced and unforced choice, for example between being forced to optimize and not being forced to do so. This distinction might for instance serve to distinguish between capitalists at different stages of capitalist development, as suggested by Weber.[5]

One may take this argument a step further. According to the "satisficing" school of theorists, not only is there no opposition between choice and necessity: choices are only made out of necessity.[6] In the normal course of events, firms follow routines that cannot in any reasonable sense be referred to as choices. Only when the current routine leads to a fall in profit below some critical level are the firms energized into actively searching for alternatives and comparing them to the *status quo.*

---

[1] "The characters who appear on the economic stage (*die ökonomischen Charaktermasken der Personen*) are but the personifications of the economic relations that exist between them" (*Capital I*, p. 85).
[2] *Capital I*, p. 152; *Zur Kritik (1861–63)*, p. 16.
[3] *Capital I*, p. 594.
[4] For this view, see for instance Shaikh, "Political economy and capitalism", effectively refuted by Steedman, "A note on the 'choice of technique' under capitalism".
[5] Weber, *The Protestant Ethic*, p. 181.
[6] For the argument in the following paragraphs, see Nelson and Winter, *An Evolutionary Theory of Economic Change* and my *Explaining Technical Change*, chs. 3 and 6.

Necessity is the mother of invention, and more generally of all active search-and-selection behaviour. This is a quite radical departure from the rational-choice model of producer behaviour. By substituting behaviour that is "good enough" for the "optimal" behaviour, the satisficing school implies that firms may often operate far away from the optimum. In my opinion this is a more attractive and realistic view than the standard neoclassical theory of the firm, although perhaps flawed by an element of *ad hoc*-ness, in that the satisficing theorists do not offer a theory of why firms have the aspiration levels they have. Be this as it may, the satisficing approach that makes necessity into a precondition for choice is certainly a more interesting alternative to the rational-choice model than the structuralist theories that substitute necessity for choice.

In particular, the satisficing model appears very attractive when we turn to the problem of explaining technical change. Since the *ex ante* possibility and profitability of innovations are so hard to assess, it makes sense to argue that innovating firms are spurred by adversity rather than lured by profits. Let me draw attention to a passage in which Marx seems to propose a similar view:

It is evident that the English legislature, which certainly no one will venture to reproach with being overdosed with genius, has been led by experience to the conclusion that a simple compulsory law is sufficient to enact away all the so-called impediments, opposed by the nature of the process, to the restriction and regulation of the working-day. Hence, on the introduction of the Factory Act into a given industry, a period varying from six to eighteen months is fixed within which it is incumbent on the manufacturers to remove all technical impediments to the working of the Act. Mirabeau's "Impossible! Ne me dites jamais ce bête de mot!" is particularly applicable to modern technology.[1]

Although one should not on the basis of this one text make Marx a precursor of the satisficing theory of innovation, there are other passages, quoted and discussed in 3.3.2 below, that point in the same direction. Since technical change is at the core of Marx's theory of capitalism, it is a point of some importance whether one finds its source in the inner drive of entrepreneurs to accumulate, or in external pressures created by the state or recalcitrant workers.

Let me add a comment on game-theoretic reasoning in Marxist economic theory. Although strategic interaction is crucial in economic life, both within and between classes, Marx took little explicit account of it. In later chapters I shall occasionally elaborate on some of his theories, using a game-theoretic framework, but in doing so I shall largely go

[1] *Capital I*, p. 477.

beyond what is to be found in his writings. As in virtually any social theorist of some stature, one finds in his work instances of the interaction structure known as the Prisoner's Dilemma. In particular this holds for his analysis of the relation between the members of the economically dominant class in a society: the class as a whole may have interests that do not coincide with those of the individual members. Yet what Marx says on this topic is hardly more coherent and systematic than what may be discovered in Hobbes, Rousseau or Tocqueville.[1] Moreover, he is sometimes confused with respect to the crucial distinction between variable-sum and constant-sum interaction, as in this passage from *Capital III*:

So long as things go well, competition effects an operating fraternity of the capitalist class, as we have seen in the case of the equalization of the general rate of profit, so that each shares in the common loot in proportion to the size of his respective investment. But as soon as it no longer is a question of sharing profits, but of sharing losses, everyone tries to reduce his own share to a minimum and to shove it off upon one another. The class, as such, must inevitably lose. How much the individual capitalist must bear of the loss, i.e. to what extent he must share in it at all, is decided by strength and cunning, and the competition between them becomes a fight among hostile brothers. The antagonism between each individual capitalist's interests and those of the capitalist class as a whole then comes to the surface, just as previously the identity of these interests operated in practice through competition.[2]

The last phrase must imply that competition – in good times as in bad – is a variable-sum game, whereas the preceding analysis can hardly be understood otherwise than as an argument for a constant-sum game.

1.2.3. Intentional explanation of political behaviour

Marx's political writings are suggestive, often brilliant, although methodologically ambiguous, hovering between the intentional and the functional modes of explanation. I shall briefly consider four questions: the logic of collective action, the theory of coalition formation, the explanation of state behaviour and the theory of international politics. With the exception of the last topic, these issues are all discussed more extensively in later chapters.

Collective action takes place when a group – for example a class – is capable of acting jointly to further its interests as a group, thus overcoming the free-rider problem (6.2.1). On general grounds, a satisfactory

---

[1] On Hobbes, see Taylor, *Anarchy and Cooperation*; on Rousseau, see Runciman and Sen, "Games, justice and the general will". For an occurrence in Tocqueville, see *Democracy in America*, p. 627 note.

[2] *Capital III*, p. 253.

explanation of collective action must provide micro-foundations for the behaviour, that is explain it in terms of the desires and beliefs that enter into the motivation of the individuals participating in it (1.1). Marx has fairly little to say about this problem. In trying to reconstruct what one might sensibly say about it, there seem to be three main avenues of research. First, the most parsimonious explanation would invoke nothing but rational and selfish motivation among the participants. Next, we may relax the assumption of selfishness and allow altruism and public-spiritedness as motives. Thirdly, as a rather desperate last-ditch attempt, we might feel compelled to assume that the agents act irrationally when engaging in collective action. In different cases different models could be appropriate. There is no reason why the same set of assumptions should explain cartel formation and union formation, peasant revolts and urban strikes. In all cases, however, the focus must be on the individuals, not on the group. The group may have an objective interest, but it has no goal. The objective interest will be realized only to the extent that it coincides with, or is made to coincide with, the interests of individual members. An extensive, if somewhat inconclusive, discussion of these issues is found in 6.2.3.

Once collective actors have been formed and have achieved some stability, we may look at the way in which they confront one another in the social and political arena.[1] Since Marx always refers to the class struggle as involving three or more classes, we at once get into the problem of class coalitions. In his writings on English politics, Marx alludes to many of the principles regulating coalition formation in triads, such as "*tertius gaudens*", "*divide et impera*", "the enemy of my enemy is my friend" and the principle of the lesser evil. They are all deeply ambiguous, suggesting both a rational-choice explanation and a functional account. The same holds for his explanation of alliance formation in French politics, as in the following case to which Raymond Aron has drawn attention.[2] In *The Eighteenth Brumaire* Marx asks why the two monarchical fractions, Legitimists and Orleanists, united around the parliamentary republic. Marx offers two answers. One is couched in terms of economic interest, and relies heavily on functional explanation. The other operates strictly at the political level: for each of the fractions a republican regime was a more acceptable solution than the monarchist option preferred by

---

[1] I am not denying that such confrontation is also a determinant of class consciousness. Yet the formation of class consciousness and the process of class struggle should be kept analytically distinct, even if they often occur *pari passu*. The former is an intra-class, the latter an inter-class, phenomenon.

[2] Aron, *Les Etapes de la Pensée Sociologique*, p. 290.

the other.[1] Unlike many other issues, the choice between two pretenders allows of no other compromise than that of choosing neither. This is a fully satisfactory rational-choice explanation, yet Marx felt a need to supplement it by a more "fundamental" account in terms of objective class interest.

A similarly ambiguous attitude is found in Marx's explanations of the policies followed by the mid-nineteenth-century European states. On the one hand he offered a straightforward intentional explanation: the behaviour of the state derives from the self-interest of the governing clique, constrained by the interest of the capitalist class. On the other hand, his basic theory told him that the state in a capitalist society had to be a capitalist state, hence he argued that ultimately everything came down to the interest of the capitalist class. More specifically, the fact that the capitalists did not seek political power could be explained by the benefits they derived from another class exercizing it. This is a purely functional account, with no attempt to provide a mechanism that could make it a plausible story. In 7.1 I argue that in his political sociology Marx allowed considerable autonomy of action to the state, explaining its behaviour in terms of the interest of the aristocratic–feudal–bureaucratic groups that were actually in charge of the government. The argument is made, moreover, that his attempt to explain this autonomy as a form of capitalist abdication was largely unsuccessful.

In his journalistic writings Marx devoted an immense energy to the study of international politics. I shall not pay a corresponding attention to these writings, which are largely devoid of theoretical interest.[2] A few methodological comments may still be in order. Like other students of the topic, he did not limit himself to explanation in terms of the officially professed motives of the actors but went beyond them in two ways. First, he occasionally explained political behaviour in terms of the larger historical goal that it served. Thus commenting on Russia's attitude to Turkey, he suggested that she was "but the unconscious and reluctant slave of the modern *fatum*, Revolution".[3] Similarly, the British rule in India was "the unconscious tool of history" in bringing about a fundamental revolution in Asia.[4] These passages are more fully cited and discussed in 2.4.2. They rely on the functionalist notion of free-floating intentions, purposes that can be imputed to no specific actor, only to

---

[1] *The Eighteenth Brumaire*, p. 166.
[2] For discussions, see Molnar, *Marx, Engels et la Politique Internationale* and Papaioannou, *De Marx et du Marxisme*, V.ii.
[3] *New York Daily Tribune* 9.6.1853.   [4] *Ibid.* 25.6.1853.

"history". Next, there is a pronounced tendency in his writings to seek conspiratorial explanations – substituting hidden intentions for the overt ones. In some cases this led him to quite extravagant views, for instance his notorious theory that Lord Palmerston was "in vassalage to Russia" while he served as British Foreign Secretary.[1] In other cases his refusal to take appearances at face value helped him to quite valuable insights, as when he explained to Engels that in matters of revolution and war, "the whole point is, who is most able to give himself the appearance of not being afraid".[2] The general point to be made here is that the distinction between functional and conspiratorial explanations is often difficult to draw in a given case, since both involve going beyond overt intentions and invoking some other purpose, the only evidence for which is typically the benefits brought about by the action to be explained.

1.3. Two varieties of causal analysis

In the three-tiered scheme of explanation suggested above, two varieties of causal analysis were involved. First, there are the causal explanations of preferences and other mental states, such as beliefs, emotions etc. I shall refer to this as explanation in terms of sub-intentional causality. Next, there are the causal explanations of aggregate social phenomena as the resultant outcome of many individual actions. This I refer to as supra-intentional causality. Metaphorically, the causal mechanisms involved in both cases can be said to operate "behind the back" of the individuals concerned. True, Marx uses that phrase only to refer to supra-intentional causality – the production of unintended consequences that thwart our efforts and subvert our aims.[3] Yet the expression is equally apt as a characterization of the psychic causality that, unbeknown to the agent, shapes his beliefs and desires. Although Marx is best known for his study of supra-intentional causality, one aim of the present work is to argue that he was also a pioneer in the study of preference formation and – especially – belief formation.

1.3.1. Sub-intentional causality

Beliefs and desires arise in an agent by the force of external circumstances mediated by internal psychic mechanisms. Cognitive psychology makes

---

[1] *Herr Vogt*, p. 136; also *New York Daily Tribune* 17.4.1854.
[2] *Marx to Engels* 2.6.1853. The mechanism has been extensively studied by Schelling, *The Strategy of Conflict*.
[3] See for instance *Grundrisse*, pp. 225, 244; *Capital I*, p. 44; *Capital III*, p. 168.

a distinction between two kinds of mechanism, called "hot" and "cold" respectively.[1] The hot mechanisms include motivationally based processes, such as wishful thinking, the reduction of cognitive dissonance and the like. The cold mechanisms rest on purely cognitive processes and biases, unrelated to motivation. An application of these ideas to Marxism might involve doing two things. First, one might try to describe the external circumstances in socio-economic terms, in order to show how differently situated individuals subject to similar psychic mechanisms will end up having different beliefs and preferences. Secondly, one might try to show how the incidence of biases and distortions is itself related to, say, class membership. Marx would no doubt have said that in post-class society these distortions will no longer be found. There is, however, no basis in his work for suggesting different sorts of biases, or different frequency of bias, among the members of different classes. Hence, in what follows, and in later chapters, I shall focus on the first problem: how to explain beliefs and desires in terms of class position and class interest, assuming identical psychic mechanisms to be operating.

Consider first the explanation of beliefs. This will be dealt with in some detail in several later chapters: in the discussion of fetishism (2.3.2), in an attempt to clarify the distinction between essence and appearance in economic life (3.1.2) and at greater length in the discussion of ideology (chapter 8). Hence the present comments will be relatively brief. Marx's most original contribution to the theory of belief formation was, in my opinion, his idea that the economic agents tend to generalize locally valid views into invalid global statements, because of a failure to perceive that causal relations that obtain *ceteris paribus* may not hold unrestrictedly. For instance, although *any* worker may be seen as the marginal worker, not *all* workers can be at the margin. This is a local–global fallacy that leads to cognitive failures, different from yet related to the local–global confusions that lead to failures of action (1.5.3). This is perhaps the most powerful part of the Marxist methodology: the demonstration that in a decentralized economy there spontaneously arises a *fallacy of composition* with consequences for theory as well as for practice.

These and other spontaneously arising illusions are the result of cold mechanisms of belief formation. Marx, of course, also insisted on – and probably is better known for – his theory of hot belief formation. Thus, he argued that the members of any given class tend to present their particular interest as the interest of society in general by a process of self-deception or

---

[1] For further discussion of these two kinds of process, linked with the names of Festinger and Tversky respectively, see my *Sour Grapes*, ch. IV, and ch. 8 below.

wishful thinking. Or again, consider his theory of religion as a form of dissonance reduction, "the sigh of the oppressed creature".[1] I argue in chapter 8 below that this part of the theory is marred by a confusion between two ways of explaining beliefs in terms of interest – as being shaped by the interest of the believer, or as serving some interest or other. The former is a causal explanation, the latter a more dubious functional one.

Consider now the explanation of desires and preferences. Among economists there is a minority who argue that preferences are identical among individuals and stable over time, appearances to the contrary notwithstanding.[2] The variance in behaviour is to be explained exclusively by the variance in opportunities, whereas the preferences themselves are presumably to be explained as a product of biological evolution. Although this approach might appear to be pleasingly "materialist", it does not fit the Marxist theory of needs (2.2.3), nor is it at all plausible taken by itself. There is, however, an important core of truth in the idea that opportunities are central in the explanation of behaviour, since preferences themselves are to a large extent shaped by what is possible. Among the many ways in which this can occur, one is especially important for our present purposes. In class societies, preferences are often shaped so that the exploited classes come to accept their fate, regarding it as inevitable or even preferable. This occurs by the mechanism of dissonance reduction or some variety thereof, such as "sour grapes".[3] Observe that this outcome clearly is beneficial for the exploiting classes, but that these benefits do not explain the preferences. Rather, they are to be explained by the benefits they bring to the exploited and dominated classes by bringing them a modicum of peace of mind. Paul Veyne has argued persuasively that this was a dominant mechanism of preference formation among subjects in the ancient world.[4] Marx to some extent agrees, while also stressing the contrast to the modern world:

In bourgeois economics – and in the epoch of production to which it corresponds – this complete working-out of the human content appears as a complete emptying-out, this universal objectification as total alienation, and the tearing-down of all limited, one-sided aims as sacrifice of the human end-in-itself to an entirely external end. This is why the childish world of antiquity appears on one side as loftier.

---

[1] "Contribution to the Critique of Hegel's Philosophy of Law. Introduction", p. 175.
[2] Kolm, *Justice et Equité*, p. 79; Stigler and Becker, "De gustibus non est disputandum"; Harsanyi, "Cardinal welfare, individualistic ethics and interpersonal comparisons of utility".
[3] For details of this mechanism, cp. *Sour Grapes*, ch. III.
[4] Veyne, *Le Pain et le Cirque*, pp. 305ff, 706ff and *passim*.

On the other side, it really is loftier in all matters where closed shapes, forms and given limits are sought for. It is satisfaction from a limited standpoint; while the modern gives no satisfaction; or where it appears satisfied with itself, it is *vulgar*.[1]

The point to be emphasized is that endogenous preference formation is not invariably a stabilizing mechanism. In most times and places, perhaps, the poor and the exploited are induced by their situation to set their sights so low that the idea of revolt is foreign to them, yet there are important exceptions. The world of industrial capitalism, in particular, creates an impatience and dissatisfaction that ultimately will undermine it (2.2.5). In addition to the passages from the *Grundrisse* to be cited in chapter 2, one may recall that in *The Communist Manifesto* Marx praised the bourgeoisie for having "rescued a considerable part of the population from the *Idiotismus* of rural life".[2]

Besides this line of argument, Marx and later Marxists have also offered a quite different explanation of the preferences and desires of the exploited classes. This explanation insists on the benefits that the preferences bring to the exploiters, not on the benefits for the exploited themselves. If subjects come to accept or even prefer their state of subjection, this must be explained by the obvious utility such attitudes have for the rulers. If the explanation stops here, we have a functional account (1.4). If it goes on to spell out a mechanism, we often get a theory of preference formation by deliberate manipulation and indoctrination, that is an intentional (or conspiratorial) explanation.

For reasons stated elsewhere,[3] I do not believe that explanations of this kind are likely to be successful. Manipulation is difficult and, more often than not, superfluous. For an instance of this kind of reasoning in Marx, we may take the following comment on Ireland:

The ordinary English worker hates the Irish worker as a competitor who lowers his standard of life. In relation to the Irish worker he feels himself a member of the *ruling nation* and so turns himself into a tool of the aristocrats and capitalists of his country *against Ireland*, thus strengthening their domination over *himself*. He cherishes religious, social and national prejudices against the Irish worker. His attitude towards him is much the same as that of the 'poor whites' to the 'niggers' in the former slave states of the USA. The Irishman pays him back with interest in his own money. He sees in the English worker at once the accomplice and the stupid tool of the *English rule in Ireland*. This antagonism is artificially kept alive and intensified by the press, the pulpit, the comic papers, in short, by

[1] *Grundrisse*, p. 488.
[2] *The Communist Manifesto*, p. 488.
[3] *Sour Grapes*, chs. II.5 and III.2.

all the means at the disposal of the ruling classes. *This antagonism is the secret of the impotence of the English working class*, despite its organization.[1]

It is not easy to know what to make of this passage. The first part suggests quite strongly that the prejudices of the English workers arose endogenously. By this I mean that given the domination of the workers by the capitalists and the presence of the Irish, there would be a natural psychological tendency at work to produce prejudice. The frustration or dissonance that comes from being dominated can be eased to some extent by the mental operation of drawing the main dividing line in society below rather than above oneself. This would not require any manipulation by the capitalist class, although the prejudices could well be intensified by their action. Towards the end of the passage, however, Marx says that the conflict between English and Irish workers is not only intensified, but "artificially kept alive" by the ruling classes, implying that it would have been absent but for their intervention. This step from *tertius gaudens* to *divide et impera* does not seem plausible to me. Ruling classes can exploit prejudices, but they cannot create them.[2]

1.3.2. Supra-intentional causality

There is a cluster of notions that more than any other has contributed to the making of modern social science – that of "private vices, public benefits" (Mandeville), "the invisible hand" (Adam Smith), "the ruse of reason" (Hegel) and "latent functions" (Merton). The common core of these ideas is that individuals, acting for some goal of their own, bring about something that was no part of their intention. I postpone to 1.4 the discussion of the idea that these consequences, even if unintended, may nevertheless enter into the explanation of the behaviour that caused them. Here I want to focus on the other part of the chain, that running from the many individual actions to the aggregate outcome.

The relation between a set of actions and their aggregate outcome may be one of the following. (i) The actors knowingly bring about the outcome, each of them choosing his course of behaviour on correct assumptions about the behaviour of others and the means–end relations involved. (ii) The actors bring about the intended outcome, but accidentally – that is not in the way they intended to bring it about. A paradigm for this

---

[1] Marx to Meyer and Vogt 9.4.1870.

[2] This might appear to be a case of blaming the victims, but as observed by Veyne (*Le Pain et le Cirque*, p. 89) it is no more flattering for the subjects if we explain their beliefs in terms of manipulation. In any case it should be remembered that capitalist domination is at the core of the process: it is not a question of voluntary servitude, but of rationalization of servitude.

case is La Fontaine's fable of the labourer and his children. Since they were too lazy to work in the fields, as their father wanted them to, he told them that there was a treasure buried in the grounds. Eager to get rich in a hurry, they overturned the soil in an unsuccessful search for the treasure, and in doing so made it so fertile that they did indeed get rich, although not in the way they had planned. (iii) The actors bring about an outcome different from the intended one – either because they made erroneous assumptions about one another, or because they misjudged the technical relations involved. In what follows I shall disregard the somewhat trivial case of defective technical insight, the better to focus on the mutually invalidating behavioural assumptions. I shall also disregard case (i) above, and offer only a brief illustration of case (ii). This draws on an important passage from the *Grundrisse* that offers a direct application of La Fontaine's fable:

The period which precedes the development of modern industrial society opens with general greed for money on the part of individuals as well as of states. The real development of the sources of wealth takes place, as it were, behind their backs, as a means of gaining possession of the representatives of wealth. Wherever it does not arise out of circulation – as in Spain – but has to be discovered physically, the nation is impoverished, whereas the nations which have to work in order to get it from the Spaniards develop the sources of wealth and really become rich. This is why the search for and discovery of gold in new continents, countries, plays so great a role in the history of revaluation, because by its means colonization is improvised and made to flourish as if in a hothouse. The hunt for gold in all countries leads to its discovery; to the formation of new states; initially to the spread of commodities, which produce new needs, and draw distant continents into the metabolism of circulation, i.e. exchange.[1]

The passage is not only of methodological interest. By placing the burden of explanation on a historical coincidence, it offers a picture of the development of capitalism rather different from the standard Marxist account (5.2.2). If individuals and states in the early modern period had not been under the sway of mercantilist illusions – likened by Marx to those of the alchemists – they would not have had the motivation to engage in the efforts that ultimately brought them real, productive wealth. The mercantile system, therefore, may well have been optimal for the development of the productive forces, but only in this Pickwickian sense.[2]

In case (iii), there is a distinction to be made between the unintended

---

[1] *Grundrisse*, p. 225.
[2] For a discussion of this non-standard sense, see Cohen, *Karl Marx's Theory of History*, pp. 169ff.

consequences that are beneficial for the agents bringing them about, and those that are harmful or detrimental to their interest. If, for convenience of exposition, we limit the attention to the unintended consequences that arise instead of – rather than in addition to – the intended ones, these subcases may schematically be indicated as follows. Let us assume that each of many similarly placed agents performs a certain action, believing that it will raise his income, utility etc. from level a_0 to a_1. We assume furthermore that this belief is technically correct, so that it is true of each agent that if he were the only one to perform the action, he would indeed get a_1. The *invisible hand* operates when the aggregate outcome of everybody acting in this way gives each of them a benefit $a_2 > a_1$. *Counterfinality*, to use Sartre's term, operates when the outcome gives to each of them $a_3 < a_0$.[1] Marx was well aware of both of these possibilities. The distinction is explicitly made in this passage from the *Grundrisse*:

> This reciprocal dependence is expressed in the constant necessity for exchange, and in exchange value as the all-sided mediation. The economists express this as follows: Each pursues his private interest and only his private interest; and thereby serves the private interests of all, the general interest, without willing or knowing it. The real point is not that each individual's pursuit of his private interest promotes the totality of private interests, the general interest. One could just as well deduce from this abstract phrase that each individual reciprocally blocks the assertion of the others' interest, so that instead of a general affirmation, this war of all against all produces a general negation. The point is rather that private interest is itself already a socially determined interest, which can be achieved only within the conditions laid down by society and with the means provided by society; hence it is bound to the reproduction of these conditions and means. It is the interest of private persons; but its content, as well as the form and means of its realization, is given by social conditions independent of all.[2]

Observe that Marx weaves together the theme of sub-intentional causality, that is the formation of private interest, with that of supra-intentional causality, that is the production of unintended consequences by individuals acting on the interests thus generated. Individuals are as it were caught in the middle, between the psychic causality that shapes their aims and desires and the social causality that thwarts and frustrates them.

Let me give some specific examples of the invisible hand and counterfinality from Marx's writings. The positive externalities, to use the

---

[1] Why not define counterfinality by $a_3 < a_1$, so as to retain the symmetry with the invisible hand? I am guided by Sartre's use of the notion, and by the discussions in Marx to which I want to apply it. They were both concerned with vicious spirals of collectively self-defeating behaviour, not just with the general notion of reciprocal blocking.

[2] *Grundrisse*, p. 156.

economist's language, include the creation of relative surplus-value and the economizing on constant capital. Concerning the first, Marx insists in the 1861–3 *Critique* that

This shortening of the necessary labour time is a consequence which redounds to the benefit of capitalist production in general and reduces the production costs of labour power as a whole because, in accordance with our assumption, the commodity produced by the machinery enters into its reproduction. However, this is not a reason for the individual capitalist to introduce machinery, merely a general consequence which does not bring him any particular benefit.[1]

Elsewhere in the manuscript, and later in *Capital I*, he simplifies the exposition by assuming that "the worker lives off the use-value that he himself produces",[2] but the above passage shows that he was fully aware of the distinction between the windfall profits that befall all capitalists as by-products of self-interested behaviour, and the immediate reward that is the motivation for the latter. This also applies to external economies in production:

The characteristic feature of this kind of saving of constant capital arising from the progressive development of industry is that the rise in the rate of profit in *one* line of industry depends on the development of the productive power of labour in *another*. Whatever falls to the capitalist's advantage in this case is once more a gain produced by social labour, if not a product of the labourers he himself exploits.[3]

The validity of such analyses depends on the presence of some reward that the individual agent can internalize and that motivates him to action – even if it falls short of the contribution he thereby makes to the general interest of his class. In 3.3.2 below I discuss an issue in the theory of labour-saving innovations which raises the difficulty that there may not be any private incentive to perform the collectively beneficial action. Without such micro-foundations, the analysis of the invisible hand easily slides into functional explanation.

For Marx, counterfinality – the negative externalities of the capitalist mode of production – was a more interesting phenomenon. He believed that capitalism systematically tends to aggravate spontaneously arising crises, since each entrepreneur reacts to them by behaviour that, even if individually rational, is disastrous in the aggregate. The main instance of this mechanism Marx found in the process that according to him tends to

---

[1] *Zur Kritik (1861–63)*, pp. 301–2.
[2] *Ibid.*, p. 215, also *Capital I*, p. 316. The latter passage is more ambiguous, and comes close to a violation of methodological individualism.
[3] *Capital III*, pp. 81–2.

generate a fall in the rate of profit. This theory is discussed in some detail in 3.4.2. Here I shall single out another instance in Marx of a theory with the same general structure, foreshadowing one of the central insights of Keynesian economics. In Joan Robinson's phrase, it is "an essential paradox of capitalism"[1] that each capitalist wants low wages for his own workers, since this makes for high profits, yet high wages for the workers employed by other capitalists, since this makes for high demand for his products. This paradox underlies the crises of effective demand studied by Keynes. Although Marx did not attach the same importance to this variety of capitalist crises (3.4.3), he was fully aware of the contradictions generated by the dual role of workers in the economy: "to each capitalist the total mass of workers, with the exception of his own workers, appear not as workers, but as consumers".[2] He recognized, moreover, that this at least creates a *potential* for crises:

[No] economist will deny that if workers *generally*, that is as *workers* (what the individual worker does or can do, as distinct from his genus, can only exist as *exception*, not as a *rule*, because it is not inherent in the character of the relation itself), that is, if they acted according to [the demand to save] as a *rule* (apart from the damage they would do to general consumption – the loss would be enormous – and hence also to production, thus also to the amount and volume of the exchanges which they could make with capital, hence to themselves as workers), then the workers would be employing means which absolutely contradict their purpose ... Each capitalist does demand that his own workers should save, but only *his own*, because they stand towards him as workers; but by no means the remaining *world of workers*, for these stand towards him as consumers.[3]

In 1.5.3 I examine more closely the logical structure of this relationship between workers and capitalists. Here I want only to emphasize that we must indeed expect something to give if each capitalist acts on an assumption – that only *his* workers should save or accept lower wages – which as a matter of logic cannot be true for all. In Marx's phrase, "each individual reciprocally blocks the assertion of the others' interest", because they act on mutually incompatible assumptions about one another.

This mechanism generates social change not only in capitalism, but in any society in which economic decisions suffer from lack of coordination. Sartre, for instance, takes erosion as his paradigmatic case of counterfinality: each peasant seeks to obtain more land by cutting down trees on his plot, but a general deforestation induces erosion, with the

---

[1] Robinson, *The Accumulation of Capital*, p. 78; see also Keynes, *A Treatise on Money*, vol. V, pp. 143–5.
[2] *Grundrisse*, p. 419.
[3] *Ibid.*, pp. 285–7.

result that less land is available to him than at the outset.[1] Marx, however, had little to say about counterfinality in pre-capitalist societies. In 2.1.2 below I cite his observation that culture, when progressing in an unconscious and unplanned way, leaves a desert behind itself, as in the ancient East.[2] This, while certainly compatible with the Sartrian idea, is not quite specific enough to count as evidence for its presence in Marx. Nor are his comments in the *Grundrisse* on the destabilizing effects of population growth in pre-capitalist societies (5.1.1) sufficient textual grounds for ascribing to him the more specific view that larger family size, while individually rational, is often collectively undesirable. Only in the case of capitalism did Marx go beyond the general notion of his predecessors, from Vico to Hegel, that history is the result of human action, but not of human design. By imposing a definite structure on that notion, he transformed it from *Weltanschauung* into a scientific methodology.

1.4. Functional explanation in Marx

Did Marx practise functional explanation? If so, was he successful? If not, could his explanations be improved? In this section I shall mainly explore the first two questions, with only brief references to the third, which I have pursued more fully elsewhere.[3] I begin by spelling out the structure of functional explanation as commonly employed, and my objections to it. I then survey the main instances of functional explanation in Marx, including his philosophy of history, the theory of the development of the productive forces, the theory of the political and ideological superstructure and miscellaneous other matters. Most of these are also more fully discussed in later chapters.

1.4.1. The nature of functional explanation

Intentional explanation cites the *intended* consequences of behaviour in order to account for it. Functional explanation cites the *actual* consequences. More specifically, to explain behaviour functionally involves demonstrating that it has *beneficial* consequences for someone or something. There is an apparent paradox in this formulation that must be removed before we proceed: how can behaviour be explained in terms of

---

[1] Sartre, *Critique de la Raison Dialectique*, pp. 232ff.
[2] Marx to Engels 25.3.1868.
[3] See especially my *Explaining Technical Change*, ch. 2 and "Marxism, functionalism and game theory".

something that occurs at a time posterior to it? The answer[1] is that the explanandum cannot be an individual event, but rather must be a persisting pattern of behaviour, so that the occurrence of the behaviour at time t_1 has consequences that contribute to its occurrence at time t_2. In other words, functional explanation presupposes the existence of a feedback loop from the explanans back to the explanandum.

In this book I shall be concerned with functional explanations of a rather crude kind. These are the attempts to explain behaviour *simply* by pointing to the fact that it has beneficial consequences for some agent or agents. Clearly, this is an extremely unsatisfactory mode of explanation. Many beneficial consequences of actions arise in a purely accidental, non-explanatory manner. Moreover, by a suitable choice of the time at which the chain of consequences is cut off, and of the group of agents that benefit from the behaviour, one will be able to generate an indefinite number of "explanations" of the same explanandum. Hence it might appear highly implausible that anyone would ever attempt to explain social phenomena in this frictionless manner. Yet I believe the book will make it clear that I am not setting up a straw man. Marx had a strong propensity to use this kind of explanation, without pausing to provide any kind of backing for it. Also, many proponents of non-Marxist functionalist sociology have offered similar explanations.[2] This practice is so puzzling that it would itself seem to call for an explanation. In my opinion its roots are to be sought both in the history of ideas and in individual psychology; but this is not the place to pursue these rather speculative ideas.[3]

Let me briefly point to some ways in which functional explanation could be made intellectually respectable. Clearly, the best way would be to provide the actual mechanism by which the consequence feeds back on the behaviour to be explained. Typically, this would either be some analogy to natural selection, explaining the presence of patterns of behaviour by the differential survival of the entities exhibiting them, or some kind of filter process, explaining the behaviour by the ability of the beneficiaries to favour it over other possible forms of action.[4] Alternatively, one might be able to give reasons for thinking that some such mechanism must be operating, even if one is not able to specify it in any

[1] Or at least one answer: for an alternative conception, see Cohen, "Functional explanation, consequence explanation and Marxism".
[2] Similarly, the tendency of many economists to assume that the proof of the existence of an equilibrium also ensures that it will be realized can be seen as a variety of functionalism.
[3] See *Sour Grapes*, ch. II.10.
[4] Cp. van Parijs, *Evolutionary Explanation in the Social Sciences*.

given case. One might argue, that is, on general theoretical grounds that there is a tendency in societies to evolve behavioural patterns that have certain stabilizing consequences, or at least do not have destabilizing effects.[1] Hence whenever behaviour with such consequences is observed, there is a presumption that it occurs *because* it has these consequences. Lastly, one might try to eliminate the possibility that the benefits arise in an accidental way by establishing a lawlike regularity between the behaviour and the consequences. Specifically, one might set out to establish a *consequence law* to the effect that whenever the explanandum would have certain beneficial consequences, then it is observed to occur.[2] Of these three forms of backing, the first is equivalent to the substitution of a non-functional explanation for the functional one. The other two retain the specifically functional form of explanation, but seek to avoid the arbitrary features spelled out in the preceding paragraph. In this book I need not discuss whether they succeed in this task, since it is certain that Marx did not propose any of these sophisticated versions of functionalism. Perhaps some of his claims could be backed by one of the sophisticated versions. I shall not discuss this possibility, except to state that I have not come across any convincing attempts to do so.

1.4.2. Philosophy of history

I discuss Marx's theory of history in 2.4 below, and then again in 5.3. Here I shall only make a few remarks on the – very intimate – relation between his philosophy of history and his predilection for functional explanation. It was certainly because Marx believed history to be directed towards a goal – the advent of communist society – that he felt justified in explaining, not only patterns of behaviour, but even individual events, in terms of their contribution to that end. Thus in 7.2.1 I argue that his attitude towards the bourgeois revolutions was deeply influenced by his belief that the bourgeoisie *had to* fulfil its historical mission of bringing about capitalism, so that the workers could be enabled to go on to communism. This, moreover, had practical as well as theoretical consequences, since Marx's own strategy in the German revolution of 1848 derived from this a priori view.

The philosophy of history warrants explanation in terms of consequences that are beneficial for the ultimate advent of communism. In other contexts, Marx argues that social institutions and forms of

---

[1] Cp. Stinchcombe, "Merton's theory of social structure".
[2] Cohen, *Karl Marx's Theory of History*, ch. IX.

behaviour are to be explained by their stabilizing effect on class domination. He can thus play on two registers, sometimes invoking the demise of capitalism and sometimes its continued existence as the explanatory benefit. This introduces an additional element of *ad hoc*-ness that plagues many varieties of functionalist Marxism. True, the two perspectives are not necessarily incompatible. If capitalism, for instance, is to dig its own grave, it must be left with rope to hang itself (if I am allowed a mix of metaphors). The subjective and objective conditions for communism are developed *pari passu* with capitalism itself, hence what benefits capitalism in the short run may undermine its reproduction in the long run. Yet, to anticipate an objection to be made in 2.4.1 below, long-term consequences do not have explanatory power unless an intentional actor is present who deliberately sacrifices short-term benefits. This point also applies to the inverse mode of reasoning: some institutions may be explained by long-term benefits to the capitalist mode of production, even if their immediate consequence is to the detriment of the capitalist class. This explanatory pattern is especially prominent in the Marxist theory of the state (7.1).

1.4.3. The development of the productive forces

G. A. Cohen has made a powerful argument for the view that, on Marx's theory, the primacy of the productive forces must be explanatory rather than straightforwardly causal, and that the explanation must in fact be a functional one. He derives this conclusion from two premises. (i) Marx asserted the primacy of the productive forces over the relations of production. (ii) Marx also admitted, in fact insisted on, the causal efficacy of the relations of production in developing the productive forces. There is no other way, Cohen submits, of rendering these compatible with one another than by explaining the relations functionally, in terms of their capacity to develop the productive forces. The relations of production obtain because and so long as they are optimal for the development of the productive forces. In a subsequent exchange with Philippe van Parijs, Cohen has made it clear that there is also a causal component in the argument for primacy. It is the level attained by the productive forces that (causally) explains why a certain set of relations of production are optimal for their further development.[1]

I return to these issues in chapter 5 below. Here I want only to warn against confusing the exegetical issue with the substantial one. I believe

---

[1] For this discussion, see Cohen, *Karl Marx's Theory of History*, ch. VI; van Parijs, "Marxism's central puzzle"; Cohen, "Reply to four critics".

Cohen has shown that the primacy of the productive forces must be understood functionally, but in doing so he has also contributed to showing how implausible the primacy thesis is. In my opinion, he does not establish that Marx provided his explanation with the kind of *backing* that would be required for taking it seriously. Moreover, even on grounds of internal consistency Marx is open to criticism. His accounts of the transitions from feudalism to capitalism and from capitalism to communism do not rest on the optimality of the new relations of production for the development of the productive forces.

1.4.4. The theory of the capitalist state
In Marx, as in later Marxist writings, this is the privileged terrain for functional explanation. It is easy to see why this came to be so. Some time around 1850 Marx abandoned his view that the state was a mere instrument in the hands of the economically dominant capitalist class. The state undeniably took some account of working-class interests, and increasingly appeared to have interests of its own as well. Yet Marx was struck by the fact that this very deviation from the instrumental pattern also seemed quite useful to the capitalist class, since a one-to-one correspondence between state action and capitalist interest could have provoked the working class to far more dangerous claims than those which were in fact granted. From recognizing the long-run benefits to the capitalist class of state actions that (in the short run) go against its interest, there was but a short step to the conclusion that the benefits *explain* the concessions made to the workers or the autonomous state policies.

According to the usual Marxist view, the state is part of the superstructure and as such is dependent on the economic structure. G. A. Cohen argues, convincingly, that this is to beg central questions. Rather it is the other way around: the state depends on the economic structure, and for that reason (and to that extent) is part of the superstructure. This allows us more precisely than the first formulation to identify the empirical issue at stake, namely whether the state does in fact depend on the economic base. Instead of the ambiguous phrase "depends on the economic base", Cohen more precisely writes "is explained by the nature of the economic structure".[1] This would suggest the following definition: the state is part of the superstructure to the extent that it can be explained by the economic structure. Later in his book Cohen proposes a more narrow definition, according to which only functional explanation can provide

[1] Cohen, *Karl Marx's Theory of History*, p. 216.

the link between base and superstructure.[1] On this view the state is part of the superstructure only to the extent that it has a stabilizing effect on the relations of production. His analysis is carried out in detail only for the legal part of the superstructure, but one definitely has the impression that it is intended to be valid for the other parts as well. In this subsection and in the following I want to question the contention that a functional explanation is needed to establish an institution as part of the superstructure. True, the institution must be linked to the base by some explanatory connection, but the explanation may be causal as well as functional.

I shall first discuss a pair of contrasting cases that would appear to support (what I take to be) Cohen's view. Consider first mid-nineteenth-century England. Here, Marx argued in the articles quoted in 6.3.3 and 7.1.4, the distribution of economic power was such that the capitalists had much, the aristocracy some and the workers none of it. On the other hand, political power was distributed so that the aristocracy had much, the capitalists some and the workers none. (This might appear to beg some questions about what constitutes political power in class societies. I return to this issue in 7.1.2.) Marx suggested that the latter distribution is to be explained, à la Cohen, by its stabilizing impact on the former. On the other hand, Marx argued that during a brief period in 1848 the French bourgeoisie held both economic and political power, the latter deriving directly from the former. This situation, however, proved unstable, whence the *coup d'état* of Louis Bonaparte whereby the bourgeoisie was "delivered from the dangers of its own rule". This tends to confirm Cohen's view, that viable political systems can be explained by their tendency to stabilize the economic structure, and that systems which are incompatible with the latter soon disappear. Yet I want to question a premise implicit in this view, namely that there is no "zone of satisfaction" between optimality and incompatibility.

Consider the political system of the Roman world,[2] a society in which economic and political superiority coincided systematically. There is a clear sense in which the latter was derived from and explicable through the former, since wealth – although often enhanced by political power – was a precondition for entering the political arena in the first place. It is arguable that this arrangement was far from optimal for the dominant class of senatorial landowners who, as politicians, were excessively

---

[1] "There is no well-stated alternative to the view that major Marxian explanatory claims are functional in character" (*ibid.*, p. 279). The following discussion is intended to point to one such alternative.

[2] The following sketch is based on my reading of Veyne, *Le Pain et le Cirque*, and Ste Croix, *The Class Struggle in the Ancient Greek World*.

influenced by short-term greed. It might well have been wiser had they left political matters in the hands of some other class or group, more capable of taking the long view; yet this they did not do. The exercise of power was a heady experience that they were not likely to give up, and in any case they could get away with being greedy. Although far from an optimal stabilizing arrangement, the system was "good enough" for the survival of the economic structure.[1] It would be strange to say that this political system cannot be explained by the economic relations, since in fact it was derived from them in a particularly simple and transparent way. Within the Marxist tradition one would certainly say that the political institutions were part of the superstructure, and yet they were not explicable by their stabilizing influence on the economic relations. The relation between economics and politics in this case was straight-forwardly *causal*. Economic wealth formed the power base for political activity. And it will not do, I think, to argue that in the very long run the Roman world was destroyed precisely because of the short-term greed of the landowners, since – unlike the French case – the outcome was the decline of the ancient mode of production altogether, rather than a change of political regime to adjust to the mode of production.

1.4.5. The theory of ideology

An argument can be made concerning belief systems that parallels the one just stated for politics. There is a strong tendency in Marxism to explain, say, religion or bourgeois political economy in terms of their stabilizing influence on the prevailing relations of production. As mentioned in 1.3.1, Marx also offers an alternative account of belief for-mation in terms of causal processes that operate "behind the back" of individuals, whereby their class position or class interest is reflected in their beliefs and values. Such beliefs and values satisfy Cohen's more general definition of superstructural entities, since they are non-economic phenomena that can be explained by the economic structure, yet they do not tend to stabilize the latter. On the contrary, since distorted and illusionary beliefs tend in general to weaken the economic position of the agents entertaining them, the ideological beliefs of the members of the ruling class tend to undermine their domination.

In conclusion, then, I cannot accept Cohen's suggestion that the super-structure is to be defined exclusively as non-economic phenomena that

---

[1] For the relation between satisficing and functional explanation, see van Parijs, *Evolutionary Explanation in the Social Sciences* §52, and my review "A paradigm for the social sciences?"

can be explained by their stabilizing influence on the relations of production. I find his first, general definition more satisfactory. Any non-economic phenomenon is part of the superstructure if it can be explained in terms of the economic structure. True, this destroys the homogeneity of the superstructure, which now becomes a hodgepodge of phenomena that relate to the economic structure in a variety of ways, without any presumption that they are in general beneficial for the latter. Still I believe that my proposal is at least as plausible exegetically,[1] and more in conformity with the later Marxist tradition. I should add that nothing important turns upon this issue, and that it would be pointless to discuss at length whether beliefs that can be explained non-functionally in terms of the economic structure belong or not to the superstructure. The substantive issue, on which Cohen and I may disagree, concerns the existence and centrality of such beliefs, not how they are to be labelled. The same holds for non-functional explanation of the state. The issue is not whether such explanations, if successful, would justify the inclusion of the state in the superstructure, but whether and how often they will prove successful.

1.4.6. Miscellanea

I have given relatively little textual evidence so far of Marx's tendency to engage in functional explanation, referring the reader to later chapters for examples and details. I now want to consider some instances of functional explanation that do not fall neatly into the later chapters, and which are for that reason treated here. There is, in fact, a set of social phenomena that do not fit into the traditional Marxist categories, such as base or superstructure. They include family life, education, social mobility, leisure activities, the distribution of mental and physical health, crime etc. Modern Marxist sociologists have provided functional explanations for most of these phenomena, almost invariably invalid.[2] Marx himself had relatively little to say about them, since his mind was focussed on

---

[1] In the Preface to *A Critique of Political Economy* Marx says that "consciousness must be explained . . . from the contradictions of material life, from the existing conflict between the social productive forces and the relations of production". This is compatible with my analysis, and incompatible with Cohen's view that the superstructure is to be explained in terms of the relations of production alone, by the stabilizing influence on the latter. The passage, however, is not incompatible with the more general view that the explanation must be a functional one. On the other hand one may invoke a passage from *Theories of Surplus-Value*, cited more fully at the end of 1.4.6, which states that "the superstructure of ideological strata" can be explained functionally. I doubt, however, whether Cohen would care to appeal to this text, since it would also justify the imputation to Marx of a crude, wholesale functionalism.

[2] For examples, see my "Marxism, functionalism and game theory".

economics, class struggle and politics, at the expense of the texture of everyday life. Among the relevant passages, at least one is quite revealing of his cavalier attitude to the canons of explanation. It occurs in *Capital III*, immediately before the true and important statement that "the more a ruling class is able to assimilate the foremost minds of a ruled class, the more stable and dangerous becomes its rule". The reasoning leading up to this conclusion is, however, more suspect:

The circumstance that a man without fortune, but possessing energy, solidity and business acumen may become a capitalist in this manner – and the commercial value of each individual is pretty accurately estimated under the capitalist mode of production – is greatly admired by apologists of the capitalist system. Although this circumstance continually brings an unwelcome number of new soldiers of fortune into the field and into competition with the already existing individual capitalists, it also reinforces the supremacy of capital itself, expands its base and enables it to recruit ever new forces for itself out of the substratum of society. In a similar way, the circumstance that the Catholic Church in the Middle Ages formed its hierarchy out of the best brains in the land, regardless of their estate, birth and fortune, was one of the principal means of consolidating ecclesiastical rule and suppressing the laity.[1]

I read this as an explanation of social mobility in terms of its beneficial consequences for the ruling class, with no attempt to suggest a mechanism beyond that of the action of "capital" or the Catholic Church. The latter, of course, was a collective actor and as such capable in principle of devising a deliberate recruitment policy for the purpose mentioned, although Marx offers no evidence that it actually did so. "Capital", however, is not a collective actor; it does not "recruit new forces". The statement is both a violation of methodological individualism and an instance of invalid functional explanation.

A second passage is more ambiguous. Some would say that it was written with tongue in cheek and does not provide evidence for any predilection for functional explanation. This is the long digression on crime and productive labour in *Theories of Surplus-Value*, from which a few passages are excerpted:

A philosopher produces ideas, a poet poems, a clergyman sermons, a professor compendia and so on . . . The criminal produces not only crimes, but also criminal law, and with this also the professor who gives lectures on criminal law and in addition to this the inevitable compendium in which this same professor throws his lectures onto the general market as "commodities" . . . The criminal produces an impression, partly moral and partly tragic, as the case may be, and in this way renders a "service" by arousing the moral and aesthetic feelings of the public . . .

[1] *Capital III*, pp. 600–1.

The criminal breaks the monotony and everyday security of bourgeois life. In this way he keeps it from stagnation, and gives rise to that uneasy tension and agility without which even the spur of competition would get blunted . . .

The effects of the criminal on the development of productive power can be shown in detail. Would locks ever have reached their present degree of excellence had there been no thieves?[1]

The argument is a parody on Mandeville's "private vices, public benefits", with the added intention of being a *reductio ad absurdum* argument against the view of some vulgar economists that all professions are productive. It certainly cannot be taken as evidence that Marx wanted to explain crime by these various benefits to the social order, in spite of the deadpan seriousness with which the passage has been read by some Marxist criminologists.[2] Yet my impression, for what it is worth, is that Marx to some extent was carried away by the exercise. In particular, the observation that crime keeps capitalism from stagnation is not dissimilar to the comments on the benefits for "capital" of social mobility. If one already believes on other grounds that Marx tended to use functional explanation in an unwarranted manner, the cited passage may be read as a half-serious explanation of crime, but, to repeat, it does not itself provide any such grounds.

To add some plausibility to this reading, I shall cite another passage from the *Theories of Surplus-Value* where Marx makes fun of an opponent while also trying to bring out the rational core in his views. The argument he attacks is that of some bourgeois economists that all activities – especially their own! – are productive labour. Marx characterizes this as "nonsense", and adds that it can be "reduced to the following":

1. that the various functions in bourgeois society mutually presuppose each other;
2. that the contradictions in material production make necessary a superstructure of ideological strata, whose activity – whether good or bad – is good, because it is necessary;
3. that all functions are in the service of the capitalist, and work out to his "benefit";
4. that even the most sublime spiritual productions should merely be granted recognition, and *apologies* for them made to the bourgeoisie, that they are presented as, and falsely proved to be, direct producers of material wealth.[3]

I believe it is plausible, but not compellingly so, to impute to Marx the views he states as the "reduction" of "nonsense" – presumably a reduction with the purpose of making sense of it. If this reading is accepted, the

---

[1] *Theories of Surplus-Value*, vol. 1, pp. 387–8.
[2] See for instance Chambliss, "The political economy of crime".
[3] *Theories of Surplus-Value*, vol. 1, p. 287.

passage supports the view that Marx had a strong functionalist methodology. It also suggests that the digression on crime may be taken somewhat more seriously than one would otherwise do. Yet as will be made abundantly clear in later chapters, I rest my case for Marx's use of functional explanation on much more solid grounds.

1.5. Dialectics

Marx, on numerous occasions, invoked the "dialectical method" as a privileged approach to the analysis of social phenomena. Did Marx practise any such method? If so, was it a help or a hindrance to understanding? It is not easy to answer these questions. When Marx explicitly refers to dialectics, it is usually in such general, even vapid terms, that it is hard to see what implications they have for more specific analyses.[1] Although he repeatedly intended to set out the rational core of the Hegelian dialectics,[2] he never got around to doing so. Any reconstruction of this method must, therefore, be very tentative. I shall discuss three strands of Hegelian reasoning in Marx, each of which has a claim to be called, if not *the* dialectical method, at least *a* dialectical method. The first is the quasi-deductive procedure used in central parts of the *Grundrisse* and in the opening chapters of *Capital I*, inspired above all by Hegel's *Logic*. The second is the dialectic as codified by Engels, including the "laws" of the negation of the negation and of the transformation of quantity into quality. The third is a theory of social contradictions, derived largely from the *Phenomenology of Spirit*. I shall argue that of these, the first is barely intelligible; the second has a certain, although somewhat limited interest; while the third emerges as an important tool for the theory of social change. In each of the more interesting interpretations, the dialectical method can be stated in ordinary "analytical" language, thus offering no brief to those who believe in a radical divide between these two modes of reasoning.

1.5.1. Dialectical deduction

Hegel, in *The Science of Logic*, derived the various ontological categories from each other according to certain deductive principles which have resisted analysis to this day. The connection is neither that of cause to effect, nor that of axiom to theorem, nor finally that of given fact to its condition of possibility. The "self-determination of the concept" appears

---

[1] In particular, the Preface to the second German edition of *Capital I* quotes approvingly a description of the dialectical method that, on closer reading, appears devoid of content.

[2] Marx to Engels 16.1.1858; Marx to Dietzen 9.5.1868.

to be nothing more than a loose *ex post* pattern imposed by Hegel on various phenomena that he found important. At the time he was working on the *Grundrisse* Marx reread Hegel's work, with a visible influence not only on that manuscript, but on parts of *Capital* as well.[1] In particular, he believed it possible to deduce the economic categories from one another in a way reminiscent of what Hegel had done for ontology. Yet, unlike the Hegelian categories, the economic ones also succeed each other chronologically, in the order of their historical appearance. Hence Marx had to confront the question of how the logical sequence is related to the historical one, without being able, however, to provide a consistent answer.[2]

If we attempt a synthesis of the *Grundrisse* and the opening chapters of *Capital I*, the logical or dialectical sequence embodies the following stages: product – commodity – exchange value – money – capital – labour. The first links in the chain are thus summarized in the *Grundrisse*:

> The product becomes a commodity; the commodity becomes exchange value; the exchange value of the commodity is its immanent money-property; this, its money-property, separates itself from it in the form of money, and achieves a general social existence separated from all particular commodities and their natural mode of existence; the relation of the product to itself as exchange value becomes its relation to money, existing alongside it; or, becomes the relation of all products to money, external to them all. Just as the real exchange of products creates their exchange value, so does their exchange value create money.[3]

Clearly, this is no explanation of what drives the process, only a fancy redescription of the successive stages. Marx himself must have felt this, since a few pages later he added that:

> It will be necessary later, before this question is dropped, to correct the idealist manner of presentation, which makes it seem as if it were merely a matter of conceptual determination and of the dialectic of these concepts. Above all in the case of the phrase: product (or activity) becomes commodity; commodity, exchange value; exchange value, money.[4]

Yet roughly the same sequence (beginning, however, with commodities rather than with products in general) is retained in *Capital I*, where it has confused and deterred innumerable readers. I argue in 5.3.3 that the sequence in its historical interpretation makes some empirical sense, but the logico-dialectical deduction remains vacuous.

---

[1] Marx to Engels 16.1.1858.

[2] For inconclusive discussions of the relation between historical and theoretical (i.e. dialectical) development, see *Grundrisse*, pp. 102, 107, 247, 276, 505, 672 and the letter to Engels of 2.4.1858.

[3] *Grundrisse*, pp. 146–7.   [4] *Ibid.*, p. 151.

The further transition from money to capital occupies some of the most dazzlingly obscure pages in the *Grundrisse*. This passage is representative:

We have already seen, in the case of money, how value, having become independent as such – or the general form of wealth – is capable of no other motion than a
quantitative one; to increase itself. It is according to its concept the quintessence of
all use values; but, since it is always only a definite amount of money (here,
capital), its quantitative limit is in contradiction with its quality. It is therefore
inherent in its nature constantly to drive beyond its own barrier ... Already for
that reason, value which insists on itself as value preserves itself through increase;
and it preserves itself precisely only by constantly driving beyond its quantitative
barrier, which contradicts its character as form, its inner generality.[1]

Marx here tries to perform with a conceptual sleight of hand the task to which Max Weber devoted vast empirical studies: to explain the emergence of the reinvestment motive in early capitalism. No short-cut, however, is possible – unless one already has the answer. The explanation of saving and investment must be found in the motives of individual economic agents. It cannot be derived from a conceptual analysis of money.

Having deduced capital – that is self-expanding value – from the con-
cept of money, Marx has to explain how the creation of a surplus is possible. In well-known dramatic pages in *Capital I* Marx sets the scene for a derivation of labour-power as the condition of possibility for the existence of a general surplus, as opposed to the surplus that any commodity-
owner may realize at the expense of others.[2] As further explained in 3.2.3, the deduction is invalid, since any commodity may be taken as the one whose exploitation makes the economy productive and hence makes a surplus possible. Yet this is a honest mistake, unlike the fundamentally misguided reasoning that underlies the attempt to deduce capital from money. Still, even had the derivation of labour from capital been successful, it is hard to see what insight would thereby have been gained. Surely the demonstration would not provide an explanation of the presence of exploited labour in the production process, since the premise – the exist-
ence of capital – is itself derived in such a shaky manner.

The defects of the conceptual deduction are linked to those of methodological collectivism. It is, in fact, difficult to decide whether the self-determination of capital is conceptual or behavioural – or whether we are meant to conclude that this very distinction is superseded. In arguing against these practices one encounters the familiar difficulty of refuting a

[1] *Ibid.*, p. 270; see also *Capital I*, pp. 151–2.   [2] *Capital I*, pp. 167ff.

confused position which, by its very incoherence, resists being pinned down sufficiently to allow a precise rebuttal. I have tried to mount attacks from several quarters, in the hope that their cumulative impact will prove persuasive.

1.5.2. The laws of dialectics

Engels, in *Anti-Dühring*, stated two dialectical laws, that of the negation of the negation and that of the transformation of quantity into quality. (In the posthumously published *Dialectics of Nature* he added a third and more general law, which I shall ignore.) Some of the illustrations he cites for these laws are quite extravagantly silly, but this does not mean that it is impossible to make sense of the laws themselves, as has often been argued by analytically-minded readers.[1] True, in order to make them appear plausible one has to reduce them from "laws" to something like "not infrequent patterns of change". Also, one must try to make these patterns the object of explicit definition, rather than having them embedded in and obscured by a welter of heterogeneous "examples". The definitions proposed below draw on a more homogeneous subset of examples, with no pretension to cover all the cases cited by Engels.

A paradigm case of the negation of the negation is the transition from capitalism to communism, cited by Engels as well as by Marx.[2] It instantiates the pattern – further discussed in 2.4.2 – of an undifferentiated unity, followed by differentiation and splitting (first negation) and then the establishment of a higher, differentiated unity (second negation). One might equally well have used the language of thesis, antithesis and synthesis, although Marx avoids this terminology and in fact scorns those who tend to search for such triads everywhere.[3] Tentatively, I suggest that the characteristic feature of this process is the presence of three successive stages – p, q and r – such that (i) they are pairwise incompatible with one another, (ii) the step from p directly to r is impossible and (iii) the step from q back to p is impossible. The pattern could also be illustrated by some instances of belief formation, beginning with dogmatic belief, passing through doubt and arriving finally at a more reflective belief.[4] It is clearly a common, but far from universal pattern of change. It is restricted in two different ways. First, the pattern is not found in the processes themselves, only in certain descriptions of them. A given process may

---

[1] For a total dismissal, see for instance Acton, "Dialectical materialism".
[2] *Capital I*, p. 763.
[3] Marx to Engels 8.1.1868; Marx to Engels 11.5.1870.
[4] Tocqueville, *Democracy in America*, pp. 186–7 has a good analysis of this process: "deep conviction lies at the two ends, with doubt in the middle".

exhibit the pattern under one description, but not under another. Secondly, the pattern does not appear to fit all processes equally well – some processes do not appear to exhibit it under any interesting description.[1]

To refer to a process as an instance of the negation of the negation, then, is *only* to draw attention to the fact that it can be interestingly described in a characterization with these features. It is emphatically not to suggest that there exists a specifically dialectical form of negation that, unlike the standard logical negation, does not cancel when iterated. I should add, however, that in one context Marx employs the phrase in a way that appears to suggest the latter, more ambitious idea. In his mathematical manuscripts he tried to make sense of the operation of differentiation as an instance of the negation of the negation. He notes first that if, in the function $y = ax$, we let x increase to x_1 and y correspondingly to $y_1 = ax_1$, the difference $y_1 - y = a(x_1 - x)$ reduces to $0 = 0$ when again we let x_1 approach x. He then adds that:

> To first posit differentiation and then again to suppress it, leads, then, literally to *nothing*. The whole difficulty of understanding the operation of differentiation – as with the *negation of the negation* quite generally – lies precisely in seeing how it differs from this simple procedure and therefore leads to real results.[2]

The idea is not taken up in the later development of the argument. Let me mention as an aside that Marx's treatment of the calculus, while not in any way original, is at least more cautious and coherent than anything offered by Engels. The latter, in some of the most reckless pages of *Anti-Dühring*, referred to the mysterious fraction $0/0$ as proof of the power of the dialectic to get something from nothing.[3] He took the differential calculus to prove the reality of contradictions, whereas Marx tried to bring out the rational form of the calculus in which it can dispense with them. He recognized that the differentials dx and dy have meaning only in a context, not in themselves; that the notion of a limit was central in demystifying the infinitesimals; that the "infinitely small" quantities should really be called "indefinitely small"; and that the rational form that d'Alembert gave to the calculus was preferable to its mystical expression in Newton or Leibniz.

From the examples given by Engels, it would appear that the transformation of quantity into quality covers two cases, one being a special instance of the other. First, the water-into-ice example suggests the notion of a *discontinuous* functional link between the independent variable

---

[1] For instance, there do not appear to be processes in inorganic or organic (non-human) nature that can be interestingly described in this way. If not, this has some relevance for the issue whether there can be a "dialectics of nature".

[2] *Mathematische Manuskripte*, p. 51.

[3] *Anti-Dühring*, p. 128.

and the dependent one. Secondly, the amusing military example that Engels takes from Napoleon, that whereas two Mamelukes are superior in combat to three Frenchmen, 1000 Frenchmen will beat 1500 Mamelukes, suggests the more general notion of a *non-linear* functional relation. The notion of economies of scale is a more familiar illustration, also employed by Marx in one of his few references to this idea.[1] It requires no lengthy argument to see that there are indeed many natural and social processes with the properties of discontinuity and non-linearity, nor to understand that not all processes have these features.[2] Yet to remind us of them may be a useful task, since it is so much easier to study the world using linear or at least continuous models, and since it is tempting to believe that features which are privileged at the level of model-building are so in reality as well.

Let me briefly comment on a more general argument often advanced in this connection: although direct references to the laws of dialectics are infrequent in Marx's work, he is known to have read the manuscript of *Anti-Dühring* and would surely have protested had he disagreed. I believe this view to be misguided. Marx was constitutionally incapable of arriving at his conclusions without deep, prolonged and independent study – always seeking out original sources and developing his own views only when he had thoroughly assimilated them. In a letter to Engels he points out with some pride that "whatever shortcomings [my writings] may have, they have the advantage of forming an artistic whole, which can only be achieved through my method of never letting them into print before they lie *wholly* before me".[3] This is indeed a good description of his published work, and a good explanation of why many of his manuscripts remained unpublished. It is an attitude wholly foreign to second-hand acceptance of ideas. He had the best of personal reasons for taking a friendly interest in Engels's work and occasionally referring to it, but this does not warrant the conclusion that he fully endorsed it. It is a fallacy to think that lack of active disagreement implies active acceptance.[4] More tentatively, I find it hard to believe that Marx would have come to accept the laws of dialectics had he

---

[1] *Capital I*, p. 309. Here (as well as in the letter to Engels of 22.6.1867) he also refers to what he thought to be an analogical phenomenon in organic chemistry, citing three chemists, one of whom he singled out as especially important. In the second edition of *Capital I* only the other two are retained, while in the third edition Engels had to explain that Marx had overestimated their importance as well. As also shown by his comments on Fraas and Trémaux, cited in 2.1 below, Marx had poor judgment with respect to the natural sciences.

[2] For an extensive discussion, see Georgescu-Roegen, *The Entropy Law and the Economic Process*.

[3] Marx to Engels 31.7.1865.

[4] Alexander Zinoviev argues that this fallacy is at the core of the regimes that claim to embody Marx's teachings, or rather what they fallaciously conclude to be his teachings, among them the laws of dialectics. For an exposition of his views, see my "Négation active et négation passive".

put his mind to them. He was invariably critical of all attempts, from Proudhon to Lassalle, to apply the Hegelian mode of reasoning in a mechanical way. Referring to Lassalle's philosophy of law, he says that "the dialectical method is incorrectly applied. Hegel never referred to the subsumption of a mass of 'cases' under a general principle as dialectics".[1] Yet Engels's attempt to formulate laws of dialectics is precisely that – the subsumption of miscellaneous cases under general principles.

1.5.3. The theory of contradictions

In *Capital I* Marx observes that J. S. Mill, while capable of contradicting himself trivially, yet "feels at sea in the Hegelian contradiction, the source of all dialectic".[2] Among analytical philosophers, the Hegelian contradiction has rather been thought to be a source of confusion.[3] In this they are no doubt largely right. Yet I shall argue that there is a sense in which one may, meaningfully, speak of "real contradictions" and that a powerful methodology may be constructed on that basis. First, however, I want to eliminate the unacceptable sense in which one sometimes speaks of contradictions in reality, implying that a statement and its negation can both be true at the same time and in the same respect. Hegel certainly appears to have believed that this state could obtain – indeed, that it had to obtain if change and motion were to be possible at all.[4] Modern logicians, with some exceptions, have dismissed the idea as ridiculous.[5] There are few passages in Marx that lend themselves to this reading, none of them very important.[6] They belong to the same residue from Hegel's *Logic* that was discussed and dismissed above.

Unlike some later Marxists, Marx did not use the term "contradiction" to denote every form of conflict, struggle or opposition. This fact has been obscured by a frequent mistranslation, whereby not only "Widerspruch" but also "Gegensatz" are rendered into English (and French) by "contradiction".[7] As a student of Hegel, Marx was extremely unlikely to use these terms interchangeably, and there are in fact clear differences in the

---

[1] Marx to Engels 9.12.1861.

[2] *Capital I*, p. 596.

[3] See for instance Popper, "What is dialectic?"

[4] Hegel, *The Science of Logic*, vol. II, p. 67.

[5] An ambitious attempt to defend the possibility of contradictory states of affairs is Routley and Meyer, "Dialectical logic, classical logic and the consistency of the world". Johansson, "Der Minimalkül", showed that in some weak logical systems contradictions can be contained, so that the admission of one contradictory statement does not commit us to the acceptance of all contradictory statements, as in the standard logical calculi.

[6] For an example see *Grundrisse*, p. 401.

[7] For examples, see Marx and Engels, *Collected Works*, vol. 5, pp. 52, 432; vol. 10, p. 589; vol. 14, p. 143; *Capital III*, pp. 386, 440.

way he uses them. Most importantly, he never to my knowledge refers to a struggle between two classes as a "contradiction", only as an "opposition".[1] I do not claim that Marx uses "contradiction" in one, unified, sense, but he certainly does not employ the term to refer indiscriminately to the broad range of phenomena covered, for instance, in Mao's essay "On contradiction".

Is it possible, then, to define a sense in which the notion of real contradictions remains firmly tied to the logical concept, without committing us to accept the truth of contradictory statements? Having explained in some detail elsewhere how this can be accomplished, I shall only briefly indicate it here.[2] Following the *Phenomenology of Spirit*, as well as the writings of Jean-Paul Sartre, I distinguish between psychological and social contradictions. The former obtain in mental states that are contradictory in their content, that is when one individual simultaneously entertains beliefs and desires from which a contradiction can be logically derived. The latter – which form my sole topic here – obtain when several individuals simultaneously entertain beliefs about each other which are such that, although any one of them may well be true, it is logically impossible that they all be. An important special case arises when a particular description that may be true of *any* agent, for purely logical reasons cannot be true of *all*. If the individuals having these mutually invalidating beliefs about each other all act as if they were true, their actions will come to grief through the mechanism of unintended consequences sketched in 1.3.2. In condensed jargon, counterfinality is the embodiment of the fallacy of composition.

The structures of this variety discussed by Marx overlap with his uses of the term "contradiction", although neither set is included in the other. I first set out the two central uses of the term "contradiction" that refer to the fallacy of composition and, in one case, to counterfinality. They are central both by virtue of their theoretical importance in Marxism, and by the fact that they occur in the title or the subtitle of a chapter, suggesting that Marx did not use them without some specific idea in mind.

In *Capital I* there is a subsection (which became a chapter in the English translation) called "The contradiction in the general formula of capital". It

---

[1] Marx does occasionally, however, refer to the relation between capital and labour as a "contradiction", contrary to what I wrote in *Logic and Society*, p. 90, note 1. See for instance *Zur Kritik (1861–63)*, pp. 2014, 2056. This, however, is not a reference to the class struggle, but a statement of the fact that capital tends both to employ as little labour as possible (to reduce the wage bill) and as much labour as possible (to increase surplus-value).

[2] For a fuller statement, see *Logic and Society*, chs. 4 and 5, as well as my "Négation active et négation passive".

appears, Marx argued, that "capital must have its origin both in circulation and yet not in circulation".[1] On the one hand, how "can surplus-value originate anywhere else than in circulation, which is the sum total of all the mutual relations of commodity-owners, as far as they are determined by their commodities"?[2] On the other hand, it can be shown that the assumption that surplus-value arises in circulation involves the fallacy of composition. Marx quotes Destutt de Tracy to the effect that "industrial capitalists make profits because 'they all sell for more than it has cost to produce. And to whom do they sell? In the first instance to one another'", and then goes on to comment that: "The capitalist class as a whole, in any country, cannot overreach themselves."[3] Any commodity-owner may profit at the expense of others, but the exchange as a whole must be constant-sum. The way out of this dilemma is given by the deduction, mentioned earlier, of the buying and selling of labour-power as the condition of possibility of surplus-value, showing that the contradiction was an apparent one only. Hence the structure of the argument is this. Surplus-value must originate in circulation, since the assumption that it does not is absurd. Yet the assumption that it does arise in circulation can be made to look plausible only by committing the fallacy of composition, generalizing the local possibility of cheating to the self-contradictory theory of a circular and universal cheating. The argument is very elaborately staged for the purpose of springing labour-power as a surprise on the stunned reader, but it is not really a substantial piece of reasoning. Whatever interest it has I find in the logical contrast between what any commodity-owner can do and what all can do.

A central chapter in *Capital III* is titled "Exposition of the internal contradictions of the law", the law being that of the tendency of the rate of profit to fall. The phrasing is unfortunate, and unfortunately appropriate, as will be seen in 3.4.2, but Marx surely intended it to convey a contradiction in the world, not in his theory. The contradiction involved in the fall of the rate of profit is a very nebulous one, but there is at least one passage that comes close to suggesting the mechanism of counterfinality:

No capitalist ever voluntarily introduces a new method of production, no matter how much more productive it may be, and how much it may increase the rate of surplus-value, so long as it reduces the rate of profit. Yet every new such method of production cheapens the commodities. Hence, the capitalist sells them originally above their prices of production, or, perhaps, above their value. He pockets the difference between their costs of production and the market prices of the same

---

[1] *Capital I*, p. 166.
[2] *Ibid.*, p. 165.   [3] *Ibid.*, p. 163.

commodities produced at higher costs of production. He can do this, because the average labour-time required socially for the production of these latter commodities is higher than the labour-time required for the new methods of production. His method of production stands above the social average. But competition makes it general and subject to the general law. There follows a fall in the rate of profit – perhaps first in this sphere of production, and eventually it achieves a balance with the rest – which is, therefore, wholly independent of the will of the capitalist.[1]

As John Roemer remarks, in his comment on this passage, it is not clear whether the last sentence should be taken to assert that the new rate of profit falls below the original one, or merely below the transitory rate.[2] As observed in 1.3.2, only in the former case would there be counterfinality.[3] The context suggests that this is the correct interpretation, since Marx in this chapter is concerned with explaining the steady downward trend in the rate of profit, not with explaining why it might rise less than anticipated. If this reading is accepted, the passage states an argument for the contradictory character of capitalist behaviour. Actions taken by the individual capitalists for the purpose of increasing the rate of profit have the aggregate result of bringing about a fall in the rate. Any capitalist might succeed in his endeavour, were he the only one to try, but when all try they all fail. Once again the contradiction turns upon the local–global opposition. In 3.4.2 I explain why the theory of the falling rate of profit is formally defective, yet this does not make the general structure of the argument less important.

I shall adduce some further instances in Marx of analyses that have the same logical structure, although he does not use the term "contradiction" in expounding them. In addition to the proto-Keynesian passages from the *Grundrisse* already cited in 1.3.2, the following may be cited as an especially striking statement:

Actually, the relation of one capitalist to the workers of *another* capitalist is none of our concern here. It only shows every capitalist's illusion, but alters nothing in the relation of capital in general to labour. Every capitalist knows this about his worker, that he does not relate to him as producer to consumer, and he therefore wishes to restrict his consumption, i.e. his ability to exchange, his wage, as much as possible. Of course he would like the workers of *other* capitalists to be the greatest consumers possible of *his own* commodity. But the relation of *every* capitalist to *his own* workers is the *relation as such of capital and labour*, the essential relation. But this is just how the illusion arises – true for the individual capitalist as distinct from all the others – that *apart from his* workers the whole remaining working class

[1] *Capital III*, pp. 264–5.   [2] Roemer, *Analytical Foundations*, p. 109.
[3] See note 1, p. 24 above.

confronts him as *consumer* and *participant in exchange*, as money-spender and not as worker.[1]

Note the important idea that certain illusions about the capitalist economy arise naturally out of its mode of operation, a theme further discussed in 2.3.2 and again in 8.2.3.

Consider also a passage from the *Theories of Surplus-Value* in which Marx effectively brings together contradictions within and between the capitalist nations:

Production and consumption are *in their nature* inseparable. From this it follows that since in the system of capitalist production they are in fact separated, their unity is restored through their opposition – that if A must produce for B, B must consume for A. Just as we find with every individual capitalist that he favours prodigality on the part of those who are co-partners with him in his revenue, so the older Mercantile system as a whole depends on the idea that a nation must be frugal as regards itself, but must produce luxuries for foreign nations to enjoy.[2]

Let me finally consider some cases of Marx using the term "contradiction" in senses that differ from that discussed here. The most central is the "contradiction between the productive forces and the relations of production", discussed at some length in 5.1.3. Both in the *Grundrisse* and in *Capital III* Marx suggests that this contradiction is the same as that underlying the falling rate of profit, but I cannot see how this can be defended. The contradiction between the productive forces and the relations of production rests on a contrast between the *actual* rate of development of the forces and the *counterfactual* rate that would have obtained under a different set of relations, whereas the fall in the rate of profit comes about because of the difference between the *intended* and the *actual* result of capitalist behaviour. The two "contradictions" might coexist and be causally related, but they are conceptually distinct. I return to this matter in 3.4.2.

The phrase that became a central element in the Marxism of the Second International, the "contradiction between social production and private appropriation", is used several times by Engels, but to my knowledge only once by Marx, in the 1861–63 *Critique*:

As capitalism develops into a *universal social power*, the contradiction between it and the *private power of the individual capitalist* over these social conditions of production becomes increasingly acute and implies the dissolution of the relationship between the two since it also implies that the material conditions of

---

[1] *Grundrisse*, p. 420.
[2] *Theories of Surplus-Value*, vol. 1, p. 283.

production will develop into universal and hence communal and social conditions of production.[1]

This contradiction, however, is a merely verbal one, like that between a tall wife and a short husband. The contrast is striking, but irrelevant – since it provides no reason why the contradiction could not go on indefinitely. The notion of a social contradiction has the theoretical function of identifying causes of instability and change, not of locating symmetry violations.

Many other occurrences could be cited, some quite insightful, others rather extravagant, but little would be achieved by doing so, since they do not appear to fall into any pattern. Marx was apt to use the term "contradiction" whenever he came across a feature of capitalism that struck him as counterintuitive, perverse or somehow heralding its doom. Most of them do not bear a great theoretical weight, hence I have concentrated on the more prominent, systematic or notorious uses. I have tried to establish (i) that there is a pattern of argument that occurs frequently in Marx and that may well be referred to as "a theory of social contradictions", and (ii) that Marx himself occasionally, but far from invariably, uses the term "contradiction" when engaged in such argument. I have not made the stronger claim (iii) that Marx explicitly entertained the theory of social contradictions, but I would assert (iv) that this way of thinking was so much part of his intellectual background and atmosphere that he had no need to spell it out in any systematic manner. The general idea that unintended consequences arise when agents entertain beliefs about each other that exemplify the fallacy of composition is an extremely powerful one. In my opinion, it is Marx's central contribution to the methodology of social science, especially when considered together with his theory of endogenous belief formation. Whether we refer to this method by the terms "dialectics" and "social contradictions" is, by comparison, a secondary matter.

[1] *Zur Kritik (1861–63)*, pp. 1672–3. Ste Croix, *The Class Struggle in the Ancient Greek World*, p. 548 note 2, cites as other instances *Capital III*, pp. 266, 440. Of these the first is ambiguous, while the second has "Gegensatz", not "Widerspruch", in the original.

Part I
Philosophy and economics

The first part of this book deals with problems that today are studied by philosophers and economists. The second part is more closely related to history, sociology and political science. The distinction is largely one of convenience, yet sufficiently robust to provide a useful way of organizing the subject-matter. It can be stated rather starkly as follows. In this first part I discuss Marx's analysis and indictment of capitalism as an economic system, and the ideal of communist society which is constantly present in the background. In the second part, social change and collective action form the focus of attention, mainly but not exclusively with a view to understanding Marx's theory of the transition from capitalism to communism. To be sure, these dynamic problems are also treated in the first part, notably in the discussion of capitalist crises (3.4), but they take second place to an equilibrium analysis of capitalism and a normative assessment of what it does to human beings.

Very broadly speaking, both the second and the fourth chapters deal with normative issues. In chapter 2 I try to bring out the complex structure of what Marx called alienation in capitalism and of the closely related phenomena of fetishism and reification. I argue that Marx's discussion of alienation only makes sense against the background of a normative view of what constitutes the good life for man. Specifically, this is a life of all-sided creative activity, of which economic production is one, but by no means the only, form. Although, for the most part, this ideal has to be reconstructed from Marx's extensive discussion of its perversion under capitalist conditions, the vision which emerges is nevertheless fairly clear. It also contains some Utopian elements, notably the assumption that anyone not only can but actually will do everything.

In chapter 4 I consider some issues of distributive justice. Exploitation is seen as a main flaw of capitalism, because it violates the principle: "To each according to his contribution." Although I do believe – contrary to several recent writers – that Marx did condemn capitalism on the grounds of distributive injustice, I also believe that this was less important in his eyes than the lack of self-realization stemming from alienation. Yet when we turn to communism, issues of distribution also arise if we admit that self-realization may be a scarce good, because it may require scarce material goods. Even assuming that *anyone* could actually do everything, it does not follow that *everyone* would be able to do so. In this context I discuss the principle "To each according to his needs" as a principle of communist justice.

The third chapter is exclusively analytical, with the purpose of setting out Marx's theory of equilibrium and disequilibrium under capitalism. This involves a critical examination of the labour theory of value, an equally critical discussion of Marx's theories of capitalist crises and a somewhat more positive evaluation of his views on accumulation and technical change. This chapter may prove disappointing to some readers, for two reasons. First, since the gist of what I have to say is largely negative, the reader who wants to find out what is worth while preserving in Marx will not find much here that speaks to him. Secondly, the discussion in this chapter is somewhat more technical than elsewhere, because of the quantitative nature of the subject-matter. To the objections to which these problems might give rise, I have an answer, or rather two. Marx's economic theory is so closely linked to the other parts of his work that a good understanding of what *is* worth preserving presupposes some acquaintance with it. To sort out what is useful from what is useless in Marx's views on exploitation, fetishism or the contradictions of capitalism, we must understand why the labour theory of value or the falling rate of profit lead us in the wrong direction. Also, it is impossible to do justice to economic problems without a minimum of formal apparatus. Marx went wrong, largely because he believed he could discuss verbally problems that can only be handled by quantitative techniques which allow us to sort out the net effect of the many opposed tendencies at work. To understand his mistakes we must first of all avoid repeating them.

2. Philosophical anthropology

The present work is largely about Marx as a social scientist, understood against a background of normative and anthropological presuppositions. These are set out in this chapter. The epistemological status of these background theories is quite varied. Some of them are largely empirical, and belong to the borderland between social anthropology, psychology and evolutionary biology. Others are more in the nature of conceptual analysis, the unravelling of what it means to act and interact. Still others appear to be speculative philosophy of a kind that is now discredited. And finally, some belong to the Aristotelian tradition within moral philosophy which tries to derive statements about the good life for man from an analysis of human nature. It will appear in each particular case how Marx may have intended his views to be understood and in which sense, if any, they can be accepted as true.

    Men interact with nature (2.1) and with one another (2.3). They do this on the basis of needs and capacities that constitute human nature (2.2).

They do so, moreover, within the framework of world history (2.4). These propositions have served to organize the present chapter. From a different perspective, one may distinguish between three sets of issues. First, there is the pathology of human nature and society under capitalism. This involves a number of different phenomena that I have tried to distinguish as carefully as is allowed by the texts. Spiritual alienation (2.2.5) arises when human needs are undeveloped or unfulfilled, social alienation (2.3.3) when the products of men's joint activities take on an independent existence and escape from the control of their makers. The theme of unnatural independence also underlies the theory of reification (2.2.6), conceived as a theory of how needs and capacities come to acquire a one-sided and even compulsive character. Fetishism (2.3.2), finally, is the cognitive process whereby relational properties of objects are falsely seen as adherent within them in the manner of natural properties.

Next I offer a discussion of Marx's conception of the good life for man, as it would be realized in communism (2.2.7). *Creation* and *community* are two key words. The essence of man is to create for the sake of others, to externalize one's creative powers in the service of humanity. I discuss the psychological basis of this ideal, as well as some empirical and logical difficulties associated with it.

Finally, there is the question of how to get from here to there (2.4). In Marx's philosophy of history – distinct from, although closely related to the empirical theories discussed in chapter 5 – capitalism was the indispensable stepping-stone to communism. Like Hegel, he saw alienation as a necessary stage in the development of the powers of mankind. Like him, moreover, he explained it teleologically, in terms of this necessity. Just as "Human anatomy contains a key to the anatomy of the ape",[1] communism provides the key to the understanding of capitalism (and capitalism to the understanding of pre-capitalist modes of production). This teleological stance is closely related to the propensity for functional explanation, discussed in 1.4.

The importance of these background presuppositions in Marx can hardly be stressed too much. Although only a small part of his written work deals with them, they gave him the essential motivation for a lifetime of hardship and struggle. There are no signs that he ever wavered in his total commitment to the ideal of communism and his firm belief that it would inevitably come about. In addition to motivation, these beliefs also provided a powerful source of bias in his thought. His theory of human

---

[1] *Grundrisse*, p. 105.

nature rests on the assumption that what is desirable is also possible; his philosophy of history on the idea that what is desirable and possible is inevitable. To wish for the same passionate energy without the distortions produced by passion is probably to ask for too much.

2.1. Man and nature

This is a topic on which not much of interest can be said, even though much has been claimed for it. Marx's views in this respect are either rambling and incoherent, or inherently trivial. A few interesting observations can nevertheless be extracted from his writings. In 2.1.1 I first consider Marx's philosophical materialism, that is, his theory of the physical world and its relation to human consciousness. In 2.1.2 I discuss his rather extravagant views of the extent to which nature has been transformed by man. In 2.1.3 I conclude with some comments on how Marx saw man as constrained by nature, with a view to discerning possible elements of geographical determinism in his thought.

2.1.1. Philosophical materialism
On this topic little more needs to be said than that Marx had no coherent materialist view, and that had he had one, it would have borne no interesting relation to historical materialism. Clearly, Marx was a materialist in the sense of believing that the external world had an existence independent of, and prior to, the existence of man,[1] even though some passages suggest a different view.[2] I do not know of any passage where Marx argues for a materialist theory of consciousness, in any one of the possible versions of such a theory. These include epiphenomenalism, that is the view that mind is ontologically independent of, but causally dependent on, matter, and the identity theory which states that mind *is* matter under a different description. When Marx occasionally asserts the primacy of being over consciousness,[3] it is unclear whether he refers to the fact of consciousness or to its content, and also what form the priority would take. I simply do not believe that any coherent doctrine can be extracted from Marx's remarks on materialism in *The Holy Family* or from his discussion of what he variously calls realism, naturalism and humanism in the

---

[1] *The German Ideology*, p. 40. Ruben, *Marxism and Materialism*, pp. 71ff lists other passages to the same effect.
[2] E.g. *Economic and Philosophical Manuscripts*, p. 305.
[3] *The German Ideology*, p. 37.

Economic and Philosophical Manuscripts, despite energetic attempts to show the contrary.[1]

On independent grounds, however, someone might come up with a defence of philosophical materialism, and argue that it bears some interesting relation to historical materialism. He might say, for instance, that Marx's theory of history is materialist, since it gives explanatory primacy to *matter*. This will not do, however, since there is no sense in which Marx's theory of history accords a privilege to the material as opposed to the mental. He invokes "spiritual" productive forces, such as science and language on a par with technology, and affirms their importance for the process of social change. As G. A. Cohen has argued, the relevant antonym for "material" is "social", not "mental".[2] If the productive forces *en bloc* are said to be material, it is in opposition to the social relations of production, not in contrast to the products and activities of the mind.

Nor will it do to say that the relation between mind and matter is analogous to that between the economic basis and the political and ideological superstructure. True, the relation in both cases might be one of explanatory primacy of the material over the non-material, yet the mechanisms underlying the primacy in the two cases would be so different that nothing but confusion could result from assimilating them to one another. Recall here the discussion in 1.4.4 and 1.4.5 of Cohen's account of the relation between base and superstructure. Even if one does not accept his view that the primacy of the base is in all cases a matter of functional explanation of the superstructure in terms of its impact on the base, I would not deny that this is true in some cases. An attempt to transfer this to the mind–matter relation would inevitably be a form of interactionism – a doctrine that cannot in the most liberal sense of the term be called materialist. In any case, even were it possible to establish a fuller analogy between philosophical and historical materialism, the validity (or invalidity) of the one would not be an argument for (or against) the other. Only if one could argue for some deductive connection could the philosophical variety serve as a basis for the historical one, or – less plausibly – the other way around. But I do not know of any theory that takes even the smallest step towards the establishment of such a deductive link.

2.1.2. The transformation of nature by man
Marx had rather extreme and exaggerated views on the extent to which nature in his time had become humanized as a result of human labour. In

---

[1] Ruben, *Marxism and Materialism*; Wood, *Karl Marx*, part IV.
[2] Cohen, *Karl Marx's Theory of History*, p. 47 and ch. IV.

The German Ideology he criticizes the contemplative and sensuous materialism of Feuerbach in these terms:

He does not see that the sensuous world around him is not a thing given direct from all eternity, remaining ever the same, but the product of industry and of the state of society . . . Even the objects of the simplest "sensuous certainty" are only given him through social development, industry and commercial intercourse. The cherry-tree, like almost all fruit trees, was, as is well known, only a few centuries ago transplanted by *commerce* into our zone, and therefore only *by* this action of a definite society in a definite age has it become "sensuous certainty" for Feuerbach . . . For that matter, nature, the nature that preceded human history, is not by any means the nature in which Feuerbach lives, it is nature which today no longer exists anywhere (except perhaps on a few Australian coral islands of recent origin) and which, therefore, does not exist for Feuerbach either.[1]

And what about the millions of solar systems existing outside the reach of man?[2] Marx's emphasis on the extent to which nature is transformed by man is both exaggerated and pointless. Yet we find him retaining the same outlook some fifteen years later, in the 1861–3 *Critique*:

Except for raw produce, the materials of labour have always undergone an earlier labour process. What looks like the materials of labour, i.e. like raw material, in one branch of industry, appears as a product in another. In the form in which they are now used and reproduced by men, the vast majority of the objects thought of as the products of nature (such as plants and animals), are the result of a process of transformation that has taken place under human supervision and as the consequence of human labour over many generations, in the course of which both their form and substance have been modified.[3]

In 1868 he praises the German agriculturalist Fraas for proving "that climate and flora changed in historic times. He is a Darwinist before Darwin and makes even the species arise in historic times."[4] This view of nature as being mediated by labour through and through was deeply entrenched in Marx. It is part of his theory of the good society that man should everywhere "see himself in a world that he has created", with nature being an endless mirror reflecting himself. This, however, presupposes that society is organized rationally so that the various activities of men do not interfere with each other and with nature in a destructive way. In the same letter to Engels Marx praises Fraas for having half-perceived this fact:

---

[1] *The German Ideology*, pp. 39–40.
[2] Papaioannou, *De Marx et du Marxisme*, p. 70.
[3] *Zur Kritik (1861–63)*, p. 50.
[4] Marx to Engels 25.3.1868. See also Lucas, "Marx und Engels' Auseinandersetzung mit Darwin", especially p. 438, note 1.

He maintains that as a result of cultivation – in proportion to its degree – the "dampness" so very much beloved by the peasants is lost (hence plants, too, emigrate from South to North) and eventually the formation of steppes begin. The first effect of cultivation is useful but is eventually devastating on account of deforestation etc . . . The sum total is that cultivation – when it progresses naturally and is not consciously controlled (as a bourgeois, of course, he does not arrive at this) – leaves deserts behind it, Persia, Mesopotamia, etc., Greece. Here again another unconscious socialist tendency!

In *Capital III* there is a similar reference to the fact that in agriculture based on private ownership, "exploitation and squandering of the vitality of the soil . . . takes the place of conscious rational cultivation of the soil as eternal communal property, an inalienable condition for the existence and reproduction of a chain of successive generations of the human race".[1] There is an interesting contrast to be made here between Marx's theory of perpetual progress of the productive forces and the more gloomy view of the perpetual destruction of nature. There might even appear to be a conflict between the two ideas, since cultivated soil should itself be seen as a productive force. There is no need, however, to ascribe to Marx the view that each component of the productive forces progresses throughout history, since it is compatible with the texts and sufficient for his purposes to take him as stating that on the whole these forces tend to increase. There remains a special problem for pre-capitalist societies. Since Marx had little faith in their technological dynamism (5.1.1), while certainly believing in their ability to destroy the environment by thoughtless and unplanned exploitation, the net effect on the productive forces might well be negative.

2.1.3. Geographical determinism

Marx was no geographical determinist in the sense in which, say, Karl Wittfogel was one.[2] Yet there are some strands of this view in his thought. Consider first Marx's view of what Wittfogel was to call "hydraulic society":

Climate and territorial conditions, especially the vast tracts of desert extending from the Sahara through Arabia, Persia, India and Tartary, to the most elevated Asiatic highlands, constituted artificial irrigation by canals and waterworks the basis of Oriental agriculture . . . This prime necessity of an economical and common use of water, which, in the Occident, drove private enterprise to voluntary association, as in Flanders and Italy, necessitated in the Orient where civilization was too

---

[1] *Capital* III, p. 812; cp. *ibid.*, p. 620 and *Capital I*, pp. 239, 265.
[2] Wittfogel, "Die natürlichen Ursachen der Wirtschaftsgeschichte"; see also his *Oriental Despotism*.

low and the territorial extent too vast to call into life voluntary association, the interference of the centralizing power of government.[1]

Although less prone to geographical determinism than the letter from Engels on which Marx's article was based,[2] the argument is ambiguous. To explain the difference between East and West, Marx invokes both the difference in the level of productive forces ("civilization"[3]) and different geographical conditions. To understand the relative importance of these two explanatory factors, we must go to an important text from *Capital I*:

Capitalist production once assumed, then, all other circumstances remaining the same, and given the length of the working-day, the quantity of surplus-labour will vary with the physical conditions of labour, especially with the fertility of the soil. But it by no means follows from this that the most fruitful soil is the most fitted for the growth of the capitalist mode of production. This mode is based on the domination of man over Nature. Where Nature is too lavish, she "keeps him in hand, like a child in leading strings". She does not impose on him any necessity to develop himself. It is not the tropics with their luxuriant vegetation, but the temperate zone, that is the mother-country of capital. It is not the mere fertility of the soil, but the differentiation of the soil, the variety of its natural products, the changes of the seasons, which form the physical basis for the social division of labour, and which, by exchange in the natural surroundings, spur man on to the multiplication of his wants, his capabilities, his means and modes of labour.[4]

The development of humanity, therefore, was in a sense an accident of geography. If there had been no intermediate zone between the luxuriant tropics and the regions of extreme harshness,[5] the need and the possibility for development would not have come together. This is not to say, however, that the development, once initiated, continued to be shaped by geography. Once the self-reinforcing process of expanding needs and productive powers had been set up (2.2.4), geography plays no further role than that of constraining the technical changes that are possible at any given stage. According to Marx, the economic structure is then explained by its tendency to develop the productive forces as much as is possible within these and other constraints. Applied to hydraulic society, this means that given a vast territory and an initially low level of the productive forces, centralized government rather than voluntary association was optimal for the further development of these forces, although

---

[1] *New York Daily Tribune* 25.6.1853.
[2] Engels to Marx 6.6.1853.
[3] Marx tended to use the word "civilization" to denote the development of the productive forces; see for instance the *Grundrisse*, pp. 308, 584ff.
[4] *Capital I*, pp. 513–14.
[5] Marx (*ibid.*) quotes N. Forster to the effect that "A soil incapable of produce by labour is quite as bad as a soil that produces plentifully without any labour."

the reverse might be true at a later stage of their development. Marx's view that the development of civilization depended on the existence of this narrow geographical ridge may be open to criticism,[1] but not on the grounds that it is incompatible with historical materialism.

In his published writings Marx held a well-balanced view concerning the importance of geographical conditions. In private he could be more reckless. The following extracts from his correspondence with Engels show that he was easily misled by passion and prejudice into attaching excessive significance to geography. They concern a book by P. Trémaux, which today is remembered exclusively because of the undeserved praise which Marx bestowed on it:[2]

In its historical and political applications, the book is much more important and copious than Darwin. For certain questions such as nationality, etc. a natural basis is found only in this work. For example, the author corrects the Pole Duchinski, whose findings in regard to the geological differences between Russia and the West Slavs he generally confirms, that, contrary to the Pole's belief, the Russians are not only no Slavs, but, rather, Tartars etc. but also that on the existing soil formation of Russia the Slavs became Tartarized and Mongolized, just as he (he has been in Africa for a long time) proves that the common Negro type is only a degeneration of a much higher one. "Outside the grand laws of nature, man's plans are mere calamities; this is shown by the efforts of the Czars to make Muscovites out of the Polish people. The same nature, the same abilities, will be reborn on the same soil . . ."[3]

Clearly, Marx embraced Trémaux's views because they allowed him to give his Russiophobia a seemingly scientific foundation in geographical determinism.[4] Earlier references to the Russian character had been straightforwardly racist,[5] whereas the appeal to geology promised a more materialist explanation. In his reply Engels brushed Trémaux aside as ridiculous,[6] but Marx, unconvinced, then came up with the following argument:

Trémaux's basic idea regarding the *influence of the soil* (although he naturally does not evaluate the historic modifications of this influence, and in these historic modifications I include also the chemical changes of the topsoil

---

[1] North, *Structure and Change in Economic History*, p. 87, objects that "This argument ignores the fundamental dilemma of growing population pressure and the common property resource problem." On his view: "It is more likely that man found rich areas where there was an abundance of wild grain that could be harvested with a sickle and then began to defend these areas against intruders."

[2] See Conry, *L'Introduction du Darwinisme en France au XIXᵉ Siècle*, p. 220.

[3] Marx to Engels 7.8.1866.

[4] For Marx's Russiophobia, see Papaioannou, *De Marx et du Marxisme*, pp. 461ff.

[5] See for instance his remarks on Russia in *The Secret Diplomatic History of the Eighteenth Century* and his letter to Engels of 24.6.1865.

[6] Engels to Marx 2.10.1866.

through agriculture, etc., and in addition the varied influence that is caused by the various methods of production of such things as coal beds, etc.) is, in my view, an idea that only has to be *expressed* in order to earn for ever a citizen's right in science, and this apart from Trémaux's method of presentation.[1]

After Engels's further, devastating reply,[2] Marx did not return to the topic.

2.2. Human nature

2.2.1. The problem

The analysis of human nature can take three forms, all of them found in Marx. First, one can ask about the features that are common to all men, barring retardation, mental illness or senility.[3] Some of these will be the features which distinguish men from animals (2.2.2), others will be common to men and (at least some) animals. Next, one may inquire into the range of features that can be developed by men, even if they have not been observed in any actual society. And finally one may ask which of the features within that range *ought* to be developed. Marx's answer to the second question must largely be reconstructed from what he says about the third, following the principle that "Ought implies can". It falls outside the scope of a theory of human nature to ask *how* the desirable features are to be developed, but it might follow from the theory that some are such that they can only arise as by-products, in the sense that deliberate attempts to bring them about might be self-defeating.[4]

Human nature, according to Marx, can be described and evaluated in terms of needs (2.2.3) and capacities. The development of humanity takes place by an interaction between needs and capacities (2.2.4), as capacities are developed so as to satisfy needs and then in turn give rise to new needs. This process can be blocked at an early stage, so that both needs and capacities remain undeveloped, as in the "luxuriant vegetation" of the tropics. The process can also be channelled so that, although never blocked, the development becomes one-sided or otherwise undesirable. Or it can occur in a desirable way, either toward some steady state or

---

[1] Marx to Engels 3.10.1866.

[2] Engels to Marx 5.10.1866.

[3] Marx never to my knowledge discussed these or other fatalities that may befall men, such as disease or accident, nor does he refer to the implications of man's mortality. Yet the limited and unknown span of human life has profound consequences for human nature, as has also the constant possibility of debilitations of various kinds. An implicit reference to man's mortality, however, underlies the view that even in communism the economization of time will remain of paramount importance.

[4] For the idea of such states that are essentially by-products, see my *Sour Grapes*, ch. II.

indefinitely. Observe that the normative assessment of needs and capacities turns upon several different issues. Some needs and capacities may remain undeveloped. Others may develop, but remain unsatisfied or not exercised. Still others may develop and be satisfied, respectively exercised, but in a way that is not integrated with the personality as a whole. The first two problems I refer to as spiritual alienation (2.2.5), further subdivided into an objective and a subjective variety. The third I refer to as reification (2.2.6). On the background of this study of the pathology of human nature, I finally try to reconstruct the positive side of the coin, that is Marx's view of what constitutes the good life for man (2.2.7).

2.2.2. Men and animals

Marx distinguishes men from other animals on the basis of (i) self-consciousness, (ii) intentionality, (iii) language, (iv) tool-using, (v) tool-making and (vi) cooperation. These are, of course, strongly interrelated, but sufficiently different to be discussed separately. Moreover, in a critical confrontation they do not all survive equally well. As one writer puts it, "we have seen in the last few decades a steady erosion of the putative hallmarks of man".[1]

Consider first self-consciousness. In the *Economic and Philosophical Manuscripts* Marx writes that:

The animal is immediately one with its life activity. It does not distinguish itself from it. It is *its life activity*. Man makes his life activity itself the object of his will and of his consciousness. He has conscious life activity. It is not a determination with which he directly merges. Conscious life activity distinguishes man immediately from animal life activity.[2]

In *The German Ideology* we find a similar formulation: "Where there exists a relationship, it exists for me: the animal does not 'relate' itself to anything, it does not 'relate' itself at all. For the animal its relation to others does not exist as a relation."[3] In the passage immediately following the first text, Marx goes on to speculate about the origin or conditions of self-consciousness.[4] One suggestion is that it is linked to production, that man becomes aware of himself by seeing himself "in a world that he has

---

[1] Beck, *Animal Tool Behavior*, p. 218.
[2] *Economic and Philosophical Manuscripts*, p. 276.
[3] *The German Ideology*, p. 44.
[4] I say "origin or condition" since it is not clear whether Marx here is proposing a causal theory of the emergence of self-consciousness or a transcendental argument about the conditions of its possibility.

created".[1] Another is that man's awareness of himself is related to his awareness of himself as a "species-being", a more obscure idea, and probably false. It could be true that man is aware of himself through his awareness that other people are aware of him, but this does not seem to be what Marx had in mind. Rather he appears to be saying that man's consciousness of himself is related to his awareness of himself as a member of humanity – not a plausible notion for the early hominids. In any case, the use of self-consciousness as a distinguishing criterion appears plausible enough, although we should add that the matter is empirical rather than conceptual. It is not too hard to think of circumstances that might lead us to impute self-consciousness to animals.[2]

In a famous passage from *Capital I* man's capacity for intentional planning is emphasized as a distinctive trait:

A spider conducts operations that resemble those of a weaver, and a bee puts to shame many an architect in the construction of her cells. But what distinguishes the worst architect from the best of bees is this, that the architect raises his structure in imagination before he erects it in reality.[3]

In the *Economic and Philosophical Manuscripts* a similar contrast is drawn between the stereotyped constructions carried out by animals and the general capacity for free construction found in man.[4] I argue below, with respect to tools, that these oppositions appear to be artificial. Animals have the ability to construct according to (or otherwise relate to) "images" of what is spatially and temporally remote. They also have the ability to invent creative solutions to novel problems.

Consider next language. Immediately before the remarks in *The German Ideology* quoted above, Marx writes that:

Language is as old as consciousness, language *is* practical, real consciousness that exists for other men as well, and only therefore does it also exist for me; language, like consciousness, only arises from the need, the necessity, of intercourse with other men.[5]

Since Marx goes on to talk about the capacity to relate to one's own relation, he must mean by "consciousness" here self-awareness, rather than awareness generally. As the passage links language to self-consciousness and argues that the latter is found only in man, this would also seem to hold for language. A similar view is stated in the *Comments on Wagner* some thirty-five years later:

[1] *Economic and Philosophical Manuscripts*, p. 277.
[2] Dennett, *Brainstorms*, pp. 273ff.   [3] *Capital I*, p. 178.
[4] *Economic and Philosophical Manuscripts*, p. 277.
[5] *The German Ideology*, p. 44.

Men do not in any way begin by "finding themselves in a theoretical relationship to the things of the external world". Like every animal, they begin by eating, drinking, etc. that is, not by "finding themselves" in a relationship (*in einem Verhältnis zu stehen*) but by behaving actively (*sich aktiv zu verhalten*), gaining possession of certain things in the external world by their actions, thus satisfying their needs. (They thus begin by production.) By repetition of this process, the property that those things have of "satisfying their needs" is impressed on their brain; men, like animals, also learn to distinguish "theoretically" the external things which, above all others, serve to satisfy their needs. At a certain point in their evolution, after the multiplication and development of their needs and of the activities to assuage them, men will baptize with the aid of words the whole category of these things that experience has enabled them to distinguish from the rest of the external world.[1]

Compared to the earlier passages, two differences stand out. Marx now imputes to animals certain cognitive, even theoretical capacities. Also the origin of language is found specifically in the production process, rather than in social interaction. It develops by the needs–capacities interaction further discussed in 2.2.4. Hence one is left with the impression that what distinguishes men from other animals is the ability to stabilize cognition through language.

Marx had a "technological conception of history". Did he also have a technological conception of human nature? If so, what relation does it bear to historical materialism? I shall first discuss the view that men uniquely employ tools to satisfy their needs, and then the idea that what characterizes them is the production rather than the use of tools.

In *The German Ideology* we read:

Men can be distinguished from animals by consciousness, by religion or anything else you like. They themselves begin to distinguish themselves from animals as soon as they become to *produce* their means of subsistence, a step which is conditioned by their physical organization . . . What they are, therefore, coincides with their production, both with *what* they produce and with *how* they produce.[2]

I shall understand this as an assertion that men distinguish themselves from animals by producing with tools. This is to go beyond what is unambiguously stated or implied by the text, but it is a possible and to my mind plausible reading. In any case the idea is sufficiently close to other views that Marx certainly did hold to merit discussion.

To evaluate this view I draw on Benjamin Beck's *Animal Tool Behavior*. He argues that the use of tools is not unique to man, nor a necessary condition for cognitive capacities. It is not unique to man, since animals

[1] Comments on Wagner, pp. 362–3.
[2] *The German Ideology*, p. 31; cp. also *Capital I*, p. 179.

even from lower taxa engage in what can only be called tool use, as when crabs use stinging anemones for offensive or defensive purposes. Some animals also engage in tool use requiring intentionality, such as carrying tools to a point invisible from the point of tool selection and even bringing spares. Moreover, it appears that at least occasionally such tool use emerges by insight rather than by trial and error. Nor is tool use necessary for cognition, since insight and intentionality may also be displayed in non-tool behaviour among animals. Gulls dropping shells to break them and get access to the edible interior do not use tools, but still "behaved adaptively with regard to spatially and temporally displaced dropping sites, and thus can be inferred to have had images of such features".[1] The Japanese monkey Imo, upon receiving a mixture of sand and wheat, threw it on the water so that the sand could sink and she could recover the grain – a behaviour that displays intentionality and insight, yet does not require tools.[2] These examples confirm my earlier assertion that Marx erred in *Capital I* when he denied to animals the capacity to work according to a mental plan. They also invalidate what might look like a promising idea – that tools are required for intentional work, be it in the sense that only tool-users can work intentionally or in the sense that intentional work always involves tools. (The view that tool behaviour preceded cognition in evolution remains possible, but speculative.) I am not saying that Marx entertained this idea, but it is certainly close to views that he did hold.

In *Capital I* Marx twice refers to Franklin's characterization of man as a "tool-making animal", once ironically[3] and once approvingly.[4] Quite independently of the importance of technology for social change, it is easy to see why tool-making might be considered important for the development of human nature, and in particular for the consciousness of *time*. The manufacture of a tool sets up a link between the present and the future, since it typically involves foregoing some consumption during the construction period in order to consume more at a later date. It is, in fact, a paradigmatic instance of the pattern "one step backward, two steps forward" that is characteristic of intentional behaviour.[5] Also, one might argue that the use of a manufactured tool creates a link between the present and the past, since it involves dead labour acting jointly with

---

[1] Beck, *Animal Tool Behavior*, p. 206.
[2] Wilson, *Sociobiology*, p. 171.
[3] *Capital I*, p. 326: this view is "characteristic of Yankeedom".
[4] *Capital I*, p. 179. The text is ambiguous, since Marx does not distinguish between tool-using and tool-making. See also *Zur Kritik* (1861–63), p. 87.
[5] Cp. my *Ulysses and the Sirens*, ch. I.3.

living labour. The use of a tool to make a tool – culminating in "the production of machines by machines"[1] – brings together the past, the present and the future in one synthesizing movement.

Consider three claims that could be made in this connection. First, is tool-making a specifically human activity? Marx appears to make this claim, but the evidence is against him. Animals engage in a variety of tool-making behaviours, as amply documented by Beck. True, there are no documented instances of an animal using a tool to make a tool, but in the first place such cases might yet be found, and in the second place their impossibility is only part of Marx's claim. Next, is tool-making a cause or condition for the consciousness of the future? So far as I know, Marx does not make this claim, but it is closely related to other claims that he does make. It is refuted by the instances cited above. Lastly, is tool-making a cause or condition for the consciousness of the past? Marx does not make this claim. In one context he argues that the only occasion we have to bring the origin of manufactured objects to mind is when they present some imperfection that reminds us of their makers.[2] He also argues that lack of awareness of the past may have disastrous consequences if the product of men's activity takes on an independent or even hostile form in which they do not recognize their own labour: this is further discussed in 2.3.3. Hence the temporal dimension of production creates the possibility that men can be enslaved by their own products, so that liberation will require the consciousness of the past activity as their own. But the production process by itself does not bring about this awareness.

Finally, consider cooperation. Marx sometimes argued that intra-species and inter-species cooperation never occurs among animals. Intra-species cooperation is denied in this passage from the *Economic and Philosophical Manuscripts*:

Animals are unable to combine the different attributes of their species, and unable to contribute anything to the *common* advantage and comfort of the species. It is otherwise with *men*, amongst whom the most dissimilar talents and forms of activity are of use to one another.[3]

Against this we may set a surprising passage from the *Theories of Surplus-Value*, to the effect that "the interests of the species in the human kingdom, as in the animal and plant kingdoms, always assert

[1] *Capital I*, pp. 384–5.
[2] *Ibid.*, pp. 182–3.
[3] *Economic and Philosophical Manuscripts*, p. 320.

themselves at the cost of the interest of individuals".[1] The two passages do not formally contradict one another, but the underlying spirit is different.

For a denial of inter-species cooperation we can go to the *Grundrisse*:

The fact that this need on the part of one can be satisfied by the product of the other, and vice versa, and that the one is capable of producing the object of the need of the other, and that each confronts the other as owner of the object of the other's need, this proves that each of them reached beyond his own particular need etc. as a *human being*, and that they relate to one another as human beings; that their common species-being is acknowledged by all. It does not happen elsewhere – that elephants produce for tigers, or animals for other animals.[2]

The contrast is somewhat strange, opposing intra-species cooperation in man to the lack of inter-species cooperation among animals. Moreover, this alleged lack is fictitious, as shown by between-species altruism, symbiosis etc.[3] More importantly, Marx is also wrong in denying intra-species cooperation, as shown massively by recent socio-biological literature.[4] It would be pointless to blame Marx for not anticipating modern biological theory, or for indulging in speculation in work not intended for publication. Yet we may question whether, on his own premises, the suggested contrasts are valid. One reason for thinking that they are not is that what Marx describes here as characteristically human is only the working of the invisible hand, not a conscious and deliberate effort of cooperation. The latter *is* uniquely human,[5] the former not. In fact, Marx himself wrote to Engels that:

Darwin recognizes among beasts and plants his English society with its division of labour, competition and opening-up of new markets, 'inventions', and the Malthusian 'struggle for existence'. It is Hobbes's *bellum omnium contra omnes*, and one is reminded of Hegel's *Phenomenology*, where civil society is described as a 'spiritual animal kingdom', while in Darwin the animal kingdom figures as civil society.[6]

The proper contrast, therefore, would seem to be between the conscious cooperative behaviour of which men are capable, and the mutual benefits that arise as unintended consequences of selfish behaviour (or "selfish genes") among men as well as animals.

---

[1] *Theories of Surplus-Value*, vol. 2, p. 118. The full passage is cited and discussed in 2.4.2 below.
[2] *Grundrisse*, p. 243.
[3] Trivers, "The evolution of reciprocal altruism".
[4] For a synthesis, see Axelrod and Hamilton, "The evolution of cooperation".
[5] Moore, *Marx on the Choice between Socialism and Communism*, p. 15.
[6] Marx to Engels 18.6.1862; cp. *Capital I*, p. 356.

To conclude, the most robust of the features that Marx cites as characteristic of man are his awareness of himself and his use of language. Intentionality, production, tool-using and tool-making are also found among animals, as is cooperation of the unconscious variety described by Marx. The fact that self-consciousness and language are cognitive capacities does not constitute an objection to historical materialism. There is no reason why the features that distinguish man from other animals should also be the features that explain the development of man throughout history. Conversely, the importance of technology in historical materialism creates no presumption that it should be equally central in a theory of how men differ from other animals. The uniquely human cognitive capacities explain why the tool-making and tool-using abilities that man shares with other animals were, in his case, capable of much greater development – given the need and the proper environmental conditions.

2.2.3. Needs

The concept of human needs is fundamental in Marx's theory of human nature. The good society, for Marx, is one in which people are rich in needs and rich in need satisfaction. Conversely, capitalism is defective both because people have few needs and because the needs they do have are not satisfied. The latter set of issues is discussed in 2.2.5; here I want only to consider Marx's conceptual analysis of the different kinds of need. I give notice here that I shall only be considering needs that, if they exist, are subjectively perceived, excluding such needs as the need for vitamin C.

Needs have objects, if the latter are taken in a general sense, so that I may have a need for books but not for any particular book. I shall refer to the attitude one has to a specific book as a *desire*, corresponding to Marx's observation that each need "forms the basis of a desire".[1] Any need, if satisfied, is satisfied by the fulfillment of a desire, but the converse need not hold. There may be desires that do not derive from any general need – desires that are directed towards specific objects that do not admit of substitution. Also, a specific desire may derive from more than one general need. Thus the desire for specific clothes might not derive from the need for clothing, but from some other need such as the need for prestige and recognition. This would be the case if the substitute for the clothes was a watch from which I could derive the same prestige, rather than some other clothes.[2]

[1] *The German Ideology*, p. 256.
[2] Cp. the theory of *characteristics* developed by Lancaster, "A new approach to consumer theory".

A typology of needs in Marx, drawing largely upon Agnes Heller,[1] includes the following. *Physical needs* are needs for physical or biological necessities.[2] Even at subsistence, such needs can be satisfied by many objects with corresponding desires, as remarked in 1.2.2. Which of the objects is then in fact chosen to satisfy the need will depend on preferences, which in turn will often depend on cultural elements. *Necessary needs* are needs that in themselves contain what Marx called a "historical and moral element".[3] They correspond to the conventional and accepted standard of living of a particular group of people at a particular time and place. Marx believed that in capitalism the value of the labour-power of the worker is uniquely defined by his necessary needs.[4] This is wrong, however, since the necessary needs can be realized by many different desires, the satisfaction of which need not all embody the same labour value. This also holds if we add the constraint of a given monetary wage, since commodity bundles that add up to the same amount of money need not have the same total labour content (3.2.2). *Luxury needs* may be defined either as needs for objects that form no part of the conventional standard of living of the workers, or as needs for objects too expensive to be brought by the workers.[5] Normally these two definitions coincide.

Social needs can, according to Heller, mean four different things in Marx. Of these I shall retain two, and then add a third meaning that, even if not explicitly present in Marx, can help us understand some of his more cryptic utterances. First, social needs are simply needs that have a social origin, that is are socially rather than biologically caused. Secondly, they are needs that, as a matter of fact or as a matter of logic, can only be satisfied communally, such as the need for education (if I cannot afford a private teacher) or the need for association with others. To these I add, thirdly, the needs whose objects essentially involve a reference to other people. They are social in content rather than in origin.[6] The needs that can only be communally satisfied overlap with this group, as shown by the need for association, but are not included in it, as shown by the need for education. Nor do they include it, as shown by the following examples. Consider first the need for positional goods, that is the need for relative excellence, to have more or to be better than other people.[7] Next,

---

[1] Heller, *The Theory of Needs in Marx.*
[2] Marx refers to these as *natural needs* (*Capital I*, p. 171), an expression that may easily be misunderstood.
[3] *Capital I*, p. 171.   [4] *Ibid.*; see also 1.2.1 above.
[5] Heller, *The Theory of Needs in Marx*, pp. 35ff; also *Capital II*, p. 403.
[6] See Cohen, *Karl Marx's Theory of History*, pp. 94–5, 103; also my *Sour Grapes*, ch. I.3.
[7] Hirsch, *Social Limits to Growth.*

consider the need to be like other people, or to differ from other people, that is conformism and anti-conformism.[1] And finally one may cite the need to impress other people, for example by conspicuous consumption. Here objects are consumed not because of the direct satisfaction they give, but for the satisfaction one gets from seeing that other people are impressed.[2] An important feature of needs that are social in this third sense is that they may be individually or collectively self-defeating.[3] The need for positional goods is collectively self-defeating, in that it may be worse for all if all are motivated by it than if none are.[4] The need to impress others often is individually self-defeating, since, notoriously, nothing is so unimpressive as the attempt to impress.[5]

Needs are interrelated. Not all needs can exist simultaneously, and not all existing needs can be satisfied simultaneously. This holds for any given individual, as well as for a group of individuals whose needs constrain one another mutually. Consider first a single person. Marx argues in *The German Ideology* – the main source for understanding his theory of needs – that communism "will make possible the normal satisfaction of all needs, i.e. a satisfaction which is limited only by the needs themselves".[6] One such limitation is that the scarcity of time may make it impossible to satisfy all one's needs. Marx notes in the *Grundrisse* that society is like an individual in that "its enjoyment and its activity depends on economization of time".[7] Another limitation is that some needs might override others, as when my need to eat a lot is restrained by my need to keep slim. These are reasons why the satisfaction of some needs might prevent the satisfaction of others. In 2.2.6 I discuss the idea that some needs might take on a compulsive character that blocks other needs from even emerging.

Consider next the relation between the needs of several persons. According to Marx:

All emancipation carried through hitherto has been based ... on restricted productive forces. The production which these productive forces could provide was insufficient for the whole of society and made development possible only if some persons satisfied their needs at the expense of others, and therefore some – the minority – obtained the monopoly of development.[8]

---

[1] *Sour Grapes*, ch. I.3.
[2] See for instance Veblen, *The Theory of the Leisure Class* and Bourdieu, *La Distinction*.
[3] For this distinction see Parfit, "Prudence, morality and the Prisoner's Dilemma".
[4] Haavelmo, "Some observations on welfare and economic growth".
[5] *Sour Grapes*, ch. II.5.   [6] *The German Ideology*, pp. 255–6.   [7] *Grundrisse*, pp. 172–3.
[8] *The German Ideology*, pp. 431–2.

It is implicit here that in the fully developed communist society there will be no such incompatibility of needs satisfaction. If we disregard the Utopian idea of communist abundance, Marx offers no argument for this view. One or two may, however, be suggested. First, while man will become "rich in needs", some needs will also disappear:

Communist organization has a twofold effect on the desires produced in the individual by the present-day relations; some of these desires – namely desires which exist under all relations, and only change their form and direction under different social relations – are merely altered by the communist social system, for they are given the opportunity to develop normally; but others – namely those originating solely in a particular society, under particular conditions of [production] and intercourse – are totally deprived of their conditions of existence.[1]

The latter group, presumably, would include the "inhuman, sophisticated, unnatural and imaginary appetites", "depraved fancies" and "morbid cravings" which Marx refers to in the *Economic and Philosophical Manuscripts*.[2] Moreover, they would include the inherently limitless need for money for its own sake, as well as the individually or collectively self-defeating needs referred to above. The disappearance of the latter is especially important, since their presence implies that full need satisfaction is inherently impossible.

A second argument is that under communism spiritual needs – the need for productive and creative activity – will assume greater importance than the need for material goods. To this it may be objected that such needs may also be quite difficult to satisfy. First, not all individuals may have the talents required to satisfy them (2.2.7); secondly, even spiritual needs may require for their satisfaction a great deal by way of material goods (4.3.3).

2.2.4. Capacities and the development of needs
Marx often refers to the self-expanding process of needs creation, whereby the satisfaction of one need gives rise to another. A mediating element in this process is the development of new human *capacities*, by which Marx appears to mean man's cognitive, creative and productive powers. In *The German Ideology* Marx, after stating that production is the "first historical act", goes on to say that "the satisfaction of the first need, the action of satisfying and the instrument of satisfaction which has been acquired, leads to new needs; and this creation of new needs is the first

---

[1] *Ibid.*, p. 256.
[2] *Economic and Philosophical Manuscripts*, p. 307.

(*sic*) historical act".[1] In *Capital I* he makes it clear, in a passage cited earlier, that there is a threshold effect operating, but that beyond the threshold man is spurred on to "the multiplication of his wants, his capabilities, his means and modes of labour".[2] In the passage from the *Comments on Wagner*, also cited above, the emergence of language is seen as part of "the multiplication and development of . . . needs and of the activities to assuage them".[3]

These statements are quite general, and we are not told exactly how the satisfaction of existing needs generates new ones. In Marx's work there appear to be two, quite different, suggestions. First, there is the idea that the exercise of a capacity may itself become a need. In the *Economic and Philosophical Manuscripts* Marx observes that "When communist *artisans* associate with one another, theory, propaganda etc. is their first end. But at the same time, as a result of this association, they acquire a new need – the need for society – and what appears as a means becomes an end."[4] Similarly, in communism "work is not only a means to life, but itself has become the prime need of life".[5] An important feature of this process is that the new needs develop in the very same individuals whose capacities had developed as a response to earlier needs.

Other passages suggest a different mechanism, emphasizing the development of humanity rather than of individual men. Consider first an important statement from the *Economic and Philosophical Manuscripts*:

The *real*, *active* orientation of man to himself as a species-being (i.e. as a human being), is only possible if he really brings out all his *species-powers* – something which in turn is only possible through the cooperative action of all mankind, only as the result of history – and treats these powers as objects: and this, to begin with, is again only possible in the form of estrangement.[6]

In the 1861–3 *Critique* this expansion of human powers is explicitly linked to the expansion of needs:

It is implicit in the laws governing human development that no sooner has one set of needs been satisfied than other needs are set free or created. Hence as capital extends labour time beyond the limits required to satisfy the natural needs of the worker, it intensifies the process of the division of social labour – of labour in society as a whole. It increases the diversity of production and expands the horizon of social needs as well as the means of satisfying them. It thereby contributes to the growth of man's productive powers and causes capacities to be

---

[1] *The German Ideology*, p. 42.
[2] *Capital I*, p. 514. The full passage was quoted in 2.1.3.
[3] *Comments on Wagner*, p. 363.   [4] *Economic and Philosophical Manuscripts*, p. 313.
[5] *Critique of the Gotha Program*, p. 21.
[6] *Economic and Philosophical Manuscripts*, p. 333.

activated in new directions. But just as surplus labour time is the precondition of free time, the expansion of the horizon of needs and the means of satisfying them is likewise dependent on shackling the worker to the basic necessities of life.[1]

Here it is clear that the persons whose needs are expanded are not the same as those whose capacities are developed. The ever-widening circle of needs within the exploiting class corresponds to an increase in the productive powers of the exploited class. Even within the latter, the multiplication of capacities is not found within each individual worker. "The one-sidedness and deficiencies of the detail labourer become perfections when he is part of the collective labourer."[2] Or again, "in order to make the collective labourer, and through him capital, rich in social productive power, each labourer must be made poor in individual productive power".[3] The same process "turns the worker into an insensible being lacking all needs",[4] in contrast to the sometimes unnatural multiplication of needs in the capitalist. The latter performs the world-historical mission of creating civilization, at the expense of the workers whose deprivation makes it possible. Ultimately both sides of the process come together in the "development of the rich individuality which is as all-sided in its production as in its consumption",[5] but this unification is made possible only by a long history of separation. To use Cohen's phrase again, the history of mankind before communism is the development of Man, not of men.

Leaving aside for later discussion (2.4) the strong teleological strand in this argument, I want to stress here that the development of productive forces is only part of the general development of man's "species-powers". The capacity for artistic creation, for instance, is equally important as part of these powers. The communist society in which men's capacities are fully developed and exercised is not one in which all individuals are engaged in promoting the growth of the productive forces, even though the latter may be expected to flourish at an unprecedented rate. Yet, although the "species-powers" form the more general and teleologically more important category, the productive powers are privileged, since they generate the free time needed for the development and exercise of species-powers generally. Their increase is both a component of the development of the species-powers, and a condition for the development of the other components. Hence historical materialism, which is largely about the growth of the productive forces,

[1] *Zur Kritik (1861–63)*, p. 175.   [2] *Capital I*, p. 349.   [3] *Ibid.*, p. 361.
[4] *Economic and Philosophical Manuscripts*, p. 308.
[5] *Grundrisse*, p. 325.

has a somewhat different focus than Marx's philosophical anthropology, which emphasized the development of man's creative powers generally.[1]

2.2.5. Spiritual alienation

The alienation generated by capitalism is a constant theme in Marx's work, from the *Economic and Philosophical Manuscripts* to the mature economic writings.[2] The notion, however, has several strands or elements, not all of which are equally prominent in Marx's writings from all periods. I shall not give much emphasis to the development of Marx's thinking on this point, since there does not seem to me to be any case to be made for a sharp contrast or break in his views.

Following John Plamenatz and Allen Wood,[3] I shall distinguish between two main concepts of alienation in Marx. First there is what one may refer to as lack of self-actualization (Wood) or spiritual alienation (Plamenatz). This is the topic of the present section. Secondly, there is the power that the products of man may acquire over their creators. This is discussed in 2.3.3.

Spiritual alienation may be seen either as a lack of a sense of meaning, or as a sense of a lack of meaning.[4] Both Marx and his commentators are ambiguous on this crucial point. In the *Economic and Philosophical Manuscripts* Marx asks:

What, then, constitutes the alienation of labour? First, the fact that labour is *external* to the worker, i.e. it does not belong to his intrinsic nature; that in his work, therefore, he does not affirm himself but denies himself, does not feel content but unhappy, does not develop freely his physical and mental energy but mortifies his body and ruins his mind. The worker therefore only feels himself outside his work, and in his work feels outside himself. He feels at home when he is not working, and when he is working he does not feel at home.[5]

Is the central fact that the worker "feels outside himself" in his work, or that "he does not feel at home"? The presence of a negative feeling, or only the absence of a positive one? In his discussion of this form of alienation, Allen Wood is similarly ambiguous, referring both to "a lack of a sense of 'meaning'",[6] and to "the experience of one's self and life as

---

[1] For a further discussion of this difference, see Cohen, "Reconsidering historical materialism".

[2] In the present chapter and again in ch. 8 many texts on alienation from the later writings are cited. Some of them could have appeared verbatim in the early manuscripts, e.g. the eloquent passage in *Results of the Immediate Process of Production*, p. 990, cited in 8.2.1 below.

[3] Plamenatz, *Karl Marx's Philosophy of Man*, p. 141; Wood, *Karl Marx*, p. 50.

[4] For a similar distinction, see Cohen, "Bourgeois and proletarians", p. 118.

[5] *Economic and Philosophical Manuscripts*, p. 274.   [6] Wood, *Karl Marx*, p. 8.

empty".[1] The failure to make this distinction is a case of a quite general tendency to confuse external and internal negation.[2] In the present context, the failure is especially fatal, since the link between alienation and collective action undertaken to overcome it depends on which of the readings is chosen.

Although Wood's discussion is ambiguous between the two readings, he opts on the whole for the objective notion of spiritual alienation, according to which "it is a matter of whether my life in fact actualizes the potentialities which are objectively present in my human essence",[3] and thus not "a matter of whether my conscious desires are satisfied or how I think about myself or my life".[4] Yet he then goes on to argue, inconsistently, that alienation thus defined can be a lever for social change:

Generally speaking, the degree of systematic, socially caused alienation in a society will be proportional to the gap which exists in that society between the human potentialities contained virtually in society's productive powers and the actualization of these potentialities by the society's members. Thus the possibilities for alienation increase along with the productive powers of society. For as these powers expand, there is more and more room for a discrepancy between what human life is and what it might be. *There is more and more pressure on social arrangements* to allow for the lives of individual human beings to share in the wealth of human capacities which belong to social labour.[5]

The passage provokes two, related, comments. First, the argument parallels one made in 5.1.3 below, with respect to the development of the productive forces. Wood argues that alienation is measured by the gap between actual and potential self-realization, the latter being defined in terms of the level of development of the productive forces. Similarly, the contradiction between the productive forces and the relations of production is measured by the gap between the actual rate of change of the productive forces and the potential rate of change that – at the given level of development of the forces – could obtain under different relations. It is a question, in one case, of the suboptimal or inhuman use of the productive forces, in the other of their suboptimal development. In 5.1.3 I argue that Marx tended to confuse these two flaws of capitalism with one another, but they are clearly distinct phenomena.

Secondly, the passage raises a problem that we shall meet repeatedly in this work. We may be able to single out some feature of capitalism by virtue of which it ought to be abolished, and to offer an argument that a

[1] *Ibid.*, p. 9.
[2] Cp. my "Négation active et négation passive" for an analysis of this distinction, and the consequences of ignoring it.
[3] Wood, *Karl Marx*, pp. 23–4.   [4] *Ibid.*, p. 23.   [5] *Ibid.*, p. 45. Italics added.

society is possible in which that feature is not found. Yet this offers no answer to the questions of how the abolition is to occur, and what causal role the feature will have in the abolition if it occurs. If we condemn capitalism by virtue of a purely objective alienation, there is no reason to expect it to set up a "pressure on social arrangements". We may, perhaps, be able to argue that capitalism will be overthrown *when* alienation (in this spiritual, objective sense) becomes sufficiently acute, but this is not to say that it will be abolished *because* of the acute alienation. We might even be able to argue for a lawlike correlation between alienation and the abolition of capitalism, in the sense that the process leading to abolition inevitably also aggravates alienation, but this would be a case of causal concomitance, not of causal production. Or finally one might be prepared to argue that objectively existing alienation at some point comes to be felt subjectively, thereby providing the motivation to abolish the system that generates it.[1] What one cannot argue is that the mere objective need for change, assessed on a certain view of what is objectively good for human beings, will in itself bring about that change. We shall see in later chapters that similar problems arise if one argues that capitalism will be abolished because it is based on exploitation, or because it generates a contradiction between the productive forces and the relations of production. In 2.4 below I suggest that Marx entertained a speculative philosophy of history that authorized him to neglect this difficulty, or at least to give it less attention than it required. The problem is also discussed in the concluding chapter.

There are, then, two different ways of looking at alienation.[2] One implies that as alienation grows, people subject to it become increasingly unhappy, discontent and prone to revolt. The other is compatible with alienation growing worse without any growing feeling of discontent. If for example the actual needs remain constant, the growth in the objective possibilities for the fulfilment of needs does not bring about an increase of misery. Increasing alienation could even go together with decreasing misery, if the needs diminish as the possibility of needs satisfaction increase. Hence alienation may be found in the non-satisfaction of actual

---

[1] G. A. Cohen points out to me that the objective alienation might also acquire subjective force in some more complex or indirect way. Speculatively, the capitalists might perceive that the workers are objectively alienated, and fearing (possibly without good reason) that they might come to recognize this, take measures that bring about a state of subjective frustration in the workers.

[2] For an analogy, cp. the two ways of looking at *suffering* in Buddhism, exemplified by Kolm, *Le Bonheur-liberté* (who takes suffering to be a subjective psychological state) and Collins, *Selfless Persons* (who takes suffering to be a theoretical construct that depends on the whole of Buddhist theory for its explication).

needs, or in the non-satisfaction of non-actual, satisfiable needs. In the first sense alienation may cause collective action, in the second it could rather be an obstacle to it.

It is not clear which of these conceptions is the more central in Marx. The *Economic and Philosophical Manuscripts* emphasize the alienation of man from his species-being, an Aristotelian ideal the deviation from which appears to be a purely objective phenomenon. In *The Holy Family*[1] and later in *The Results of the Immediate Process of Production*[2] Marx draws a contrast between the capitalist who finds satisfaction in his state of alienation, and the worker who feels indignation in it and experiences it as a form of enslavement. This points to a subjective conception of alienation, at least as far as the workers are concerned. Similarly, the *Grundrisse* praises capitalism for creating rich needs which it cannot satisfy.[3] In this work Marx also suggests an important contrast between the pre-capitalist modes of production, in which men felt relatively content within a small circle of needs, and the capitalist mode that multiplies needs beyond the creation of means of satisfying them.[4] There is much that the workers want to do and to have; and they believe it would be possible for them to do and to have what they want if only society were so organized that the productive forces could be rationally utilized. Hence they feel frustrated and unhappy, that is alienated in the subjective, spiritual sense of the term.

In pre-capitalist society men were not objectively alienated, since even with a reorganization of the production it would not have been possible to satisfy needs much wider than those actually satisfied.[5] Rather they suffered from what I have elsewhere proposed to call "adaptive preferences", that is adaptation of wants to what is possible.[6] This distinction suggests the following table:

	Actual needs	Satisfied needs	Satisfiable needs
Adaptive preferences	small	small	small
Subjective spiritual alienation	large	small	large
Objective spiritual alienation	small	small	large
Utopian preferences	large	small	small
Communism	large	large	large

---

[1] *The Holy Family*, p. 35.
[2] *Results of the Immediate Process of Production*, p. 990.
[3] *Grundrisse*, pp. 283, 325, 409.   [4] *Ibid.*, pp. 162, 488.
[5] As far as I know, Marx never employs the term "alienation" with respect to pre-capitalist societies. Nor do I know of any passage where he explicitly affirms that alienation only exists under capitalism.   [6] Cp. my *Sour Grapes*, ch. III.

Given the constraints that actual needs cannot be smaller than satisfied needs and the latter not larger than the satisfiable ones, these cases exhaust all possibilities. Utopian preferences may lead to premature revolutions, while objective alienation may block feasible revolutions. By contrast, adaptive preferences and subjective alienation are in a sense more adequate to the situation. (Even in pre-capitalist society there may have been a gap between the actual and the satisfiable needs, since the adaptation of preferences to what is possible often tends to overshoot the mark.[1] To the extent that this occurs, adaptive preferences are not adequate.)

2.2.6. Reification

I use this as a technical term for the tendency of needs and capacities to become fixed, isolated and independent within the individual, instead of being integrated with the personality as a whole. The corresponding German term would be "Verselbständigung", but there does not appear to be any English equivalent. Marx often uses the German equivalents of "reification", such as "Verdinglichung", "Versachlichung" and "Verknöcherung",[2] but mainly to refer to social alienation (2.3.3). The use of the term "reification" to denote the compartmentalization of individual psychology was first, as far as I know, introduced by Lukacs.[3] I shall first discuss the reification of needs, that is the process whereby they take on a one-sided, compulsive character. I shall then go on to discuss the reification of capacities, including language.

A need – or the desire corresponding to it – is reified if "it assumes an abstract, isolated character, if it confronts me as an alien power, if, therefore, the satisfaction of the individual appears as the one-sided satisfaction of a single passion".[4] Whether this happens

depends not on consciousness, but on being; not on thought, but on life; it depends on the individual's empirical development and manifestation of life, which in turn depends on the conditions obtaining in the world. If the circumstances in which the individual lives allow him only the one-sided development of one quality at the expense of all the rest, if they give him the material and time to develop only that one quality, then this individual achieves only a one-sided, crippled development.[5]

---

[1] Veyne, *Le Pain et le Cirque*, p. 313; *Sour Grapes*, pp. 118–19.
[2] See especially the discussion of "Revenue and its sources" in *Capital III* and in vol. 3 of the *Theories of Surplus-Value*.
[3] "Die Verdinglichung und das Bewusstsein des Proletariats", pp. 263ff.
[4] *The German Ideology*, p. 262.   [5] *Ibid.*

In particular, needs in capitalism are all needs for consumption, for passive enjoyment, whereas the need to develop and exercise one's capacities is stifled. This diagnosis is also an indictment. It does not presuppose the strong thesis that in the good society work itself should become a need, but requires only that the good life for man is one of active creation – within or outside working hours – rather than of passive consumption. Given this ideal (and its feasibility), Marx can criticize capitalism as a one-sided "consumer economy":

> every person speculates on creating a *new* need in another, so as to drive him to fresh sacrifice, to place him in a new dependence and to seduce him into a new mode of *enjoyment* and therefore economic ruin. Each tries to establish over the other an *alien power*, so as thereby to find satisfaction of his own selfish need. The increase in the quantity of objects is therefore accompanied by an extension of the realm of the alien powers to which man is subjected, and every new product represents a new *potentiality* of mutual swindling and mutual plundering. Man becomes poorer as man, his need for *money* becomes ever greater if he wants to master the hostile power.[1]

In other words, the one-sided craving for material consumption breeds an obsessional need for money. This is the "true need" and the "only need" developed by the economic system.[2] "All passion and all activity must be submerged in avarice."[3] Marx notes, however, that the abstract greed for money as an end in itself tends to undermine the system that gives rise to it. Avarice interferes with the effective demand for goods, so that "a controversy now arises in the field of political economy"[4] between those who recommend thrift and those who advocate luxury.

An ambiguity should be mentioned before I proceed. Although Marx in his early writings emphasized the need for money in the *consumer*, who came to substitute exchange-value for use-value as the object of his desire, he later found it mainly in the *producer*, for whom the production of surplus-value rather than use-value became the dominant end. The abstract need for money was first linked to the hoarding of income, later to the reinvestment of profits. The miser's thirst for money that he never spends on consumption is only a psychological quirk, while the capitalist's need to reinvest follows from his role as the "functionary of capital".[5] In Marx's later phrase, "that which in the miser is a mere idiosyncracy, is, in the capitalist, the effect of the social mechanism, of which he is but one of the wheels".[6] I have discussed this questionable formulation in 1.2.1 above. Here I want only to give notice that my present concern is with the

---

[1] *Economic and Philosophical Manuscripts*, p. 306.
[3] *Ibid.*, p. 307.   [3] *Ibid.*, p. 309.   [4] *Ibid.*   [5] *Capital III*, p. 264.   [6] *Capital I*, p. 592.

repercussions of capitalism on the individual as consumer, as discussed in the early manuscripts.

In the passages quoted above two main themes appear. In capitalism needs are *one-sided*, being directed towards passive consumption rather than active creation. Also, they take on a *compulsive* character, when appearing as alien powers to the individual who has them. Or rather, metaphorically speaking, the needs have him, rather than the other way around. The two themes are not only logically but empirically distinct, since people can wallow non-compulsively in material wealth. If we ask what Marx meant by compulsion or, in his language, needs and desires that "confront me as an alien power", some answers might be the following. There may be desires derived from no need, that is desires that are directed towards specific objects and not towards objects as means of satisfying a need. It is characteristic of desires derived from needs that they allow of substitutes, so that under different circumstances the need would be satisfied by desires directed towards different objects. By contrast, a reified or compulsive desire might be one that has no rationale, but is arbitrarily attached to an object that serves no purpose. Fetishism, in the Freudian rather than the Marxist sense, could be an example. Also, compulsive needs could be identified by their insatiable character, or by not being subject to diminishing marginal utility. If my need is never satisfied, not even approximately, I may have to engage in the same behaviour over and over again, compulsively. The main example in Marx is the limitless thirst for money: "the desire after hoarding is in its very nature insatiable".[1] On one occasion he also refers to the "limitless waste, which logically attempts to raise consumption to an imaginary boundlessness, by gulping down salads of pearls etc.".[2] Similarly, the need for positional goods or the need to impress others might, because of their self-defeating character, appear as compulsive. Lastly, compulsion may be understood in terms of the rigid character traits that often appear as a result of overly successful attempts to curb impulsiveness.[3]

The reification of capacities implies, mainly, a one-sided development of some abilities at the expense of others. The earlier stage of capitalism, based on manufacture and division of labour, tended systematically to cripple the worker and to develop some capacities to the point of hypertrophy, whereas others atrophied. This system "converts the labourer into a crippled monstrosity, by forcing his dexterity at the

---

[1] *Ibid.*, p. 133.   [2] *Grundrisse*, p. 270.
[3] Cp. Ainslie, "A behavioral economic approach to the defence mechanism".

expense of a world of productive capabilities".[1] In a later stage capitalism, now based on machinofacture, is compelled

under penalty of death, to replace the detail-worker of today, crippled by life-long repetition of one and the same trivial operation, and thus reduced to the mere fragment of man, by the fully developed individual, fit for a variety of labours, ready to face any change of production, and to whom the different social functions he performs are but so many modes of giving free scope to his own natural and acquired powers.[2]

It is clear from the context that Marx believed this was already taking place within capitalism, since the need for the many-sided worker is explained by the incessant technical change it had set in motion. This analysis is not so much Utopian as downright silly, as is the belief evinced by Marx that the factory system was already at his time bringing about the unity of work and education[3] and of work and family life[4] that would obtain under communism. These views cannot have derived from observation or from sociological theorizing. Rather they express a speculative Hegelian assumption that capitalism must create the conditions for its own abolition not only *en gros*, but also *en détail*.

In *The German Ideology* Marx argued that the very idea of an "occupation" corresponds to a reified conception of man:

with a communist organization of society, there disappears the subordination of the artist to local and national narrowness, which arises entirely from the division of labour, and also the subordination of the individual to some definite art, making him exclusively a painter, sculptor etc.; the very name aptly expresses the narrowness of his professional development and his dependence on the division of labour. In a communist society there are no painters but only people who engage in painting among other activities.[5]

Marx's theory of language can also be seen in this perspective. Language is a specifically human capacity, which is developed as well as distorted by the successive class societies. At a superficial level, Marx's critique of the abstract language of the philosophers appears quite similar to that of the later Wittgenstein. "The philosophers have only to dissolve their language into the ordinary language from which it is abstracted, in order to recognize it as the distorted language of the actual world."[6] And further on: "Language, of course, becomes a phrase as soon as it acquires an independent existence."[7] Stirner, for example, is criticized for substituting etymology for argument, and verbal similarities for real con-

---

[1] *Capital I*, p. 360.   [2] *Ibid.*, pp. 487–8.   [3] *Ibid.*, p. 484.   [4] *Ibid.*, p. 489.
[5] *The German Ideology*, p. 394.
[6] *Ibid.*, p. 447.   [7] *Ibid.*

nections.[1] But there is a crucial difference. Marx wanted above all to criticize the ordinary language of capitalist society, not only to expose the philosopher's language as ordinary language isolated from context:

For the bourgeois it is all the easier to prove on the basis of this language the identity of commercial and individual, or even universal, human relations, as this language is itself a product of the bourgeoisie, and therefore both in actuality and in language the relations of buying and selling have been made the basis of all others.[2]

Marx cites the similarity between *Eigentum* (property in the sense of possession) and *Eigenschaft* (property in the sense of feature or quality). It is no accident that these words have a common root, but the connection is historical and transient, not essential. At a certain stage in their development men come to think of individual relations in commercial terms. At the same stage they tend to believe in the essential similarity of phenomena denoted by similar terms. As a consequence they wrongly conclude that individual qualities and relations are essentially linked to property and commerce. An example, which Marx may well have had in mind even though he does not cite it, could be Hegel's view that private property is an essential condition for individuality.[3]

The basic reification of language is the process that creates nouns out of verbs: "the original roots of all words are *verbs*".[4] When verbs are congealed into nouns, we come to speak of painters, and not only of people who, among other things, also paint. This linguistic reification corresponds to the actual reification of man's capacities, so that language is no more than faithful to reality when it refers to the reified activity by a reified verb such as a noun. (I note parenthetically that in Romance as well as Germanic languages the very word for *thing* ["causa", "Sache", 'Ding''] originally meant *process* or *deliberation*. The word "thing" itself is a reified process![5])

2.2.7. The good life for man

Marx advocated communism, because he believed it would in important ways be a better society than any capitalist society could be. Yet not all of the advantages of communism were equally central in his argument for it. No doubt he believed that communism would be better at developing the productive forces (5.2.3), and superior from the point of view of distribu-

---

[1] *Ibid.*, pp. 229–30, pp. 275–6. A full discussion is in Erckenbrecht, *Marx's materialistische Sprachtheorie*, I.3.

[2] *The German Ideology*, p. 231.   [3] Hegel, *The Philosophy of Right*, p. 236.

[4] *The German Ideology*, p. 276. It is difficult to reconcile this with the theory of the origin of language found in the "Comments on Wagner", quoted in 2.2.2.

[5] I am indebted to Kostas Papaioannou and Rodney Needham for this observation.

tive justice (4.3). Yet I believe these arguments in terms of efficiency and justice were secondary to him. True, such considerations may motivate people living in capitalism to overthrow that system, and provide – if valid – perfectly good reasons for doing so. But Marx himself condemned capitalism mainly because it frustrated human development and self-actualization. Correlatively, he saw communism as a society in which men could become fully human, that is fully realize their potential as all-around creators. The problem of efficiency would be solved as a by-product, since one of the ways in which people will realize their potential is through scientific and technical work that will raise productivity far beyond anything seen before. It is less obvious how the problem of distributive justice is to be solved, or dissolved.

The two passages that most strikingly bring out Marx's vision of communism are, in my opinion, the following:

Communism differs from all previous movements in that it overturns the basis of all earlier relations of production and intercourse, and for the first time consciously treats all naturally evolved premises as the creation of hitherto existing men, strips them of their natural character and subjugates them to the power of the united individuals ... The reality which communism creates is precisely the true basis for rendering it impossible that anything should exist independently of individuals, insofar as reality is nevertheless only a product of the preceding intercourse of individuals.[1]

In fact, however, when the limited bourgeois form is stripped away, what is wealth other than the universality of individual needs, capacities, pleasures, productive forces etc. created through universal exchange? The full development of human mastery over the forces of nature, those of so-called nature as well as of humanity's own nature? The absolute working-out of [the human being's] creative potentialities with no presupposition other than the previous historic development, which makes this totality of development, i.e. the development of all human powers as such the end in itself, not as measured on a *predetermined* yardstick? Where he does not reproduce himself in one specificity, but produces his totality? Strives not to remain something he has become, but is in the absolute movement of becoming?[2]

The first passage states that in communism there will be no social alienation (2.3.3) nor any reification of the needs and capacities of the individual. No sub-individual or supra-individual entities will be allowed to assume an independent existence, contrary to what occurs in capitalism, where the individual is "caught in the middle" (1.3) between these two extremes. The second passage identifies communist individuality and

---

[1] *The German Ideology*, p. 81.   [2] *Grundrisse*, p. 488.

creativity. It argues not only that under communism there will be no spiritual alienation, that is no gap between actual and potential self-actualization, but also that the potential itself is boundless.

In connection with these views, I want to raise some questions. Why did Marx place so much emphasis on creation, as opposed to the more passive forms of enjoyment? Did Marx really believe that each and any individual could achieve self-actualization through creative work at a high level of excellence? If so, was he right? Is this form of self-actualization compatible with the idea of having a broad range of activities? I postpone to 4.3.3 the further question whether all individuals can achieve self-realization in this way, even assuming that any individual can.

Consider first the vexed issue whether Marx believed that in communism man would realize himself in work or outside of it. The texts are ambiguous and allow of no definite answer. Three suggestions can be distinguished in Marx. According to the first, work will become "the prime need of life",[1] as it was perhaps to the skilled artisan that William Morris held up as the socialist ideal.[2] The *Economic and Philosophical Manuscripts* and the contemporary *Comments on James Mill* also express this view.[3] According to the second, work will become superfluous in communism. The production process will be largely automated, with men relating to it in a more indirect or general way:

Labour no longer appears so much to be included within the production process; rather, the human being comes to relate more as watchman and regulator to the production process itself ... No longer does the worker insert a modified natural thing as middle link between the object and himself; rather, he inserts the process of nature, transformed into an industrial process, as a means between himself and inorganic nature, mastering it. He steps to the side of the production process instead of being its chief actor. In this transformation, it is neither the direct human labour he himself performs, nor the time during which he works, but rather the appropriation of his own general productive power, his understanding of nature and his mastery over it by virtue of his presence as a social body – it is, in a word, the development of the social individual which appears as the great foundation-stone of production and of wealth.[4]

---

[1] *Critique of the Gotha Program*, p. 21.
[2] Cp. Thompson, *William Morris*, pp. 641ff; cp. also pp. 751ff for the relation between Marx and Morris.
[3] *Economic and Philosophical Manuscripts*, pp. 296ff; *Comments on James Mill*, pp. 227–8 (partly quoted below).
[4] *Grundrisse*, p. 705.

Finally, there is the view that man will realize himself outside work, which remains an indispensable task to be reduced and humanized as much as possible:

[The] realm of freedom actually begins only where labour which is determined by necessity and mundane considerations ceases; thus in the very nature of things it lies beyond the sphere of actual material production. Just as the savage must wrestle with Nature to satisfy his wants, to maintain and reproduce life, so must civilized man, and he must do so in all social formations and under all possible modes of production. With his development this realm of physical necessity expands as a result of his wants; but, at the same time, the forces of production which satisfy these wants also increase. Freedom in this field can only consist in socialized man, the associated producers, rationally regulating their interchange with Nature, bringing it under their common control, instead of being ruled by it as by the blind forces of Nature; and achieving this with the least expenditure of energy and under conditions most favourable to, and worthy of, their human nature. But it nonetheless remains a realm of necessity. Beyond it begins that development of human energy which is an end in itself, the true realm of freedom, which, however, can blossom forth only with this realm of necessity as its basis. The shortening of the working-day is its basic prerequisite.[1]

A reasonable synthesis could be the following. In communism, all individuals will realize themselves by creative activities of one form or another. Some will do so in the process of material production, by using and developing their scientific and technical skills. Others will do so outside production, by engaging in artistic pursuits or pure science. Some drudgery for at least some individuals will, however, inevitably remain. The problem is further discussed in chapter 9.

I now turn to the priority of creation over consumption, of activity over passivity. I shall consider various arguments for this view, some of them derived directly from Marx, others more conjectural. First, there is the idea classically expressed by Leibniz: "je trouve que l'inquiétude est essentielle à la félicité des créatures".[2] Not tranquillity and contentment, but the overcoming of obstacles makes for happiness. This is a source of satisfaction eminently found in creative work:

It seems quite far from [Adam] Smith's mind that the individual, 'in his normal state of health, strength, activity, skill, facility', also needs a normal portion of work and of the *suspension of tranquillity*. Certainly, labour obtains its measure from the outside, through the aim to be attained and the obstacles to be overcome in attaining it. But Smith has no inkling whatsoever that *this overcoming of obstacles is in itself a liberating activity* . . . [Labour] becomes attractive work, the individual's self-realization, which in no way means that it becomes mere fun, mere amusement, as Fourier, with grisette-like naiveté, conceives it. Really free working, e.g.

---

[1] *Capital III*, p. 820.   [2] Leibniz, *Nouveaux Essais*, p. 175.

composing, is at the same time precisely the most damned seriousness, the most intense exertion.[1]

The two phrases I have italicized may be understood as saying that frustration is an indispensable part of happiness. Indeed, one could well speak of *optimal frustration*[2] as the amount of tension that, when released, gives the greatest net satisfaction. In this sense, however, passive consumption may also bring happiness, not perhaps by eating a meal, but surely by reading a novel. One reason why novels are more satisfactory than daydreams is precisely that we do not know beforehand how they will turn out, so that there takes place a build-up and then a release of tension.[3] If the release from tension is made into a main criterion for happiness, we must reject both the societies that generate too much frustration – that is frustration that is never resolved or resolved too late – and the societies in which there is too little frustration because needs are so modest that they are immediately satisfiable. These, for Marx, correspond to the capitalist and the pre-capitalist societies respectively. In the latter we have "satisfaction from a limited standpoint; while the [former] gives no satisfaction".[4] All this makes good utilitarian sense.

Yet we must be allowed to doubt whether this reading corresponds to Marx's intentions, since it places (some forms of) consumption on a par with active creation. To argue for communism in terms of pleasurable mental states is foreign to his basic aspirations for that society. An additional argument against the utilitarian view is provided by Ronald Dworkin.[5] Consider the great artist or scientist who throughout his life is desperately unhappy, because on the one hand he cannot help doing what he does, while on the other hand he suffers from not attaining the standards he sets for himself. It is precisely because of his great power and insight that he is capable, far more than others, of seeing how far his work falls short of that ideal. His work may remain as a lasting achievement of humanity, but his life may have been one of subjective misery. It is implicit in Marx's psychology that he did not believe such cases would arise in communism, but had he recognized the possibility my conjecture is that he would have counted them as lives of self-realization.

Another argument for the priority of creation derives from Hegel. To know who and what he is, man must externalize himself in word or work so that his inner nature can become accessible to others and take its place

---

[1] *Grundrisse*, p. 611.   [2] Cp. my *Sour Grapes*, p. 138.
[3] See Ainslie, "Beyond microeconomics".
[4] *Grundrisse*, p. 488.
[5] Dworkin, "What is equality? Part 1", pp. 211, 222.

in the common world. A life of pure consumption would be a life without substance, at best the life of the aesthete, the "beautiful soul" who is afraid that any attempt to externalize his nature might betray its ineffable essence.[1] Creative work allows for the kind of existence-for-others that is necessary for individuation. This in itself does not bring us to communism. In capitalism one can also observe the process of intense competition among artists or scientists who try to gain recognition by their fellow workers.[2] In communism, however, creation and production is also undertaken for the sake of others, that is, the purpose of the creative process is to bring forth products that can be enjoyed by others. Hence there is no opposition between individuality and community, as in capitalism, but a full complementarity:

Let us suppose that we had carried out production as human beings. Each of us would have *in two ways affirmed* himself and the other person. (1) In my *production* I would have objectified my *individuality*, its *specific* character, and therefore enjoyed not only an individual *manifestation of my life* during the activity, but also when looking at the object I would have the individual pleasure of knowing my personality to be *objective, visible to the senses* and hence a power *beyond all doubt*. (2) In your enjoyment or use of my product I would have the direct enjoyment both of being conscious of having satisfied a *human* need by my work, that is, of having objectified *man's* essential nature, and of having thus created an object corresponding to another *man's* essential nature ... Our products would be so many mirrors in which we saw reflected our essential nature.[3]

There is, however, the germ of an internal inconsistency in this argument; at least it does not add up to a reason for preferring creation over consumption. If creation is to be valued mainly because it is creation *for others*, then in a sense it is parasitic on consumption and cannot avoid being contaminated by the low value attached to the latter. To put the matter starkly: in a society entirely made up of active, creative individuals nobody would be bothered to read, watch or otherwise enjoy what others are producing, except to learn from them. As one writer is supposed to have said: "If I want to read a book, I write one myself." I do not want to carry this argument too far, but neither do I consider it a mere fancy. In all social movements emphasizing altruism and action for the sake of others there lurks the difficulty that other-regarding behaviour is logically impossible unless there are some individuals who at least some of the time act in a self-interested manner. "Do not act for your own sake, but for that of the community" is a self-defeating instruction when issued to everybody, as shown perhaps in some of the excesses of the Chinese

[1] Hegel, *The Phenomenology of Spirit*, pp. 399ff; cp. also p. 187.
[2] *Ibid.*, pp. 237ff.   [3] *Comments on James Mill*, pp. 227–8.

Cultural Revolution. Similarly, Marx's emphasis on creation and production may in the final analysis be difficult to reconcile with his emphasis on community.

Under capitalism, the self-actualization of man occurs at the expense of that of individual men. The collective labourer achieves perfection at the expense of the crippling of the individual worker. In communism self-actualization of men is the supreme value, and no such sacrifices can be tolerated. "Above all we must avoid postulating 'society' again as an abstraction *vis-à-vis* the individual."[1] Yet Marx clearly believed that through the self-actualization of the individuals under communism there would also occur an unprecedented flowering of humanity. Moreover, he seemed to take it for granted that under communism there could be no conflict or trade-off between these two goals. I want to question this view.

The objection assumes, as will be further explained below, that talents are unequally distributed. Not anyone can achieve anything he sets his mind to, not even under the most favourable conditions. It is not quite clear what was Marx's view on this problem. In *The German Ideology* we find him arguing against Stirner's misunderstanding of Fourier and other "organizers of labour". It "was not their view, as Stirner imagines, that each should do the work of a Raphael, but that anyone in whom there is a potential Raphael should be able to develop himself without hindrance".[2] And Marx goes on to argue for himself that "whether an individual like Raphael succeeds in developing his talents depends wholly on demand, which in turn depends on the division of labour and the conditions of human culture resulting from it".[3] This is most plausibly, perhaps, read as a recognition that talents are unequally distributed; but this is not the only way to understand the passage. In the *Grundrisse* Marx suggests both that work in production will become increasingly intellectual and scientific, and that this, by reducing the necessary labour time, will allow the "artistic, scientific etc. development of the individuals in the time set free".[4] Again it is not clear whether this is predicated of man or of men, but here the most plausible reading is that Marx thought it to be true of each and every individual. This is also the view that fits best with the corpus as a whole, which never to my knowledge refers to differences in natural talents.

If Marx, thus understood, is right, there is no conflict between the self-actualization of man and that of men. But if he is wrong, as appears

---

[1] *Economic and Philosophical Manuscripts*, p. 299.   [2] *The German Ideology*, p. 393.
[3] *Ibid.*
[4] *Grundrisse*, p. 706.

overwhelmingly probable, the following difficulty arises. If only those engage in creative and intellectual work who are certain *ex ante* to succeed, then fewer will do so than are required for the social optimum.[1] If no potential Raphael is to be blocked, then many who wrongly believe themselves to be potential Raphaels will be frustrated. This is not the frustration of the successful creative artist who despairs over the flaws that perhaps only he is able to perceive in his work, but the much more widespread frustration of those who fail because their work is all too visibly flawed. If Marx did not conceive of artistic or scientific work as a gamble in which the chances of success are highly uncertain, it may have been because he considered only those who actually succeeded. He wrote that "Milton produced *Paradise Lost* for the same reason that a silk worm produces silk. It was an activity of *his* nature."[2] Yet this presumably was not true of Milton at all stages in his development. With some exceptions – Mozart comes to the mind – artists and scientists initially engage in an uphill struggle or, to change the metaphor, go against the grain. The satisfaction of finding which way the grain goes does not come to all, and may come late in life if it comes.

Let me use this example to introduce another objection: I would like to question Marx's view that in a communist society needs and capacities will never become one-sided. If Milton wrote *Paradise Lost* as a silk worm spins silk, in some sense he could not have done otherwise. Surely he could not have taken time off in the afternoon to be a fisherman or in the evening to be a critical critic.[3] Marx thought that under communism creative work, while remaining "damned serious", would not come to dominate the individual. A communist Milton would not be a writer, only a person who among other activities also writes – a highly implausible view. The same holds for the successful, but miserable, artist or scientist envisaged above. The fact that such a person would pursue a career that brought him nothing but misery can hardly be understood otherwise than as a sign that his need to create is almost compulsive. Marx does not appear to have considered this possibility. His model for communist man is not, in fact, so much Raphael or Milton as Leonardo da Vinci – an individual capable of excelling in many arts and crafts, turning from one to another as his fancy takes him. It is an attractive idea, but somewhat

[1] "We probably would have few novelists, actors, or scientists if all potential aspirants to these careers took action based on a normatively justified probability of success. We also might have few new products, new medical procedures, new political movements, or new scientific theories" (Nisbett and Ross, *Human Inference*, p. 271).
[2] *Theories of Surplus-Value*, vol. 1, p. 401.
[3] Cp. *The German Ideology*, p. 47.

unreal. The problem is not quite that Marx believed that "le malheur vient de l'étroitesse de l'existence, non de son manque de profondeur".[1] Rather it is that Marx did not believe there was any trade-off between breadth and depth, no more than between the self-actualization of man and that of men.[2]

The above comments have been concerned mainly with problems related to the second of the two passages quoted at the beginning of this subsection. I want to add a few words about a problem raised by the first. This passage has a negative emphasis rather than a positive: communism is the state of affairs in which no product of the activity of individuals can assume an independent existence. In 2.3.3 I return to the most important implication of this view, the idea that the product of men's joint activities will be under their joint control and not be allowed to dominate them. Here I want to make a few remarks about the implications for individual psychology.

Is it really possible for the individual to be at all times unfettered by his own past behaviour, as distinct from the constraints that may have been set up by that behaviour? When acting, one often sets in motion a process in the external world that at a later time may constrain one's behaviour, but one often also establishes a *habit* or disposition to act that way. Marx seems to be committed to the view that a fully human life should not in any way be constrained by habits or, more generally, by character traits resulting from past behaviour. This extreme, somewhat Sartrian, view is implausible both because it seems impossible to envisage a creature totally without habits, and because the attempt to do away with habits may, to the extent it succeeds, be harmful rather than beneficial.[3]

The involuntary emergence of habits should be distinguished from the deliberate process of character planning that has been advocated by many philosophers, psychologists and economists.[4] It is not clear that Marx ought to have been equally hostile to such methods for self-control, for if one's earlier self tries to limit or shape a later self, this is not a process going on "behind the back" of the person, but a conscious and (let us assume) rational activity. In the only place where Marx touches upon this problem, he nevertheless appears to be rather sceptical about the idea.

---

[1] Papaioannou, *De Marx et du Marxisme*, p. 110.

[2] A case might be made for a more plausible version of Marx's view. *Ex ante* anyone is free to develop himself in whatever direction he wants, but once the choice is made a change to a different profession is difficult or impossible. This "putty clay" model of human malleability was suggested to me by Dagfinn Føllesdal.

[3] Rorty, "Akrasia and self-deception", argues that although these phenomena largely stem from the existence of habits, the latter are nevertheless essential to the coherence of a life.

[4] For surveys, see my *Ulysses and the Sirens*, ch. II and *Sour Grapes*, ch. II.

True, this mainly holds with respect to the political analogy, that "in a democracy individuals only exercise their sovereignty for a moment and then at once relinquish their authority".[1] He notes that this view has "been put forward both by revolutionaries and reactionaries", and dismisses it as an "idealistic conception of the state". From Marx's argument against this conception it appears probable that he would also have dismissed the need for an individual to bind himself: "Whether or not tomorrow the self-will of an individual will feel oppressed by the law he has helped to make, depends on whether new circumstances have arisen and whether his interests have changed." This, however, is to ignore a third reason why the individual might feel oppressed by a law he has helped to make: he may be tempted, through caprice[2] or weakness of will, to perform the action that the law was designed to exclude. Marx did not believe either that weakness of will might be a general predicament of human life, or that strategies for self-control might be necessary to cope with it. To the belief in the transparency of social relations under communism[3] he added faith in the autonomy of individual human beings – an autonomy so unconditional that it would not even have to protect itself against backsliding.

To conclude, it appears that the core of Marx's indictment of capitalism is not so much his normative view of human nature as his theory of the range of possibilities that are open to man. The Utopian character of his views is due to his reluctance to admit that even under communism some hard choices might have to be made, and that conflicts between values might persist. Since the cutting edge of a normative theory only appears when such conflicts arise, it is hard to assess his view that self-actualization is the supreme human good. Summing up, I believe the main weaknesses of his theory are the following. (i) He ignores the conflict between the self-actualization of man and of men that could arise because the frustration of unsuccessful individuals is an inevitable by-product of a system that allows a full development of human talents. (ii) He similarly ignores the conflict that might arise between the objective self-realization of the individual and the subjective feeling of happiness. (iii) He also neglects the conflict between the all-sided development of the individual and the one-sided devotion to one activity characteristic of very creative persons. (iv) Lastly he overlooks both the problem of excessive impulsiveness, and the danger that the devices people invent to cope with it might lead to excessive

---

[1] *The German Ideology*, p. 333. For himself, Marx thought that in a democracy the representatives should be removable and revocable at all times (7.3.1).

[2] For a discussion of a law designed to protect the individuals against their own caprice, see *Contribution to the Critique of Hegel's Philosophy of Law*, pp. 100ff.

[3] Cp. Cohen, "Karl Marx and the withering away of social science".

rigidity of character. The communist individual would appear to have neither id nor superego.

Marx's psychological theory, then, is largely based on wishful thinking. It was only by denying or ignoring important features of human nature that he was able to set up the stark contrast between individual fulfilment in class societies and in communism. This is not to say that one could not defend some more sober versions of his claims. The emphasis on *homo faber* can be retained even if one discards the more extravagant notions about human malleability and omni-competence. The critique of consumer society remains valid and important in many respects. Autonomy, creativity and community are all values that command the highest respect. Other things being equal, each of them ought to be promoted as much as possible. When other things are not equal, we must look elsewhere for guidance.

2.3. Social relations

In this section I discuss Marx's theory of social relations: their real nature and their distorted appearance in capitalist society. In 2.3.1 I first set out, with little reference to Marx, a general theory of social relations. This will also prove useful for the analysis of exploitation and class in later chapters. In 2.3.2 I turn to Marx's theory of fetishism, that is the view that under capitalism the social relations between men appear as natural properties of objects. In 2.3.3 I finally survey what, following Plamenatz, I call "social alienation" – the fact that the products of human activity may take on an independent and even hostile form *vis-à-vis* their creators.

2.3.1. A theory of relations[1]

Leibniz wrote that "relations either are relations of comparison or of connection".[2] Another frequently invoked distinction is that between external and internal relations.[3] I shall argue that it is useful to distinguish between the two distinctions, although they are also closely related. Both turn out to be helpful for the understanding of Marx's social theory.

Some statements by Marx are relevant in this connection. One – quoted in 2.2.2 above – appears in the *Marginal Notes on Wagner*, where Marx makes a distinction between "to stand in a relationship" and "to relate

---

[1] The following draws heavily on my *Logic and Society*, pp. 20ff, with a simplification suggested by G. A. Cohen.
[2] Leibniz, *Opuscules et Fragments Inédits*, p. 355.
[3] I should give notice that my definition of external and internal relations has nothing in common with those of Ollmann, *Alienation*, and Gould, *Marx's Social Ontology*.

actively". Another, more explicit, is found in the *Economic and Philosophical Manuscripts*:

The antithesis (*Gegensatz*) between *lack of property* and *property*, so long as it is not comprehended as the antithesis of *labour* and *capital*, still remains an indifferent antithesis, not grasped in its *active connection*, in its *internal relation*, not yet grasped as a *contradiction* (Widerspruch).[1]

The relation between property and the lack of it, in other words, is a mere quantitative difference – a relation of comparison, not of a real connection. It is only when they are described as capital and labour that the mutual dependence becomes clear.[2]

As preliminary paradigms for external and internal relations we may take the following statements:

(1) A has more money than B

(2) A exploits B.

Here the first statement is predicated on the basis of a comparison between A and B, who need not interact in any way. The second statement, by contrast, points to a direct, causal link between A and B. We might want, therefore, to propose the following

> *Tentative definition*: '*Rab*' expresses an external relation if and only if there exist predicates $F_1 \ldots F_n$ and $G_1 \ldots G_m$ such that '*Rab*' can be inferred from a truth function of 'F_1a', 'F_2a' $\ldots$ 'F_na' and 'G_1b', 'G_2b' $\ldots$ 'G_mb'.

On this definition statement (1) expresses an external relation, since it can be inferred from the statements 'A has 10 dollars' and 'B has 5 dollars'. On the other hand we may defy anyone to come up with a similar reduction of the relational statement (2) to statements only ascribing monadic predicates to the relata.[3]

This account, however, proves unsatisfactory. Let us compare (1) with

---

[1] *Economic and Philosophical Manuscripts*, pp. 293–4.

[2] To avoid misunderstanding: the mutual dependence is causal, not conceptual. Marx often refers to what, following Hegel, he calls "Reflexionsbestimmungen" (e.g. *The German Ideology*, p. 440 and *Capital I*, p. 57). These correspond to what is also called "polar concepts", illustrated by the opposition between true and false coins – a purely conceptual dependence with no real connections being presupposed.

[3] The point of insisting on a *truth-functional* reduction can be seen from an example that will also occupy us in chs. 4 and 6 below. It is shown there that the predicates "being an exploiter" and "being exploited" can be defined independently of any relation of exploitation. Hence, following a suggestion by Leibniz (*Opuscules et Fragments Inédits*, p. 287), we might try to define that relation in terms of these predicates, by reducing "A exploits B" to "A is an exploiter, and by that very fact (*eo ipso*) B is exploited". The connective "eo ipso" is not, however, a truth-functional one, hence the relation of exploitation is not shown to be an external relation.

(3) A is taller than B.

According to the tentative definition, both (1) and (3) are external relations. The reducing predicates, however, differ importantly in their logical form. The predicate "having n dollars", unlike the predicate "being n
centimetres tall", is *relationally defined*. If we spell out what it means to
possess a certain amount of money, we cannot avoid making a reference
to other people. This, perhaps, is made even clearer by the following:

(4) A has more power than B

(5) A has power over B.

Here (5) is an internal relation between A and B, whereas (4) would be an
external relation according to the tentative definition. Yet any attempt to
define what it means to have power must involve a reference to other
people. In one simple conceptualization of power, my amount of all-
round power is defined as the number of people *over whom* I have control,
so that the relational character of power appears explicitly. In another,
more complex characterization my power depends on my control over
resources in which other people have an interest – also a relationally
defined property.[1] Similarly, the possession of money must also, if spelled out, involve a reference to other people who are prepared to accept my
money as payment for goods. Wittgenstein remarks somewhere that it is
impossible to make sense of the statement "It is five o'clock on the sun",
and it would also be nonsensical to say that Robinson Crusoe on his island
could be rich by the mere possession of gold coins.

In statements (1) and (4) the person B will frequently be one of those by
virtue of whom we ascribe wealth or power to A. This means that we
cannot first describe A and B in terms of monadic predicates and only later
relate them to one another, since they are already connected to each other
through the predicates. This suggests the:

> *Revised definition*: 'Rab' expresses an external relation if it does so
> according to the tentative definition, and in addition no F_i has a
> hidden relational structure with a bound variable among whose
> values is b, and no G_j has a hidden relational structure with a bound
> variable among whose values is a.

The more general conclusion is that in the analysis of society one cannot –
except for such trivial cases as (3) – begin by describing isolated individuals and then go on to define the (comparative) relations between them,

---

[1] For the first definition, see Kemeny, Snell and Thompson, *Introduction to Finite Mathematics*, p. 384; for the second, Coleman, *The Mathematics of Collective Action*.

since an (interactional) relation must be present from the outset.[1] In the study of society, relations are prior to predicates. An empiricist methodology of social science is one that rests on the opposite priority. This is not the occasion to go more deeply into this issue.

The contrast between external and internal relations, then, is exemplified by (3) as against (2). Yet the difference between (1) and (2) also remains important, for reasons explained in 6.1.3. If A exploits B, it means that these two individuals actually interact with one another. If A has more money than B, it need not mean more than that A and B are part of a network of potentially interacting individuals: B would be prepared to accept A's money as payment were they to meet, which they might never actually do. I shall, therefore, bring out the distinction between (1) and (2) by the terms *relations of comparison* and *relations of interaction*. Any relation of interaction is also an internal relation, but as just explained the converse need not hold.

2.3.2. Fetishism

By this Marx means that the social relations of men come to appear as the (natural) properties of objects. The *locus classicus* for this view is in *Capital I*:

A commodity, therefore, is a mysterious thing, simply because in it the social character of men's labour appears to them as an objective character stamped upon the product of that labour; because the relation of the producers to the sum total of their own labour is presented to them as a social relation, existing not between themselves, but between the products of their labour . . . [The] existence of things *qua* commodities, and the value-relation between the products of labour which stamps them as commodities, have absolutely no connexion with their physical properties and with the material relations arising therefrom . . . It is a definite social relation between men, that assumes, in their eyes, the fantastic form of a relation between things. In order . . . to find an analogy, we must have recourse to the mist-enveloped regions of the religious world. In that world the productions of the human brain appear as independent beings endowed with life, and entering into relations both with one another and with the human race. So it is in the world of commodities with the products of men's hands. This I call Fetishism which attaches itself to the products of labour, so soon as they are produced as commodities, and which is therefore inseparable from the production of commodities.[2]

[1] This is a purely methodological statement, which does not prejudge any substantial issues. Although it shows, if correct, that statement (4) in the text cannot be a primitive statement, it does not create any presumption that the proper reduction must be in terms of (5). Similarly for the relation between (1) and (2): the former presupposes *some kind* of interactional relation, of which the latter is one instance, but not necessarily the relevant one for this reduction.
[2] *Capital I*, p. 72.

This passage does not quite support the definition given above, since it defines fetishism as the metamorphosis of relations between men into relations between things, not into properties of things. Other texts, however, assert the latter. One refers to the "fetishism which metamorphoses the social, economic character impressed on things in the process of production into a natural character stemming from the material nature of those things".[1] Or again, "the participants in capitalist production live in a bewitched world and their own relationships appear to them as properties of things".[2] In other places Marx refers to fetishism as the process whereby the social relations between men are turned into properties of things *and* into relations between things.[3] He also asserts that Bailey "is a fetishist in that he conceives value, though not as a property of the individual object (considered in isolation), but as a *relation of objects to one another*, while it is only a representation in objects, an objective expression, of a relation between men".[4] The difference between the two definitions is not important. The central fact underlying both is that the relation between objects is one of comparison, based upon what appears to be their monadic predicates. The fetishism thesis can in fact be stated as follows: relations of interaction between men appear as relations of comparison between objects. Even more sharply: they appear as external relations, since the properties by which the objects are compared do not appear to have a relational component (i.e. to embody a reference to the relations between men), but to inhere in the objects as natural qualities. The most general and parsimonious way of stating the thesis is that *in commodity-producing societies there is a tendency to overlook the implicitly relational character of certain monadic predicates*. Whether or not these monadic predicates are then made the basis for a further comparison, conceived of as an external relation, is less essential.

Although commodity fetishism is the best-known variety of fetishism, because of its prominent place in Marx's best-known work, it is by no means the only or even the most important case. The following categories are all subject to fetishism: commodities, money, industrial capital and interest-bearing capital. The fetishism of commodities is, as we have seen, the belief that commodities *have* value in the same sense as they *have* weight or colour. One may well ask who ever held this absurd belief.[5] Marx was aware that the "mystification is still a very simple one in the case of a commodity. Everybody understands more or less clearly that the

---

[1] *Capital II*, p. 225.   [2] *Theories of Surplus-Value*, vol. 3, p. 514.   [3] *Ibid.*, pp. 130, 137.
[4] *Ibid.*, p. 147.
[5] As does Cohen, *Karl Marx's Theory of History*, p. 127, note 1.

relations of commodities as exchange-values are really the relations of people to the productive activities of one another."[1] The real mystery appears only with money, as we shall see. First, however, we should note that although Marx was correct in saying that commodities have exchange value only by virtue of their relations to persons and the relations between persons, he erred when locating these relations in the process of production. In the imaginary case of a fully automated economy, or in the case of rare objects found by accident, things may have exchange value although not produced by a social process of production. They have value because they are valued, that is because of their capacity to satisfy human wants. And this in fact holds universally. True, in most cases the cost of production also is a determinant of value, but this does not hold universally. I discuss these matters further in 3.2.3.

Money fetishism is the next step in the hierarchy:

> The semblance of simplicity [found in commodity fetishism] disappears in more advanced relations of production. All the illusions of the Monetary system arise from the failure to perceive that money [or gold[2]], though a physical object with distinct properties, represents a social relation of production.[3]

In fact, "the riddle presented by money is but the riddle presented by commodities; only now it strikes us in its most glaring form".[4] Glaring, and therefore blinding: the monetary illusion is much harder to see through than the commodity illusion. As vividly described by Eli Heckscher, mercantilist policy and theory were driven to absurdities because of the confusion of money with real wealth.[5] The psychological roots of this confusion are at least partly to be found in the role of money as interest-bearing capital, further discussed below. Partly the illusion may also be connected with the tendency for money to become the object of compulsive hoarding, as if it were an end in itself (2.2.6). I add a note on the complex, and only moderately interesting, issue of the relation between money fetishism and the reification of language.[6]

---

[1] *A Contribution to the Critique of Political Economy*, p. 22.
[2] In his personal copy of the book Marx substituted "Gold" for "Geld".
[3] *A Contribution to the Critique of Political Economy*, p. 22.
[4] *Capital I*, p. 93.
[5] Heckscher, *Mercantilism*, vol. II, p. 202 and *passim*.
[6] There is a long tradition for comparing money and language. Both are useful symbols for, respectively, non-monetary and non-linguistic reality. Both, moreover, may induce errors if the symbol is invested with some of the qualities of the real thing, or vice versa. Marx, however, explicitly rejects the analogy between money and language (*Grundrisse*, pp. 162–3), because he examined the relation of language to thought rather than that of language to the world. Elsewhere, in a passage on fetishism, he notes that this "paradox of reality is also reflected in paradoxes of vulgar speech" (*Theories of Surplus-Value*, vol. 3, p. 137), coming close to suggesting a connection between fetishism and the reification of

Adam Smith, the "Luther of political economy"[1] denounced the mercantilist fetishism of money. Yet, Marx argues, "As soon as the modern economists, who sneer at the illusions of the Monetary System, deal with the more complex economic categories, such as capital, they display the same illusions."[2] To say, for instance, that "instruments of labour are fixed capital" is to give a scholastic definition that "brings to completion the fetishism peculiar to bourgeois Political Economy".[3] That capital is a relation rather than a thing is incomprehensible to the economist: since he "only knows tangible things and ideas, relations do not exist for him".[4]

Capital fetishism, in G. A. Cohen's phrase, occurs when "capital's power to produce . . . appears to be a faculty inherent in it, not one it owes to the labour process".[5] This holds with respect to both the production of use-values and the production of surplus-value or profit.

With respect to the production of use-values, Marx argues that because the extra productive power of bringing many workers together "costs capital nothing, and because . . . the labourer himself does not develop it before his labour belongs to capital, it appears as a power with which capital is endowed by nature".[6] *To whom* does it appear in this way? Mainly to the workers, as argued in chapters 4 and 8 below.

The other form of capital fetishism takes shape as an illusion that constant and variable capital are equally productive of profit, whereas in reality only the variable capital generates a surplus. Since profit accrues equally to constant and variable capital, it appears to be created equally by both. Appears to whom? To the capitalist, certainly, since to him all the factors of production "contribute equally to the formation of the cost-price".[7] Marx no doubt was correct in imputing this view to the capitalist, but wrong in thinking that the view is incorrect. The premise that only living labour contributes to the surplus is untenable (3.2.3). In another

language. Other passages (extensively cited in Erckenbrecht, *Marx's materialistische Sprachtheorie* I.5) point in the same direction, many of them suggesting that the price is the "money-name" of the commodity. Some questions may be raised. Is there a link between the tendency of fetishism to turn relations into monadic predicates, and the tendency of reification to turn verbs (the bearer of relations) into nouns? Is linguistic reification a causal expression of the economic fetishism, or does it rather tend to stabilize it? In other words, assuming that we want to explain linguistic reification in terms of fetishism, should we invoke causal or functional explanation? I am not at all certain that these are issues worth looking into, but then again they might be.

[1] *Economic and Philosophical Manuscripts*, p. 290. The passage is cited in full in 8.3.2.
[2] *A Contribution to the Critique of Political Economy*, p. 22.
[3] *Capital II*, p. 225.   [4] *Zur Kritik (1861–63)*, p. 133.
[5] Cohen, *Karl Marx's Theory of History*, p. 117. In the following I draw extensively on Cohen's analysis.
[6] *Capital I*, p. 333.
[7] *Capital III*, p. 35; cp. also *Grundrisse*, p. 759 and Cohen, *Karl Marx's Theory of History*, p. 123.

passage Marx argues, puzzlingly, that the non-proportionality of profit and surplus-value in the different spheres of production "completely conceals the true nature and origin not only from the capitalist, who has a special interest in deceiving himself on that score, but also from the labourer".[1] The puzzle is why Marx here links fetishism to self-deception. As further argued in 8.2.3, it is a cognitive illusion, not a motivationally based process.

"The relations of capital assume their most externalized and most fetish-like form in interest-bearing capital."[2] If money can multiply and fructify itself independently of the production process, it is indeed tempting to conclude that it is, mysteriously, productive. In reality it is productive only when and because it is invested and put to productive use, but for the financial capitalist this may not be visible. He may even conclude, absurdly, that money capital would yield an interest "even if all capitalists only loaned their capital, and none used it productively".[3] Again I refer to chapter 8 for further discussion.

Marx's theory of fetishism is an important contribution to psychological economics, although to some extent vitiated by its dependence on the labour theory of value. It is also somewhat exaggerated, in the sense that not all the claims made are equally plausible. Economic agents do not invest commodities and instruments of production with the full panoply of mysterious powers that Marx describes in such detail. Money is indeed a mysterious entity, but only in part for the reasons brought out by Marx. In addition the opacity of money arises from the ever-more fictitious and intangible forms that it tends to assume. One may know *a priori that* the properties of money derive from social relations between men, and yet remain mystified because one is unable to show *how* they derive from them. Yet the history of economic doctrine and policy shows that money fetishism has indeed existed in the form Marx described it. It may also be argued that the neoclassical notion of "aggregate capital" as a factor of production also embodies a kind of fetishism, as shown in the "capital controversy".[4]

---

[1] *Capital III*, p. 168.   [2] *Capital III*, p. 391.
[3] Cohen, *Karl Marx's Theory of History*, p. 118.
[4] For this controversy, see Harcourt, *Some Cambridge Controversies*, and Bliss, *Capital Theory and the Distribution of Income*. The various fallacies of aggregation that formed the object of the capital controversy are related to fetishism as follows: statements that are true at most by virtue of relations that obtain between the disaggregated entities are taken to be true of the aggregate entities as such.

2.3.3. Social alienation

Perhaps the most central single theme in Marx's thinking, from the *Economic and Philosophical Manuscripts* to *Capital*, is the idea that under capitalism the products of men gain an independent existence and come into opposition to their makers. Religion, the State and Capital are the three main examples of this process. The general logic of the "subject–object inversion" is discussed in 8.2.1. Here I shall only focus on the alienation that takes place in the economic sphere. This involves several aspects, since men "produce" social relations no less than material objects and, among the latter, instruments of production no less than objects of consumption. The alienation from social relations is closely linked to the supra-intentional and dialectical processes discussed in 1.3.2 and 1.5.3, while the alienation from the means of consumption is related to spiritual alienation as defined in 2.2.5. The alienation from the means of production is the central problem of the mature economic writings.

In *The German Ideology* Marx introduced a quite general notion of alienation, involving men's alienation from social institutions and other aggregate phenomena:

This fixation of social activity, this consolidation of what we ourselves produce into a material power above us, growing out of our control, thwarting our expectations, bringing to naught our calculations, is one of the chief factors in historical development up till now. The social power, i.e. the multiplied productive force, which arises through the cooperation of different individuals as it is caused by the division of labour, appears to these individuals, since their cooperation is not voluntary but has come about naturally, not of their own united power, but as an alien power existing outside them, of the origin and goal of which they are ignorant, which they are no longer able to control, which on the contrary passes through a peculiar series of phases and stages independent of the will and the action of man, nay even being the prime governor of these.[1]

Marx here argues that men are alienated ("to use a term which will be comprehensible to the philosophers"[2]) from the aggregate result of their activities when (i) they do not realize that these aggregates are the result of their own activities and (ii) they are unable to control or to change the outcome. He also adds, more obscurely, that they are alienated because they ignore the goal of these aggregates – a notion that immediately invites the question: goal for whom? I postpone this issue to 2.4. It should be emphasized that even when (i) does not obtain, (ii) may be true. Men may well know that their own social environment is the product of their own behaviour, and yet be unable to control it. This can happen if they

[1] *The German Ideology*, pp. 47–8; see also p. 245.
[2] *Ibid.*, p. 48.

know *that* but not *how* their actions generate the aggregate features that they deplore. This is not a trivial insight. When farmers stop blaming the weather or the government for the price fluctuations of their products, and realize that they are caught in a web of their own making,[1] they have taken a large step forward even if they can neither specify exactly what they are doing wrong, nor *a fortiori* take steps to remedy the situation. In other cases the agents may even understand the causal mechanism and yet be unable to do anything about it, because it is in the private interest of no one to do so and they are unable to act in concert (6.2).

In the *Grundrisse*, conditions (i) and (ii) are not invariably assumed to go together. Individual agents may acquire information about the economic system that helps them to improve their individual position and even to anticipate the outcome; yet the latter is not in any real sense under their control:

Since ... the autonomization of the world market (in which the activity of each individual is included) increases with the development of monetary relations (exchange value) and vice versa, since the general bond and all-round interdependence in production and consumption increase together with the independence and indifference of the consumers and producers to one another; since this contradiction leads to crises etc. hence, together with the development of this alienation, and on the same basis, efforts are made to overcome it: institutions emerge whereby each individual can acquire information about the activity of all others and attempt to adjust his own accordingly, e.g. lists of current prices, rates of exchange, interconnections between those active in commerce through the mails, telegraphs etc. ... (This means that, although the total supply and demand are independent of the actions of each individual, everyone attempts to inform himself about them, and this knowledge then reacts back in practice on the total supply and demand. Although, on the given standpoint, alienation is not overcome by these means, nevertheless relations and connections are introduced thereby which include the possibility of suspending the old standpoint.)[2]

Two lessons can be drawn from this remarkably suggestive passage. First, there may be social alienation without fetishism. The opacity of social relations and their "transubstantiation" into natural properties of things may lead to the production of collectively undesirable consequences, but the latter can also arise when social relations are perfectly transparent. The problem then is not one of information but of coordination. Secondly, the alienation discussed here arises from interaction within classes, not from struggle between classes. Problems of collective action, in fact, arise within the working class as well as within the class of capitalists (6.2).

[1] For the "cobweb" as a paradigm of counterfinality, see my *Logic and Society*, pp. 111ff.
[2] *Grundrisse*, pp. 160–1.

Yet the working class is also subject to alienation in a more specific sense that does not apply to the capitalist class. This is related to the role of the worker as *producer* of means of consumption and production. Consider first an early statement from the *Economic and Philosophical Manuscripts*:.

the worker is related to the *product of his labour* as to an *alien* object. [On] this premise it is clear that the more the worker spends himself, the more powerful becomes the alien world of objects which he creates over and against himself, the poorer he himself – his inner world – becomes, the less belongs to him as his own. It is the same in religion. The more man puts into God, the less he retains in himself. The worker puts his life into the object; but now his life no longer belongs to him, but to the object. Hence the greater this activity, the more the worker lacks objects. Whatever the product of his labour is, he is not. Therefore, the greater this product, the less he is himself. The *alienation* of the worker in his products means not only that his labour becomes an object, an *external* existence, but that it exists *outside him*, independently, as something alien to him, and that it becomes a power on its own confronting him. It means that the life which he has conferred on the object confronts him as something hostile and alien.[1]

Considered as an argument this is a series of *non sequiturs*, culminating a few pages later in the deduction of the capitalist and of private property from the fact of alienated labour.[2] It makes more sense as a mere description of the worker's plight, but even as such it remains vague. We can get it better in focus by distinguishing between two classes of objects from which the worker is alienated: consumption goods and instruments of production. The distinction is briefly made once in the early manuscripts: "the worker is robbed of the objects most necessary not only for his life but for his work".[3] The emphasis appears to be on the means of consumption, with the means of production added as an afterthought. In a text written some fifteen years later the emphasis is reversed: "All the objective elements required by labour for its realization appear to him as alienated, as standing on the same side as the capitalist, the means of subsistence no less than the means of production."[4] It is the alienation from the means of production that is by far the more important theme in these later economic writings.

The worker's alienation from the objects of consumption he has created is closely linked to his spiritual alienation. The production of objects of

---

[1] *Economic and Philosophical Manuscripts*, p. 272.
[2] *Ibid.*, pp. 278–9. Marx here performs a quite extraordinary sleight of hand, using the (dubious) logico-dialectical deduction of private property from alienated labour to argue that the latter is also the *cause* of the former. Cp. also 1.5.1 above.
[3] *Economic and Philosophical Manuscripts*, p. 272.
[4] *Zur Kritik (1861–63)*, p. 119.

consumption goes together with the creation of a need for them – a need that is often frustrated in the capitalist mode of production. This is a fairly transparent connection. It is less obvious why the worker should be frustrated by the alienation from the means of production, since he can hardly be said to need them in the same sense. This form of alienation is in fact less superficially evident, but also more profound in its implications. The alienation from the means of production is the crucial structural fact that underlies the alienation from the means of consumption, since it deprives the worker of his claim on the whole net product. Also, the dispossession from the means of production excludes the worker from full control of the work process and prevents him, therefore, from fully exercising his creative capacities. Let me elaborate on these statements.

In the capitalist process of production, living labour is dominated by dead labour, the worker by the means of production with which he produces and which are themselves the product of past labour. This domination has a rather complex structure. Three aspects at least can be distinguished, and will be brought out by citing at some length three passages from the *Grundrisse*. First, the worker is dominated by constant capital because he is made into a mere appendix of the machine:

The appropriation of living labour by objectified labour – of the power or activity which creates value by existing for-itself – which lies in the concept of capital, is posited, in production resting on machinery, as the character of the production process itself, including its material element and its material motion. The production process has ceased to be a labour process in the sense of a process dominated by labour as its governing unity. Labour appears, rather, merely as a conscious organ, scattered among the individual living workers at numerous points of the mechanical system; subsumed under the total process of machinery itself.[1]

This is related to the spiritual alienation of the worker who is subjectively or objectively impoverished by what Marx calls "his real subsumption under capital".[2] In early capitalism the worker is only formally subsumed under capital, that is dominated by capital only in the sense of being exploited by capital. This is in one sense the fundamental form of capitalist domination, since it is what makes the real subsumption possible. What goes on "at the point of exchange" between labour and capital determines what goes on "at the point of production" (4.1.5). Yet subjectively or phenomenologically the loss of control over the production process whereby the worker is turned from a producer into a mere *instrumentum vocale* may be as intolerable as the fact of being exploited. The

[1] *Grundrisse*, p. 693.
[2] Cp. especially the *Results of the Immediate Process of Production*.

power of decision in work provided an – admittedly limited – means of self-realization, the loss of which left the worker poorer in needs or in needs satisfaction.

The second aspect of the domination is quantitative rather than qualitative. To state it, I must briefly anticipate the discussion in chapter 3 of Marx's economic theory. A central notion of Marxist economics is the organic composition of capital, or the ratio of the value of constant capital to that of variable capital: c/v. Assuming that labour-power with a value v produces a surplus-value s, we may also define the value composition of capital as $c/(v + s)$. Unlike the first ratio, this is determined solely by technology. It expresses the ratio of dead labour to living labour in the production process, whereas the organic composition of capital expresses the ratio of dead labour to the value of the labour-power used in the production. In the following passage Marx must be taken to argue that an increase in the value composition of capital takes place *pari passu* with increased qualitative domination of capital over labour:

> The fact that in the development of the productive powers of labour the objective conditions of labour, objectified labour, must grow relative to living labour – this is actually a tautological statement, for what else does growing productive power of labour mean than that less immediate labour is required to create a greater product, and that therefore social wealth expresses itself more and more in the conditions of labour created by labour itself? – this fact appears from the standpoint of capital not in such a way that one of the moments of social activity – objective labour – becomes the ever more powerful body of the other moment, of subjective living labour, but rather ... that the objective conditions of labour assume an ever more colossal independence represented by its very extent, opposite living labour, and that social wealth confronts labour in more powerful portions as an alien or dominant power.[1]

Marx also believed that the rise in the organic composition of capital was brought about by a rise in the value composition.[2] He argued, moreover, for a link between an increasing organic composition of capital and a fall in the rate of profit (3.4.2). Hence there emerges a connection between two major flaws of capitalism – the spiritual alienation created by the real subsumption of labour under capital and the economic crises due the falling rate of profit. Increased alienation or impoverishment of the worker who is reduced to an appendage to his own product goes together with a rising value composition of capital, hence with a rising organic composition, hence with a fall in the rate of profit. The rise of capital at the expense of the worker is detrimental to the worker – but also to capital

[1] *Grundrisse*, p. 831.   [2] *Capital III*, p. 212.

since in the last analysis all profit comes from living labour. This vision is admirably "dialectical", but unfortunately logically incoherent. There may be increased qualitative domination without a rise in the value composition if the machines are sufficiently devaluated by technical progress. There may be a rise in the value composition without a rise in the organic composition, if the value of the labour-power is sufficiently devaluated through falling real wages or increased productivity. And there may be a rise in the organic composition without a fall in the rate of profit if (for instance) there is a rise in the rate of exploitation. These matters are further discussed in 3.4.2.

Thirdly, the domination of dead labour over living labour may be linked to the phenomenon of exploitation, another major flaw of capitalism. It is in fact only by virtue of the capitalist's possession of the means of production that he can exploit the workers without the use of force or violence, beyond that necessary to protect private property in general. Or, more correctly: he can exploit them because they believe that his possession is legitimate, which they do because of their alienation from the means of production. This alienation may be taken to mean that the workers unthinkingly accept the currently used means of production as being the property of the current generation of capitalists, ignoring that they are also the product of past labour. Or, more plausibly,[1] although aware that the means of production are the product of past workers, they accept the present capitalist possession as legitimate because the earlier generation of workers produced them with the help of means of production held to be the legitimate possession of the earlier generation of capitalists. On this view, alienation and exploitation reinforce each other in a *steady-state* process that has been well described by Mario Nuti:

Attention is focussed not on past labour but on the present value of the embodiment of past labour, and its current productiveness can be taken to provide a justification for the attribution of the surplus of current output over the wage bill to those who have appropriated the embodiment of past labour, thereby providing the current basis of future appropriation.[2]

As I understand it, alienation from the means of production is not constituted by the workers feeling oppressed in the knowledge that they are *unjustly* dominated by the products of their own labour. It is rather that while knowing themselves to be dominated by the products of their past

[1] I owe this amendment to Cohen's "Reply" to my "Marxism, functionalism and game theory".
[2] Nuti, "Capitalism, socialism and steady growth", p. 57.

labour,[1] they do not see that the possession of these products by the capitalist is illegitimate. Hence they also accept the appropriation by the capitalist of part of the current net product as legitimate. True, there may be grumbling at the lack of satisfaction of satisfiable needs, but this is a far cry from rejecting the current state of affairs as fundamentally unjust. Thus, if I am right in my analysis, even subjective spiritual alienation may not be much of a lever for change in the presence of alienation from the means of production.

The emphasis on the *injustice* of alienation may prove controversial. I postpone to 4.3 the presentation of my reasons for thinking that Marx had a theory of justice, but one central piece of evidence will be given here, since it fits in with the argument of the last paragraph. In the *Grundrisse* we find the following passage:

> The recognition by labour of the products as its own, and the judgment that its separation from the conditions of its realization is improper (*ungehörig*) – forcibly imposed – is an enormous awareness (*enormes Bewusstsein*), itself the product of the mode of production resting on capital, and as much the knell to its doom as, with the slave's awareness that he *cannot be the property of another*, with his consciousness of himself as a person, the existence of slavery becomes a merely artificial vegetative existence and ceases to be able to prevail as the basis of production.[2]

Now one may argue that the word "ungehörig" is ambiguous, and need not be taken in the sense of "unjust". Also, the passage would appear to be quite atypical, almost unique in its insistence on the cognitive conditions for revolution. Both of these objections evaporate in the face of the remarkable fact that in the 1861–3 *Critique*, written a few years after the *Grundrisse*, Marx repeats the same passage almost verbatim, with one main exception. This is that the separation from the means of production that in the *Grundrisse* was referred to as "ungehörig", in the later manuscript is called "ein Unrecht".[3] If Marx had not believed in the injustice of capitalist property he would hardly, when singling out this passage for excerption, have sharpened the "improperness" of alienation into "injustice". And had it not been representative of his thinking, it would hardly have been singled out in the first place.

I conclude that the alienation of the workers from the means of production has the consequence of making exploitation appear as legitimate.

---

[1] *Whose* past labour? In reality, of course, the workers use means of production in the production of which they have not been involved themselves; hence their claim to the whole net product cannot be based on historical considerations. Rather it must be based on the lack of entitlement of the capitalist, as argued in 4.3.2.

[2] *Grundrisse*, p. 463.   [3] *Zur Kritik* (1861–63), p. 2287.

Were one to sum up Marx's analysis and critique of capitalism in one sentence, I do not believe one could do better than to say that *alienation prevents the workers from perceiving the injustice of exploitation*. This captures both the normative view that exploitation *is* unjust, and an explanatory claim about the appearance of justice. It is instructive to compare capital fetishism with capital as alienated labour. Although both rest on illusions, the nature of the illusory beliefs differs. Capital fetishism, like fetishism in general, is an illusory perception of how the economy works. Capital as alienated labour is possible because the workers have an unfounded belief about the entitlement of the capitalist to the means of production. The first is an illusion about causality, the second an illusion about morality. Both illusions are natural, almost compelling, within the framework of a capitalist economy.

2.4. Philosophy of history

Marx had a theory of history, of the successive modes of production based on class domination. This is the topic of chapter 5 below. Here I want to consider his non-empirical philosophy of history. This is the view that before the rise of modes of production based on class division, society existed in a form of undifferentiated unity, and that after the demise of class society there will again be unity, but now in a differentiated form that allows full scope for the development of the individual. True, this view need not be based on *a priori* assumptions. One might well argue on empirical grounds that the advent of a communist society is highly probable, given certain trends in capitalism. My contention, however, is that Marx believed in the necessity of this development on non-empirical, speculative grounds. Many of the texts I shall cite are open to different interpretations, but in my opinion their cumulative impact leaves little doubt that Marx was indeed guided by a teleological view of history.

I shall first and very briefly sketch the historical background of the problem, with emphasis on the philosophies of history proposed by Leibniz and Hegel (2.4.1). I then discuss in their chronological order the central passages in Marx, especially in the early manuscripts, the political journalism and the mature economic writings (2.4.2). I end by drawing some distinctions that suggest themselves on the basis of these texts, and by offering some conclusions on the importance of Marx's philosophy of history for his explanatory and political purposes (2.4.3).

2.4.1. The background

Marx was, of course, steeped in Hegel, but also in Leibniz.[1] If I draw attention to Leibniz it is not, however, because of his direct influence on Marx, but because of his key role as an influence on Hegel. Leibniz's philosophy of history was part of his general theodicy, his view that the actual world is the best of all possible worlds.[2] Logically speaking, there is no reason why the best of all possible worlds should also contain the best of all possible societies; or the best of all possible temporal sequences for the universe as a whole the best of all possible histories of humanity. The general logic of the theodicy is that the over-all optimum may require suboptimality in the parts, either as a necessary means to the optimum or as an inevitable by-product of it. Leibniz held the first of these two versions of the theodicy, Malebranche the second. On either version it could be the case that the optimality of the universe as a whole requires suboptimality in the small corner where human history unfolds itself. Yet Leibniz apparently also believed that the course of all human history was the best of all possible courses, and this is in any case how he was generally understood.

Leibniz made a distinction between two ways in which an optimal development may require suboptimal intervals. The first was later and independently developed by Tocqueville[3] and Schumpeter:[4] a system that at any given moment exploits its possibilities maximally, may over time perform less well than a system that does so at no given moment. The patent system is an instructive example: by restricting the diffusion of knowledge, it ensures that there will be more knowledge to diffuse.[5] The second is what Leibniz referred to as "reculer pour mieux sauter": it may be necessary at some point to take one step backwards in order to be able later on to take two steps forwards.[6] An instance of this pattern is investment – consuming less now in order to be able to consume more later on. Now the crucial point is that both of these optimizing methods requires an intentional agent. The first requires the ability to say No to favourable opportunities in the present in order to be able to say Yes to even more favourable ones later on, the second an ability to say Yes to unfavourable options now in order to be able to say Yes to very favourable ones in the

---

[1] For details, see my "Marx et Leibniz".
[2] The following draws heavily on my *Leibniz et la Formation de l'Esprit Capitaliste*, ch. VI and *passim*.
[3] Tocqueville, *Democracy in America*, p. 224.
[4] Schumpeter, *Capitalism, Socialism and Democracy*, p. 83.
[5] Robinson, *The Accumulation of Capital*, p. 87.
[6] References in *Leibniz et la Formation de l'Esprit Capitaliste*, pp. 233ff.

future. In both cases the suboptimal action only makes sense in view of the future gains that it makes possible. But to act in the light of the future is to act intentionally.[1] In Leibniz's philosophy this made perfectly good sense, since on his view the course of human history was decided by God when he chose the actual world among the many possible worlds. God is the intentional agent whose goal – to create the best of all possible worlds – makes sense of the local and temporary defects of the universe.

For Leibniz, then, history had a goal and a creator. These two, of course, go together. Hegel, disastrously, retained the idea that history had a goal, yet did not invoke any intentional agent whose actions were guided by that goal.[2] Hegel's philosophy of history is a secular theodicy, which is to say that it is nonsense. His *Lectures on the Philosophy of History* and (to a much smaller extent) the *Phenomenology of Spirit* rest on disembodied intentions, actions in search of an actor, verbs that are attached to no subject. His idea of "the ruse of reason" is related to Mandeville's "private vices, public benefits" and Adam Smith's "invisible hand", but unlike them he thought that the consequences which are unintended by the actors nevertheless have a meaning or a purpose. In his notes on the neo-Confucian philosophers, Leibniz observed that if they believe in an orderly universe, they must also believe in a divine creator. "I strongly doubt whether they have the vain subtlety of admitting sagacity without admitting also a sage."[3] This, however, is exactly what Hegel did, and I shall argue that Marx to some extent took over this pattern of thought. They remained imprisoned in a halfway house, between a fully religious and a fully secular view of history.

2.4.2. The texts

Marx had a fairly consistent teleological attitude towards history, but with some variations over time. It is occasionally present in the *Economic and Philosophical Manuscripts*, strongly rejected in *The German Ideology*, and then again quite prominent in the writings from the 1850s and the 1860s. I have no explanation for the stark contrast between *The German Ideology* and the other works, except possibly in the influence of Engels. Although capable of wild flights of fancy, Engels may have had a more sober attitude towards history than did Marx, corresponding to his

---

[1] See my *Ulysses and the Sirens*, ch. I.2.
[2] I refuse, that is, to take "Spirit" and "Reason" as agents in a non-metaphorical sense. For a critical discussion, see Grégoire, *Etudes Hégéliennes*.
[3] Bodemann, *Die Leibniz-Handschriften*, p. 105.

better judgment concerning specific historical events.[1] This, however, remains somewhat speculative.[2]

In the *Economic and Philosophical Manuscripts* Marx asks: "What in the evolution of mankind is the meaning (*Sinn*) of this reduction of the greater part of mankind to abstract labour?"[3] He does not immediately provide an answer, but returns to the question later:

> The *real*, active orientation of man to himself as a species-being . . . is only possible if he really brings out all his *species-powers* – something which in turn is only possible through the cooperative action of all mankind, only as the result of history – and treats these powers as objects: and this, to begin with, is again only possible in the form of alienation.[4]

Otherwise the emphasis in these manuscripts is on the suffering involved in alienation, not on its broader historical meaning. In *The German Ideology* any such meaning is dismissed out of hand:

> History is nothing but the succession of the separate generations, each of which uses the materials, the capital funds, the productive forces handed down to it by all the preceding generations, and thus, on the one hand, continues the traditional activity in completely changed circumstances, and, on the other, modifies the old circumstances with a completely changed activity. This can be speculatively distorted so that later history is made the goal of earlier history, i.e. the goal ascribed to the discovery of America is to further the eruption of the French Revolution.[5]

Other passages are equally explicit, including an amusing refutation of Stirner's tendency to see every positive event, like the invention of the railroad, as the removal of its absence.[6]

In 1852–3 Marx wrote four newspaper articles in which we find various assertions that lend themselves to a teleological reading. The most explicit, and the least important, is the conclusion of a discussion of the Russian attitude to Turkey: "Does Russia act on her own free impulse, or is she but the unconscious and reluctant slave of the modern *fatum*, Revolution? I believe the latter."[7] The passage is too rhetorical to carry much weight. Another may be too brief. In explaining that the English bourgeoisie would rather avoid a forcible collision with the aristocracy, Marx argues that "historical necessity and the Tories press them onwards".[8] I attach more importance to an article where Marx argues that

---

[1] Anderson, *Lineages of the Absolutist State*, p. 23, note 12.
[2] The conjecture is supported by the fact that in one of Engels's contributions to *The Holy Family* (p. 93) there is a similar anti-teleological statement.
[3] *Economic and Philosophical Manuscripts*, p. 241.   [4] *Ibid.*, p. 333.
[5] *The German Ideology*, p. 50.
[6] *Ibid.*, pp. 302ff.   [7] *New York Daily Tribune* 9.6.1853.   [8] *Ibid.* 25.8.1852.

the alternative rise and fall of wages, and the continual conflicts between masters and men resulting therefrom are, in the present organization of industry, the indispensable means of holding up the spirit of the labouring classes, of combining them into one great association against the encroachment of the ruling class, and of preventing them from becoming apathetic, thoughtless, more or less well-fed instruments of production ... Without the great alternative phases of dullness, prosperity, over-excitement, crisis and distress, which modern industry traverses in periodically recurring cycles, with the up and down of wages result-ing from them, as with the constant warfare between masters and men closely corresponding with those variations in wages and profits, the working classes of Great Britain, and of all Europe, would be a heart-broken, a weak-minded, a worn-out, unresisting mass, whose self-emancipation would prove as impossible as that of the slaves of Ancient Greece and Rome.[1]

The passage is characteristic in the tension between the two ways of looking at the ills of capitalism: as an instrumental "means" for the emancipation of the worker, and as merely a necessary condition for it. On the former view the periodical crises can actually be *explained* by their favourable impact on working-class combativity, on the latter no such implication can be drawn. Similarly ambiguous, although leaning more strongly to the instrumental and teleological view, is the concluding pas-sage from the article on "The British Rule in India":

England, it is true, in causing a social revolution in Hindostan, was actuated only by the vilest interests, and was stupid in her manner of enforcing them. But that is not the question. The question is, can mankind fulfil its destiny without a fun-damental revolution in the social state of Asia? If not, whatever may have been the crimes of England she was the unconscious tool of history in bringing about that revolution. Then, whatever bitterness the spectacle of the crumbling of an ancient world may have for our personal feelings, we have the right, in point of history, to exclaim with Goethe:

> Sollte diese Qual uns quälen
> Da sie unsre Lust vermehrt,
> Hat nicht myriaden Seelen
> Timurs Herrschaft aufgezehrt?[2]

Again we might want to dismiss the text as rhetorical, but in the light of similar texts not intended for publication, I do not find this plausible. Before I quote these texts, I want to make two, related comments on the cited passage. First, it is not clear to me whether Marx saw the suffering of India as the inevitable by-product of progress or as the causal condition for (or instrumental means to) progress. When Marx writes about English capitalism, it is clear that working-class suffering is a condition for pro-gress, in two ways. First, as suggested by the passage on the trade cycle,

[1] *Ibid.* 14.7.1853.   [2] *Ibid.* 25.6.1853.

the periodically recurring misery of the workers is a causally necessary condition for revolution. Also, the exploitation of the workers is a causal condition for the creation of free time and the development of civilization. The passage on India, however, could equally well be taken as a comment on omelette-making and egg-breaking.

Secondly, it is in fact only "in the point of history" that one can invoke Goethe's verse to justify the ills of capitalism. Marx quotes the quatrain a few years later, but then in an ironic vein, directed against the "Manchester school" which – rather improbably – might use it to justify their exploitation of the workers.[1] Although Marx can see the capitalist exploiter as the agent of progress, this does not mean that the latter can justify his actions by the same argument. It is not just that such an argument would be obviously self-serving and hypocritical. More fundamentally, there might be many events that one would welcome were they to happen, yet one might not want to be the person by whose agency they come about.[2]

If we search for teleological statements in the mature economic writings, we find them clustered mainly in the 1861–3 *Critique*, including the *Theories of Surplus-Value*. In the *Grundrisse* there are many passages where Marx argues that capitalist alienation is a necessary condition for communism, but in general they do not have instrumental or teleological overtones. An important exception is the following passage, which forms the immediate continuation of an argument quoted in 2.3.3 above:

The emphasis comes to be placed not on the state of being *objectified*, but on the state of being *alienated*, dispossessed, sold; on the condition that the monstrous objective power which social labour itself erected opposite itself as one of its moments belongs not to the worker, but to the personified conditions of production, i.e. to capital. To the extent that, from the standpoint of capital and wage labour, the creation of the objective body of activity happens in antithesis to the immediate labour capacity – that this process of objectification in fact appears as a process of dispossession from the standpoint of labour or as appropriation of alien labour from the standpoint of capital – to that extent, this twisting and inversion is a *real* [*phenomenon*], not a merely *supposed one* existing merely in the imagination of the workers and the capitalists. But obviously this process of inversion is a merely *historical* necessity, a necessity for the development of the forces of production solely from a specific historic point of departure, or basis, but in no way an *absolute* necessity of production; rather, a vanishing one, and the result and the inherent purpose of this process is to suspend this basis itself, together with the form of the process.[3]

---

[1] *Neue Oder Zeitung*, 20.1.1855.   [2] Cp. Williams, "A critique of utilitarianism".
[3] *Grundrisse*, pp. 831–2, following the text belonging to note 1, p. 104 above.

Here the ambiguity is definitely resolved. The creation of communism is not only the "result" of capitalist alienation, but also "the inherent purpose of the process".

In the *Grundrisse* we also find a clear statement of the periodization of history into three stages, which correspond to the pattern of the negation of the negation:

Relations of personal dependence (entirely spontaneous at the outset) are the first social forms, in which human productive capacity develops only to a slight extent and at isolated points. Personal independence founded on *objective* dependence is the second great form, in which a system of general social metabolism, of universal relations, of all-round need and universal capacities is formed for the first time. Free individuality, based on the universal development of individuals and on their subordination of their communal, social productivity as their social wealth, is the third stage. The second stage creates the conditions for the third.[1]

As is clear from the context, the pre-capitalist modes of production belong to the first stage. In the *Theories of Surplus-Value* a somewhat different periodization is presented, with all class societies incorporated in the second stage:

The original unity between the worker and the conditions of production (abstracting from slavery, where the labourer himself belongs to the objective conditions) has two main forms: the Asiatic communal system (primitive communism) and small-scale agriculture based on the family (and linked with domestic industry) in one form or another. Both are embryonic forms and both are equally unfitted to develop labour as *social* labour and the productive power of social labour. Hence the necessity for the separation, for the rupture, for the antithesis of labour and property (by which property in the conditions of production is to be understood). The most extreme form of this rupture, and the one in which the productive forces of social labour are also most powerfully developed, is capital. The original unity can be re-established only on the material foundations which capital creates and by means of the revolutions which, in the process of this creation, the working class and the whole society undergo.[2]

Like Weber and Durkheim, Marx thus saw the progress of history up to the present as one of constant differentiation. Unlike them, he did not see this as an irreversible process, but predicted that there would occur a final stage of integration or loss of differentiation. Thus, for instance:

Capitalist production completely tears asunder the old bond of union which held together agriculture and manufacture in their infancy. But at the same time it creates the material conditions for a higher synthesis in the future, viz. the union

---

[1] *Grundrisse*, p. 158.
[2] *Theories of Surplus-Value*, vol. 3, pp. 422–3.

of agriculture and industry on the basis of the more perfected forms they have acquired during their temporary separation.[1]

In this integrated society men would not, however, be absorbed without remainder in the community, as was the case in the earliest forms. They would retain and in fact develop the individuality that is fostered by class society, but without the agonistic and antagonistic character which prevails in the "spiritual animal kingdom" (2.2.7). The individual no less than the society would be rendered whole again, enriched by the middle passage through separation and alienation.

There can be little question that this was Marx's vision of world history. Does it qualify as a teleological view, in which the earlier stages are seen as tending irresistibly towards the latter and as being explained by their contribution to the latter? Or did Marx simply state a series of necessary conditions for the successive stages to emerge? In my opinion the texts to be quoted below all point towards the first interpretation. In the *Results of the Immediate Process of Production* Marx argued that the capitalist inversion of subject into object and vice versa

is the indispensable transition without which wealth as such, i.e. the relentless productive forces of social labour, which alone can form the material base of a free human society, could not possibly be created by force at the expense of the majority. This antagonistic stage cannot be avoided.[2]

In the 1861–3 *Critique* Marx again quotes the verse from Goethe, immediately after the remark that "It is, in fact, only at the greatest waste of individual development that the development of general men is secured in those epochs of history which prelude to a socialist constitution of humanity."[3] This phrase, which is repeated almost verbatim in *Capital III*,[4] hardly makes sense outside the teleological frame of mind. Like the preceding passage, it is marked by the characteristic use of the passive, subjectless voice of the verb. The antagonistic stage "cannot be avoided" – avoided by whom? The development of mankind "is secured" – secured by whom?

Consider finally two more passages from the 1861–3 manuscript:

Surplus labour is the labour of the worker, of the individual, beyond the limits of his own needs. It is truly labour for the benefit of society, even though, initially, the capitalist *collects* the proceeds of this surplus labour in the name of society. As we have pointed out, this surplus labour is, on the one hand, the basis of society's

---

[1] *Capital I*, p. 505.
[2] *Results of the Immediate Process of Production*, p. 990.
[3] *Zur Kritik (1861–63)*, p. 327 (English in the original).
[4] *Capital III*, p. 88.

free time, and, on the other, it provides the material basis for the entire development of society and of culture in general. By forcing the great mass of society to
carry out this work which goes beyond its immediate needs, the coercive power of
capital creates culture: it fulfils an historical and social function.[1]

[Although] at first the development of the capacities of the *human species* takes
place at the cost of the majority of human individuals and even classes, in the end
it breaks through this contradiction and coincides with the development of the
individual; the higher development of the individual is thus only achieved by a
historical process during which individuals are sacrificed, for the interests of the
species, as in the animal and plant kingdoms, always assert themselves at the cost
of the interest of individuals, because these interests of the species coincide only
with the *interests of certain individuals,* and it is this coincidence which constitutes
the strength of these privileged individuals.[2]

The first text is a quite extraordinary homage to the capitalist as the
unconscious agent of humanity and civilization. The second contains a
blatantly teleological statement to the effect that the interests of the
species always assert themselves. True, Marx also appears to suggest a
mechanism through which the species interest can assert itself, namely
by coinciding with the private interest of certain individuals. But since
nothing is said about why this coincidence should enable those private
interests to get the upper hand, we are left with an unsubstantiated
postulate.[3]

2.4.3. Discussion

I have been concerned to bring out Marx's teleological view of history,
closely linked to the functional mode of explanation discussed in 1.4. The
central event in the development of humanity – the rupture occurring
with the emergence of class society, culminating in capitalism – was
explained by its indispensable place as a stepping-stone to communism.
One could object that Marx's goal was rather to explain that rupture in
ordinary causal, or causal-cum-intentional language. His aim was to
explain how individuals and classes, in trying to promote their own interest, came to realize changes that were no part of their purpose – nor of any
other purpose. This objection, however, misses the mark. It is part and
parcel of the teleological tradition that all events can be explained twice
over, causally as well as teleologically. "There are two realms, that of

---

[1] *Zur Kritik (1861–63)*, p. 173.
[2] *Theories of Surplus-Value*, vol. 2, p. 118.
[3] True, Marx may be read as saying here that *when* the interest of the species asserts itself, it
does so at the expense of individuals, not that it always asserts itself, but I find this less
plausible in the light of the passage as a whole. In any case the explanatory power of the
coincidence would still remain mysterious.

efficient causes and that of final causes, and each is sufficient to explain everything in detail, as if the other did not exist."[1] When God created the universe, he set up the causal chain that would best bring about his goal, so that any event can be explained both as the effect of its predecessor in the causal chain and as part of an optimal chain. It takes some mental effort to understand how this view could survive in a secular view of history, yet it certainly did so in Hegel and to a large extent in Marx.

Marx's most explicitly teleological statement is the postulate that the interest of the species always asserts itself. *Humanity* was for Marx what Spirit or Reason was for Hegel – the supra-individual entity whose full development is the goal of history, even though it is not endowed with the qualities of an intentional agent who could *act* to bring about that goal. According to methodological individualism, humanity as such cannot act, at least not before the emergence of communist society that turns it into a collective actor. In that society men will in fact be able to control their own development, but one cannot coherently assume that the development of humanity up to that stage will occur as if it had already been reached. The fact that one possible development has as its end result the emergence of a collective actor that could have guided the process towards that end had it been present from the beginning is no guarantee that history will in fact evolve in that direction.

Even assuming that the presence of teleology in Marx is granted, its importance might still be questioned. One might deny, that is, that Marx's speculative philosophy of history has consequences for his other writings and activities. Later chapters in this book will refute this view, and show that the teleological attitude was far from inconsequential – both as concerns Marx's explanation of historical events and with respect to his own political practice. Thus his explanation of the French Revolution and his own strategy in the German Revolution of 1848 were both shaped by his philosophy of history (7.2.1), as was his implausible belief that the subjective and the objective conditions for a communist revolution would come together in one and the same country (5.2.3).

A political theorist who is also a political organizer may easily find himself in a situation where his theory tells him to pursue or approve a course of action whose immediate consequences are undesirable as evaluated by the same theory. Marx, for instance, found himself compelled to "say to the workers and the petty bourgeois: it is better to suffer in modern bourgeois society, which by its industry creates the material

---

[1] Leibniz, "Considérations sur les principes de vie", p. 542.

means for the foundation of a new society that will liberate you all, than to revert to a bygone form of society which, on the pretext of saving your classes, thrusts the entire nation back into medieval barbarism".[1] Substitute the peasantry for the petty bourgeoisie, and primitive socialist accumulation for modern bourgeois society, and you have the classic justification for Stalinism.

Let us assume that our political theorist employs a straightforward utilitarian framework. This implies, among other things, that he does not believe that the current generation has *rights* that constrain the intertemporal calculus of benefits, nor that there is a distinction between first-person and third-person morality – between what ought to be done and what one ought to do. The right thing to do is then simply whatever contributes most to total happiness over time. The question then arises how one is to know what action this criterion favours. If one is very confident of the truth of one's political theory, one will unhesitatingly accept the sacrifice of those now living for the sake of later generations. This kind of confidence is strongly encouraged by a speculative philosophy of history, and quite difficult to sustain without one. Usually, if a person acts on his beliefs about the future course of history, his actions will take account of the uncertainty surrounding those beliefs. This will inspire caution, a preference for reversible choices and a greater reluctance to impose certain suffering for the sake of uncertain benefits. But if the belief is held in the mode of total certainty, there will be nothing to restrain one from taking drastic action. This holds even more strongly if the philosophy of history goes together with a form of functional explanation that can justify the notion of "objective complicity".[2] From Stalin to the Red Guards this outlook has led to a disregard for individuals that goes far beyond the denial of *methodological* individualism.

The main objection, therefore, to speculative theories of history resting on the notion of "reculer pour mieux sauter" is practical, not theoretical. Their intellectual shortcomings, though serious when measured by intellectual standards, are of little import compared to the political

---

[1] *Neue Rheinische Zeitung*, 22.1.1849.

[2] Tsou, "Back from the brink", p. 63, argues that "functional analysis can be placed in the service of radicalism as well as conservatism". In China, for instance, the "misuse of functional analysis as a political weapon contributed to the loss of a generation of educated youth, scientists, engineers, physicians, humanists, social scientists, writers, artists and other specialists".

disasters they can inspire. We should retain the respect for the individual that is at the core of Marx's theory of communism, but not the philosophy of history that allows one to regard pre-communist individuals as so many sheep for the slaughter.

3. Economics

In this chapter I set out the main tenets of Marx's analysis of capitalism as an economic system. This analysis rests on two main pillars: the labour theory of value and the theory of the falling rate of profit. Both have conclusively been shown to be invalid. Yet their centrality in Marx – and in later Marxist work – warrants and indeed requires the attention given to them here. Moreover, the framework of Marx's economic theory could perhaps be used to develop more robust propositions than he was able to advance himself. I shall provide, therefore, a fairly exhaustive, although compact, discussion of Marx's economic theories. I shall first in 3.1 touch upon some problems of method. In 3.2 I define the basic notions of the theory, and discuss Marx's attempt to explain prices and profit in terms of labour value. In 3.3 I consider what in my view remains the most valuable part of Marx's economics, his theory of accumulation and technical change. In 3.4 I conclude with a survey of the main theories of crises proposed by Marx. With a very few exceptions nothing I shall have to say in this chapter is original. The work of Okishio, Morishima, von Weizsäcker, Samuelson, Steedman and Roemer over the last decades has clarified the issues to a point where little is left to be added beyond some exegetical comments.

For many readers, Marxist economics will be more or less synonymous with the labour theory of value. That theory does indeed have a central place in the following exposition, not only in 3.2 where it is formally stated and discussed, but in other sections as well. I argue that the theory is useless at best, harmful and misleading at its not infrequent worst. Specifically, the labour theory of value is incapable of explaining the formation of equilibrium prices and the equilibrium rate of profit (3.2.2). Nor does the claim that labour is the source of exchange value and of profit survive a critical examination (3.2.3). Labour values as conceived by Marx confuse the analysis of balanced growth (3.3.1), and are misleading as a tool for the theory of resource allocation and technical choice (3.3.2). In addition, adherence to the labour theory of value led Marx to adopt an invalid explanation of capital fetishism (2.3.2). On the other hand, labour values have a place in the theory of exploitation (4.1), although even in this role they are open to serious objections.

3.1. Methodology

Many of the discussions in chapter 1 apply immediately to Marx's economic theory, such as the analysis of rational-choice theory (1.2.1) and the comments on the methodology of unintended consequences (1.3.2). Some additional problems also arise, however, that are more specifically related to his economic writings. In 3.1.1 I first consider the appropriateness of talking about Marx's economic "models", in the modern sense of that term. Under this heading I also discuss Marx's use of "tendency laws" to explain economic relations. In 3.1.2 I comment on Marx's attempt to apply the Hegelian distinction between essence and appearance to economic life, notably to the relation between values and prices. I argue that while this particular application fails, others hold out more promise. This discussion is closely related to the analysis of fetishism (2.3.2) and of ideology (notably 8.2.3).

3.1.1. "Models" in Marx

Marx had an economic theory, but it is not clear whether he also minted it out in economic models.[1] This involves the use of deliberately simplifying, quantitative assumptions – achieving precision at the expense of realism. Some of the – interrelated – advantages of models are the following. (i) They make it possible to assess the consistency of a theory and to derive testable implications from it. As long as a theory is offered

---

[1] For perceptive comments on the relation between theory and models in Marxism, see Roemer, *Analytical Foundations*, pp. 1ff and especially *A General Theory*, pp. 152–3.

merely in verbal terms, it is impossible to determine the net equilibrium effect of all the relations involved. (ii) They allow economies of exposition. If, for instance, we want to provide a counterexample to some proposition, it does not matter if it is very abstract or starkly implausible as long as it satisfies the antecedents of the proposition. (iii) Models enable us to play the devil's advocate. When it is difficult to arrive at exact estimates of an empirical relation, one can tip the scales against oneself by assuming the hypothesis that is least favourable to what one wants to prove. (iv) Finally, models are indispensable in that they allow us to talk of one thing at a time. True, there is the danger that one may believe that a general-equilibrium theory can be constructed by adding together conclusions derived from partial-equilibrium or *ceteris paribus* models. Yet science has to begin somewhere, and as long as one is aware of the limitations of such local studies they are an invaluable tool for the advance of knowledge.

Marx was well aware of these advantages, although his Hegelian training sometimes led him astray. His attempts to provide algebraic or arithmetic proofs of his main assertions show that he recognized the power of mathematics in this respect,[1] even though today his efforts appear extremely clumsy. Unlike Hegel, he did not relegate mathematics to the platitudinous level of the "understanding", as opposed to "reason". Nor did he join Engels in the attempt to make mathematics into a mysteriously "dialectical" discipline (1.5.2). Marx was also aware of the need to tackle problems one at a time, to reduce complex economic systems to more manageable proportions. In a letter to Engels he states that in his planned discussion of "capital in general" he will assume that

the wage of labour is set at its minimum. The movements of wages and the rise and fall of this minimum itself belong to the analysis of wage labour. Moreover I assume that landed property = 0, i.e. land as a particular economic relation does not yet concern us. Only by this procedure does one avoid the necessity of bringing everything to bear upon everything.[2]

In a contemporary passage from the *Grundrisse* he also states (somewhat ambiguously) that "All of these fixed suppositions themselves become fluid in the further course of development. But only by holding them fast at the beginning is their development possible without confounding everything."[3]

His actual practice also conforms to this principle. Thus in *Capital I* he assumes that prices are directly proportional to labour values, giving notice that this is only a temporary simplification that will be abandoned

[1] Cp. Smolinski, "Karl Marx and mathematical economics".
[2] Marx to Engels 2.4.1858.   [3] *Grundrisse*, p. 817.

later, as indeed it is in *Capital III*.[1] In *Capital II* he notes that in the analysis of simple reproduction one must disregard foreign trade: it "can only confuse without contributing any new element of the problem or of its solution".[2] In *Capital I* he similarly argues that "In order to examine the object of our investigation in its integrity, free from all disturbing subsidiary circumstances, we must treat the whole world as one nation, and assume that capitalist production is everywhere established and has possessed itself of every branch of industry."[3] A similar abstraction underlies the vast project from 1858, of which the *Grundrisse* was to form only one of six parts. Here the purely economic categories of capital, land and labour were to be treated before the state. The latter was to be discussed first in its internal and then in its external aspects, and only thereafter would the whole edifice be crowned by an analysis of the world market.[4] This method of successive approximations is in no way remarkable in itself, but shows that Marx did not fall into the trap of premature totalization which from Lukacs onward has plagued Western Marxism.[5]

Marx also appreciated the advantage of models in mounting his attack on capitalism. He wanted to show that the flaws of capitalism were inherent in the system, not imperfections that could be removed by minor, reformist change. In the 1861–3 *Critique* he gives notice that he shall not take account of temporary depressions in the value of labour-power, or of the use of women and children in production. "Thus we give capital a *fair chance*, by assuming the non-existence of its most horrible aspects."[6] In the *Grundrisse* he argues that one "must always presuppose here that the wage paid is *economically* just, i.e. that it is determined by the general laws of economics. The contradictions have to follow from the general relations themselves, and not from fraud by individual capitalists."[7] Marx is leaning over backwards to make his indictment of capitalism as general and powerful as possible. The same motivation, I believe, underlies his tendency to assume competitive conditions, and to disregard monopolistic and monopsonistic practices.

Still I do not believe that Marx had rid himself completely of the Hegelian outlook that is well summarized in a passage from the *Philosophy of Right*: "All else, apart from this actuality established through the

---

[1] *Capital I*, pp. 166, 216.   [2] *Capital II*, p. 470.   [3] *Capital I*, p. 581.

[4] For a full discussion of Marx's successive plans for his major work, see Rubel, "Plan et méthode de l' 'Economie'".

[5] Lukacs, "Die Verdinglichung und das Bewusstsein des Proletariats", part III; cp. also Sartre, "Question de méthode".

[6] *Zur Kritik* (1861–3), p. 41; "fair chance" in English in the original.

[7] *Grundrisse*, p. 426; see also *Capital I*, p. 314.

working of the concept itself, is ephemeral existence, external contingency, opinion, unsubstantial appearance, falsity, illusion and so forth."[1] On this view, the aspects of reality that are not captured by our theory are *ipso facto* not worth considering. In Marx's work this attitude comes to the surface when he denies the possibility of determining a "natural" rate of interest:

If we inquire further as to why the limits of a mean rate of interest cannot be deduced from general laws, we find the answer lies simply in the nature of interest. It is merely a part of the average profit. The same capital appears in two roles – as loanable capital in the lender's hand and as industrial or commercial capital in the hands of the functioning capitalist. But it functions just once, and produces profit just once. In the production process itself, the nature of capital as loanable capital plays no role. How the two parties who have claim to it divide the profit is in itself just as purely empirical a matter belonging to the realm of accident as the distribution of percentage shares of a common profit in a business partnership.[2]

Marx here makes the very same error that J. Pen has criticized in connection with the last-mentioned problem, that of dividing the benefits from cooperation. Pen observes that if a situation such as bilateral monopoly is indeterminate according to one particular model, this does not mean that the situation is indeterminate *in itself*.[3] Indeed, the last notion is devoid of sense, at least outside quantum mechanics. In the social sciences we never encounter phenomena that are accidental in an absolute sense, only theory-relative accidents.

Marx referred to the law of the falling rate of profit as a "tendency law". As pointed out by Mark Blaug, this can to some extent be defended as a claim that the law is valid only under the simplifying assumptions of a model.[4] Let me distinguish between three cases here. First, it is quite reasonable to disregard counter-tendencies that are totally exogenous to the main tendency. This might well be the case, for instance, with foreign trade, which can legitimately be disregarded in order to bring out the internal dynamic of capitalism as a self-contained system. (On the other hand, of course, such "safety-valves" could make a great deal of difference if we are concerned with predicting the course of actual economies.) Secondly, but more questionably, one might disregard counter-tendencies that are causally generated by the main tendency. The capitalists, observing the fall in the rate of profit, might take measures that

---

[1] Hegel, *Philosophy of Right*, § 1.
[2] *Capital III*, p. 364. See also Panico, "Marx's analysis of the relationship between the rate of interest and the rate of profit", who arrives at a similar conclusion.
[3] Pen, *The Wage Rate under Collective Bargaining*, pp. 91ff.
[4] Blaug, *The Methodology of Economics*, pp. 66ff and *A Methodological Appraisal of Marxian Economics*, pp. 41ff.

partly or completely offset it. The opening of foreign markets might in fact be motivated by such considerations. In this case we can still refer to a *main* tendency because of its causal primacy, but this does not prove that it is also the main tendency in the sense of being quantitatively dominant. It might well generate counter-tendencies that completely annul it. In that case we might still want to study the main tendency in isolation, precisely to bring out that it will not be allowed to remain in isolation. Hegel's analysis in the *Philosophy of Right* of the internal contradictions of capitalism has exactly this hypothetical structure.[1]

Thirdly, and less justifiably, one might disregard the counter-tendencies that are causally correlated with the main tendency, because they stem from the same causes. This is what Marx proposed to do: "We have thus seen in a general way that the same influences which produce a tendency in the rate of profit to fall, also call forth counter-effects, which hamper, retard, and partly paralyse this fall."[2] In particular, this holds for the rise in the rate of surplus-value and the fall in the value of the elements of constant capital: these have the same cause as the "main" tendency of the rate of profit to fall, namely technical progress. Under this circumstance the only interesting question concerns the net effect produced by that common cause, while the splitting up into a main tendency and a countertendency becomes quite artificial.[3] In Marx this procedure is related to his general teleological outlook. The tendency of capitalism to destroy itself was for him a tangible fact, given prior to the analysis of the specific mechanism whereby it comes about.

3.1.2. Essence and appearance

Marx frequently referred to a distinction between "Wesen" and "Erscheinung", essence and appearance, in economic life. I shall not go deeply into the darkly Hegelian origin of these notions, except to suggest that in his best-known application of them Marx may have misunderstood Hegel quite radically.

The appearance, that which appears, allows for two different antonyms. First, it may be contrasted with what is hidden, and accessible only by the mediation of thought. In this sense one may say that behind the

---

[1] In the *Philosophy of Right* (§§ 244ff) Hegel explains the existence of the state by pointing to the social contradictions (1.5.3) that would arise in its absence.

[2] *Capital III*, p. 239.

[3] The same ambiguity surrounds the proposal by Guy Bois that the decline of feudalism can be explained by the "tendency of the rate of feudal levy to fall" (*Crise du Féodalisme*, pp. 203–4, 354–5). The use of the word "tendency" presumably implies that there were also countertendencies; if so, one would want to know what was their causal relationship (correlation or causation) and what was the net effect of the various forces.

appearance of a table is the atomic structure that forms its essence. This, broadly speaking, is how Marx conceived of the relation between labour values and prices. The former are of a different and more fundamental ontological order than the latter, which, however, are the only ones that appear to the economic agents. Prices are on the surface of things, in the double sense of being immediately observable and of being explicable in terms of a deeper and more fundamental structure. Secondly, one may focus on the *local* character of the appearance – since what appears always appears to a person occupying a particular standpoint and observing the phenomena from a particular perspective. Hence any given appearance may be contrasted with the *global network* of appearances that is not tied to any particular standpoint. As far as I understand Hegel's theory of essence and appearance, the second interpretation is the correct one. It says that the essence is *the totality of interrelated appearances*, not something that is "behind" them and of a different ontological order.[1] An example is the relation of partial-equilibrium to general-equilibrium analysis in economics.

In 3.2 I argue that labour values are not in any way prior to prices. Hence Marx's theory should be dismissed because it is incorrect, not because it rests on a faulty understanding of Hegel. Yet because this understanding was an important part of his motivation for insisting on the primacy of labour values, an extended quotation of his views may be in order:

It is then only an accident if the surplus-value, and thus the profit, actually produced in any particular sphere of production, coincides with the profit contained in the selling price of a commodity. As a rule, surplus-value and profit, and not their rates alone, are then different magnitudes. At a given degree of exploitation, the mass of surplus-value produced in a particular sphere of production is then more important for the aggregate average profit of social capital, and thus for the capitalist class in general, than for the individual capitalist in any specific branch of production. It is of importance to the latter only in so far as the quantity of surplus-value produced in his branch helps to regulate the average profit. But this is a process which occurs behind his back, one he does not see, nor understand, and which indeed does not interest him . . .

The fact that this intrinsic connection is here revealed for the first time; that up to the present time political economy . . . either forcibly abstracted itself from the distinctions between surplus-value and profit, and their rates, so it could retain value determination as a basis, or else abandoned this value determination and with it all vestiges of a scientific approach, in order to cling to the differences that strike the eye in this phenomenon – this confusion of the theorists best illustrates

---

[1] I owe this understanding of Hegel to lectures by Jean Hyppolite at the Collège de France in 1966.

the utter incapacity of the practical capitalist, blinded by competition as he is, and incapable of penetrating its phenomena, to recognize the inner essence and inner structure of this process behind its outer appearance.[1]

Whatever else it is, this contrast between the inner and the outer is bad Hegelianism,[2] and not the better for being *bad* Hegelianism. Yet the reference to the blinding effects of competition suggests the second – more authentic and intrinsically more interesting – reading of the distinction. The appearance, one might say in Leibnizian terms, reflects the essence from its point of view, which may well be a distorted or one-sided one.

Marx employs the distinction in this second sense in *Capital I,* when he comes to the analysis of wages. He took great pride in his distinction between labour and labour-power,[3] and strongly objected to the expression "value of labour". In the latter phrase,

the idea of value is not only completely obliterated, but actually reversed. It is an expression as imaginary as the value of the earth. These imaginary expressions arise, however, from the relations of production themselves. They are categories for the phenomenal form of essential relations. That in their appearance things often represent themselves in inverted form is pretty well known in every science except Political Economy.[4]

A few pages later this is spelled out in a sociologically more interesting way:

The wage form thus extinguishes every trace of the division of the working-day into necessary labour and surplus-labour, into paid and unpaid labour. All labour appears as paid labour. In the corvée, the labour of the worker for himself, and his compulsory labour for his lord, differ in space and time in the clearest possible way. In slave-labour, even that part of the working-day in which the slave is only replacing the value of his own means of existence, in which, therefore, in fact he works for himself alone, appears as labour for his master. All the slave's labour appears as unpaid labour. In wage-labour, on the contrary, even surplus-labour, or unpaid labour, appears as paid. There the property relation conceals the labour of the slave for himself; here the money relation conceals the unrequited labour of the wage labourer.[5]

We are dealing here with a generalized form of fetishism, that is structurally induced illusions about how the economy works. One might be tempted to conclude that the proper place for the essence–appearance distinction is not in economic theory proper, but in the sociology of

---

[1] *Capital III*, pp. 167–8.
[2] Cp. Hegel, *The Phenomenology of Spirit, passim.* A vigorous criticism of a similar fallacy in Chinese thought is given by Levenson, *Confucian China and its Modern Fate*, vol. I, ch. iv.
[3] See Engels, Preface to the 1891 edition of *Wage Labour and Capital.*
[4] *Capital I*, p. 537.   [5] *Ibid.*, pp. 539–40.

economic thought, and this is indeed to some extent the case. Hence the problem is also discussed, in 8.2.3, as a sub-variety of ideological thinking. Yet to insist on this labelling would be to miss the important point that economic theory should also aim at explaining the formation of economic beliefs. The sociology of knowledge may be helpful in explaining the beliefs of the economic agents, hence also their actions, and hence in fact the aggregate structure that generates the beliefs in the first place. The – systematically distorted – beliefs about the structure (i) are to be explained by the structure and (ii) enter into the explanation of its persistence. I submit that this is a central and valuable insight of Marx's economic theory, perhaps derived from and at least compatible with the Hegelian view that the essence is upheld by the very appearance it generates. Hence, I believe, the centrality of the term "critique" in the title or subtitle of Marx's major economic works. To explain the economy, one must also explain how the economic agents – and, following them, the political economists – arrive at incorrect beliefs about how it works.

3.2. The labour theory of value

As a preliminary to the exposition of the labour theory of value, and to the later parts of this chapter, I first in 3.1 set out the basic notions of Marxian economics. I then go on to consider several interpretations of – and possible arguments for – the labour theory of value. The theory has been understood as explaining: first, relative prices and the rate of profit in equilibrium; secondly, the condition of possibility of exchange value and profit; and lastly, the rational allocation of goods in a planned economy. Of these, the first two form the object of 3.2.2 and 3.2.3 respectively, while the third is postponed to 3.3.2.

3.2.1. Basic notions[1]

Marx conceived of the economy as divided into two or three sectors. The best-known model involves a capital goods sector and a consumption goods sector, while another splits the latter into one sector producing necessities for the workers and one producing luxury goods for the capitalists. Modern treatments use the more general n-sector approach, and I shall mostly use the same procedure, except when a two-sector model is better suited for illustrative purposes. To describe the sectors and their interrelations, we must know the productive technology and the real

---

[1] I shall not give references for these definitions. The reader can find the sources by looking at the index to the editions of *Capital I* and *Capital III* in *Marx–Engels Werke*.

wage, from which – given the institutional assumptions of profit maximization and perfect competition – labour values, equilibrium prices and the equilibrium rate of profit can be derived. I postpone to 3.2.2 the deduction of prices and the profit rate, while the derivation of labour values will be given here.

I assume, then, that the economy is divided into n sectors, each of which produces a single homogeneous good.[1] I also rely on the twin assumptions of constant returns to scale and fixed coefficients of production, implying that factor input per unit of product is independent both of the scale of production and of factor prices. These assumptions are usually imputed to Marx on insufficient textual evidence. I have argued elsewhere that in his verbal discussions Marx recognized the obvious facts that there is often a choice between labour-saving and labour-using techniques, and that production at a large scale is more efficient.[2] Yet in his numerical models Marx retained the two assumptions, and I shall do the same here. It is also difficult to derive robust results in models that do not rely on these assumptions. Treatments of Marxist economics that abandon the assumption of fixed coefficients are available,[3] as are also discussions that allow for constant or decreasing returns to scale,[4] but none to my knowledge that admit increasing returns.

Given these preliminaries, we can characterize the technology of sector j in the economy by noting that the production of one unit of good j requires a_{oj} units of labour (assumed for the present to be homogeneous, and measured in, say, hours of labour time) and a_{ij} units of good i as inputs. The *labour value* of one unit of good j is the amount of labour that is needed to produce it – needed directly (i.e. a_{oj}) as well as indirectly (i.e. the labour value of non-labour inputs). The apparent circularity of this definition is circumvented by the method of simultaneous equations. Setting x_j for the labour value of one unit of good j, the principle that value in must equal value out leads to the following equations:

---

[1] This involves excluding the case of joint production, of which much has been made in recent Marxist work; see Pasinetti (ed.), *Essays on the Theory of Joint Production*. The main use of this notion has been to conceptualize fixed capital, which in depreciated form is produced jointly with the main product. As shown by Sraffa, *Production of Commodities by Means of Commodities*, p. 95, there are passages in which Marx appears to think of fixed capital in this way, but in my opinion they are far too slender to allow us to say that he fully adopted this theory, let alone that he drew the full consequences of it. In any case I assume throughout that all constant capital is circulating capital, i.e. completely used up in the course of the production process, since at the chosen level of abstraction the discussion does not require the more complex idea of durable capital.

[2] *Explaining Technical Change*, ch. 7.

[3] Roemer, *Analytical Foundations*, ch. 2.   [4] *Ibid.*

$$x_j = a_{0j} + a_{1j}x_1 + a_{2j}x_2 + \ldots + a_{nj}x_n, \quad \text{with } j = 1, 2, \ldots, n \tag{1}$$

Given certain conditions on the coefficients,[1] this system allows of an economically meaningful solution that defines the labour values of all goods. The method of simultaneous equations corresponds to the fact that labour values are determined by what are currently the most efficient techniques of production, and not by the techniques that as a matter of historical fact were used in producing the means of production a_{ij}. "What determines value is not the amount of labour time incorporated in products, but rather the amount of labour time necessary at any given moment."[2] The fact that the currently used means of production were produced by labour in the past may or may not be relevant for the purpose of normative analysis (4.3.2), but is surely irrelevant for the analytical task of estimating current labour values.[3]

I should add, however, that the simultaneous method is equivalent to a procedure that regards current value as the sum of an infinite series of labour inputs in the past. To avoid complex matrix algebra, I shall show this for a simple one-sector model in which corn and labour are used to produce corn. Specifically, we assumed that a units of seed corn and b units of labour are needed to produce one unit of corn. Setting x for the unknown labour value of one unit of corn, we immediately have

$$ax + b = x \tag{2}$$

which gives $x = b/(1-a)$. We can also, however, reach the same result by another route. Let us ask, namely, how much direct labour and seed corn was needed to produce the seed corn itself, assuming that the same technique was employed. The answer emerges by multiplying each of the inputs in equation (2) by the proportionality factor a, giving a^2 units of corn and ab units of labour. We then ask the same question about the seed corn a^2, and get the answer that it was produced by the help of a^3 corn and a^2b labour. Continuing in this way, we can determine the labour value of one unit of corn as the sum of all labour inputs in the (infinite) past: $x = b + ab + a^2b + \ldots = b/(1-a)$. This might appear to be a historical determination of value, but of course the whole operation takes place in logical, not historical time, hence it cannot be taken literally as an argument for the causal importance of the past in determining current values. I shall make use of this construction in the discussion of economic planning (3.3.2).

The assumption that labour is homogeneous clearly must be justified,

[1] *Ibid.*, p. 36.   [2] *Grundrisse*, p. 135.
[3] Cp. my "Note on hysteresis in the social sciences".

as Marx well knew. In one well-known passage he expresses himself in a way that appears to suggest that skilled labour can be reduced to unskilled labour by comparing the wage rates.[1] This, however, was not his position. Rather he argued that skilled labour be conceived as unskilled labour plus an amount of invisible or human capital, that is skill, which is produced in much the same way as any other commodity:

> In order to modify the human organism, so that it may acquire skill and handiness in a given branch of industry, and become labour-power of a special kind, a special education or training is requisite, and this, on its part, costs an equivalent in commodities of a greater or less amount. This amount varies according to the more or less complicated character of the labour-power. The expenses of this education (excessively small in the case of ordinary labour-power) enter pro tanto into the total value spent in its production.[2]

This, however, remains ambiguous, as observed by Bob Rowthorn.[3] The passage may be taken to say that the value of the labour-power of the skilled worker be construed as the sum of the value of his means of subsistence and the value expended in his education. The second component of the sum is further defined as the value of the means of subsistence of the educational workers plus the value of the educational means of production. The reduction to unskilled labour takes place by comparing these "inclusive values". This construction, however, suffers from the defect that a change in the real wage may influence the reduction rate and hence the labour values of all commodities, not only the value of labour-power. If we regard it as desirable that the labour value of commodities other than labour-power reflect nothing but technical conditions of production, and in particular that they be independent of the class struggle as part-determinant of the real wage, this counts decisively against the proposed method. And surely it was Marx's intention that labour values of commodities should be definable in terms of labour expenditure only, and not be sensitive to changes in the reward of labour.

Another way of reading the passage was suggested by Hilferding and further elaborated by Rowthorn. It involves looking at the value created in the educational sector, rather than the value of the constant and the variable capital employed in it. This allows us to determine the reduction rates independently of the wage level, and – as shown by Rowthorn – also permits a more fruitful discussion of the importance of education in a capitalist economy.

Yet this construction does not solve the problem of heterogeneous

---

[1] *Capital I*, p. 44.   [2] *Ibid.*, p. 172; cp. also p. 198.
[3] Rowthorn, "Skilled labour in the Marxist system".

labour. Two important, unresolved and probably unresolvable difficulties remain. First, there is the issue of non-producible skills.[1] These include natural talents as well as skills whose acquisition at some point becomes irreversibly blocked, notably verbal skills that are acquired in the family at an early age. This leads to truly heterogeneous labour, which cannot be circumvented in the way just described. At times Marx appears to have believed that the problem could be neglected, because of a tendency of all labour to become unskilled labour,[2] but this is flatly contradicted by other passages that suggest that all labour will become highly specialized and scientifically trained.[3]

Secondly, Ian Steedman has drawn attention to a different source of heterogeneity in labour.[4] Different forms of labour may – quite independently of the level of skill – vary according to the unpleasantness of the work to be performed. In a competitive labour market this will give rise to wage differentials that lead to serious problems for the labour theory of value. Steedman has shown that given such wage differences, central claims of Marx's theory can be upheld only if the different forms of concrete labour are aggregated via the relative wage rates of those different kinds of labour.[5] On the other hand the spirit of the latter solution is quite contrary to the intentions behind the labour theory of value. Surely Marx would not have admitted that the labour content of commodities could depend on the subjective disutility derived from certain forms of work, any more than it could depend on the outcome of the class struggle.

I conclude that the presence of genuinely and irreducibly heterogeneous labour is a major stumbling-block for Marxist economics. If taken seriously, it prevents the labour theory of value from even getting off the ground, since the basic concepts cannot be defined. In 3.2.2 I go on to argue that even if we disregard these difficulties, so that the *concept* of labour value can be defined, the *theory* of labour value fails because there is no use to which the concept can be put. In the next chapter I discuss the difficulties that heterogeneous labour poses for the theory of exploitation.

Assuming, henceforward, that there is only one form of worker and only one form of work (i.e. that there are no differences in skill and no differences in the unpleasantness of work), we can define the *value of*

---

[1] This difficulty is emphasized by Blaug, "Another look at the reduction problem in Marx", and by Roemer, *A General Theory*, ch. 6.
[2] E.g. *Capital I*, p. 198.   [3] E.g. *Grundrisse*, pp. 705–6.
[4] Steedman, "Heterogeneous labour, money wages and Marx's theory".
[5] For instance, this aggregation is required if we want to retain Marx's view that with zero profits or equal organic compositions of capital, prices are proportional to values.

labour-power as $v = b_1 x_1 + b_2 x_2 + \ldots + b_n x_n$, where b_i is the amount of commodity i that enters into the daily consumption of the worker. If the worker works h hours a day, the *surplus-value* generated is $h - v$. This is the difference between the value created by the worker and the value of his consumption. Increasing the surplus-value by increasing h gives rise to *absolute surplus-value*, whereas an increase that occurs by a lowering of v creates *relative surplus-value*. The latter may in turn occur by a change in the value of commodities, or by a change in the real wage, or both. In 4.1.4 I discuss in some detail these determinants of *the rate of surplus-value* (h/v), also referred to as *the rate of exploitation*. In the present chapter I shall consider the value of labour-power as given.

Capital consists of factors of production bought by a capitalist and operated for the purpose of "valorization" or profit-making. *Variable capital* is the labour-power employed, whereas *constant capital* is made up of non-human factors of production. I shall assume, as I did implicitly in equation (1) above, that the constant capital is completely used up in the process of production. This does not seriously affect the conclusions.[1] Hence the value of the output in a given sector may be decomposed into three elements. First, there is the value of the constant capital – that is the value of the means of production – employed in the sector; secondly, the value of the variable capital, that is the value of the labour-power; and thirdly the surplus-value created in the sector. This value decomposition is usually written $C_j + V_j + S_j$ for sector j. A similar decomposition may be made for the individual unit of good j or for an individual firm in sector j. The *organic composition of capital* in sector j is the ratio C_j/V_j. This is not a purely technical notion, since it depends not only on the number of workers employed relative to the capital, but also on the value of their labour-power. A purely technical notion of capital intensity would be given by the ratio $C_j/(V_j + S_j)$, which we might call the *value composition of capital*. Marx, however, does not use this concept. Instead he refers to the *technical composition of capital* as the ratio of the "mass of the means of production" employed to the amount of labour employed. This, however, is an ill-defined notion, since Marx does not tell us how to measure the "mass" of means of production. Perhaps the phrase is best understood to refer to the set of coefficients $(a_{0j}, a_{1j}, \ldots, a_{nj})$ rather than to a ratio of any kind.

---

[1] For a full treatment of the more general case, see Roemer, *Analytical Foundations*, ch. 2.

3.2.2. Derivation of prices and the rate of profit[1]

I now consider what use, if any, these concepts might be put to. I first state what has some claim to be called the *fundamental equation of Marxist economics*. Following Marx, we define the rate of profit as the ratio of surplus-value to the total capital employed: $r = S/(C + V)$. For the time being we leave it unspecified whether these magnitudes refer to a given sector, or to the economy as a whole. We then divide both numerator and denominator by V, obtaining the fundamental equation:

$$r = \frac{S/V}{C/V + 1} \tag{3}$$

In words, the rate of profit equals the rate of exploitation divided by the organic composition of capital increased by 1. The two central theories of Marxist economics may both be discussed in terms of this relationship. The labour theory of value deals with the problems that arise when the fundamental equation is disaggregated, so that we compare the rates of profit of different sectors of the economy. The theory of the falling rate of profit looks at the dynamic aspect of the equation by studying the trends in the rate of exploitation and the organic composition of capital, and their implication for the rate of profit.

Here, the equation will be used to give a *reductio ad absurdum* proof that equilibrium prices cannot be proportional to labour values in the general case. Assume, namely, that this proportionality obtained. A capitalist in sector *j* would then realize the profit given by the fundamental equation, with all magnitudes defined with respect to that sector. Having paid the constant and the variable capital with amounts C_j and V_j he would be left with S_j and the rate of profit defined by the fundamental equation. Now Marx assumed the rate of exploitation to be the same in all sectors, an assumption that follows immediately when we assume that all workers receive the same real wage and work the same number of hours. Hence different organic compositions of capital will give different rates of profit in different sectors. Since there undeniably are differences in organic composition across the sectors, we may conclude that there will be a plurality of rates of profit in the economy. This, however, violates the equilibrium condition that the rate of profit must be the same in all sectors. As noted earlier, when Marx in *Capital I* assumed the proportionality of values and prices, he well knew that this was a simplification to be abandoned later.

---

[1] For more elaborate versions of the following, see Morishima, *Marx's Economics*, ch. 7; Steedman, *Marx after Sraffa*, chs. 3 and 4; Roemer, *Analytical Foundations*, ch. 1. The textual evidence is found mainly in chs. IX and X of *Capital III*.

When Marx in *Capital III* attempted a more sophisticated derivation of prices from values, he proceeded in two steps. First, he derived the average rate of profit from the fundamental equation, with all magnitudes defined with respect to the economy as a whole. There is no justification for this procedure, and it does in fact give the wrong result. The fundamental equation holds only when values and prices coincide because the organic composition is the same in all sectors, or when there is no surplus value. Next, Marx in a numerical example in *Capital III* derived the prices by multiplying the values of the inputs by $(1 + r)$, that is by using the average rate of profit as a mark-up on values.[1] This, however, can only be called a howler, since the values are unknown magnitudes and hidden to the capitalist; hence they cannot enter into his calculations. To confuse value and profits is to commit the dialectical sin of mixing essence and appearance. The equilibrium condition must be that the capitalists in all sectors calculate the same rate of profit on the price costs of the factors of production, not on their costs in value terms. The mathematical curiosity, reported by Morishima, that Marx's incorrect procedure converges towards the correct result when iterated, has no exegetical or substantive significance.[2]

The correct procedure uses simultaneous equations. Let us write p_j for the unit price of commodity j and take commodity 1 as a numéraire, so that $p_1 = 1$. Let us write, moreover, b_i' for b_i/h, so that b_i' is the amount of commodity i that the worker receives in return for one hour's work. We can then derive the rate of profit, r, and the relative prices from the following equations:

$$(a_{oj} (b_1' + b_2'p_2 + \ldots + b_n'p_n) + a_{1j} + a_{2j}p_2 + \ldots + a_{nj}p_n) (1 + r) = p_j; j = 1,2, \ldots, n \qquad (4)$$

Here the first parenthesis within the large left-hand parenthesis gives the monetary wage for one hour's work, as the cost of the commodities that the worker receives in return for this work. The large parenthesis as a whole gives the total outlays for the capitalist per unit of good produced. These form the basis on which the profit is calculated. The equilibrium condition is that outlays plus the average rate of profit on them must equal selling price. It is easy to show by means of an example that this gives a different result from the procedure proposed by Marx.[3]

[1] *Capital III*, pp. 155ff.   [2] Morishima, *Marx's Economics*, pp. 60, 77.
[3] In a two-sector example, we set $a_{o1} = 1$, $a_{11} = \frac{1}{2}$, $a_{21} = 0$, $a_{o2} = 1$, $a_{12} = \frac{1}{4}$, $a_{22} = 0$, $b_1 = 0$, $b_2 = \frac{1}{3}$. Following Marx's method, we first find the values by the equations corresponding to (1) above, i.e. $1 + x_1/2 = x_1$ and $1 + x_1/4 = x_2$. This gives $x_1 = 2$ and $x_2 = \frac{3}{2}$. We then assume that both processes are operated at a scale that gives one unit of

I now turn to some more fundamental issues of interpretation. I shall distinguish between four different interpretations of the labour theory of value, considered as a theory of price formation:

1. *The local identity interpretation.* Prices are proportional to values.
2. *The global identity interpretation.* (a) The sum of all prices equals the sum of all values. (b) The totality of surplus-value equals the totality of profit.
3. *The Hegelian interpretation.* (a) Values can be determined independently of prices, but (b) prices cannot be determined independently of values.
4. *The Ricardian interpretation.* Prices are independent of the composition of final demand.

All of these have some textual support in Marx. As mentioned earlier, the local identity thesis was asserted in *Capital I* as a convenient simplification only, and little time need be spent on it, except to say that it is valid only with the same organic composition of capital in all sectors or with zero surplus-value ("simple commodity production"). The two varieties of the global interpretation may be dismissed as confused or trivial,[1] various attempts to show the contrary notwithstanding.[2]

Nothing quite as specific as statements (3a) and (3b) is found in Marx, but in the later Marxist tradition they are certainly taken as fundamental. Marx's incorrect derivation of prices from values could – if correct – have shown that prices can be derived from values, but not that they can only be reached via this route. Later Marxists have offered a deduction of prices from values that is formally correct, but of no avail in proving (3b).[3] The

output of each commodity. Hence the total amount of value created in this economy is 2. The total value of the variable capital is equal to the value of $\frac{2}{3}$ unit of the consumption commodity (good 2), or 1. Hence the surplus equals 1, and the average rate of profit is $r = 1/(1 + (\frac{1}{2} + \frac{1}{4})2) = 0.4$. The price of one unit of good 1 is the value of the inputs $(\frac{1}{3} \times \frac{3}{2} + \frac{1}{2} \times 2)$ multiplied by 1.4, or 2.1. That of one unit of good 2 similarly equals $(\frac{1}{3} \times \frac{3}{2} + \frac{1}{4} \times 2) \times 1.4 = 1.4$. Using commodity 1 as numéraire we find p_2 = approximately 0.67. The correct procedure starts from the equations corresponding to (4): $[p_2/3 + \frac{1}{2}] \quad (1 + r) = 1$ and $[p_2/3 + \frac{1}{4}] \quad (1 + r) = p_2$, from which we derive approximately $r = 0.39$ and $p_2 = 0.65$.

[1] Steedman, *Marx after Sraffa*, p. 61.

[2] E.g. Morishima, *Marx's Economics*, ch. 7 or Lipietz, "The so-called 'transformation problem' revisited". Morishima's result is obtained under quite restrictive assumptions that do not seem to have any interesting relation to what Marx wrote or how the world is. Lipietz arrives at his result by taking the rate of exploitation rather than the real wage or the monetary wage as given – an approach that completely neglects the need for micro-foundations.

[3] Thus Sweezy, *The Theory of Capitalist Development*, pp. 116ff first derives values from the technical coefficients and thereafter uses the price-value ratios as unknowns in an equation system in which the values appear as their coefficients. This is a mere sleight of hand, with no substantive implications.

correct procedure set out above shows irrefutably that one can derive prices directly from the technological coefficients, hence the second part of the Hegelian interpretation is false.

What about the first half (3a)? Given the assumption of fixed co-efficients of production, the values can indeed be determined independently of prices, as in equation (1) above. The assumption, however, is a very dubious one, and in fact not consistently held by Marx. Once one admits a choice of techniques, it must be made by comparing the costs at the ruling prices, hence prices and technology must be determined simultaneously, both of them prior to the labour values.[1] Hence there are two theoretical pressures that may have led Marx and later Marxists to rely on the assumption of fixed coefficients. First, it emphasizes the role of structural constraints, as opposed to the more subjective entrepreneurial choice (1.2.1). Also, it allows one to assert at least one half, albeit by far the least interesting one, of the Hegelian interpretation. It is indeed hard to see what is proved by showing that values do not depend on prices, when there is nothing that depends on values.

The following statement may, perhaps, be seen as a statement of the Ricardian interpretation of the labour theory of value:

The law of value dominates price movements with reductions or increases in required labour time making prices of production fall or rise. It is in this sense that Ricardo (who doubtlessly realized that his prices of production deviated from the value of commodities) says that "the inquiry to which I wish to draw the reader's attention relates to the effect of the variations in the relative value of commodities, and not in their absolute value".[2]

I believe that Marx intended to say not only what he actually states in the first sentence, that changes in labour values are a sufficient condition for price changes, but that they are a necessary condition as well. A standard, if vulgar, objection must be met here: is it not obvious that prices will rise for a good in great demand and fall if the demand falls? This completely misses the point. Marx, following Ricardo, distinguished between short-term and long-term (or equilibrium) prices. If demand shifts so that consumers want more of a good at the ruling prices than is produced, the price will go up and so will the rate of profit in the sector producing it. Attracted by the higher rate of profit, other capitalists will start production of the same good, the capital inflow continuing until once again the profit rate equals that of other sectors. The labour theory of value, in this

---

[1] A related and more powerful argument for the same conclusion is offered by Roemer, *A General Theory*, ch. 5.
[2] *Capital III*, p. 179.

Ricardian interpretation, states that with the market once again in equilibrium, the price of the good will be the same as before the demand shift.

Even with this objection rebutted, however, the Ricardian view fails, since demand also enters the system at another point, through working-class consumption.[1] In the equations (4) from which the rate of profit and the prices were derived, the consumption coefficients b_i' appear as coefficients of the unknown price variables. Hence a shift in demand will affect the solution of the system, contrary to the Ricardian view. That view, in fact, is valid only on the assumption – contrary to Marx's general procedure – that the workers are *paid* a monetary wage rather than *produced* by consumption commodities. If in equations (4) the first parenthesis within the large left-hand parenthesis is replaced with an exogenously given wage rate, w, the composition of final demand cannot influence equilibrium prices. This holds even when there is a choice of techniques: when labour is the only scarce (i.e. non-producible) good, the choice of input combinations is independent of demand.[2] (We may note, however, that when there are several scarce factors, e.g. land and labour, demand *will* affect prices.)[3]

As noted in 1.1.2, Marx generally took the workers' consumption bundle rather than the monetary wage as given, although he occasionally recognized that this was deeply misleading as a characterization of the capitalist mode of production. This enabled him to speak of *the* value of labour-power, a phrase that would be devoid of meaning if the workers could spend a given wage on many different bundles that, even if they do add up to the same price, need not add up to the same value (since prices in general are not proportional to values). On the other hand, this procedure also prevented him from securing a firm foundation for the labour theory of value in the Ricardian interpretation.

In summary, the Marxist view may be contrasted with the standard or non-Marxist view with the help of a diagram (fig. 1), where arrows indicate explanatory primacy and two-way arrows explanatory simultaneity. It will be appreciated that in the correct deduction of the prices and the rate of profit, values have no role whatsoever. They appear as a mere appendix, and are about as useless as that organ. This confirms a remark made in 3.2.1: even assuming (contrary to fact) that the notion of labour value is well defined, there is no purpose it can serve.

[1] Hence the prices are not affected by changes in demand stemming from a change in *capitalist* consumption. This, however, is insufficient as support for the Ricardian interpretation.

[2] For this "non-substitution theorem", see for example von Weizsäcker, *Steady-State Capital Theory*, p. 11.

[3] *Ibid.*, p. 12.

The Marxist Model

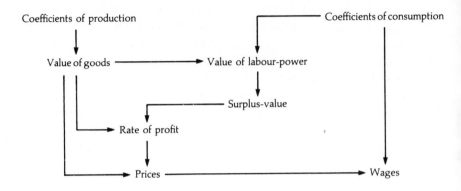

The non-Marxist Model

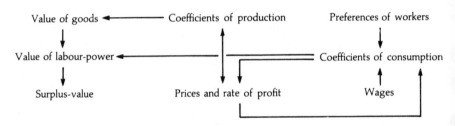

Fig. 1

3.2.3. Two transcendental arguments

To "explain" prices and profit can mean several distinct things. First, the explanation may involve a formal model that permits determination of the exact numerical magnitudes of these variables. We have seen that labour values play no role in this explanation. Secondly, however, it may address the more fundamental question of how prices and profits are at all possible. As noted by Robert Nozick,[1] this is a "Kantian-type" question usually referred to as a transcendental argument. It starts from the factually given, and works backwards to deduce the conditions of its possibility. If the labour theory of value is useless in determining the quantitative magnitudes, does it fare better in answering this qualitative question?

[1] Nozick, *Anarchy, State and Utopia*, pp. 261–2.

In the opening chapters of *Capital I*, Marx offers two arguments of this general form. The first begins with the fact of exchange, and deduces labour as a condition of possibility:

Let us take two commodities, e.g. corn and iron. The proportions in which they are exchangeable, whatever those proportions may be, can always be represented by an equation in which a given quantity of corn is equated to some quantity of iron: e.g. 1 quarter corn = x cwt iron. What does this equation tell us? It tells us that in two different things – in 1 quarter of corn and x cwt of iron, there exists in equal quantities something common to both. The two things must therefore be equal to a third, which in itself is neither the one nor the other. Each of them, so far as it is exchange value, must therefore be reducible to this third ... This common "something" cannot be either a geometrical, a chemical, or any other natural property of commodities. Such properties claim our attention only in so far as they affect the utility of those commodities, make them use-values. But the exchange of commodities is evidently an act characterized by a total abstraction from use-value. Then one use-value is just as good as another, provided only it be present in sufficient quantity ... As use-values, commodities are, above all, of different qualities, but as exchange values they are merely different quantities and consequently do not contain an atom of use-value. If, then, we leave out of consideration the use-value of commodities, they have only one property left, that of being products of labour.[1]

This famous passage can be broken down in two steps. (i) For exchange to be possible, the goods exchanged must have some common element. (ii) This common element can only be the property of being products of human labour. The first statement is quite ambiguous. In the beginning of the passage Marx refers to a common element that must "exist in" each of the commodities, but towards the end he says only that they must have a "common property", which could well be relationally defined. The property of being made by labour is, in fact, a relational one, as is the property of satisfying human needs. Taken in this latter, broader sense, the first statement appears to be true. If definite proportions of two goods regularly exchange against one another, this must be due to some – possibly relational – feature that they both possess. The second statement, by contrast, appears to be false. First, labour is not necessarily a component of all goods; secondly, there may be other common features that in fact explain the exchange.

As to the first objection, an economy worked by highly trained monkeys could have well-defined relative prices and a well-defined rate of

[1] *Capital I*, p. 37.

profit, with no labour being used. The von Neumann growth model can in fact be understood in this light.[1] More specifically, imagine a fully automatized economy, with a class of capitalists and a class of badly paid soldiers making up a standing army. Here goods would be transferred between firms and from firms to consumers, according to well-defined notional prices, yet no labour would enter into the production of goods. There would be no exploitation, although there could well be social conflict. One might object that such an economy would have had to be set up by human labour in the first place, but I do not think this would invalidate my point – unless the phrase "being products of labour" is taken in an extended historical sense that Marx probably did not intend.

Concerning the second objection, there are several other candidates for the status of "common feature of all goods". In any actual economy there would be some "basic commodities" in Sraffa's sense, that is commodities that directly or indirectly enter into the production of all others. With the exception of energy, however, these do not qualify for the status in question, since they are open to the same objection made above with respect to labour, namely that they are not essential in all possible economies, although they are so in the actual one. More centrally, the common "something" could be the potential for human want satisfaction, or utility or use-value. Marx's statement that "the exchange of commodities is evidently an act characterized by a total abstraction from use-value" is hardly compatible with another passage to the effect that "the labour spent upon the commodities counts effectively only in so far as it is spent in a form that is useful for others".[2] Here Marx himself appears to give a reason for singling out utility as the common feature of all goods.

One might argue, however, that Marx's position is not refuted if one takes the modified view that what goods have in common when they exchange is the complex property of being *useful* products of human labour, since labour then remains part of the transcendental condition, even if not all of it. The question, however, is whether goods with these two properties exchange *by virtue of* having both. The argument made in the first objection above shows that goods that only possess utility (in the more general sense that also includes usefulness for productive purposes that ultimately are directed to want satisfaction), without being products

---

[1] This is well brought out in the exposition of this model in Kemeny, Snell and Thompson, *Introduction to Finite Mathematics*, pp. 434ff. In their chicken–egg example no labour appears as input, and yet relative prices and the rate of profit (i.e. the rate of growth) are well defined.   [2] *Capital I*, p. 85.

of human labour, nevertheless can exchange in definite proportions. True, in addition to being useful, the goods must also be scarce, but they can be this by virtue of other things than being the product of human labour. The scarcity of non-human natural resources may be the cause of the scarcity of goods. Hence it appears reasonable to say that when goods in fact possess the property of being useful products of human labour, they exchange by virtue of being useful and scarce. The former complex property is a sufficient condition for the latter, but not a necessary one.

Another transcendental argument was briefly discussed in 1.5.1. It concerns the deduction of surplus-value and exploitation as a condition of possibility of profits. Morishima has proved as a "fundamental theorem" of Marxist economics that positive profits are possible if and only if there is a positive rate of exploitation.[1] This equivalence, however, does not show that exploitation is a condition for the possibility of profit, no more than correlation in general can show the presence of causation. In fact, similar "fundamental theorems" can be proved with respect to steel or any other basic commodity.[2] The central fact underlying these theorems is that profit, interest and economic growth are possible only because man can tap external sources of raw material and energy. It follows from the second law of thermodynamics that an economy based exclusively upon recycling would have a negative growth rate.[3] True, for any given state of the economy we can imagine a level of workers' consumption that leaves no room for profits; but then, for any given level of workers' consumption, we can imagine a state of the economy, and in particular of the technology, that allows for a positive rate of profit.[4] Obviously and tautologically, profits are possible only because workers do not consume the whole net product, which in some circumstances amounts to their being exploited. This, however, does not prove that the workers have a mysterious capacity to create *ex nihilo*. To summarize, man's ability to tap the environment makes possible a surplus over and above any given consumption level. Whether this surplus should be used for more workers' consumption, for capitalist consumption or for investment is a further question that bears no relation to the issue of "the ultimate source of profits".

[1] Morishima, *Marx's Economics*, ch. 5; generalized in his "Marx in the light of modern economic theory"; further generalized in Roemer, *Analytical Foundations*, ch. 2.4.
[2] Roemer, *A General Theory*, Appendix to ch. 7.
[3] Georgescu-Roegen, *The Entropy Law and the Economic Process*.
[4] True, this may be limited by $E = Mc^2$ and other constraints, but I assume that the economy is operating well within these limits.

3.3. Accumulation and technical change

The issues discussed above are compatible with the assumption of a static, unchanging economy. True, there is a surplus, but nothing was said to exclude this being entirely devoted to capitalist consumption. I now turn to some dynamic issues. I shall first discuss the concept of extended reproduction, or balanced quantitative growth on a constant technical basis (3.3.1). I then go on to consider the causes, the nature and the consequences of technical change under capitalism (3.3.2), a discussion that is continued in 3.4.2.

3.3.1. Simple and extended reproduction

The notion of equilibrium is at the heart of economic theory as usually conceived.[1] In 3.2.2 it was shown how to derive equilibrium prices from the equilibrium conditions (i) that the rate of profit be the same in all sectors and (ii) that in any given sector the sum of expenditures and profit equal income. This, however, leaves the relative size of the sectors undetermined, hence a separate argument is needed to establish the physical equilibrium, as distinct from the price equilibrium. In *Capital II* Marx, following Quesnay, pioneered in the investigation of physical equilibrium. He distinguished between simple reproduction, in which no net investment takes place, and extended reproduction in which part of the surplus is reinvested on a constant technical basis. While this volume is certainly one of the most boring works ever written by a major author, these analyses of physical equilibrium were strikingly original, even if technically flawed.

To discuss physical reproduction we use Marx's two-sector model. Sector I is the capital goods sector, while sector II produces consumption goods for workers and capitalists alike. The value decomposition of the output of the sectors is $C_1 + V_1 + S_1$ and $C_2 + V_2 + S_2$. Since we assume that the constant capital is completely used up in the production process, the output of sector I must in equilibrium be exactly equal to the constant capital employed in both sectors: $C_1 + V_1 + S_1 = C_1 + C_2$. Also, the output of sector II must in equilibrium be exactly sufficient to cover workers' consumption (corresponding to the variable capital) and capitalist consumption (which corresponds to the surplus since there is no net investment): $C_2 + V_2 + S_2 = V_1 + V_2 + S_1 + S_2$. Both of these reduce to the same formula: $C_2 = V_1 + S_1$. The physical equilibrium for simple reproduction is that the value of constant capital used in the consumption

---

[1] For a major exception see Nelson and Winter, *An Evolutionary Theory of Economic Change.*

sector equals the value added in the capital sector. Of course, this is not a sufficient condition for equilibrium to obtain, since it is formulated at a highly aggregate level that leaves much room for disequilibrium at lower levels. Also, similar conditions might have been formulated using prices instead of values as aggregators.

Consider now what happens when part of the surplus is reinvested. I shall not here repeat the objections stated in 1.5.1 to the dialectical argument whereby Marx deduced the self-expansion of value, but simply take it as an assumption that some net investment takes place. Marx's way of handling this case is very strange.[1] He first assumes that a certain proportion of the surplus-value created in sector I is reinvested, and then simply fiddles with the surplus in sector II until he finds an amount that will allow balanced growth. Thus different proportions of the surplus are reinvested in the two sectors. This, in itself, is not objectionable. There is no mechanism whereby capitalists in the two sectors would invest the same proportion of the *surplus*, which is a value magnitude and hence unobservable.[2] What is objectionable is the lack in Marx of any connection between saving behaviour in the two sectors. The obvious assumption would be that of equal rates of saving out of *profits*, but this would necessitate a flight from the pure world of values. When we turn to dynamic considerations to find the "balanced path" of a growing economy, the value accounting becomes not only superfluous, but a hindrance to understanding.

3.3.2. Technical change
We may now turn to more exciting matters. Marx believed, paradoxically, both that technical change was the central fact in all world history, and that it was a phenomenon uniquely characterizing capitalism. In 5.1.1 I return to this antinomy, and discuss in some detail whether it can be resolved. Here I consider Marx's theory of technical change under capitalism.[3] What are the causes of – and motivation for – technical change in this system? At what rate does innovation take place? Is that rate an optimal one, or are there obstacles in capitalism to the full use of the

---

[1] *Capital II*, p. 512.
[2] Tsuru, "Keynes versus Marx", p. 185; Bronfenbrenner, "*Das Kapital* for modern man", and (more ambiguously) Blaug, *Economic Theory in Retrospect*, p. 263 all assume that the rate of saving out of surplus-value is the same in both sectors. For a correct exposition, see Morishima, *Marx's Economics*, ch. 12. The error involved is the same as that committed by Marx in his derivation of prices from values – that of assuming that labour values have behavioural significance for the agents.
[3] The following draws on ch. 7 of my *Explaining Technical Change*.

innovative potential? Is there any consistent bias in technical change – towards labour-saving or labour-using innovations?

The motivation behind innovations – as distinct from the external economies stemming from them – is stated in the chapter on relative surplus-value in *Capital I*. A capitalist who introduces a new and superior technique can sell the commodities

above their individual, but under their social value ... This augmentation of surplus-value is pocketed by him, whether his commodities belong or not to the class of necessary means of subsistence that participate in determining the general value of labour-power. Hence, independently of the latter circumstance, there is a motive for each individual capitalist to cheapen his commodities, by increasing the productiveness of labour.[1]

As noted in 1.3.2, Marx took this as an example of "the invisible hand", creating surplus-value for the class of capitalists as a whole out of actions motivated by individual profits. It is indeed true that profit-maximization may have this by-product, but it need not have it.[2] To show this I shall make use of a two-sector model that will also prove useful in the later discussion of the suboptimal character of capitalism innovation.

In this model we set the price of the capital good equal to 1 by convention. The real wage, in units of the consumption good, is w. The rate of profit is r, the price of the consumption good is p. The conditions for price equilibrium given in equation (4) then take the following form:

$$\left.\begin{array}{l}(a_{01} \times w \times p + a_{11})(1 + r) = 1 \\ (a_{02} \times w \times p + a_{12})(1 + r) = p\end{array}\right\} \tag{5}$$

From these equations we can obtain r as an explicit function of w. In a coordinate system with w measured along the horizontal axis and r along the vertical axis, this function will have a downward-sloping graph. In fig. 2 I have drawn two such curves, shown as straight lines for simplicity.[3] They correspond to two different techniques, I and II, that is two sets of coefficients of production. At any wage rate below w_0, technique I is the most profitable and will be chosen by an entrepreneur who wants to maximize the rate of profit on capital. At wages above w_0, technique II is preferred. Now observe that the distance OA (respectively OB) can be interpreted as the net product per worker when technique I (respectively II) is employed: when there is no profit, wages exhaust the

[1] *Capital I*, p. 317.
[2] I am indebted to Robert van der Veen for drawing my attention to this problem.
[3] For the significance of this "straight-line assumption" in the capital controversy, see Harcourt, *Some Cambridge Controversies*. The point made here is not affected if this simplification is dropped.

total product. Also note for later reference that the labour content of each unit of product must therefore be smaller when technique II is employed, since this allows for a larger product per worker.

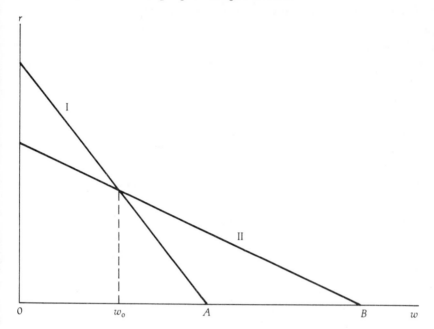

Fig. 2

Consider now two possibilities. (i) $0 < w < w_0$ and technique II is the only known technique. If technique I is introduced, capitalists will switch to it immediately, since it is associated with a higher rate of profit (at that wage level). The switch, however, entails a fall in the rate of surplus-value, which under technique II was wB/Ow and now becomes wA/Ow. (ii) $w_0 < w < A$ and technique I is the only known technique. If technique II is introduced it will be preferred on profit-maximizing grounds, and will also lead to an increase in the rate of surplus-value. Hence it is shown that profit-motivated innovation can bring about a rise in the rate of surplus-value, but – contrary to what Marx asserted – need not do so.

I should add that this argument, while valid, needs to be disambigu-ated in an important respect. The diagram demonstrates the possibility of an inverse relationship between the rate of surplus-value and the equilib-rium rate of profit. The capitalists, however, are not motivated by the equilibrium rate, that is the profit that can be made at the new equilibrium prices, but by the profit that can be made with the new technique at the time it is introduced, at pre-innovation equilibrium prices. It can be shown, however, that at a constant real wage all innovations that are profitable at pre-innovation prices remain so at post-innovation prices.[1] Hence the conclusion of the preceding paragraph should be restated as follows: profit-motivated innovation must bring about a rise in the equilibrium rate of profit, and may or may not lead to an increase of the rate of surplus-value. In fact, we can be more specific than this. Case (ii) above suggests that the rate of surplus-value rises with the rate of profit when the innovation has the property of reducing the labour content of the product, and it has in fact been shown that this is the case quite generally.[2] As we shall see, Marx believed that this property was the socially desirable criterion on which innovations should be judged; also that it could deviate from the profitability criterion. Hence he cannot also insist that the invisible hand will ensure the coincidence of profitability and the creation of surplus-value.

I now return to the motivation behind capitalist innovation. If we assume that the capitalist is a consistent profit-maximizer, he will innovate maximally within the feasible set to the extent that it is known to him. Marx has little to say about the determinants of the latter. In particular, he does not mention the vast extension of the set of economically – as distinct from technically – profitable inventions that were brought about by the introduction of the patent system.[3] He does offer, however, some comments on the motivation behind capitalist innovation that are more specific than the rather general statement quoted above. These concern, first, the impact of technical change on the class struggle, and, secondly, the suboptimal consequences of the profit-maximizing criterion of innovation. The first problem is also linked to the issue of "maximizing vs. satisficing" discussed in 1.2.1.

As further explained in 4.1.4, the wage rate is in part determined by the class consciousness and combativity of the workers, which in turn is influenced by such elements as factory design, skill of the work-force and mode of cooperation in the work process. All of these are in part

---

[1] Okishio, "Technical change and the rate of profit"; see also Roemer, *Analytical Foundations*, ch. 4.

[2] Roemer, *Analytical Foundations*, ch. 4.3.

[3] As far as I know Marx's only reference to the patent system occurs in *Zur Kritik* (1861–3), p. 1682, where he suggests that it may have the effect of delaying rather than accelerating technical progress. This is in a sense a false dilemma, since the paradox of the patent system is that by delaying the diffusion of innovations it ensures that there will be more innovations to diffuse. There is no sign that Marx was aware of this trade-off between the use and the development of the productive forces (further discussed in 5.1.3).

determined by the choice of technique.[1] Hence a rational and far-sighted capitalist will search for the innovation that has the best net effect on the profit rate, taking account of both the impact on productivity and on the wage rate.[2] This idea, that has been much discussed lately,[3] has a precursor in *Capital I*:

But machinery acts not only as a competitor who gets the better of the workman, and is constantly on the point of making him superfluous. It is also a power inimical to him, and as such capital proclaims it from the roof tops and as such makes use of it. It is the most powerful weapon for repressing strikes, those periodical revolts of the working class against the autocracy of capital. According to Gaskell, the steam engine was from the very first an antagonist of human power, an antagonist that enabled the capitalist to tread under foot the growing claims of the workmen, who threatened the newly born factory system with a crisis. It would be possible to write quite a history of the inventions made since 1830 with the sole purpose of supplying capital with weapons against the revolts of the working class. At the head of these in importance stands the self-acting mule, because it opened up a new epoch in the automatic system.[4]

Let me first spell out what this means in the maximizing framework. As a maximizer, the capitalist will normally innovate to the hilt in all circumstances, because as a rule increased technical efficiency leads to higher profits. The class struggle argument, however, provides a reason why these two might diverge, hence why the capitalist might not go all the way to the "innovation possibility frontier".[5] Or, alternatively, the class struggle might make him search systematically for some kinds of innovation rather than others, perhaps hitting the frontier at a point that is not optimal at the pre-innovation wage level. The class struggle, however, could never make them innovate *more* than they would otherwise have done.[6] This, on the other hand, is exactly what we would expect to occur

[1] For a formal model of the relation between technology and working-class combativity, see Roemer, *Analytical Foundations*, pp. 55ff.

[2] In addition to rationality and foresight one might have to postulate a measure of solidarity with other capitalists to overcome the free-rider problem that could arise in this connection.

[3] See Braverman, *Labor and Monopoly Capital* and Marglin, "What do bosses do?" Later developments include special issues of *Monthly Review* (1976), *Cambridge Journal of Economics* (1979) and *Politics and Society* (1980).

[4] *Capital I*, pp. 435–6; see also *The Poverty of Philosophy*, p. 207. Moene, "Strike threats and the choice of production technique", argues that machinery *invites* strikes by making it more costly for the employer to have capital idling.

[5] For this notion, see Kennedy, "Induced bias in innovation and the theory of distribution". I argue in ch. 4 of *Explaining Technical Change* that it is a highly dubious construct, yet some notion of this kind is needed to explain technical change within the neoclassical framework. This points to an inherent weakness of that approach.

[6] This assumes that innovation is costless. If there are costs of research and development, the expected value of an innovation could change from negative to positive when the impact on the workers is taken into account. (I owe this point to Aanund Hylland.)

in a satisficing framework. Following the observation made in 1.2.1 that Marx occasionally suggested that "necessity is the mother of invention", the quoted passage might be read as saying that the capitalists were driven by the workers to introduce machinery that otherwise they would have had no incentive to acquire. This view would have important political consequences. On the maximizing approach, the class struggle would tend to be a fetter on the development of the productive forces, while on the satisficing view it is part and parcel of the process of accelerated technical change under capitalism. Hence the latter conception makes the working class more instrumental in creating the technical basis for communism than the accepted view, according to which the profit motive is a constant, almost compulsive force that needs no spur from adverse circumstances, such as recalcitrant workers or state regulation. I do not believe, however, that the texts allow us to impute either view to Marx with any certainty.

Whether the capitalist is a maximizer or a satisficer, he will in all cases be *profit-oriented*. Given the choice between two techniques he will prefer the one associated with the highest expected profit, quite irrespective of how the two have been developed. Marx argued that this choice criterion is socially suboptimal, compared to the socially desirable criterion of choosing the technique that minimizes the labour time needed to produce the output. The latter criterion is socially preferable because it restricts "the realm of necessity" and hence increases the "realm of freedom" (2.2.7). Yet in capitalism only the former can motivate the individual capitalist. In the *Grundrisse* Marx was still confused with regard to this distinction. He writes that by the employment of machinery,

the amount of labour necessary for the production of a given object is indeed reduced to a minimum, but only in order to realize a maximum of labour in the maximum number of such objects. The first aspect is important, because capital here – quite unintentionally – reduced human labour expenditure of energy to a minimum. This will redound to the benefit of emancipated labour, and is the condition of its emancipation.[1]

In the 1861–3 *Critique* he came to see that this view is not correct. True, he still argued that technical progress under capitalism creates free time for the development of civilization, as in the texts cited in 2.4.2. Yet in addition to arguing that this occurs only as an incidental by-product of profit-maximization, he also claimed that this led to technical change on a smaller scale than could have been possible:

[1] *Grundrisse*, p. 701.

Here once again we perceive the limits of bourgeois production and discover that it is not the ultimate form appropriate to the development of the forces of production. On the contrary, it becomes plain that the two come into conflict at a certain point. One aspect of this conflict takes the form of the recurrent crises, etc. which break out when one or the other sector of the working class finds that its traditional occupation has become superfluous. Its outer limit is the surplus time of the workers; the absolute surplus time that society gains, is of *no concern* to them. Hence *the development of the forces of production* is only important to the extent to which it increases the workers' surplus labour time, and not because it reduces the labour time required for material production in general.[1]

In *Capital I* Marx asserts that the capitalist profit comes "not from a diminution of the labour employed, but of the labour paid for".[2] In a footnote added in the second edition he draws the conclusion that "Hence in a communistic society there would be a very different scope for the employment of machinery than there can be in a bourgeois society." New techniques that are superior from the point of view of labour-minimizing need not be so from the point of view of profit-maximizing.

For a full discussion of the relation between "viable" or cost-reducing, and "progressive" or labour-reducing, technical change, the reader is referred to the recent work of John Roemer.[3] The central idea can be conveyed in terms of fig. 2 above. Recall that technique II is superior on labour-minimizing criteria, yet technique I will be chosen for wage levels below w_0. At these wage levels, the social and the individual criteria for choice of technique give different results.

To this argument, however, an important proviso must be added.[4] To state it, we go back to the argument following equation (2) in 3.2.1, where it was observed that the labour value of any commodity can be expressed as the sum of an infinite series of dated labour inputs. This, as was noted, holds with respect to a given technique. Assume now that there exist two techniques, both of which can be resolved into such infinite series. According to the simple criterion of labour-minimization, only the sums of the series are relevant for the choice of technique. Under some conditions, however, this does not give the socially desirable outcome. Rather, one must also take into account the temporal distribution of the inputs, if we are dealing with a growing economy. In that case, labour in the distant past is more scarce than labour in the recent past, hence preference

---

[1] *Zur Kritik (1861–3)*, pp. 1670–1.   [2] *Capital I*, p. 393; see also *Capital III*, p. 262.
[3] Roemer, *Analytical Foundations*, ch. 4.
[4] The following draws on von Weizsäcker, *Steady-State Capital Theory*, part II.3; Wolfstetter, "Surplus labour, synchronized labour costs and Marx's labour theory of value" and Roemer, *Analytical Foundations*, ch. 4.4.

should be given to the technique that employs more labour in the recent past and less in the distant past.

This argument may be clarified if reformulated with respect to the current stage of a steady-state economy, that is an economy in extended reproduction on a constant technical basis. Such an economy

is as it were working at the production of consumption goods for many future periods simultaneously. The economy is at the same time engaged in the last stage of production of the consumption goods to be available in the coming period, in the last but one stage of production for the consumption goods to be available one period later and so on. That is it synchronizes the production of consumption goods for different future periods.[1]

Taking g to be the rate of growth of the system, the author goes on to observe that "because we consider steady state situations an additional provision of consumption good i today implies that we provide $(1 + g)$ additional units of good i tomorrow, $(1 + g)^2$ additional units of the same good the day after tomorrow, and so on".[2] Hence corresponding amounts of labour must be allocated today to ensure this future provision. If we take a_n to be the direct labour input required n periods in the past to produce one unit of the good today, we must allocate a_n labour units today to make one unit available n periods in the future and $a_n(1 + g)^n$ labour units to make $(1 + g)^n$ units available at the same future date. Hence the total amount of labour that will have to be allocated today to ensure the steadily increased supply of the good in the future is given by the infinite series of labour inputs with each term weighed by the compound growth rate. To choose between techniques, then, will involve comparing these compound sums of labour inputs, rather than the simple sums. It can then be shown that if the rate of growth equals the rate of profit, the profit-maximization criterion is equivalent to the minimization of the compound sum of labour inputs. Hence in this case individual profit-seeking will bring about the socially desirable outcome, the reduction of human drudgery. Paul Samuelson has argued that this shows "the normative inferiority of Marx's *values* paradigm".[3] To this John Roemer has countered that the objection holds only under conditions of accumulation. There are circumstances under which the two criteria diverge: the technique that maximizes the rate of profit is not necessarily the one

[1] Von Weizsäcker, *Steady-State Capital Theory*, p. 23.   [2] *Ibid.*, p. 25.
[3] Samuelson, "The normative and positivistic inferiority of Marx's *values* paradigm". The "positivistic inferiority" is related to the problems discussed in 3.2.2.

chosen by rational agents.[1] Yet one must recognize that the objection takes some of the bite out of the alleged suboptimality of capitalism with respect to the choice of socially desirable techniques. Exactly how much of Marx's argument is left remains an empirical issue.

This discussion of the motivation behind innovation in a capitalist economy has provided two reasons why it might proceed less rapidly than is desirable and possible. First, an innovation that is cost-reducing in terms of the current wage level might not be so when its impact on wages is taken into account. Secondly, with the important proviso just stated, an innovation that reduces the total labour time expended on the product need not be a cost-reducing one. (The two mechanisms might interact. In fig. 2, if the firm is currently operating the labour-minimizing technique II at wages above w_0, it might embrace technique I if this has the effect of pushing wages down below w_0.) In addition there is a possibility that capitalism might in some cases lead to *too much* innovation by neglecting "producers' preferences" about how the work should be performed.[2] Technical efficiency need not coincide with social welfare, if the extra utility derived from the increased number of goods produced is smaller than the loss of utility associated with a more disagreeable way of producing them. In 5.1.3 I return to some of these questions concerning the non-optimal rate of technical change under capitalism.

From the rate of technical change I turn to a discussion of its direction – whether it is labour-saving, neutral or capital-saving. There can be no doubt that Marx believed that innovation has a pronounced tendency to be labour-saving. The question is whether he also provided an explanation for this alleged tendency. In particular, did he seek an explanation in rational choice on the part of capitalists? In the wake of John Hicks's theory of labour-saving innovation, many Marxists have argued that Marx held a similar theory. On this view, capitalists systematically seek labour-saving innovations as a rational response to an increase in the price of labour-power.[3] I believe there is only one passage that supports this understanding of Marx:

---

[1] Roemer, "Choice of technique under capitalism, socialism and 'Nirvana'". Here he shows that the choice of technique when capital is concentrated in a few hands *may* differ from the choice that will be made when it is equally distributed. This even holds when the individuals have the same preferences in both cases: to work as little as possible, subject to a consumption constraint, and to accumulate when they can do so without further work.

[2] See Pagano, *Work and Welfare in Economic Theory* for an exhaustive discussion; also Nove, *The Economics of Feasible Socialism*, pp. 199ff.

[3] Dobb, *Political Economy and Capitalism*, p. 125; Sweezy, *The Theory of Capitalist Development*, p. 88.

Between 1848 and 1859, a rise of wages practically insignificant, though accompanied by falling prices of corn, took place in the English agricultural districts ... This was the result of an unusual exodus of the agricultural surplus-population caused by the demands of war, the vast extension of railroads, factories, mines etc. ... What did the farmers do? Did they wait until, in consequence of this brilliant remuneration, the agricultural labourers had so increased and multiplied that their wages must fall again, as prescribed by the dogmatic economic brain? They introduced more machinery, and in a moment the labourers were redundant again in a proportion satisfactory to the farmers. There was now "more capital" laid out in agriculture than before, and in a more productive form. With this the demand for labour fell, not only relatively, but absolutely.[1]

Sweezy, who cites this passage, adds the following comment:

So far as the individual capitalist is concerned, each takes the wage level for granted and attempts to do the best he can for himself. In introducing machinery he is therefore merely attempting to economize on his own wage bill. The net effect of all the capitalists' behaving in this way, however, is to create unemployment which in turn acts upon the wage level.[2]

This "invisible hand" analysis, while compatible with the passage from Marx, is more precise than anything found in the latter. Moreover, the excerpt from Sweezy fails to demonstrate that the introduction of machinery is *the* individually rational response to wage rises. There is in fact no reason why the rational response to a wage increase should be an attempt to economize on wages.[3] It has been proposed that the capitalist would have grounds for tilting his innovative search in a labour-saving direction if he believed that wages would continue to rise in the future.[4] This, while true, comes up against the objection that he would have no rational grounds for holding this belief. In fact, wages will rise only if other capitalists are less rational than himself and do not economize on labour – but this is an irrational assumption to make.[5]

In any case I do not think these were the grounds on which Marx held the labour-saving view of innovation. First, there are passages in the *Grundrisse* that explicitly repudiate the Hicksian view. Moreover, both in that work and in *Capital* we find statements that point to a quite different explanation. In the *Grundrisse* Marx quotes Ravenstone to the effect that:

Machinery can seldom be applied with success to abridge the labour of an individual; more time would be lost in its construction than could be saved by its application. It is only really useful when it acts on great masses, when a single

---

[1] *Capital I*, p. 638.   [2] Sweezy, *The Theory of Capitalist Development*, p. 88.
[3] Salter, *Productivity and Technical Change*, pp. 43–4.
[4] Fellner, "Two propositions in the theory of induced innovations".
[5] Cp. also ch. 4 of my *Explaining Technical Change*.

machine can assist the labour of thousands. It is accordingly in the most populous countries where there are most idle men that it is always abundant. It is not called into action by the scarcity of men, but by the facility with which they are brought together.[1]

A few pages later he asserts this view as his own:

The employment of machinery itself historically presupposes – see above, Ravenstone – superfluous hands. Machinery inserts itself to replace labour only where there is an overflow of labour powers ... It enters not in order to replace labour power where this is lacking, but rather in order to reduce massively available labour power to its necessary measure.[2]

This argument is quite compatible with the preponderance of labour-saving innovations. It excludes only a certain type of explanation of this tendency, one linking the introduction of labour-saving machinery to the scarcity of labour. Marx's own explanation – if that word is not too strong – is that technical progress is by its very nature labour-saving. In the *Grundrisse* he goes so far as to assert that this is a mere tautology:

The fact that in the development of the productive powers of labour the objective conditions of labour, objectified labour, must grow relative to living labour – this is actually a tautological statement, for what else does growing productive power mean than that less immediate labour is required to create a greater product, and that therefore social wealth expresses itself more and more in the conditions of labour created by labour itself?[3]

A somewhat less obscure statement in *Capital III* is too long to be usefully cited here.[4] It can be broken down into the following propositions. (i) Economic growth implies or is synonymous with more output per worker. (ii) If more is produced per worker, each worker must be able to handle more raw material. (iii) In order to be able to handle more raw material, the worker needs more machinery. (iv) Since constant capital mainly consists of raw material and machinery, it follows that the amount of capital per worker must rise – that is that technical progress is inherently labour-saving. Premises (ii) and (iii) may appear compelling, but in fact are not. They embody a narrow vision of technical change, that excludes among others such dramatic capital-saving innovations as explosives or the wireless. Marx's argument for the preponderance of labour-saving inventions is invalid, and the conclusion quite possibly wrong.[5]

This discussion of technical change has mainly been concerned with

---

[1] *Grundrisse*, p. 690, also quoted in *Capital I*, p. 430.
[2] *Grundrisse*, p. 702.   [3] *Ibid.*, p. 831.   [4] *Capital III*, p. 212.
[5] Blaug, "Technical change and Marxian economics".

the intended consequences of technical change, and only incidentally with the actual consequences. In particular, the notions of capital-saving and labour-saving innovations have been taken in the *ex ante* sense of methods that modify the value (or the price) of the constant capital relative to the number of workers when it is evaluated in terms of the pre-innovative equilibrium. This is indeed the relevant notion in a discussion of the motivation behind innovations. In 3.4.2 I consider the *ex post* view, and discuss whether innovations that are labour-saving at pre-innovation values (or prices) remain so in the post-innovative equilibrium.

3.4. Theories of capitalist crises

No problem is more central to Marxism than the mechanism whereby capitalism destroys itself. At the most general level, this comes about by the "contradiction between the productive forces and the relations of production" (5.1.3). Yet in his economic writings Marx did not devote much attention to this idea. Or rather, he wrongly thought that some of his more specific views on capitalist crises instantiated that general theory. Of these views, the best-known and the most articulate is the theory of the falling rate of profit (3.4.2). More diffuse are a variety of other theories that may be loosely collected together as "theories of insufficient demand" (3.4.3). Before I examine these theories in detail, I state some of the features that a Marxist theory of crises should exhibit.

3.4.1. Desiderata for a Marxist theory of crises
Given the general methodological remarks made in chapter 1 and in 3.1, as well as the function of crisis theory in Marx's political argument, the capitalist crises should be shown to have the following features. (i) They should be *system-immanent*, in the sense of being generated neither by exogenous shocks nor by monopoly or other avoidable malpractices. (ii) They should have *micro-foundations*, in the sense that the globally irrational outcome should be shown to derive from the local rationality of the individual agents.[1] (iii) They should be *irreversible*, in the sense of not being amenable to political regulation from within the capitalist system. (iv) They should provide a *motivation for political action* with the purpose of abolishing capitalism. Only if these conditions are fulfilled do we obtain a

---

[1] Strictly speaking, this is requiring too much. Methodological individualism does not demand rationality in the motivation of the individuals (1.1). Yet in the present case I believe that the demand for micro-foundations amounts to a demand for rational-choice explanation.

theory of crises that is satisfactory both from the point of view of economic theory and from that of revolutionary action.

Let me briefly indicate how the theories discussed here fare in these respects. As further argued in the next chapter, the contradiction between productive forces and relations of production fails to provide a robust motivation for revolutionary action. A less-than-optimal rate of technical change will hardly incite to revolution if that rate is high and even increasing. Demand crises of various kinds (3.4.3) have proved eminently amenable to political reforms that do not touch the foundations of the capitalist mode of production. The theory of the falling rate of profit, being linked to irreversible technical change, is more satisfactory in this respect. It fails, on the other hand, to provide micro-foundations, since it takes "the tendency of the rate of profit to fall" as an immanent property of the capitalist mode of production.

3.4.2. The theory of the falling rate of profit[1]

Like the classical economists before him, Marx believed that the rate of profit tended to fall, but he provided a very different explanation of this alleged fact. The difference is obvious from a look at the table of contents of *Capital III*, compared to the *Principles* of Ricardo or Malthus. In their exposition profit is treated after ground rent, and the fall in the rate of profit deduced as a consequence of diminishing productivity in agriculture. Marx, on the other hand, completes the analysis of the falling rate of profit before he comes to ground rent. In the *Grundrisse* he accuses Ricardo of fleeing "from economics to seek refuge in organic chemistry",[2] as if the falling rate of profit was a natural fact rather than a social one. Moreover, while his predecessors saw technical progress as a force counteracting the tendency of the rate of profit to fall, Marx argued that innovations were the very vehicle of that tendency. Carey, he remarks, correctly stated that "the rate of profit falls as a result, not of a decrease but rather of an increase of the productive force".[3] We shall see that his view was contrary not only to intuition, but to truth as well.

In the *Grundrisse* we find Marx arguing or suggesting that the falling rate of profit was an instance of the contradiction between the productive forces and the relations of production. In particular we find this assertion

---

[1] The law itself and the countertendencies that impede its operation are treated in chs. XIII and XIV of *Capital III*. Ch. XV treats the law in a more general perspective – too general, in fact, to be very helpful. An analysis of the many pseudo-issues that have confused the later debate is van Parijs, "The falling-rate-of-profit theory of crises". Roemer, *Analytical Foundations*, ch. 5 has the fullest recent discussion.

[2] *Grundrisse*, p. 754.   [3] *Ibid.*, p. 558.

in a passage that is worth quoting at some length. It is quite probably the most forceful statement that Marx ever made of his theory – or visionary image – of the decline and fall of the capitalist mode of production. When reading the apparently more sober statements in *Capital*, it is useful to have this apocalyptic passage in mind:

[The law in the decline in the rate of profit] is in every respect the most important law of modern political economy, and the most essential for understanding the most difficult relations. It is the most important law from the historical standpoint. It is a law which, despite its simplicity, has never before been grasped and, even less, consciously articulated. Since this decline in the rate of profit is identical in meaning (1) with the productive power already produced, and the foundation formed by it for new production; this simultaneously presupposing an enormous development of scientific powers; (2) with the decline of the part of the capital already produced which must be exchanged for immediate labour, i.e. with the decline in the immediate labour required for the reproduction of an immense value, expressing itself in a great mass of products, great mass of products with low prices, because the total sum of prices is = to the reproduced capital + profit; (3) [with] the dimension of capital generally, including the portion which is not fixed capital; hence intercourse on a magnificent scale, immense sum of exchange operations, large size of the market and all-sidedness of simultaneous labour; means of communication etc. presence of the necessary consumption fund to undertake this gigantic process (workers' food, housing etc.); hence it is evident that the material productive power already present, already worked out, existing in the form of fixed capital, together with population etc. in short all conditions of wealth, that the greatest conditions for the reproduction of wealth, i.e. the abundant development of the social individual – that the development of the productive forces brought about by the historical development of capital itself, when it reaches a certain point, suspends the self-realization of capital, instead of positing it. Beyond a certain point, the development of the powers of production becomes a barrier for capital; hence the capital relation a barrier for the development of the productive powers of labour. When it has reached this point, capital, i.e. wage labour, enters into the same relation towards the development of social wealth and of the forces of production as the guild system, serfdom, slavery, and is necessarily stripped off as a fetter . . .

The growing incompatibility between the productive development of society and its hitherto existing relations of production expresses itself in bitter contradictions, crises, spasms. The violent destruction of capital not by relations external to it, but rather as a condition of its self-preservation, is the most striking form in which advice is given it to be gone and to give room to a higher state of social production. It is not only the growth of scientific power, but the measure in which it is already posited as fixed capital, the scope and width in which it is realized and has conquered the totality of production. It is, likewise, the development of the population etc. in short, of all moments of production; in that the productive power of labour, like the application of machinery, is related to the population; whose growth in and for itself already the presupposition as well as the result of the growth of the use values to be reproduced and hence also to be consumed.

Since this decline of profits signifies the same as the decrease of immediate labour relative to the size of the objectified labour which it reproduces and newly posits, capital will attempt every means of checking the smallness of the relation of living labour to the size of the capital generally, hence also of the surplus value, if expressed as profit, relative to the presupposed capital, by reducing the allotment made to necessary labour and by still more expanding the quantity of surplus labour with regard to the whole labour employed. Hence the highest development of productive power together with the greatest expansion of existing wealth will coincide with depreciation of capital, degradation of the labourer, and a most straitened exhaustion of his vital powers. These contradictions lead to explosions, cataclysms, crises, in which by momentaneous suspension of labour and annihilation of a great portion of capital the latter is violently reduced to the point where it can go on ... Yet these regularly recurring catastrophes lead to their repetition on a higher scale and finally to its violent overthrow.[1]

In 2.3.3 I argued that Marx attempted to demonstrate a connection between three major flaws of capitalism: exploitation, alienation and the "social contradiction" involved in the falling rate of profit. In the passage just quoted he also tries to link the last of these with the more general thesis of historical materialism, that all modes of production come to an end because of a contradiction between the productive forces and the relations of production. Clearly, the forging of such a link would be highly desirable. In its absence, historical materialism and the economic theory of capitalism would remain separate bodies of analysis, each of them offering an explanation of the downfall of capitalism unrelated to that proposed by the other.[2]

A possible link could be the following. As the crises of capitalism become increasingly more severe, by the fall in the rate of profit which is only partly checked by the periodic remissions, the capitalist motivation to invest wears off. Profit is the "vital flame" and the "motive power" of capitalist production. With less investment goes a lower rate of technical change – the "fettering of the productive forces" involved in the contradiction between productive forces and relations of production. Yet this view appears to be inherently muddled, and inconsistent with other passages from the *Grundrisse*. The muddle is this. If the rate of profit falls because of an increase in the productive powers, then presumably the fall should be halted when technical stagnation sets in. It might be possible to construct a model in which this consequence does not follow, but it *is* a

---

[1] *Ibid.*, pp. 748ff.
[2] Thus Kolakowski, *Main Currents of Marxism*, vol. 1 writes first that technical progress leads to a falling rate of profit (p. 297) and then that capitalism is destroyed because it becomes a brake on technical progress (p. 301) – without noting the need to relate these two tendencies to one another.

prima facie consequence and Marx does not tell us how to avoid it. The textual difficulty is this. In passages cited in 5.1.3 and 5.2.3 Marx states that capitalism will disappear not when and because it becomes incapable of developing the productive forces, but when and because its inherently limited way of doing so is no longer required for their further progress. The emphasis here is on the limits of capitalism, not on its impotence. The limits are permanent features of the capitalist mode of production, but assume historical importance only when the material possibility emerges of another mode of production not subject to them. Hence capitalism creates the conditions for its own destruction, not by curtailing its own powers, but by enabling the establishment of another, more powerful system.

Note the importance of the idea that capitalism will disappear when *and because* it ceases to be the best system for developing the productive forces. It is the explanatory claim of historical materialism that enters into conflict with the explanatory claim of the theory of the falling rate of profit, not the respective predictions of the theories. It might well be true that capitalism disappears *when* it is no longer optimal, and *because* the rate of profit falls below the minimum level that is acceptable to the capitalists. Conversely, but less plausibly, the suboptimality might be the causally important fact and the fall in the rate of profit merely a concomitantly occurring process. The argument of the preceding paragraph was directed against the idea that the fall in the rate of profit could bring about the fettering of the productive forces, in which case the two explanatory claims could be reconciled. Of course, they could also be reconciled by assuming that the downfall of capitalism is causally over-determined, so that two individually sufficient forces are at work. This, however, seems to be an explanation of last resort.

So much for context – let me now turn to the theory itself. I shall first state it in informal, persuasive terms, and then go on to point out why this is treacherous language that does not survive a more rigorous statement. The source of all surplus labour and hence of profit – so the argument goes – is living labour. It is in the collective interest of the capitalist class to keep alive the goose that lays the golden eggs. Yet it is also in the interest of each individual capitalist to substitute dead labour for living labour, machinery for workers. By using more productive methods he can realize for a while supernormal profits, while the fall in the average rate of profit that comes about as a result of his innovation, even when generalized, is too insignificant to deter him from introducing it. Yet the aggregate effect of all entrepreneurs in all industries behaving similarly is significant indeed, leading to the steady erosion in the rate of profit. As shown by the fundamental equation of Marxist economics (3.2.2), the rising organic composition of capital associated with the introduction of machinery leads to a fall in the rate of profit, assuming the rate of exploitation to be constant.

One basic flaw in this argument is the assumption that living labour is the ultimate source of profit (3.2.3). Yet it is not clear in exactly which way the fallacy in this assumption enters the argument. Hence a more specific refutation is needed. Let us accept for the sake of simplification that the fundamental equation is valid, thus disregarding the problems created by the divergence of prices from values. The emphasis here is on the trend in the average organic composition of capital, not on the sectoral differences that make prices deviate from values.[1] On this assumption, three objections will be made to Marx's theory of the falling rate of profit.

First, it turns crucially on the assumption that innovations as a rule are labour-saving in the *ex ante* sense. As pointed out above, Marx assumed this more or less unthinkingly, without realizing that an argument was needed. Moreover, there does not appear to exist any argument that we could feed into his theory to justify the assumption. No doubt we could tell a story in which extended reproduction on a constant technical basis comes up against a scarcity of labour-power (assuming that the working force grows more slowly than the rate of expansion of the economy) and in which capitalists are therefore motivated to substitute machinery for labour. I have argued, however, that this Hicksian argument is invalid. Moreover, even were we to accept it, the rate of growth of the working force, divided by the rate of savings out of profit, would provide a floor below which the rate of profit would not fall, and this might well be high enough to ensure the continuance of the system.

Secondly, even accepting the preponderance of labour-saving inventions in the *ex ante* sense, there is no reason why they should in general remain labour-saving when evaluated in the post-innovation values (or prices). One would commit the fallacy of composition if, from the fact that a given innovation is labour-saving when all other things are constant, one concludes that this remains true when all innovations are considered simultaneously. Innovation in sector A, which produces constant capital for sector B, might lead to a lowering of the value of each physical unit of

---

[1] Yet sectoral differences could be important in non-steady-state growth. There might be an increase in the organic composition of capital in each sector, and yet the average organic composition might fall if the sectors with low organic composition expand sufficiently faster than the sectors with high organic composition.

capital in sector B, even if labour-saving innovations in B lead to an increase in the number of such units per worker.[1] The net effect of these two, opposed tendencies could go either way. Marx simply has no argument for the implicit contention that the pre-innovative trend would remain dominant. This conclusion is not affected by the additional complication that the (*ex ante* and *ex post*) notions of labour-saving innovations are defined in terms of the value compositions of capital, while the fundamental equation is stated in terms of the organic composition. True, the latter might rise more rapidly than the former if there also takes place a fall in the value of labour-power, but, first, we would still be unable to say anything *a priori* about the net effect, and, secondly, a fall in the value of labour-power would go against the assumption of a constant rate of surplus-value.

The third objection is directed against that last assumption itself. Under conditions of technical change that also affect the industries producing consumption goods for the workers, the assumption of a constant rate of surplus-value implies a rise in the real wage. Clearly, the more labour-saving are the inventions, the less is the aggregate demand for labour and the smaller will be the rise in the real wage – and the larger the rise in the rate of surplus-value. Hence on grounds of internal consistency it is hard to assert both strongly labour-saving innovations and a constant rate of exploitation. Marx did not in fact assert the latter, but offered an obscure argument to show that the increasing rate of surplus-value could never offset the "main" tendency of the rate of profit to fall. Once again this is a quite arbitrary contention. Recall also the fact that if the real wage is constant, the average rate of profit can *never* fall as a result of *ex ante* profitable inventions.[2] In this case the fall in the rate of profit as the result of technical change is an impossibility, in the general case it is merely a non-necessity. Marx, of course, wanted it to be a necessary process rooted in the nature of capitalist relations of production.

To conclude, we cannot assert that there is a tendency for the denominator in the fundamental equation to increase over time, nor, were this to happen, that it would not be offset by a rise in the numerator. If we want to speculate about what led Marx into this multiply confused argument, we might invoke wishful thinking, an uncertain grasp of mathematics or, more fundamentally, a confusion between the quantitative and the qualitative aspects of the domination of capital over labour, the objective spirit

---

[1] Clearly, this is only a crude way of stating the point, chosen for heuristic purposes only. Capital-using innovations typically imply different machinery, not more of the same.
[2] See references in note 1, p. 146 above.

over the subjective spirit (2.3.3). Also, the dialectical twist of having capital develop by a process that eliminates the very source of progress must have appealed strongly to Marx. Quoting Juvenal, Marx captured the political dilemma of the capitalist class in the phrase "Et propter vitam vivendi perdere causas" – for the sake of life to sacrifice life's only end.[1] In the theory of the falling rate of profit he found a similar predicament at the economic level.

3.4.3. Theories of insufficient demand

It is clear from the long passage from the *Grundrisse* cited above, and from the prominent place it has in *Capital III*, that Marx believed the fall in the rate of profit to be the central mechanism in the economic breakdown of capitalism. This theory also has the virtue of being stated in terms sufficiently precise to allow discussion and, in fact, refutation. This is not true of the various other theories of capitalist crises scattered around in his writings. They tend to be trivial, or rambling and repetitive, or obscure. They may contain isolated phrases that can be used to justify the term "Marxist" as a characterization of some subsequently proposed theory, but the ensuing war of quotations has tended to distract attention from the substantive issues. I shall briefly discuss three such theories in Marx: a disproportionality theory, an overproduction theory and an underconsumption theory. For convenience I have grouped them all together under the heading of theories of insufficient demand, but they are really quite distinct suggestions. (I shall not consider the proto-Keynesian theory of over-saving (1.3.2 and 1.5.3), since Marx did not intend this as an explanation of the actual crises, only as an analysis of what would happen if the exhortation to the workers to save part of their wage were taken seriously.) In what follows, the term "crisis" must be understood quite broadly, ranging from mere disequilibrium through cyclical fluctuations to the ultimate breakdown of capitalism.

The disproportionality theory and the overproduction theory are both linked to the separation of sale and purchase in capitalism. This, Marx says in *Capital I*, implies "the possibility, and no more than the possibility, of crises".[2] Let me first focus on the disproportionality crises that stem from this separation. In a decentralized economy there is no guarantee that producers will find a market for their products, nor that goods in demand will be produced in sufficient quantity. There may be imbalance between the capital and the consumption sectors, that is violation of the

---

[1] *Neue Oder Zeitung*, 12.6.1855.
[2] *Capital I*, p. 114. For discussion, see Kenway, "Marx, Keynes and the possibility of crisis".

conditions of simple or extended reproduction, and also imbalance within the capital sector, due to the uneven rate of depreciation of fixed capital.[1] In *Capital II* this disproportionality between sectors is almost made into a rule:

[Inasmuch] as only one-sided exchanges are made, a number of mere purchases on the one hand, a number of mere sales on the other – and we have seen that the normal exchange of the annual product on the basis of capitalism necessitates such one-sided metamorphosis – the balance can be maintained only on the assumption that in amount the value of the one-sided purchases and that of the one-sided sales tally. The fact that the production of commodities is the general form of capitalist production implies the role which money is playing in it not only as a medium of circulation, but also as money-capital, and engenders certain conditions of normal exchange peculiar to this mode of production and therefore of the normal course of reproduction, whether it be on a simple or an extended scale – conditions which change into so many conditions of abnormal development, into so many possibilities of crises, since – owing to the spontaneous nature of this production – a balance is in itself an accident.[2]

The last phrase suggests the influence of Sismondi, "the patron saint of all those 'explanations' that are content to talk about the anarchy of capitalist production, the lack of knowledge of what the other fellow does and what buyers want, and so on".[3] Elsewhere Marx made it clear, however, that he did not believe the equilibrium to be a mere accident, a knife-edge property as it were. In *Capital I* he contrasts the anarchy of the division of labour in society with the despotism of division of labour in the workshop, but adds that the lack of regulation in the former is only an apparent one:

The different spheres of production . . . constantly tend to an equilibrium: for, on the one hand, while each producer of a commodity is bound to produce a use-value, to satisfy a particular social want, and while the extent of these wants differs quantitatively, still there exists an inner relation which settles their proportions into a regular system, and that system one of spontaneous growth; and, on the other hand, the law of the value of the commodities ultimately determines how much of the disposable working-time society can spend on each particular class of commodities. But this constant tendency to equilibrium, of the various spheres of production, is exercised only in the shape of a reaction against the constant upsetting of the equilibrium.[4]

Marx was quite fond of this idea, that in capitalism equilibrium is attained only by the "negation of the negation"[5] – by the constant overcoming of deviations from equilibrium rather than in the direct way that would be

[1] *Capital II*, pp. 468–9.   [2] *Ibid.*, pp. 494–5.
[3] Schumpeter, *History of Economic Analysis*, p. 741.   [4] *Capital I*, pp. 355–6.
[5] *Grundrisse*, p. 137; see also *ibid.*, p. 148 and *Theories of Surplus-Value*, vol 2, p. 500.

possible in a planned economy. In retrospect we can say that the attainment of equilibrium by out-of-equilibrium trading is a much more complex process than Marx and the classical economists believed, and that the dynamic process of mutual adjustments may well fail to bring about an equilibrium.[1] Marx, in this case, credited capitalism with more collective rationality than it does in fact possess. Generally, he seems to have vacillated among the views that in capitalism disequilibrium is a mere possibility, that it obtains as a rule and that it tends to be eliminated by market adjustments. Nowhere does he come close to suggesting that it could be self-reinforcing.

In the *Theories of Surplus-Value* Marx discusses at some length the possibility of a "general glut" in all markets. While the disproportionality theory did not go beyond the idea of local overproduction, the general glut involves simultaneous overproduction in all sectors of the economy. One might think that the assertion of general overproduction involves the fallacy of composition, but Marx effectively disarms this objection by pointing out that it is valid only under conditions of barter, unmediated by money:

Let us examine this fantasy more closely: It is admitted that there can be overproduction in *each particular* industry. The only circumstance which could prevent overproduction in *all* industries simultaneously is, according to the assertions made, the fact that commodity exchanges against commodity – i.e. recourse is taken to the supposed conditions of barter. But this loop-hole is blocked by the very fact that trade under capitalist conditions is not barter, and therefore the seller of a commodity is not necessarily at the same time the buyer of another. This whole subterfuge then rests on abstracting from *money* and from the fact that we are not concerned here with the exchange of products, but with the circulation of commodities, an essential part of which is the separation of purchase and sale.[2]

Elsewhere in the same manuscripts the role of money is more specifically explained in terms of what Keynes was to call liquidity preference:

At a given moment, the supply of all commodities may be greater than the demand for all commodities, since the demand for the *general commodity*, money, exchange-value, is greater than the demand for all particular commodities, in other words the motive to turn the commodity into money, to realize its exchange-value, prevails over the motive to transform the commodity again into use-value.[3]

---

[1] On this issue, see Weintraub, *Microfoundations*.
[2] *Theories of Surplus-Value*, vol. 2, pp. 532–3.   [3] *Ibid.*, p. 505.

These observations, while true and potentially important, do not lead us beyond the "possibility of crises". Once again, there is no hint at a dynamic mechanism by which the crisis, once set in motion, could become self-reinforcing. In this crucial respect the theory of the falling rate of profit, whatever its other flaws, is more satisfactory.

Overproduction is not synonymous with underconsumption, since the latter term refers exclusively to lack of effective demand for *consumption* goods. Crises of underconsumption must also be distinguished from the (hypothetical) crises that could arise from over-saving. In *Capital II* Marx explicitly distinguishes between these two "contradictions of capitalism":

Contradiction in the capitalist mode of production: the labourers as buyers of commodities are important for the market. But as sellers of their own commodity – labour-power – capitalist society tends to keep them down to the minimum price. Further contradiction: the periods in which capitalist production exerts all its forces regularly turn out to be periods of over-production, because production potentials can never be utilized to such an extent that more value may not only be produced but also be realized; but the sale of commodities, the realization of commodity-capital and thus of surplus-value, is limited not by the consumer requirements of society in general, but by the consumer requirements of a society in which the vast majority are always poor and must always remain poor.[1]

In *Capital III* Marx refers in passing to this "further contradiction" as "the ultimate reason for all real crises".[2] If taken literally, this would dethrone the theory of the falling rate of profit from its place as Marx's principal theory of capitalist crises. In the chapter on the "internal contradictions of the law" of the falling rate of profit in *Capital III* there is, however, a more nuanced statement of the relation between these two mechanisms:

The creation of this surplus-value makes up the direct process of production, which, as we have said, has no other limits but those mentioned above. As soon as all the surplus-labour it was possible to squeeze out has been embodied in commodities, surplus-value has been produced. But this production of surplus-value completes but the first act of the capitalist process of production – the direct production process. Capital has absorbed so and so much unpaid labour. With the development of the process, which expresses itself in a drop in the rate of profit, the mass of surplus-value thus produced swells to immense dimensions. Now comes the second act of the process. The entire mass of commodities, i.e. the total product, including the portion which replaces the constant and variable capital, and that representing surplus-value, must be sold. If this is not done, or done only in part, or only at prices below the prices of production, the labourer has indeed been exploited, but his exploitation is not realized as such for the capitalist, and

---

[1] *Capital II*, p. 316.
[2] *Capital III*, p. 484. For a discussion of this and related texts, see Bleaney, *Underconsumption Theories*, ch. 6.

this can be bound up with a total or partial failure to realize the surplus-value pressed out of him, indeed even with the partial or total loss of capital. The conditions of direct exploitation, and those of realizing it, are not identical. They diverge not only in place and time, but also logically. The first are limited only by the productive power of society, the latter by the proportional limits of the various branches of production and the consumer power of society. But this last-named is not determined either by the absolute productive power, or by the absolute consumer power, but by the consumer power based on antagonistic conditions of distribution, which reduce the consumption of the bulk of society to a minimum varying within more or less narrow limits.[1]

It is, in fact, possible for a fall in the *rate* of profit to go together with a rise in the *mass* of surplus-value. The former constitutes the "first act" of the breakdown of capitalism, while the underconsumption crises generated by the latter form the "second act". This sounds like an interesting scenario, but it suffers from a fatal defect: Marx nowhere tells us how the limited consumption power can act as a barrier to the realization of surplus-value. Note that we are not dealing here with a general glut caused by liquidity preference, nor with a sectoral disequilibrium, nor with lack of effective demand caused by workers' over-saving. As far as we can tell, Marx had in mind something different from all of these – but it is impossible to know what. This third variety of the "effective demand" theories is even more nebulous and opaque than the first two. They at least had the virtue of pointing to a causal mechanism, even if its detailed mode of operation was left unspecified. The underconsumption theory of crises is virtually devoid of content, beyond the pre-analytical notion that capitalism creates wealth which must remain barren because of the restricted consumption power of the workers.

[1] *Capital III*, p. 244.

4. Exploitation, freedom and justice

The theory of exploitation was centrally important in Marx, and remains a focus of intense work today. Unlike most of his analytical economics, it is worth examining for itself, not just for its place in the history of thought. The importance of exploitation in Marxism is twofold. First, the presence of exploitation in a society provides the outside observer with a ground for normative criticism. Exploitation is wrong; exploiters are morally condemnable; a society that tolerates or generates exploitation ought to be abolished. Secondly, exploitation can provide the exploited with a ground for taking individual or collective action against the system, and hence enters into the explanation of such action. When constructing a more elaborate theory of exploitation, one may face the problem that the normatively relevant concept is one that does not have much explanatory significance. Workers may be exploited by shareholders, yet direct their action against the managers.[1] In the present chapter I am mainly concerned with the normative theory of exploitation, while the explanatory issue is discussed in 6.1 below.

    In 4.1 I discuss the nature and causes of exploitation, as seen by Marx and later Marxist writers. In particular I draw heavily on the recent work by John Roemer, *A General Theory of Exploitation and Class*. In 4.2 I discuss

---

[1] Weber, *Economy and Society*, vol. 1, p. 305.

whether the workers under capitalism are coerced or forced into selling their labour-power, and if so what relation this bears to their being exploited. This also occasions a more general discussion of Marx's conception of freedom. In 4.3 I consider the question of the injustice of exploitation, arguing that Marx had a theory of justice that supported both his condemnation of exploitation and his conception of communism. Many ideas in the latter two sections derive from work by G. A. Cohen.

4.1. The nature and causes of exploitation

Being exploited means, fundamentally, working more hours than are needed to produce the goods one consumes. This apparently simple formulation hides a number of conceptual problems that are explored in the present section. The most fundamental is posed by the existence of heterogeneous labour: if it is impossible to define the labour content of goods, it is also impossible to compare labour expended with "labour commanded" in the form of goods. I postpone discussion of this difficulty to 4.1.5. Another central problem concerns the relation between exploitation through direct (extra-economic) coercion and exploitation in the market. The former is the object of 4.1.1, the latter of 4.1.2. Together, these make up the discussion of what exploitation *is*. In the following subsections I discuss the *causes* of exploitation. In 4.1.3 I consider a variety of markets that may give rise to exploitation. In 4.1.4 I discuss the determinants of the *rate* of exploitation, in the canonical case of exploitation through the labour market in a capitalist economy.

4.1.1. Non-market exploitation
There is a tension in the concept of exploitation, as employed both within and outside Marxism. On the one hand there is a suggestion that exploitation differs from (extra-economic) *coercion*. Being exploited is being "taken unfair advantage of", a much subtler form of suffering harm than being the object of physical coercion. We probably would not say that the victim of a protection racket is exploited, and we certainly would not say this of the victim of an armed robbery. On the other hand it would be contrary to usage to deny that the slave or the serf is exploited – even though feudal exploitation may not differ much from a protection racket.[1] If, as seems to be the case, our linguistic intuitions are inconsistent in this way, there is a choice to be made concerning the direction in which one wants to go.

---

[1] North, *Structure and Change in Economic History*, p. 130.

Earlier, I proposed to define exploitation as extraction of surplus labour through market transactions, thus effectively denying that the slave is exploited.[1] I now believe this was a mistake. At least within the Marxist tradition, and probably also outside it, the case for saying that there is exploitation outside the market is overwhelmingly strong, even though it remains difficult to separate it clearly from robbery and similar phenomena.

Yet this terminological issue is less important than the underlying substantive one. There are important differences between extraction of surplus labour through extra-economic coercion and exploitation in the market. I shall first consider what the two have in common, and then go on to Marx's theory of non-market exploitation.

The feature common to all class societies is that extraction of surplus labour takes place. Marx defines surplus labour generally as labour beyond what is needed to reproduce the labour-power of the worker:

That portion of the working-day, then, during which this reproduction takes place, I call *"necessary"* labour time, and the labour expended during that time I call *"necessary"* labour . . . During the second period of the labour process, that in which his labour is no longer necessary labour, the workman, it is true, labours, expends labour-power; but his labour being no longer necessary labour, he creates no value for himself. He creates surplus-value which, for the capitalist, has all the charms of a creation out of nothing. This portion of the working-day I name surplus labour-time, and to the labour expended during that time, I give the name of surplus-labour. It is every bit as important, for a correct understanding of surplus-value, to conceive of it as a mere congelation of surplus labour-time, as nothing but materialised surplus-labour, as it is, for a proper comprehension of value, to conceive it as a mere congelation of so many hours of labour, as nothing but materialised labour. The essential difference between, for instance, a society based on slave-labour, and one based on wage-labour, lies only in the mode in which this surplus-labour is in each case extracted from the actual producers.[2]

Capital has not invented surplus-labour. Wherever a part of society possesses the monopoly of the means of production, the labourer, free or not free, must add to the working-time necessary for his own maintenance an extra-working time in order to produce the means of subsistence for the owners of the means of production, whether this proprietor be the Athenian [aristocrat], Etruscan theocrat, civis Romanus, Norman baron, American slave-owner, Wallachian Boyard, modern landlord or capitalist.[3]

I have discussed in 2.5 the world-historical importance of surplus-labour that makes possible the advance of civilization by creating free time for a small class of non-producers. I insist on the word "possible" in

---

[1] In my "Exploitation, freedom and justice".   [2] *Capital I*, pp. 216–17.
[3] *Ibid.*, p. 235.

the preceding sentence. Some writers, such as V. G. Childe, have tried to explain the emergence of classes and exploitation by the presence of a technology allowing a surplus. This explanation, however, is invalid, since the producers always have the option of working less to achieve the same consumption level, rather than working more in order to create a surplus. The choice of the latter rather than the former must be explained by the nature of the social relations, and hence cannot explain them, as Marx well knew:

[The] natural conditions or limits of rent, being those of surplus-value in general, are plainly clear. The direct producer must (1) possess enough labour-power, and (2) the natural conditions of his labour, above all the soil cultivated by him, must be productive enough, in a word, the natural productivity of his labour must be big enough to give him the possibility of retaining some surplus-labour, over and above that required for the satisfaction of his own indispensable needs. It is not this possibility which creates the rent, but rather compulsion which turns this possibility into reality.[1]

It is misleading, therefore, to say that "as long as there is some surplus, class society is possible".[2] Rather, it is the possibility of a surplus that makes class society possible. The economy *has* no surplus.[3] In 5.3 I consider the sequence of events that, according to Marx, led to the actualization of surplus, as distinct from its mere possibility.

Surplus labour can be extracted by (extra-economic) force, or by the market. The most important passage in which Marx explains the need for direct force occurs in *Capital III*:

It is furthermore evident that in all forms in which the direct labourer remains the "possessor" of the means of production and labour conditions necessary for the production of his own means of subsistence, the property relationship must simultaneously appear as a direct relation of lordship and servitude, so that the direct producer is not free; a lack of freedom which may be reduced from serfdom with enforced labour to a mere tributary relationship. The direct producer, according to our assumption, is to be found here in possession of his own means of production, the necessary material labour conditions required for the realization of his labour and the production of his means of subsistence. He conducts his agricultural activity and the rural home industries connected with it independently . . . Under such conditions the surplus-labour for the nominal owner of the land can only be extorted from them by other than economic pressure, whatever the form may be assumed to be. This differs from slave or plantation economy in that the slave works under alien conditions of production and not independently. Thus, conditions of personal dependence are requisite, a lack of personal

---

[1] *Capital III*, p. 792; also *Capital I*, p. 514.
[2] Cohen, *Karl Marx's Theory of History*, p. 198. A more accurate statement occurs on pp. 61–2.
[3] Cp. Pearson's essay thus entitled.

freedom, no matter to what extent, and being tied to the soil as its accessory, bondage in the true sense of the word.[1]

Unlike the slave, the feudal serf or Asiatic peasant owns part of his labour-power and can dispose of it independently (5.1.2). Unlike the wage labourer, he owns the means of production needed to produce his own subsistence. Hence surplus labour can only be extracted from him by making him unfree, that is by the lord gaining possession of part of his labour-power.[2]

Rent in kind, on the other hand,

presupposes a higher stage of civilisation for the direct producer, i.e. a higher level of development of his labour and of society in general. And it is distinct from the preceding form in that surplus-labour needs no longer be performed in its natural form, under the direct supervision and compulsion of the landlord and his representatives; the direct producer is driven rather by the force of circumstances than by direct coercion, through legal enactment rather than the whip, to perform it on his own responsibility ... In this relation the direct producer more or less disposes of his entire labour-time, although, as previously, a part of his labour-time, at first practically the entire surplus portion of it, belongs to the landlord without compensation; except that the landlord no longer directly receives this surplus-labour in its natural form, but rather in the products' natural form in which it is realized.[3]

I take this to state, or to imply, that there now exists a market in tenancies. Since the labourer "more or less" owns all of his labour-power, the surplus labour can be extracted from him only by virtue of his lack of access to the means of production. This lack of access constitutes "the force of circumstances", as opposed to the "direct coercion" characteristic of labour rent. In 4.2.3 I discuss this contrast in some detail. Here I want to observe that what Marx here says seems to be contradicted by what he states in a later section on money rent:

the basis of this type of rent ... remains the same as that of rent in kind, which constitutes its point of departure. The direct producer as before is still possessor of the land, either through inheritance or some other traditional right, and must perform for his lord, as owner of his most essential condition of production, excess corvée labour, that is unpaid labour for which no equivalent is returned, in the form of a surplus-product transformed into money.[4]

It is difficult to make unambiguous and consistent sense of these two passages. The distinction between possession and ownership is not clarified. In the first passage it is clear that possession is not an empty

---

[1] *Capital III*, pp. 790–1.   [2] Cp. Cohen, *Karl Marx's Theory of History*, p. 65.
[3] *Capital III*, pp. 794–5.   [4] *Ibid.*, p. 797.

phrase, since it is what makes direct compulsion necessary for the extraction of surplus labour. The second similarly shows that ownership has a substantial meaning, since it is what allows the landlord to extract the surplus from the direct producer. Hence, when a given land is simultaneously possessed by the direct producer and owned by the landlord, the extraction of surplus labour appears to be explained twice over – once by the landlord's use of force and then by his legal rights which obviate the need for force.[1]

We must ask what difference it makes whether we say that the producer has full ownership of the land and part-ownership of his labour-power, or part-ownership of the land and full ownership of his labour-power. Labour rent can arise in both cases: in the first because the lord can compel the peasant to work part of his time on the demesne land, in the second because the labour rent is payment for the right to work on the plot that is part-owned by the lord. A difference would arise if land is abundant relative to labour, for then, in the second case, competitive bidding by landlords for tenants would drive rents down, contrary to what would be observed in the first case. It has in fact been argued that when land has been abundant relative to labour, either the class of non-working landowners or the class of free peasants had to disappear.[2] Marx, however, ignores this issue, as he also neglects to explain the distinction between possession and ownership. As a result, his account of exploitation in non-market economies remains vague, except for the case of slavery, which does not pose these conceptual difficulties.

4.1.2. Market exploitation: the canonical case

The distinction between non-market and market economies is not the same as that between pre-capitalist and capitalist modes of production. It is an important fact about pre-capitalist economies that they often contained pockets of market exchange that could give rise to exploitation "by the force of circumstances". Capitalism is, however, historically the central form of the market economy, characterized by the fact that even labour-power is a commodity that is bought and sold on the market. In the present discussion I shall only consider the forms of exploitation that arise under these conditions. Other varieties of market exploitation are discussed in 4.1.3.

---

[1] The fact that legal rights are effective only when backed by the force of the state is irrelevant here, since I am asking whether the *landowner* needs to use force to extract the surplus.

[2] Domar, "The causes of slavery and serfdom".

I shall rely heavily on the models of labour-market exploitation offered by John Roemer. These appear to me faithful to the central intuitions in *Capital*, while also sufficiently precise to allow us to detect and discuss problems that could not come to the surface in Marx's own analysis. In his book, Roemer offers one model in which the agents minimize their labour time subject to a constraint on consumption ("a capitalist subsistence economy") and one in which they maximize their revenue subject to a constraint on their labour time ("a capitalist accumulation economy"). In what follows I focus mainly on the latter, which is closer to actual capitalist economies.

Even the accumulation model, however, is too stark, since it has no scope for a trade-off between labour time and wealth. In recent work Roemer has explored the more general case, in which agents have a supply function of labour that depends on their wealth. Under reasonable assumptions about these supply functions, the results of the pure accumulation model are shown to be robust. Under non-standard assumptions – when the agents perversely want to work longer hours the richer they are – the results do not hold. Specifically, under the latter circumstances poor agents may exploit the rich, if the latter want to work more than their large stock of capital allows them to do, while the former do not even want to utilize all of what little they have got, and hence hire the rich to work for them.[1] The result is mainly of conceptual interest, in that it shows that from the ethical point of view exploitation cannot be a fundamental concept. If the rich want to be exploited, the poor ought not to take any blame. If there is anything wrong with the situation, it is to be found in the unequal distribution of wealth, not in the forms of exploitation that arise in it because of this peculiar supply function of labour. I return to the issue in 4.3.2, but for the time being I shall disregard this complication.

Imagine a set of individuals all equipped with the same amount of labour-power (of the same skill), but differently endowed with other factors of production. In addition to the individuals we must postulate the presence of a state that guarantees property rights and enforces contracts. There are well-defined techniques for producing all goods except labour-power which is assumed to be the only non-producible good. Since there is a labour market,

an agent can engage in three types of economic activity: he can sell his labour power, he can hire the labour power of others, or he can work for himself. His constraint is that he must be able to lay out the operating costs, in advance, for the

[1] Roemer, "Should Marxists be interested in exploitation?"

activities he chooses to operate, either with his own labour or hired labour, funded by the value of his endowments.[1]

Here the endowments and the labour-power are evaluated at the prices and wage rate that obtain at equilibrium, calculated in a manner broadly similar to that sketched in 3.2.2. In addition to the capital constraint, Roemer assumes that there is a constraint on the length of the working day. Finally, the agents are supposed to maximize their net revenues. With respect to a given equilibrium, we can ask three questions with respect to the agents:

(i) What is the monetary value of their endowments?
(ii) Do they work for themselves, sell their labour-power or buy labour-power?
(iii) Do they work longer hours than are embodied in the commodities they can buy with their revenue?

The first question concerns the *wealth* of the economic agents, the second their *class* membership and the third their *exploitation* status. Roemer proves in important theorems that these are highly correlated.[2] The individuals who must hire labour-power to optimize are exploiters, those who must sell their labour-power to optimize are exploited. In the class of those who can optimize by working for themselves, some are exploiters, some are exploited, while some belong to a "grey area" characterized by the fact that some of the commodity bundles they can buy with their revenue embody more labour time than they work, while others embody less. The existence of this grey area is due to the non-proportionality of prices and values (3.2.2). Moreover, the ordering of individuals in terms of wealth correspond in the expected way to ordering in terms of class or in terms of exploitation status. Some further features of the model are discussed in 6.1.

Although highly abstract, Roemer's model brings out very well some central features of the Marxist theory of exploitation. Because it is so explicit in its assumption, it also forces us to consider some questions that otherwise might have escaped our attention. I want to discuss four striking features of the model. (i) Exploitation and class are *modally* defined, so that exploitation status and class membership cannot be established just by looking at actual behaviour. (ii) Exploitation appears as a *property* of individuals or of whole economies, not primarily as a relation between individuals. (iii) Exploitation is restricted to a purely *static* setting, ignoring both the past history of the individual endowments and

---

[1] Roemer, *A General Theory*, p. 113.   [2] *Ibid.*, Theorems 4.3, 4.6 and 4.7.

the future use of the revenues derived from them. (iv) It is also restricted to a fully *competitive* setting, ignoring what forms exploitation takes in "thin markets".

(i) Both class membership and exploitation are defined modally. Roemer does not say that someone is a member of the capitalist class simply because he hires labour. A capitalist is someone who *must* hire labour in order to optimize. Arguably, he is not "forced by circumstances" to hire labour, because, unlike the worker in most circumstances, he is not forced to optimize (4.2.3). Yet if he wants to optimize, he can do so only by hiring labour. I return to the rationale for this definition in 6.1.1.

Similarly, Roemer does not say that an agent is exploited simply by virtue of the fact that the labour embodied in the commodities he buys is less than what he expends. He is exploited when the labour content of any commodity he *can* buy is less than the labour he expends. This definition has two implications, one mentioned by Roemer, the other not. He stresses that by adopting this modal definition, exploitation status becomes independent of consumption preferences, which he regards as a desideratum of the theory. In this he seems justified, at least if we want to retain the moral relevance of exploitation. If an agent could change from being exploited into being an exploiter simply as a result of a change of tastes, some of the moral connotations of exploitation would be lost. Another consequence of the definition is that it allows Roemer to disregard what actually happens to the net revenue that is earned, and in particular to disregard the issue of reinvestment vs. consumption. This is further discussed in comment (iii) below.

(ii) The model defines exploitation as a *property*, not as a relation. The central fact about exploitation is not a face-to-face relation between an exploiter and an exploited agent; rather it is the property of either being an exploiter or being exploited. Consider the following example from Roemer:

There are two technologies for making corn: the farm, which requires only direct labour, and the factory, which uses labour plus seed corn as capital. To reproduce a worker (which requires one bushel of corn) using the farm requires six days' labour, while using the factory technology only three days' labour is needed, plus some capital. Suppose that the society in question has exactly enough capital for it to reproduce one-half of its members using the factory, and that capital stock is distributed in an egalitarian manner among all producers. Suppose producers desire only to subsist. Then each producer will work $4\frac{1}{2}$ days in each week ... [There] are several ways of achieving this result; the simplest is the autarchic solution where each producer works up his seed corn in the factory in $1\frac{1}{2}$ days, thereby producing one-half his subsistence requirement, and then travels to the farm and produces the other half of his subsistence needs in 3 days' work on the farm. Now consider a second arrangement which achieves the same results, but with a social division of labour. Two-thirds of the society, whom we will call coalition A, will contract to hire the other one-third, coalition B. Each agent in B will work up his own stock of seed corn, plus the stock of two agents in A, his employers. Thus, a typical agent in B works $4\frac{1}{2}$ days a week. He produces $1\frac{1}{2}$ bushels of corn, and pays as profit to his employers $\frac{1}{2}$ bushels ($\frac{1}{4}$ bushel to each of them). Thus, he works precisely $4\frac{1}{2}$ days and receives his subsistence needs. Each agent in A works only on the farm for $4\frac{1}{2}$ days, thus producing $\frac{3}{4}$ bushel of corn there; the other $\frac{1}{4}$ bushel he requires he receives as profits from his employee in B. Thus each agent in A works precisely $4\frac{1}{2}$ days and receives his subsistence needs.[1]

Under the second arrangement, as under the first, the net outcome is that no one is exploited. Yet the second arrangement might easily give the impression that the agents in A exploit those in B, if we only consider the interactions that take place between them. The "micro" approach to exploitation is misleading in such cases, and in other cases as well. Thus a capitalist might optimize by hiring a member of the petty bourgeoisie, that is someone who can optimize by working for himself but also by buying or selling labour-power. It might look as if the latter is exploited by the former, but the petty bourgeois might in fact be an exploiter himself, in the sense of commanding more labour with his income than he performs.[2] We cannot tell who is exploited and who is an exploiter simply by looking at who extracts surplus labour from whom. On the other hand, as further argued in 6.1, the latter relation might be central for an understanding of the class struggle.

The shift from exploitation as a relation between individuals to exploitation as a property of individuals involves a certain dilution of the Marxist notion. A further dilution takes place when we consider the problem of *multiple price equilibria*. This issue arises in Roemer's model of exploitation through the commodity market in a subsistence economy, but presumably it could also emerge in the canonical case of accumulation with a labour market. In that latter model we observe the existence of a "grey area" of agents created by the non-proportionality of prices to values and by the consumer's choice. In the subsistence model there is a given consumption bundle that is consumed by all agents, but another indeterminacy arises through the following mechanism:

Consider a reproducible solution p for a precapitalist subsistence economy . . . at which producer u exploits producer v. How does it come about that u can exploit v? Perhaps it is because u worked harder in the (prehistorical) past and built up a

---

[1] *Ibid.*, pp. 234–5. [2] *Ibid.*, pp. 131–2.

bigger endowment, so that today he can reap the fruits of his past labour. But suppose there is another reproducible solution $\hat{p}$ for the same economy, at which v exploits u. (That is, the same data of the economy are consistent with at least two equilibria p and $\hat{p}$.) Then we would be forced to maintain that v must have worked harder in the past, if this is our explanation of the source of exploitation. It is, however, impossible that u and v each worked harder in the past than the other. Hence, the exhibiting of such a "reswitching" phenomenon will show that there is no intrinsic property of the producer's behaviour, such as working harder in the past, or risk taking, which can be claimed responsible for his ability to exploit another.[1]

This example may lead us in one of two directions. On the one hand we might define an exploited agent as one who works excess hours *at all equilibria*, not only at the one that happens to obtain; similarly for the exploiters. This creates a *new grey area* of agents that are neither exploited nor exploiters, namely those who work more than they get at some equilibrium and less at another. In Roemer's numerical example the new grey area coincides with the set of all agents in the economy. On the other hand we might want to consider exploitation a property of the economy as a whole, not just of individuals. We might say that there is *economy-wide exploitation* if any equilibrium has some agents that work excess hours, even if there are no agents that work excess hours at all equilibria. Roemer asserts that he has examples of "weak reswitching" in which one equilibrium has some agents working excess hours while another has all agents getting the equivalent of their labour time.[2] Even if the former state is the one that happens to obtain, there is then no economy-wide exploitation. Finally, we might combine the two suggestions. Cases of economy-wide exploitation in which the new grey area coincides with the set of all agents could make sense of Roemer's statement (made in a different context) that "exploitation [is] a social phenomenon, and the existence of exploitation need not imply, in principle, the existence of individual exploiters or exploited".[3]

Clearly, this "possible-world" account of exploitation has no explanatory relevance. No agents would ever be motivated to action by arguments about the state that would obtain at a different equilibrium.[4] It does, however, have some normative significance. As further argued in 4.3.2, an exploitative arrangement might be justified if the endowment structure generating it has come about in a "clean" way. This argument, however, is weakened if *luck* intervenes between the endowment structure and the distribution of exploitation statuses. The presence of one

[1] *Ibid.*, p. 44.   [2] *Ibid.*, p. 45.   [3] *Ibid.*, p. 136.
[4] Contrary to what is argued in Bowles and Gintis, "The power of capital", pp. 239ff.

price equilibrium rather than another will in fact be a matter of chance, which does not create any deserts or entitlements.

(iii) *Accumulation and technical change* create difficulties for Roemer's theory of exploitation. As indicated, this holds in two respects. First, unequal endowments may reflect unequal savings in the past. If the latter reflected nothing but free choices of the agents, there may be nothing objectionable to exploitation generated by the former. I postpone discussion of this issue to 4.3.2. Secondly, the use made of the revenues may be relevant to the moral status of their distribution. Here I offer comments on this second issue.

Consider first an economy in simple reproduction, in which the capitalists consume all profits. Then the following two measures of the rate of exploitation will coincide:

$$e_1 = \frac{\text{surplus-value}}{\text{value of labour-power}}$$

$$e_2 = \frac{\text{value of capitalist consumption}}{\text{value of labour-power (= value of workers' consumption)}}$$

In extended reproduction, the first measure may not be a good indicator of exploitation, conceived as a form of distributive injustice.[1] Part of the surplus is then used for investment in future production, and part of that future production will benefit the workers. The part of the future product that does not immediately benefit the workers will in part be consumed by the capitalists, but also in part reinvested and then benefit later generations of workers. Marx writes in *Capital I* that "the greater part of the yearly accruing surplus-product [is] embezzled, because abstracted without return of an equivalent".[2] If this is what constitutes the moral wrongness of exploitation, the return later of part of the surplus would appear to make it less wrong. The fact that it is not returned to the *same* individuals need not be an objection, since those currently living benefit similarly from investments made possible by the surplus extracted from earlier workers. Nor does it count as an objection that the investment does not bring about an increase in the real wage, only an increase in the number of workers earning it, since in the absence of the investment some of these workers would have been unemployed.

[1] It may, of course, be a good indicator if we understand exploitation as lack of power over investment decisions, as in Kolakowski, *Main Currents of Marxism*, vol. 1, p. 333. This usage is, however, distinctly unusual.
[2] *Capital I*, p. 611.

To define a suitable measure of exploitation that includes this temporal dimension, let us set $t = 1$ today and x_t and y_t for the consumption made possible at time t in the future for workers and capitalists respectively by one unit of labour today. We then define

$$e_3 = \frac{y_1 + y_2 + \ldots +}{x_1 + x_2 + \ldots +}$$

To simplify we set $x_1 = 1$. Moreover, we set the economy-wide organic composition of capital equal to k and the rate of savings out of profit equal to s. The rate of surplus-value equals e_1, which is also the amount of surplus-value created in the first year. Out of this, the capitalists consume $e_1 (1 - s) = y_1$ and invest $e_1 s$, allocating $(k/(k + 1)) e_1 s$ to constant capital and $x_2 = (1/(k + 1)) e_1 s$ to variable capital. This variable capital creates a surplus-value equal to $(e_1/(k + 1)) e_1 s$, out of which the capitalists consume $y_2 = (e_1/(k + 1)) (1 - s) e_1 s = (e_1 s/(k + 1)) y_1$. This shows that x_t and y_t grow with the same factor of proportionality $e_1 s/(k + 1) = q$, so that we have

$$e_3 = \frac{y_1 (1 + q + q^2 + \ldots +)}{x_1 (1 + q + q^2 + \ldots +)} = y_1 = e_2$$

The ratio between capitalist and working-class consumption at one point of time also measures the intertemporal rate of exploitation. Clearly, we have $e_1 > e_2 = e_3$. Also, in the limiting case of zero capitalist consumption, there is zero exploitation.[1] Nevertheless the relevant (explanatory) variable for the class struggle might be e_1 rather than e_2. The extraction of a surplus is tangible in the capitalist profit, which could have been used to alleviate the fate of the workers here and now. By contrast, the fate of future workers might count less in the balance. Hence, in addition to the "micro bias" discussed under (ii) above, there could be a "myopic bias" that prevents the normatively relevant concept of exploitation from having motivational force.

A somewhat different conclusion follows if we introduce technical progress. In that case, the surplus reinvested might actually benefit the workers in the form of an increase in the real wage. If initially workers live by bread alone, reinvestment of the surplus may in part go to caviar for the capitalist, but in part also to butter for the workers, not only to bread

---

[1] For a more elaborate version of this argument, see von Weizsäcker, "Modern capital theory and the concept of exploitation".

for more workers. This is recognized by Marx in the manuscript on "Wages" from 1847:

A main condition for the rise of wages is the growth of the productive capital, and its most rapid possible growth. The main condition for the worker to be in a passable position is, therefore, to depress his position in relation to the bourgeois class more and more, to increase as much as possible the power of his opponent, capital. That is, he can only be in a passable position provided he creates and reinforces the power which is hostile to him, his own opposite.[1]

The idea may be compared to the "Lancaster model" of capitalism as a dynamic game, in which the workers out of self-interest drive a less hard wage bargain than they could have done in order to ensure a sizeable capitalist profit, on which depends reinvestment and the future welfare of the workers.[2] Marx, of course, had nothing like this in mind. It is only in retrospect that we can detect the germ of strategic thinking. Yet even if Marx did not believe that the workers would deliberately ask for less than they could get, the passage suggests that the anticipation of future benefits might make them accept getting less than what they ask for. As in the case of extended reproduction, the rate of exploitation under conditions of technical change is smaller when seen in the dynamical perspective that appears to be the proper one for normative purposes.[3] Even in this case there could be myopia that would give the exploitation rate e_1 greater motivational force than normatively warranted – unless one argues that the normative concept itself should incorporate the time preferences of the workers.[4]

When interpreted dynamically, in the sense of e_2, the rate of exploitation may not be very large, especially in modern capitalist economies. Capitalist consumption, over and above what is paid out of (non-exploitative) "wages of superintendence" is probably a smallish magnitude compared to working-class consumption. Yet this does not imply that the injustice of capitalist exploitation is correspondingly small.[5] The amount of injustice created by capitalist exploitation is a function not only of aggregate capitalist consumption, but also of per capita expenditures. Independently of the numerical size of the two classes, "the difference in per capita personal income remains massive, and it matters a great deal to the self-perception and sense of dignity of working people".[6] Yet this

---

[1] "Wages", p. 428; see also pp. 420, 435.
[2] Lancaster, "The dynamic inefficiency of capitalism".
[3] Von Weizsäcker, "Modern capital theory and the concept of exploitation".
[4] On this issue, see *Ulysses and the Sirens*, ch. II.5.
[5] In what follows I disregard the issue of capitalist *entitlement*, discussed in 4.3.2 below.
[6] Cohen, "Reply to Elster", p. 494.

does not affect the main point I am making here, since the part of the surplus that is reinvested does not in the same way offend the self-esteem of the workers. It may offend it in another way, since they are excluded from the investment decisions, but to the extent that they benefit from the investments it does not add to the injustice derived from the income effect of exploitation.

(iv) The *competitive* nature of Roemer's model can be defended in several ways. For one thing, it highlights the contrast with the neoclassical theory of exploitation, according to which exploitation can only occur in the *absence* of perfect competition.[1] In this it captures Marx's intention to show that the flaws of capitalism are inherent in it, and do not arise because of imperfections such as oligopolies or cartels (3.1.1). For another, the class–exploitation–wealth theorems can be proved only with respect to a given equilibrium. Since there is no general-equilibrium theory applicable to conditions of imperfect competition, we just cannot tell what is the optimizing behaviour of the agents and the value of their endowments in this case.

On the other hand there can be no doubt that imperfections of competition are massively important in actual capitalist economies, and that the Marxist theory of exploitation ultimately will have to consider the implications of this fact. I shall not here pursue the issue, but indicate where some further discussions are found. In 4.1.4 I consider collective bargaining as a determinant of the rate of exploitation. In particular, I discuss a passage from *Capital III* that has been adduced as evidence that Marx believed the wage bargain to rest on bilateral monopoly. In 4.3.3 I propose a distinction between force and coercion in the labour market, the latter involving the exercise of (economic) power. And in 6.2.1 I discuss how capitalist divide-and-conquer tactics may also affect the rate of exploitation.

4.1.3. Varieties of market exploitation

Exploitation can arise in several markets. In an analysis of class that also applies to exploitation, Weber wrote that "the struggle in which class situations are effective has progressively shifted from consumption credit toward, first, competitive struggles in the commodity market and then toward wage disputes on the labour market".[2] Roemer similarly distinguishes between exploitation arising in labour markets, commodity

---

[1] For the neoclassical theory see Bronfenbrenner, *Income Distribution Theory*, ch. 6.
[2] Weber, *Economy and Society*, vol. II, pp. 930–1.

markets and credit markets, although by the latter he has in mind credit for production rather than for consumption. I shall consider these varieties in turn.

In an early part of his book Roemer shows the logical possibility of exploitation arising through the exchange of commodities, without labour-power itself being a commodity. By virtue of the unequal distribution of endowments, the end result of the exchange between the producers is that some work more than is necessary to produce their subsistence bundle and others less. This immediately shows that there is at least no logical necessity for exploitation to take place at "the point of production", since here it manifestly takes place only at "the point of exchange".[1] In 4.1.5 I argue that this holds also in the case of exploitation through the labour market. This argument, however, may not convince all readers, whereas I believe that Roemer's argument is an irrefutable objection to the "fundamentalist" view that exploitation *must* be mediated by domination in the labour process.[2]

Roemer does not claim that the model has important applications to national economies. To understand why it does not, we may begin by citing Marx's claim that "It is just as pious as it is stupid to wish that exchange value would not develop into capital, nor labour which produces exchange into wage labour."[3] From the context it is clear that he has in mind not production of commodities generally, such as may also occur in a slave economy, but commodity production in an economy of independent producers. The statement may then be read as asserting the inherent instability of an economy with exploitation without class divisions. The market economy removes the psychological or institutional barriers that might otherwise prevent the agents from selling their labour-power in order to optimize.[4]

National boundaries, however, form a more impenetrable barrier. Hence the main application of the model of exploitation by exchange of (non-labour) commodities has been to the theory of international trade.[5] Marx himself remarked that in international trade, "the richer country exploits the poorer one, even where the latter gains by the exchange",[6] and certainly did not mean that the rich country does so by hiring the

---

[1] Roemer, *A General Theory*, pp. 39–40.
[2] For this view see Marglin, "What do bosses do?" or Bowles and Gintis, "The Marxian theory of value and heterogeneous labour".
[3] *Grundrisse*, p. 249.
[4] For a good account of this process, see Polanyi, *The Great Transformation*. Marx's own account is discussed in 5.3 below.
[5] Roemer, *A General Theory*, Appendix 1.1.   [6] *Theories of Surplus-Value*, vol. 3, p. 106.

workers of the poor. The latter form of "unequal exchange" between countries developed mainly after his time.[1] Nor did Marx consider the possibility of an international capital market that would be the functional equivalent to an international labour market.[2]

I have already discussed exploitation through the labour market as the canonical form of exploitation, yet some further nuances may be added. In Roemer-like models capitalists exploit workers by virtue of their control over capital goods, but this is not the only source of capitalist exploitation. Capitalists can also exploit workers by virtue of the isolation and lack of organization of the latter. Consider the following passage from the chapter in *Capital I* on "Cooperation":

> The labourer is the owner of his labour-power until he has done bargaining for its sale with the capitalist; and he can sell no more than what he has – i.e. his individual, isolated labour-power. This state of things is in no way altered by the fact that the capitalist, instead of buying the labour-power of one man, buys that of 100, and enters into separate contracts with 100 unconnected men instead of with one. He is at liberty to set the 100 men to work, without letting them co-operate. He pays them the value of 100 independent labour-powers, but he does not pay for the combined labour-power of the hundred. Being independent of each other, the labourers are isolated persons, who enter into relations with the capitalist, but not with one another. This cooperation begins only with the labour process, but they have then ceased to belong to themselves. On entering that process, they become incorporated with capital. As co-operators, as members of a working organism, they are but special modes of existence of capital. Hence, the productive power developed by the labourer when working in co-operation is the productive power of capital. This power is developed gratuitously, whenever the workmen are placed under given conditions, and it is capital that places them under such conditions. Because this power costs capital nothing, and because, on the other hand, the labourer does not develop it before his labour belongs to capital, it appears as a power with which capital is endowed by Nature – a productive power that is immanent in capital.[3]

The salient features of this situation are the increasing returns to scale, individual wage bargaining and the workers' inability to advance their own wages. To bring out my point as clearly as possible, I assume – contrary to what Marx had in mind – that each worker is paid the full value of what he could produce by working with his proportional share of the means of production. More specifically, we may imagine that the workers own their means of production and bring them to the work-place. Since they negotiate individually with the capitalist, without entering into relations with one another, he need not pay them more than they could get on

---

[1] For an analysis, see Roemer, "Unequal exchange, labour migration and international capital flows".
[2] *Ibid.*   [3] *Capital I*, pp. 332–3.

their own, and hence is enabled to derive "pure entrepreneurial profits" from employing them.

If the workers were able to act in concert (and to advance their own wages), they would not have to subject themselves to this exploitation. The capitalist has no physical capital by virtue of which he exploits them, only money capital to advance wages and his organizational ability, including the ability to prevent the workers from organizing themselves. Whatever the historical importance of this form of exploitation,[1] it differs from the canonical case of labour-market exploitation, in which the capitalist also owns the constant capital without which the workers would not be able to employ themselves gainfully. In this case, even an organized working class would do worse working for themselves without access to physical capital than working at a wage for a capital-owner. In the absence of control over physical capital, both increasing returns to scale and a fully competitive labour market are needed to generate exploitation. With control over capital, neither is necessary.

In many traditional societies, exploitation through the credit market has been the central form of surplus-labour extraction. Roemer has shown that credit market exploitation and labour market exploitation are isomorphic in a precise sense, thus confirming the neoclassical adage that it does not matter whether capital employs labour or labour capital.[2] Marx makes essentially the same statement in *The Class Struggles in France*:

> The condition of the French peasants, when the republic had added new burdens to their old ones, is comprehensible. It can be seen that their exploitation differs only in *form* from the exploitation of the industrial proletariat. The exploiter is the same: *capital*. The individual capitalists exploit the individual peasants through *mortgages* and *usury*; the capitalist class exploits the peasant class through the state taxes.[3]

The problem of exploitation by taxation is discussed in 4.1.5. One should note that exploitation of the peasants through mortgages, while in one sense equivalent to the exploitation of wage labour, elsewhere in the same work is called one of "capital's secondary modes of exploitation",[4] presumably because it is dissociated from the dynamic core of the capitalist mode of production. "Usurer's capital . . . paralyses the productive forces instead of developing them."[5] In *Capital III*, Marx extends the term "secondary exploitation" to cover credit for consumption purposes as

---

[1] For a controversial account, see Marglin, "What do bosses do?", further discussed in 5.2.2.

[2] Roemer, *A General Theory*, ch. 3.   [3] *The Class Struggles in France*, p. 122.

[4] *Ibid.*, p. 57.   [5] *Capital III*, pp. 595–6.

well. In a discussion of the illusion that interest-bearing capital is the fundamental form of capital, he writes that:

It is still more irrelevant and meaningless to drag the lending of houses etc. for individual use into this discussion. That the working-class is also swindled in this form, and to an enormous extent, is self-evident; but this is also done by the retail dealer, who sells means of subsistence to the worker. This is secondary exploitation, which runs parallel to the primary exploitation process taking place in the production process itself.[1]

Elsewhere in the same chapter a different formulation is used: "Usurer's capital employs the method of exploitation characteristic of capital yet without the latter's mode of production."[2] In both formulations it is clear that there can be exploitation that does not take place "at the point of production", contrary to the fundamentalist view.

Marx also discussed credit market exploitation in pre-capitalist economies. In *Capital III* he makes a distinction between two forms that usurer's capital can take in these economies:

These two forms are: *first*, usury by lending money to extravagant members of the upper classes, particularly landowners; *secondly*, usury by lending money to small producers who possess their own conditions of labour – this includes the artisan, but mainly the peasant, since particularly under pre-capitalist conditions, in so far as they permit of small independent individual producers, the peasant class necessarily constitutes the overwhelming majority of them.[3]

Of these, only the second leads to exploitation in the strict sense. Marx goes on to say that "the indebted slaveholder or feudal lord becomes more oppressive because he is himself more oppressed",[4] and that "the place of the old exploiter, whose exploitation was more or less patriarchal because it was largely a means to political power, is taken by a hard money-mad parvenu".[5] But, significantly, he does not say that the slaveowner or lord is *exploited*. Hence the following well-known passage from *Capital I* is somewhat misleading:

The class struggles of the ancient world took the form chiefly of a contest between debtors and creditors, which in Rome ended in the ruin of plebeian debtors. They were displaced by slaves. In the middle ages the contest ended with the ruin of the feudal debtors, who lost their political power together with the economic basis on which it was established. Nevertheless the money relation of debtor and creditor that existed at these two periods reflected only the deeper-lying antagonism between the general economic conditions of existence of the classes in question.[6]

---

[1] *Ibid.*, p. 609.   [2] *Ibid.*, p. 597.   [3] *Ibid.*, p. 594.   [4] *Ibid.*, p. 596.   [5] *Ibid.*, p. 597.
[6] *Capital I*, p. 135.

Although somewhat excessive, the claim that the class struggle in antiquity became manifest in the credit market is not implausible.[1] Since Marx elsewhere says that it took place between the rich and the poor,[2] or between large and small landed property,[3] we may infer that he thought these to be equivalent partitions of society. (A class–exploitation–wealth correspondence statement.) Presumably the property difference is the "deeper-lying antagonism" that explains both the wealth and the class differences. Note that he does not suggest (and elsewhere denies explicitly[4]) that the slaves took any part in the class struggle. I return to these issues in chapter 6 below. Here I want to argue that the third sentence of the quoted passage, and correlatively part of the final one, are misleading, given the passage from *Capital III* which emphasizes the extravagant consumption of the upper classes as the cause of their debts. True, it has been argued that in economies based on personal power relationships the consumption expenditures of the upper classes may be classified among the costs of production, to the extent that they vary with the scale of production and not with the size of the surplus.[5] Also, the argument has been made that the feudal lords went into debt because of military expenditures that were closely related to their economic situation.[6] Neither suggestion, however, is found in Marx.

I need not say much by way of conclusion. Since capitalism is the most highly developed market economy, and wage labour the central institution of capitalism, we may expect that labour market exploitation is the most important form of market exploitation. The formally equivalent exploitation through the credit market is less important in capitalism, because it does not tend to develop the productive forces, but it is the most important form of market exploitation in pre-capitalist economies, interacting with non-market exploitation in various ways. Exploitation in the (non-labour) commodity market shows the logical possibility of exploitation without class divisions. The main application of the idea is in international trade.

4.1.4. Determinants of the rate of exploitation

I now turn to a discussion announced in 3.2.2, the analysis of the rate of surplus-value under capitalism. While the discussion in 4.1.3 was

---

[1] See Ste Croix, *The Class Struggle in the Ancient Greek World*, pp. 162–70. Finley, *Politics in the Ancient World*, pp. 107ff argues that social conflict in antiquity was about two main issues: formal privileges and material gains. Among the latter, debt cancellation and land redistribution were the most important.

[2] Preface to the 2nd edition of *The Eighteenth Brumaire of Louis Bonaparte*, p. 359.

[3] Marx to Engels 8.3.1855.   [4] In the text cited in note 2 above.

[5] Cp. my "Some conceptual problems in political theory", pp. 260ff.

[6] Cp. Brenner, "The agrarian roots of European capitalism".

concerned with the qualitative issue of how exploitation comes about, I now want to consider the quantitative issue of what determines the rate of exploitation, in the canonical case of labour market exploitation.

Recall that the rate of exploitation is the ratio $(h - v)/v$, where h is the number of hours worked per day and v the value of the consumption goods needed to reproduce the labour-power of the worker for one day. The latter is in turn determined by the real wage and the labour content of the commodities that constitute it. Hence the rate of exploitation is a function of three independent variables. Of these, the labour value of commodities is not the object of economic bargaining or political struggle, as are the other two determinants of the rate of surplus-value.

Consider first the length of the working day, which is extensively discussed in one of the most forcefully brilliant chapters of *Capital I*. Marx's analysis is not strictly economic in character, but refers also to the class struggle and to politics. In Marx's whole corpus it is probably the most important detailed discussion of how economic exploitation, collective action and political intervention relate to one another. This justifies the marshalling of numerous, long quotations to bring out the logic, to some extent the illogic, of Marx's thought on this issue. He seems in fact to have hesitated between an explanation of the shortening of the working day in terms of working-class interest, capitalist interest and the interest of "society". The discussion below will not exhaust the problem, which is taken up again in chapters 6 and 7.

The following is probably intended as a major theoretical statement:

[Apart] from extremely elastic bonds, the nature of the exchange of commodities itself imposes no limit on the working-day, no limit to surplus-labour. The capitalist maintains his rights as a purchaser when he tries to make the working-day as long as possible, and to make, whenever possible, two working-days out of one. On the other hand, the peculiar nature of the commodity sold implies a limit to its consumption by the purchaser, and the labourer maintains a right as seller when he wishes to reduce the working-day to one of definite normal duration. There is, therefore, an antinomy, right against right, both equally bearing the seal of the law of exchanges. Between equal rights force decides. Hence it is that in the history of capitalist production, the determination of what is a working-day presents itself as the result of a struggle, a struggle between collective capital, i.e. the class of capitalists, and collective labour, i.e. the working-class.[1]

This can be read as a statement about collective bargaining, or about

---

[1] *Capital I*, pp. 234–5.

political struggle with the state as the arena. As Marx made clear in *Wages, Price and Profit*, he did not believe the English workers obtained a reduction of the working-day by "private settlement between the working men and the capitalists". Rather "general political action" and "legislative interference" were necessary.[1] I turn in a moment to Marx's ambiguous view concerning these political events. First, however, I want to cite a text in which Marx explains why in his economic capacity the capitalist has every incentive to increase the working day as much as possible, although in the long run this behaviour may prove to be self-defeating:

Capital that has such good reasons for denying the sufferings of the legions of workers that surround it, is in practice moved as much and as little by the sight of the coming degradation and final depopulation of the human race, as by the probable fall of the earth into the sun. In every stock-jobbing swindle everyone knows that some time or other the crash must come, but every one hopes that it may fall on the head of his neighbour, after he himself has caught the shower of gold and placed it in safety. *Après moi le déluge!* is the watchword of every capitalist and of every capitalist nation. Hence Capital is reckless of the health or length of life of the labourer, unless under compulsion from society. To the out-cry as to the physical and mental degradation, the premature death, the torture of over-work, it answers: Ought these to trouble us since they increase our profits? But looking at things as a whole, all this does not, indeed, depend on the free will of the individual capitalist. Free competition brings out the inherent laws of capitalist production, in the shape of external coercive laws having power over every individual capitalist.[2]

Here the curbing of capitalist greed is explained by the compulsion of "society", not by the struggle of the workers. Marx also refers to "factory legislation, that first conscious and methodical reaction of society against the spontaneously developed form of the process of production".[3] In the 1861–3 *Critique* he similarly argues that:

These excesses led to the outbreak of epidemics whose severity threatened the existence of capitalist and worker alike. In consequence the state was forced to introduce normal [working] days in the factories despite the bitter opposition of the capitalist class.[4]

Still further passages argue that the limitation of the length of the working day can be explained by the collective interest of the capitalist class, as distinct from that of its individual members. The short-term greed of the

---

[1] *Wages, Price and Profit*, p. 74.
[2] *Capital I*, pp. 269–70. Note the reference to Goethe's verse (2.4.2).
[3] *Capital I*, pp. 480; cp. also p. 409.   [4] *Zur Kritik (1861–3)*, p. 193.

latter is explained in a comparison with the equally irrational character of capitalist agriculture:

Capital cares nothing for the length and life of labour-power. All that concerns it is simply and solely the maximum of labour-power, that can be rendered fluent in the working-day. It attains this end by shortening the extent of the labourer's life, as a greedy farmer snatches increased produce from the soil by robbing it of its fertility.[1]

The same comparison is also used to show the need for collective action by the capitalist class, to restore the forces of the nation:

[The English Factory Acts] curb the passion of capital for a limitless draining of labour-power, by forcibly limiting the working-day by state regulations, made by a state that is ruled by capitalist and landlord. Apart from the working-class movement that daily grew more threatening, the limiting of factory labour was dictated by the same necessity which spread guano over the English field. The same blind eagerness for plunder that in the one case exhausted the soil, had, in the other torn up by the roots the living force of the nation. Periodical epidemics speak on this point as clearly as the diminishing military standard in Germany and France.[2]

It is not clear how the crucial second sentence is to be read. It may be taken as saying that both the workers' class struggle and collective capitalist interest formed separate, sufficient conditions for the Factory Acts, which would be a case of causal overdetermination. Or Marx may have meant that the causes were singly necessary and jointly sufficient for the Act. It is unclear, moreover, how the "necessity" to curb capitalist greed is translated into behaviour. The passage suggests a form of functional explanation, invoking the interests of "capital in general".[3]

It might be thought that I am reading too much into this passage. Marx does not say in so many words that the collective interest of the capitalist class explained the Factory Acts, although it is natural to understand him in this way when he refers to the actions of a "state that is ruled by capitalist and landlord". An important passage from the 1861–3 *Critique*, while still not unambiguous on this point, at least leaves no room for doubt as to the conflict between the collective and the individual interests of the capitalists:

As we know, whether a commodity is sold at a price above or below its value depends in practice on the relative power of the buyer and the seller (a power which is always determined by economic factors). Similarly, whether or not a

---

[1] *Capital I*, p. 265; cp. *Capital III*, pp. 620, 812.   [2] *Capital I*, p. 239.
[3] In *Capital I*, p. 270, note 2, there is a reference to a petition for legislative enactment by 26 firms in the pottery industry. This, however, occurred in 1863, and is irrelevant for the explanation of the Factory Acts.

worker supplies more than the normal amount of surplus labour will depend on the strength of the resistance he is able to offer to the boundless demands of capital. The history of modern industry teaches us, however, that the boundless demands of capital can never be restrained by the isolated efforts of the worker. Instead his opposition has to take the form of class struggle and only when this has led to the intervention of the state has it become possible to set certain limits to the overall length of the working day . . . It may perhaps be thought that just as the slaveowner is forced to purchase new negroes, to replace those he has used up every seven years, the same would apply to capital, since it is predicated on the uninterrupted existence of the working class and must therefore pay for wearing the workers out so quickly. But Capitalist A may be able to grow rich on the policy that this "killing is no murder", while Capitalist B, or the generation of Capitalists B, may have to foot the bill. For the individual capitalist is in constant rebellion against the general interests of the capitalist class as a whole. On the other hand, the history of modern industry has shown that a constant over-population is a possibility, even though it is composed of a succession of human generations, each of which fades swiftly from the scene, as it were untimely plucked.[1]

Even disregarding the last sentence, which if accepted would undermine the "necessity" of curbing capitalist greed,[2] the passage offers plenty of food for thought. First, note the explicit reference to the relative power of the parties as an explanation of the length of the working day, and the observation that only when organized can the workers offer any resistance to the capitalists. Secondly, observe that nothing is said about a similar organization on the part of the capitalists to overcome that resistance. Thirdly, it is even suggested that were the capitalists to organize themselves, it would be in their collective interest to join forces with the working class in the struggle for a shorter working day, rather than to oppose them. Fourthly, the passage makes explicit the important distinction between the individual–collective and short-term–long-term oppositions (6.2.1). Clearly, it might be easier for the capitalist class to act in its collective short-term interest than to act for the survival of capitalism as a system, even though the former also is a threat to individual profit-maximization. Fifthly, the contrast with the slaveowner is surely intended to bring out the difference between individual and collective rationality, and to suggest that it would be a fallacy to conclude that the capitalist class, like the individual slaveowner, will always ensure the reproduction of the labour-power of the producers. Lastly, the opaque reference to state intervention may be linked to this collective rationality, but need not be so.

Other passages suggest a different explanation altogether, by interpreting these events in the light of the theory of class coalitions further

---

[1] *Zur Kritik (1861–3)*, p. 162.
[2] This idea is also suggested in *Wages, Price and Profit*, p. 72.

discussed in 6.3.3. Consider first the following appeal to worker–capitalist coalitions:

The factory hands, especially since 1838, had made the Ten Hours' Bill their economic, as they had made the Charter their political, election-cry. Some of the manufacturers, even, who had managed their factories in conformity with the Act of 1833, overwhelmed Parliament with memorials on the immoral competition of their false brethren whom greater impudence, or more fortunate local circumstances, enabled to break the law. Moreover, however much the individual manufacturer might give the rein to his old lust for gain, the spokesmen and political leaders of the manufacturing class ordered a change of front and of speech towards the workpeople. They had entered upon the contest for the repeal of the Corn Law, and needed the workers to help them to victory. They promised, therefore, not only a double-sized loaf of bread, but the enactment of the Ten Hours' Bill in the Free-trade millenium.[1]

Further on Marx invokes the worker–landowner alliance:

The time just before the repeal of the Corn Laws threw new light on the condition of the agricultural labourers. On the one hand, it was to the interest of the middle-class agitators to prove how little the Corn Laws protected the actual producers of the corn. On the other hand the industrial bourgeoisie foamed with sullen rage at the denunciations of the factory system by the landed aristocracy, at the pretended sympathy with the woes of the factory operatives, of those utterly corrupt, heartless and genteel loafers, and at their "diplomatic zeal" for factory legislation. It is an old English proverb that "when thieves fall out, honest men come by their own", and, in fact, the noisy passionate quarrel between the two fractions of the ruling class about the question, which of the two exploited the labourers more shamefully, was on each hand the midwife of truth. Earl Shaftesbury, then Lord Ashley, was commander-in-chief in the aristocratic, philanthropic anti-factory campaign.[2]

Compare this with Karl Polanyi's curt comment: "The Ten Hours Bill of 1847, which Karl Marx hailed as the first victory of socialism, was the work of enlightened reactionaries. The labouring people themselves were hardly a factor in this great movement the effect of which was, figuratively speaking, to allow them to survive the Middle Passage."[3] These enlightened reactionaries were "Evangelicals consciously doing the Lord's work against the hosts of Satan and industrialism".[4] According to Polanyi, they ensured the "self-protection of society" – an idea also expressed by Marx in passages quoted above, although quite different from the one stated in the last-quoted text.

Hence we see Marx asserting, or suggesting, the following views.

---

[1] *Capital I*, p. 281.   [2] *Ibid.*, p. 675; see also p. 494.
[3] Polanyi, *The Great Transformation*, p. 166.
[4] Perkin, *The Origins of Modern English Society*, p. 363.

(i) There is an implacable conflict of interest between organized capital and organized labour over the length of the working day. (ii) There is a total conflict at the level of individual interests, but a partial coincidence at the collective level, since the capitalists do not want to kill the goose that lays the golden eggs any more than the goose wants to be slaughtered. (iii) There is a conflict of interest at the collective level, but the capitalists temporarily set it aside as long as they have an even stronger conflict of interest with the landowners. (iv) The state is the tool of the collective interest of the capitalist class, as defined by (ii) above. (v) On the contrary, the state represents the interest of "society", as opposed to that of particular classes. The landowners present themselves as the carriers of this general interest, but this is only a disguise for their interest in maintaining the Corn Laws, with the help of the workers.

Prima facie, these various views contradict one another in a number of ways. I am not saying that some of the contradictions could not be removed by a more refined analysis, but it would be an abuse of the principle of charity in textual interpretation to absolve Marx of responsibility for these confusions. He seems to overlook the fact that at this time in the history of capitalism it was in the interest of *everybody* to limit the length of the working day – with the exception of the individual entrepreneur out to maximize his short-term profits come what may. The landowners were disturbed at the possibility of social unrest, the government by the prospect of plague and depletion of the vital forces of the nation, the capitalist class by the undermining of future profits by present greed, and the working class not only disturbed, but vitally threatened in all the ways so well described by Marx. Instead of attacking the analytically important task of determining which of these interests actually explain the events in question (and which could have caused them had they not been preempted by the actually operating ones), he emphasizes now one, now another of these factors, at each occasion appearing to think that it must operate to the exclusion of, and even in conflict with, the others. One is struck by admiration for the brilliant way in which each of these mechanisms is described, and dumbfounded by the apparent lack of concern for consistency.

Marx, incidentally, misses a possibility that has been raised in recent work: that regulation was in the interest of the manufacturers because the curtailing of production enabled them to make monopoly profits.[1] For the reasons mentioned in 3.1.1, Marx was not very interested in monopoly in

---

[1] Marvel, "Factory regulation: an interpretation of the early English experience".

the product market as a determinant of the rate of exploitation. To the extent that the effect operates via the price of consumption goods,[1] such a monopoly tends to increase the rate of exploitation. The effect that operates via a reduction of production – assuming this to be brought about by a shortening of the working day – does, however, tend to bring it down.

The intensity of work may also be seen as a determinant of the rate of exploitation. Even if the time from the beginning to the end of the working day is a certain number of hours, these may be more or less "porous", and the effective labour time may therefore be smaller or greater as a result. Hence it is in the interest of the capitalist – other things being equal – to increase the intensity of labour by filling up these pores in the labour process. This can either be conceptualized as a kind of technical change (Taylorism etc.) or as the creation of absolute surplus-value. "This condensation of a greater mass of labour into a given period thenceforward counts for what it really is, a greater quantity of labour."[2] Marx never explains, however, how more and less intensive labour can be reduced to a common standard of labour time.

Marx's discussion of what in turn determines the intensity of labour is strangely incomplete, since he does not discuss the collective capacity of the working class to resist intensification. If the length of the working day is the object of class struggle, it is hard to see why this should not also be true of the intensity of labour. Perhaps the subtleties of the pressures involved make it difficult to equalize degrees of intensity across firms and industries, so that political action by the working class would be hard to undertake, but one might at least expect that the workers in a given firm would be able to act in concert. Be this as it may, Marx recognizes that an intensification of labour meets with the obstacle that the worker has an incentive to shirk, if he can get away with it. On the one hand the capitalist solves this problem by a system of fines, so that "a violation of his laws is, if possible, more profitable to him than the keeping of them"[3] – a rather implausible suggestion. On the other hand it is solved by the introduction of piece-wages, "the form of wages most in harmony with the capitalist mode of production".[4] "Since the quality and intensity of the work are here controlled by the form of the wage itself, superintendence of labour becomes in great part superfluous."[5] This is one of the rare contexts in which Marx discusses the enforcement costs associated

[1] Rowthorn, "Marx's theory of wages", pp. 216–17.   [2] *Capital I*, p. 410.
[3] *Ibid.*, p. 424.   [4] *Ibid.*, p. 556.   [5] *Ibid.*, p. 553.

with various industrial systems. He does not recognize, however, the tension between the productivity gains from specialization and the enforcement costs arising from specialization.[1] Other things being equal, piece-wages are superior because they entail smaller enforcement costs; but they may only be possible with technologies that are inferior in other respects.

Finally, Marx recognized that intensification is limited by the sheer physical strength of the worker, and that this in turn varies inversely with the length of the working day. The shortening of the working day creates an incentive for the capitalist to step up the pace of production – and it also makes this possible by creating a reservoir of strength on which he can draw. Marx argues, however, that this reaction will typically tend to overshoot:

> There cannot be the slightest doubt that the tendency that urges capital, so soon as a prolongation of the hours of labour is once for all forbidden, to compensate itself, by a systematic heightening of the intensity of labour, and to convert every improvement in machinery into a more perfect means of exhausting the workman, must soon lead to a state of things in which a reduction of the hours of labour will again be inevitable.[2]

Consider finally the determinants of the value of labour-power, that is the real wage and the labour content of the goods that enter into it. I shall discuss these two variables in turn.[3] In the short run, the second may be taken as given, and the first is then determined by the balance of forces in the class struggle. In the long run, the second falls with increasing productivity, and this in turn influences the bargaining over the real wage.

An early manuscript on "Wages" is remarkable because of its introduction of the proto-Lancaster model, in the passage cited in 4.1.2 and several other places. As we have just seen, the capitalists have a vested interest in keeping alive and healthy the workers on whom they depend for their profits, and similarly the workers respect the capitalist profit to the extent needed for future wage raises. Note that these are temporally defined relationships. When maximizing myopically, the capitalists want to exploit labour as much as possible while the workers want to raise their wages as much as possible. In their more farsighted moments, however, they both pull their punches.[4] Yet these are secondary or peripheral

---

[1] North, *Structure and Change in Economic History*, p. 209 and *passim*.
[2] *Capital I*, p. 417.
[3] For a more extensive discussion, see Rowthorn, "Marx's theory of wages".
[4] I should add, however, that one can find, at most, half of the Lancaster model in Marx. Although that model also has a temporal dilemma for the capitalist class, it has nothing to do with the need to ensure the physical reproduction of the working class.

elements in Marx. The main thrust of his argument, as stated in *Wages, Price and Profit*, is that "the capitalist constantly strives to reduce the wage level to its physical minimum, while the worker constantly pushes in the opposite direction".[1] And Marx adds that "The question resolves itself into the power relations of the combatants", as in the above-cited passage on the length of the working day. This refers clearly to a one-shot struggle, not to a protracted conflict in which present gains must be weighted against future ones.[2]

Marx hesitates between explaining the wage rate as the result of supply and demand in competitive markets, and as the outcome of bargaining between collective actors. The texts are confused, perhaps irremediably so. Tentatively, one may distinguish between three strands in Marx's thought on this point. First, there is the view of *Capital I* that "the general movements of wages are exclusively regulated by the expansion and contraction of the industrial reserve army",[3] except to the extent that the workers succeed in organizing "a regular co-operation between employed and unemployed in order to destroy or to weaken the ruinous effect of this law of capitalist production on their class".[4] Marx overestimated the likelihood of success in this endeavour (and underestimated the success of closed-shop policies as a less solidary means to the same end). Next, there is the view of *Wages, Price and Profit* that the wage "settlement always depends upon supply and demand",[5] modified by collective bargaining. The latter, however, can at most resist the general tendency of the real wage to fall; any increase in the wage rate brought about by their action can only be a transient one.[6] (The reader should recall the argument in 3.4.2, that with a constant – and a fortiori with a falling – real wage, it is logically impossible for the rate of profit to fall as the result of *ex ante* profitable innovations.) Lastly, there is the view that Gerard Maarek finds in *Capital III* – that Marx considered the wage contract to be the outcome of a bilateral monopoly.[7] He cites as evidence a passage that deals with competition quite generally, and that should also be applicable to the labour market:

The side of competition which happens for the moment to be weaker is also the side in which the individual acts independently of, and often directly against, the mass of his competitors, and precisely in this manner is the dependence of one

---

[1] *Wages, Price and Profit*, p. 74.
[2] Cp. also my "Marxism, functionalism and game theory" and its sequel, "Further thoughts on Marxism, functionalism and game theory".
[3] *Capital I*, p. 637.   [4] *Ibid.*, p. 640.   [5] *Wages, Price and Profit*, p. 74.   [6] *Ibid.*, p. 78.
[7] Maarek, *An Introduction to Karl Marx's* Das Kapital, pp. 130–1.

upon the other impressed upon them, while the stronger side always acts more or less as a united whole against its antagonist. If the demand for this particular kind of commodity is greater than the supply, one buyer outbids another – within certain limits – and so raises the price of the commodity for all of them above the market-value, while on the other hand the sellers unite in trying to sell at a high market price. If, conversely, the supply exceeds the demand, one begins to dispose of his goods at a cheaper rate and the others must follow, while the buyers unite in their efforts to depress the market-price as much as possible below the market-value. The common interest is appreciated by each only so long as he gains more by it than without it. And unity of action ceases the moment one or the other side becomes the weaker, when each tries to extricate himself on his own as advantageously as possible . . . If one side has the advantage, all belonging to it gain. It is as though they exerted their common monopoly. If one side is weaker, then one may try on his own hook to become the stronger (for instance who works with lower costs of production), or at least to get off as lightly as possible, and in such cases each for himself and the devil take the hindmost, although his actions affect not only himself, but also his boon companions.[1]

Like a similar passage cited in 1.2.1, this text is both suggestive and tantalizing, because it is so hard to pin down exactly what it states. It appears to rest on a confusion between gains from cartellization – "unity of action" – and the disequilibrium gains that may accrue to either buyer or seller under competitive conditions. If, say, buyers "have the advantage" (i.e. if the price is below the equilibrium price), they do indeed gain, but they could have gained even more by exerting their common monopoly. Moreover, the argument that cartels tend to form in good times and not in bad is either false or questionable. It is false if Marx thought that in good times there is no conflict of interest between capitalists, and empirically questionable if he thought that the conflict of interest (created by the free-rider problem) was more easily solved in good times than in bad. The last issue is discussed in 6.2.2. In any case the passage is too general to be taken as evidence for the idea of bilateral monopoly in the *labour* market; and even accepting the application to the labour market, it rather states that one side of the market will be organized and the other not.

Consider, finally, the determinants of the value of the consumption goods that enter into the real wage. Little need be added to what has been said in 1.3.2 and in chapter 3. The central idea is that a cheapening of the consumption goods due to technical progress leads to the production of relative surplus-value. This is an externality that cannot motivate the individual capitalist to innovate. Rather he innovates to get the temporary super-profits during the period he had a monopoly on the new methods. The fall in the value of consumption goods and hence – assuming a

[1] *Capital III*, p. 193–4.

constant real wage – the increase in the rate of exploitation are general-equilibrium phenomena, unlike the changes that are due to individual or collective confrontation between capitalist and workers.

Yet the capitalist must *impose* this increase no less than the others, since he has to make the workers accept a fall in their monetary wage. If workers were paid in goods, the steady increase in the productivity of labour would automatically bring about a steady increase in the rate of exploitation. Since, however, they are paid in money, no such automatism exists. Marx was led to ignore this problem because of his insistence on the notion of a historically determined real wage that at any time is required for the reproduction of the labour-power. For instance, "the cheapened commodity . . . causes only a pro tanto fall in the value of labour-power, a fall proportional to the extent of that commodity's employment in the reproduction of labour-power".[1] The notion of fixed coefficients of consumption here leads to mechanistic thinking, and to a neglect of the class relations that mediate between technical progress and the real wage.

Let me try to bring together some strands in the discussion. The behavioural explanations of the rate of surplus-value are the following. (i) Confrontation between the individual capitalist and his workers, notably with respect to the intensification of labour. (ii) The operation of supply and demand in the competitive labour market, with the industrial reserve army exerting a downward pressure on wages. (iii) Collective bargaining between organized workers and organized capitalists. (iv) Indirect, general-equilibrium effects of technical progress that, by lowering the value of the commodities that enter into the consumption bundle of the workers, lead to an increase in the rate of exploitation. (v) Intervention by the state, on behalf either of the capitalist class or of "society". (vi) Political alliance formation, which induces the capitalists to give concessions to the workers in order to get their support for measures against the landowners. Clearly, this picture, for all its complexity, is a realistic one. In broad outline it is an impressive achievement, and we should not fault Marx too much for defects of detail.

4.1.5. Exploitation, power and counterfactuals

Here I discuss some thorny conceptual questions that arise in the analysis of exploitation. What is the relation between exploitation and power? What is the alternative to being exploited? Does the characterization of a

[1] *Capital I*, p. 315.

state as exploitative require that there is some feasible state in which the exploited would be better off? Could one even *define* exploitation by the presence of such states? These questions are also pursued in 4.2.3, 4.3.3 and 6.1.1.

In non-market exploitation power is involved in an essential and obvious way. Hence I focus here on the relation between power and market exploitation. I discuss three ways in which market exploitation involves power relations: through the power of the state to enforce property rights; through the presence of monopoly power; and through domination in the production process.[1] In connection with the first issue I also discuss whether the state itself can be an exploiter.

In the traditional formulation, the power of the state is needed to guarantee property and enforce contracts. This appears to be tautologically true, but G. A. Cohen has argued that behind this appearance there is a substantive problem.[2] Although *legal* control over the means of production must be enforced by the state, there may exist non-legal or pre-legal control that has a similar effect. In principle, there could be a capitalist economy where the capitalist's factory is protected by his private thugs, much as the feudal lord's retinue would expel anyone who tried to settle on the demesne. To this it may be answered that in capitalism the state also guarantees the control of the worker over his own labour-power. The worker has no non-labour wealth with which he could hire protection. The control must be backed by the power of someone else, and that can hardly be a would-be employer and his thugs. The state is the third party that guarantees the control of the worker over his labour-power. Again, this is not a conceptual necessity. One's property to one's own labour-power could be protected by a libertarian ideology to which the gangster-employing capitalists also subscribed. Such counterexamples aside, however, the link between market exploitation and a state that guarantees the formal freedom of the transactions would appear to be very close.

Could the state itself be an exploiter? Hitherto I have tacitly assumed that exploiters as well as exploited are individuals, but could one extend the notion so that either or both are collectivities? In G.E.M. de Ste Croix's study of exploitation in classical antiquity, all four possibilities appear:[3]

– exploitation of individuals by individuals (slave and slaveowner)

---

[1] For a related analysis, see Roemer, "Should Marxists be interested in exploitation?"

[2] Cohen, *Karl Marx's Theory of History*, ch. VIII (and personal communication).

[3] Ste Croix, *The Class Struggle in the Ancient Greek World*, pp. 205–6.

- exploitation of individuals by collectivities (state-owned slaves and exploitation of peasants through taxation)
- exploitation of collectivities by individuals (a village collectively responsible for rent)
- exploitation of collectivities by collectivities (a village collectively responsible for taxes).

We saw that Marx similarly referred to the taxation of the French peasantry as a form of capitalist exploitation.

First, let us note that if the state exploits the citizen, it is not a form of market exploitation, barring the unlikely case that all nations have free emigration and immigration.[1] The state, if it exploits, does so through its monopoly over the means of violence. To make some headway on this issue, let us distinguish between five cases. (i) Taxes are used to produce public goods that benefit all members of the population directly, such as health and education, social security,[2] national defence[3] or internal peace.[4] (ii) Taxes are used to produce public goods that promote capital accumulation, such as improved means of communication, basic research etc. (iii) Taxes are used to maintain a repressive apparatus that keeps the exploited classes from organizing themselves. (iv) Taxes are siphoned off to the economically dominant class, providing them with additional revenue for consumption purposes. (v) Taxes are retained by the state officials for consumption purposes. Of these, the first does not give rise to any exploiters, nor does the second to the extent that the economic growth is to the benefit of all. (Cp. the discussion of reinvestment and exploitation in 4.1.2.) Case (iv) seems to have obtained in the Roman world,[5] while case (v) may correspond to the Asiatic mode of production or to the Bonapartist state.

Case (iii) is more difficult to classify. It involves extraction of surplus labour in one form for the purpose of making another form possible and

---

[1] Cp. Hirschman, "Exit, voice and the state".

[2] Some writers (e.g. O'Connor, *The Fiscal Crisis of the State*) argue that welfare expenses are the modern equivalent of repression, to be explained by their effects on the class consciousness of the workers. For a critique of this functionalist approach, see my "Marxism, functionalism and game theory".

[3] Imperialist expansion has – analogously to the argument mentioned in the preceding note – been explained as a way of substituting nationalistic sentiments for class consciousness in the working class. More plausibly, wars could be a means for one nation to exploit another, by imposing unfavourable terms of trade. This, of course, is a different issue than that raised by the question of whether the state is an exploiter of its own citizens.

[4] Again, the prevention of crime has been seen as a technique of class rule by many writers; for a critical discussion, see "Marxism, functionalism and game theory".

[5] Ste Croix, *The Class Struggle in the Ancient Greek World*, ch. VIII and *passim*.

profitable, but it is not profitable in itself. Hence it does not qualify as exploitation if we require that the loss of the exploited equals the gain to the exploiters, with no deadweight expenses. This, however, is not a reasonable constraint to impose on the analysis. Even within the factory there are costs of enforcement that reduce the rate of exploitation below what it would have been had the workers been perfectly docile and cooperative. Marx refers to the work of the agents engaged in such enforcement as "necessary but unproductive".[1] They are *agents of exploitation* who need not themselves be exploiters, since they can be quite badly paid. Hence the last three cases differ as follows. In case (iii) taxation is a precondition for the existence of a class of exploiters, and gives directly rise to a class of agents of exploitation. In case (iv) taxation adds to the benefit of the exploiters. In case (v) it gives rise to a separate class of exploiters. The class status of the agents of exploitation and of the exploiters created by taxation is further discussed in 6.1.2.

A second way in which power intervenes in exploitation is by the existence of "thin markets", that is in the presence of monopoly power. I argue in 4.2.3 that in such cases the exploited are not only driven "by the force of circumstances" to sell their labour-power, but may actually be coerced into doing so. More frequently, perhaps, the rate of exploitation – as distinct from the presence of *some* degree of exploitation – can be shaped in this way. Clearly, this is a form of market exploitation that is in some ways related to non-market exploitation, while also differing importantly from it.

Thirdly, it has been argued that power relations enter into exploitation via the coercive supervision and discipline needed to keep the worker from shirking. No contract can specify in full detail what the worker is to do, hence supervision is needed to fill the gap. Moreover, unless there is supervision, the worker has an incentive to violate the letter of the contract as well as its spirit by arriving late to work, taking frequent breaks etc. Hence domination in the labour process is of the essence of exploitation, which takes place "at the point of production", not "at the point of exchange".[2]

I do not believe these features of the wage contract make it any different from any other contract. Quality control is always necessary to ensure that the buyer gets what he has contracted to get. True, in this case the commodity sold – labour-power – is inseparable from the seller, so that

---

[1] *Theories of Surplus-Value*, vol. 1, pp. 175, 287. In the *Grundrisse*, p. 533, the phrase is used in a somewhat different sense, to cover the production of public goods.
[2] See the references in note 2, p. 181 above.

the buyer must relate to the person of the seller in order to control the quality of what he sells. This is indeed an important fact, with far-reaching consequences for the class struggle (6.1). Yet it is misleading to say that this control is an exercise of power, if by that we mean something different from the economic power wielded by the capitalist by virtue of his possession of the means of production. The exercise of power occurs when the contract is signed, by the capitalist taking advantage of the lack of property of the worker. The enforcement of the contract is not then a further exercise of power. "What brings the seller into a relationship of dependency is *solely* the fact that the buyer is the owner of the conditions of labour."[1] Normally, the contract is enforced by the worker's knowledge that he will be fired if he violates it.[2] Direct supervision may also be needed to detect violations that otherwise could not be imputed to specific workers, but this form of quality control could well be, and often is, incorporated into the wage agreement itself. It is simply not true that "Authority at the point of production must be used to *evince* worker behaviour not guaranteed by the wage labour contract",[3] since the use of such authority may be a clause in the contract itself. To avoid misunderstanding, let me state again that this conceptual issue does not prejudge the causal question of what are the mainsprings of social conflict in capitalism. It could well be that the confrontation in the production process has greater motivational force than the property relations which make it possible.

I now turn to the relation between statements about exploitation and counterfactual statements about non-exploitative states of affairs. I shall consider two distinct, partially related issues. First, what are the implications of the dictum "Ought implies can" for the theory of exploitation? More specifically, what are the feasibility constraints that we must impose on the counterfactual alternative to exploitation in order to retain the moral connotations of that term? Secondly, I shall take up an issue briefly mentioned at the beginning of the chapter: how should we treat exploitation when the labour content of goods cannot be defined because of the problem of heterogeneous labour? Could we – as suggested by John Roemer – then *define* exploitation by the presence of some state of affairs in which the exploited would have been better off?

Consider the following, well-known argument. The term exploitation

---

[1] *Results of the Immediate Process of Production*, pp. 1025–6; italics by Marx.
[2] *Ibid.*, p. 1031.
[3] Bowles and Gintis, "The Marxian theory of value and heterogeneous labour", p. 177.

carries connotations of injustice. To say that exploitation is unjust is to say that it ought to be abolished, which only makes sense if it can be abolished. Historical evidence and theoretical argument suggest that abolition of capitalist exploitation would make not only the exploiters, but also the exploited, worse off, mainly because of incentive problems (4.3.2). In that case we are condemned to say either that a change to a state in which all are worse off could be an improvement in distributive justice, or that there is nothing morally wrong with so-called "exploitation", which should be referred to by some other term, such as "socially necessary inequality". Neither option is attractive to someone who would argue for the injustice of exploitation. It would appear that the exploitation that "ought" to be abolished is not one that "can" be abolished.

Let us accept, for the sake of argument, that the incentive problem is as serious as this objection presupposes. I still do not believe that it succeeds. It rests on a historical notion of feasibility that is not the relevant one in the present context. Abolishing exploitation without making the exploited worse off may not be feasible in the present historical situation, but it surely is feasible in a different and more relevant sense, which we may refer to as physical feasibility. Since workers under capitalism work hard, entrepreneurs use their managerial skills and capital-owners reinvest part of their profit, we know that there are no physical barriers to implementing the non-exploitative alternative. The proposal is not Utopian in the sense in which it is Utopian to assert that everybody could be a Raphael or even a Leonardo (2.2.7). I suggest that "Ought implies can" holds only if "can" is taken in this narrow sense of physical (or biological) feasibility. If it is taken in the broader sense of historical possibility, the principle can be turned around: that something is perceived as morally obligatory may contribute to making it historically feasible, given its physical possibility. Historical feasibility is a relative and highly volatile notion. It should not be absolutized to serve as an argument for inequalities that may be unavoidable today, but need not remain so indefinitely.

Counterfactual alternatives are central to John Roemer's "general theory of exploitation", which seeks to dispense with the notion of labour content of goods.[1] As explained in 3.2.1, the presence of non-producible skills prevents us from speaking of *the* labour content of commodities, and hence from comparing the labour time expended by an agent and the labour time he receives in the form of commodities. In this case the

---

[1] Roemer, *A General Theory*, part III; see also his "Property relations vs. surplus-value in Marxian exploitation".

"labour theory of exploitation" breaks down, as does the labour theory of value. There is, however, a difference between the two theories. From a normative point of view, one could argue that the amount of labour time expended is the only relevant fact, irrespective of the skill with which the labour is performed. Nobody deserves to be rewarded for his natural talents,[1] whereas those who work longer hours deserve a greater part of the net social product. Hence it is possible to characterize as unjust a situation in which two persons work the same number of hours, but earn different (monetary) incomes. From the analytical or explanatory point of view, no similar significance can be attached to an undifferentiated measure of labour time. This defence of the labour theory of exploitation breaks down, however, when we consider the other source of heterogeneous labour, namely the different degrees of disutility of work, which do indeed justify differential payment to persons working the same number of hours.

I return to these issues in 4.3. It is clear, in any case, that there are good reasons for trying to define a concept of exploitation that does not presuppose that all labour is homogeneous. Roemer proposes to do this by postulating that a coalition of agents S in the economy are *capitalistically exploited* if:

(1) If S were to withdraw from the society, endowed with its per capita share of society's alienable property (that is, produced and nonproduced goods), and with its own labour and skills, then S would be better off (in terms of income and leisure) than it is at the present allocation;

(2) If [the complementary coalition] S' were to withdraw under the same conditions, then S' would be worse off (in terms of income and leisure) than it is at present;

(3) If S were to withdraw from society with its *own* endowments (not its per capita share), then S' would be worse off than at present.[2]

On this definition, a group of workers that lack both capital and skills need not be capitalistically exploited, since without skill they might not be able to make good use of their per capita share of the means of production. This is somewhat surprising. Presumably a motivating force behind "the general theory" was to show that skilled capitalists exploit unskilled workers, an idea that cannot be stated within the labour theory of exploitation. It now turns out that the idea, though statable, need not be true

---

[1] This is not the place to defend this stark postulate. For a good discussion of the view that distribution ought to be "ambition-sensitive", but not "endowment-sensitive", see Dworkin, "What is equality?", part 2.

[2] Roemer, "Property relations vs. surplus-value in Marxian exploitation", p. 285, corrected for an obvious misprint.

within the general theory. Roemer's way out of this problem involves a distinction between capitalist exploitation (defined above) and socialist exploitation:

> Let a coalition withdraw, taking with it its per capita share of *all* endowments, alienable and inalienable. If it can improve the position of its members, and if the complementary coalition is worse off under such an arrangement, then it is socialistically exploited at the allocation in question.[1]

In capitalism, there can be socialist exploitation by the skilled as well as capitalist exploitation by the capital owners. In socialism, capitalist exploitation is eliminated, only socialist exploitation remains, to be eliminated under communism. I do not think this re-conceptualization of exploitation is very helpful. It replaces the ill-defined notion of labour content by another that is hardly in better shape, namely the idea of "withdrawing with one's per capita share of society's intangible assets", that is skills. Even as a thought experiment, it remains unclear how the workers are to take with them their share of the managerial skill, while leaving the managers behind them.[2]

In addition to this objection, I believe that Roemer's approach is inadequate in a more fundamental way.[3] Intuitively, exploitation has a causal as well as a moral aspect. The fact that some end up as exploiters and others as exploited must be due to some interaction between them (or to some network of interaction through which they are linked to one another). Now it is generally true that causal statements cannot be captured exhaustively by counterfactual statements: "A caused B" is neither a sufficient nor a necessary condition for the truth of "If A had not occurred, B would not have occurred."[4] Hence we know in advance that Roemer's attempt to capture the causal notion of exploitation by statements about hypothetical withdrawal rules is bound to fail. It is easy, moreover, to provide counterexamples to the proposed definition.[5]

This is not to say that Roemer's general theory is without merit. It enables us to characterize quite compactly the main varieties and sources of exploitation. Thus *feudal exploitation* is defined by the possibility for the

---

[1] Roemer, *A General Theory*, p. 212.
[2] Roemer (*ibid.*) provides a model in which the agents differ in their knowledge of the production possibilities, and "each member of a withdrawing coalition is assigned the ability to operate each individual's technology for $1/N$ of the day", N being the number of individuals in the society. Unlike the withdrawal rules for feudalism and capitalism, this assignment has no independent appeal. In fact, it would be pointless for the withdrawing individuals not to employ the union of all individual technologies during the whole day.
[3] The following is developed more extensively in my "Roemer vs Roemer".
[4] See my *Explaining Technical Change*, p. 34.   [5] See "Roemer vs Roemer".

coalition to improve its lot by withdrawing and taking with it its *own* endowments.[1] Clearly, for this to be possible, the feudally exploited agents must be restricted in their personal freedom. Hence we can say that in feudalism, exploitation occurs because some individuals do not control their own labour-power; whereas socialist exploitation occurs because some individuals (the skilled exploiters) *do* control their own labour-power. In capitalism, exploitation occurs because some individuals control *only* their own unskilled labour-power. We can see that these are distinct, and important, varieties of distributive injustice. Exactly what is gained by referring to them as exploitation, and by using the framework of withdrawal rules, remains unclear.

On the other hand I would argue that the problem of heterogeneous labour should not lead us to discard the labour theory of exploitation. It remains a useful, although special, case on which we can test some of our ethical intuitions. A remotely analogous case is the assumption of non-increasing returns to scale, standardly made in non-Marxist as well as Marxist economic theory. Although everyone recognizes the massive importance in the real world of increasing returns to scale, they are analytically intractable and often set aside. If we make the more special assumption of constant returns to scale, the analogy becomes slightly less remote. This assumption is a *homogeneity* postulate that disregards some of the baffling, qualitative phenomena that abound in reality. Like the assumption of homogeneous labour, also an enormous simplification, it helps us to get an analytical grip on problems that at present are too complex for more adequate understanding.

4.2. Freedom, coercion and force

Market exploitation rests on exchanges that in one sense are free and voluntary, rather than forced. Marx argued, however, that in another and more important sense the selling of labour-power *is* forced. Hence there is a need to examine in which sense Marx understood the notions of freedom, force, coercion and compulsion. In 4.2.1 I first discuss Marx's notion of positive freedom, or freedom as autonomous self-realization, and how it is related to the formal freedom of choice. In 4.2.2 I consider the senses in which – and the limits within which – capitalism offers a freedom that was absent in earlier societies. In 4.2.3 I first discuss whether

---

[1] Roemer, *A General Theory*, pp. 199ff. Recall, however, the ambiguities in the notion of peasant ownership or possession (4.1.1).

the worker in capitalism is *coerced* into selling his labour power, and then the weaker claim that he is *forced* to do so. I also discuss the link between these features of wage labour and the fact that labour is exploited.

4.2.1. Freedom as autonomy

With one possible exception (cited below) Marx never explicitly makes the contrast between positive and negative freedom. Both notions, however, can be found in his work. He refers to the former as "formal freedom", as when the worker is said to be formally free to leave his master.[1] The latter he calls "real freedom", which he also equates with self-actualization:

Smith has no inkling whatever that this overcoming of obstacles is itself a liberating activity – and that, further, the external aims become stripped of the semblance of merely external natural urgencies, and become posited as aims which the individual himself posits – hence as self-realization, objectification of the subject, hence real freedom.[2]

This is a conception of freedom as autonomy, the positive ability to choose one's aims, rather than the negative freedom from interference in the attempt to realize whatever aims one happens to have. The theme is also prominent in *The German Ideology*. "Free activity", for the communists, is "the creative manifestation of life arising from free development of the abilities of the 'whole fellow'."[3] Conversely, he refers to "the fact that one desire of an individual in modern society can be satisfied at the expense of all others, and that this 'ought not to be' and that this is more or less the case with all individuals in the world today and that thereby the free development of the individual as a whole is made impossible".[4] A similar point is made, although more ambiguously, in a passage from the *Grundrisse* that constitutes the possible exception mentioned above. Here Marx first contrasts the freedom of exchange found in capitalism with the various forms of unfree labour found in pre-capitalist economies:

[When] the economic form, exchange, posits the all-sided equality of its subjects, then the content, the individual as well as the objective material which drives towards the exchange, is *freedom*. Equality and freedom are thus not only respected in exchange based on exchange values but, also, the exchange of exchange values is the productive, real basis of all *equality* and *freedom* ... Equality and freedom as developed to this extent are exactly the opposite of the freedom and equality in the world of antiquity, where developed exchange was not their basis, but where, rather, the development of that basis destroyed them. Equality and freedom presuppose relations of production as yet unrealized in the ancient

---

[1] *Grundrisse*, p. 464. The passage is cited in full below.   [2] *Ibid.*, p. 611.
[3] *The German Ideology*, p. 225.   [4] *Ibid.*, p. 256.

world and in the Middle Ages. Direct forced labour is the foundation of the ancient world; the community rests on this as its foundation; labour itself as a 'privilege', as still particularized, not yet generally producing exchange values, is the basis of the world of the Middle Ages. Labour is neither forced labour; nor, as in the second case, does it take place with respect to a common higher unit (the guild).[1]

Marx probably meant that equality and freedom in the ancient world existed only at the political level, as the equality of free citizens.[2] If so, this is "real freedom" at the level of the community, collective self-determination.[3] This freedom is destroyed by the exchange economy, which, however, makes possible a new kind of economic freedom (4.2.2). Having made the point about this new freedom, Marx goes on to add a comment that may be understood as an assertion of lack of real freedom (at the individual level):

Now, it is admittedly correct that the [relation between those] engaged in exchange, in so far as their motives are concerned, i.e. as regards natural motives falling outside the economic process, does also rest on a certain compulsion; but this is, on one side, itself only the other's indifference to my need as such, to my natural individuality, hence his equality with me and his freedom, which are at the same time the precondition of my own; on the other side, if I am determined, forced by my needs, it is only my own nature, this totality of needs and drives, which exert a force upon me; it is nothing alien.[4]

The reason why the passage cannot unambiguously be read as a contrast between formal freedom and real unfreedom is the very last remark, which seems to affirm the autonomy of the agents involved in exchange. Yet this is probably a mere terminological difficulty, reflecting the fact that autonomy may be threatened from within as well as from outside. Although only the latter threat is mentioned here, the early manuscripts show that Marx also considered "being forced by one's needs" as an obstacle to real freedom.

Generally speaking, Marx emphasized the negative effects of the formal freedom in the market. Full self-actualization requires a community with others that is incompatible with the arm's length transactions in the market (2.2.7). Also, formal freedom tends to create an ideological illusion about the extent to which the worker has genuine scope for choice (4.2.2). Yet he also suggested that the formal freedom of the worker to some extent tends to make him autonomous, by making him responsible for his choices. This holds for his freedom as consumer,

[1] *Grundrisse*, p. 245.
[2] Cp. also Constant, "De la liberté des anciens comparée à celle des modernes".
[3] Cp. Finley, "Politics".   [4] *Grundrisse*, p. 245.

his freedom as producer and his freedom in the labour market. Postponing the last issue to 4.2.2, some texts relevant for the first two will be cited here.

In the "Reflections" from 1851 Marx notes that the formal freedom of the worker is extended by his mode of payment, but he does not see this as a positive accomplishment of capitalism. "The worker can squander his wages on liquor for himself instead of buying meat and bread for his children, a thing he cannot do when he is paid in kind. His personal freedom has thereby been extended, i.e. more latitude has been allowed to the rule of liquor."[1] A passage from the *Results of the Immediate Process of Production* suggests a quite different perspective:

The slave receives the means of subsistence he requires in the form of *naturalia* which are fixed both in kind and in quantity – i.e. he receives *use-values*. The free worker receives them in the shape of *money, exchange value*, the abstract social form of wealth. Even though his wage is in fact nothing more than the *silver* or *gold* or *copper* or *paper* form of the necessary means of subsistence into which it must constantly be dissolved – even though money functions here only as a means of circulation, as a vanishing form of exchange-value, that exchange-value, abstract wealth, remains in his mind as something more than a particular use-value hedged round with traditional and local restrictions. It is the worker himself who converts the money into whatever use-values he desires; it is he who buys commodities as he wishes and, as the *owner of money*, as the buyer of goods, he stands in precisely the same relationship to the seller of goods as any other buyer. Of course, the conditions of his existence – and the limited amount of money he can earn – compel him to make his purchases from a fairly restricted selection of goods. But some variation is possible as we can see from the fact that newspapers, for example, form part of the essential purchases of the English worker. He can save or hoard a little. Or else he can squander his money on drink. But even so he acts as a free agent; he must pay his own way; he is responsible to himself for the way he spends his wages. *He learns to control himself, in contrast to the slave*, who needs a master.[2]

This firm Victorian attitude differs strikingly from the earlier passage, which held the personal freedom of the worker up to ridicule and equated it with the rule of liquor. True, in the later passage Marx suggests that the autonomy of the worker is also useful for capital, but it is no less autonomy for that.

The freedom of the consumer is a permanent feature of capitalism. A similar freedom of the worker as producer is limited to the stage of merely formal subsumption of labour under capital, that is the putting-out system and similar arrangements under which the producer works for a

[1] "Reflections", p. 591.
[2] *Results of the Immediate Process of Production*, p. 1033.

wage, but has full control over the production process. Under these circumstances, "The consciousness (or better: the *idea*) of free self-determination, of liberty, makes a much better worker" of him than the slave.[1] This is a weaker form of self-determination than what is involved in consumer purchases, since it requires control only over behaviour, not over wants as well. In any case it disappears with the real subsumption of labour under capital that comes about with the machine technology (2.3.3).

4.2.2. Formal freedom in capitalism
Outside the factory gate, no one can tell the worker what to do. He can purchase the goods he wants to, within the limits of his wage. He can change employer, within the limits of alternative employment. He may even try to become self-employed or an employer himself, and sometimes succeed. This freedom, while ultimately a danger to capitalism, has useful short-term ideological consequences, since it creates an appearance of independence not only from any particular capitalist, but from capital itself. I shall cite and discuss some passages where these points are made.

The idea that the freedom of the worker to change employer makes him free in a way not found in earlier modes of production was a commonplace one at Marx's time. He himself cites Linguet[2] and Edmonds;[3] Tocqueville also makes much of this fact.[4] When Marx refers to it, he unfailingly adds (i) that the worker depends on capital even if he does not depend on any particular capitalist and (ii) that the independence in the latter sense hides the real dependence in the former sense. The most explicit statement, perhaps, occurs in the *Grundrisse*:

The first presupposition, to begin with, is that the relation of slavery or serfdom has been suspended. Living labour capacity belongs to itself, and has disposition over the expenditure of its forces, through exchange. Both sides confront each other as persons. *Formally*, their relation has the equality and freedom of exchange as such. As far as concerns the legal relation, the fact that this form is a mere *semblance*, and a *deceptive semblance*, appears as an *external* matter. What the free worker sells is always nothing more than a specific, particular measure of force-expenditure; labour capacity as a totality is greater than every particular expenditure. He sells the particular expenditure of force to a particular capitalist, whom he confronts as an independent *individual*. It is clear that this is not his relation to the existence of capital as capital, i.e. to the capitalist class. Nevertheless, in this

[1] *Ibid.*, p. 1031; cp. also *Capital I*, p. 555.
[2] *Theories of Surplus-Value*, vol. 1, p. 229.
[3] *Results of the Immediate Process of Production*, p. 1027.
[4] Tocqueville, *Democracy in America*, p. 557.

way everything touching on the individual, real person leaves him with a wide field of choice, of arbitrary will, and hence of formal freedom.[1]

The deceptive character of formal freedom is also asserted in *Capital I*:

The Roman slave was held by fetters: the wage-labourer is bound to his owner by invisible threads. The appearance of independence is kept up by means of a constant change of employers, and by the fictio juris of a contract.[2]

The reproduction of a mass of labour-power, which must incessantly re-incorporate itself with capital for that capital's self-expansion; which cannot get free from capital, and whose enslavement to capital is only concealed by the variety of individual capitalists to whom it sells itself, this reproduction of labour-power forms, in fact, an essential of the reproduction of capital itself.[3]

The observation that the formal freedom of the worker in the labour market has the ideological effect of creating an appearance of independence parallels the comment (cited in 4.2.1) that the freedom of the producer creates an "idea of self-determination" that makes him work harder. Hence one might think that for Marx the freedom of the worker was valuable only to the capitalist. It is true that Marx did not stress that such freedom is an inherently valuable achievement (since it is a good thing in itself not to be under the domination of another[4]). His mind was too concerned with the society of the future to be much concerned with second-best arguments about the situation of the worker under capitalism. He did believe, however, that the formal freedom – by its impact on autonomy – had instrumental efficacy in enabling the workers to bring about that future. This is brought out by a passage in the *Results of the Immediate Process of Production* immediately preceding the text cited in 4.2.1:

Certain though it be that the mass of work must be performed by more or less unskilled labour, so that the vast majority of wages are determined by the *value of simple labour-power*, it nevertheless remains open to individuals to raise themselves to higher spheres by exhibiting a particular talent or energy. In the same way there is an abstract possibility that this or that worker might conceivably become a capitalist and the exploiter of the labour of others. The slave is the property of a particular *master*; the worker must indeed sell himself to capital, but not to any particular capitalist, and so within certain limitations he may choose to sell himself to whomever he wishes; and he may also change his master. The effect of all these differences is to make the free worker's work more intensive, more continuous, more flexible and skilled than that of the slave, quite apart from the fact that they fit him for a quite different historical role.[5]

---

[1] *Grundrisse*, p. 464.   [2] *Capital I*, p. 574.   [3] *Ibid.*, pp. 613–14.
[4] Simmel, *The Philosophy of Money*, p. 200.
[5] *Results of the Immediate Process of Production*, pp. 1032–3.

Because Marx then goes on to discuss the freedom of the worker as consumer, it is not clear whether the last phrase refers to this or to freedom in the labour market. Perhaps Marx had both kinds of freedom in mind as preconditions for the "historical role" of the worker. Taken together thèse passages imply the following view. On the one hand, the freedom of the worker–consumer creates in him a *capacity* for the historical action of overthrowing capitalism. The conditions for the "real freedom" in communism are created by workers who to some extent already partake in it, as a result of the formal freedom that compels them to be responsible for their choices. On the other hand, the formal freedom also blunts the *motivation* to undertake such action, since it conceals the oppressive nature of capitalism. Of these two themes, the second is by far the most heavily emphasized by Marx, yet the first ought at least to be noticed.

In the last-quoted passage Marx refers briefly to the freedom of the worker to become an exploiter – his partial independence not only of any specific capitalist, but of capital as capital. In a passage from *Capital III* quoted in 1.4.6 Marx suggested that such upwards mobility is doubly useful to capitalism, because of its ideological value and because of its strengthening effect on the capitalist class. (He might have added a third consequence – the correlative weakening of the working class, which in this way loses its potential leaders.) In the preparatory manuscripts he insists on the limits inherent in this mobility:

The truth is this, that in this bourgeois society every workman, if he is an exceedingly clever and shrewd fellow, and gifted with bourgeois instincts and favoured by an exceptional fortune, can possibly be converted himself into an *exploiteur du travail d'autrui*. But where there was no *travail* to be *exploité*, there would be no capitalist nor capitalist production.[1]

The definedness of individuals, which in [pre-capitalist societies]appears as a personal restriction of the individual by another, appears in [capitalism] as developed into an objective restriction of the individual by relations independent of him and sufficient unto themselves. (Since the single individual cannot strip away his personal relations, but may very well overcome and master external relations, his freedom *seems* to be greater in case 2. A closer examination of these external relations, these conditions, shows, however, that it is impossible for the individuals of a class etc. to overcome them en masse without destroying them. A particular individual may by chance get on top of these relations, but the mass of those under their rule cannot, since their mere existence expresses subordination, the necessary subordination of the mass of individuals . . .).[2]

---

[1] *Ibid.*, p. 1079.   [2] *Grundrisse*, p. 164.

Both the freedom to change employer and the freedom to become an employer oneself give rise to ideological illusions that embody the fallacy of composition.[1] The first is the inference from the fact that a given worker is independent of *any* specific employer, to the conclusion that he is free from *all* employers, that is independent of capital as such. The second is the inference from the fact that *any* worker can become independent of capital as such, to the conclusion that *all* workers can achieve such independence. It might look as if the conclusion of the first inference follows validly from the premise of the second, but this is due merely to the word "can" being employed in two different senses. The freedom of the worker to change employer depends, for its realization, mainly on his decision to do so. He "can" do it, in the sense of having the real ability to do so should he want to. The freedom to move into the capitalist class, by contrast, can only be realized by the worker who is an "exceedingly clever and shrewd fellow". Any worker "can" do it, in the sense of having the formal freedom to do so, but only a few are really able to.

Hence the worker possesses the least important of the two freedoms – namely the freedom to change employer – in the strongest of these two senses of freedom. He can actually use it should he decide to. Conversely, the more important freedom to move into the capitalist class obtains only in the weaker, more conditional sense: "every workman, *if* he is an exceedingly clever and shrewd fellow ... *can* possibly be converted into an *exploiteur du travail d'autrui*". Correlatively, the ideological implications of the two freedoms differ. With respect to the first, the ideologically attractive aspect is that the worker is free in the strong sense, while the second has the attraction of making him free with respect to an important freedom. If the two are confused, as they might easily be, the idea could emerge that the worker remains in the working class by choice rather than by necessity. This way of summarizing Marx's analyses goes beyond what is strictly warranted by the text, but seems to reflect the spirit of his argument.

4.2.3. Is wage labour forced labour?

The unexceptional worker, then, is not free to set himself up as a capitalist and hire the labour-power of others, if by freedom we mean some kind of real ability. Does this imply that he is forced to sell his labour-power? If so, should we say that he is coerced into selling it? I want to distinguish between force and coercion, taking coercion to imply the presence of an

---

[1] See my *Logic and Society*, pp. 97ff.

intentional agent or coercer, while force need not imply more than the presence of constraints that leave no room for choice. I am forced to live in my native town if I cannot get a job elsewhere, but I am coerced to live there if I would be arrested were I to try to leave. I shall first discuss whether the worker can be said to be coerced, and then, to the extent that he is not, whether it is at least plausible to say that he is forced to sell his labour-power.

Coercion may take various forms. First, there is the open use of threats, whether physical or not, whether in the form of inflicting punishment or in the form of withholding benefits. Next, there is manipulation of the external environment, that is depriving the coerced person of some options that he would otherwise have had. This may, but need not, go together with adding an extra option – for example an offer – to the original feasible set. Lastly, more controversially, there is manipulation of the beliefs and desires of the coerced agent. The common features of these cases are the following:

> A coerces B into doing Y if A performs an action X that has the intended and actual consequence of making B do Y, which differs from the action Z that B would have performed had A instead pursued his "normal" course of action W.[1]

In addition we must stipulate that B prefers the counterfactual situation in which A does W and he does Z to the one in which A does X and he does Y. (If the coercion takes the form of preference manipulation, this must be understood with reference to the pre-coercion preferences.[2]) We need not, I think, stipulate that A prefers the actual situation to the counterfactual one. A may coerce B just to flex his muscles. Standardly, however, A will indeed coerce B for his own benefit, broadly conceived.[3]

Clearly, much depends on how we define A's "normal" course of action. A moralized definition – where the normal course is the action that A *ought to* have taken – is clearly inadequate in some cases. It would, for instance, prevent us from saying that the police justly coerce people into abstaining from crimes. In some cases the relevant baseline would seem to be what A usually does; in other cases it may be what he would have done in B's absence (not from the universe, but from A's field of influence). And in some cases a moralized conception of the baseline may

---

[1] And we may add the standard clause that the consequence be brought about in the intended way, i.e. not by fluke
[2] See my *Ulysses and the Sirens*, pp. 82ff.
[3] The need for a broad conception of what benefits A may be seen by considering paternalistic coercion.

be unavoidable. I am far from confident that our intuitions are fully consistent in this regard.[1] In what follows, the normal course of action will be understood as that which A would have undertaken in B's absence.

For capitalist A to coerce worker B into selling his labour-power, there must be some alternative, preferred course of action Z that the worker would have chosen had it not been for the capitalist's intervention X. This alternative to wage labour could be self-employment, setting up a workers' cooperative or becoming a capitalist employer. The capitalist intervention might take the form of interference in the credit market, a threat to undersell the worker or – in the case of the cooperative – the use of "divide-and-conquer" tactics to blunt the class consciousness of the workers (6.2.2). Of these ways of coercing the workers to sell their labour-power, the first two involve deviation from perfect competition, while the last rests on a somewhat different principle. In all cases the situation can be characterized by a Roemer-like withdrawal statement: the workers would have done better for themselves by withdrawing with their own means of production. Their real option, however, is not one of total withdrawal, but one of setting up a business of their own within a capitalist environment. The capitalists may be able to block them from doing so by virtue of economic power, in a manner analogous to the feudal lord's use of physical power to stop the peasants from becoming independent producers.

Whatever the empirical importance of such coercion,[2] Marx did not pay much attention to it. When he opposed the "direct coercion" of non-market exploitation to the "force of circumstances" that leads to capitalist exploitation, it is natural to understand him as saying that the latter does not rest on coercion. Similarly, the "dull compulsion of economic relations" is opposed to "direct force, outside economic conditions" – which excludes the possibility of direct force within economic conditions. Marx

---

[1] For more far-reaching conceptual discussions the reader is referred to Nozick, "Coercion" and Frankfurt, "Coercion and moral responsibility". Recent discussions with application to the wage contract are Zimmerman, "Coercive wage offers"; Alexander, "Zimmerman on coercive wage offers", and Zimmerman's "Reply".

[2] Nozick, *Anarchy, State and Utopia*, pp. 252–3 argues that since capitalists "act in their personal and not their class interest", they would not interfere with worker-controlled firms. As a general statement it is certainly false that capitalists are unable to act according to their common interests (6.2). In this particular case, however, it seems that the reason why almost all workers' cooperatives in the nineteenth century failed had more to do with internal decay than with external interference; see Miller, "Market neutrality and the failure of co-operatives". Miller also offers good arguments against taking such failures as evidence of the non-viability of market socialism, defined as an economy-wide system of worker-owned, worker-managed firms.

would not have denied that the capitalist has the means to coerce the worker, but it was a much more important part of his vision that capitalist exploitation is anonymous and mediated through the impersonal, competitive market. Moreover, he preferred to operate on this assumption for methodological reasons, giving capital a "fair chance" rather than assuming the presence of monopoly power (3.1.1).

He did believe, on the other hand, that the worker is forced to sell his labour-power. This statement can be understood in various ways. First, given the constraints facing him, the worker has only two options: to starve to death or to sell his labour-power. Secondly, while the worker can survive without selling his labour-power, he can do so only under conditions so bad that the only acceptable course of action is to sell his labour-power. Thirdly, the worker must sell his labour-power to optimize, but there may be acceptable ways of surviving that do not involve wage labour. This third way of understanding the force exerted on workers may be set aside as spurious. An agent may have robbery as an optimizing strategy, but he is not forced into crime if he can easily find a well-paid job. Closer to the present topic, a capitalist is not forced to hire labour, even if he can only optimize by doing so.[1] And the worker who has well-paid self-employment as an alternative is not forced to take a better-paid job as a wage labourer.

Before I turn to the other senses, let me cite an important argument by G. A. Cohen that stands the last sentence on its head.[2] The workers may be forced to sell their labour-power even when they would optimize by moving out of the working class. This paradoxical statement turns upon a distinction between individual and collective unfreedom. Cohen argues – contrary to Marx – that *any* worker, not just the exceptionally gifted ones, has moving out of the working class as a real option. At least, he argues this to be the case in contemporary Britain, and it is certainly a conceivable state of affairs. Yet the reason why all workers have this option is that so few of them take it, fewer in fact than the number of available exits from the working class. It is then true of each individual worker that he is free not to sell his labour-power, but true of the working class as a whole that it is collectively forced to sell its

---

[1] True, Marx writes in *The Holy Family*, p. 33 that "the capitalist is compelled to fix the wage as low as possible", but this can only hold in the sense that the capitalist is compelled to act in this way *if* he wants to remain a capitalist. But he is typically not forced to remain a capitalist.

[2] This argument is set out in three related articles: "Capitalism, freedom and the proletariat", "Illusions about private property and freedom" and "The structure of proletarian unfreedom".

labour-power. Moreover, a possible explanation of their not using the option could be solidarity, that is that no worker wants to use a freedom not open to all. This is an ideologically important argument, since it allows a refutation of the defence of capitalism that appeals to the freedom of the workers to set up a business of their own. Yet, to repeat, it is a different refutation from the one offered by Marx, who appealed to the distinction between unconditional and conditional freedom, not between individual and collective freedom.

To my knowledge Marx never says that the worker is forced to sell his labour-power in the strong sense that the alternative is starvation. Observe that this view is not equivalent to the idea that wages are at subsistence level. Wages could be above subsistence, and yet the only alternative to wage labour could be below subsistence, if the worker has no access to capital. Conversely, wages might be at subsistence because of the existence of a mass of peasants similarly living at subsistence, forcing wages down to their level but also providing an alternative occupation to wage labour. Hence evidence concerning Marx's view on the trend in the actual wage level is not evidence for his view on the counterfactual issue whether workers have to sell their labour-power or starve. Nor are the chapters in *Capital I* on primitive accumulation relevant here, since their main thrust is that the ruling class *coerced* the agricultural population to turn to wage labour by deliberately making it impossible for it to survive on its own land.[1]

The most reasonable way of understanding Marx's contention that the worker is forced to sell his labour-power is by taking it in the second sense. The existence of alternative courses of action that might allow him to survive is irrelevant if they are so unattractive that no man in his senses would choose them. This, of course, turns completely on how we define what is acceptable and what is not.[2] Clearly, it will have to be defined both in relative and in absolute terms. If wages are high, a person may be said to be forced to sell his labour-power if the alternative barely allows him to survive, but if wages, too, are at survival levels, the existence of such an alternative implies that he is not forced to sell his labour-power. On the other hand some alternatives are so good that even were the wage offer raised to astronomical levels, the worker would not be forced to take it.[3] This suggests that the worker is forced to sell his labour when (i) the offered wage rate is above the alternative and (ii) the alternative is below

[1] See notably *Capital I*, p. 726.
[2] See Cohen, "The structure of proletarian unfreedom".
[3] Frankfurt, "Coercion and moral responsibility" discusses this issue.

some critical level. Neither condition is sufficient by itself. The critical level remains to be determined. If we look at force as a purely causal notion, then the critical level should not be the subject of a moralized definition.[1] I suspect, however, that our intuitions about force – like those concerning coercion or power – are a confused amalgam of causal and moral notions. If so, the notion of a universal criterion of acceptability may prove chimerical.

In conclusion, let me summarize the relation between the notions of exploitation, coercion and force as they apply to wage labour. I shall do so in terms of Roemer-like withdrawal statements – not because I think we can use them to define these concepts, but because they provide compact, useful characterizations of standard cases:

> A worker is *exploited* if he would be better off were he to withdraw with his per capita share of the means of production.

> A worker is *coerced to sell his labour power* if he would be better off were he to withdraw with his own means of production.

> A worker is *forced to sell his labour-power* if he would be unacceptably worse off were he to withdraw with his own means of production.

Clearly, a worker can be exploited without being either coerced or forced to sell his labour-power. Hence, whatever is morally wrong with exploitation cannot stem from the forced nature of the wage contract – unless one is prepared to say that exploitation is morally unobjectionable when the contract is unforced.

4.3. Is exploitation unjust?

The word "exploitation" is highly value-laden, with overtones of moral wrongness and unfairness. Yet Marx, while writing extensively about exploitation, was apt to dismiss talk about justice and fairness as bourgeois ideology. This tension in Marx's thought has received much attention in recent years. I shall argue that despite many statements by Marx to the contrary, both the theory of exploitation in *Capital* and the theory of communism in the *Critique of the Gotha Program* embody principles of justice. Like M. Jourdain, he did not know how to describe correctly what he was doing; unlike him, he actually went out of his way to deny that the correct description was appropriate. In 4.3.1 I first survey the relativistic

[1] Cohen, "Capitalism, freedom and the proletariat".

texts in which Marx denies the existence of objective, transhistorical criteria of justice. In 4.3.2 I discuss the texts in which he refers to the idea that property is theft – an idea that appears to presuppose such criteria. I conclude in 4.3.3 with a discussion of the principles "To each according to his contribution" and "To each according to his needs", and their application to capitalism and the two stages of communism.

4.3.1. Marx against justice

Marx's critique of justice can best be introduced in the context of his more general remarks about the view that communism is to be adopted because of the *ideals* it seeks to realize. Two questions must be firmly distinguished. One concerns the *status* of the ideals, that is their transhistorical or merely relative validity. Another concerns the political *efficacy* of the ideals, that is whether the workers in their revolutionary struggle will be motivated by ideals or by more narrowly defined class interest.[1] Marx's views on these issues are quite bewilderingly ambiguous. It is no great exaggeration to say that the texts allow us to impute to him any of the four possible combinations of answers to these questions.

Consider first *The German Ideology*. Here Marx dismisses talk about ideals in the following terms: "Communism is not for us a *state of affairs* which is to be established, an ideal to which reality will have to adjust itself. We call communism the *real* movement which abolishes the present state of things."[2] This is an expression of the Hegelian aversion against mere "ought" (*Sollen*), already found in a letter to Arnold Ruge from 1843.[3] It should not, however, be read as a statement about the political inefficacy of ideals, at least not if we want to impute to Marx a minimum of consistency. Elsewhere in the same work he writes that

[Stirner] presents the proletarians here as a "closed society", which has only to take the decision of "seizing" in order the next day to put a summary end to the entire hitherto existing world order. But in reality the proletarians arrive at this unity only through a long process of development in which the appeal to their

---

[1] Buchanan, *Marx and Justice*, p. 77, adds a third question: will the concept of justice have a place in communist life? One should consider the possibility, that is, that "in communist society, persons will have rights, but will employ no conception of rights". (For an analogy, consider societies in which persons get what they need of Vitamin C, but do nothing in order to get it, because they do not have – nor need – the concept.) I believe that on any non-Utopian interpretation of the needs principle (4.3.3), it will actually play a role in distribution under communism.
[2] *The German Ideology*, p. 49.
[3] "Letters from the *Deutsch-Französische Jahrbücher*", p. 144.

right also plays a part. Incidentally, this appeal to their right is *only* a means of making them take shape as "they", as a revolutionary, united mass.[1]

Appeal to rights is *only* a means to class consciousness, hence rights have no objective status. The appeal, however, *is* a means to class consciousness, hence rights have political efficacy. A somewhat different view is suggested by a well-known passage in the published version of *The Civil War in France*:

> The working-class did not expect miracles from the Commune. They have no ready-made utopias to introduce *par décret du peuple*. They know that in order to work out their own emancipation, and along with it that higher form to which present society is irresistibly tending by its own economical agencies, they will have to pass through long struggles, through a series of historical processes, transforming circumstances of men. They have no ideals to realize, but to set free elements of the new society with which old collapsing bourgeois society itself is pregnant.[2]

This certainly conveys the impression that ideals are superfluous for the advent of communism, since the process is governed by an objective necessity independent of the will of men. This is what came to be called "scientific socialism", a disastrous teleological conception, the very opposite of scientific thought.[3] Yet in a draft to the same work Marx expresses a quite different attitude:

> All the Socialist founders of Sects belong to a period in which the working class themselves were neither sufficiently trained and organized by the march of capitalist society itself to enter as historical agents upon the world's stage, nor were the material conditions of their emancipation sufficiently matured in the old world itself. Their misery existed, but the conditions of their own movement did not yet exist. The Utopian founders of Sects, while in their criticism of present society clearly describing the goal of the social movement, the supersession of the wages system with all its economical conditions of class rule, found neither in society itself the material conditions of its transformation nor in the working class the organized power and the conscience of the movement. They tried to compensate for the historical conditions of the movement by phantastic pictures and plans of a new society in whose propaganda they saw the true means of salvation. From the moment the workingmen class movement became real, the phantastic utopias evanesced, not because of the working class had given up the end aimed at by these Utopists, but because they had found the real means to realize them, but in their place came a real insight into the historic conditions of the movement and a more and more gathering force of the military organization of the working class. But the last 2 ends of the movement proclaimed by the Utopians are the last ends proclaimed by the Paris Revolution and by the International. Only the means are

---

[1] *The German Ideology*, p. 323; my italics.   [2] *The Civil War in France*, p. 143.
[3] For a forceful critique of this conception, see the chapter on Lukacs in vol. 3 of Kolakowski, *Main Currents of Marxism*.

different and the real conditions of the movement are no longer clouded in Utopian fables.[1]

This is a much more straightforward view of politics, as finding the best means to realize a given end. The utopians are criticized for believing that merely preaching the ideal would bring about its realization, not for believing in the ideal itself. On the contrary, the ideal is shared, "only the means are different".

Finally, consider the extraordinary passage cited towards the end of 2.3.3, in which Marx says that the recognition by labour that its separation from the means of production is unjust is the knell of doom to capitalist production. The fact that Marx uses the term "recognition" (*Erkennung*) rather than some subjective term such as "belief", shows that he believed the injustice to be a *fact* about capitalism. Also, the passage shows that the perception of this fact is at least a concomitant of the abolition of capitalism, and quite plausibly part of the motivation for abolishing it.

Consider now more specifically the status of different kinds of ideals. It has been argued, notably, that the ideal of self-actualization for Marx had an absolute, transhistorical character, while the ideal of justice does not.[2] On the face of it, the textual evidence appears to support this view. There can be little doubt that Marx throughout his life adhered to a quasi-Aristotelian ideal of the good life for man (2.2.7). Although the extent to which it is realized differs in different epochs, the ideal itself is transhistorically valid. On the other hand, there are a number of texts affirming that "right" has meaning only with respect to a given society, more precisely with respect to a given class society. With communism, right is transcended, not transformed. I first discuss some passages that affirm the relative character of rights in class societies, and then an important text affirming the absence of rights under communism.

In *Capital III* Marx cites a certain Gilbart to the effect that it is "a self-evident principle of natural justice" that "a man who borrows money with a view of making a profit of it, should give some portion of his profit to the lender". Marx comments that:

To speak here of natural justice, as Gilbart does, is nonsense. The justice of the transaction between agents of production rests on the fact that these arise as natural consequences out of the production relationship. The juristic form in which these economic transactions appear as wilful acts of the parties concerned, as expressions of their common will and as contracts that may be enforced by law

---

[1] First draft to *The Civil War in France*, pp. 66–7.
[2] Brenkert, "Freedom and private property in Marx", pp. 135–6; Wood, *Karl Marx*, pp. 126ff.

against some individual party, cannot, being mere forms, determine this content. They merely express it. This content is just whenever it corresponds, is appropriate to the mode of production. It is unjust whenever it contradicts that mode. Slavery on the basis of capitalist production is unjust; likewise fraud in the quality of commodities.[1]

A related passage occurs in *Wages, Price and Profit*:

To clamour for *equal or even equitable retribution* on the basis of the wages system is the same as to clamour for *freedom* on the basis of the slavery system. What you think just or equitable is out of the question. The question is: What is necessary and unavoidable with a given system of production?[2]

A further passage, more immediately relevant for the theory of exploitation, occurs in *Capital I*:

The circumstance that, on the one hand the daily sustenance of labour-power costs only half a day's labour, while on the other hand the very same labour-power can work during a whole day, that consequently the value which its use during one day creates, is double what he pays for that use, this circumstance is, without doubt, a piece of good luck for the buyer, but by no means an injustice to the seller.[3]

It has been argued that Marx in these passages does not assert that capitalist exploitation *is* just, only that it appears to be so.[4] Now I believe that Marx held the view that capitalist transactions generate the appearance that they are transhistorically just, and that he wanted to denounce this as mere appearance. Yet that denunciation does not imply that he took these transactions to be transhistorically unjust. When denying their transhistorical justice, he denied the "transhistorical" not the "justice" part. This, in my view, is the only unstrained interpretation of the passages cited.

These passages offer no *argument* for the relative nature of rights and justice. For this, we must turn to the *Critique of the Gotha Program*, with the distinction between two stages of communism (7.3.2). In the first, the producers are paid according to the labour time they contribute, a principle of "equal right" that is a definite advance on the capitalist mode of production. Yet it falls short of communism in the full sense, in which rights are transcended:

In spite of this advance, this equal right is still constantly stigmatized by a bourgeois limitation. The right of the producers is proportional to the labour they supply; the equality consists in the fact that measurement is made with an equal standard, labour.

---

[1] *Capital III*, p. 339–40.   [2] *Wages, Price and Profit*, p. 46.   [3] *Capital I*, p. 194.
[4] Husami, "Marx on distributive justice".

But one man is superior to another physically or mentally and so supplies more labour in the same time, or can labour for a longer time; and labour, to serve as a measure, must be defined by its duration or intensity, otherwise it ceases to be a standard of measurement. This equal right is an unequal right for unequal labour. It recognizes no class differences, because everyone is only a worker like everyone else: but it tacitly recognizes unequal individual endowments and thus productive capacity as natural privileges. It is, therefore, a right of inequality, in its content, like every right. Right by its very nature can consist only in the application of an equal standard; but unequal individuals (*and they would not be different individuals were they not unequal*) are measurable only by an equal standard in so far as they are brought under an equal point of view, are taken from one definite side only, for instance, in the present case, are regarded only as workers and nothing more is seen in them, everything else being ignored.

Further, one worker is married, another not; one has more children than another, and so on and so forth. Thus, with an equal performance of labour, and hence an equal share in the social consumption fund, one will in fact receive more than another, one will be richer than another, and so on. To avoid all these defects, right instead of being equal would have to be unequal.

But these defects are inevitable in the first phase of communist society as it is when it has just emerged after prolonged birth pangs from capitalist society. Right can never be higher than the economic structure of society and its cultural development conditioned thereby.[1]

Marx here purports to offer a general argument against theories of justice – "contending that any institutions are inequitable to the extent that they operate through general rules".[2] Any general rule must neglect relevant differences between individuals. Let me try to reconstruct the argument more fully. On the one hand, no two individuals are identical. The phrase that I have italicized in the cited text clearly is a statement of Leibniz's principle of the identity of indiscernibles, which Marx also refers to elsewhere.[3] On the other hand, no set of (written) principles can distinguish fully between individuals, since language is essentially poorer than the world.[4] Any principle stating that individuals fulfilling certain conditions have the right to certain goods flounders at the fact that there can be morally relevant differences between persons who fulfil the conditions. (This presupposes that the set of potentially relevant features is also inexhaustible.) Hence there is a choice to be made between justice and

---

[1] *Critique of the Gotha Programme*, p. 21.
[2] Moore, *Marx on the Choice between Socialism and Communism*, p. 45.
[3] See my "Marx et Leibniz".
[4] This statement can be defended by various arguments. In this context we may understand it in the light of the traditional Chinese mistrust of written, legal codes – epitomized in the proverb that "For each new law, a new way of circumventing it will arise" (Needham, *Science and Civilisation in China*, vol. II, p. 522).

individuality as the foundation of communism. Marx, having chosen the self-actualization of the individual as the supreme value, cannot also propose strict criteria of justice.

The argument is not without interest, but fails because of an obvious internal inconsistency. When referring to the "defects" of the contribution principle, Marx is implicitly invoking a higher principle of justice. In fact, after the quoted passage, the text goes on to spell out what this principle is: To each according to his needs (4.3.3). No doubt Marx believed that in this passage he had set out a devastating argument against any abstract theory of justice, and did not notice that in doing so he invoked a theory of the kind he wanted to dispense with. Marx, posing as M. Jourdain, argues in prose against the possibility of talking prose.

This survey of Marx's dicta on ideals, right and justice has been somewhat inconclusive. In my opinion this reflects vacillations in Marx's thinking, rather than any difficulty in understanding it. Although most of the cited passages are evidence for his intermittent hostility to talk about justice and rights, others reflect the opposite attitude. I now go on to consider some passages that more strongly support the view that Marx did condemn capitalism on grounds of distributive injustice.

4.3.2. Is property theft?

Marx often refers to the transaction between capitalist and worker as "robbery", "embezzlement", "theft" etc. This constitutes prima facie evidence that he believed capitalism to be an unjust system, even if he does not in these passages use that term. Yet the matter is more complex, as Marx also recognized. In what follows I shall pursue both the exegetical task of finding out what were Marx's views on the topic and the substantive one of discussing whether they were justified.

We may first note that some forms of property are literally due to theft, namely those originating in so-called primitive accumulation. In *Capital I* Marx refers to the clearing of estates effectuated by the Duchess of Sutherland as an example of such forcible expropriation.[1] The passage draws on a newspaper article written some fifteen years earlier, in which he refers to the Proudhonian notion that property is theft:

If of any property it ever was true that it was *robbery*, it is literally true of the property of the British aristocracy. Robbery of Church property, robbery of commons, fraudulous transformation accompanied by murder, of feudal and patriarchal property into private property – these are the titles of the British aristocrats to their possessions.[2]

[1] *Capital I*, pp. 729–30.   [2] *New York Daily Tribune* 9.2.1853.

One possible argument, along Nozick-like lines, would be that the property of contemporary capitalists is unjust because derived from this forcible, rights-violating appropriation by earlier capitalists.[1] This would not be restricted to direct inheritance. The unjust primitive accumulation made it possible for individuals other than the primitive accumulators and their descendants to enrich themselves in ways that would otherwise have been unavailable, for example by trading with the accumulators and thus getting a share of their wealth. This argument might cover a good deal of modern capitalist property, although it is impossible to tell exactly how much. It is not, however, an argument found in Marx. When he refers to the theft or robbery involved in capitalist–worker exchange, he usually does so with respect to current transactions only, without going back to the historical past in order to justify this characterization. True, he often refers to the fact that capital is only a form of past labour, but this is not meant to suggest that the capitalist has forcibly robbed earlier workers of their product. He has robbed them, or someone has robbed them, but only in the same sense that the capitalist is currently robbing his own workers. This self-perpetuating or steady-state process (2.3.3) should not be confused with primitive accumulation.

In the *Grundrisse* Marx refers to "*the theft of alien labour-time on which the present wealth is based*" as a "miserable foundation" compared to the new basis created by modern large-scale industry.[2] In *Capital I* he similarly asserts that the "yearly accruing surplus-product [is] embezzled because abstracted without return of an equivalent".[3] In the *Grundrisse* the last phrase is elaborated to the appropriation of "alien labour *without exchange, without equivalent*, but with the semblance of exchange".[4] (This is not representative. Usually Marx says: exchange, without an equivalent, but with the semblance of an equivalent.) Another passage from *Capital I* merits a fuller quotation. It occurs in a discussion of extended reproduction, where Marx supposes the existence of an "original capital" of £10 000, which creates a surplus of £2000. Even if the former were acquired honestly, the latter, according to Marx, is not:

The original capital was formed by the advance of £10 000. How did the owner become possessed of it? "By his own labour and that of his forefathers", answer unanimously the spokesmen of Political Economy. And, in fact, their supposition appears the only one consonant with the laws of the production of commodities.

[1] One might extend this from actions violating the rights of others, to include as well actions that constitute an abuse of one's own rights, a form of coercion through economic power. For this important category, see Liebermann and Syrquin, "On the use and abuse of rights".
[2] *Grundrisse*, p. 705.   [3] *Capital I*, p. 611.   [4] *Grundrisse*, p. 551.

But it is quite otherwise with regard to the additional capital of £2000. How that originated we know perfectly well. There is not one single atom of its value that does not owe its existence to unpaid labour. The means of production, with which the additional labour is incorporated, as well as the necessaries with which the labourer is sustained, are nothing but component parts of the surplus-product, of the tribute annually exacted from the working-class by the capitalist class. Though the latter with a portion of that tribute purchases the additional labour-power even at its full price, so that equivalent is exchanged for equivalent, yet the transaction is for all that only the old dodge of every conqueror who buys commodities from the conquered with the money he has robbed them of.[1]

The argument is somewhat disingenuous or question-begging. To see this, consider G. A. Cohen's gloss on the last sentence: "capitalists pay wages with money they get by selling what workers produce".[2] But of course workers produce with the help of capital goods, that by the assumption of the argument are the legitimate possession of the capitalist. I return to this substantive issue shortly. Here I want to consider the passage as evidence that Marx believed the capitalist appropriation of surplus-value an unjust one. Cohen, in his further comment, convincingly argues that it must indeed be understood in this sense:

Now since ... Marx did not think that by capitalist criteria the capitalist steals, and since he did think he steals, he must have meant that he steals in some appropriately non-relativist sense. And since to steal is, in general, wrongly to take what rightly belongs to another, to steal is to commit an injustice, and a system which is "based on theft" is based on injustice.[3]

An objection to this view is that one can steal only what rightly belongs to another, while Marx argued that the very notion of such possession is a bourgeois category. In a letter on Proudhon he says that the view that property is theft is confused, "since 'theft' as a forcible violation of property presupposes the existence of property".[4] This in my opinion is not a decisive objection. By extension, "theft" may denote wrongly taking from someone what belongs to him by natural law, independently of whether it also belongs to him by bourgeois law.

Another piece of exegetical evidence, that also raises serious substantive difficulties, is found in the *Marginal Notes on Wagner*, in which Marx discusses the view imputed to him by Wagner, namely that the capitalist robs the worker:

This obscurantist foists on me the view that "surplus-value, which is produced by the workers alone, remains with the capitalist entrepreneurs in a *wrongful* manner". But I say the direct opposite: namely, that at a certain point, the

---

[1] *Capital I*, p. 582.   [2] Cohen, Review of Wood: *Karl Marx*.   [3] *Ibid*.
[4] Marx to Schweitzer 24.1.1865.

production of commodities necessarily becomes "capitalistic" production of commodities, and that according to the *law of value* which rules that production, "surplus-value" is due to the capitalist and not to the worker.[1]

In my presentation, the earnings on capital are not in fact "only a deduction or 'robbery' of the worker". On the contrary, I present the capitalist as a necessary functionary of capitalist production, and show at length that he does not only "deduct" or "rob" but forces the production of surplus-value, and thus helps create what is to be deducted; further I show in detail that even if in commodity exchange *only equivalents* are exchanged, the capitalist – as soon as he pays the worker the actual value of his labour-power – earns *surplus-value* with full right, i.e. the right corresponding to this mode of production.[2]

Exegetically, the passages can be taken to support the relative as well as the absolute view of justice. The first interpretation is suggested by the last phrase, and also by the first passage as a whole. The second draws strength from the fact that Marx says that the capitalist does not *only* rob the worker, which presupposes that he *does* rob him. We can then apply Cohen's argument to infer that Marx had in mind a non-relative conception of injustice.

We should note, however, that the robbery involved differs from standard cases of theft. As usually employed, the notion of theft presupposes that the stolen object exists prior to the act of stealing it. It is because the object exists that someone might want to steal it. In capitalist exploitation it is the other way around: it is because the surplus can be appropriated and robbed that the capitalist has an incentive to create it. Had there been no capitalist, the workers would not have been robbed, but they would also have nothing that anyone could rob them of. (At least this is true under certain special conditions, further indicated below.) Hence the terminology of robbery is somewhat misleading, since it suggests that from the moral point of view such cases can be assimilated to straightforward theft. They may in the end turn out to be similar, but the question should be confronted explicitly, not obscured, as it is by this terminology.

On the basis of this discussion, I shall consider two reasons why the capitalist appropriation of surplus-value may be considered unjust – and two correlative objections to this characterization. I shall consider two polar cases; actual cases frequently have some elements of both.

First, consider the pure capitalist coupon-clipper, who hires a manager at a poor wage to exploit the workers for him. Disregarding for the time being how the capitalist came to acquire his capital, this is unjust, since the capitalist makes no contribution *in terms of work*, yet receives an

---

[1] *Marginal Notes on Wagner*, p. 382.   [2] *Ibid.*, p. 359.

income. Capitalist profit violates the principle "To each according to his contribution". This, while not the supreme principle of justice (4.3.3), is at least a principle of justice. It may be overridden, but in the present case there are no reasons for violating it. (To say that the capitalist contributes capital is relevant only if this is accumulated by "his own labour and that of his forefathers", which is the issue I prefer to postpone for a moment.) This does not mean that the working class is somehow entitled to the product because directly or indirectly its labour accounts for all that is produced. The "indirect" contribution of past workers to currently used capital is irrelevant if they are no longer alive. The "working class" is not a historical subject with a collective claim on "its" product. The issue is exclusively one of the distribution of the current product among those currently living. Of the latter, only the workers make a contribution, hence they are entitled to share the product between them.

At the other pole, consider the pure capitalist entrepreneur, who has no capital, but who exploits the workers by virtue of his organizational skill, under conditions of increasing returns to scale (4.1.3). By bringing together workers whose abilities complement one another, he makes them much more productive collectively than they could be in isolation. He "helps create what is to be deducted". Yet this does not entitle him to an income vastly greater than that of his workers. One is not morally entitled to everything one is causally responsible for creating. In particular, a broker or mediator has no claim to the entire gain that he makes possible by bringing people of complementary skills together. He should be rewarded for his job, not for theirs. Similarly, a skilled manager should be rewarded for the actual work of bringing workers together, not for the work done by those whom he assembles.

To these polar cases correspond two widespread and important objections. With respect to the first, we must face the problem whether there could not be a "clean path" to capitalist accumulation.[1] If some workers, who for the sake of argument we may assume to differ from others only in their time preferences, choose to save and invest rather than to consume, could anyone object if they induce others to work for them by offering them a wage above what they could earn elsewhere? (To simplify matters, let us assume that our self-made capitalist arises within an initially egalitarian communist economy, not within a capitalist economy in which the alternative wage would be determined in part by past and

---

[1] For statements of this problem, see Cohen, "Freedom, justice and capitalism", p. 13; Arneson, "What's wrong with exploitation?", p. 204; Roemer, "Are socialist ethics consistent with efficiency?"

current injustice.[1]) This is a variant of the "Wilt Chamberlain" argument: can anyone forbid consenting acts between capitalistic adults?[2]

This is a powerful objection, that must be taken seriously by anyone who sets out to defend Marx's theory of exploitation. Some counter-arguments are the following. First, curtailment of inheritance rights might be *somewhat* easier to defend than an interdiction against Pareto-improving wage contracts.[3] Secondly, even if it could be in the interest of individuals to accept the offer, it might be in their collective interest not to do so.[4] Hence much would turn upon people's organizational ability. At the very least the would-be capitalist is not entitled to profit if he uses his wealth to make such organization difficult – even if he does so without violating any laws.[5] Thirdly, it might not even be in the interest of the individual person to accept the offer, but he might do so because he was unaware of the consequences of taking it. Again, a sufficient condition for refusing to grant any profit to the capitalist would exist if he uses his resources to keep people ignorant about the consequences of taking his offer.[6] These, clearly, are arguments that need book-length exposition. The present remarks are intended to be no more than the sketch of a research programme.

The second case raises the *incentive problem* that is at the heart of current discussions about the viability of socialism. How could it be unjust to reward someone for a task that he would not have undertaken in the absence of the promise of a reward? Again the objection can be stated in terms of Pareto-efficiency: no one is made worse off by people reaping a reward for skills that would otherwise have lain dormant. The practical importance of this objection is undeniable. Yet as a conceptual argument against the view that appropriation of surplus-value is unjust, it fails, for the reasons given in 4.1.5. Even if there is currently no way of overcoming the incentive problem, I have yet to see any satisfactory argument that it will indefinitely remain an obstacle to efficient redistribution. Moreover, we should beware of an ideological bias in the argument. Marx believed, and I agree with him, that the exercise of skills is in most cases highly rewarding in itself. Hence the fact that the possessors of such skills can hold society to ransom and threaten to withhold them unless they are

---

[1] This is how the problem is stated by Nozick, *Anarchy, State and Utopia*, pp. 160ff and by Nove, *The Economics of Feasible Socialism*, p. 110.

[2] Nozick, *Anarchy, State and Utopia*, p. 163.

[3] Roemer, "Are socialist ethics consistent with efficiency?"

[4] Cohen, "Robert Nozick and Wilt Chamberlain".

[5] Cp. note 1, p. 223 above.   [6] *Ulysses and the Sirens*, p. 82.

highly paid should not lead us to believe that a payment is necessary to elicit their use.

Let me conclude by relating these problems to the issue of exploitation. The case of "clean capital accumulation under socialism" places us in the following dilemma. Either the discrepancy between labour expended and labour received in the form of consumption commodities should not be called exploitation, since there is nothing morally objectionable about it, or we must admit the presence of morally unobjectionable forms of exploitation. The latter option is so contrary to intuition and usage that we are almost compelled to prefer the former. In either case, it is clear that the labour discrepancy in itself does not constitute a rock-bottom moral objection to a distribution of income. (Recall that the same conclusion was reached in 4.1.2, by a different route.) The labour discrepancy can be unjust for two reasons: it may stem from an unjust distribution of endowments or it may arise in an unjust way from the distribution of income.[1] The first of these corresponds to property acquired by illegitimate means, for example forcible primitive accumulation. The second corresponds to cases where justly acquired wealth is unjustly used to trap people into selling their labour-power, for example by preventing them from organizing themselves or by keeping relevant information from them. More controversially, we might include cases where people are unorganized and uninformed for no fault of their own – *nor of anyone else.*

The incentive problem is difficult to treat within the exploitation framework, since it presupposes that the entrepreneur has some non-producible managerial skills by virtue of which he earns more than the workers. As observed in 4.1.5, this allows us to compare his income with theirs, and to characterize the difference as unjust. It does not, however, allow us to compare the labour equivalent of his income with the labour he performs and characterize the discrepancy as exploitative, since there is no common standard that we can use for a comparison. I should repeat that a basic premise in the argument that the income difference is unjust is that skilled work is rewarding in itself, or at least does not have any greater disutility than other work. If this fails to hold, it may indeed be just to pay the skilled manager for the (to him) unpleasant task of putting his rare skills at the service of society.

To summarize, there are three basic reasons why exploitation cannot be a fundamental notion in moral theory. They are all related to the fact that

---

[1] These correspond to Nozick's "justice in acquisition" and "justice in transfer". To accept his way of stating the problem is not, of course, to accept his specific account of what acquisitions and transfers *are* just.

people differ. They differ in their inborn skills, hence the labour theory of exploitation does not even clear the first, definitional hurdle. They differ in their leisure–income preferences, hence the theory can in certain cases support the counterintuitive conclusion that the poor exploit the rich.[1] And finally individuals differ in their time preferences, which may lead some of them to accumulate wealth and hire others to work for them to the benefit of all parties. Exploitation can be a useful concept in broad historical overviews where these difficulties can be neglected, but it is an ill-suited tool for a more fine-grained investigation into moral theory.

4.3.3. Contribution and need
In the *Critique of the Gotha Programme* Marx makes a distinction between the principles of distribution that will obtain under the first and the final stages of communism. The first principle can be stated as follows: to each proportionally to his labour contribution, after funds are set aside for investment, public goods, funds for those unable to work etc. The second principle is stated in the culminating part of this famous statement:

In a higher phase of communist society, after the enslaving subordination of the individual to the division of labour, and therewith also the antithesis between mental and physical labour, has vanished; after labour has become not only a means to life, but life's prime want; after the productive forces have also increased with the all-round development of the individual, and all the springs of cooperative wealth flow more abundantly – only then can the narrow horizon of bourgeois right be crossed in its entirety, and society inscribe on its banners: from each according to his ability, to each according to his needs.[2]

As stated by Marx (see the passage cited in 4.3.1) the contribution principle requires that skilled and unskilled labour have been reduced to a common measure that takes account of this difference, so that the man who is "superior to another physically or mentally and so supplies more labour in the same time, or can labour for a longer time" is correspondingly better paid. I need not belabour the problems involved in this statement. I shall simply assume that the reduction has been accomplished, and that a similar operation can be carried out for capitalism.

The contribution principle then appears as a Janus-like notion. Looked at from one side, it serves as a criterion of justice that condemns capitalist exploitation as unjust. Looked at from the vantage point of fully

---

[1] Roemer, "Should Marxists be interested in exploitation?" Strictly speaking, it is not necessary for people to be different for this paradox to be possible. As observed in 4.1.2, it suffices that people have identical, perverse supply curves for labour as a function of wealth.

[2] *Critique of the Gotha Program*, p. 21.

developed communism, it is itself condemned as inadequate by the higher standard expressed in the needs principle. An able-bodied capitalist who receives an income without working represents an unjustified violation of the contribution principle – a violation, that is, which is not justified by the needs principle. By contrast, an invalid who receives welfare aid without contributing anything in return represents a violation of the contribution principle that *is* justified by the needs principle. Hence Marx had *a hierarchical theory of justice*, by which the contribution principle provides a second-best criterion when the needs principle is not yet historically ripe for application.[1] Capitalist exploitation is doubly unjust, since it obeys neither principle. The "equal right" of the first stage of communism, is also unjust, but less so, since only the needs principle is violated.

I believe this interpretation makes sense both of Marx's critique of capitalism and the theory of the two stages of communism. Needless to say, it is an analytical reconstruction that bears only an indirect relation to the texts. *No* interpretation of Marx's various remarks on justice and rights can make them all consistent with one another, but I believe that the one presently proposed is compatible with most of the central texts. The theory that we can impute to Marx on this interpretation is not a compellingly plausible one. If we assume that the needs principle embodies some form of egalitarianism (see below), the contribution principle is presented as a second-best substitute for equality. I believe that Rawls' difference principle would serve better as such a substitute. The spirit underlying this principle is that we should seek as much equality as possible, up to the point where the pursuit of more becomes pointless, by making the worst off even worse off. Here the first-best ideal of equality does in itself guide the search for a second-best way of approximating it. We do not know the range of inequalities compatible with the contribution principle, since we do not know how the different forms of skill can be reduced to a common standard. It is clear, however, that the contribution principle is in no way designed with the minimization of inequality in mind. It ensures that no one will earn an income without working, but does nothing to narrow down the range of incomes accruing to those who do in fact work.

Consider finally the needs principle itself. Given the brevity of Marx's discussion in the *Critique of the Gotha Programme*, the principle lends itself to several interpretations. First, the reference to abundance has been

---

[1] For a similar argument, see Roemer, *A General Theory*, pp. 265ff.

taken to imply that Marx believed the "circumstances of justice" would no longer obtain under communism.[1] Following Hume, these circumstances include moderate scarcity and limited sympathy between men: "'tis only from the selfishness and confin'd generosity of man, along with the scanty provision nature has made for his wants, that justice derives its origin".[2] Of these two conditions, scarcity of resources is really the important one. Even were men perfectly public-spirited, there would still have to be principles of distribution to regulate the use of scarce resources.[3]

Abundance, in the sense of suppression of scarcity, means that all goods under communism would be free goods, that is that demand for all goods would be saturated. When everyone had taken what he wanted from the common consumption stock, there would be something of each good left over. This state of affairs could be approximated by two kinds of development: increased productivity and reduced wants. Of these, Marx certainly affirms the former (5.2.3). It might appear as if he is also asserting the diminution of wants under communism, in the references to the "unnatural needs" that exist under capitalism (2.2.3). Also, when work becomes "life's prime want", the need for consumption goods, for the production of which scarce resources are needed, will presumably become smaller. On the other hand we should set Marx's reference to the "rich individuality which is as all-sided in its production as in its consumption"[4] and many similar utterances in the *Grundrisse*. Moreover, there is the problem, further discussed below, that self-actualization through work may also require scarce resources as a material condition. Considering Marx's work as a whole, there is no doubt that he could not rest any hope for abundance on a limitation of human wants. He may have believed that the flowering of the productive forces under communism would create abundance in an absolute sense. In that case there is nothing more to say, except to write this part of his theory off as hopelessly Utopian.[5] I am not quite prepared, however, to do this. The texts are sufficiently vague to allow us to explore other possibilities.

Marx's comments on the "defects" of the contribution principle (4.3.1) point to an interpretation of the needs principle in terms of equality. When he states as a defect of the contribution principle that it will lead to a

---

[1] Buchanan, *Marx and Justice*, p. 57; Lukes, *Marxism and Morality*, ch. 3.
[2] Hume, *A Treatise on Human Nature*, p. 495.
[3] Nove, *The Economics of Feasible Socialism*, p. 17.
[4] *Grundrisse*, p. 325; see also pp. 409, 711.
[5] Nove, *The Economics of Feasible Socialism*, pp. 15ff. An economic analysis of abundance that well brings out the absurdity of the concept is in Tartarin, "Gratuité, fin du salariat et calcul économique dans le communisme".

worker with many children receiving the same income as a worker with few, it is presumably because it will lead to between-family inequality in per capita income or welfare. The defect may be eliminated by creating a system where inequality ceases to matter, because no one would want to have more of anything than they have: this is the Utopian interpretation. Or it might be got rid of by a principle of equal distribution. Equality of what? In the light of Marx's theory of the good life for man (2.2.7), the most plausible suggestion is that the needs principle should ensure *equality of self-realization*. If the highest value is the self-realization of men, rather than of Man as a species-being, it should be realized for each and every individual to the highest extent compatible with its realization to the same extent for everyone else.

Ronald Dworkin has shown that the problem of *expensive needs* makes this ideal a rather unattractive one.[1] Some ways of self-actualization are inherently more expensive than others. To write poems requires little by way of material resources, to direct epic films a great deal more. If free rein was given to the development of the need for self-actualization, with a guarantee that it would be fulfilled to an extent compatible with the same level of self-actualization for all, expensive preferences might emerge in a quantity that would make it only possible to satisfy them very partially. Everyone might be allowed to direct ten seconds of an epic movie, as in Andy Warhol's image of the future society. This anarchy of preferences would recreate the Prisoner's Dilemma that exists in the first stage of communism, but in a more subtle form. In the first stage the dilemma leads to an incentive problem. If there is no correlation between individual effort and individual reward, selfishly motivated individuals – "economically, morally and intellectually still stamped with the birth marks of the old society" – will try to shirk and get their share of the social product created by the effort of others. Any given person is but marginally hurt by his own shirking, while the gain in leisure is highly valued. In the higher stage this problem no longer will exist, because the desire to create for the community will be paramount in individual motivation (2.2.7). Yet this desire on the part of individuals might turn out to be collectively self-defeating. Any given individual will be but marginally hurt by the constraints his use of scarce resources creates for the self-actualization of others, while the gain to himself is highly valued.

In 2.2.7 I argued that there was a tension between the values of creativity and community, in that a society of highly creative individuals

[1] Dworkin, "What is equality?", part 1.

might not be very interested in one another's creations. The argument of the preceding paragraph adds an additional source of conflict between the two ideals. Creation for the sake of the community might be to the detriment of the community, if the self-realization of the individual becomes prohibitively expensive. As explained in 2.4, Marx believed that communism would realize a synthesis of the community found in pre-class or pre-capitalist society and the unbridled individualism developed by capitalism. Perhaps, instead of a synthesis, he would have done better looking for a viable compromise between these values.

Let me recall another difficulty stated in 2.2.7. Even if society were able to provide everyone with what they need to realize themselves, they might be frustrated when they discover that they are not very good at it. It would be facile and Panglossian to suggest that the frustration due to lack of resources has the useful consequence of preventing people from experiencing a more profound frustration due to lack of talent. The persons who are blocked by the first constraint are not necessarily the same as those who would in any case be blocked by the second. Yet ignorance about which constraint is really the binding one may be a condition for self-respect in many cases. In other cases the constraint due to lack of resources may lead to waste of human talent. Nothing can be said a priori about the net effect of these two opposed tendencies, and given the unavoidable scarcity of resources there may be little point in speculating about what would happen were they to become available in abundance. Could it, however, be an important consequence of human finitude that our failures would be unendurable if we had only ourselves to blame for them?

Part II
Theory of history

Part I has been concerned mainly with Marx's economic theory of capitalism – its physiology (chap. 3) and pathology (chaps. 2 and 4). This was
indeed one of his two main theoretical concerns, the other being the
broader theory of history which is the object of Part II. This change of
focus involves a twofold extension of our perspective – from capitalism to
the full range of historical phenomena, and from the economic domain to
the full range of social phenomena. In chapter 5 I discuss the first extension: Marx's theory of economic history. The following chapters consider
the second extension: his theory of class struggle, politics and ideology in
capitalism.

As a general theory, historical materialism was clearly intended to
cover both of these extensions simultaneously. If we go to the 1859 Preface to the *Critique of Political Economy*, generally and rightly considered
the most authoritative compact presentation of the theory, we find statements about the relation between the economic basis and the politico-
ideological superstructure that claim unrestricted application to all historical modes of production. But this declaration of intention was never
carried out in detailed historical research. Marx wrote virtually nothing
about non-economic phenomena in pre-capitalist societies, the main
exception being some remarks about the class struggle in the ancient
world and the role of the state in the Asiatic mode of production. By
contrast, his works contain numerous, though scattered, remarks on
pre-capitalist economic systems and they also include a large body of
writings on the non-economic features of capitalism.

Lukacs and, following him, Finley have argued that pre-capitalist societies differed from capitalism with respect to the relation between
economic and non-economic domains.[1] And one might conjecture that
Marx's silence about the superstructural phenomena of earlier societies
reflected his recognition that they did not really conform to the general
theory. This conjecture would be wrong, as the following passage from
Capital I shows:

[1] Lukacs, "Funktionswechsel des historischen Materialismus"; Finley, *The Ancient Economy*, p. 50.

I seize this opportunity of shortly answering an objection taken by a German paper in America, to my work "Zur Kritik der pol. Ökonomie, 1859". In the estimation of that paper, my view that each special mode of production and the social relations corresponding to it, in short, that the economic structure of society, is the real basis on which the juridical and political superstructure is raised, and to which definite social forms of thought correspond; that the mode of production determines the character of the social, political, and intellectual life generally, all this is very true for our own times, in which material interests preponderate, but not for the middle ages, in which Catholicism, nor for Athens and Rome, where politics, reigned supreme. In the first place it strikes one as an odd thing for any one to suppose that these well-worn phrases about the middle ages and the ancient world are unknown to anyone else. This much, however, is clear, that the middle ages could not live on Catholicism, nor the ancient world on politics. On the contrary, it is the mode in which they gained a livelihood that explains why here politics, and there Catholicism, played the chief part.[1]

The last phrase suggests a notion of "derived autonomy", of which much has been made.[2] In 7.1 I discuss a related idea in Marx's theory of the capitalist state and argue that it does not make much sense.[3] Here I cite the passage as evidence that in 1867 Marx retained his belief in the general character of his theory of the superstructure. Whatever prevented him from applying it to pre-capitalist societies, it was not any doubt about its applicability.

The chapters in Part II fall into a pattern which may be described as one of successive overlapping. Chapters 5 and 6 are both concerned with the "fundamental motive force in history". In Marxism, bewilderingly, two candidates vie for this status; their relation to one another is a major unresolved problem. On the one hand, all history is the history of the relation between productive forces and relations of production. The relations of production that distinguish modes of production from one another rise and fall according to their tendency to promote or hinder the growth of the productive forces. This is the central message of the 1859 Preface, already stated in all essentials in *The German Ideology*. On the other hand, "The history of all hitherto existing society is the history of class struggles."[4] The problem is not that classes go unmentioned in the 1859 Preface. This omission may have a simple explanation in Marx's anticipation of Prussian censorship.[5] The difficulty is that Marx never

[1] *Capital I*, p. 82 note.
[2] See notably Balibar, "Les concepts fondamentaux du matérialisme historique".
[3] If the argument here is to be understood in light of the penultimate sentence of the passage, it is in any case a piece of vulgar Marxism, not unlike Brecht's "Erst kommt das Fressen, dann kommt die Moral."
[4] *The Communist Manifesto*, p. 482.
[5] Printz, "Background and ulterior motives of Marx's 'Preface' of 1859".

indicates how the class struggle is instrumental in mediating between the "need" for new relations of production and their actual establishment. Given his general predilection for functional explanation, supported by his speculative philosophy of history, he may not have thought this an important problem, but it is one that has rightly worried his successors.

A central topic in both chapter 6 and chapter 7 is the social and political struggle between the main classes in the main European countries around 1850. Marx commented extensively on these events, in his journalistic writings and in *The Eighteenth Brumaire of Louis Bonaparte*. In chapter 6 his views are discussed in the context of a more general analysis of class and class consciousness, while in chapter 7 they are related to the problem of state autonomy. I argue in these chapters that Marx's outstanding achievement was the development of a valuable theory of *class coalitions*. I also claim that he overestimated the centrality of class – both with respect to other springs of collective action and with respect to the power of the state apparatus.

Finally, chapters 7 and 8 also overlap in their concerns. Just as a major problem in 7.1 is how to understand and delimit the autonomy of politics with respect to economics and the class struggle, the issue of the autonomy of thought is raised in 8.1. In my struggle with Marx's writings on ideologies, I have been constantly exasperated by their elusive, rhetorical character. In order to pin them down, I have insisted on the methodological individualism set out in 1.1, with results that may appear incongruous to some readers. Yet I fail to see any satisfactory alternative. A frictionless search for the "function" of ideologies or the "structural homologies" between thought and reality has brought this part of Marxism into deserved disrepute. To rescue it – and I strongly believe there is something here to be rescued – a dose of relentless positivism seems to be called for.

5. Modes of production

Marx's theory of the rise and fall of modes of production, as set forth in the 1859 Preface and elsewhere, explains the relations of production in society in terms of their tendency to maximize the *rate of growth of the productive forces*. New relations arise when and because the existing ones are no longer optimal for this development. It may be useful to state at the very outset two alternative approaches, each of which substitutes another maximand for the one proposed by Marx. First, it has been argued that the property rights system can be explained by its tendency to maximize *the net social product at any given moment*.[1] This theory differs from Marx's because it emphasizes the optimal use of the productive forces, not their optimal development. True, we shall see that Marx also considered this static criterion; but I believe his main commitment was to the dynamic one. Secondly, many authors have argued that the property rights system can be explained by its tendency to maximize *the surplus that accrues to the ruling class or dominant group in society*.[2] This would appear consistent with Marx's emphasis on the class struggle as the basic force in history. On the

---

[1] See, for instance, Posner, *Economic Analysis of Law*. A useful criticism of the implicit functionalism of this approach is Field, "The problem with neoclassical institutional economics".

[2] For different versions of this approach see North, *Structure and Change in Economic History* and Marglin, "What do bosses do?".

other hand, it does not support his view that the productive forces tend to progress throughout history.

It cannot be assumed without argument that these three objectives tend to be maximized simultaneously; on the contrary, there are good reasons why, under certain conditions, they tend to diverge from one another. A conflict between optimal development and optimal use underlies the paradox of the patent system, to which reference has been made several times in earlier chapters. Current output would be maximized if technical knowledge were freely available, but this unrestricted availability would reduce the incentives for the production of new knowledge. A conflict between maximizing net output and maximizing surplus occurs when the property rights that are optimal for the former also make the surplus extraction difficult or costly. Thus "forms of organization that have low measurement costs to the rulers for tax collecting will persist even though they are relatively inefficient (monopoly grants in Colbert's France, for example)".[1]

In 5.1 I first set out the general theory from the 1859 Preface, interpreted in the light of various other writings. Here I rely heavily on G. A. Cohen's path-breaking work, although I shall also have occasion to disagree with some of its conclusions. In particular, I do not believe the conflict between Marx's general theory and his account of the dynamics of pre-capitalist societies is resolvable in the way Cohen proposes (or in any other manner). In 5.2 I compare more systematically Marx's general theory with his account of the various historical modes of production. I argue that in his explanation of the transition from feudalism to capitalism Marx relies on the notion of surplus-maximization, while in his predictions about the transition from capitalism to communism he emphasizes output-maximization. In neither case does the maximization of the rate of growth of the productive forces play any major explanatory role. I try, nevertheless, to reconstruct an argument for the idea that communism will come about when and because capitalist relations of production cease being optimal for the development of the productive forces. It turns out to be difficult to make a plausible case for this idea. In 5.3 I finally consider Marx's periodization of history, and its relation to the speculative philosophy of history discussed in 2.4. I argue that Marx also proposed, in addition to the well-known sequence of modes of production, a periodization in terms of the *goals* of production that are dominant in various epochs: production for use, for exchange or for profits.

[1] North, *Structure and Change in Economic History*, p. 43.

5.1. The general theory of modes of production

The authoritative text from the 1859 Preface to a *Critique of Political Economy* contains the following statements:

In the social production of their life, men enter into definite relations that are indispensable and independent of their will, relations of production that correspond to a definite stage of development of their productive forces … At a certain stage of their development, the material productive forces of society enter into contradiction with the existing relations of production, or – what is but a legal expression for the same thing – with the property relations within which they have been at work hitherto. From forms of development of the productive forces these relations turn into their fetters. Then begins an epoch of social revolution. … No social formation ever perishes before all the productive forces for which there is room in it have developed; and new, higher relations of production never appear before the material conditions for their existence have matured in the womb of the old society itself.[1]

The present section is devoted to the main ideas expressed in this text. In 5.1.1 and 5.1.2 I discuss the notions of productive forces and relations of production which form the basic building blocks of the theory. In 5.1.3 I consider various ways of understanding the "correspondence" and "contradiction" between the productive forces and the relations of production. In 5.1.4 I discuss the sense in which the productive forces may have "primacy" over the relations of production.

5.1.1. The productive forces

In G. A. Cohen's exposition, the forces of production are circumscribed intensionally, extensionally and theoretically. Intensionally, "to qualify as a productive force, a facility must be capable of use by a producing agent in such a way that production occurs (partly) as a result of its use, and it is someone's purpose that the facility so contributes to production".[2] Extensionally, they include means of production (notably instruments of production and raw materials) and labour-power with its various attributes such as skill, strength or knowledge. Theoretically, the notion of productive forces is constrained by the more general theory in which it is embedded, The productive forces must be (i) ownable, even if not necessarily owned; (ii) developing throughout history, in the sense (broadly speaking) of reducing the labour content of the goods produced; (iii) capable of explaining the form of the relations of production and (iv) capable of being fettered by these relations.[3] I shall refer to these as the constraints of ownability, development, explanation and fettering.

---

[1] *Critique of Political Economy*, pp. 8–9.   [2] Cohen, *Karl Marx's Theory of History*, p. 32.
[3] *Ibid.*, p. 41. For the ownability constraint, see also p. 43.

Cohen's approach is characteristically lucid. It enables the construction of a coherent theoretical system that bears some relation to what Marx wrote. Yet I shall argue that Marx was less lucid and coherent and also more concerned with the complex historical development. I shall explain and exemplify by considering some recalcitrant cases: social relations, science and population. I then conclude with a discussion of an ambiguity in the notion of the *development* of the productive forces.

Marx sometimes appears to use the term "productive force" and its equivalents[1] in a more general sense: anything that is causally efficacious in enhancing the productivity of the workers or the size of total output counts as a productive force. In the *Grundrisse*, for instance, he refers to the increase in the productive forces that "results from science, inventions, division and combination of labour, improved means of communication, creation of the world market, machinery etc.".[2] Here what *constitutes* an increase in the productive forces (narrowly conceived), such as an invention, is put on a par with what *causes* such increase, for example the development of the world market. One could then understand Marx as saying that the latter in itself is an increase in the productive forces and, more generally, that the social relations of production *are* productive forces to the extent that they promote the (optimal?) development of the productive forces. Similarly, in *The German Ideology* Marx argues that "machinery and money" under certain conditions may turn into "destructive forces", suggesting that otherwise they would both be productive forces.[3] Even more generally, one might argue that such superstructural practices as religion should be included among the productive forces, to the extent that they increase the productivity of labour.

As Cohen observes, this broader understanding of the notion makes no sense.[4] Even if Marx sometimes expresses himself in a way that might point in this direction, the theoretical constraints on the notion exclude it. In particular, social relations of production cannot be explained by the productive forces if they are themselves such forces. The explanatory link presupposes the conceptual distinction, as noted by Marx himself when referring to the "*Dialectic of the concepts productive force (means of production) and relations of production, a dialectic whose boundaries are to be*

---

[1] *The German Ideology* on one occasion (p. 35) clearly uses the term "Produktionsverhältnisse" in the sense of productive forces. More generally, this work uses the composite expressions "Produktions- und Verkehrsverhältnisse" (pp. 176, 209, 416), "Produktions- und Verkehrsweise" (pp. 88, 159, 247, 367) and "Produktions- und Verkehrsbedingungen" (pp. 85, 418) in a way that suggests that he intends to refer to what in the later terminology became "forces and relations of production".

[2] *Grundrisse*, p. 308.   [3] *The German Ideology*, p. 52.

[4] Cohen, *Karl Marx's Theory of History*, pp. 32ff.

determined, and which does not suspend the real difference."[1] In one context, however, Cohen makes a remark that – if suitably generalized – allows for the insertion of a *cognitive equivalent* of these wider phenomena among the productive forces. Following Marx,[2] he makes a distinction between a purely technical division of labour and a specifically capitalist form. In his terminology, the former belong to the material work relations, the latter to the social relations of production.[3] Being relations, they cannot be used or owned, and hence do not qualify as productive forces. Yet, to accommodate our intuition that material work relations may enhance the productivity of labour, he adds the following comment:

We agree that *something* in this conceptual area is a productive force, but not the work relations themselves. On our account, knowledge of ways of organizing labour is a productive force, part of managerial labour power, but the relations established when that knowledge is implemented are not productive forces. It is necessary to distinguish the blueprint for the set of relations from the relations themselves, and it is the first which is a productive force.[4]

Although Cohen does not make a similar comment on the specifically capitalist division of labour, one might ask whether the same cognitive analogy could not apply here. Consider a passage from *Capital I*:

Although then, technically speaking, the old system of division of labour is thrown overboard with machinery, it hangs on in the factory, as a traditional habit handed down from Manufacture, and is afterwards systematically re-moulded and established in a more hideous form by capital, as a means of exploiting labour-power. The life-long speciality of handling one and the same tool, now becomes the life-long specialty of serving one and the same machine. Machinery is put to the wrong use, with the object of transforming the workman, from his very childhood, into a part of a detail-machine. In this way, not only are the expenses of his reproduction considerably lessened, but at the same time his helpless dependence on the factory as a whole, and therefore upon the capitalist, is rendered complete. Here as everywhere else, we must distinguish between the increased productiveness due to the development of the social process of production, and that due to the capitalist exploitation of that process.[5]

The passage is ambiguous, and interestingly so. Up to the final sentence, the only natural reading is to understand it as asserting that the specifically capitalist organization of production was motivated by profit, not by efficiency or productivity. More precisely, it suggests that the capitalists deliberately opted for technically inferior methods in order to

---

[1] *Grundrisse*, p. 109.
[2] *Capital I*, p. 420; cp. also p. 419 for an analysis of how the specifically capitalist division of labour is superimposed upon the technical division of labour required by "every possible employment of machinery on a large scale".
[3] Cohen, *Karl Marx's Theory of History*, ch. IV.   [4] *Ibid.*, p. 113.   [5] *Capital I*, p. 422.

subdue the worker, paralleling an argument set out in 3.2.2. It then comes as a surprise when Marx concludes by saying that the capitalist organization also increased productivity. I shall return to the first reading in 5.2.2. Here I want to focus on the second reading, suggested by the final sentence, and ask whether the entrepreneurial knowledge that the capitalist division of labour is more productive does not count as a productive force – analogously to knowledge about material work relations that enhance productivity. Should not Taylorism count as a productive force? And if this is accepted, what blocks the generalization to managerial knowledge about the efficacy of religion in making the workers work harder than they would otherwise have done (as distinct from its possible role in restraining their wage claims)? Since knowledge about social relations is in itself neither social nor a relation, why could it not enter into the productive forces?

I feel confident that Marx would have resisted this conclusion. Yet it is not clear where in the following chain the cut-off point should be made: machinery – technical division of labour – capitalist division of labour – Taylorism – Human Relations – morning prayers in the factory – Sunday school for factory children – Sunday church services for factory workers. The most natural solution seems to be by adding a theoretical constraint: the productive forces should be *neutral* with respect to the relations of production. By this I mean that the productive forces should be defined so that, when the relations of production change, there is no *immediate* change in the productive forces employed. Changes may occur later on, as new and superior productive forces develop, but in the immediate aftermath technical rationality dictates that the existing productive forces should be retained. While not without problems,[1] this proposal seems faithful to one central idea in Marx's thinking – that the development of the productive forces reflects the progressive mastery of nature by man, not the more efficient exploitation of man by man.

Now consider *science*, uncontroversially a productive force according to Marx.[2] One may ask whether science, being a mental creation, can be a *material* productive force. To this two answers may be given, and it does

---

[1] An exegetical difficulty is that, in the "Commentary on List" (p. 285), Marx refers to productive forces in a very broad sense: "If the monotony of an occupation makes you better suited for that occupation, then monotony is a productive force." A substantive problem is created by producers' preferences (3.2.2): a technique that is optimal in terms of efficiency may not be so in terms of welfare. Finally there is a theoretical difficulty in adopting a neutral definition of the productive forces, since non-neutral methods of organization may enter into the explanation of the relations of production.

[2] See especially *Grundrisse*, pp. 690ff and *Zur Kritik (1861–63)*, pp. 2060ff.

not matter much which we choose. Either, following Marx, we can say that some productive forces are "spiritual", others "material".[1] Or, following Cohen, that the antonym to "material" is "social" rather than "mental", so that a productive force can be spiritual and material at the same time.[2] Nothing important turns upon this question. Note, however, that the science of social relations would *not*, according to the argument of the preceding paragraph, be a productive force.

Another difficulty is more serious. A productive force, according to Cohen, must be ownable, but scientific knowledge often resists being legally possessed. A person can have a *de facto* monopoly on some specific knowledge simply by keeping it to himself, but an attempt to claim legal possession will often be self-defeating. To claim a legal monopoly in information requires making it public and hence often available to others free of cost. Information has the peculiar feature "that its value for the purchaser is not known until he has the information, but then he has in effect acquired it free of cost".[3] The patent system overcomes this problem in some, but far from all, cases. Basic knowledge in mathematics and the natural sciences in many, perhaps most, cases cannot be patented. Such non-patentable knowledge satisfies the development constraint, but not the ownability constraint. It may satisfy the fettering constraint, if scientists are wholly or partly motivated by the profit they can make from their discoveries, as suggested by Marx in the 1861–3 *Critique:*

Inasmuch as these sciences serve as a means for the enrichment of capital and thereby as a means of enriching their practitioners, the men of science compete with each other to discover *practical applications* of their science.[4]

Yet typically Marx does not emphasize this motivation. His general attitude is better summed up when he says that "capital does not create science, but exploits it".[5] There occurs a growth in non-patentable knowledge on which capital can draw, without being instrumental in creating it. Hence it is also doubtful whether science can satisfy the explanatory constraint. It is inherently implausible to suggest that the private ownership of the means of production can be explained by its impact on the development of non-ownable productive forces. True, Marx emphasizes that the historical task of capitalism is to create *free time* in which a minority can devote themselves to artistic and scientific activities that will lay the foundations for the society of the future (2.4.2), but he no-

---

[1] *Grundrisse*, pp. 223, 502.   [2] Cohen, *Karl Marx's Theory of History*, p. 47.
[3] Arrow, *Essays in the Theory of Risk-Bearing*, p. 152.
[4] *Zur Kritik (1861–63)*, p. 2062.   [5] *Ibid.*, p. 2060; cp. also *Capital I*, p. 386 note.

where explains why the capitalist relations of production should have this result, nor how they could be explained by having this consequence. Moreover, the development of science is in the *collective* interest of the capitalist class, not in the interest of each individual entrepreneur. Hence it is hard to see how it could enter into an explanation of *private* ownership of the means of production. The collective interests of the capitalist class are mainly promoted by political means, but a reference to political institutions would be out of place in an explanation of the relations of production, since these in turn are invoked to explain why the political system takes the form it does.

To complete – and complicate – the picture, I should add that Cohen's notion of ownability is only legal shorthand for the more fundamental relation of effective control. On his view, legal ownership relations stabilize pre-juridical relations of effective control.[1] For some comments on this view, see 7.1.1 below. Here I want to point out that if the ownability constraint is replaced by a constraint of effective controllability, even non-patentable knowledge might satisfy it.[2] On the other hand, the legal stamp would not stabilize this pre-juridical control, but destroy it by making the information publicly available. Hence Cohen is faced with a dilemma. If he insists on the legal ownability of the productive forces, he must accept that basic science is not part of the productive forces, contrary to a view strongly held by Marx. If instead he insists on the effective controllability of the productive forces, he must accept that some forms of effective control cannot be stabilized by the stamp of the law, contrary to his own theory.[3]

The conceptual status of social relations and of science, therefore, is somewhat ambiguous. They satisfy some of the theoretical constraints on the productive forces, but not others. This is not to say that they constitute fundamental difficulties in Marx's project. Rather, they represent substantive, medium-sized problems of the kind that will arise in any comprehensive theory of social change. A deeper flaw in the theory arises in Marx's treatment of *population*. In accordance with the mercantilist

---

[1] Cohen, *Karl Marx's Theory of History*, ch. VIII.

[2] Yet even in that case a question would remain whether the knowledge could both be controlled *and* used, since it is often possible to reconstruct from the final product the knowledge that has gone into its construction.

[3] True, Cohen's stated view is only that for every right there exists a matching power. This is disproved by patentable knowledge, if the conditions cited in the preceding note obtain. Non-patentable knowledge disproves the converse claim, that for every power there exists a right which it matches. Although Cohen does not explicitly make this claim, it is implicit in his account and in the theory he is interpreting.

tradition,[1] but contrary to his own general theory, he tended to include population among the productive forces. In doing so he confused the extensive and the intensive forms of economic growth, that is growth of the total product and growth of product per capita.

Consider first a passage from the 1861–3 *Critique* in which population is included among the many productive forces that the capitalist can acquire free of cost:

One form of machinery which costs the capitalist nothing is the division of labour and the combination of labour within the production process. What he pays for is the labour power of the individual workers, not their combination and not the social power of labour. A further productive force that costs him nothing is scientific power. Population growth is another such force of production which comes to him gratis. But it is only through the ownership of capital – above all in the form of machinery – that he is able to appropriate these free forces of production. The same holds good for the latent wealth of nature, the forces of nature as well as every other social labour power arising from the growth of the population and the historical development of society.[2]

The last sentence suggests that when classifying the population as a productive force, Marx simply meant that the growth of the total mass of workers also tends to enhance the productivity per worker. If so, he was only guilty of a momentary confusion between what constitutes a growth in the productive forces and what causes such growth. Population growth, on this reading, would not *be* a development of the productive forces, but it would – given capitalist conditions – lead to such development by permitting an increased division of labour. Elsewhere in the same manuscript Marx does in fact assert this explicitly: "with the growth of the population, the [workers'] skill increases, division of labour grows, the possibility [for using] machinery grows, constant capital grows, in short, the productivity of labour grows".[3]

According to Marx, it is only under capitalist conditions that population increase leads to a growth in the productivity of labour. Under pre-capitalist conditions there is a negative rather than a positive correlation between population size and product per capita:

---

[1] Within the mercantilist and neo-mercantilist tradition, population was considered a most important productive force of the nation, as succinctly stated by Leibniz: "Kräfte sind Fruchtbarkeit, Volk und Geld" (cited after Sombart, *Der moderne Kapitalismus*, vol. II, p. 934). Here Leibniz confuses not only productive forces in the intensive sense (fertility) and in the extensive sense (population), but also productive forces in the narrow sense (what is used in production) and productive forces in the broad sense (what has the effect of increasing production). Marx never liberated himself fully from either fallacy.
[2] *Zur Kritik (1861–63)*, p. 2047.   [3] *Theories of Surplus-Value*, vol. 3, p. 244; cp. p. 259.

In the ancient states of Greece and Rome, compulsory emigration, assuming the shape of the periodical establishment of colonies, formed a regular link in the structure of society. The whole system of those states was founded in certain limits to the numbers of the population, which could not be surpassed without endangering the condition of antique civilization itself. But why was it so? Because the application of science to material production was utterly unknown to them. To remain civilized, they were forced to remain few. Otherwise they would have had to submit to the bodily drudgery which transformed the free citizen into a slave. The want of productive power made citizenship dependent on a certain proportion in numbers not to be disturbed. Forced emigration was the only remedy. It was the same pressure of population on the powers of production that drove the barbarians from the high plains of Asia to invade the Old World. The same cause acted here, although under a different form. To remain barbarians, they were forced to remain few. They were pastoral, hunting, war-waging tribes, whose manner of production required a large space for every individual, as is now the case with the Indian tribes in North America. By augmenting in numbers, they curtailed each other's field of production.[1]

This fits in with the view that population growth *under certain conditions* causes an increase in the productive forces, but does not in itself constitute such an increase. According to Marx these conditions were limited to capitalist production. In this he may have been wrong,[2] but this is irrelevant for the exegetical issue now under consideration.

The outcome of the foregoing exegetical discussion is that no compelling grounds exist for attributing to Marx the view that population is a productive force. Yet the problem of the dissolution of the ancient world forces us to reconsider that conclusion. Marx did not believe that any technical change occurred in pre-capitalist societies (5.2.1). Hence it is hard to see how these societies could break down as the result of a development of the productive forces, if this is taken in the intensive sense of increased productivity per worker. On the other hand Marx does assert that they broke down because of an increase in population, and in doing so he comes very close to saying that population is a productive force:

The survival of the commune in the old mode requires the reproduction of its members in the presupposed objective conditions. Production itself, the advance of population (this too belongs with production) necessarily suspends these conditions little by little; destroys them instead of reproducing them etc., and, with that, the communal system declines and falls, together with the property relations on which it was based.[3]

[1] *New York Daily Tribune* 22.3.1853.
[2] See Boserup, *Population and Technological Change* for an argument that population growth was the main cause of technical change in pre-capitalist societies.
[3] *Grundrisse*, p. 486.

Since in all [pre-capitalist] forms of production the development of the productive forces is not the basis of appropriation, but a specific relation to the conditions of production (forms of property) appears as *presupposed barrier* to the productive forces, and is merely to be reproduced, it follows that the development of the population, in which the development of all productive forces is summarized, must even more strongly encounter an *external barrier* and thus appear as something to be restricted. The conditions of the community [were] consistent only with a specific amount of population. . . . Overpopulation and population, taken together, are *the* population which a specific production basis can create. The extent to which it goes beyond the barrier is given by the barrier itself, or rather by the same base which posits the barrier.[1]

I believe that Marx in these texts from the *Grundrisse* was led to include the population among the productive forces because (i) it fitted the theoretical constraint that the explanation of social change should be found in the development of the productive forces and (ii) it could – consistently with the mercantilist tradition – be seen as a main source of wealth. He must have overlooked that population growth and technical change cannot enter into the explanation of social change in the same way, and that an increase of population need not go together with an increase in per capita production.

Admittedly, this is a somewhat speculative reconstruction. Ideally, one would want to find in Marx both a general theory of social change and a consistent application of it to pre-capitalist societies as well as to capitalism. My interpretation is motivated by the idea that it is more charitable to attribute to Marx a confused attempt to apply the general theory, than to say that he did not even try. The ambiguous understanding of the development of the productive forces – as an extensive process of population growth or an intensive process of productivity growth per capita – enabled him to bridge, however inconsistently, the gap between the general theory and his investigation of pre-capitalist societies.

The problem of population growth enables us to detect another ambiguity in the notion of the development of the productive forces, considered now as a purely intensive process. Imagine the following scenario. At an initial stage there is sparse population, engaged in slash-and-burn agriculture with fairly high productivity per worker. In a second stage productivity declines as population grows, no change of agricultural technique having occurred. In a final stage the population has switched to more intensive forms of agriculture that raise productivity, but not up to the initial level. Comparing the first and the third stages, has there taken place a "development of the productive forces"?

[1] *Ibid.*, p. 605.

The answer clearly turns upon the counterfactual efficiency of the newer methods under the initial conditions of resources and population. If they would have enabled a larger product per worker in that situation, their emergence constitutes a development of the productive forces. Against this, Cohen argues that "the level of development of the productive forces is said to determine the shape of the economic structure, and the economic structure will not be responsive to anything so counterfactual".[1] But consider the three-stage scenario again. In the second stage, the intensive methods of cultivation would be superior to the slash-and-burn techniques. If the new methods can be introduced and developed only by the establishment of new relations of production, this fact might explain why such relations are subsequently established. (I do not believe in this story, but I am accepting it here for the sake of argument.) There is nothing counterfactual in this statement. The counterfactual comparison is needed only for deciding whether the new methods constitute a development of the productive forces, not for deciding whether they determine the shape of the economic structure.

Hence, in this hypothetical case we can say both that the productive forces develop, and that they explain the change in the relations of production. What we cannot say, however, is that the change in the relations is explained by the development of the forces.[2] (The forces might explain the change in the relations without developing at all, in the case where the new methods would have been inferior to the old in the initial situation, yet are adopted because they are superior to the old under changed environmental and demographic conditions.) This may be the substance of Cohen's objection. I believe, however, that it ought to be rephrased so that it does not turn upon the meaning of the "development" of the productive forces, but on the issue of whether Marx believed that a change in the relations of production always is explicable by a preceding development of the productive forces.

A final point is also relevant to this issue. Let us ask *by virtue of which feature* the productive forces at a certain level of their development require new relations of production for their further, optimal growth. The

---

[1] Cohen, *Karl Marx's Theory of History*, p. 61.

[2] We may say, nevertheless, that the development of the forces *causes* the change in the relations. The process referred to as "the development of the productive forces" may serve as a cause for the change in the relations, even when it does not do so by virtue of being a *development*. One may refer to a cause in a way that is irrelevant for the way it acts as a cause. See Beauchamp and Rosenberg, *Hume and the Problem of Causation*, pp. 93ff.

standard answer points to the level of surplus[1] as the relevant feature. This was certainly Marx's view with respect to the transition from capitalism to communism (5.2.3). One could also argue, however, that when the productive forces embody techniques or knowledge that are sufficiently sophisticated, their further, optimal development requires new relations of production. For instance, there may be inherent limits to the development of the productive forces within a system based on slavery. One can imagine bountiful natural conditions under which slavery produced a huge surplus, but prevented further technical advance. Conversely, less plausibly perhaps, population growth and dwindling resources under capitalism might force surplus per worker or total surplus down to pre-capitalist levels, without pre-capitalist relations of production becoming optimal.

In most cases, these various senses of "development" of the productive forces go together. A larger potential surplus goes together with a larger actual surplus, and so does increased technical sophistication (an elusive concept, but surely not a meaningless one). Even so, it remains to single out the feature which is most relevant for the explanation of changes in the economic structure. To avoid *ad hoc*-ness, this should be the same feature in all cases. It would not be satisfactory to explain the breakdown of slavery by the inherent limits to the use of skilled labour within that system, and the breakdown of capitalism by the (dynamically) inefficient use it makes of the surplus it has created. I am not saying this is how Marx explained the decline of slavery; in fact, he did not offer any explanation at all (5.2.1). But it is an explanation with some appeal to Marxists, because it sounds like an instance of the contradiction between the productive forces and the relations of production.

5.1.2. The relations of production
Again I begin with Cohen's valuable discussion, and then go on to supplement it in some ways. Since the property relations are "but a legal

---

[1] More specifically, to the level of surplus per capita. Not infrequently, however, one encounters the view that the total surplus was the relevant feature of the development. According to Boserup, *Population and Technological Change*, p. 65 and *passim*, the typical form of technical progress in pre-capitalist societies involved a fall in surplus per capita and an increase in total surplus. The latter allowed the emergence of a class of specialists who could take the progress still further, whereas rising surplus per capita in itself had no such consequences. I do not believe Marx had any such view in mind, but later Marxists have certainly adopted it from time to time. This view in my opinion is quite plausible, although insufficiently worked out. It remains unclear, for instance, why population growth without technical change could not have the same effect, if the marginal productivity of labour does not decline too rapidly.

expression for" the relations of production, we can characterize the latter in terms of ownership and non-ownership of the factors of production. Following Cohen, we may distinguish between three degrees of ownership: full, partial or none. (A less crude approach is used in 6.1.1 for the purpose of defining classes.) Also, we may distinguish between two kinds of factors of production: human (i.e. labour-power) and non-human (i.e. means of production). This gives the following table:[1]

		Does the producer own his labour-power?		
		Yes	Partly	No
Does the producer own his means of production?	Yes	independent producers	impossible	impossible
	Partly	transitional forms to capitalism	serfdom	improbable
	No	capitalism	improbable	slavery

For the impossible and improbable cases, I refer to Cohen. Some of the remaining entries in the table call for comments that will motivate a broader conceptualization of the relations of production.

Independent producers. This category has two radically different subclasses. The first is production for subsistence, the other "simple commodity production". In both cases the producers own their means of production and operate them without the help of hired labour. In the first, the productive unit is self-sufficient, in the second it is integrated in a commodity market. Production for subsistence has been the rule in most traditional peasant societies. To a variable extent it has been mixed with some extraction of surplus labour in the form of taxation. It is then usually better characterized as dependent production, as in the Asiatic mode of production. The mere fact that taxation takes place is not, however, sufficient to allow us to assert that the producers have less than full ownership of their means of production. (See the discussion in 4.1.5 of the relation between taxation and exploitation.)

Simple commodity production is a more fragile structure. As explained in 4.1.3, with unequal endowment of resources this system would involve exploitation without class formation, thus showing the logical separability of these two phenomena. Marx argued that in actual cases a society based on simple commodity production would soon develop a credit market or a labour market, thus transforming it into capitalism or one of the transitional forms discussed below. Whereas formerly all worked for themselves with their own capital, there now emerge buyers

[1] Constructed from table 1 and table 2 in Cohen, *Karl Marx's Theory of History*, pp. 65–6.

and sellers of labour-power, as well as lenders and borrowers of capital. This change occurs because "the maintenance or loss of the means of production on the part of small producers depends on a thousand contingencies, and every one of these contingencies or losses signifies impoverishment and becomes a crevice into which a parasitic usurer may creep".[1] Or – we might add – into which an enterprising capitalist may creep offering a contract for wage labour, or a merchant offering a putting-out contract. Simple commodity production is inherently unstable.

Transitional forms. Marx distinguishes between two main forms of transition to capitalism: exploitation through usurer's capital and through merchant's capital.[2] It is not clear whether these are transitional in the developmental sense, or only in the sense of being intermediate categories in a classificatory scheme. The latter appears to be the case for usurer's capital, an inherently stagnant form of exploitation with no potential for development:

This form intensifies the exploitation of the producers, and drives it to an extreme. [The usurer] thus introduces a capitalist mode of production – albeit to begin with only in the form of the formal subsumption of labour under capital – without doing anything to foster the intensified productivity of labour associated with it or the transition to the capitalist mode of production proper. It is rather a form which makes labour sterile.[3]

What Marx calls "*Debt-Slavery* in distinction to *Wage-Slavery*"[4] can take two forms. Either the means of production are used as collateral, as when the French peasantry are exploited through the mortgage.[5] Or the producer pawns the future product in order to get working capital, as is the case with the Indian ryot.[6] In both cases the producer's ownership of the means of production is only partial, since some of the rights of ownership – the right, respectively, to dispose freely of what one owns and to dispose fully of the fruits of what one owns – are absent.

Merchant capital leads to putting-out as a transitional form to capitalism. The producers own some of their means of production, but the merchant provides them with raw materials and buys their product at an agreed price. As with exploitation through usurer's capital, this is neither a real subsumption of labour under capital, corresponding to a change in technique, nor even a formal subsumption. And, as in that case, although

---

[1] *Capital III*, p. 599.   [2] See especially *Zur Kritik (1861–63)*, pp. 2152ff.
[3] *Ibid.*, p. 2155; see also *Capital III*, p. 596.   [4] *Zur Kritik (1861–63)*, p. 2155.
[5] *The Class Struggles in France*, pp. 57, 122.   [6] *Zur Kritik (1861–63)*, p. 2155.

much more ambiguously, merchant capital appears to be transitional in a classificatory rather than in a developmental sense:

The transition from the feudal mode of production is two-fold. The producer becomes merchant and capitalist, in contrast to the natural agricultural economy and the guild-bound handicrafts of the medieval urban industries. This is the really revolutionizing path. Or else, the merchant establishes direct sway over production. However much this serves historically as a stepping-stone – witness the English seventeenth-century clothier, who brings the weavers, independent as they are, under his control by selling his wool to them and buying their cloth – it cannot by itself contribute to the overthrow of the old mode of production, but tends rather to preserve and retain it as its precondition.[1]

Capitalism. I need not add much to the analyses of chapters 3 and 4, except to make a conceptual point that is brought out by considering the place of *guilds* within Marx's theory. Although a medieval phenomenon, it would be inappropriate to describe this institution in terms of feudalism or serfdom. On the contrary: historically the guilds represented the liberation of labour from landed property, and led – during their progressive phase – a constant struggle against feudal and royal power.[2] Not only was the guild system not feudal; in one place Marx even suggests that it was capitalist:

[The guild system] involves relations between buyers and sellers. Wages are paid and masters, journeymen and apprentices encounter each other as free persons ... The master does indeed own the conditions of production – tools, materials etc. (although the tools may be owned by the journeyman too) – and he owns the product. To that extent he is a *capitalist*.[3]

In fact, on the structural definition of capitalism proposed by Cohen,[4] the medieval master *was* a capitalist. At any given time one could observe private property of the means of production on the one hand, private property of labour-power on the other. This definition, however, is too narrow, since the relations of production must be defined dynamically.[5] In addition to private property and wage labour, capitalism is characterized by the free mobility of capital and labour, which is precisely what was lacking in the guild system. To differentiate between the two systems, one must consider not only their possible states, but also the possible changes that can occur from one moment to another.

---

[1] *Capital III*, p. 334.   [2] *Zur Kritik (1861–63)*, p. 1975.
[3] *Ibid.*, pp. 2131–2 (= *Results of the Immediate Process of Production*, p. 1029).
[4] Cohen, *Karl Marx's Theory of History*, pp. 73ff.
[5] On this, see also my review of Cohen's book in *Political Studies*, pp. 122–3, as well as 6.1.4 below.

Marx did not ignore the restrictions on the guild system. The *numerus clausus* on the number of apprentices prevented "the transformation of the master of a trade into a capitalist".[1] Also, the "capital" of the master cannot be transferred freely to any branch of production, but is restricted to the trade in which he is established.[2] This does not confirm the idea that the master was a capitalist (which in any case is affirmed by Marx only "to the extent that" the master owns the means of production and the final product). Elsewhere Marx makes it very clear that the guild relations of production differ from the capitalist ones, and in fact form a unique system that can be put on a par with the other pre-capitalist relations. In the *Grundrisse* he refers to "the guild system, serfdom and slavery" as successive fetters on the productive forces before the advent of capitalism.[3] And in the opening sentences of the *Communist Manifesto* the pre-capitalist struggles are enumerated as "freeman and slave, patrician and plebeian, lord and serf, guild-master and journeyman".[4] Cohen's table does not respect this text, one of the two most famous succinct statements by Marx of his theory of history. Nor, as we shall see, does it respect the other.[5]

The specific conclusion is that the guild relations must be considered *sui generis*, and not subsumable under the capitalist relations of production. My more general conclusion is that the relations of production cannot be defined in terms of temporal cross-sections of the ownership structure. To fully grasp the pattern of ownership, we must know how it is acquired and divested. The implications of this fact for class formation are discussed in 6.1.4.

Serfdom. The consideration of this category points to another set of relations that are mentioned by Marx, yet omitted from Cohen's table. In the 1859 Preface Marx says that "In broad outlines Asiatic, ancient, feudal, and modern bourgeois modes of production can be designated as progressive epochs in the economic formation of society."[6] Of these, the first has no place in Cohen's table. True, Marx does not refer often to the Asiatic mode,[7] but its place in this highly programmatic passage suggests

---

[1] *Capital I*, p. 309.   [2] *Capital III*, pp. 377–8; see also *Zur Kritik (1861–63)*, pp. 2132, 2353.
[3] *Grundrisse*, p. 749.   [4] *The Communist Manifesto*, p. 482.
[5] In itself this is no criticism of the table, which is only intended to cover the ownership position of the immediate producers. The phenomena neglected in the table are also, however, neglected in Cohen's book as a whole.
[6] *Critique of Political Economy*, p. 9.
[7] There are in Marx's work only 2.5 explicit references to the Asiatic mode of production. In addition to the passage cited in the preceding note, the term occurs in *Zur Kritik (1861–63)*, p. 2269. In *Capital I*, p. 79 the term "altasiatische Produktionsweise" is used.

that he believed it to be an economic structure quite distinct from, and conceptually on a par with, the other three. His ideas concerning it were confused and largely wrong,[1] but this does not entitle us to say that he accorded as little significance to it as we may want to do in the light of later knowledge.

It could be argued that the Asiatic mode occurs in Cohen's table as a sub-variety of serfdom. And it is true that from the point of view of the immediate producers, the two may have been indistinguishable, much as Trotsky argued that there was capitalism in Russia around the turn of the century by virtue of the presence of wage labour, even though the employer was the state rather than private capital.[2] Yet to omit the Asiatic mode on these grounds would be unsatisfactory. There is not only a need to respect the textual evidence, but there are also important theoretical constraints which must be considered. The nature of the non-producing owners would presumably enter importantly into any analysis of the furthering or fettering of the productive forces by the relations of production. Also, if the politico-legal superstructure is to be explained, à la Cohen, by its stabilizing impact on the relations of production, the latter must be defined so as to make clear what is the economically dominant class. Hence, the table must be supplemented by an explicit account of the nature of the non-producing owners – whether these are individuals, intermediate collectives or the state bureaucracy as a whole.

Summing up, the relations of production are defined in terms of (i) the relation of the producers to the means of production and their own labour-power, (ii) the nature of the non-producing owners, if any, and (iii) the rules governing acquisition and transfer of property. Hence both the Asiatic mode of production and the guild system are specific forms of the relations of production that differ from the usual triad of slavery, serfdom and capitalism. The Asiatic mode differs from serfdom with respect to the nature of the non-producing owner, and the guild system differs from capitalism with respect to the mobility of capital and labour.

5.1.3. Correspondence and contradiction

Within each mode of production, the relations of production first "correspond" to the productive forces, and then enter into a "contradiction" with them. The task of clarifying what this means is quite complex, hence it may be useful to sketch the structure of the argument that follows.

---

[1] See the appendix on the Asiatic mode of production in Anderson, *Lineages of the Absolutist State*.

[2] See Knei-Paz, *The Social and Political Thought of Leon Trotsky*, p. 117.

The general theory set out in the 1859 Preface and elsewhere is ambiguous. It can be read as stating that the relations of production contradict the productive forces when the latter are in a state of stagnation, or that the contradiction obtains when other relations of production would be superior for the further development of the forces. To disambiguate, we must consider what Marx says about specific modes of production, and notably about capitalism. This points decisively to the second interpretation. The difficulty then arises that some of the other things he says about capitalism are inconsistent with the general theory, on either interpretation. I shall cite several passages that suggest that the contradiction arises when the relations of production prevent the optimal *use* – as distinct from the optimal *development* – of the productive forces. Hence there are three main interpretations of what the contradiction means:

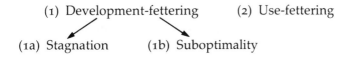

   (1) Development-fettering   (2) Use-fettering

  (1a) Stagnation   (1b) Suboptimality

Of these, I believe that (1b) is at the core of historical materialism, whereas (2) was more prominent in Marx's thinking about the transition from capitalism to communism. In 5.2.3 I discuss whether a theory for that transition could be constructed that is more compatible with historical materialism.

The statements from the 1859 Preface cited in the introduction to 5.1, as well as several similarly worded passages in *The German Ideology*,[1] lend themselves naturally to the following interpretation. At the initial stage of each mode of production there occurs a rapid development of the productive forces. The relations of production are then "forms of development" for the forces – they "correspond" to one another. Later, stagnation of the productive forces sets in: the relations then "fetter" their development. Hence correspondence and contradiction are interpreted as, respectively, technical progress and technical stagnation. This interpretation has in its favour the Preface statement that "No social formation ever perishes before all the productive forces for which there is room in it has developed." Also, it fits in well with intuitive notions about decreasing marginal productivity: modes of production eventually exhaust their creative potential. For the case of capitalism at least, one can also construct a plausible scenario to flesh out this abstract scheme: competition

---

[1] *The German Ideology*, pp. 88, 432.

leads to rapid technical change that, by the concomitant economies of scale, creates oligopolies and a slowing-down of the innovative process.[1]

Although this interpretation is the most plausible reading of the Preface taken in isolation, and has been held more or less clearly by a majority of the commentators,[2] broader considerations force us to reject it. Instead we must choose an interpretation that is also consistent with the Preface statements (with the exception of the one cited in the preceding paragraph) and is required by numerous other texts. On this reading, the change from correspondence to contradiction occurs when the relations of production become suboptimal for the development of the forces, not when that development is being decelerated. The relations become suboptimal when another set of relations of production would develop the forces more rapidly, hence the implied comparison is with a counterfactual set of relations, not with the same relations at an earlier stage. This does not exclude the idea that suboptimality might coincide with technical stagnation. Moreover, if stagnation should set in, this would be a sign of suboptimality, assuming that technical progress has not come to an end. On the other hand we may have suboptimality without stagnation. This is the case for capitalism, which exhibits uninterrupted and in fact *accelerating* technical change throughout its existence, even after the "contradiction" has set in.

A model for the development of the productive forces under capitalism is given in 5.2.3. Some of the textual evidence for that model is given here, since it is also evidence against the traditional interpretation. Although Marx never to my knowledge says in so many words that the productive forces will increase ever more rapidly under capitalism, this view can be deduced from other statements. He asserts that in the course of capitalist development "the rapidity of the change in the organic composition of capital, and in its technical form increases".[3] Moreover, "the level of productivity attained is manifested in the relative preponderance of constant over variable capital".[4] Taken together, these statements imply that the rate of technical change is increasing.

A second, more decisive piece of evidence is provided by the numerous texts in the 1857–8 and 1861–3 manuscripts, where Marx refers to the double tendency of capital to *develop and fetter* the productive forces. In some cases this refers to use-fettering, further discussed below. In other

[1] See my *Explaining Technical Change*, p. 215.
[2] See for instance Plamenatz, *German Marxism and Russian Communism*, pp. 20, 28; Kolakowski, *Main Currents of Marxism*, vol. 1, p. 375 and Cohen, *Karl Marx's Theory of History*, p. 173, Proposition 4.
[3] *Capital I*, p. 631.   [4] *Capital III*, p. 759. Other passages are cited in 3.3.2.

cases Marx clearly has development-fettering in mind. In the 1861–3 manuscript Marx even refers to a specific form of development-fettering – the choice of techniques according to profit-maximization instead of labour-minimization (3.3.2). He refers to this as a "barrier" on capitalism[1] and as an instance of its contradictions.[2] Such fettering does not, however, exclude the tendency of capitalism to stimulate the development – in one place Marx even refers to the "unrestrained" and "unfettered" development[3] – of the productive forces. This double tendency is asserted in two important passages from the *Grundrisse*:

First of all, there is a limit, not inherent to production generally, but to production founded on capital. This limit is double, or rather the same regarded from two directions. It is enough here to demonstrate that capital contains a *particular* restriction of production – which contradicts its general tendency to drive beyond every barrier to production – in order to have uncovered the foundation of *overproduction*, the fundamental contradiction of developed capital; in order to have uncovered, more generally, the fact that capital is not, as the economists believe, the *absolute* form for the development of the productive forces – not the absolute form for that, nor the form of wealth which absolutely coincides with the development of the productive forces. The stages of production which precede capital appear, regarded from its standpoint as so many fetters upon the productive forces. It itself, however, correctly understood, appears as the condition of the development of the productive forces as long as they require an external spur which appears at the same time as their bridle. It is a discipline over them, which becomes superfluous and burdensome at a certain level of their development, just like the guilds etc.[4]

There appears here the universalizing tendency of capital, which distinguishes it from all previous stages of production. Although limited by its very nature, it strives towards the universal development of the productive forces, and thus becomes the presupposition of a new mode of production, which is founded not on the development of the productive forces for the purpose of reproducing or at most expanding a given condition, but where the free, unobstructed, progressive and universal development of the productive forces is itself the presupposition of society and hence of its reproduction.[5]

The capitalist relations of production are both a spur and a bridle on the development of the productive forces. This can be elaborated as follows. According to the view of human nature worked out in the *Economic and Philosophical Manuscript*, innovative and creative activity is natural for man. Contrary to the usual approach in political economy, the problem is not one of creating incentives to innovation, but of removing the obstacles to the

[1] *Zur Kritik (1861–63)*, p. 1671; *Theories of Surplus-Value*, vol. 3, pp. 116, 120.
[2] *Zur Kritik (1861–63)*, p. 1653 (corrupted text).
[3] *Theories of Surplus-Value*, vol. 3, pp. 55–6.
[4] *Grundrisse*, p. 415.   [5] *Ibid.*, p. 540.

natural creative urge of the individual "in whom his own realisation exists as an inner necessity".[1] Special incentives are needed only under conditions of scarcity and poverty, in which the needs of the individual are twisted and his capacities developed only in a one-sided way. In the early stages of capitalism there was indeed a great deal of scarcity and poverty, and unavoidably so, since the material conditions for a high level of want satisfaction were not yet created. Under those conditions, capitalism was the best and most progressive arrangement, even though it subordinated progress to profits. The system, however, created the conditions for its own demise. In later phases of capitalism there is still a great deal of poverty, but avoidably so. Given the technology developed by capitalism itself, it is materially feasible to install a regime in which the level of want satisfaction is so high that innovation as a spontaneous activity comes into its own – as part of the general self-actualization of individuals. The result will be a rate of innovation far in excess of anything seen before.

The "spur-and-bridle" argument may also be stated as follows. The rate at which innovations are forthcoming can be seen as the result of search followed by selection.[2] Up to a certain level of the productive forces, capitalism is an indispensable spur on the search for new methods, while at all times it is a bridle on the selection, for example by substituting profit-maximization for labour-minimization. In the initial stage the net effect of these opposing tendencies is positive, compared to the feasible alternatives, but from a certain point onwards the possibility emerges of a new set of relations of production that will both provide a superior spur and remove the bridle. In 5.2.3 I shall discuss whether it is plausible that the workers will make a revolution for the purpose of bringing about these changes. Here I wish to add some sceptical comments on the plausibility of the changes themselves. We saw in 3.2.2 that the importance of profit-maximization as a bridle on technical change is doubtful. There may be other fetters, but if so Marx has nothing to say about them. Also, the creation of a new, powerful spur is purely speculative. In particular, if the self-actualization of men is the supreme value, that of man may be fettered (2.2.7). This being said, the idea of a new motivation for innovation should not be dismissed out of hand. The history of art and science shows well enough that the creative urge does not need the stimulus of material gain. Yet we might want to question whether innovation constrained by profitability (or by the minimization

---

[1] *Economic and Philosophical Manuscripts*, p. 304.
[2] See Nelson and Winter, *An Evolutionary Theory of Economic Change*; also my *Explaining Technical Change*, ch. 6.

of compounded labour values) offers the same outlet for individual self-realization. Technical perfectionism and elegance are often the enemy of economic rationality. Here, if anywhere, the best can be the enemy of the good.[1] Hence what makes innovative work valuable for the individual does not immediately coincide with what makes it useful for society. To the problems of communism discussed in 2.2.7 and 4.3.3 we must now add the question whether it will attract too many scientists and too few engineers.

I now turn to the texts that suggest a quite different interpretation of the contradiction between the productive forces and the relations of production, as *suboptimal use* rather than suboptimal development. Independently of Marx, how can one understand the notion that techniques are used in a suboptimal way? First, there may be inefficient static resource allocation because of cartels, oligopolies etc. Secondly, there may be suboptimal provision of public goods because of externalities, free-rider problems etc. Thirdly, there may be unemployment, unused productive capacities and goods that meet no effective demand, all because of the lack of coordination that characterizes market decisions. Lastly, the productive forces may be used in an inhuman way – either because the workers do not fully exercise their capacities or because production caters only to their baser needs.

Of these, Marx had little to say about the first, for the methodological reasons set out in 3.1.1. As further explained in 7.1.1, he was not fully aware of the importance of the second category of problems. He did, however, consider both the third and the fourth categories as cases of "contradiction" between the relations of production and the productive forces.

Consider first a passage from *The Class Struggles in France* where Marx discusses the conditions for revolution:

With this general prosperity, in which the productive forces of bourgeois society develop as luxuriantly as is at all possible within bourgeois relationships, there can be no talk of a real revolution. Such a revolution is only possible in the periods when *both these factors*, the *modern* productive *forces* and the *bourgeois forms of production*, come in *collision* with each other . . . *A new revolution is possible only in consequence of a new crisis. It is, however, just as certain as this crisis.*[2]

Observe the curious contraposition of "development" and "crisis". One might have expected a contrast between development and fettered development, or between equilibrium and its interruption, but not this mixed pair. This heterogeneous contrast occurs frequently in Marx's

---

[1] A case study in the pointless search for generality is that of Leibniz as engineer, sketched in ch. III of my *Leibniz et la Formation de l'Esprit Capitaliste*.

[2] *The Class Struggles in France*, p. 135.

writings. In the *Grundrisse* and the 1861–3 manuscript Marx regularly contrasts the development of the productive forces by capitalism in its heyday, and the crises of overproduction that increasingly plague it from a certain point onwards.[1] In fact, this "mixed" interpretation, in which "correspondence" is understood in terms of optimal development and "contradiction" in terms of suboptimal use, is perhaps more plausible textually than either of the "pure" interpretations (1b) or (2) (see p. 259). It is, however, too blatantly inconsistent to deserve a central place in the reconstruction of the general theory.

The equating of the contradiction between forces and relations of production with the dehumanizing aspects of capitalism is most explicitly found in an article in *The People's Paper* from 1856:

In our days, everything seems pregnant with its contrary. Machinery gifted with the wonderful power of shortening and fructifying human labour, we behold starving and overworking it. The new-fangled sources of wealth, by some strange weird spell, are turned into sources of want. The victories of art seem bought by the loss of character. At the same pace that mankind masters nature, man seems to become enslaved to other men or to his own infamy. Even the pure light of science seems unable to shine but on the dark background of ignorance. All our invention and progress seem to result in endowing material forces with intellectual life, and in stultifying human life into a material force. This antagonism between modern industry and science on the one hand, between misery and dissolution on the other hand; this antagonism between the productive powers and the social relations of our epoch is a fact, palpable, overwhelming, and not to be controverted.[2]

This is perhaps the most succinct and eloquent indictment of capitalism ever made by Marx. Nearly every sentence reflects deep theoretical preoccupations. The contrast between labour and science reappears in the 1861–3 *Critique*,[3] whereas the immediately following sentence is an early

---

[1] *Grundrisse*, pp. 541, 748ff; *Theories of Surplus-Value*, vol. 3, p. 56.

[2] *People's Paper* 19.4.1856.

[3] "Science appears as a *force alien* and *inimical* to *work and dominating it*. Its applications entail the consolidation on the one hand, and the development into science, on the other, of the mass of individual pieces of received knowledge, observations and tricks of the trade with which to analyse the process of production, and to apply the natural sciences to the process of material production. These applications are based wholly on the separation of the intellectual powers of the process from the knowledge, experience and expertise of the individual workers, just as the consolidation and development of the conditions of production and their transformation into capital is based on depriving the worker of them and parting him from them. Instead, work in the factory leaves the worker with the knowledge of only a few manipulations; hence along with knowledge the apprenticeship laws were abrogated too. And the campaign waged by the state to ensure that factory children should at least learn to read and write shows how this 'application of science to the process of production' coincides with the suppression of all intellectual development in the actions which make up the process. It remains true, of course, that a small class of higher

statement of the idea of fetishism. The "antagonism" – a few lines later it is referred to as a "contradiction" – between the productive forces and the relations of production clearly resides in the inhuman use of the productive forces. The contrast is between their potential liberating power and their actual enslaving consequences, not between a high potential rate of change and the lower actual rate. Hence the contradiction between the productive forces and the relations of production is identified here with spiritual alienation (2.2.5).

I remarked earlier that *The German Ideology* contains passages that lend themselves naturally to interpretation (1). This is indeed the case if they are read in the light of the 1859 Preface. If, however, they are seen in the light of the *Economic and Philosophical Manuscripts*, interpretation (2), and more specifically the understanding of the contradiction as the inhuman use of the productive forces, is equally plausible. First, there is the suggestion that the contradiction appears when the productive forces turn into "destructive forces":

[Large-scale industry] produced a mass of productive forces, for which private property became just as much a fetter as the guild had been for manufacture and the small rural workshop for the developing handicrafts. These productive forces receive under the system of private property a one-sided development only, and for the majority they become destructive forces; moreover, a great many of these forces can find no application at all within the system of private property.[1]

The implication seems to be that fettering means suboptimal or inhuman use. Further, one may point to two places where Marx argues that what is fettered by the "form of intercourse" (as Marx at this time called what he was later to call "relations of production"[2]) is the "self-activity" of the individual. They are too long to be cited here, and anyway somewhat inconclusive. In one of them self-activity is clearly conceived as the full self-actualization of the individual,[3] while in the other an "advanced mode of self-activity" is linked to "more developed productive forces".[4] With respect to communism, the two views of self-activity are, of course, compatible, but with respect to earlier modes of production they are not. The development of man and that of men do not progress *pari passu*. The transition from one set of relations of production to another is certainly

workers is formed, but this is minute in comparison with the mass of workers who have been deprived of all knowledge ['entkenntnisst']." (*Zur Kritik (1861–63)*, pp. 2061–2.) The passage is unique in Marx's writings in suggestion that *knowledge* may create an internal cleavage within the working class.
[1] *The German Ideology*, p. 73.   [2] See note 1, p. 244 above.
[3] *The German Ideology*, pp. 87–8.   [4] *Ibid.*, p. 82.

linked to the development of the productive forces, that is to the self-actualization of mankind, but not necessarily to a higher degree of self-actualization of the individual (5.3.2).[1]

In conclusion, let me try to assess the strengths and the weaknesses of the view that the contradictions of a mode of production are defined in terms of the suboptimal use of the productive forces. Clearly, there are strong theoretical pressures that favour this conception. For one thing, it allows Marx to bridge the gap between philosophical anthropology and historical materialism by identifying spiritual alienation and the contradiction between productive forces and relations of production. For another, it suggests a mechanism by which the contradiction could motivate to political action, since if perceived it could set up a pressure for more efficient and human use of the productive forces. As further argued in 5.2.3, a weakness of interpretation (1b) is that the link between the contradiction and political action remains obscure.

The glaring weakness of interpretation (2) is that it does not point to any dynamic mechanism. It is a theoretical constraint on the notion of correspondence between productive forces and relations of production that it must be possible for the correspondence to turn endogenously into contradiction. If the correspondence is understood as in interpretation (1b), that is as a maximal rate of change of the productive forces, this constraint is satisfied. If it is understood merely as full utilization of the forces, it is not. If we opt for interpretation (2), we may be able to understand why the contradictions lead to political action and ultimately to the establishment of new relations of production, but not why this should go together with faster technical progress.

In fact, there is a famous argument that a system that allows for a better utilization of the productive forces may lead to a *lower* rate of technical change. Joseph Schumpeter believed that communism would be superior to capitalism in avoiding waste and cycles, but that it would be less good in developing new techniques. This is an illustration of the general proposition that "A system – any system, economic or other – that at *every* given point of time fully utilizes its possibilities to the best advantage may yet in the long run be inferior to a system that does so at *no* given

---

[1] Ste Croix, *The Class Struggle in the Ancient Greek World*, p. 112, is guilty of a confusion between these two senses of development. He cites Marx on the "civilizing [aspect] of capital that it enforces surplus-labour in a manner and under conditions which are more advantageous to the development of the productive forces, social relations, and the creation of the elements for a new and higher form than under the preceding forms of slavery etc." (*Capital III*, p. 819). He wrongly takes this to imply that the "hired labourer [has] a position superior to that of the slave or the serf". See also 5.3 below on the underlying distinction between progress and development.

point of time, because the latter's failure to do so may be a condition for the level or speed of long-run performance."[1] Hence, if better use of the productive forces is the motive behind changes of property rights, there can be no presumption that this will maximize the rate of change of the productive forces.

I return to these problems in 5.2.3. Here I want to draw together some of the strands in the preceding argument by observing that the rate of growth of the net product in society can be seen as a (broadly speaking) multiplicative function of three variables: the intensity of search for new techniques, the efficiency of selecting new techniques among those thrown up by the search and the efficiency with which the selected techniques are used in production. When we compare social systems, this rate of growth should be the relevant criterion. The rate of technical progress is relevant only to the extent that it influences the rate of growth of the net social product. Hence in principle there may be trade-offs between the three variables; a system that fares better in one respect may do worse in another. As already observed in 2.2.7, Marx was little inclined to consider such trade-offs between values. He believed that communism would be superior on all three counts, and capitalism consistently inferior. This a priori belief that all good things go together is a major weakness of his social theory.

5.1.4. The primacy of the productive forces
Marx's son-in-law Paul Lafargue is said to have exclaimed one day: "Dieu, ce sont les forces productives." Kostas Papaioannou, who cites this phrase,[2] finds the same cult of the productive forces in Marx himself. On his interpretation, Marx believed that men could realize themselves only through productive work, narrowly conceived as the transformation of nature by the help of science and technology.[3] This must be a mistake. Marx certainly believed that self-actualization through *art* was as rewarding as engineering or scientific work. *Creation*, not production, is at the centre of Marx's philosophical anthropology (2.2.7). Yet in historical materialism, the productive forces hold the centre of the stage.[4] In communism, the expansion of the productive forces will take place as a part of the general flowering of human creativity, but in the process leading up to this stage the productive forces have a privileged position. It is their forced development, at the expense of all other values, that creates the

---

[1] Schumpeter, *Capitalism, Socialism and Democracy*, p. 83. See also 2.4.1 above.
[2] Papaioannou, *De Marx et du Marxisme*, p. 59.   [3] *Ibid.*, pp. 78ff, 89ff.
[4] On this see Cohen, "Reconsidering historical materialism".

material conditions for a society in which their development is only one value among others.

These are grand, speculative issues. They enter into the background of the more sober claim that forms my topic here: that the productive forces have some kind of primacy with respect to the relations of production. To understand why the relations obtain when they obtain, and change when they change, we must look to the productive forces.

If Marx believed in this primacy of the productive forces, he faced the following dilemma.[1] On the one hand he was then committed to the view that

(1) The level of development of the productive forces in a society explains the nature of its economic structure.

On the other hand there is abundant evidence that he also believed that

(2) The economic structure of a society promotes the development of its productive forces.

At least this holds to the extent that the relations of production correspond to the productive forces; and when they do not, there is set up a pressure to change them so as to bring about a new set of relations.

The apparent contradiction between these two statements has created an enormous amount of confusion in Marxism. It was difficult to reconcile the alleged primacy of the productive forces with the massive influence of the relations on the forces, hence various pseudo-solutions have been proposed to the problem (and to the formally similar problem concerning the relation between the economic structure and the superstructure).[2] Perhaps the greatest achievement of Cohen is the demonstration that statements (1) and (2) can be reconciled in an unstrained manner by understanding the explanatory primacy asserted in (1) in terms of *functional* explanation. The relations of production can be explained by their impact on the productive forces. They obtain because and so long as they are optimal for the development of the forces; they change when and because they no longer are optimal. Since the explanans in general has primacy with respect to the explanandum, this shows that the two assertions are compatible with one another.

As a result of exchanges with Philippe van Parijs, Cohen's position

---

[1] See especially Cohen, "Functional explanation, consequence explanation and Marxism" for a clear statement of the dilemma and its solution.

[2] The analogous statements here are (3) The economic structure in a society explains the nature of its superstructure and (4) The superstructure of a society stabilizes its economic structure.

has been further clarified.[1] Consider the question *why* the relations of production at some point cease being optimal for the development of the productive forces. According to Cohen, Marx believed that the answer to this question is found in the level of development of the productive forces. This is most strikingly seen in Marx's argument for the eventual superiority of communism: capitalism develops the productive forces to a point where communist relations become superior for their further development. Hence the productive forces enter doubly into the explanation of the relations of production: first because they determine what relations are optimal, and secondly because they constitute the element for (the development of) which the relations are optimal. Or again: both the *level* and the *rate of change* of the productive forces enter into the explanation of the relations of production. The level attained by the forces explains why certain relations rather than others maximize the rate of change of the forces. Logically speaking, something else than the productive forces could occupy either place in the argument,[2] but, according to Cohen, Marx believed that the productive forces filled both places.

This interpretation is a very attractive one. It enables us to bring together in one fell swoop two kinds of statement found in Marx. On the one hand there are the teleological assertions to the effect that the relations of production must disappear when they no longer perform the historical task of developing the productive forces to a maximal degree. On the other hand there are the more straightforwardly causal statements that changes in the productive forces bring about a change in the relations of production. The former are taken care of by Cohen's original interpretation, the latter by the modified view that emerged from the confrontation with van Parijs. This revised interpretation has the immense advantage that Marx appears much more consistent than on any other reading. Since this part of Marx's theory is second to none in importance, this advantage should not be lightly abandoned.

I shall, however, adduce some evidence against such a reading. I believe that when Marx refers to the changes in the relations of production that are caused by the productive forces, he does not have in mind changes that are due to new relations having become optimal. Rather, he

---

[1] See van Parijs, "Marxism's central puzzle" and Cohen, "Reply to four critics".

[2] Van Parijs, "Marxism's central puzzle", suggests that the location of a country on the centre-periphery dimension of the world economy might determine which relations are optimal for the forces; conversely the forces might determine which relations were optimal for social cohesion. These are hypothetical examples, cited for the sake of clarifying the distinction. In 5.2.2 I suggest that Marx's theory of the transition from feudalism to capitalism can be read as stating that the level but not the rate of change of the forces were decisive for the new relations.

seems to refer to something more trivial or straightforward. The textual evidence is given below. First, however, I want to spell out, by means of an analogy, what I think Marx did have in mind when he made causal statements of this kind. Consider the social consequences of the computer revolution. One could argue, in the grand manner, that computer technology for the first time makes a planned economy an optimal arrangement for the development of the productive forces, and that this will in fact lead to the emergence of new relations of production. Yet by the "social consequences" of computers one can also refer to the wide-ranging changes in work habits, relations of authority and dependence within the firm etc. that they are bringing about. To some extent these changes may be explained functionally: they are required for the *optimal use* of the new technology. But this of course has nothing to do with the idea that a change in the economy-wide relations of ownership are necessary for the *optimal development* of the technology. My contention is that when Marx makes causal statements about the impact of new technology on social relations, it is more plausible to understand him in this second way. This may not be a compelling interpretation, but I would at least like to offer it for consideration.

The main evidence for my view is taken from the recently published 1861–3 *Critique*. First, however, I shall cite some well-known passages from *The Poverty of Philosophy*. In one place Marx refers to the fact that "a change in men's productive forces necessarily brings about a change in their relations of production".[1] There is no suggestion that this change is mediated by a change in what relations are optimal for the further development of the productive forces. True, the text is compatible with this view, but it would not come to the mind of any reader who was not already persuaded of its importance. Elsewhere he argues that

Social relations are closely bound up with productive forces. In acquiring new productive forces men change their mode of production; and in changing their mode of production, in changing their way of earning their living, they change all their social relations. The hand-mill gives you society with the feudal lord; the steam mill, society with the industrial capitalist.[2]

The same comments apply to this text. (It is also historically absurd, as Marx later came to realize. See the texts cited in 5.2.1.) A neutral reader would never contemplate the idea that the hand-mill "gives" us feudalism because feudal relations of production are better suited for the development of the steam-mill. He might consider various other ideas,

---

[1] *Poverty of Philosophy*, p. 175.   [2] *Ibid.*, p. 166.

such as the link between small-scale technology and decentralized production, or between low productivity and the impossibility of capitalist production. Neither would be an obligatory reading, but both would be more plausible than the teleological interpretation.

This passage points to an important conceptual distinction between "productive forces" and "mode of production". The latter term, as showed by Cohen,[1] is used by Marx both in a material and in a social sense. When he refers to the "capitalist mode of production", as distinct from serfdom or slavery, he is using the term in a social sense. When he refers to the "specifically capitalist mode of production", he is using it in the material sense of factory production, as distinct from manufacture or handicraft production.[2] When Marx states that the impact of the productive forces on the social relations is mediated by the mode of production, that term must be taken in the material sense.

Marx may also appear to suggest that any change in the productive forces leads to a change in the mode of production, but I do not believe that this was his intention. The example of the hand-mill and the steam-mill does not refer to any mere quantitative increase in productivity, but to a dramatic discontinuity in the organization of work. In the 1861–3 *Critique* Marx states explicitly, apropos the introduction of machinery, that "this does not involve a clearcut demarcation at the level of technology but a revolution in the application of the means of labour which transforms the mode of production and with it the relations of production".[3] There can be technical change without a change in the mode of production, but only such technical change as is also accompanied by the latter brings about a change in the relations of production. In the same manuscript we also find a significant comment on a passage from a Factory Inspection Report:

"There has been no *mechanical invention* of recent years which has created so great a *revulsion in the mode of manufacture, and eventually in the habits of the operatives, as the spinning jenny and the throstle frame did.*"

This makes the right connection. The "mechanical invention". It has created a "revulsion in the *mode of manufacture*" and hence in the relations of production, in social relations and "eventually, in the *habits* of the operatives".[4]

If this is the "right connection" between technical change and a change in the relations of production, we are a far cry from the teleological interpretation. Marx is here referring to such changes in the relations of

---

[1] Cohen, *Karl Marx's Theory of History*, pp. 79ff.
[2] *Capital I*, pp. 510, 624, 629, 738. See also note 3, p. 282 below.
[3] *Zur Kritik (1861–63)*, p. 1915.   [4] *Ibid.*, p. 2002.

production that can occur *within* capitalism, not the change that takes place when we go from capitalism to communism. In the discussion of the relations of production in 5.1.2, the level of abstraction was such that there was no room for intra-system variations. Yet it is clear that the concrete modalities of ownership and control can change without the changes amounting to a change of regime. It is plausible, moreover, that such changes may come about as a result of changes in the work process. The "primacy" of the productive forces that obtains in such cases has little if anything to do with the teleological primacy.

I return to the primacy issue in 5.2 when discussing specific historical processes. The best case for the Cohen–van Parijs interpretation is Marx's theory of the transition from capitalism to communism (5.2.3). Here it is possible to link together the level and the rate of change of the productive forces in the way required by their interpretation. On the other hand, the theory of the transition from feudalism to capitalism (5.2.2) is most naturally understood in a way that gives primacy to the relations of production, not to the productive forces. The growth of the productive forces here appears as a by-product of the establishment of capitalist relations of production, not as an element in the explanation of that event.

5.2. The historical modes of production

Marx's general theory must be confronted with his account of specific modes of production, not only to test for consistency, but also in the hope that the more concrete analyses can help us locate the most plausible reading of the general theory when it is ambiguous, as is frequently the case. In some cases the general theory points to a specific implication for how it is to be applied, and we can then see whether Marx consistently respected this implication. In other cases the general theory can be understood in several ways, with different implications for applications, and by looking at the more specific analyses we can reconstruct the reading of the general theory that on the whole makes Marx as consistent as possible. To some extent I have already followed these procedures in 5.1. I now proceed more systematically. In 5.2.1 I consider Marx's view of the various precapitalist modes of production, with surplus extraction by extra-economic coercion and stagnant techniques as the main common features. In 5.2.2 I look at Marx's explanation of the transition from feudalism to capitalism or, more precisely, his account of the relation between "the rise of capitalism" and "the industrial revolution". In 5.2.3 I consider Marx's various writings on the predicted transition from capitalism to communism. A formal model is offered to show the existence of different criteria for the "optimal time of transition" to communism. Here I also discuss the connection between "the rise and fall of nations" and "the rise and fall of property right structures", a topic that is further pursued in 5.3.2. A summary of the argument is found in 5.2.4.

5.2.1. Pre-capitalist modes of production

These are often considered together by Marx, as in the long section in the *Grundrisse* on "Forms which precede capitalist production". From the present perspective, their most important common feature is the stagnation of the productive forces. In *Capital I* Marx writes that "The technical basis of modern industry is therefore revolutionary, while all earlier modes of production were essentially conservative."[1] In a footnote he then cites a passage from the *Communist Manifesto:*

> The bourgeoisie cannot exist without continually revolutionising the instruments of production, and thereby the relations of production and all the social relations. Conservation, in an unaltered form, of the old modes of production was on the contrary the first condition of existence for all earlier industrial classes.[2]

In 5.1.1 passages from the *Grundrisse* in the same vein were quoted to support my view that Marx explained the dynamics of pre-capitalist societies in terms of the extensive development of the productive forces, as opposed to the intensive development implied by the general theory.

To see how other interpretations could appear plausible, consider another passage from the *Grundrisse*, in which Marx argues that these early communities

> necessarily correspond to a development of the productive forces which is only limited, and indeed limited in principle. The development of the productive forces dissolves these forms, and their dissolution is itself a development of the human productive forces. Labour begins with a certain foundation – naturally arisen, spontaneous at first – then historic presupposition. Then, however, this foundation or presupposition is itself suspended, or posited as the vanishing presupposition which has become too confining for the unfolding of the progressive human pack.[3]

This could appear to support G. A. Cohen's view that the pre-capitalist relations of production stimulate the productive forces indirectly, much as a constitutional monarch, by opposing democracy, might actually

---

[1] *Capital I*, p. 486.
[2] *The Communist Manifesto*, p. 487. We may note in passing that the passage supports the view of the "primacy" thesis stated towards the end of 5.1.4.
[3] *Grundrisse*, pp. 496–7.

encourage it.[1] But that view is implausible on other grounds. Marx asserts not only that pre-capitalist relations of production opposed technical change, but also that technology *was* basically unchanged from antiquity to the early modern age (5.2.2). It would also be possible to read the passage as affirming an *autonomous* tendency of the productive forces to develop in history, and to destroy any relations of production that might oppose them.[2] The last sentence in particular can be read in this way. It can also, however, be seen as a statement about the destabilizing effects of population growth. In any case, this strongly teleological reading is also blocked by the statements about technical stagnation in the ancient world.

The three pre-capitalist modes of production differ in their internal structure and dynamics. With respect to the *Asiatic mode of production* it has been suggested that the relation between irrigation techniques and a centralized bureaucracy (mentioned by Marx in a passage cited in 2.1.3) is an instance of the primacy of the productive forces.[3] In the first place, this suggestion does not fit the general theory, since there is no dynamic element in this relation between the economic structure and the productive forces. Moreover, even if explanatory primacy is taken in a static sense, it does not necessarily obtain. When Marx in the quoted passage says that in the Orient the need for water "necessitated' government intervention in the economy, he may have meant only that a centralized authority was a necessary condition for irrigation, not that it owed its existence to this need. True, if X is indispensable for Y, and Y is an important economic function in the society, this may tend to stabilize X and reduce the chances of an alternative emerging. This, for instance, seems to have been the case for the Chhin state as it achieved imperial unification in the fourth century BC, through its ability to stop competition for irrigation water.[4] Yet in other cases X may have such a strong basis, prior to (or in the hypothetical absence of) the function Y, that the latter contributes little to explaining its presence. The man who is strong and generous may be but marginally more powerful than the man who is strong and mean.[5]

From what Marx says about the Asiatic mode of production, it appears as unchanging from time immemorial. Often we find statements to the

[1] Cohen, *Karl Marx's Theory of History*, p. 170.
[2] In his review of Cohen's book Joshua Cohen implausibly takes this to be Cohen's interpretation.
[3] Cohen, *Karl Marx's Theory of History*, p. 201.
[4] Needham, *Science and Civilisation in China*, vol. IV:3, pp. 254ff and especially p. 265.
[5] Veyne, *Le Pain et le Cirque*, pp. 404ff and *passim*.

effect that "the Oriental empires always show an unchanging social infrastructure coupled with unceasing change in the persons and tribes who managed to ascribe to themselves the political superstructure".[1] In the Asiatic mode of production even population growth does not have the disruptive impact it has elsewhere: "if the population increases, a new community is founded, on the pattern of the old one, on unoccupied land".[2] This mode is a blind alley of history, capable of changing only under the shattering impact of British colonialism. I return briefly to this issue in 5.3.2.

Consider next *ancient slavery*. Marx believes that this system was inherently flawed by the low productivity of labour. In *Capital I* he cites as a characteristic feature of capitalism the avoidance of waste of raw materials, instruments and labour. He then adds that:

This is one of the circumstances that makes production by slave labour such a costly process. The labourer here is, to use a striking expression of the ancients, distinguishable only as instrumentum vocale, from an animal as instrumentum semi-vocale, and from an implement as instrumentum mutum. But he himself takes care to let both beast and implement feel that he is none of them, but is a man. He gives himself the satisfaction (*Selbstgefühl*) of knowing that he is different, by treating the one unmercifully and damaging the other con amore. Hence the principle, universally employed in this mode of production, only to employ the rudest and heaviest implements and such as are difficult to damage owing to their sheer clumsiness.[3]

This construction explains the low level of slave productivity in terms of social psychology: it was necessary for the self-respect of the slaves to treat animals and tools badly, since in so doing they could perceive themselves as human beings. (Cp. also the comments in 1.3.1 on endogenous preference formation.) Elsewhere Marx writes of wage labour that "in contrast to the slave, this labour becomes more productive because more intensive, since the slave works only under the spur of external fear, but not for his *existence* which is *guaranteed* even though it does not belong to him".[4]

To this we may add a complementary reluctance on the part of slaveowners to invest the surplus in new production. Marx's writings are

---

[1] *Die Presse* 7.7.1862; see also *Capital I*, p. 358. An exception is the statement that the Indian communities "transformed a self-developing social state into never changing natural destiny" (*New York Daily Tribune* 25.6.1853), suggesting that there had been some development before stagnation set in.

[2] *Capital I*, p. 358.

[3] *Capital I*, p. 196 note (modified translation). See also Finley, *Ancient Slavery and Modern Ideology*, pp. 111, 175 (Note 71).

[4] *Results of the Immediate Process of Production*, p. 1031.

somewhat ambiguous on this point. On the one hand he refers to "the transformation of a patriarchal slave system devoted to the production of immediate means of subsistence into one devoted to the production of surplus-value"[1] as the result of commerce and the development of merchant's capital. This view is further discussed in 5.3.3. The passage is somewhat atypical. More frequently, Marx emphasizes the tendency of the ruling classes in all pre-capitalist modes of production to prefer consumption over investment. In the *Grundrisse* Marx observes that the "*specific advances* which capital makes signify nothing more than that it *realizes* objectified surplus labour – surplus product – in new living surplus labour, instead of investing (spending) it, like, say, Egyptian kings or Etruscan priest–nobles for pyramids etc.".[2] A few lines later he argues that "*production for luxury* as it presents itself in antiquity is a necessary result of the slave relation. Not over-production, but *over-consumption* and *insane consumption*, signifying, by its turn towards the monstrous and the bizarre, the downfall of the old system of states".[3] In the *Theories of Surplus-Value* we find a more general statement. Discussing the fact that under capitalism the great majority of the producers are excluded from the consumption of wealth, Marx observes:

This was indeed also the case, and to an even higher degree, in the ancient mode of production which depended on slavery. But the ancients never thought of transforming the surplus-product into capital. Or at least only to a very limited extent. (The fact that the hoarding of treasure in the narrow sense was widespread among them shows how much surplus-product was completely idle.) They used a large part of the surplus-product for unproductive expenditure on art, religious works and public works. Still less was their production directed to the release and development of the material productive forces – division of labour, machinery, the application of the powers of nature and science to private production.[4]

As Finley puts it, the psychology of the slaveholders was that of the rentier. "Their energies went into spending their wealth, not making it."[5] One may disagree over the reasons behind this choice. Following Marx, one may find them in the demonstrative attitude of slaves towards the means of production. If slaves could be expected to treat their tools badly, there was no point in investing in improved means of production. Or, following Hegel and Genovese, one may explain the lack of investment by the demonstrative attitude of the slaveowner towards his slaves.[6] He

---

[1] *Capital III*, p. 332. The passage is also discussed in 5.3.3.
[2] *Grundrisse*, p. 433.   [3] *Ibid.*, p. 434.
[4] *Theories of Surplus-Value*, vol. 2, p. 528.
[5] Finley, "Technical innovation and economic progress in the ancient world", p. 188.
[6] On this, see my "Some conceptual problems in political theory".

had to consume unproductively in order to display his superiority over them. One could of course also argue that the slaveowners lacked *both* profitable objects of investment and the motivation to invest. On any of these views it seems hard to explain the slave relations of production in terms of their impact on the productive forces.

A more nuanced view emerges, however, when we ask how Marx explained the *origin* of slavery. Once again, a basic mechanism is population increase:

> After the *city of Rome* had been built and the surrounding countryside cultivated by its citizens, the conditions of the community were different from what they had been before. The aim of all these communities is *survival*, i.e. *reproduction of the individuals who compose it as proprietors, i.e. in the same objective mode of existence as forms the relation among the members and at the same time therefore the commune itself. This reproduction, however, is at the same time necessarily new production and destruction of the old form.* For example, where each of the individuals is supposed to possess a given number of acres of land, the advance of population is already under way. If this is to be corrected, then colonization and that in turn requires wars of conquest. With that slaves etc.[1]

Elsewhere, Marx elaborates this "conquest theory of slavery" by adding that "the production of the country for which the slave is stolen must be structured to allow of slave labour".[2] It is not clear what he means by this, but a plausible reading is that he had in mind the level achieved by the productive forces, in the sense of their degree of sophistication (5.1.1). An industrial nation could not use slave labour to man advanced factories, even were it to become available as a result of conquest. Hence the slave relations of production are doubly related to the productive forces. First, the growth of the population – that is development of the productive forces in the extensive sense – necessitates conquests and hence makes slavery a possible option by creating a mass of cheap slave labour. Next, the character of the productive forces is what determines whether that option will in fact be taken up. Observe that the latter connection has nothing whatsoever to do with the ability of slavery to *develop* the productive forces (in the intensive sense). Once again, Marx's general theory is not instantiated in this historical application.

With respect to *feudalism*, Marx is virtually mute. The reference to the hand-mill and the feudal lord can hardly be taken seriously. In the 1861–3 *Critique* there is a lengthy and much more substantial discussion of the various kinds of mill. There is no suggestion that the hand-mill was characteristic of feudalism or serfdom. Having explained why the use of

[1] *Grundrisse*, pp. 493–4.   [2] *Ibid.*, p. 98.

the mortar led to the invention of the rotating hand-mill, Marx adds that "At first slave women were given the task of grinding the corn; later on this was done by serfs."[1] He then goes on to explain how the various types of mill fitted into the feudal property structure:

Middle Ages. Hand mills, animal mills and *water mills.* (Windmills invented in Germany in the tenth or eleventh Century. No serious-use made of them before the twelfth Century. Then used exclusively until *mid-sixteenth Century.*) Typical that the German nobility, and after them the priests, claimed the wind as their own property. In 1159 Frederick I declared watermills the property of the Crown. This was later extended to windmills. Seigneurial *right* or *forced-labour mills.* Moses says, "Thou shalt not muzzle the ox when he treadeth out the corn." But their Christian–Germanic lordships assert, "During work the serfs shall have a large wooden collar placed round their necks so that their hands cannot reach to put the flour into their mouths."[2]

These observations from the history of technology are fascinating, in particular the reference to the attempt of the German nobility to appropriate the wind as private property.[3] They do not, however, add up to a theoretical account of the feudal relations of production and their impact on the productive forces. Nor does Marx in any other work discuss or even mention this issue. He never refers to the agricultural technology of the Middle Ages, nor to the subtle varieties of serfdom discussed by Marc Bloch and others. Nor is there any hint of a dynamic mechanism internal to serfdom that could explain the commutation of rent into labour or kind into money rent.

5.2.2. The transition from feudalism to capitalism

In the historical chapters of *Capital I* and *III*, as well as in the preparatory manuscripts, Marx offers a highly complex account of this process. Broadly speaking, he argues that the creation of the world market and the transformation of traditional agriculture created both a capitalist system of industrial production and the inner market that was the condition for its further expansion. It is far from clear how this corresponds to the general theory, that is to the requirement that the new relations of production arise when and because they are required for the further, optimal development of the productive forces. I discuss this in some detail below. First, however, I shall cite a passage from *Capital I* that shows clearly that

---

[1] *Zur Kritik (1861–63)*, p. 1918.   [2] *Ibid.*, p. 1925.
[3] See also the passage referenced in note 2, p. 249 above. Natural forces, like basic science, are non-ownable productive forces. To the extent that science is directed to harnessing natural forces for human purposes, the non-ownability of the knowledge of how to do this would not eliminate the incentive to develop such knowledge if the natural forces themselves could be privately owned.

Marx intended to explain the rise of capitalism by pointing to the fettering of the productive forces by previous relations of production:

The private property of the labourer in his means of production is the foundation of petty industry, whether agricultural, manufacturing or both; petty industry, again, is an essential condition for the development of social production and of the free individuality of the labourer himself. Of course, this petty mode of production exists also under slavery, serfdom and other modes of dependence. But it flourishes, it lets loose its whole energy, it attains its adequate classical form, only where the labourer is the private owner of his own means of labour set in action by himself; the peasant of the land which he cultivates, the artisan of the tool which he handles as a virtuoso. This mode of production presupposes parcelling of the soil, and scattering of the other means of production. As it excludes the concentration of these means of production, so also it excludes cooperation, division of labour within each separate process of production, the control over, and the productive application of the forces of Nature by society, and the free development of the social productive powers. It is compatible only with a system of production, and a society, moving within narrow and more or less primitive bounds. To perpetuate it would be, as Pecqueur rightly says, "to decree universal mediocrity". At a certain stage of development it brings forth the material agencies for its own dissolution. From that moment new forces and new passions spring up in the bosom of society; but the old social organisation fetters them and keeps them down. It must be annihilated; it is annihilated.[1]

Although the passage is somewhat ambiguous, and by itself does not allow deduction of the general principles of the 1859 Preface, it is more than just compatible with that text. The gist of the argument is that "simple commodity production", from being "an essential condition for the development of social production", at a certain stage becomes a fetter for the further development of the forces that have been created within its womb. Then, "it must be annihilated; it is annihilated". The difficulty is that Marx never spells out exactly how these processes occur, and that some texts suggest a quite different picture.

"In England, serfdom had practically disappeared in the last part of the fourteenth century. The immense majority of the population consisted then, and to a still larger extent in the fifteenth century, of free peasant proprietors, whatever was the feudal title under which their rights of property was hidden."[2] There obtained, in other words, a form of simple commodity production (see also 5.3.3). Yet for political as well as economic reasons this system as doomed to destruction. In *Capital I* Marx leaves "on one side the purely economic causes" of the production of small-scale property, and deals "only with the forcible means

---

[1] *Capital I*, pp. 761–2.   [2] *Ibid.*, p. 717.

employed".[1] These were, notably, the expropriation of peasant property through the sixteenth- and eighteenth-century enclosure movements, the first carried out in violation of the law and the second with its assistance – that is through illegal and legal violence respectively.[2] In *Capital III* the "purely economic causes" are enumerated.[3] They include destruction of rural domestic industry through competition with large-scale industry; a gradual impoverishment of the soil due to the primitive character of small-scale cultivation; competition with the plantation system and with large-scale capitalist agriculture; improvements in agriculture that led to falling prices of agricultural products and to greater capital requirements; vulnerability to all sorts of contingencies and hence to usurer's capital; and finally – as a more political measure – taxation. Most of these causes presuppose that capitalism is already established, in agriculture or elsewhere, and hence cannot enter into an explanation of how it came to be established. By themselves, economic causes operating independently of capitalism would tend towards a low-productivity agriculture exploited by usurer's capital and taxation, as in France.

The divergent development in England must, therefore, be explained by the political means employed, hence the prominent place of the latter in Marx's discussion of primitive accumulation in England. According to Marx, the enclosure movements here had the effect of throwing onto the market a vast mass of landless labourers, and thereby creating an essential precondition of urban capitalism.[4] This view is no longer held today.[5] The enclosure movement absorbed more workers than it separated from the land,[6] hence the urban labour supply must rather have grown as part of a general population increase.

The alleged release of labour was not, however, the only effect of the enclosures that Marx mentions. They also led to increased profitability of agriculture by allowing economies of scale and by depressing the agricultural wage level. Let us focus for the moment on the first of these mechanisms, which appears to make some sense of the idea that the rise of capitalism was linked to the unfettering of the productive forces. We may conjecture that small-scale property was progressive as long as it tended

---

[1] *Ibid.*, p. 723.   [2] For this distinction, see *ibid.*, p. 724.   [3] *Capital III*, p. 807.
[4] *Capital I*, p. 725.
[5] See Chambers and Mingay, *The Agricultural Revolution 1750–1880*, ch. 4, and Collins, "Marx on the English agricultural revolution". The latter, despite some exaggerations, is valuable in showing that Marx's account was not only factually wrong, but internally inconsistent.
[6] For a partial acknowledgement of this fact, see *Capital I*, p. 329, note 1.

to develop the "free individuality of the labourer".[1] Yet the potential for increased productivity in simple commodity production was soon exhausted. Although the free peasant is much more careful and attentive to his work than the slave or the serf, he is nevertheless limited by the small scale of production. To overcome these limits, large-scale landed production – and not merely large landed property – was necessary. In England this took the form of consolidations carried out by enclosure. If this explanation can be imputed to Marx (and we shall see that it is not certain that it can), it lacks microfoundations. It is not a trivial matter to state the conditions under which entrepreneurs are able to exploit potential gains from institutional change.[2]

Before I discuss whether this view can in fact be attributed to Marx, I shall discuss a closely related argument concerning the independent artisan who is replaced by manufacture. Marx, in fact, explicitly compares this process with the enclosure movement:

It can be seen that for the contemporaries of this *process*, which plays such a crucial role in the *original accumulation* of capital, the *characteristic feature* is the separation of *the earth from its industrious children* (quote Steuart later), namely the formation of large farms or what is called 'ingrossing' (which is just another term for the concentration of many small farms in *a single hand*). Just as in Mirabeau, where the large manufacturing workshops are called 'fabriques réunies' in a single hand, concentrated little manufacturing concerns.[3]

The creation of manufacture was a decisive step in the rise of capitalism; as argued below, Marx probably thought of it as *the* decisive step. Its preconditions were, on the one hand, the presence of urban workers not bound by the guild restrictions, and, on the other hand, a potential capitalist to employ them. In *Capital I* and *Capital III* Marx gives rather different accounts of the latter of these preconditions. In the chapter on "The genesis of the industrial capitalist" in *Capital I* he says that the transformation of the guild-master or artisan into a capitalist was a process that proceeded at a "snail's pace",[4] and suggests that the investment of capital created by overseas trade and various political measures was much more important. In the passage from *Capital III* cited in 5.1.2 he argues in the opposite manner: the transformation of the producer into a merchant is

---

[1] According to Macfarlane, *The Origins of English Individualism*, pp. 43, 195, Marx neglected the individualistic character of English agriculture, wrongly believing it to be similar in all respects to conditions on the continent. He does not mention, however, this reference to the free individuality of the petty producer in England, nor a similar passage in *Capital III*, p. 807.

[2] See notably North, *Structure and Change in Economic History*.

[3] *Zur Kritik (1861–63)*, p. 2298.   [4] *Capital I*, p. 750.

the "really revolutionizing path", whereas merchant capital had scant impact on the actual process of production. The two views could be reconciled by introducing credit and banking, channelling capital from trade into productive activities,[1] but Marx has surprisingly little to say about this mediating mechanism.[2]

Manufacture is the first, but not the complete, form of capitalist production. In all his mature works Marx distinguishes between two stages of capitalism. The first he variously refers to as "production of absolute surplus-value" or "formal subsumption of labour under capital", the second as "production of relative surplus-value", "real subsumption of labour under capital" and "the specifically capitalist mode of production". Although he explicitly asserts the identity of these different ways of making the distinction,[3] he employs it inconsistently. In *Capital I*, cooperation, division of labour and machinofacture are all discussed in Part IV on "Production of relative surplus-value", but only the last is referred to as the "specifically capitalist mode of production". He very explicitly says that relative surplus-value can only be created by revolutionizing the mode of production,[4] and that manufacture initially did not represent any change in the mode of production, compared to the handicraft methods used by the guilds.[5] Yet he also asserts that the mere bringing-together of many workers in one place allows for economies of constant capital and hence increased productivity of labour.[6]

These various views may be reconciled as follows. There are two distinct sources of increased productivity: economies of scale within a given technology, and technical change. Of these, only the latter amounts to a change in the (material) mode of production (5.1.4). In an initial phase the mere setting-up of capitalist relations of production permitted the

[1] See Crouzet, "Capital formation in Great Britain during the Industrial Revolution" for the substantive issues involved.
[2] The chapter in *Capital III* on the role of credit in capitalist production is silent about its possible role in the early stages of capitalism. In *Capital I*, p. 309 there is a brief reference to the fact that "certain spheres of production demand, even at the very outset of capitalist production, a minimum of capital that is not as yet found in the hands of single individuals". Among the possible remedies Marx mentions state subsidies to private persons and the formation of societies with legal monopoly for the exploitation of certain branches of industry and commerce – but he does not cite banking and private credit institutions.
[3] For the equivalence of production of relative surplus-value and the specifically capitalist mode of production, see *Capital I*, p. 510. For the equivalence of real subsumption of labour under capital and the specifically capitalist mode of production, see *Capital I*, p. 738 and *Zur Kritik (1861–63)*, p. 2145. The equivalence of formal subsumption and production of absolute surplus-value is asserted in *Zur Kritik (1861–63)*, p. 2130 and in *Results of the Immediate Process of Production*, p. 1021. In the 1861–3 *Critique* he also states the contrast between formal and real subsumption as one of "Gegensatz" or "Entfremdung" vs "Widerspruch" or "Feindlichkeit" (pp. 2014, 2057–8).
[4] *Capital I*, p. 510.   [5] *Ibid.*, p. 310.   [6] *Ibid.*, pp. 324–5.

creation of relative surplus-value by exploiting the hitherto untapped economies of scale of the old techniques. Conceptually, it is debatable whether this amounts to a development of the productive forces, or only to an improvement in their use. My intuition is that economies of scale constitute an improvement solely in the *use* of the forces. They are contingent upon a sufficient demand, and hence may be lost if demand falls, for instance because of population decrease. The development of the productive forces, by contrast, is supposed to be irreversible in a way that is inconsistent with such dependence on demand. In any case, the growth potential of economies of scale is soon exhausted. In the next stage relative surplus-value can only be created by technical change proper. This, moreover, is an inexhaustible source of surplus-value – hence its importance in the "specifically capitalist mode of production".

Yet Marx also states that capitalist relations can be established merely on the basis of its superior use of force:

Within the process of production . . . capital acquired the command over labour. i.e. over functioning labour-power or the labourer himself. Personified capital, the capitalist takes care that the labourer does his work regularly and with the proper degree of intensity. Capital further developed into a coercive relation, which compels the working-class to do more work than the narrow round of its own life-wants prescribes. As a producer of the activity of others, as a pumper-out of surplus-labour and exploiter of labour-power, it surpasses in energy, disregard of bounds, recklessness and efficiency, all earlier systems of production based on directly compulsory labour. At first, capital subordinates labour on the basis of the technical conditions in which it historically finds it. It does not, therefore, change immediately the mode of production. The production of surplus-value – in the form hitherto considered by us – by means of simple extension of the working-day, proved, therefore, to be independent of any change in the mode of production itself. It was not less active in the old-fashioned bakeries than in the modern cotton factories.[1]

A passage suggesting a similar view was cited in 5.1.1.[2] It is also predominant in the discussion of formal subsumption in *Results of the Immediate Process of Production* and in the 1861–3 *Critique*. From the latter, the following passage stands out as an explicit affirmation of the two-way causal relationship between the change in the relations of production and the change in the (material) mode of production:

With the real subsumption of labour under capital all the changes which we have set out enter into the technological process, the labour process. At the same time there are concomitant changes in the worker's relation to his own production and to capital. And finally there is a change in the productive power of labour, since

[1] *Ibid.*, pp. 309–10.   [2] *Ibid.*, p. 422.

we can see the development of the productive powers of social labour and not until then do we witness the large-scale application of the forces of nature, of science and machinery to the immediate process of production. Hence what changes here is not just the formal relation as such, but the actual process of labour. On the one hand, the capitalist mode of production – which appears here for the first time as a mode of production in its own right – changes the shape of material production. On the other hand, this change forms the basis for the development of the capitalist relations of production whose adequate shape, therefore, presupposes a given stage in the development of the material forces of production. We have explained how all this alters the nature of the worker's condition of dependence in the production process. This is the first point to be emphasized. This increase in the productivity of labour and in the scale of production is partly the consequence and partly the foundation of the development of the capitalist relations of production.[1]

In the *Results of the Immediate Process of Production* Marx, uncharacteristically, emphasizes that capitalist relations of production need, for their introduction,

that a certain historical level of social production has been attained. Even within the framework of an earlier mode of production certain needs and certain means of communication and production must have developed which go beyond the old relations of production and coerce them into the capitalist mould. But for the time being they need to be developed only to the point that permits the formal subsumption of labour under capital. On the basis of that change, however, specific changes in the mode of production are introduced which create new forces of production.[2]

The claim that the needs and means of production "coerce" the relations of production into the capitalist mould remains obscure. It certainly cannot mean that capitalism is necessary for the further development of the productive forces. This, while no doubt part of Marx's view, does not enter into his explanation of the rise of capitalism – except at the level of general theory, as in the 1859 Preface. In the more detailed discussions of the emergence of capitalism, he argues that the real subsumption of labour under capital, with the concomitant development of the productive forces, was a mere, non-explanatory by-product of the process. Later, I suggest an interpretation of the first part of the passage, where Marx says that the introduction of capitalism is possible only at a certain level of social production. Here I emphasize the latter part, which leaves little doubt that the emergence of capitalist relations occurred prior to, and independently of, the development of the productive forces.

If this is accepted, we must attribute to Marx the view that Stephen

---

[1] *Zur Kritik (1861–63)*, p. 2142; see also p. 2160.
[2] *Results of the Immediate Process of Production*, p. 1064.

Marglin has forcefully asserted in his study "What do bosses do?", subtitled "The origins and functions of hierarchy in capitalist production". In his view, both manufacture and machinofacture were introduced with a view to subduing the worker – the first to destroy his control over the product and the second to take away his control over the work process. The purpose was to break down the resistance of the workers, not to make productivity gains. Marglin implausibly denies that the manufacturing system involved any such gains, even as by-products.[1] (He does of course acknowledge that machinofacture led to immense technical progress, but argues that this was unrelated to its rise. The first stage, however, is the crucial one.) Even if we accept, as did Marx, that the manufacture system created economies of scale, we may still hold (i) that these do not constitute a development of the productive forces and (ii) that in any case they were secondary compared to the gains due to increased efficiency of exploitation. I believe that on general theoretical grounds we should attribute (i) to Marx and that there is direct evidence that he accepted (ii).

On this interpretation, the general theory is not instantiated in the account of the transition from feudalism to capitalism. The capitalist relations of production emerged because they allowed more surplus, not because they favoured a more rapid development of the productive forces, although that was in effect a consequence. Before this conclusion is embraced, we must ask whether the theory of the agricultural revolution could not provide a better link between the general theory and the particular case. If the enclosure movement was motivated by the gains from consolidation, and if capitalist agriculture depended on the enclosures, could not this provide the connection between increased productivity and social change?

There are, however, several objections to this argument, paralleling those just made with respect to manufacture. First, it is not clear that Marx believed gains in productivity to be the main motivation behind the enclosures. With respect to the sixteenth-century enclosures he says that "the capitalist system demanded . . . a degraded and almost servile condition of the mass of the people, the transformation of them into mercenaries, and of their means of labour into capital".[2] This suggests a functional explanation of the enclosures in terms of the separation of the worker from his means of production, required for the further development of capitalism. With respect to the second wave of enclosures, the

---

[1] Marglin, "What do bosses do?", pp. 20ff. For objections, see *Explaining Technical Change*, pp. 172ff.
[2] *Capital I*, p. 720.

emphasis is also on the fact that they "'set free' the agricultural population as proletarians for manufacturing industry".[1] Secondly, even if the
motivation is assumed to have been the increased productivity gained
from consolidation, it remains doubtful whether such economies of scale
count as "development of the productive forces". Lastly, it was Marx's
explicitly stated view that "agriculture can never be the sphere in which
capital starts".[2] In *Capital III* this view is defended at some length:

> As soon as rent assumes the form of money-rent, and thereby the relationship
> between rent-paying peasant and landlord becomes a relationship fixed by con-
> tract – a development which is only possible generally when the world-market,
> commerce and manufacture have reached a certain relatively high level – the
> leasing of land to capitalists inevitably also makes its appearance. The latter
> hitherto stood beyond the rural limits and now carry over to the country-side and
> agriculture the capital acquired in the cities and with it the capitalist mode of
> operation developed.[3]

True, the chapter in *Capital I* on "The genesis of the capitalist farmer"
suggests a different origin of capitalist agriculture, prior to or at any rate
independent of the rise of urban capitalism. On balance, I believe this is
less weighty than the evidence that Marx held the opposite view. In any
case, the first two objections also undermine the idea that Marx explained
the rise of capitalist relations of production by the increases in productivity they allowed in agriculture. Yet I do not say that this view can be
ruled out of court – it is a sign of the elusiveness of Marx's thought that
almost no interpretation can be definitely eliminated.

I have been arguing that the *rate of change* of the productive forces plays
no role in Marx's explanation of the emergence of capitalist relations of
production. It is quite understandable that Marx did not find any specific
mechanisms by which his general theory – that has the rate of change at
the very core – could be implemented. The rise of capitalist relations of
production must be explained by the gains to be made at the time of
introduction, not by the later gains in productivity that were arguably
unforeseeable, almost certainly unforeseen, in any case, too remote in
time to motivate profit-seeking individuals, as well as being subject to
various sorts of free-rider problems.[4]

Yet the *level* of the productive forces might still play a role in the explanation. We might consider the suggestion by Philippe van Parijs that the

---

[1] *Ibid.*, p. 725.   [2] *Grundrisse*, p. 669.   [3] *Capital III*, p. 799.
[4] The role of the state in financing basic science has already been mentioned (5.1.1). In
addition there is the problem that if, as argued by Cohen (*Karl Marx's Theory of History*, p.
292), the class best placed to develop the productive forces gains dominion by attracting
allies from other strata, it must be shown that it is more rational for each of these allies to
join the coalition than to hope for free-rider gains.

level of productive forces could determine which set of relations of production are optimal, but that something else than the rate of change of the
productive forces could be the maximand (5.1.4). More specifically, the
maximand could be the surplus to be extracted from the immediate producers. The passage from the *Results of the Immediate Process of Production*
cited on page 284 could give some support to this view, as does also the
following passage from the 1861–3 *Critique:*

Gunpowder, the compass and printing, the three great inventions which ushered in
bourgeois society. Gunpowder blew the world of knighthood to pieces; the compass discovered the world market and established the colonies; and printing
furnished Protestantism with the tools it required and paved the way for the
regeneration of science in general; it was the most powerful instrument with
which to build the essential intellectual foundations.[1]

This oft-cited trio of inventions form an apparent exception to the view
that there occurred virtually no change in the productive forces from
antiquity to the early modern age. On reflection, it is doubtful whether
they *constituted* an increase in the productive forces, although they may
well have been important *causes* of such increase. On no conception is
gunpowder a productive force. The printing press did not exert its importance *qua* profitable outlet for investment, but as the presupposition for
the requisite spiritual development. The compass, finally, may or may
not be seen as a productive force, depending on how goods are individu-
ated. If goods are identified by the time and place at which they are made
available, as well as by their inherent qualities, any improvement in the
means of communication is an increase in the productive forces.

Hence the van Parijs' suggestion would have to be understood somewhat liberally, in the following sense. As a result of technical change in
the early modern period, there occurred fundamental changes in the
organization of society. New military technology did away with the
power of the knights. Improved maritime technology created a world
market and led, among other things, to the discovery of the gold mines in
America. (I want to recall here a passage cited in 1.3.2, for a purely
methodological purpose. In this text from the *Grundrisse* Marx suggests
that the belief that real wealth could be created by gold mining was at once
illusory and self-fulfilling, as in La Fontaine's fable of the labourer and his
children.) Finally, the printing press was a material condition for the
diffusion of the Bible that was at the heart of the Protestant revolution,
and for the closely related scientific revolution. In this radically changed

[1] *Zur Kritik (1861–63)*, p. 1928.

context, capitalist relations of production became superior for the extraction of surplus labour. To repeat, the *level* of the productive forces has only a subsidiary character in this explanation. Rather it is the specific qualitative character of the inventions that has the central explanatory function.

I am not making any strong claims about the attribution of this view to Marx. It is a plausible sort of theory, of the kind that can be held by non-Marxists as well as Marxists. Moreover, the plausibility of this diluted Marxist theory may count for something in explaining the widespread acceptance of the undiluted theory (set out in 5.1.3). The undiluted theory can be summarized as saying that "technology is the main determinant of social change". That phrase, of course, is much more vague than the undiluted theory, and lends itself to many interpretations, one of which is the diluted theory just set forth. It is certain that later Marxists have been led into thinking that evidence for the diluted theory also counts as evidence for the undiluted one. Whether Marx himself confused the two is less clear. Confused he certainly was, as this chapter shows – confused to the point of making it difficult to identify his confusions with precision.

5.2.3. The transition from capitalism to communism
In 5.1.3 I discussed the idea that the communist revolution will occur "when and because" the capitalist relations of production become less good at developing the productive forces than communist relations would be. I pointed to a tension in Marx between this view, to which he was committed by his general theory, and the view that capitalism would break down because of its suboptimal *use* of the productive forces. I now pursue these themes, within a slightly more formal framework that will allow us to distinguish between several possible interpretations of Marx's thought. I first discuss the strong version of the theory, that communism will come when and because it is needed to develop the productive forces. Having argued that this proposition is quite implausible, I consider some weaker claims. First, the temporal clause is dropped, so that the revolution could occur before the relations actually become suboptimal. Next, a more drastic modification is suggested, by weakening the causal force of "because" to a mere correlation between the development of the productive forces and the revolution. This version also turns out to be implausible, because one of its basic premises has not been verified by history. Nor does Marx succeed in making it more persuasive by taking into account the relation between centre and periphery in capitalism. As

we shall see below, and again in 5.3.2, there are elements in Marx of a theory of "combined and uneven development", in which the relation between advanced and backward capitalist nations has a central role. In the present discussion I focus on the idea that the revolution might occur in the East and then spread to the West, whereas in 5.3.2 I consider the possibility that there might be instead a diffusion of technology from the West to the East. I shall argue that neither theory makes out a plausible case for a successful transition to communism – successful in the double sense of setting up communist relations of production and of developing the productive forces faster than would be possible under capitalism.

I first sketch a formal model, more fully presented elsewhere,[1] of the transition to communism. It assumes that the following time trajectories can be defined. First, we need to know the level of the productive forces under capitalism as a function of time. This function, $f(t)$, must be defined both for the actual capitalist past and for a – possibly hypothetical – capitalist future. If the communist revolution occurs because capitalism has become suboptimal for the development of the productive forces, we must be able to say something about how they would have developed under a continued capitalist regime. Next, assuming that a communist revolution occurs at time s, $f_s(t)$ denotes the level of productivity that would then obtain at time t. The notions of correspondence and contradiction between the forces and relations of production can now be made more precise by considering various possible relations between such time profiles.

In addition to various continuity and consistency requirements, the model rests on two substantive assumptions: the initial indispensability of capitalism and the ultimate superiority of communism. The first can be formally stated as follows: there exists a time s and a number A such that for all t, $f_s(t) < A$. There is a strong textual basis in Marx for this assumption. In *The German Ideology* he warns against a premature revolution: "this development of the productive forces . . . is an absolutely necessary practical premise, because without it privation, *want* is merely made general, and with *want* the struggle for necessities would begin again, and all the old filthy business would necessarily be restored".[2] (See 7.3.2 for some further comments on the character of such premature communism.) In the *Grundrisse* he refers to attempts to create a classless society without the requisite material conditions as "quixotic",[3] while in the *Theories of Surplus-Value* he notes that if the workers are to employ the

[1] *Explaining Technical Change*, Appendix 2.   [2] *The German Ideology*, p. 49.
[3] *Grundrisse*, p. 159.

means of production as autonomous *subjects*, 'it is of course assumed . . . that capitalist production has already developed the productive forces of labour to a sufficiently high degree for this revolution to take place".[1] As to the assumption of the ultimate superiority of communism, it has been amply documented in 5.1.3. In formal terms, it states that there exists a time s such that for all $t > s$, $f_s(t) > f(t)$.

To say that the revolution will occur when and because capitalist relations become suboptimal, is to say that it will occur at the earliest time s satisfying the last-mentioned condition. Let us call this time T_1. It is not obvious that transition at time T_1 is very attractive as an ideal, independently of the capacity of the suboptimality to motivate the workers to action. If this transition time is advocated, it must be because the growth of the productive forces is seen as the only superiority of communism over capitalism. This, however, is contrary to Marx's view. He stressed the free and full development of the individual as the main reason for preferring communism (2.2.7). It is quite conceivable that the time at which communism would be superior to capitalism in this respect is earlier than the time at which it becomes technically superior. Hence it would seem reasonable to allow the revolution to occur earlier than T_1 – if one were certain that the development of the productive forces would ultimately overtake that which would have occurred under capitalism. Formally, we ask whether there is a time $s < T_1$ and a time $s' > s$ such that for all $t > s'$, $f_s(t) > f(t)$, even if by assumption $f_s(s) < f(s)$. If this is the case, we define T_2 as the earliest such s. Clearly, for any s between T_2 and T_1, $f_s(T_1) < f_{T_1}(T_1)$: preferring an earlier transition time will postpone the time at which communism becomes superior. Hence there is a trade-off to be considered. Should the material conditions for communism be developed by capitalism, which is the more rapid way, or should one prefer the slower development whereby communism itself creates the conditions for its own future blossoming?

If communism can promote the self-realization of the individual even with a less-than-maximal rate of technical change, the latter option ought to be preferred. Yet one might not want to have the revolution occur as early as T_2, if that implies a very long time to catch up with (the counterfactual) capitalism. It might be better (on grounds of maximizing the total amount of self-realization over time) to have a few generations endure the hardship of capitalist alienation than to have many generations live under comparatively poor communist conditions.

[1] *Theories of Surplus-Value*, vol. 2, p. 580.

I should briefly mention a third criterion for the optimal transition time. If we go back to the formal statement of the indispensability of capitalism, we see that it ceases to be indispensable whenever communism can generate unbounded technical progress. Let us refer to the earliest time at which this becomes possible as T_3. If the communist revolution occurs between T_3 and T_2, then communism will never overtake capitalism, although any level of technical development reached by capitalism will ultimately also be reached by communism. This would at least avoid one form of premature revolution, the one that would condemn communism to everlasting "privation". Yet it would not of course satisfy Marx's view that communism would ultimately become superior to capitalism. The relation between the various transition times is shown in Fig. 3.

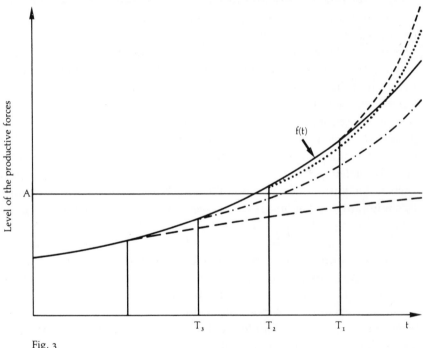

Fig. 3

Needless to say, these distinctions have at best a tenuous relevance for political action. Some considerations of this kind may have been behind the debate between Mensheviks and Bolsheviks about the proper communist strategy in a country which had not developed an industrial capitalism; but one would not expect to find precise statements of these alternative options. The discussion is mainly relevant from the welfare-theoretical point of view: how should we evaluate the various transition times with respect to the communist goal of promoting maximal and equal self-realization for individuals? Different theories of intergenerational justice will support different answers to this question. There is a real possibility that one plausible theory might conflict with the desideratum of creating ultimate superiority. If, namely, one refuses the sacrifice of those currently living for the sake of later generations, the transition to communism ought to be made at the earliest point T_4 at which the chances of self-realization for the individual would be improved. On a priori grounds, nothing excludes the possibility that $T_4 < T_3$, so that communism would indefinitely remain a state of moderate bliss.

Consider now the political relevance of suboptimality. I assume the validity of Marx's basic assumption concerning the ultimate superiority of communism, in spite of the objections made in 5.1.3. (One should note, however, that the failure of actual communist countries to overtake capitalism is not directly relevant. In the model this can be interpreted by saying that the revolution in these countries occurred too early – earlier than T_1 and possibly than T_2.) Yet even an objectively valid theory needs subjective acceptance if it is to become a revolutionary force. I submit that it is highly implausible that the workers will accept the assumption to the extent of acting on it. The counterfactual nature of the base-line for evaluating capitalist performance makes the theory too abstract to serve as a basis for action. If one could point to a declining performance over time, this might provide an incentive to change the system, but I have argued that according to Marx the contrary is the case. If one could compare the existing capitalist system in one country with an existing communist system in another, then the proven superiority of the latter might motivate the transition to communism in the former, but this argument would be of no avail in explaining the transition in the crucial first country to set up communist relations of production. Internal crises or external examples may suffice to topple a regime, but not the abstract possibility of a superior way of doing things.[1] Both uncertainty and the costs of transition would deter workers from taking the plunge.

Let me, however, pursue the motivation provided by an external example. The idea would be that the superiority of communism would

---

[1] As an anecdotal illustration, due to Francis Sejersted, I may cite the fact that the Norwegian Conservative Party in 1961 understandably had little success when *in opposition* they adopted the slogan that the British Conservatives and later the Danish Social Democrats successfully used *in power*: "Make good times better."

explain the communist revolution in all countries but the first in which it occurred. In this case, the explanation must be a different one, that need not concern us here. The first appearance of communism on the historical world scene could be more or less accidental, but its subsequent diffusion would be rationally grounded.[1] An obvious condition is that the revolution should not occur too early in the first country. Having dismissed the proposal that communism will occur in the pioneer country *because* it is more efficient, it remains essential that it should be introduced at a moment *when* communism – immediately or ultimately – can develop the productive forces more rapidly than capitalism, since otherwise there will be no success to inspire the latecomers. "But societies are not so rational in building that the dates for proletarian dictatorship arrive exactly at that moment when the economic and cultural conditions are ripe for socialism."[2] In fact, I shall argue that they are so irrational in building that these two factors tend systematically not to coincide.

Communism is desirable only when that system would be (or become) optimal for developing the productive forces. Call this the objective condition for communism. Communism is possible only when the development of capitalism creates a motivation for people to abolish it. Call this the subjective condition for communism. Clearly, Marx needs a theory that ensures the simultaneous presence of these two conditions. I have been arguing against the view that a perception of the objective condition could provide the subjective condition – the view that communism is brought about "when and because" it is becoming superior for the development of the productive forces.[3] A weaker claim could be that the subjective and objective conditions are causally correlated – both being the result of the development of the productive forces to a certain level. Immediately before the passage in *The German Ideology* where Marx warns against a premature transition to communism, he argues that

This "alienation" (to use a term which will be comprehensible to the philosophers) can, of course, only be abolished given two *practical* premises. In order to become an "unendurable" power, i.e. a power against which men make a revolution, it must necessarily have rendered the great mass of humanity "propertyless", and moreover in contradiction to an existing world of wealth and

---

[1] This would make the presently considered argument compatible with the functional explanation of the relations of production offered by Cohen in *Karl Marx's Theory of History*. It is not, however, compatible with the mechanism he suggests to back up the explanation (see note 4, p. 286 above).

[2] Trotsky, *History of the Russian Revolution*, p. 334.

[3] Actually, the "when and because" theory could also be spelled out in other ways. See note 1, p. 76 above for discussion of an analogous problem.

culture; both of these premises presuppose a great increase in productive power, a high degree of its development.[1]

Elsewhere in the same work Marx refers to "the material elements of a complete revolution" as "on the one hand the existing productive forces, on the other hand the formation of a revolutionary mass".[2] Taking these passages together, they imply the following view. For a revolution to be possible there must exist a revolutionary mass. It is created by the accumulation of wealth among some, and of poverty among others – presumably because it is relative rather than absolute poverty that motivates people to action. Poverty no less than wealth presupposes highly developed productive forces. These, in turn, also create the objective conditions for communism.

The same idea can also be expressed in the terms used in 5.1.3. The capitalist relations of production become suboptimal for the development of the productive forces at the very moment when they also become increasingly suboptimal with respect to their human use. The former guarantees the viability of communism, the latter provides the motivation for the communist revolution. This view can also be integrated with the distinction between pioneers and latecomers. Communism initially comes about because workers revolt against the use-fettering, whereas subsequent countries can also be motivated by the development-fettering that is demonstrated by the success of communism in the pioneer country. Moreover, even in the first country the transition would not be accidental, since the use-fettering would be causally correlated with the development-fettering.

This might appear to be a viable synthesis of Marx's apparently conflicting statements. It does, however, have a weak point – the assumption that the development of the productive forces will generate an increasing gap between wealth and poverty that will motivate the workers to action. Besides not being borne out by the historical record, this postulate is inherently implausible. If the real wage increases with the gap, the latter cannot be expected to have much motivating power (see also 6.2.2). If, on the other hand, the gap widens while the workers remain as poor as ever, it will be impossible also to observe a fall in the rate of profit (3.3.2). Moreover, capitalism is simply not so perverse that it will generate universal misery while developing productive forces that allow for universal self-fulfilment. If intelligent capitalists, paternalistic landowners or statesmen acting on behalf of "society" saw the need for the Factory Acts

---

[1] *The German Ideology*, p. 48.   [2] *Ibid.*, p. 54.

(4.1.4), they could presumably also see the need to give the workers a share – perceived as fair or at least adequate – of the social wealth.

The idea of a successful communist revolution can be taken in two distinct senses. First, it may mean the successful establishment of communist relations of production; secondly, the successful realization of the goal of the revolutionaries.[1] We assume that this goal is to overtake capitalism with respect to the rate of technical change. We have seen that to ensure success in the second sense, the revolution must occur after T_1 if the criterion is instantaneous superiority, after T_2 if it is ultimate superiority. Similarly we may define a time T_5 in the development of capitalism which is the earliest time when the subjective conditions for a communist revolution are present. In particular, there must obtain "the very first prerequisite of a proletarian revolution ... namely the existence of an *industrial* proletariat in a national scale".[2] Following the line of argument of the preceding paragraph, we may also define a time T_6 that represents the latest time at which these subjective conditions are present. The development of capitalism at some time creates a general level of welfare which is such that the motivation for revolution can no longer be sustained. We may now consider various possibilities and problems.

First, the time between T_5 and T_6 might be very short, even vanishingly so. The emergence of a nation-wide proletariat could occur *pari passu* with the improvement in its living conditions, so that the working class would first be too small and then too affluent to make a revolution. Next, consider the possibility that the revolution does occur, but prematurely. If $T_5 < T_1$, the revolution might occur too early according to the criterion of instantaneous superiority; if $T_5 < T_2$, too early even by the weaker criterion of ultimate superiority. It might, but it need not. The task of the proletarian leadership would be to stave off the revolution until the time when the objective conditions have been created. If, however, $T_6 < T_2$, any revolution would have to be premature, in the strong sense that it would never lead to a superior communist system. With $T_2 < T_6 < T_1$, the revolution would be premature only in a weaker sense.

Marx, I believe, was aware of these problems. Anticipating Trotsky's theory of combined and uneven development, he tried to resolve them by suggesting a division of revolutionary labour among the various capitalist countries. At a given time, different countries find themselves

---

[1] See Dunn, "The success and failure of modern revolutions".
[2] *Herr Vogt*, p. 91; cp. *The Class Struggles in France*, p. 56.

at different levels of capitalist development, hence the objective conditions for revolution can be present in some and the subjective conditions in others. Consider first a text from *The German Ideology:*

Thus all collisions in history have their origin, according to our view, in the contradiction between the productive forces and the form of intercourse. Incidentally, to lead to collisions in a country, this contradiction need not necessarily have reached its extreme limit in that particular country. The competition with industrially more advanced countries brought about by the expansion of international intercourse, is sufficient to produce a similar contradiction in countries with a less advanced industry (e.g. the latent proletariat in Germany brought into more prominence by the competition of English industry).[1]

Despite some ambiguity, the trust of the passage seems clear. In England, the productive forces have developed so far that capital is no longer optimal for their further development. In Germany this is not yet the case, but nevertheless her backward situation exposes her to revolution, possibly more so than England. A few years later these tentative propositions harden into a general theory:

Just as the period of crises occurs later on the Continent than in England, so does that of prosperity. The original process always takes place in England; it is the demiurge of the bourgeois cosmos. . . . While, therefore, the crises first produce revolutions in the Continent, the foundation for these is, nevertheless, always laid in England. Violent outbreaks must naturally occur rather in the extremities of the bourgeois body than in its heart, since the possibility of adjustment is greater there than here.[2]

In itself this does not solve the problem. Even accepting that development of the productive forces in the advanced countries brings about hardship for the backward ones, it might not be the case that these hardships become "unendurable" only when the development has advanced to the point of making communism better suited for the further development. Moreover, one may ask what difference it would make if the events were synchronized in the required manner. A viable communism in a given country requires a communist revolution in *that* country. Nothing so far would exclude the conclusion that England in 1850 was too advanced for a successful communist *revolution*, and France and Germany too backward for a successful *communist* revolution. If so, there would seem to be an impasse.

The first objection can be met, I believe, only by assuming as an accidental fact that the development in one country of the productive forces to the level necessary for a viable communism also leads to conditions in

---

[1] *The German Ideology*, pp. 74–5.   [2] *The Class Struggles in France*, p. 134.

other countries that are conducive to revolution. Clearly, that revolution would not occur *because* of the suboptimality of the capitalist relations in the first country. Nor does Marx offer any argument for a *lawlike correlation* between events in the two camps.

The second objection can be met in two ways. In 1850 Marx argued that the revolution will spread from the backward countries in which it occurs to the advanced countries in which it can lead to durable results. Immediately after the last-quoted passage, Marx goes on to say that "the degree to which the Continental revolution reacts back on England is at the same a thermometer which indicates how far these revolutions really call in question the bourgeois conditions of life, or how far they only hit their political formations". Elsewhere in the same work he prophecies that "the class war within French society turns into a world war, in which the nations confront one another. Accomplishment begins only when, through the world war, the proletariat is pushed to the fore in the nation which dominates the world market, to the forefront in England."[1] Marx, of course, was thinking in terms of the French Revolution and the counterrevolutionary wars it unleashed. This is explicitly stated in an article written on the last day of 1848 and published in the *Neue Rheinische Zeitung* on the first day of 1849:

The liberation of Europe, whether brought about by the struggle of the oppressed nationalities for their independence or by overthrowing feudal absolutism, depends therefore on the successful uprising of the French working class. Every social upheaval in France, however, is bound to be thwarted by the English bourgeoisie, by Great Britain's industrial and commercial domination of the world. Every partial social reform in France or in the European continent as a whole, if designed to be lasting, is merely a pious wish. And only a *world war* can overthrow the old England, as only this can provide the Chartists, the party of the organised English workers, with the conditions for a successful rising against their gigantic oppressors. Only when the Chartists head the English Government will the social revolution pass from the sphere of utopia to that of reality. But any *European war* in which England is involved is a world war, waged in Canada as in Italy, in East Indies as in Prussia, in Africa or on the Danube. A European war will be the first result of a successful workers' revolution in France. England will head the counter-revolutionary armies, just as it did during the Napoleonic period, but through the war itself will be thrown to the head of the revolutionary movement and will repay the debt it owes in regard to the revolution of the eighteenth century.

It is difficult to know how seriously this phantasmagoria was intended. Bias there surely is, but is it the bias of wishful thinking or the bias of exhortation (7.2.2)? I tend to believe that it is the latter. Yet the general

[1] *Ibid.*, p. 117.

scenario of a revolution starting on the continent and then spreading to England was probably a more serious proposal. Observe that the advanced–backward contrast is not the same as the pioneer–latecomer distinction used earlier. The former refers to the level of development of the productive forces, the latter to the time of transition to (viable) communism.

In his later years Marx suggested another way of meeting the objection. Instead of putting his trust in the diffusion of the revolution westwards, from the European continent to England, he now argued that the revolution in a backward country could lead to a viable communism if there took place a diffusion of technology eastwards, from Western to Eastern Europe. I return to this argument in 5.3.2.

How should we assess the first answer to the objection? The aftermath of the October Revolution is of some relevance here. The Western powers did not fulfil their historical mission by engaging in a large-scale counterrevolutionary war. True, they remained far from passive, but their support to the anti-communist forces surely did not amount to what Marx would have expected. Their reasons for acting as they did do not concern us here. We can, however, suggest a reason that Marx ought to have considered. If Marx, or the socialist movement, was able to foresee what the outcome would be of a counterrevolutionary war, then surely the powers that were supposed to carry it out could also anticipate it. By attributing to himself greater insight and sophistication than his adversaries, Marx violated an important canon of rational behaviour, or at least of political prudence. In 7.2.1 I discuss another case in which Marx violated this principle of "mutual rationality".[1]

I conclude with a comment on the case that $T_5 < T_2 < T_6$. I asserted above that this may, but need not, lead to an irreversible and premature commitment to communism. I now want to add a reason why this might be expected to happen, if the country in question is a backward one. In such countries the development of working-class organizations will often be in advance of the development of capitalism. The implantation of socialist ideas can proceed more rapidly than the accumulation of capital. Trotsky explained very well why this was so:

[In] Russia the proletariat did not arise gradually through ages, carrying with itself the burden of the past as in England, but in leaps involving sharp changes of environment, ties, relations, and a sharp break with the past. It is just this fact –

---

[1] On this principle see Harsanyi, *Rational Behavior and Bargaining Equilibrium in Games and Social Situations*, ch. 6.

combined with the concentrated oppression of czarism – that made the Russian workers hospitable to the boldest conclusions of revolutionary thought.[1]

More specifically, he argued that the political importance of the proletariat depended not only on the proportion it formed of the nation, but also on "the amount of productive forces it sets in motion" – that is on the capital-intensity and hence on the size of the firms. Russia, being a latecomer to industrialization, was free to use the most advanced methods of large-scale production, requiring huge numbers of workers. Such concentration in itself facilitates class consciousness, which is further helped by the absence of a reformist past and the possibility of drawing on the stock of socialist ideas developed in the West.[2]

Under such conditions there will typically be a great deal of impatience among the workers. Their leaders, assuming them to understand the predicament, have the choice between two alternatives. One is to stave off the revolution to T_2 (or to some acceptable time between T_2 and T_1). The other is to speed up the economic development to bring T_2 (or that acceptable date) closer to T_5. For easily understood reasons, Marxists have usually chosen the second, less quietist alternative. This was Marx's policy in 1848, or at least one of his policies (7.2). It was also that of the Mensheviks before the October Revolution and of the Chinese communists up to the Shanghai massacre. For equally obvious reasons, it has invariably failed. For one thing, once the workers have successfully engaged in a struggle against the feudal–absolutist–colonial regime, it will be hard to stop them from turning – prematurely – against their former ally, the bourgeoisie. For another, the bourgeoisie will recognize this danger, and therefore be quite circumspect about any alliance with their future enemies. The only scenario that would satisfy the Marxist is one in which the workers successfully help the bourgeoisie to power, and then unsuccessfully try to replace them. This defeat will provide time for capitalist development, and harden the class consciousness of the workers for later struggles.[3] A delicate balance is needed. The workers must be strong, yet not too powerful. The bourgeoisie must be so weak they need the help of the workers, yet not so weak that they cannot resist them. In practice it has not worked out.

[1] Trotsky, *History of the Russian Revolution*, p. 33.
[2] See also Knei-Paz, *The Social and Political Thought of Leon Trotsky*, p. 117 and *passim*.
[3] On the function of defeats in bringing social relations "to the point of sharp class antagonisms", see *The Class Struggles in France*, p. 47.

5.2.4. Summing-up on the modes of production

Marx's theory of the modes of production is something of a conceptual jungle. Hence a summary of the main propositions and distinctions made in 5.1 and 5.2 may be in order.

(1) On any interpretation, the theory of modes of production says that the relations of production can be explained in terms of the productive forces. This constitutes the *primacy* of the productive forces.

(2) The primacy thesis may involve the *level* of development of the productive forces, their *rate of change*, or both. In the last version, the theory says that the level of the productive forces determines which relations are optimal for their further development. It says, moreover, that optimal relations tend to be realized. This is probably the version that best captures Marx's more general, theoretical statement.

(3) When the relations are suboptimal for the forces, they are *fetters* on them. There is, however, another interpretation of fettering with some support in Marx. This says that the relations fetter the forces when the forces cease to develop. Such *absolute stagnation*, however, is on balance less plausible than *suboptimality* as an interpretation of fettering.

(4) There is another alternative way of understanding fettering, as the suboptimal *use* of the productive forces. This amounts to proposing *another maximand* for the historical process. Instead of arguing that history is to be seen as the maximization of the rate of change of the productive forces, this alternative says that property right structures rise and fall according to their capacity for maximizing the net product. Once again, this is less plausible exegetically than the interpretation stated in (2).

(5) The notion of *development* of the productive forces is multiply ambiguous. It is unclear whether the exploitation of economies of scale counts as such development. Also, it is unclear whether the productive forces develop when they allow for a greater surplus under constant environmental and demographic conditions, or when they allow for a greater surplus under the actual, possibly changed conditions.

(6) At the level of the general theory, as stated in (2), Marx does not specify any *mechanism* whereby optimal relations of production come to be realized. In particular, he does not suggest any link between this process and the class struggle. To some extent his teleological view of history may have led him to neglect this problem.

(7) *The dynamics of pre-capitalist society*, as discussed by Marx, do not fit the general theory, on any interpretation. Marx argued that population growth rather than the development of the productive forces was the cause of the breakdown of these earlier modes of production.

(8) *The transition from feudalism to capitalism* does not fit the general theory as stated in (2). This statement must be modified in two ways. First, the *level* of the productive forces does enter into the explanation of the rise of capitalism, although the maximand would seem to be surplus-extraction rather than the development or the use of the productive forces. Next, the exploitation of economies of scale made possible by capitalism can be seen as promoting the use of the productive forces; even, but less plausibly, as promoting their development.

(9) *The transition from capitalism to socialism* was the object of a political struggle, not of historical analysis. If construed in the light of the general theory as set out in (2), the transition appears as highly unlikely. It is somewhat more plausible if both use-fettering and development-fettering are introduced. This modified theory, in turn, achieves maximal plausibility if we further distinguish between advanced and backward capitalist countries. Yet even in this improved version the theory fails to convince.

(10) *The transition from socialism to communism*, or from the first stage of communism to the higher stage, has not been discussed in this chapter. It is taken up in 7.3.2 below. It should be noted, however, that Marx owes us an account of the dynamics of this transition, not only a conceptual discussion of the difference between the two stages.

5.3. Marx's periodization of history

In addition to his theory of the internal dynamics of each mode of production, Marx had a theory of world history, of the order and way in which the modes of production succeed one another on the historical scene. It is sometimes assumed that this theory was "uni-linear", meaning (i) that all countries go through the same sequence and (ii) that the sequence is consistently progressive. In 5.3.1 I sketch a conceptual framework that allows a discussion of this view. In 5.3.2 I consider the sequence of modes of production from this perspective. In 5.3.3 I argue that Marx also employed a periodization of history in terms of the changing purposes underlying the productive activities – production for use, for exchange and for surplus.

5.3.1. Development and progress in history

A theory of economic development involves a series of stages or states through which the process must necessarily, or normally, pass. There are two questions we can ask of a theory of this kind. First, we may ask whether the development is in some sense also a progress – that is if each state ranks higher than its predecessor on some scale of perfection. Secondly, we may ask whether the theory of stages applies to each exemplar (e.g. each nation-state) of the entity undergoing development.

The main answers to the first question can be stated using geometrical metaphors. The successive stages may form a linear, a circular or a spiral movement. The spiral for our purpose is a combination of line and circle: it returns toward the origin, but at ever-higher levels. It may also be expressed as a cycle superimposed on an upwards trend, or as a progression of the form "One step backward, two steps forward" (2.4.1). Vico is often credited with the invention of the spiral image of history, but the view was stated before him, with unsurpassable precision, by Leibniz.[1]

Observe that a given sequence of stages may be linear, circular or spiral according to the chosen criterion of progress. Economic growth is a linear progress if we consider production per capita, but a spiral – one step backward, two steps forward – if we consider consumption per capita. If the development is progressive in the long term, but with temporary setbacks, an ambiguity arises in the contrast between advanced and backward countries. It can be understood either as a contrast between countries that are more or less advanced along the sequence of developmental stages, or as a contrast between countries that score more or less highly on the scale for progressiveness. A given country may be advanced in one sense and not in another, if it is in the process of taking a step backward as part of the preparation for further advance. For countries in the process of modernization this may cause considerable intellectual confusion, with simultaneous feelings of inferiority and superiority with respect to the more developed countries.[2]

The second question also allows of three main answers. (i) All nations go through the same stages in the same order, even though different nations will reach a given stage at different times. This is the *model of*

---

[1] See references in *Leibniz et la Formation de l'Esprit Capitaliste*, especially pp. 216, 229–30.
[2] See Feuerwerker, "China's modern economic history in communist Chinese historiography" for a vivid description.

unique development. (ii) For one country to be in stage n, at least one country, not necessarily the same, must already have passed through stage n − 1. We may refer to this as the *bloc model of development*, since the group of nations as a whole is the bearer of the development. (iii) If one country is the first to arrive at stage n, then it is necessarily another country that is the first to arrive at stage n + 1. Following Ernest Gellner, we may refer to this as the *torch-relay model of development.*[1] Of these the first and the third are polar cases. The second is compatible with both, but may also take a form that differs from each.

There is no point in crossing these trichotomies with each other, but some connections may be noted. The rarely defined expression "unilinear development" can plausibly be understood as a form of unique development exhibiting uninterrupted progress. The combination of the torch-relay model and a development of the form "One step backward, two steps forward" corresponds to the notion of *sacrifice* in history. One country takes the burden of regression so that others can progress to further heights. Finally, there can be a tension between the model of unique development and the idea of progress interrupted by temporary setbacks. This is related to the second point: if one nation has gone through Purgatory, must others follow in its steps – or can they enjoy the advantages of backwardness?

5.3.2. The sequence of modes of production

"In broad outlines Asiatic, ancient, feudal and modern bourgeois modes of production can be designated as progressive epochs in the economic formation of society." This statement from the 1859 Preface can be read either as asserting a theory of development or as ranking these modes of production according to a criterion of progress. The Preface as a whole almost irresistibly suggests that Marx had both ideas in mind, but other texts leave room for doubt. I shall discuss progress and development in turn, relating the modes of production based on exploitation to one another as well as to the pre-class society preceding them and the post-class society which was to follow.

Marx, it is usually said, believed the uninterrupted progress of the productive forces to be a fundamental fact about history.[2] There is no doubt that he often expressed himself in a way that supports this view, notably in *The German Ideology.*[3] The acknowledgment of local or

[1] Gellner, "A Russian Marxist philosophy of history".
[2] See notably Cohen, *Karl Marx's Theory of History*, ch. VI.   [3] *The German Ideology*, p. 82.

temporary setbacks[1] does not make this reading less plausible, since they are described as accidents rather than parts of a developmental scheme. On the other hand, Marx also insisted on the lack of technical progress from antiquity to the early modern age (5.2.1). Nor does he mention any technical advances linked to the transition from pre-class to class society. While his general theory (5.1.3) suggests uninterrupted progress, at least within the modes of production based on exploitation and class, the accounts of the specific modes of production rather suggest a constant level of productivity up to the early modern age and then a sudden "take-off" into sustained and even accelerating technical progress.

Another possible criterion for asserting the progressive character of historical development could be the size of the surplus extracted from the immediate producers. As observed more than once, a larger surplus may, but need not be accompanied by an increase in the productivity of labour. The surplus may also be increased by forcing the producers to work longer hours, or more intensively or for a smaller subsistence. Hence there could be an uninterrupted increase in the size of the surplus without a corresponding trend in productivity. On this view, history would be the succession of ever more powerful institutions for extracting the surplus from the immediate producers. This is an inherently more plausible view than the one emphasizing an unbroken progress of the productive forces, since it can be directly linked to the class struggle. Classes confront one another over surplus extraction, not over the rate of technical change (6.1.3). On the other hand Marx never explicitly affirms this view. It is implicit in his account of the transition from feudalism to capitalism, but never stated as a general theory.

Marx did not see history as simply a form of linear progress. It also exhibited the spiral form discussed in 2.4: class society in general, and capitalism in particular, represent the step backward that humanity must take in order to move forwards to communism. Here the criterion for progress is not productivity or size of surplus, but rather the degree of social integration. The primitive unity that characterized pre-class society must be broken up in order to achieve the higher unity of post-class society. The individuals themselves must lose their original capacity for all-sided work and become specialized before they can regain and expand their all-round versatility. Hence the best summary of Marx's theory of history would appear to be: uninterrupted progress of the productive forces, interrupted progress of human development and social integration.

[1] Ibid., pp. 34, 67.

The issue of development is more complex. There is room for doubt as to the presence of a developmental scheme in Marx's writings. Thus, Umberto Melotti argues that the Asiatic mode of production was in no way a predecessor of ancient slavery.[1] Rather the Asiatic commune and the classical commune were two independently arising forms of pre-class society. This view, I think, cannot be accepted in full. In *Capital I* Marx asserted that the classical commune, based on private property of land, grew out of the oriental commune based on common property of land.[2] Yet I agree that Marx nowhere suggests that the Asiatic mode of production was a precursor of ancient slavery. Rather the picture which emerges is that the oriental commune is the ancestral form both of the Asiatic mode of production and – via the classical commune – of ancient slavery. If this is accepted, we get one main line of historical development – including the oriental commune, the classical commune, slavery, serfdom and capitalism. The side development from the oriental commune into the Asiatic mode of production appears to be a blind alley.

Did Marx believe in the model of unique development? An early text (from the commentary on List) denies this in the most explicit terms one could wish for. Having first observed that "industry can be regarded as a great workshop in which man first takes possession of his own forces and the forces of nature", he adds a warning against the theory of unique development:

To hold that every nation goes through this development internally would be as absurd as the idea that every nation is bound to go through the political development of France or the philosophical development of Germany. What the nations have done as nations, they have done for human society; their whole value consists only in the fact that each single nation has accomplished for the benefit of other nations one of the main historical aspects (one of the main determinations) in the framework of which mankind has accomplished its development, and therefore after industry in England, politics in France and philosophy in Germany have been developed, they have been developed for the world, and their world-historic significance, as also that of these nations, has thereby come to an end.[3]

Read against the background of Marx's denunciation, in the same work and elsewhere, of the industrial conditions in England, this amounts to saying that England has sacrificed herself for the sake of humanity. Other nations can dispense not only with the early industrial development, but also with capitalist relations of production that in England were the condition for that development. This is the torch-relay model of development.

[1] Melotti, *Marx and the Third Word*, p. 26 and *passim*.   [2] *Capital I*, p. 334.
[3] "Commentary on List", p. 281.

Against this we may set the Preface to *Capital I*, in which the model of unique development is asserted no less explicitly:

In this work I have to examine the capitalist mode of production and the conditions of production and exchange corresponding to that mode. Up to the present time, their classic ground is England. That is the reason why England is used as chief illustration in the development of my theoretical ideas. If, however, the German reader shrugs his shoulders at the condition of the English industrial and agricultural labourers, or in optimist fashion comforts himself with the thought that in Germany things are not nearly so bad, I must plainly tell him, *"De te fabula narratur!"* Intrinsically, it is not a question of the higher or lower degree of development of the social antagonisms that result from the natural laws of capitalism. It is a question of these laws themselves working with iron necessity towards inevitable results. The country that is more advanced industrially only shows, to the less developed, the image of its future. ... One nation can and should learn from others. And even when a society has got upon the right track for the discovery of the natural laws of its movement – and it is the ultimate aim of this work, to lay bare the economic laws of motion of modern society – it can neither clear by bold leaps, nor remove by legal enactments, the obstacles offered by the successive phases of its normal development. But it can shorten and lessen the birth-pangs.[1]

This passage combines a certain kind of scientism with a model of unique development, modified only by the possibility that latecomers may spend less time in the capitalist Purgatory. It may be objected that the modification throws doubt upon the alleged "iron necessity" of the process. One apple falling to the ground cannot learn from another and thereby be enabled to fall faster or slower. Nor, to take an example closer to the present discussion, can an adolescent learn from the mistakes of innumerable generations of adolescents before him. He may no doubt try to learn from their mistakes, and skip adolescence altogether, but will fail with virtually "iron necessity". Adolescence is a series of unsuccessful attempts to skip adolescence. It is only by the failures met with in these attempts that one gathers the experience that finally allows one to leave that stage behind. If, however, there is a real possibility of shortening the transition period by learning from others, one might ask whether the necessity could not be attenuated to the point where it becomes possible to skip the stage altogether.

To this objection one may answer, on behalf of Marx, that the ability to learn already presupposes a fairly advanced stage of development, which can only be reached endogenously. There is a parallel here to the notion of appropriation by conquest, which can succeed only if the conquering

---

[1] *Capital I*, pp. 8–10.

country is adapted to (or adapts itself to) the conditions in the conquered nation:

Nothing is more common than the notion that in history up till now it has only been a question of *taking*. The barbarians *take* the Roman empire, and this fact of taking is made to explain the transition from the old world to the feudal system. In this taking by barbarians, however, the question is whether the nation which is conquered has evolved productive forces, as is the case with modern peoples, or whether its productive forces are based for the most part merely on their concentration and on the community. Taking is further determined by the object taken. A banker's fortune, consisting of paper, cannot be taken at all without the taker's submitting to the conditions of production and intercourse of the country taken. Similarly the total industrial capital of a modern industrial country. And finally, everywhere there is very soon an end to taking, and when there is nothing more to take, you have to set about producing. From this necessity of producing, which very soon asserts itself, it follows that the form of community adopted by the settling conquerors must correspond to the stage of development of the productive forces they find in existence; or, if this is not the case from the start, it must change according to the productive forces. This, too, explains the fact, which people profess to have noticed everywhere in the period following the migration of the peoples, namely that the servant was master, and that the conquerors very soon took over language, culture and manners from the conquered.[1]

Learning and borrowing have this in common with stealing, that one cannot make good use of what is taken over if one is too far behind the level of development attained by the possessor. It follows that one cannot in such cases use borrowed knowledge (or conquered means of production) to narrow the gap. What would be useful is knowledge or technology corresponding to a stage that the advanced country has left behind, and that is more appropriate to the stage attained by the backward country. It is in the nature of the case, however, that such outdated knowledge rarely exists in suitable form, and in addition the pride of the borrower may prevent adoption of any but the most modern techniques.

Marx had to confront this problem in a practical form when Russian writers drew the conclusion from his work that Russia had to pass through the stage of capitalism before socialism could be developed. In 1877 he drafted a letter to the editors of a Russian journal that had published an article asserting this view. Marx first refers to Chernyshevsky, who "in remarkable articles has discussed the question whether Russia must begin, as the liberal economists demand, with the destruction of the peasant community, and then make the transition to a capitalist regime, or whether on the contrary it can appropriate all the fruits of the latter

---

[1] *The German Ideology*, pp. 84–5; see also *Grundrisse*, pp. 97–8.

system without going through all its tortures (*Qualen*)". He answers that "If Russia continues to pursue the path she has followed since 1861, she will lose the finest chance ever offered by history to a people and undergo all the fatal vicissitudes of the capitalist regime." In denying that his work offers any grounds for the view that Russia must enter upon the capitalist path, he first refers to the chapter on primitive accumulation in *Capital I* and then adds:

Which application to Russia could my critics make of this historical sketch? Only this: if Russia is tending to become a capitalist nation after the example of the West-European countries – and during the last few years she has been taking a lot of trouble in this direction – she will not succeed without having first transformed a good part of her peasants into proletarians; and after that, once taken to the bosom of the capitalist regime, she will experience its pitiless laws like other countries.[1]

This may or may not be compatible with the chapter on primitive accumulation, but hardly with the Preface to *Capital I*. In any case, Marx does not here enter into the substance of the problem and offer *arguments* for the view that Russia can skip the capitalist stage. This he did a few years later, when drafting a reply to Vera Zasulich who had asked for his opinion on the path of Russia to socialism. Her concern was strictly practical: should the Russian socialists direct their energy to the liberation and development of the rural commune, or to propaganda among the urban workers?[2]

Marx's brief reply is rather tentative, but in the various drafts there is a more extensive discussion. He admits that if Russia were isolated from the world, it would have to undergo all the stages of capitalist development, with the inevitable disappearance of the commune. He also admits that there are strong forces in Russia that conspire towards the elimination of the commune, notably the alliance between the state and the capitalist class supported by the state at the expense of the peasantry. Yet the existence of capitalism also holds out a hope for the commune, which can take over the advanced methods (notably in agriculture) developed in Western Europe. "It can obtain the fruits with which capitalist production has enriched humanity without passing through the capitalist regime." He raises and attempts to answer various objections to this idea. To those who point to the universal elimination of all earlier communes, he says that the Russian commune is more flexible because liberated from the bonds of kinship, and more individualistic because containing an element of private property. Concerning the isolation of the communes from one

---

[1] Marx to Mikhailovsky November 1877.   [2] "Briefwechsel mit Vera Sasulich".

another, he argues that it can be suppressed by the simple administrative measure of creating a peasant assembly. To an implied objection concerning the lack of capital for transformation of the commune, he answers by saying that the Russian society "owes" it to the commune, at whose expense it has been living.[1]

These are not powerful arguments. In fact, they are so weak that they underline the essential correctness of the *Capital* Preface. Neither moral argument nor political reforms can create the conditions for successful borrowing if the level of material development is too low. "In the course of their development [men] first have to *produce* the *material conditions* of a new society itself, and no exertion of mind or will can free them from this fate."[2]

This objection, if accepted, reinforces the argument of 5.2.3. I argued there that the subjective and the objective conditions for communism would rarely be united in one country. I discussed and dismissed the idea that the revolution can spread from the countries where the subjective conditions are present to those where the objective conditions are more favourable. The converse view would be that the objective conditions themselves can be diffused by borrowing, so that there is no need for a revolutionary class consciousness and an advanced technology to develop *pari passu* in one country. This suggestion, however, comes up against the fact that successful borrowing also requires fairly advanced objective conditions, that typically will not be conducive to revolution. To enjoy the advantages of backwardness in the field of technology a country must not be so backward that it can also be a breeding-ground for revolution. In particular, this holds if the revolution is itself caused by relative backwardness, in the sense mentioned at the end of 5.2.3. It is much easier to borrow and absorb socialist ideals than to borrow and make good use of advanced technology.

When referring to the "essential correctness" of the *Capital* Preface I had in mind only the view that the conditions for a viable communism must emerge endogenously if they are to emerge at all. I did not underwrite the view that these conditions must develop. Marx of course could deduce the latter idea from this general teleological premise. Communism will occur, hence any necessary conditions for its emergence will also occur. In this sense Marx's developmental scheme works from the future to the present, not the other way round. He did not consider the possibility that communism might occur prematurely, and like the Asiatic mode of production become a dead end of history.

---

[1] *Ibid.*   [2] *Deutsche-Brüsseler-Zeitung* 11.11.1847.

5.3.3. An alternative periodization

The sequence of modes of production has a prominent place in the 1859 Preface and in many other passages. It is certainly Marx's best-known periodization of history. There is, however, an alternative conceptualization that is equally important in his work taken as a whole. I touched upon this view in 1.5.1 when discussing Marx's "dialectical deduction" of the economic categories from one another. While rejecting this deduction as mysterious and misleading, I remarked that it makes better sense if taken as a historical sequence, generated by ordinary causal processes rather than by dialectics. I now consider this in more detail.

The sequence I shall consider has three main stages: production for use, production for exchange and production for surplus-value. The passage from the first to the second stage is mediated by external trade, that between the second and the third by internal trade. Hence we may also consider the process as consisting of five successive stages, as I do in the following.

In the *first stage* production occurs only for the subsistence needs of the producers. Production and consumption can be organized more or less communally, more or less on an individual basis, but the purpose is always satisfaction of the immediate needs of the producers. There may be private property, but neither trade nor investment nor extraction of surplus labour takes place.

The *second stage* is marked by the emergence of trade among these communities. In the *Grundrisse* Marx distinguishes between two origins of trade. Either "there is at first interposition by trading peoples, or else tribes whose production is different by nature enter into contact and exchange their superfluous products".[1] Although he then goes on to say that "the former case is a more classical form", this cannot be taken in the sense of having historical primacy, since the origin of the trading people is left in the dark. Rather we must assume that the second is the historically prior form, and this is in fact what Marx invokes in numerous other passages touching upon the origins of trade.[2] The reference to differences in production corresponds to the remark in *Capital I* that "it is not the mere fertility of the soil, but the differentiation of the soil, the variety of its natural products, the changes of the seasons, which form the physical basis for the social division of labour".[3] In a completely homogeneous

---

[1] *Grundrisse*, p. 256.
[2] *Grundrisse*, pp. 159, 204, 873; *Critique of Political Economy*, pp. 35–6; *Zur Kritik (1861–63)*, p. 249; *Capital I*, pp. 87–8; *Capital III*, p. 177.
[3] *Capital I*, pp. 513–14.

environment there might still occur differentiation of production, but it is more likely to occur with differentiated production possibilities.

How do primitive communities enter into contact with one another? Marx invariably says that this originally occurs at their borders, as a result of accidental encounters between members of different communities.[1] A plausible cause of such meetings would be population growth, but to my knowledge Marx never mentions this. It could also be a mere chance phenomenon, likely to occur when individual members stray outside their communities. We may note, parenthetically, that Marx elsewhere refers to *war* as a possible outcome of the contact between expanding communities, adding that

If human beings themselves are conquered along with the land and soil as its organic accessories, then they are equally conquered as one of the conditions of production, and in this way arises slavery and serfdom, which soon corrupts and modifies the original forms of all communities, and then itself becomes their basis.[2]

Hence the contact between primitive communities is the starting-point for the sequence of modes of production as well as for the presently considered sequence. I shall have to return to the relation between these two sequences.

The *third stage* is reached when trade, from being accidental, becomes regularized. This implies that the goods exchanged become *commodities:*

With barter ... the product is exchange value only *in itself*; it is its first phenomenal form; but the product is not yet posited as exchange value. Firstly, this character does not yet dominate production as a whole, but concerns only its superfluity and is hence itself more or less *superfluous* (like exchange itself); an accidental enlargement of the sphere of satisfactions, enjoyments (relations to new objects). It therefore takes place at only a few points (originally at the borders of the natural communities, in their contact with strangers), is restricted to a narrow sphere, and forms something which passes production by, is auxiliary to it; dies out just as much by chance as it arises. ... But if it should happen to continue, to become a continuing act which contains within itself the means of its renewal, then little by little, from the outside and likewise by chance, regulation of reciprocal exchange arises by means of regulation of reciprocal production, and the costs of production, which ultimately resolve into labour time, would thus become the measure of exchange.[3]

Part of the production has now become production of commodities, or of exchange value. The proximate *purpose* of production has changed: it is no longer directed towards immediate satisfaction, but towards exchange.

[1] This is stated in most of the passages cited in note 2, p. 310.
[2] *Grundrisse*, p. 491.   [3] *Ibid.*, p. 204.

Needs satisfaction remains, however, the ultimate purpose of the exchanges thus undertaken.

In the *fourth stage* commodity production is generalized. The inter-community exchange "reacts back upon"[1] the community itself and gives rise to intra-community exchange. The agent catalysing this process is merchant's capital. Having developed out of external exchange, concomitantly with the emergence of money as a means for stabilizing such exchange,[2] it "bites deeper and deeper" into internal production as well.[3] The most detailed description is given in the *Grundrisse:*

> At first the effect is of a more physical kind. The sphere of needs is expanded; the aim is the satisfaction of the new needs, and hence greater regularity and an increase of production. The organization of domestic production is already modified by circulation and exchange value; but it has not yet been completely invaded by them, either over the surface or in depth. This is what is called the *civilizing influence* of external trade. The degree to which the movement towards the establishment of exchange value then attacks the whole of production depends partly on the intensity of this external influence and partly on the degree of development attained by the elements of domestic production – division of labour etc. In England, for example, the import of Netherlands commodities in the sixteenth century and at the beginning of the seventeenth century gave to the surplus of wool which England had to provide in exchange, an essential, decisive role. In order then to produce more wool cultivated land was transformed into sheep-walks, the system of small tenant-farmers was broken up etc., clearing of estates took place etc. Agriculture thus lost the character of labour for use value, and the exchange of its overflow lost the character of relative indifference in respect to the inner construction of production.[4]

As will be shown shortly, Marx believed that this process had taken place twice, once in antiquity and then again in the Middle Ages. It is not clear that he was right in either case. Karl Polanyi, who has been the foremost champion of the "priority of the external over the internal development of trade",[5] did not think that the former gave birth to the latter. In antiquity, in his view, a national market never developed – there were only local markets and international trade.[6] In the Middle Ages the towns were the focus of both local and international trade, but prevented the formation of a national market until their resistance was broken by the state.[7] Broadly

---

[1] For this phrase see *Critique of Political Economy*, p. 36; *Zur Kritik (1861–63)*, p. 249; *Capital I*, p. 87; *Capital III*, p. 330.

[2] On the relation between commodity production and money see ch. 1 of *Capital I* as well as the "Chapter on money" in the *Grundrisse*.

[3] *Capital III*, p. 330.   [4] *Grundrisse*, p. 256.

[5] This phrase is taken from Polanyi, *The Livelihood of Man*, p. 78. He credits Weber with the invention and Thurnwald with the development of this idea, apparently ignoring its importance in Marx.

[6] Polanyi, *The Livelihood of Man*, ch. 13.   [7] Polanyi, *The Great Transformation*, ch. 5.

speaking, these views have been upheld by other scholars as well.[1] In one case, Marx exaggerated the extent to which an internal market was present, in another he misidentified the mechanism by which it emerged. True, in his articles on revolutionary Spain he also states that "absolute monarchy presents itself as a civilizing centre, as the initiator of social unity",[2] instead of emphasizing "the civilizing influence of foreign trade". (See also 7.1.5.) The two views could be partly reconciled if absolute monarchy stabilized rather than created the national market.

The *fifth stage* is the emergence of production for surplus-value. This transition occurs differently in the dialectical and the historical developments. From the dialectical point of view, the important feature of the fourth stage is that production for exchange value is also production for *money*. According to the argument set forth in 1.5.1, money has an inherent need for self-expansion: "value which insists on itself as value preserves itself through increase".[3] From the historical point of view, the fourth stage is unstable for the reasons given in 5.1.2. A system of simple commodity production can exist only in a knife-edge equilibrium, and will be upset by any accident of endowment or fortune. In the chapter on usurer's capital in *Capital III* the outcome is described as follows:

Both the ruin of the rich landowners through usury and the impoverishment of the small producers lead to the formation and concentration of large amounts of money-capital. But to what extent this process does away with the old mode of production, as happened in modern Europe, and whether it puts the capitalist mode of production in its stead, depends entirely upon the stage of historical development and the attendant circumstances.[4]

With respect to antiquity, Marx describes this process in two different ways. First he says that "As soon as the usury of the Roman patricians had completely ruined the Roman plebeians, the small peasants, this form of exploitation came to an end and a pure slave economy replaced the small peasant economy".[5] A few pages later he argues that

The indebted slave-holder or feudal lord becomes more oppressive because he is himself more oppressed. Or he finally makes way for the usurer, who becomes a landed proprietor or a slaveholder himself, like the knights in ancient Rome. The place of the old exploiter, whose exploitation was more or less patriarchal because it was largely a means to political power, is taken by a hard, money-mad parvenu.[6]

---

[1] On antiquity, see Garnsey, Hopkins and Whittaker (eds.), *Trade in the Ancient Economy.* On the unifying role of the mercantilist state, see Heckscher, *Mercantilism.*
[2] *New York Daily Tribune* 9.9.1854.
[3] *Grundrisse*, p. 270.   [4] *Capital III*, p. 594.   [5] *Ibid.*, p. 595.   [6] *Ibid.*, pp. 596–7.

Whereas the first passage says that the effect of the ruin of the small producers was the *creation* of a slave economy, the second says that it led to the *transformation* of the slave economy from a patriarchal system into a money-oriented one. The latter characterization is more consistent with the view that production for exchange value tends to turn into production for surplus-value. The second view is also confirmed in an important passage from the historical chapter on merchant's capital in *Capital III*. Here Marx telescopes the fourth and the fifth stages into one process:

The development of commerce and merchant's capital gives rise everywhere to the tendency towards production of exchange-values, increases its volume, multiplies it, makes it cosmopolitan, and develops money into world-money. Commerce, therefore, has a more or less dissolving influence everywhere on the producing organisation, which it finds at hand and whose different forms are mainly carried on with a view to use-value. To what extent it brings about a dissolution of the old mode of production depends on its solidity and internal structure. And whither this process of dissolution will lead, in other words, what new mode of production will replace the old, does not depend on commerce, but on the character of the old mode of production itself. In the ancient world the effect of commerce and the development of merchant's capital always resulted in a slave economy; depending on the point of departure, only in the transformation of a patriarchal slave system devoted to the production of the immediate means of subsistence into one devoted to the production of surplus-value. However, in the modern world, it results in the capitalist mode of production.[1]

I have cited two passages where Marx affirms the existence in antiquity of a slave system devoted to money-making, or the production of surplus-value. As noted in 5.2.1, this is not the way in which Marx usually characterizes slavery, but the view is hard to avoid given his need to graft the presently considered sequence onto the sequence of modes of production. Tentatively, his thinking may be reconstructed as follows. On "dialectical" grounds he was persuaded that production for exchange value must lead to production for surplus-value. This conviction may have originated in the study of capitalism, and then acquired the status of a general proposition. He was then driven to postulate the existence of slavery oriented towards surplus-value, in spite of his sound observations elsewhere that slavery was unfavourable to the transformation of surplus product into capital.

The five-stage sequence occurs twice in the history of mankind. The first time around it begins (we must assume) in the oriental commune, with the second, third and fourth stages corresponding to various stages in early Graeco-Roman history, and the fifth being commercial slavery. This

[1] *Ibid.*, pp. 331–2.

presupposes that non-commercial or patriarchal slavery had arisen earlier, through conquest and subsequent enslavement of conquered peoples. If we make the plausible assumption that Marx believed population growth to have been at the origin of trade no less than of war, the following scenario emerges. When the original communities expand and enter into contact with one another, the outcome in some cases is war and the enslavement of one people by another. In other cases the result is the emergence of trade between them. A community that has successfully enslaved another, and also entered into trade with third parties, will find that external trade reacts back upon internal production, so that the slave economy ultimately comes to be oriented towards trade and money-making. Conquest led to an economy *based on* the extraction of surplus labour through cheap slaves. Trade transformed that system into one of slavery *devoted to* surplus labour extraction.

The second time the sequence is realized in a quite different way. Once again Marx has little to say about the origins of the process, but we must assume that it began with the subsistence production of isolated peasant communities attached to a manor. Long-distance trade – in this case plausibly mediated by trading peoples – arises, and as before reacts on internal production. The outcome is the creation of a class of independent artisans and peasants producing for the market. This brief moment of simple commodity production – a transitional stage between feudalism and capitalism – cannot, however, last for long. The system tends to generate cumulative inequalities, and in time the separation of the producers from their means of production. The conditions for the emergence of capitalism are united.

At this point we may quote a remark by Marx in a draft letter from 1877:

In several parts of *Capital* I allude to the fate which overtook the plebeians of ancient Rome. They were originally free peasants, each cultivating his own piece of land on his own account. In the course of Roman history they were expropriated. The same movement which divorced them from their means of production and subsistence allowed the formation not only of big landed property, but also of big money capital. And so one fine morning there were to be found on the one hand free men, stripped of everything except their labour power, and on the other, in order to exploit this labour, those who held all the acquired wealth in their possession. What happened? The Roman proletarians became not wage-labourers but a mob of do-nothings more abject than the former 'poor whites' in the South of the United States, and alongside of them there developed a mode of production which was not capitalist but based on slavery.[1]

[1] Marx to Mikhailovsky November 1877.

The last phrase may be read as suggesting that slavery did not exist prior to the expropriation of the plebeians, but also as saying that slavery underwent further development after that event. I shall assume the latter reading as most compatible with the other texts cited here. The reason for the non-development of capitalism may then be sought in the simple fact that slavery already existed as a massive source of surplus labour, so that the newly created fortunes would naturally seek this mode of expansion rather than invent a wholly new form of surplus labour extraction. Two thousand years later, however, there was no such pre-existing system onto which the desire for surplus-value could latch. (At least this was the case in Western Europe. Marx to my knowledge does not discuss the "second serfdom" in Eastern Europe, based on production for the market.)

A puzzle remains: the decline of slavery and the subsequent rise of serfdom. This massive fact of world history is surprisingly neglected by Marx. I know of only one attempt to explain how this transition took place:

If Antiquity started out from the *town* and its small territory, the Middle Ages started out from the *country*. This different starting-point was determined by the sparseness of the population at that time, which was scattered over a large area and which received no large increases from the conquerors. In contrast to Greece and Rome, feudal development, therefore, begins over a much wider territory, prepared by the Roman conquests and the spread of agriculture first associated with them. The last centuries of the declining Roman empire and its conquest by the barbarians destroyed a considerable part of the productive forces; agriculture had declined, industry had decayed for want of a market, trade had died out or been violently interrupted, the rural and urban population had decreased. These conditions and the mode of organisation of the conquest determined by them, together with the influence of the Germanic military constitution, led to the development of feudal property.[1]

One receives the impression here that the decline of the Roman Empire preceded the German conquests, although possibly reinforced by them. There is no hint at the mechanism by which the decline, if endogenous, took place.

We must conclude that in addition to the linear theory of modes of production, Marx offered a cyclical periodization of world history in terms of the changing purposes of productive activity. Production for immediate subsistence turns into production for exchange, which in turn becomes production for surplus-value. After one run of this sequence, ending with slavery, serfdom marks the beginning of the second. Broadly

[1] *The German Ideology*, pp. 33–4.

speaking, the first run corresponds to the Asiatic and the ancient modes of production, the second to feudalism and capitalism. This provides a rationale for the frequent comparisons in Marx's work between slavery and capitalism,[1] and the (less frequent) comparisons between the Asiatic and the feudal modes of production.[2]

The dynamic element of this process is external and internal *trade*, neither class struggle nor the development of the productive forces. This "neo-Smithian"[3] or proto-Hicksian[4] theory of history is not usually associated with Marx. And it is of course only part of his theory. Yet, as I said, it is no less central than the better-known theory of the rise and fall of property right structures in accordance with their ability to promote the productive forces. Marx owes us an account of how these two views are to be welded into one coherent theory. Some links are readily discernible, and have been noted above. They do not, however, amount to a full integration of the two periodizations, each with its own internal dynamics. Some will conclude that Marx, a true historian, kept an open mind and avoided all dogmatism. Others will argue that the presence of these two, prima facie incompatible views shows a deplorable lack of intellectual discipline. Most probably, there is an element of truth in both assertions.

---

[1] See for instance his remarks on the insights of the Greek into the nature of political economy ("Aus der 'kritischen Geschichte'", p. 213) and on the relation between Roman law and capitalism (*Grundrisse*, pp. 245–6 and letter to Lassalle of 22.7.1861).
[2] See for instance the section on labour rent in ch. 47 of *Capital III*.
[3] See Brenner, "The origins of capitalist development: a critique of neo-Smithian Marxism".
[4] See Hicks, *A Theory of Economic History*, ch. III and *passim*.

6. Classes

In chapter 5 I have discussed the view that history is the history of the development of the productive forces. I now turn to the other major strand of Marx's thought, that "the history of all hitherto existing society is the history of class struggle".[1] The lack of integration of these two views is, as I said earlier, a major difficulty in Marxism.[2] There is no hint of any mechanism by which the class struggle promotes the growth of the productive forces. Marx's overall theory of history is strangely disembodied, while his theory of collective action is no less strangely myopic. Once again, the explanation must be sought in his teleological view of history, which, by working backward from end result to preconditions, could dispense with actors and their intentions.

In 6.1 I consider the meaning of "class" in Marx. In reconstructing the notion I have kept in mind what I believe was Marx's main use for the concept – to explain the incidence and the forms of collective action. I examine attempts to define class in terms of property endowments, exploitation, market behaviour and power – concluding that none of these by itself will give us what we want. Rather, a more complex definition is

---

[1] *The Communist Manifesto*, p. 482.
[2] Cp. Cohen, "Reply to Elster" and Roemer, "Methodological individualism and deductive Marxism" for opposed views on the relative importance of these two theories.

needed, defining class membership in terms of "endowment-necessitated behaviour". I also consider the question of what relations obtain between the classes thus defined, with special emphasis on exploitation and power relations.

In 6.2 I consider the notion of class consciousness and the conditions for its emergence – both with respect to general background conditions and with respect to specific motivational mechanisms. Although I am unwilling to abandon the idea of explaining collective action in terms of individual goals (rational or irrational), the attempt may, for the time being, be premature. Marx, in any case, did not offer plausible micro-foundations for class consciousness. Rather, he appeared to argue that collective action can be explained teleologically.

In 6.3 I turn to the class struggle – from latent conflict through overt confrontation to coalition formation. The study of class alliances is perhaps Marx's most suggestive contribution to the theory of social conflict – anticipating Simmel and Caplow. I return to the political aspects of coalition formation in chapter 7.

6.1. Defining classes

Marx never defined what he meant by class.[1] Yet by a triangulation method similar to that employed in 5.1.1 it is possible to reconstruct how the term is to be understood in his writings. In 6.1.1, I cite the main texts in which Marx indicates what social groups he took to be classes and then propose a notion that is extensionally adequate to this enumeration and also theoretically satisfactory. In 6.1.2 I compare the notions of class and *status*, in the sense of estate or order. In 6.1.3 I discuss what on this conception are the main relations between classes. This will also occasion a comparison between the Marxist theory of class and the theory of social stratification. In 6.1.4 I discuss mobility as a – possibly definitional – feature of class. The analysis in this section, while largely conceptual, is also implicitly theoretical. In deciding between various interpretations, I try to choose the one that is most plausible in the light of Marx's theory of the class struggle.

6.1.1. An analytical reconstruction

We know what Marx took to be the main classes of pre-capitalist societies: "freeman and slave, patrician and plebeian, lord and serf, guild-master

---

[1] A useful attempt to collect and organize the main texts where Marx discusses classes in general terms is found in ch. I of Dahrendorf, *Class and Class Conflict in Industrial Society*. For a survey of his more detailed analyses, Draper's encyclopaedic *Karl Marx's Theory of Revolution*, vol. II, is invaluable.

and journeyman".[1] In capitalism, "wage labourers, capitalists and land-lords constitute the three great social classes".[2] In England, the most advanced capitalist country, these are also the *only* classes, with the exception of the occasionally mentioned class of finance capitalists; in France, Marx also refers to the peasantry and the petty bourgeoisie as important classes.[3]

This enumeration suggests some preliminary comments. First, we are left in the dark about the class structure of the Asiatic mode of production. Secondly, each of the other modes of production is said to include three or more classes, thus excluding any kind of dichotomous class structure, such as the haves vs. the have-nots.[4] Next, the category of freeman is an incongruous element, since his relations to the factors of production is not fully specified. The free man owns his labour-power, he may or may not own the means of production and the labour-power of others. Finally, patricians and plebeians would seem to form status groups rather than classes. I return to this problem in 6.1.3. It suggests that it may not be possible to construct a Marxist notion of class that is fully consistent with both Marx's actual usage and his theoretical purposes.

Some other texts will be cited, and interpreted according to the following principle. If Marx refers to X, Y and Z as somehow being on a par, and if we already know from other works that he considered X to be a class, then there is a presumption that Y and Z also are classes on his view. The principle is not self-evidently correct, and there are cases where it hardly works.[5] Yet handled with caution it provides a useful guide. Consider, for instance, the passages in *Capital III* where Marx refers to "the slave-owner, the feudal lord and the state (for instance the oriental despot)",[6] and then again "the slave-owner, the feudal lord and the tribute-collecting state"[7] as the owners of the surplus under, respectively, "slavery, feudalism and tributary relations".[8] It is hard not to conclude that the tribute-collecting state, or at least some members of its

---

[1] *The Communist Manifesto*, p. 482.   [2] *Capital III*, p. 886.

[3] Of these, the class status of the financial capitalists may be the most controversial. In *The Class Struggles in France* (pp. 48ff) Marx refers to them as "the ruling class"; see also 6.3.3 below.

[4] For such dichotomous views, see Ossowski, *Class Structure in the Social Consciousness*, ch. II.

[5] See for instance *Grundrisse*, p. 87 where Marx asserts that "the conqueror who lives from tribute, or the official who lives from taxes, or the landed proprietor and his rent, or the monk and his alms, or the Levite and his tithe, all receive a quota of social production, which is determined by other laws than that of the slave's etc.". It would be foolhardy to conclude on this basis that Marx considered the mendicant friars to form a social class.

[6] *Capital III*, p. 331.   [7] *Ibid.*, p. 326.   [8] *Ibid.*

apparatus, constitute a class. Other passages point in the same direction.[1]
A more complex statement is the following:

The entire contents of the relation, as well as the way in which the conditions of
his labour appear as something alienated from that labour itself, manifest themselves in their naked economic form, without any political, religious or other
trimmings. It is a pure money relation. Capitalist and worker. Objectified labour
and living labour power. Not master and servant, priest and layman, feudal lord
and vassal, master craftsman and journeyman, etc. In all social formations the
class (or classes) which rules is always the class which has the objective conditions
of labour in its possession; and its representatives work, if at all, then not as
workers, but as owners. And the serving class is always the class which finds itself
or its labour power in the hands of the property-owners (slavery) and never
controls more than its own labour-power. (Even where it may seem, as in India,
Egypt, etc., that it owns landed property, the true owner is really the king or a
caste, etc.) But all these formations differ from capitalism inasmuch as the relation
is disguised as one of the master to his servants, the freeman to the slaves,
demi-gods to ordinary mortals, etc. and exists as such a relation in the consciousness of both parties. Only in capitalism have all these political, religious and other
ideal disguises been cast off.[2]

This appears to suggest that (Catholic or heathen) priests may constitute a
ruling class, and, a fortiori, a class. In a passage from *Capital III* cited in 1.4.6
Marx also comes close to stating that the Catholic Church formed a class
during the Middle Ages.[3] As in the last-quoted passage, he refers to the
suppression of the laity by the church, and cites its practice of opening its
ranks to "the best brains in the land" as a means of consolidating its
"rule". And the passage ends with a general comment on the usefulness
of such practices for the ruling *class*. Similarly, Marx's references to the
Etruscan "theocracy"[4] or "priest–nobles"[5] provide support for this view.

  Altogether these passages mention some fifteen groups that appear as
classes in the various modes of production: bureaucrats and theocrats in
the Asiatic mode of production; slaves, plebeians and patricians under
slavery; lord, serf, guild-master and journeyman under feudalism; industrial capitalists, financial capitalists, landlords, peasants, petty bourgeoisie and wage labourers under capitalism. The task is to construct an
intensional definition consistent both with this enumeration and with the
theoretical constraints on the notion. In particular, classes must be
defined so as to be at least potential collective actors. Also, the interests

[1] See notably *Grundrisse*, pp. 87, 433 and *Capital I*, pp. 334, 598. Useful discussions are found
  in Melotti, *Marx and the Third World*, ch. 8 and Draper, *Karl Marx's Theory of Revolution*, vol.
  I, ch. 22.
[2] *Zur Kritik (1861–63)*, p. 116.   [3] *Capital III*, p. 600–1.   [4] *Capital I*, p. 334
[5] *Grundrisse*, p. 433.

they have as collective actors must somehow emerge out of their economic situation. These are broad constraints, but they serve to rule out of court at least some proposals. Income groups are not classes, nor are groupings defined by ethnic, religious or linguistic criteria.

I shall proceed by discussing *four possible definitions* of class, in terms of, respectively, property, exploitation, market behaviour and power. We shall not find what we want in any single criterion, but discussion of them will enable us to construct a notion that appears fairly adequate, even if also quite complex. Part of the complexity stems from the need to take account of the difference between market and non-market economies. Also, the distinction between private and corporate ownership of the means of production creates difficulties for any attempt to construct a simple definition.

The view most frequently attributed to Marx is probably that a class is a group of persons who stand in the same relation of property or non-property to the factors of production, that is labour-power and means of production.[1] This proposal comes up against several difficulties. By themselves, property and non-property are too crude as indicators of class membership. They do not, for instance, allow us to distinguish between landlords and capitalists, nor between a small capitalist and a wage labourer who owns some of the means of production (e.g. in the putting-out system). And Marx warns against any attempt to define classes in terms of the *kind* or the *amount* of property owned. The first proposal would have the absurd consequence that "owners of vineyards, farm owners, mine owners and owners of fisheries"[2] form separate social classes, whereas the second would lead to an "infinite fragmentation"[3] of classes. The trichotomy of property into full, partial or none (5.1.2) may be useful as a first approximation, but there is really no reason to think that people who own nine-tenths of their means of production and those who own one-tenth are more similar to one another than are the former to those who have full ownership and the latter to those who have none. True, as a matter of empirical fact property might be discontinuously distributed, for example in an hour-glass distribution. Since, however, distribution in many modern societies is rather diamond-shaped or pyramid-shaped, this would limit the applicability of the notion in a rather unsatisfactory way. Moreover, even when property as a matter of

---

[1] This seems to be the central criterion in the reconstruction proposed by Dahrendorf, *Class and Class Conflict*, pp. 11ff. Many authors use property as one, possibly the most important criterion, without articulating the relation to other criteria.

[2] *Capital III*, p. 886.   [3] *Ibid.*

fact is bimodally distributed, we would need a non-arbitrary division of the continuum between the extremes. To study social mobility, for instance, we would have to be able to tell when an individual has acquired enough property so that he is no longer a worker but has become a capitalist.

A final problem for this proposal is created by corporate property, for example church and state land. The managers of such property form a class, but not by virtue of property-ownership, since in a real sense the property belongs to the corporation rather than to any individual or individuals.[1] As argued later, they form a class by virtue of their power to decide how the factors of production shall be used, that is by their ability to issue legitimate commands. Their command over property emerges as a result of attaining a certain class position, and is not a prior fact explaining their class membership.

The second proposal I shall consider is that classes be defined in terms of exploitation.[2] Observe that this is not the same as to say that a relation of exploitation tends to obtain between members of different classes, as defined by some independent criterion. It is reasonable on Marxian grounds to state as a theoretical constraint that there should be a broad correlation between class status and exploitation status, but this need not take the form of postulating a definitional connection. And it is in fact easy to see that this will not do as a definition, being either too coarse-grained or too fine-grained to generate the classes cited by Marx.

The proposal is too coarse-grained if it locates all exploiters in one class and all exploited agents in another. This does not allow us to distinguish between different exploiting classes, for example between landlords and capitalists, nor between different exploited classes, such as slaves and poor freemen in societies where they have coexisted.[3] Moreover, exploitation status does not serve as a motivation for collective action, since no one in a society knows exactly where the dividing line between exploiters and exploited should be drawn. The labour-value calculations that would be necessary to determine this line would be horrendously complex, assuming that the presence of heterogeneous labour does not make them downright impossible (3.2.2).

---

[1] On this, see Coleman, *Power and the Structure of Society*, ch. 1. Contrary to appearances, this is not in conflict with the tenets of methodological individualism (1.1). Corporate property must be explicated in terms of variables ranging over individuals, which is compatible with no reference being made to specific individuals ("individual constants" in the language of logic).

[2] This is the central criterion in Ste Croix, *The Class Struggle in the Ancient Greek World*, pp. 43ff and Wright, *Class Structure and Income Determination*, pp. 14ff.

[3] For Marx on the "poor whites" in the Old South, see *Die Presse* 25.10.1861.

On the other hand the proposal is too fine-grained if classes are to be distinguished in terms of the *degree* of exploitation.[1] It then becomes analogous to the proposal to define classes as income groups. Since degree of exploitation, like income (or property), is a continuously variable criterion, we are again led to postulate an "infinite fragmentation" of classes. I return to this issue in 6.1.3.

The third proposal is to define classes in terms of market behaviour.[2] In economies with a labour market, this gives us three basic classes: those who buy labour-power, those who sell labour-power and the petty bourgeois who do neither. We may subdivide the first and the second class according to whether the agents, in addition to buying and selling labour-power, also work some time for themselves.[3] In economies with credit markets, similar classes can be defined with respect to the lending and borrowing of money. An obvious objection is that the definition is unhelpful in the study of non-market economies. I shall argue, however, that a broad analogy to the present proposal, or rather to a reconstructed version of the present proposal, can also be applied to non-market economies.

The need for a reconstruction arises because the proposal overemphasizes actual behaviour and neglects its causal grounding in the endowment structure. Classes should be defined by what people (in some sense) *have to* do, not by what they actually do. Xenophon's gentleman-farmer who works on the farm "for pleasure and for the sake of the physical and moral benefits such exercise can bestow, and not because economic necessity obliges him to work"[4] does not belong to the same class as someone who *must* work his land himself. A Rockefeller does not turn into a worker simply by taking a salaried job, unless he also gives away his fortune. A self-proletarianized student does not become a member of the working class if the option of becoming self-employed remains open. These observations flow from the constraint that the notion of class is ultimately to be used in a theory of social conflict. We would not expect the agents who have to work or to sell their labour-power to align themselves with non-compulsory workers or sellers of labour-power.

[1] Ste Croix, *The Class Struggle in the Ancient Greek World*, p. 116 suggests that classes may be distinguished by "*the scale on which exploitation of the labour of others takes place*"; cp. *ibid.*, p. 471.

[2] As shown in 6.1.2, this was Max Weber's position. It is also the view put forward in Roemer, *A General Theory*. Roemer, unlike Weber, agrees that there are classes in non-market economies, but they are not covered by his conceptualization.

[3] See Roemer, *ibid.*, chs. 2 and 4.

[4] Ste Croix, *The Class Struggle in the Ancient Greek World*, p. 121.

We know from 4.1.2 what compels some agents to sell their labour-power, and what allows others to hire them (in fact compels them to do so if they are to optimize). The cause is to be found in the endowment structure. Agents with endowments that have little value at the equilibrium prices are forced to sell their labour-power to optimize. Typically, although not invariably, they are also forced to optimize (4.2.3). This suggests an integration of the first and the third approaches to class. Although the ownership of endowments may be continuously distributed, the owners will naturally sort themselves into a small number of classes when they try to optimize by engaging in market exchanges. *Endowment-necessitated behaviour* then becomes the criterion for class.

As with the other proposals, we must consider the extensional adequacy of the definition. Once again, the landlord–capitalist distinction is a recalcitrant case. The landlord is anomalous from the present point of view, since he earns an income without working *and* without hiring labour. He does not produce anything, but lives off the rent from his land. In the type of models found in Roemer's *General Theory*, this is not conceivable, since here labour is the only non-depreciating asset and agents are not allowed to eat up their capital. In a model with both land and labour as non-produced, non-depreciating assets,[1] landlord behaviour would be feasible, and in fact optimal, with a suitably chosen objective function.[2] Hence, with a suitable extension of the conceptual apparatus the presently considered definition could be made to generate the landlord–capitalist distinction, and no doubt the distinction between independent peasants and independent artisans as well.[3] There are, however, several objections that can be made to this solution, since it may involve postulating different objective functions for landlords.[4] On ideal Marxist grounds, one would want members of different classes to have similar objective functions and different endowments. Attitudes towards work or consumption should stem from class position, not cause it. On general methodological grounds one should beware of the risk of *ad*

---

[1] See Roemer, "Why labor classes?" for one such model.
[2] Landlord behaviour could be optimal, for instance, if the objective is to minimize working hours subject to a consumption constraint, and then to consume as much as possible if it involves no labour.
[3] Yet observe that one consequence of admitting both labour and land as scarce resources is to take the bottom out of the labour theory of value. With two or more scarce factors the equilibrium prices are not independent of final demand (3.2.2). Hence there is a conflict between Marx's theory of value and his theory of classes, in that the only valid ground for distinguishing landlords from capitalists also has the effect of destroying the privileged character of labour.
[4] I am indebted to Michael Wallerstein for this point.

hoc-ness. Almost any behaviour can be seen as optimal if one is allowed to manipulate the goals of the agents. The objections may not be insuperable, but any further development of the theory ought to confront them.

In market economies, then, *classes are characterized by the activities in which their members are compelled to engage by virtue of the endowment structure*. These are the activities of working or not working, buying and selling labour-power, lending and borrowing capital, hiring and renting land. With the exception of the first, these conceptual pairs all involve *relations* between economic agents. Moreover, the property of working or not working does not constitute a complete class characterization. This would rather be something like "working and selling one's labour-power" or "not working and renting land". Hence any class characterization is necessarily relational, excluding, for instance, "blue collar" and "white collar" as class criteria.

If taken in a suitably general sense, the italicized phrase in the last paragraph can also serve to define classes in non-market economies based on private property in the factors of production. Observe, namely, that in such economies the producing agents have no or only partial control over their labour-power. This lack of control is part of the property endowment structure, and by definition is what enables the controllers to compel producers to work for them. Of course, the relation between the property structure and the activities in which the agents engage compulsorily differs fundamentally in the two cases. In market economies the distribution of agents into classes is not immediately given by the endowment structure. It must be derived from it by assuming that agents enter into market transactions. Moreover, the derivation is non-unique, as shown by the possibility of multiple equilibria (4.1.2). In non-market economies, on the other hand, who compels whom to do what is an institutional fact, given prior to any actual transactions. Also, the compulsion means different things in the two cases. The extra-economic coercion of non-market economies must be distinguished from the "dull compulsion of economic relations". These differences notwithstanding, the italicized formula is sufficiently general to cover both cases. It links what agents *do* to what they *have*, by defining classes in terms of what they must do to make the best use of what they own.[1] Neither behaviour nor endowments by themselves will give a concept that is both extensionally and theoretically adequate.

A further generalization of the concept is proposed below. First, however, we must consider a final proposal, that classes be defined in terms of

---

[1] Although the working out of this idea is mainly due to Roemer, it was suggested independently by Cohen, *Karl Marx's Theory of History*, pp. 70ff ("Redefining the proletarian").

power relations – as one criterion among others or as *the* criterion.[1] I shall discuss this idea with respect to the four possible cases that arise by distinguishing, first, between market and non-market economies and then between private and corporate property of the means of production.

(i) In market economies based on private ownership of the means of production, power is not constitutive of class. There may but need not obtain pre-political or personal power relations between members of different classes. Thus a worker is subject to domination within the labour process by virtue of his need to sell his labour-power (4.1.5). This, however, is not what makes him a worker. Rather, it is a fact that follows from what makes him a worker: his need to sell his labour-power. By contrast, a small peasant who has mortgaged his holding to a bank does not stand in a similar relation of personal subordination.[2] Finally, there may but need not exist political power relationships between the various classes. The extent to which the state in a capitalist society is also a capitalist state is an empirical matter (7.1), and certainly not one that enters into the definition of classes.

(ii) In non-market economies with individual ownership, power relations *are* constitutive of class membership. The endowment structure that gives rise to classes includes the fact that some individuals have full or partial ownership of the labour-power of others. But to own the labour-power of another *conceptually* implies that one has power over him. (By contrast, the ownership of means of production in a market economy has at most a *causal* connection with the emergence of power relations.) Here the definition of class in terms of endowment-necessitated behaviour coincides with the definition in terms of power. Ownership of persons *is* power.

These personal power relations may but need not rest on legal and political domination. The Roman law of slavery was not primarily designed to keep the slave in his place, but to regulate his status in commercial transactions with free men.[3] (Slavery in the American South differed in this respect.[4]) Similarly, power and dependency relations in the Middle Ages did not always require the sanction of the law. It is useful to keep in mind Marc Bloch's comment that "in social life is there any more elusive

[1] On his own behalf Dahrendorf proposes this as the main criterion for class. I do not think anyone has suggested that *Marx* thought of classes primarily in terms of power.
[2] But see Roemer, *A General Theory*, p. 95, note 1 for some doubts.
[3] Finley, *The Ancient Economy*, p. 63, with reference to Buckland, *The Roman Law of Slavery*.
[4] Genovese, *Roll, Jordan, Roll*, pp. 25ff.

notion than the free will of a small man?"[1] And he goes on to say that "In this troubled society, whose central authority could not get into effective touch with the masses, violence helped to transform social conditions the more effectively because, through the play of custom an abuse might always by mutation become a precedent, a precedent a right".[2]

(iii) Consider next the class status of those involved in handling corporate property in non-market economies, that is the theocrats and bureaucrats discussed by Marx. Clearly, to characterize the functionaries as *one* class would obfuscate the important distinction between different ranks of the hierarchy. A definition of class that has the Vatican's janitor and the Pope becoming members of the same class does not seem very useful. The line of cleavage within the bureaucracy might be drawn by using either exploitation status or power status as the criterion. The first would draw the line between the net exploiters and the net exploited, the second between those who control the labour-power of others and those who do not.[3] This may also be extended into a trichotomy, differentiating between those who only control (upper managers), those who only obey (workers) and those who have someone above them as well as below them in the command hierarchy (lower managers).[4]

In general, we may expect the upper managers to be exploiters, the workers to be exploited, and the lower managers to be bisected by the "net exploitation" line. Hence the arguments made above against defining classes in terms of exploitation carry over to the present case. Let me try to make these arguments somewhat more explicit and general. First, if we want classes to be relevant for social struggle and collective action, they should not be defined in terms of exploitation, since no one knows exactly where the dividing line between exploiters and exploited is to be drawn and since there is no non-cognitive way in which the line could make a difference for behaviour. By contrast, it is easy to perceive who hires labour and who sells it, who gives commands and who receives them.[5] Secondly,

---

[1] Bloch, "The rise of dependent cultivation and seignorial institutions", p. 239.

[2] *Ibid.*, p. 240.

[3] This is Dahrendorf's proposal in *Class and Class Conflict*. Intended by him as a replacement of Marx's notion, it has been used by several Marxist writers to supplement it. See for instance Wright and Perrone, "Marxist class categories and income inequality".

[4] See Robinson and Kelley, "Class as conceived by Marx and Dahrendorf".

[5] Observe, however, that the *modal* character of the definition of classes, in terms of optimizing rather than actual behaviour, has the consequence of making them less than immediately observable. One can observe what agents do, not what they *must* do to optimize. I believe, however, that in most cases those who behave in a certain way because this is their optimal solution are able to perceive if others behave similarly for non-optimizing reasons, which is sufficient to generate class consciousness out of modally defined classes.

were one to define classes in terms of their exploitation status, one would not be able to predict that some agents have an ambiguous alliance behaviour.[1] The lower managers have some positive traits in common both with the upper managers and the workers, namely the giving and receiving of commands respectively. Similarly, the petty bourgeois have some negative features in common both with the capitalists and the workers, namely the non-selling and the non-buying of labour-power respectively. Hence the lower managers and the petty bourgeois can be expected to show ambiguous coalition behaviour, as may the foremen who channel the surplus from workers to capitalists. It is not possible to respect these intuitions if class is defined in terms of exploitation.

(iv) The definition of classes in terms of a command hierarchy within the management of corporate property can also be applied to the modern business corporation. According to James Coleman, Marx's failure to look at the corporation as a juristic person with power in its own right "led to the central flaw in his analysis of capitalism".[2] This is an exaggeration, given the number of flaws in Marx's analysis of capitalism; but it is certainly true that his failure to take account of the increasingly corporate nature of capitalist property led him to overestimate property and underestimate power as a criterion for class. True, one might argue that what holds for church and state property does not automatically hold for the business corporation, which is, after all, owned by individual shareholders. The importance of this difference may, however, be questioned,[3] and in any case it is hard to see what implications it would have for the class status of the managers. The manager of the Vatican's bank and of a privately owned bank must belong to the same social class, or else the concept loses all social significance.

When I say that Marx overestimated property and underestimated power as criteria of class, I do not mean that he failed to conform to some independently defined notion of class. Rather, the statement is made on grounds of internal consistency and theoretical intuitions. Marx admitted the class character of corporate bureaucracies, at least with respect to the state and probably with respect to the church. Our theoretical intuitions about the purpose ultimately to be served by the notion of class then

---

[1] Wright, *Class Structure and Income Determination*, speaks of "contradictory class locations" to describe this ambiguity. In 6.2 and 6.3 below I neglect the important and difficult issue of the class consciousness and coalition behaviour of such ambiguously placed agents. Perhaps one might conjecture that their subjective perception of their interest is an outcome of the class struggle, not (as in the case of unambiguous classes) a cause of it?

[2] Coleman, *Power and the Structure of Society*, p. 37.   [3] Cp. p. 323, note 1 above.

compels us to search for some line or lines of internal class division, lest the pettiest functionary be admitted to the dominant class in bureaucratic or theocratic societies. On various theoretical grounds it was then argued that these lines must be drawn in terms of power relations rather than in terms of exploitation. On grounds of internal consistency, I then argued for a similar distinction in terms of power within the modern business corporation. By adding managers of the capitalist firm as a separate class we get the minimal consistent extension of Marx's list of classes.

Even if this reasoning is accepted, it does not follow that the concept of class thus imputed to Marx is wholly satisfactory. The definition of class in terms of domination and subordination is too behavioural and insufficiently structural. By this I mean that the classes of upper and lower managers are defined only by what they actually do, not – as in the case of capitalists and workers – by what they must do by virtue of what they have. It still holds that a Rockefeller cannot change his class status by taking a subordinate management job. It would be highly desirable to find a structural foundation for domination and subordination, similar to property in the case of hiring and selling labour-power. This foundation would presumably include "cultural capital",[1] inborn skills[2] as well as the opportunity of education.[3] (There might also be an important element of chance. The rise, say, from lower to upper manager does not depend solely on personal ability, but also on the number of superior positions available, which in turn depends on the market success of the firm.[4]) From innumerable studies it is known that achievement and occupation are correlated with ability, father's occupation and father's education. Yet little is understood of the exact mechanism by which these variables interact to sort people into classes, in the way Roemer's models explain how differential tangible endowments bring it about that economic agents spontaneously sort themselves into different classes. Yet even in the absence of such knowledge, the desideratum can be clearly stated and classes defined with respect to what the personal and socio-cultural endowments of agents compel them to do if they want to optimize.

This, finally, allows us to propose a general definition of class, in terms of endowments and behaviour. The endowments include tangible property, intangible skills and more subtle cultural traits. The behaviours

---

[1] See Bourdieu, *La Distinction*, for this notion.
[2] See Roemer, *A General Theory*, pp. 212ff.
[3] See for instance Boudon, *Education, Opportunity and Social Inequality*.
[4] I owe this observation to Erik Wright.

include working vs. not working, selling vs. buying labour-power, lending vs. borrowing capital, renting vs. hiring land, giving vs. receiving commands in the management of corporate property. These enumerations are intended as exhaustive. *A class is a group of people who by virtue of what they possess are compelled to engage in the same activities if they want to make the best use of their endowments.* Although I believe this definition is quite satisfactory both from the extensional and the theoretical point of view, it is somewhat defective on the methodological side. The admission of variable objective functions is one weakness, the admission of non-tangible endowments another. Also, of course, it may turn out that the notion thus constructed is less useful in explaining social conflict than Marx expected it to be. This issue, however, I postpone to 6.3.

6.1.2. Class and status

In much of current sociology the notion of status group is more frequently invoked than that of class. Max Weber, who is at the origin of this notion, defined it as follows: "In contrast to the purely economically determined 'class situation', we wish to designate as a *status situation* every typical component of the life of men that is determined by a specific, positive or negative, social estimation of *honour*."[1] Or again, "classes are stratified according to their relations to the production and acquisition of goods, whereas status groups are stratified according to the principles of their *consumption* of goods as represented by special styles of life".[2] His main emphasis was on groups as closed *Gemeinschaften*, "based on a subjective feeling of the parties, whether affectual or traditional, that they belong together",[3] and with deliberate exclusion of outsiders as the other side of the coin.[4] On this basis he distinguished between societies based predominantly on class and societies based mainly on status.[5] Since, unlike Marx, he defined classes exclusively in terms of market position,[6] this contrast follows in a fairly natural way.

We shall see that Marx also felt the temptation of status. He did so in two distinct ways: sometimes by including status groups among the classes, at other times by distinguishing between status societies and class societies. Before I cite and discuss the texts, however, we should ask

---

[1] Weber, *Economy and Society*, vol. 2, p. 932.   [2] *Ibid.*, p. 937.   [3] *Ibid.*, p. 40.
[4] *Ibid.*, pp. 341ff. Proposals to define *classes* in terms of exclusion are made by Bourdieu, "Condition de classe et position de classe" and Parkin, *Marxism and Class Theory*. These are, in a way, neo-Weberian theories of class, although they bear no relation to what Weber referred to as class.
[5] Weber, *Economy and Society*, vol. 1, p. 306.
[6] *Ibid.*, p. 928. There is a slight inconsistency when elsewhere (*ibid.*, p. 305) he refers to the (non-market) struggle between peasants and manorial lords as a *class* conflict.

exactly what the temptation is. To locate it, we may consider social conflicts in classical antiquity. Here we are in the fortunate situation of being able to compare the work of an outstanding Weberian historian – Moses Finley – with that of an equally outstanding Marxist historian – G.E.M. de Ste Croix. The former strongly denies while the latter equally vehemently affirms the centrality of class in the ancient world.

In Finley's *The Ancient Economy* we read the following:

There is little agreement among historians or sociologists about the definition of "class" or the canons by which to assign anyone to a class. Not even the apparently clearcut, unequivocal Marxist concept of class turns out to be without difficulties. Men are classed according to their relation to the means of production, first between those who do and those who do not own the means of production; second, among the former, between those who work themselves and those who live off the labour of others. Whatever the applicability of that classification in present-day society, for the ancient historian there is an obvious difficulty: the slave and the free wage labourer would then be members of the same class, on a mechanical interpretation, as would the richest senator and the non-working owner of a small pottery. That does not seem a very sensible way to analyse ancient society.[1]

One can only agree with the last sentence, while adding that Finley's is not a very sensible way to understand the Marxist concept of class. Since ownership of labour-power is a main determinant of class, the slave and the free wage labourer do not belong to the same class. The other example represents a more interesting challenge, and I shall return to it in a moment. First, however, we should note that Finley contrasts class not only with status groups, but also with orders (or estates). "An order or estate is a juridically defined group within a population, possessing formalized privileges and disabilities on one or more fields of activity, governmental, military, legal, economic, religious, marital, and *standing in a hierarchical relation to other orders*."[2] Although he does not offer an equally explicit definition of status groups, his gloss on the concept suggests that he had in mind something quite similar to Weber's notion. Clearly, an order will tend to be a status group, while the converse need not hold.

What does it mean to say that order or status is more central than class? Clearly we must specify: central for what purpose? Assuming that we are dealing only with explanatory purposes, this means that we must indicate the explanandum in which we are interested. If order or status are to represent a challenge to class, they must address the same explanandum, namely collective action. To explain individual-level behaviour in

[1] Finley, *The Ancient Economy*, p. 49.   [2] *Ibid.*, p. 45.

terms of these variables does not invalidate Marxist class theory. Pierre Bourdieu, for instance, argues that cultural behaviour can be explained in terms of the Weberian status groups, so that the new rich behave systematically differently from old wealth.[1] Finley makes a similar observation apropos the upstart Trimalchio, in Petronius's *Satyricon*.[2] I fail to see that these plausible views impugn Marx's theory of class. If Finley's senator and pottery-owner differ only in such respects, the contrast is irrelevant for the point he wants to make.

An example of social conflict organized around order rather than class was the struggle between patricians and plebeians in Rome. It has often been taken to show the lack of centrality of class in the ancient world,[3] and there certainly is a prima facie case to be made for this view. As observed by P. A. Brunt, "the conflict of the orders was unintelligible unless there were rich plebeians",[4] hence one cannot say in any simple, immediate sense that the struggle was waged between economically defined classes. Nor do I think Ste Croix's attempt to show that the struggle "really" was about class is successful.[5] The fact that the rich plebeians could exploit the class grievances of the poor plebeians, and induce them to join in an alliance against the patricians, does not show that the class grievances were the essence of the struggle. One should not confuse the relevance of class with the centrality of class. The latter requires that non-class alliances will not override class solidarity.

Marx, I noted earlier, referred to freemen, patricians and plebeians as classes. These are, however, legal orders, not classes in the sense I have tried to reconstruct. Does his calling them classes constitute an objection to my reconstruction? I do not think it does. The politico-legal superstructure is to be explained in terms of classes, and hence cannot enter into their constitution. This basic tenet of Marxism must override a few texts[6] pointing in a different direction. Marx knew that social conflicts in the Roman republic largely turned around the struggle between patricians and plebeians, and that class was not irrelevant to that struggle. From that, and his general commitment to the centrality of class, it was only a short step to asserting that the conflict was a class struggle.

In other works Marx attempts to solve the problem in a way more akin to Weber's distinction between status societies and class societies. This

---

[1] Bourdieu, *La Distinction*.   [2] Finley, *The Ancient Economy*, pp. 50–1.
[3] See notably Papaioannou, *De Marx et du Marxisme*, pp. 193ff.
[4] Brunt, *Social Conflicts in the Roman Republic*, p. 47.
[5] Ste Croix, *The Class Struggle in the Ancient Greek World*, p. 336.
[6] In addition to the opening sentences of the *Communist Manifesto* one may cite *The German Ideology*, p. 33.

view is adumbrated in the *Contribution to the Critique of Hegel's Philosophy of Law*:

The estates of civil society likewise were transformed in the process: civil society was changed by its separation from political society. *Estate* in the medieval sense continued only within the bureaucracy itself, where civil and political society are directly identical. As against this stands civil society as *civil estate*. Difference of estate is here no longer a difference of *needs* and of *work* of independent bodies. The only general, *superficial and formal* difference still remaining here is that of *town* and *country*. Within society itself, however, the difference was developed in mobile and not fixed circles, of which *free choice* is the principle. *Money* and *education* are the main criteria ... The estate of civil society had for its principle neither need, that is, a natural element, nor politics. It consists of separate masses which form fleetingly and whose very formation is fortuitous and does *not* amount to an organization.[1]

The contrast between fixity and mobility – for which see also 6.1.4 – is not here stated as one between estates and classes. Rather the estate society is opposed to one in which stratification on the basis of income and education is fundamental.[2] Later Marx came to repudiate that view of modern societies, substituting class for income groups (6.1.3). At the same time he also elaborated the view that classes and class conflict were central throughout history, not only in modern societies. *The German Ideology*, in particular, is replete with references to classes in pre-capitalist societies.[3] Yet, by a strange feat of theoretical compartmentalization, that work also makes a distinction between status societies and class societies. With respect to the modern distinction between the personal and the professional life of the individual, Marx writes that

In the estate (and even more in the tribe) this is as yet concealed: for instance, a nobleman always remains a nobleman, a commoner always a commoner, a quality inseparable from his individuality irrespective of his other relations. The difference between the private individual and the class individual, the accidental nature of the conditions of life for the individual, appears only with the emergence of the class, which is itself a product of the bourgeoisie.[4]

Later in the same work there is a reference to the countries "where the estates have not yet completely developed into classes".[5] In the somewhat obscure "Reflections" on money from 1851 this is also a major theme, as in the following contrast:

---

[1] *Contributiton to the Critique of Hegel's Philosophy of Law*, p. 80.
[2] I believe it is plausible to read "money" as indicating *income* rather than *wealth*, given the emphasis on the fluidity of modern societies.
[3] *The German Ideology*, pp. 33ff, 64ff, 176.   [4] *Ibid.*, p. 78.
[5] *Ibid.*, p. 90. See also *Neue Rheinische Zeitung*, 21.1.1849.

In the case of the estate system, the consumption of the individual, his material exchange, depends on the particular division of labour to which he is subordinated. In the class system it depends only on the universal medium of exchange which he is able to acquire. In the first case, he as a socially circumscribed person takes part in exchange operations which are circumscribed by his social position. In the second case he as an owner of the universal medium of exchange is able to obtain everything that society can exchange for this token of everything.[1]

The text goes on to emphasize the link between money and freedom of choice, a connection that is also stressed in the later economic writings (4.2). There, however, the opposition between estate and class is no longer present.

It is not clear what to make of these texts. They may reflect a mere terminological hesitation, or a more substantial doubt about the centrality of economically defined classes in pre-capitalist societies. In favour of the second reading is the opposition between "nobleman" and "commoner", and the emphasis on the "social position" as a main determinant of behaviour. Two facts, however, appear well established. For one thing, social conflict in pre-capitalist societies poses a serious problem for the Marxist theory of class. For another, Marx himself was inconsistent in what he said about classes in these societies. It is not implausible to seek the explanation of the latter fact in the former.

6.1.3. Relations between classes

To bring out the relations that can exist between classes, it is useful to compare Marxist class theory and the theory of social stratification. The latter – paradigmatically represented by *The American Occupational Structure* by Peter Blau and Otis Dudley Duncan – uses an "index of occupational socioeconomic status" to rank individuals.[2] Their index is constructed on the basis of income and education, but is intended to serve also as an estimate of the prestige ranking of occupations. Although the groups defined by such criteria are sometimes referred to as status groups, they lack many of the characteristics by which Weber defined status. In particular, it does not follow that individuals who are all rated (by others!) at the same prestige rank should also feel a subjective bond of "honour" among themselves.

The main difference between class theory and social stratification has to do with the purpose for which they were constructed. The latter mainly tries to explain properties and behaviour at the individual level by status

---

[1] "Reflections", pp. 590–1.
[2] Blau and Duncan, *The American Occupational Structure*, pp. 118ff.

variables. The former, by contrast, attempts to explain collective action in terms of the class position of the individuals engaging in it.[1] With different explananda, it is no surprise that the explanatory variables differ, nor does this show that the approaches are incompatible with one another. True, later Marxists have tried to use class theory to explain other phenomena than the ones on which Marx centred his attention, and then the theories may indeed become rival rather than complementary.[2] It is also true, and demonstrated in chapter 8 below, that Marx himself tried to explain some individual-level phenomena in terms of class. This, however, is a far cry from attempting to explain all such phenomena in terms of class membership. There is, for instance, nothing in Marx that indicates how criminality, morbidity or cultural behaviour could be explained in this way.

Yet there is no doubt that Marx was hostile to the stratification approach, notably in the following passage:

"Grobianist" common sense transforms the distinction between classes into the "distinction" between the size of the purses and class conflict into "craft bickering". The size of one's purse is a purely quantitative distinction, whereby any two individuals of the *same* class may be *incited* against one another at will.[3]

This can plausibly be read as stating that the notion of income group, and more generally any quantitative criterion, is inadequate for the analysis of social conflict – or at least for understanding the more enduring forms of such conflict. To discuss this contention I shall compare the relations between strata with the relations which obtain between classes. I shall use income groups as my example of social strata, although what follows also applies to strata defined in terms of education, prestige, etc.

The main relation between income groups is the purely quantitative comparison along the dimension defining them, that is the relation "earning at least as much as". Clearly this is a relation of comparison, not of interaction (2.3.1). The relation induces a ranking of the groups that is *complete* and *transitive*.[4] I now consider whether the relations that obtain

---

[1] Again, this is not a violation of methodological individualism, only a convenient shorthand. In 6.2.3 I argue that collective action should indeed be understood in terms of the propensities of individuals to engage in it, hence the contrast in the text may be more rigorously stated as one between different kinds of individual-level explananda.

[2] At least they become rival if each insists on explaining the whole variance of the phenomenon under study. They are complementary if class and status are seen as explanatory variables each of which is part-determinant of the explanandum. This is the approach taken in Kalleberg and Griffin, "Class, occupation and inequality in job rewards" or Wright and Perrone, "Marxist class categories and income inequality".

[3] *Deutsche-Brüsseler-Zeitung* 18.11.1847.

[4] Writing R for the relation, completeness means that for all a and b, either aRb or bRa; transitivity that aRb and bRc implies aRc.

between classes have similar properties. I have been discussing two main relations between classes: power and exploitation. In fact, two separate notions of exploitation have been considered. Exploitation is most frequently seen as a relation of interaction, based on the extraction of surplus labour. In Roemer's work, however, the relation is one of comparison, based on the net exploitation status of the agents. I shall discuss these relations in turn, beginning with the last.

We may say that A stands to B in a comparative relation of exploitation if either A is an exploiter and B is not, or B is exploited and A is not. (This allows for exploitation-neutral agents.) The relation is not complete, since it cannot relate two exploiters to one another, nor two exploited agents. It is, however, transitive. Consider now a complete extension of this relation, founded on the quantitative ratio of the number of hours worked to the number of hours embodied in what one consumes (or could consume). This ratio varies continuously from zero (a non-working exploiter) through 1 (exploitation-neutral agents) to indefinitely large positive numbers. According to this extended relation, one would be able to compare not only workers and capitalists, but also, say, landlords and capitalists or different categories of workers with one another. One would in fact obtain a stratification scheme in terms of degrees of exploitation. This would not coincide with stratification in terms of income. Some groups, notably the self-employed, tend to work much longer hours than others without earning correspondingly more. Hence they would have a lower place on the exploitation scale than on the income scale.

Now it might be claimed that the construction is devoid of interest for the same reason that made Marx reject the other stratification schemes, namely that such quantitative relations cannot explain social conflict or collective action. Discrete and stable collective actors cannot emerge out of a continuous stratification scheme. I return to this contention below. Here I want only to observe that the first (incomplete) comparative relation of exploitation is not necessarily more suitable in this respect. The issue of comparison vs. interaction is more central than that of discreteness vs. continuity. Conflicts tend to arise out of interaction, not out of mere comparison. Interacting with a common enemy galvanizes solidarity more than merely comparing oneself with other, more favourably placed, agents.

Hence I do not think the agents below the zero line of exploitation share a feeling of being unjustly treated that would lead them to being opposed *en bloc* to those above the line. One objection is the difficulty, already mentioned, of identifying the zero line. Another is that in the absence of other considerations, relative status may be as important as absolute status in determining the object of one's resentment. A harshly exploited agent might well feel more hostile towards one who is barely below the zero line, than the latter towards one who is barely above it. I am not saying that such comparisons could form the basis for stable collective actors, only that the resentment which one could feel towards other agents at the same side of the exploitation line could prevent it from becoming the focus of the formation of collective actors. To repeat, this holds only in the absence of other reasons for identifying more with agents at the same side of the line, for example class position as defined in 6.1.1.

The general idea behind the preceding remarks is that feelings of resentment and hostility do not lead to social conflict unless the object of these feelings appears as causally responsible for one's situation. Fleshing out this intuition, one might try to argue that social conflict arises out of *exploitation as interaction*. This again may be defined as follows in terms of exploitation status: A stands to B in an interactive relation of exploitation if (i) A is an exploiter, (ii) B is exploited and (iii) A is an exploiter *by virtue of* B being exploited.[1] I shall argue that this is inadequate. The relevant notion for the analysis of social conflict is not exploitation, but the closely related idea of transfer of surplus labour.

In 4.1.2 I emphasized, following Roemer, that exploiters and exploited need not interact directly. In *Capital III* this idea is expressed by a distinction between direct and indirect exploitation: "capital as an independent source of surplus-value is joined by landed property, which acts as a barrier to average profit and transfers a portion of surplus-value to a class that neither works itself nor directly exploits labour".[2] The landlord is an exploiter, but he does not interact directly with any exploited agent,[3] only with his co-exploiter the capitalist tenant. Exploiters and exploited are linked in a chain or network of transactions, but to the extent that they do not confront one another face to face, the potential for social conflict is much reduced. In his analysis of nineteenth-century England, Marx argued that the workers were opposed economically to the capitalists, but only politically to the landowners, *qua* managers of the state, despite the fact that the latter no less than the former depended on the surplus-value they created. (See also 6.3.3 and 7.1.)

---

[1] See p. 93, note 3.   [2] *Capital III*, p. 829.

[3] See also the *Deutsche-Brüsseler-Zeitung* 11.11.1847: "the *English* agricultural day labourer ... has no relationship with the landowner at all. He merely has a relationship with the tenant farmer, in other words, with the industrial capitalist who is practising agriculture in factory fashion. This industrial capitalist in turn, who pays the landowner a rent, has on the other hand a direct relationship with the landowner."

A similar problem arises in the hierarchical exploitation which is created by certain forms of piecework:

Since the quality and intensity of the work are here controlled by the form of wage itself, superintendence of labour becomes in great part superfluous. Piece-wages therefore lay the foundation of the modern "domestic labour" . . . as well as of a hierarchically organised system of exploitation and oppression. The latter has two fundamental forms. On the one hand piece-wages facilitate the inter-position of parasites between the capitalist and the wage-labourer, the "sub-letting of labour". The gain of these middlemen comes entirely from the difference between the labour-price which the capitalist pays, and the part of that price which they actually allow to reach the labourer. In England this system is characteristically called the "Sweating system". On the other hand piece-wage allows the capitalist to make a contract for so much per piece with the head labourer – in manufactures with the chief of some group, in mines with the extractor of the coal, in the factory with the actual machine-worker – at a price for which the head labourer himself undertakes the enlisting and payment of his assistant workpeople. The exploitation of the labourer by capital is here effected through the exploitation of the labourer by the labourer.[1]

The head labourer in the latter case may or may not be an exploiter, but this in any case is irrelevant for the class struggle. His assistants might well feel that he exploits them, even if in fact he is not an exploiter. Conversely, he might feel exploited by the capitalist, even if he is an exploiter himself. In both cases the belief in the presence of exploitation would be unfounded – but it might be no less effective for that.

Hence I suggest that the most relevant notion for understanding class conflict is the relation of *immediate transfer of surplus-value*. This relation obtains between worker and head labourer; between head labourer and capitalist; between capitalist and landlord. For Marx, the core of the class struggle concerned the forced transfer of surplus-value, instantiated in the hiring and selling of labour-power or land. The net exploitation status of the agents after these transactions is by comparison a secon-dary matter. The transfer can take place between two exploiters, between two exploited agents or between an exploiter and an exploited agent. The latter is as it were at the centre of the core, but the importance of other transactions should not be slighted. In particular, the form of the class struggle between exploiters and exploited is strongly shaped by the struggles between exploiters, as will be shown below.

The relation of immediate transfer of surplus-value is neither complete nor transitive. Its ancestral extension,[2] however, is transitive.

---

[1] *Capital I*, pp. 553–4.
[2] See Quine, *Methods of Logic*, pp. 228ff for a definition of this term which is, however, largely self-explanatory.

This extension defines a *chain* of transfers of surplus-value that relates the landlord to the worker by the intermediaries of the capitalist and the head labourer. In this sense the capitalist class of early capitalism was indeed a "middle class", many remarks to the contrary notwithstanding.[1] The sense in which this term applies is of course different from the one in which it applies to the petty bourgeoisie, which again differs from the sense in which it applies to lower managers. The petty bourgeoisie is only an intermediate class that does not actively mediate between other classes.

The ancestral extension of the relation of immediate transfer of surplus-value is not complete, nor a fortiori is that relation itself, nor is the relation of exploitation. The petty bourgeoisie and the small peasantry do not enter into any chain of transfer, to the extent that they are free of debts. In some societies there have been several such chains, that may or may not have intersected at the top, but certainly not at the lower levels. Both slaves and wage labourers were exploited in the American South, sometimes by the same agents, but this did not in itself create any relation between them. True, the degree to which one class was exploited may have affected – negatively or positively – the degree of exploitation of the other, but this does not set up any relation of exploitation between them. I return to the "divide-and-conquer" issue in 6.2.1.

As also emphasized in 4.1.2, the immediate transfer of surplus-value is not an important notion from the moral point of view. It has a double bias in being both too myopic and too micro-oriented. From the moral viewpoint we are mainly interested in the *long-term net effect* of the transfers.[2] Hence the moral and the explanatory aspects of Marxism diverge rather sharply at this point.[3] It would have been theoretically satisfactory to argue that the grounds on which capitalism is to be condemned are also those that will motivate the struggle to abolish it. Marx, however, does not succeed in showing that this connection obtains.

Consider finally power relations between classes. These obtain per definition between the classes defined in terms of the giving and the receiving of commands, or between classes defined in terms of the ownership of alien labour-power. They may, but need not, obtain

---

[1] Ossowski, *Class Structure in the Social Consciousness*, pp. 79ff refers to the landowner–capitalist–worker as "a trichotomous functional scheme without an intermediate class". Similarly Cole, *Studies in Class Structure*, p. 91, asserts that the middle classes of classical capitalism "were not in the middle of anything".

[2] True, this does not hold if we consider unequal distribution of *power* as a source of injustice. The lack of control over work or over the investment process is not, however, at the heart of the classical Marxian notion of exploitation that I have tried to explicate in 4.1.

[3] See also on this point my "Roemer vs Roemer".

between classes defined in terms of market behaviour. This relation is one of interaction, not of comparison. It is, moreover, one of face-to-face interaction, capable of motivating social conflicts. *Autonomy* rather than *income* is what is at stake in such struggles.

The power relation is neither complete nor transitive. The incompleteness follows from the fact that some classes do not stand in any (prepolitical) power relations at all to other classes. This is the case, for instance, for English landowners as described by Marx or for the French peasantry. The intransitivity follows from the general fact about power hierarchies that superiors *de facto* and often *de jure* have to delegate power irrevocably. The Roman law of slavery, for example, knew the category of a *vicarius*, the slave of a slave. While a slave had no general power of manumission with respect to his *vicarii*, he could, if manumitted himself, also free his wife if she was part of his *peculium*.[1] Thus the master could not fully treat any slave of his slave as his own slave. Similarly, a feudal lord "in the event of a dispute, could move only against his tenant and not his tenant's tenant".[2] Analogous restrictions exist in the large business corporations, for instance regarding the power to hire and fire personnel. It is in the nature of the case that such limitations on two-step exercises of power are often overridden, but this does not mean that they are totally ineffective.

Thus, if my understanding of Marx is correct, *the central relations between classes are the transfer of surplus from below and the exercise of power from above.* These often go together, as in the case of the slave, the serf and the wage labourer who as part of the contract has to agree to take orders. There may, however, be transfer of surplus without exercise of power, as in the case of the capitalist who pays rent to the landlord or the small producer who is exploited by the bank. Conversely, there may be exercise of power without any surplus being transferred, as in the relation between upper and lower managers. These relations are all highly specific, unlike such relations as "earns less than" which link the agent to the diffuse group of people who stand on one side of him in the relevant dimension of stratification. The incompleteness and intransitivity of the relations between classes reflect this specificity. Although such relations as 'earning less than" or "being more exploited than" can give rise to resentment and hostility, they will not have the same power to generate enduring social conflict as the relations of surplus-transfer and command-giving, precisely because they do not have this specific focus. This is not to say that

[1] Barrow, *Slavery in the Roman Empire*, p. 188.
[2] North and Thomas, *The Rise of the Western World*, p. 63.

social stratification cannot generate conflicts, or "craft-bickering" in Marx's phrase, only that these will not have the same stability as class struggles. Such, at any rate, is my reconstruction of the arguments that led Marx to single out social classes as the most significant social groups – at least the most significant for the study of social change.

6.1.4. Class mobility

At any given moment of time, classes can be defined and related to one another by the categories defined above. Yet one might wish to add a dynamic element to the definition, as was also proposed in 5.1.2 with respect to the relations of production. The degree to which it is possible to move out of one's class, and into another, is an important fact about the class structure that cannot be captured by instantaneous cross-sections. As in other cases, the question is whether the ease of mobility is something that should be predicated of classes defined on other grounds, or that should enter into the definition itself.

There seem to be two opposing intuitions at work here. On the one hand, there is the tendency to oppose class to caste or estate on the basis of the greater mobility associated with class. In Schumpeter's formulation, a "class resembles a hotel or an omnibus, always full, but always of different people".[1] In 6.1.2 I cited some texts where Marx similarly contrasts the mobility of classes with the fixity of estates. On the other hand there is the idea that a class system cannot be completely fluid, since this would destroy the substance of the phenomenon. Marx refers to "the United States of North America, where, though classes already exist, they have not yet become fixed, but continually change and interchange their component elements in constant flux".[2] Marx here asserts the existence of classes, but also their insubstantiality, suggesting that full-blooded classes must be less than completely fluid. Hence it is tempting to make it part of the definition of classes that they should allow some intermediate degree of mobility – more than caste or estate, less than would be expected on random assortment.

This proposal would restrict classes to capitalism, an idea that must be rejected on exegetical grounds. Although, as noted in 6.1.2, Marx occasionally entertains this idea, his main position is that classes also exist in non-market, pre-capitalist societies. The important core of truth behind

---

[1] Schumpeter, *Imperialism and Social Classes*, p. 165.

[2] *The Eighteenth Brumaire*, p. 111. See also Tocqueville, *Democracy in America*, p. 557: "although there are rich men, the class of the rich does not exist at all" (because of the high turn-over).

the proposal is that only with an intermediate degree of social mobility can we expect classes to crystallize into collective actors and to play a role in social conflicts. I shall return to this issue in 6.2.2. Here I only note, in a preliminary manner, that with very little mobility the idea of improving one's lot is hard to conceive, whereas very high mobility prevents agents from linking individual improvement to that of a class. Since in my opinion one important task of the theory of class is to explain when classes turn into collective actors, the conditions for this event should not be made part of the definition of class.

Yet the degree of social mobility may usefully be made part of the definition of *class structure*. To see this, consider the disagreement between E. P. Thompson and G. A. Cohen over the definition of class. According to Thompson, "if we stop history at a given point, then there are no classes, but simply a multitude of individuals with a multitude of experiences".[1] In his view, "class itself is not a thing, it is a happening".[2] Cohen objects to this processual definition, and argues for a structural definition of classes in terms of the relations of production. We should not say that class *is* process, but that classes *undergo* "a process of cultural and political formation".[3] I agree with Cohen that for process to occur there must be an underlying structure which is the bearer of that process – an entity of which the change can be predicated. I would add, however, that there may be sub-processes going on within the structure that contribute to its constitution and distinguish it from other structures. Imagine two economies that at any given moment of time have identical distributions of individuals over class positions, and yet differ because the turnover rate of the one is much higher than that of the other. If one of these economies undergoes change so as to become similar to the other – a class society turning into a caste society, at the limit – it would be strange to say that no structural change had taken place. Yet this is what Cohen is committed to saying when he argues that "there is no difference of economic structure, despite movement within the economy, as long as there are the same relations in the same frequency bound into the same network".[4]

This is not merely a quarrel over words. Cohen's structuralist approach is inadequate because it leads to the "pile of snapshots" view of social change, as opposed to the longitudinal "bunch of life histories" view. On his conception we aggregate over individuals before we study social

---

[1] Thompson, *The Making of the English Working Class*, p. 11.   [2] *Ibid.*, p. 939.
[3] Cohen, *Karl Marx's Theory of History*, p. 77.   [4] *Ibid.*, p. 85.

change, whereas I believe it more adequate to consider change before we aggregate. If we begin by aggregating over individuals, we lose track of them forever and so cannot tell if a given class position is occupied by the same individuals or not. As Rosa Luxemburg argued against Eduard Bernstein, one can be led seriously astray by neglecting class metabolism as a variable.[1] My proposal, therefore, is to accept a time-independent definition of class, but insist that the class structure is more than the sum of classes thus defined. The class structure involves the classes *and* the rates of flow between them. Or, following a useful terminology suggested by Gudmund Hernes,[2] we could distinguish between output structure and process structure. Two different process structures may well generate the same output structure.

Why should there be mobility between classes? The definition proposed in 6.1.1 suggests two sources of mobility. First, the endowment of the individual might change. Secondly, for a given endowment, his optimizing behaviour might change. The latter might occur because of a change in the endowments of other individuals, but also because of changes in technology or in demand. Such changes tend to bring about a change in relative prices, favouring some agents and disadvantaging others. In all societies we may expect some mobility due to changing endowments. Some individuals will increase their holdings – by luck[3] or by thrift.[4] Others will become impoverished for symmetrical reasons. Mobility due to changes in optimizing behaviour for given assets is restricted to modern societies, characterized by technical change.

6.2. Class consciousness

Classes, as defined, form a social category that may or may not represent a non-arbitrary division of society into separate groups. The Marxist *theory* of class asserts that agents who belong to one class also tend to have other common properties and to behave in certain common ways. In particular, it asserts that classes are *real* in the sense that under certain conditions they tend to crystallize into collective actors, that is to achieve class consciousness. In 6.2.1 I discuss the meaning of class consciousness,

---

[1] See my *Logic and Society*, p. 143 for a summary and further references.
[2] Hernes, "Structural change in social processes".
[3] Luck may include political windfalls, as explained in Bardhan, "Class formation in India".
[4] This implies that I am not treating a low rate of time preference as an asset; it is part of what the person *is*, not of what he *has*. Independently of the philosophical arguments for this view, it is quite compelling in the present context. If a low rate of time preference improves the class position of the agent, it does so via the impact on tangible assets, not directly.

including its relation to class interest and class organization. In 6.2.2 I propose a "black-box theory" of the development of class consciousness, that is an account of the facilitating and obstructing conditions which does not go into the issue of individual motivation. In 6.2.3 I turn directly to this issue, and consider the role of selfishness, solidarity and rationality in explaining collective action. This subsection is both tentative and somewhat less exegetical than most other parts of this work. Yet the fundamental importance of the problem seems to warrant a fairly lengthy discussion.

6.2.1. The meaning of class consciousness

I have been discussing class in merely distributive terms, which do not imply any interaction between class members. In Weber's words, the "social action that brings forth class situation is not basically action among members of the identical class; it is an action among members of different classes".[1] But although intra-class interaction is not part of the definition of class, such action may and does occur in forms ranging from warfare through competition to mutual support. A major task of class theory is to explain when one or another of these will take place. Before I can turn to this task, however, I must try to make clear the notion of class consciousness. The canonical text is in *The Eighteenth Brumaire*:

The small-holding peasants form a vast mass, the members of which live in similar conditions but without entering into manifold relations with one another. Their mode of production isolates them from one another instead of bringing them into mutual intercourse. The isolation is increased by France's bad means of communication and by the poverty of the peasants. Their field of production, the smallholding, admits of no division of labour in its cultivation, no application of science and, therefore, no diversity of development, no variety of talent, no wealth of social relationships. Each individual peasant family is almost self-sufficient; it itself directly produces the major part of its consumption and thus acquires its means of life more through exchange with nature than in intercourse with society. A smallholding, a peasant and his family; alongside them another smallholding, another peasant and another family. A few score of these make up a village, and a few score of villages make up a department. In this way, the great mass of the French nation is formed by simple addition of homologous magnitudes, much as potatoes in a sack form a sack of potatoes. Insofar as millions of families live under economic conditions of existence that separate their mode of life, their interests and their culture from those of the other classes, and put them in hostile opposition to the latter, they form a class. Insofar as there is merely a local interconnection among these small land-holding peasants, and the identity of their interests

---

[1] Weber, *Economy and Society*, vol. 2, p. 929.

beget no community, no national bond and no political organization among them, they do not form a class.[1]

Here class consciousness – although the term is not used – is both defined and explained. It is defined in terms of "community", "bond" and "organization". In the Hegelian language sometimes affected by Marx, these elements make the difference between a class "in itself" and a class "for itself".[2]

Before I turn to class for itself, I want to dwell on the intermediate case of "class for others". A class may achieve existence and significance for others before it attains existence for itself. An analogous case is found in social anthropology: 'A man of one tribe sees the people of another tribe as an undifferentiated group to whom he has an undifferentiated pattern of behaviour, while he sees himself as a member of a segment of his own tribe".[3] There is no tribe consciousness, no tribe-for-itself, and yet tribes have social reality beyond that of the tribe-in-itself, since they are perceived as tribes by members of other tribes. Similarly Marx suggested that the English working class passed through a phase in which it was "already a class as against capital, but not yet for itself".[4] Referring to the German bourgeoisie, he writes that it "already finds itself in conflict with the proletariat even before being politically constituted as a class".[5] Rodney Hilton refers to this phenomenon as "negative class consciousness", found in a group of people united by a common opposition to another group collectively perceived as one class.[6] In 2.2.2 I mentioned the speculative notion that self-consciousness may arise posterior to, and as a result of, the consciousness of other people. My awareness of myself may arise because I become aware that you are aware of me. The analogous idea in the case of class consciousness is more amenable to empirical study. The members of a class-in-itself may become conscious of themselves as members of a class by observing that they are treated as members of one class by other agents whom *they* perceive as members of

---

[1] *The Eighteenth Brumaire*, p. 187.

[2] It is widely assumed that Marx himself used these terms to distinguish between classes that lack and classes that possess class consciousness. As far as I know, he never actually uses the term "in itself" (*an sich*).

[3] Evans–Pritchard, *The Nuer*, p. 120. In the language of status, "the typical actor makes finer discriminations in nearby positions than in positions more distant in the social ordering" (Fararo, *Mathematical Sociology*, p. 347). The empirical issue is whether the subjective image of class is discontinuous, as in the case of the Nuer, or gradational, as suggested by the last text.

[4] *The Poverty of Philosophy*, p. 211. [5] *Deutsche–Brüsseler–Zeitung* 18.11.1847.

[6] Hilton, *Bond Men Made Free*, p. 130.

one class.[1] In 6.3.1 the notion of class-for-others is linked to that of "latent class conflict".

There is another intermediate category that should be mentioned here. Class consciousness often – although not always – takes the form of *solidarity*. By acting together the members of a class can obtain more than they could by acting in isolation. Hence, for instance, collective as opposed to individual wage bargaining is a sign of class consciousness. Yet these two cases – collective action and individual bargaining – do not exhaust all possibilities. We may also observe the formation of a coalition between one class and *part* of another class, to the benefit of the former. Lloyd Shapley and Martin Shubik have proposed a model of such "divide and conquer" tactics.[2] Here there is one agent who owns the means of production and confronts a number of unorganized workers. With individual bargaining between the capitalist and the workers the rate of exploitation, in their numerical example, is 100 per cent. If, however, one admits coalitions between the capitalist and the workers, one of the solution concepts for cooperative games predicts a rate of exploitation of 200 per cent.[3] The behavioural adequacy of this concept is uncertain, but the model serves to highlight a notion that is independently plausible, namely that the workers will fare worse under individual bargaining than under collective bargaining, and worse under "coalitional bargaining" than under individual bargaining. We may consider it a sign of incipient or rudimentary class consciousness if the workers refuse to be drawn into coalitional bargaining, even if they are unable to engage in collective bargaining.

I define (positive) class consciousness as *the ability to overcome the free-rider problem in realizing class interests*. As further explained in 6.2.2, collective action is beset by the difficulty that it often pays to defect. The individual can reap a greater reward if he abstains from the action to get the benefits without the cost. This generates a conflict between the interest of the individual class member and that of the class as a whole. Marx writes, for instance, that the "organization of the proletarians into a class, and consequently into a political party, is continually being upset by the competition between the workers themselves".[4] Similarly, the capitalists are "false

---

[1] Bardhan, "Class formation in India", provides an example of this unifying force of repression which constitutes a permanent dilemma to any would-be repressor; cp. also my "Négation active et négation passive".

[2] Shapley and Shubik, "Ownership and the production function".

[3] This concept ("the Shapley value") rests on the idea that each agent will be rewarded according to his average contribution to all the potential coalitions of which he could be a member.

[4] *The Communist Manifesto*, p. 493. Marx's most extensive discussion of competition among the workers occurs in the manuscript on "Wages", pp. 424ff.

brothers"[1] or "hostile brothers"[2] who as individuals may be opposed to measures that benefit their class. This was shown in 4.1.4 with respect to the length of the working day. Quite generally, there are always private costs associated with organization, whereas the benefits typically are public goods that cannot be restricted to members.[3]

The free-rider problem can be understood in two ways.[4] First, the individual agent is tempted to act as a free-rider with respect to his class. Secondly, the class as a whole, supposing it to be organized, is tempted to act as a free-rider with respect to its long-term interests.[5] Writing about the Ten Hours Bill, Marx made a distinction between capitalist A benefiting at the expense of capitalist B, and generation A of capitalists benefiting at the expense of generation B.[6] Similarly, the working class has to overcome not only the free-rider activity of scabs, but also the tendency to *activism* that always tries to exploit to the hilt the political possibilities of the moment, at the expense of the creation of new possibilities in the future. A mature working class, that is, should be capable of *waiting*.[7] In one of his more extravagant statements Marx said to his political opponents that

Whereas we tell the workers: "You have fifteen, twenty, fifty years of civil war and peoples' struggles to go through, not only to change the conditions but in order to change yourselves and make yourself fit for political rule", you say on the contrary: "We must come to power right away, or else we might as well go to sleep."[8]

I return to the paradoxical implications of this statement in 6.2.3. Here I cite it as an example of Marx's warning against ultra-leftism or impatience in the workers' movement. Other passages to the same effect are given in chapter 7 below.

I have defined class consciousness in terms of class interest. The latter notion, however, is in acute need of clarification. First, we must ask

---

[1] *Capital III*, p. 198.   [2] *Ibid.*, p. 253.

[3] On this general theme see Olson, *The Logic of Collective Action* and Hardin, *Collective Action*.

[4] For an elaboration, see my *Logic and Society*, pp. 127ff.

[5] Related to the second problem is the following issue. If latent interest groups solve their free-rider problem and succeed in organizing themselves, there can arise a higher-order free-rider problem between the groups. Each group has an incentive to increase its share of the social product, even if it thereby reduces the total to be shared, by the deadweight losses associated with monopolies, bargaining costs etc. (See Olson, *The Rise and Decline of Nations*, for an exposition.) Marx never foresaw this eventuality.

[6] *Zur Kritik (1861–63)*, p. 162.

[7] On this theme, see notably Meisner, *Li Ta-chao and the Origins of Chinese Communism*, p. 169.

[8] *Revelations concerning the Communist Trial in Cologne*, p. 403.

whether Marx had in mind class interest in terms of the actual preferences and goals of the members, or in terms of goals that are somehow imputed to the members, such as the goals they would have had if fully aware of the causes of, and possible remedies to, their situation. When Marx writes that the emancipation of labour "is not a question of what this or that proletarian, or even the whole proletariat, at the moment *regards* as its aim",[1] he seems to espouse the latter conception. On this view, the development of class consciousness is a two-stage process, in which the emergence of the "real interests" of the class precedes their organization. Actually, Marx believed that the two processes were fused into one. Setting up an organization to promote actual interests would also bring about a change in those interests themselves by clarifying the nature of the opposition. Thus only by engaging in an economic struggle against the capitalists will the workers understand that a political struggle is necessary. Again I refer to 6.2.3 for further discussion.

Secondly, the temporal structure of class interest must be spelled out carefully. Whether a given action is or is not in the interest of a given class depends on the consequences that flow from it, evaluated according to the (actual or imputed) preferences of the class members, including their time preferences. Much, however, turns on the exact time at which one breaks off the chain of consequences. What is in the interest of a class in the medium term may not be so in the long run. Cartel behaviour, for instance, while in the interest of an industry of capitalist firms for some time, may in the end undermine itself.[2] To the extent that the state is supposed to represent the interest of the capitalist class, this distinction could be crucial (7.1.3). Similarly, a definition of working-class interests in terms of the steady-state consequences of the action[3] would unjustifiably neglect what happens to whom during the transitional period. It is not clear that it is in the interest of currently living workers that their unborn descendants should experience socialism. To impute intergenerational altruism would be a pseudo-solution, in the absence of *actually* altruist preferences.

6.2.2. The conditions for collective action
In this section I discuss the conditions that promote or hinder the emergence of collective action. In 6.2.3 I consider some mechanisms by which these conditions could shape the individual motivation to engage

---

[1] *The Holy Family*, p. 37.   [2] See my *Logic and Society*, p. 129.
[3] For this notion, see my *Explaining Technical Change*, pp. 43ff.

in collective action, but here I mainly look at the "black-box" correlations. Most of what I shall say concerns collective action under capitalism, since Marx had little to say about what forms it took in earlier modes of production. I first look at various cognitive conditions for collective action, and then at some determinants of the motivation to engage in it. This includes a decomposition of the motivational structure into several components, as well as a discussion of the broader conditions that determine their efficacy.

The cognitive conditions of collective action include, first, the understanding that class members have of the causal context in which they are placed, and of the identity of the opposed class or classes. In Weber's phrase, class action "is especially linked to the transparency of the connections between the causes and the consequences of the class situation".[1] In particular, one should not confuse symptoms and cause. In *Wages, Price and Profit* Marx warns against this confusion with respect to the efficacy of trade unions:

[The] working class ought not to exaggerate to themselves the ultimate working of these every-day struggles. They ought not to forget that they are fighting with effects, but not with the cause of those effects; that they are retarding the downward movement [of wages], but not changing its direction; that they are applying palliatives, not curing the malady. They ought, therefore, not to be exclusively absorbed in these unavoidable guerilla fights incessantly springing up from the never-ceasing encroachments of capital or changes of the market. They ought to understand that, with all the miseries it imposes upon them, the present system simultaneously engenders the *material conditions* and the *social forms* necessary for an economic reconstruction of society.[2]

These are cognitive exhortations to the workers, enjoining them to understand the insufficiency of the wage struggle and the possibility of radical change. The need for such exhortations stems from the fact that the central class relations (6.1.3) rest on face-to-face or class-to-class interaction, whereas the more fundamental forms of class conflict may involve classes that do not interact directly. The workers and the owners of a firm, for instance, may be separated from one another by the class of managers. Ultimate causal responsibility is less perceptible, and has less motivating power, than immediate confrontations. Another cognitive obstacle is the lack of precise knowledge of where class frontiers are to be drawn. According to Tocqueville, for instance, "The reason why the English middle class, far from being actively hostile to the aristocracy,

---

[1] Weber, *Economy and Society*, vol. 2, p. 929. Foster, *Class Struggle and the Industrial Revolution*, ch. 4 has useful discussions of this cognitive issue.

[2] *Wages, Price and Profits*, p. 152.

inclined to fraternize with it was not so much that the aristocracy kept open house as that its barriers were ill defined; not so much that entrance into it was easy as that you never knew when you had got there".[1] In such cases the resentment will tend to be diffuse rather than specific, with correspondingly less motivating power. To probe the opaque social causality, workers need learning, education, leadership, whence the need for intellectuals in the working-class movement.[2]

Leadership also has the role of ensuring that the relevant information requirements for collective action are fulfilled. A more formal statement of these requirements is found in 6.2.3. Here I only insist on the fact that every incipient strike or revolution must overcome the natural scepticism and suspicion of the would-be participants. Each individual may be willing to do his share, on the condition that others will do theirs – and good leadership may be necessary to persuade him that this condition is in fact met. The need for such reassurance will depend on how much the individual stands to lose from engaging unilaterally in the relevant behaviour. I now turn to these issues of motivational strength.

The motivation to engage in collective action involves, centrally, the structure of the gains and losses associated with it for the individual. It also depends on the absolute level of welfare of the agents, to the extent that this influences their beliefs and motives, as well as their organizational ability. Relative welfare levels may also prove relevant, in two ways. First, the change of welfare over time might provide the impetus to revolt; secondly, one's status relative to that of others could act as a spur.

The gains and losses associated with collective action must, for the present purposes, be measured in terms of expected utility. Hence they depend both on the individual's estimate of the likelihood of success and failure and on the degree of risk aversion. For the time being I assume that the utility derives from the *material* gains and losses for the individual himself, postponing to 6.2.3 the question whether he might also be motivated by gains accruing to others. On these assumptions, then, the utility calculus of collective action is captured in three variables. The first is the *gain from cooperation*, defined as the difference between what accrues to the individual if all engage in the collective action and what accrues to him if none does. The second is the *free-rider gain*, that is the difference between what he gets if all but him engage in

---

[1] Tocqueville, *The Old Régime and the French Revolution*, pp. 88–9.
[2] See Draper, *Karl Marx's Theory of Revolution*, vol. II, ch. 18 for a survey of Marx's *obiter dicta* on intellectuals.

collective action and what he gets if everyone does so. Finally, there is the *loss from unilateralism* – the difference between what he gets if no one engages in collective action and what he gets (such as punishment or costs of engaging in useless individual action) if he is the only one or among the few to do so.

Other things being equal, the probability of collective action increases with the first of these variables and decreases with the second and third. Frequently, however, they do not vary independently of one another. If the gain from cooperation is large, one may expect that the loss from unilateralism is also large if the opposed class has the power to punish a behaviour that, if generalized, would cost them a great deal. If the gain from cooperation is large, the free-rider gain may or may not be large, depending among other things on the efficacy with which the participants in the collective action can impose penalties on would-be parasites. There may be cases in which the gains from cooperation are large, while the free-rider gain and the loss from unilateralism are both small. An example is cited in 6.2.3. Nevertheless I believe this will only occur exceptionally. In general, collective action will either be *individually unstable* (large free-rider gains), *individually inaccessible* (large losses from unilateralism) or both. Since nevertheless such action does occur, we must try to understand how these obstacles are overcome – a task that is postponed to 6.2.3.

Consider next poverty or hardship as a spring of collective action. Do trade unions form in good times or in bad? Does the frequency of peasant revolts vary inversely with the size of the harvest? The evidence seems ambiguous,[1] as might be expected. There is a useful analogy here with technical change. The idea that "Necessity is the mother of invention" (3.3.2) would seem to imply that technical change should occur more frequently in hard times than in periods of boom. This, however, is only one side of the coin. Innovation does indeed require the motivation to innovate, but it also requires resources with which to innovate. In particular, it minimally demands some free time, which may not be available in periods of extreme hardship.[2] Hence the relation could be non-monotonic,

---

[1] On peasant rebellions, interesting evidence on the ambiguous relation between hardship and collective action has been offered by James Tong of the University of Michigan in unpublished work. See also Popkin, *The Rational Peasant*, ch. 6. Concerning union formation, it appears that "mobilization often began defensively, in the course of a losing battle with employers" (Tilly, *From Mobilization to Revolution*, p. 74), but against this there is "the well-documented tendency of strikes to become more frequent and more demanding in times of prosperity, when workers have more slack resources to devote to acting together" (*ibid.*, p. 76).

[2] For a suggestive biological analogy, see Fagen, *Animal Play Behaviour*, p. 195, and the comments in my *Explaining Technical Change*, pp. 131ff.

leading to an internal maximum. The rate of innovation can be expected to be greatest in periods of intermediate hardship – sufficiently hard to create an inducement to innovate, but not so hard as to do away with the capacity to innovate. Similar comments apply to the idea that "Necessity is the mother of collective action". Collective action is costly, in terms of the time and energy that must be spent on organization. In periods of extreme misery, every ounce of energy will be spent seeking sources of very short-term subsistence, little being left over for organizing collective action.[1]

It may be useful to point out briefly the impact of hardship on the motivational structure. The main effect is to reduce the loss from unilateralism. For those who "have nothing to lose but their chains", that problem simply does not arise. They may be damned if they do engage in collective action, but certainly if they don't.[2] It should be added, however, that rulers often make it their business to ensure that there is a fate *worse* than death in store for those who are caught out in rebellion.[3] In that case, the loss from unilateralism can be substantial. Absolute hardship levels can also influence the probability for collective action by distorting belief formation, so that the chances of success appear to be unrealistically high.[4] The tendencies to wishful thinking that under normal conditions are kept well under control, may, in extreme circumstances, become more prominent.

Relative levels of welfare may enter in several ways. First, people may directly compare their welfare to that of other people and feel resentful if the gap becomes too large. According to Tocqueville, this is felt only with regard to medium-size differences;[5] once again the maximal probability of collective action is linked to an intermediate value of the independent variable. Or else, the trend in welfare levels over time – their own and that of other people – may induce certain expectations

---

[1] The converse of this idea is the following. If the ability of the exploiting class to extract a surplus is a (multiplicative) function of the volume of production above subsistence and the resistance of the exploited, we may also get a non-monotonic relation, since the first of these varies positively and the second negatively with general prosperity. When labour is abundant relative to land, landlords can squeeze peasants with little resistance – but there is not much there to be squeezed out of them.

[2] This will notably be the case if the outcome of doing nothing is death (for individuals) or bankruptcy (for firms). How bankruptcy makes the loss from unilateralism an irrelevant variable is well brought out by Bowman, "The logic of capitalist collective action".

[3] In the unpublished work cited in note 1, p. 352, Tong illustrates this proposition with gruesome examples from Chinese peasant rebellions.

[4] Some of the findings in Thompson, "The moral economy of the English crowd in the eighteenth century", may be interpreted in this light.

[5] Tocqueville, *Democracy in America*, p. 538.

about the level next to be attained, and resentment arises if the expectation is not fulfilled.[1] Again, the influence of this factor on collective action may operate through the estimation of the likelihood of success. When the traditional income distribution is no longer taken for granted, a first reaction may be the formation of unrealistic expectations about how rapidly it will change. When these are frustrated, a next reaction may be the formation of unrealistic expectations about the probability that collective action will succeed.

I now turn to the more remote determinants of motivation, those that are connected with the interaction structure in which the agents find themselves. I shall single out five variables: group size, the distance between group members, the turn-over rate in group membership, the degree of group homogeneity and the technology of collective action. In addition I shall briefly discuss the emergence of "self-respect" as a condition for collective action.

The standard view in the literature on collective action is that it becomes less probable the larger the group in question.[2] The free-rider benefit increases with group size, since the loss to each agent of his non-participation goes down. (But cp. the discussion below of the technology of collective action.) There is, however, also a tendency that works in the opposite direction.[3] For a given repressive force, the loss from unilateralism that is connected with the risk of punishment goes down when the size of the group increases. When the police or the army has to spread itself more thinly, the risk to each individual is smaller. Once again we can expect to find an internal maximum, that is the probability of collective action is highest for some intermediate group size.

Isolation is an obstacle to collective action, whereas proximity is a favourable condition. Here isolation should not be taken as spatial distance, but as a more general "communicational distance", depending not only on geography, but also on the means of communication. "A relatively thinly populated country, with well-developed means of communication, has a denser population than a more numerously populated country, with badly developed means of communication".[4] In the passage from *The Eighteenth Brumaire* quoted above Marx affirms that isolation in this sense is an obstacle to class consciousness and to collective action. The same view is asserted in *The German Ideology*:

---

[1] See Boudon, *Effets Pervers et Ordre Social*, ch. VI and Hirschman, "The changing tolerance for inequality" for some ways in which this effect could arise.

[2] Olson, *The Logic of Collective Action*, p. 28; Hardin, *Collective Action*, ch. 3 (but see p. 49 for some doubts).

[3] This idea was suggested to me by Mr S. Kareh Mirani.   [4] *Capital I*, pp. 352–3.

Competition separates individuals from one another, not only the bourgeois but still more the workers, in spite of the fact that it brings them together. Hence it is a long time before these individuals can unite, apart from the fact that for the purpose of this union – if it is not to be merely local – the necessary means, the big industrial cities and cheap and quick communications, have first to be produced by large-scale industry. Hence every organized power standing over against these isolated individuals, who live in conditions daily reproducing this isolation, can only be overcome after long struggles. To demand the opposite would be tantamount to demanding that competition should not exist in this definite epoch of history, or that the individuals should banish from their minds conditions over which in their isolation they have no control.[1]

In contrast to the isolation of the peasantry, the physical proximity of the workers to each other in the factory enhances their solidarity and overcomes the mutual competition. They are "disciplined, united, organized by the very mechanism of the process of capitalist production itself".[2] Marx also states that "the dispersion of the rural labourers over large areas breaks down their power of resistance while concentration increases that of the town operatives",[3] and more generally that "the power of resistance of the labourers decreases with their dissemination".[4] He does not say explicitly that it is the concentration in the work-place, rather than in housing and residence, that is the decisive factor, but from what he says elsewhere about the importance of trade unions this can reasonably be inferred.[5]

Improved means of communications have, however, an ambiguous effect on class consciousness. By bringing class members together, they favour solidarity; by enabling geographical mobility they undermine it. In the manuscript on "Wages", Marx remarks that "All improvements in the means of communication, for example, facilitate the competition of workers in different localities and turn local competition into national".[6] The net effect is in general indeterminate, but once again we may expect maximal solidarity to be produced by an intermediate degree of development of the means of communication.

This also holds, more generally, for all forms of mobility. Very little mobility tends to make social barriers appear absolute, and the idea of

---

[1] *The German Ideology*, p. 75; cp. also *The Communist Manifesto*, p. 493.
[2] *Capital I*, p. 763; cp. also *The Communist Manifesto*, p. 496, with the reference to the bourgeoisie digging its own grave.
[3] *Capital I*, p. 506.   [4] *Capital I*, p. 462.
[5] An account of working-class solidarity with much emphasis on residential patterns is Hanagan, *The Logic of Solidarity*; see also Thernstrom, "Working class social mobility in industrial America" according to whom mobility in and out of the *city* rather than the factory is the main obstacle to the formation of working-class consciousness.
[6] "Wages", p. 423.

tearing them down unthinkable.[1] Very high mobility, on the other hand, makes the system so fluid and the groups so impermanent that no durable collective actors will emerge.[2] It is unclear to what extent Marx recognized this obstacle to collective action, but apparently he believed that in this respect inter-class mobility was more important than intra-class change of occupation. In a passage from *The Eighteenth Brumaire* cited in 6.1.4 he refers to the "constant flux" of the American class structure, implying that this is an obstacle to organized action among class members. In the *Communist Manifesto* he refers to the peculiar character of the modern petty bourgeoisie: "ever renewing itself" as a class, while "the individual members of this class, however, are constantly being hurled down into the proletariat".[3] No implications for the capacity for collective action are suggested, however. In an article from 1856 such consequences are, however, stated:

The concentration of capital has been accelerated, and, as its natural corollary, the downfall of the small middle class. A sort of industrial kings have been created, whose power stands in inverse ratio to their responsibility – they being responsible only to the amount of their shares, while disposing of the whole capital of the society – forming a more or less permanent body, while the mass of shareholders is undergoing a constant process of decomposition and renewal.[4]

Finally, I have several times referred to the passage in *Capital III* that cites upwards mobility into the capitalist class as stabilizing its rule – one reason presumably being that the working class thereby loses some of its potential leaders. On the other hand, Marx rarely refers to such negative consequences of intra-class mobility, the only exception to my knowledge being the passage from "Wages" just cited. Rather, he dwells on the positive effects of such mobility for the workers, since it tends to create "the fully developed individual, fit for a variety of labours".[5] He neglects the idea that mobility, while possibly good for the worker, might weaken the resistance of the workers as a class.

The cultural heterogeneity of class members may also be an obstacle to collective action. In 1.3.1 I cited a passage on Ireland in which Marx implausibly suggests that the opposition between English and Irish workers was deliberately created, or at least artificially maintained by the English capitalists, as part of a "divide and conquer" strategy. More

---

[1] Veyne, *Le Pain et le Cirque*, pp. 314ff; Tocqueville, *Democracy in America*, p. 549.
[2] This is why Tocqueville did not believe class to be an important factor in America (see note 2, p. 342 above).
[3] *The Communist Manifesto*, p. 509.   [4] *New York Daily Tribune* 11.7.1856.
[5] *Capital I*, p. 488.

plausible is the suggestion that exploiters can turn pre-existing differences to their benefit, for example by deliberately creating a mixed work-force (6.3.1). True, cultural differences can be overcome – but the time needed for class solidarity to override other loyalties may be quite long, and if there is much mobility in and out no such time may be available. I give notice that in 6.2.3 I comment on a different kind of heterogeneity among group members, related to motivation rather than cultural background.

By the "technology of collective action" I refer to the functional relationship between the input (total participation) and the output (benefit to the individual of collective action).[1] Three main possibilities can be distinguished. (i) The relationship is that of a step-function, so that the marginal productivity of participation is zero "almost everywhere". Up to the critical threshold it is pointless to contribute, beyond the threshold it is superfluous. Only when the behaviour of one individual brings one up to the threshold does contribution make a difference. While this model may be adequate for some cases of collective action,[2] it will hardly do in the present case.[3] If more people join the strike, the chances of success go up. (ii) The functional relationship may be concave, so that initial contributions have a small impact, whereas later contributions are increasingly effective. This will typically reflect some kind of discontinuity in the organizational practices. The efficacy of revolutionaries may increase dramatically when they get sufficiently numerous to afford a machine gun. (iii) The relationship may be convex, so that the impact of early contributions exceeds that of later ones. One hunger strike may have a huge impact, but the second one may not catch the media's attention at all. Clearly, technology and motivation interact in complex ways to shape the probability of collective action. For instance, with a concave technology there is a need for some members who are highly motivated, in the sense of attaching little weight to free-rider gains or losses from unilateralism.

---

[1] This paragraph draws heavily on Marwell, Oliver and Teixeira, "Group heterogeneity, interdependence and the production of collective goods".

[2] Hardin, *Collective Action*, pp. 55ff.

[3] Buchanan, *Marx and Justice*, p. 89, assumes without justification that threshold technology is the proper model for collective action. Moreover, he draws from this assumption the unwarranted conclusion that even with altruistic motivations collective action cannot occur with this technology. With threshold technologies the probability of one person's behaviour influencing the outcome is very small, but in the rare cases that he has an influence (through being pivotal) the influence is very large. Hence the expected utility of participating for the individual could well be sufficient to motivate him to do so. See Parfit, *Reasons and Persons*, ch. 3.

A final, quite different issue is the following. What are the conditions under which the members of an oppressed or exploited group come to see themselves as active beings, capable of shaping their environment rather than passively accepting whatever happens or is done to them? Or again, what are the conditions for the emergence of self-respect? Marx, we shall see (6.2.3), argued that self-respect was largely an outcome of the class struggle, but a minimum of this attitude is also needed for the struggle to get started. We saw in 4.2.1 that he singled out the *market* as the birthplace of working-class self-respect. In a capitalist economy the labour market and the market for consumer goods forces the worker to *choose*, and with choice goes responsibility for one's actions. Hence capitalism provides the worker both with a reason for collective action *and* with a trained capacity to carry it out. In the latter respect, it differs crucially from earlier economic systems.

Marx apparently saw the chain of causes as going from the market through economic struggle to political struggle. It is instructive to compare this with E. P. Thompson's account in *The Making of the English Working Class*. In his chapter "Planting the liberty tree" he makes it clear that the origin of working-class self-respect was to be found in the political struggles during the Revolutionary and Napoleonic years. Later came the rise of industrial capitalism, with the devastating consequences on "Standards and experiences", the title of another chapter of his book. The collective reaction of the workers against the abuses was fuelled by the political Radicalism: "at any time before the 1840s it is a mistake to segregate in our minds political disaffection and industrial organization".[1] In Thompson's work there is no suggestion that the market produced the remedy along with the malady – that the freedom of choice characteristic of a market economy also contributed to the self-respect of the worker and thus enabled him to offer some resistance to the market forces. On the other hand, his argument is not incompatible with that view, since the rise of the market antedates the emergence of industrial capitalism. The liberating effect of the market could have worked its way *before* the failures of the market came to be felt on a large scale. Be this as it may, Thompson's emphasis on politics does seem incompatible with Marx's theory of the primacy of economic struggles.

6.2.3. The rationality of collective action

I have not proposed any theory of collective action, only a list of variables that at best correlate *ceteris paribus* with collective action. ("At best",

---

[1] Thompson, *The Making of the English Working Class*, p. 546.

because in some cases the net effect of the several ways in which the independent variable influences the dependent variable turned out to be ambiguous.) In this subsection I shall consider some attempts to anchor these correlations in a theory of individual behaviour. In doing so, I shall have to proceed by stark simplification; most of the variables discussed in 6.2.2 will simply be neglected. In the main I shall proceed independently of Marx, although towards the end I survey some of Marx's writings on the rationale for trade unions.

Let me recall some general points made in 1.1 and 1.2. On first principles, one should seek for micro-foundations for collective action.[1] To explain the collective action simply in terms of the benefits for the group is to beg all sorts of questions, and in particular the question why collective action so often fails to take place even when it would greatly benefit the agents. The individual-level explanations should be constructed according to the following heuristic principle: first assume that behaviour is both rational and self-interested; if this does not work, assume at least rationality; only if this is unsuccessful too should one assume that individual participation in collective action is irrational. Finally the danger of premature reductionism should be constantly kept in mind. Collective action may simply be too complex for individual-level explanations to be feasible at the current stage. In that case, the best research strategy would seem to be a further refinement of the gross correlations drawn above.

The basic problem confronting any group of people trying to organize themselves is that of the Prisoner's Dilemma.[2] In its simplest form it is a strategic game between any given individual and "Everyone else". To each of these actors, two strategies are available: to engage in the collective action or to abstain. For any pair of strategies chosen by the actors, there is a well-defined payoff (in expected material welfare) to each of them. In the matrix below the first number in each cell represents "my" payoff and the second the payoff to each of the individuals included in "everyone else".

Table 6.1

		Everyone else	
		Engage	Abstain
I	Engage	b, b	e, f
	Abstain	c, d	a, a

[1] For some recent trends in this direction, see M. Hechter (ed.), *Microfoundations of Macrosociology*; Popkin, *The Rational Peasant*; Stroebe and Frey, "Self-interest and collective action".

[2] On the two-person Prisoner's Dilemma see Rapoport and Chammah, *Prisoner's Dilemma*. For the *n*-person case see Taylor, *Anarchy and Cooperation*.

Here $b-a$ represents the gain from cooperation, as defined in 6.2.2. Similarly $c-b$ represents the free-rider gain and $a-e$ the loss from unilateralism. Clearly, whatever everyone else does, it is in my interest to abstain. If all others engage in collective action, I can get the free-rider benefit by abstaining and if everyone else abstains I can avoid the loss from unilateralism by abstaining too. Since the reasoning applies to each agent, in the place of "I", all will decide to abstain and no collective action will be forthcoming.

In one sense the logic is compelling. If (i) the game is played only once, (ii) the actors are motivated solely by the payoff in the matrix and (iii) they behave rationally, collective action *must* fail. By contraposition, we might look into the possibilities for collective action if the interaction is repeated several times; if the payoffs that motivate the actors differ from the material reward structure; and if the behaviour is less than fully rational. It turns out that under all these conditions, collective action does become possible. The three cases correspond to what was referred to earlier as rationality-cum-selfishness; rationality simpliciter; and irrationality.

Consider first repeated interactions. Capitalists in an industry or workers in a firm interact over long periods of time. What they choose to do at one moment is one determinant of what others will do at later moments, so that threats or promises – implicit or explicit – become possible. These can be formalized into such meta-strategies as "always choose the same strategy as your opponent did in the preceding game", that is retaliate with abstention against abstention and answer cooperation with cooperation. It can be shown that if all parties adopt this meta-strategy, the ensuing situation may be stable against defectors. The free-rider gains will not tempt the individual to break out of the collective action.[1]

The idea makes good intuitive sense. It was stated among others by Descartes long before the advent of formalized game theory,[2] on the basis of the observation that we often find it prudent to help others who one day may be in a position to do us a favour in return. Yet game theory can help us bring out some limitations on the theory that are not obvious from common sense observations. First, the rationality of participating in collective action depends on the extent to which present gains are preferred over future gains. More precisely, it depends on the specific quantitative relationship

[1] For details, see Taylor, *Anarchy and Cooperation*.
[2] See the letters from Descartes to Princess Elisabeth cited and discussed in my *Ulysses and the Sirens*, ch. II.4.

between the time rate of discounting and the parameters that define the gain from cooperation, the free-rider benefit and the loss from unilateralism.[1] Next, the individual rationality of collective action breaks down if the number of interactions is finite and known in advance by the players. This is so because it can never be rational to cooperate in the last game, since behaviour at that stage cannot influence future payoffs. Hence all parties will know that all will abstain in the last period. This however, means that the next-to-last period appears in the same light, since the choices made in this game will not have any consequence for the final game. And so the argument continues back to the first period of interaction. Hence collective action can only be rational if the number of interactions is either determinate and unknown, or a stochastic variable. Lastly, the meta-strategy of doing to your opponent what he did to you is never a dominant strategy, that is it is not the best response to every meta-strategy that the opponent can choose, only to his choice of the same meta-strategy. This entails that one will only choose this strategy if one has grounds to believe that the opponent will behave similarly. For this, quite stringent information requirements must be fulfilled, that is one must have grounds for thinking that the opponent is as rational and well informed as oneself. If there is doubt about his rationality or information, abstention is the rational choice.[2]

These facts can enter into an explanation of why sometimes collective action is not forthcoming. The agents may simply be too greedy to be deterred by threats of retaliation. There may be a known terminal date to the interaction. Or the agents may have incomplete information about one another. The frequency with which these conditions are satisfied, and the fact that any one of them by itself will block collective action, go a long way towards explaining the many failures of cooperation. Or, to put it the other way around, for collective action to take place so many conditions must be fulfilled that it is a wonder it can occur at all. The window of acceptable parameter values may be very narrow indeed. These statements, however, depend on the assumption that collective action must flow from selfishly rational behaviour. I now turn to explanations that do not rest on this assumption.

Agents do not choose in total isolation from one another. What an agent does is observed by others, and this fact is known to him. Also, he

---

[1] Taylor, *Anarchy and Cooperation*, ch. 3.
[2] Needless to say these are simplified statements. In a more adequate formulation one would have to take account of the number of other people expected to join the collective action and the strength of one's expectation.

is in a position to observe what others do and ultimately what they get. These externalities may influence motivation and choice in several ways. First, the agent may feel guilt and shame about abstaining, based on an anticipation of the informal social sanctions that can be brought to bear on him. For all practical purposes this is equivalent to imposing a utility fine on the choice of the abstention strategy – but only if others choose to cooperate. This will reduce or eliminate the free-rider gain, without affecting the loss from unilateralism. Secondly, the agent may derive some positive utility from the gains that accrue to others. If by engaging in collective action he can raise their utility level to some extent, this may partially or wholly offset the loss to himself, that is the free-rider benefits foregone. (I make the assumption, discussed later, that the externalities do not affect the loss from unilateralism.) Thirdly the agents may value equality as such, and derive negative utility whenever the numbers in any given cell of the payoff matrix differ. Once again this will reduce the free-rider gain, without any reduction of the loss from unilateralism. If anything, the latter will be raised by a preference for equality.

Assuming that these externalities completely do away with the free-rider benefits, cooperation appears as the solution to the game. Once more, however, this is not a dominant strategy. Since I assume that the loss from unilateralism remains, it is not rational to take the first step towards collective action. As before, stringent information requirements must be fulfilled. We are dealing, in fact, with a *conditional preference for cooperation*. Each agent prefers to cooperate if the others can be expected to do likewise, but if he suspects they will not, he won't either.

There might be two reasons for failure of collective action in such cases. For one thing, the information requirements may not be satisfied. For another, the agents might not be sufficiently motivated by the externalities in question. Here the relevance of some of the conditions mentioned in 6.2.2 appears clearly. If the agents are not too numerous, are sufficiently close to one another, sufficiently similar in background and interact for a sufficient period of time, they will come to know one another and to care for one another – so that both the information requirement and the motivation requirement tend to be fulfilled. The second part of this statement is controversial, for several reasons. First, we would not expect it to be equally true of all classes. We would not expect, for instance, capitalists to be motivated by concern for each other's profit. More generally, we may conjecture that the exploiting classes are less likely to harbour such feelings than the exploited classes. True, the fear of social sanctions should not be underestimated as a motivating force among the exploiters,[1] but they will typically be more effective in stabilizing collective action than in generating it.[2] Secondly, prolonged interaction between the same individuals may transform indifference into hostility and envy rather than solidarity, generating negative rather than positive externalities.[3] Presumably Marx thought that cooperation between the workers in the production process also predisposed them towards cooperation in class action.

By implication, I have suggested that capitalist collective action rests on selfish rationality in iterated games, whereas working-class collective action rests on externalities in the utility function. Would it not be more parsimonious to assume that the logic of the iterated Prisoner's Dilemma is at work in both cases? Workers no less than capitalists might engage in collective action because they find it selfishly rational. I find it hard to reconcile this idea with the extensive literature on working-class culture, but on the other hand the elusiveness and subtlety of these problems of individual motivation should make us wary of dismissing it out of hand. The ideas of implicit exchange and of conditional solidarity are sufficiently close to each other to generate the same political rhetoric. One could try to test the hypothesis by looking at situations in which interaction between workers does have a known terminal date, for example in road construction and similar ventures, to see whether this had a negative impact on the solidarity of the workers. Workers involved in such industries do not, however, form a stable and enduring community, hence any failure of collective action could also be imputed to the high turn-over rate. In any case, itinerant workers in construction industries often are among the most radical segments of the working class – but then one might want to question whether the radicalism is a sign of highly developed class consciousness, given its strongly activist character.[4] Hence, whatever the result turns out to be, it is likely that it can be fitted in with either hypothesis. The concepts are not sufficiently precise, and the theory not robust enough, to allow for a clear-cut confrontation. It is indeed possible that the attempt would involve premature reductionism.

Note that in both models, participation in the collective action is only conditional on the participation of others. Cooperation is never a dominant strategy. Could one conceive of models in which cooperation

---

[1] See for instance Veyne, *Le Pain et le Cirque*, pp. 230ff.
[2] van Parijs, *Evolutionary Explanation in the Social Sciences*, pp. 132ff.
[3] March and Lave, *Introduction to Models in the Social Sciences*, p. 15.
[4] See my *Logic and Society*, pp. 144–5.

is unambiguously best, whatever others do? One rationale for this view could be to assume that individuals act ethically, for example in accordance with the categorical imperative, which positively forbids one to base one's choice on what others are likely to do. Another would be to assume that individuals sometimes derive direct utility from the participation, so that by virtue of the "in-process benefits"[1] cooperation might be a dominant strategy. Both proposals involve departures from consequentialism, in different ways. The first argues in terms of the consequences that would ensue if everyone acted in a certain way, while consequentialism as usually understood is the view that the individual should act in light of the consequences brought about by *his* action. The second does not invoke consequences at all.

I am of two minds concerning the first idea. On the one hand working-class history shows that individual acts of heroism or sacrifice may be *worse* than useless, namely if they give authorities or employers an excuse to crack down on the workers.[2] The infrequency with which unconditional altruism is observed may not only be due to the superhuman demands it makes on individuals, but also to a sound insight into its moral shortcomings. On the other hand a hard core of unconditional cooperators may make it easier for others to join, if the technology of collective action is concave. One may imagine a snowball effect, where a hard core of 5 per cent unconditional cooperators attract another 10 per cent who need at least 5 per cent already cooperating, thus making it possible to attract another 30 per cent who need at least 15 per cent cooperators, etc.[3] If for some agents, that is, the loss from unilateralism is zero, their action may bring it down to zero for the next set of entrants, and so on. I am fairly convinced that this also corresponds to important episodes in working-class history. Presumably the moral strictures on unilateral action are pertinent only if no such snowball effect is operating. Note, however, that the reference to the snowball effect is a form of consequentialist reasoning.[4] The agents themselves may not think of their participation in this way, but nevertheless that is the form a justification would take. The importance of the unconditional cooperators in collective action may be precisely that they have no need to calculate whether others will follow suit – and this non-consequentialist attitude can then after the fact be consequentially justified by its effect in

---

[1] Buchanan, *Marx and Justice*, pp. 92ff; see also Hirschman, *Shifting Involvements*.

[2] See Margalit, "Ideals and the second-best", for a good account of this problem.

[3] For such mixed-preference cases see Marwell, Oliver and Teixeira, "Group heterogeneity, interdependence and the production of collective goods"; Schelling, *Micromotives and Macrobehaviour*.

[4] My thinking on this point has been helped by discussions with Charles Silver.

making others follow suit. The question remains when and under what conditions moral condemnation of unilateralism is pertinent *before* the fact.

The other rationale for thinking that cooperation could be a dominant strategy is more questionable. The benefits from participation are essentially by-products.[1] Anyone who joined or initiated collective action *solely* to get these benefits would not get them. Nor, I submit, would they be very likely to succeed in realizing the goal by which the collective action itself is defined. To organize a strike demands hard, sustained effort, hardly compatible with the narcissistic attitude of those who engage in collective action just for the kick it gives them. I am not saying that such individuals could not, by their sheer numerical presence, enhance the efficacy of an already-organized action, but I do affirm that a group only or mainly made up in this way would be singularly lacking in staying power.

It remains to discuss explanations of collective action that present individual participation as essentially irrational. (In principle one might want to distinguish between action taken on irrational beliefs and action that is irrational *given* the beliefs, but in actual cases we will rarely be able to decide whether we are observing the one or the other.) I shall briefly mention two such explanations. The first takes off from the observation that in very long runs of the Prisoner's Dilemma, players cooperate for a long time even when the terminal date is known, although they switch to defection towards the end.[2] It has been argued that such behaviour is actually rational,[3] but I am not convinced by this view. Rather we seem to be dealing with some cognitive analogy to weakness of will: the distant future simply does not enter into our calculations in the same way as do the near future and the present. Whereas weakness of will in the sense of a high rate of time discounting makes cooperation more difficult, the presently discussed inability to take account of the future makes it more accessible.

The other explanation rests on an ingenious experiment carried out by Amos Tversky and George Quattrone.[4] They found that when asked about voting behaviour in various hypothetical cases, the subjects

---

[1] Concerning this, see my *Sour Grapes*, ch. II.9.

[2] Rapoport and Chammah, *Prisoner's Dilemma*, p. 29, write that "Evidently the run-of-the-mill players are not strategically sophisticated enough to have figured out that [the strategy of non-cooperation] is the only rationally defensible strategy, and this intellectual shortcoming saves them from losing."

[3] Hardin, *Collective Action*, pp. 146ff.

[4] Quattrone and Tversky, "Self-deception and the voters' illusion".

would answer in a way that confirms the following hypothesis. If an individual thinks of himself as somehow representative or typical of a certain group, he will tend to argue that "If I act in a certain way, others like me are likely to behave similarly." Moreover, there is a tendency for this unobjectionable piece of diagnostic reasoning to become transformed into causal thinking. Individuals decide to vote because they believe, magically, that this will lead others like them to do the same. The tail believes it can wag the dog. This could also apply to the forms of collective action discussed here. The tendency is related to the conundrum known as Newcomb's problem,[1] as well as to certain modes of reasoning in Calvinism.[2] Clearly, it can be very beneficial socially. It is, as it were, the psychological implementation of the categorical imperative. I feel convinced that in certain cases this form of irrationality enters into the explanation of individual decisions to participate in collective action, but I have no idea as to how to circumscribe this class of cases.

A priori there is no reason to believe that any single model for individual-level behaviour will be the best in all cases of collective action. Explanatory pluralism should not be eschewed. On the other hand, one should beware of the dangers of *ad hoc*-ness. I believe the best strategy for further research may be a mixed one, with about 70 per cent of the effort going into further exploration of macro-correlation and 30 per cent into the formulation of models that offer micro-foundations. Surely there is no problem in the social sciences that is more important than that of explaining why people cooperate.

Before I turn to Marx, let me add a few words about the role of *leadership* in collective action. Obviously, leaders are always necessary, regardless of the motivation of individuals, to coordinate collective action. If the motivations also are such that individuals must be assured of each other before they act, leadership takes on the additional function of providing such assurance. If one individual knows and is trusted by one hundred people, he can create the information conditions by two hundred transactions – first asking each of them about their willingness to join the collective action and then telling each about the willingness of everybody else. By contrast, bilateral

---

[1] See Nozick, "Newcomb's problem and two principles of choice".

[2] Although taken from a later period, the following statement from a Baptist leaflet illustrates perfectly the Calvinist mode of reasoning: "Every soul that comes to Christ to be saved ... is to be encouraged ... The coming soul need not fear that he is not elected, for none but such would be willing to come." (Cited in Thompson, *The Making of the English Working Class*, p. 38.)

communication between the hundred will require about five thousand acts of communication. The information gains from leadership can be quite substantial.

A further role for leadership can be identified by considering a special case of the payoff matrix in table 6.1. Assume that these payoffs do not form a Prisoner's Dilemma, but are defined by $b = c$, $e = a$ and $b > a$. There is no individual interest for or against the collective action, but there is a collective interest in its favour.[1] Since the individuals are indifferent, regardless of what others do, they might just toss a coin or follow custom, but an enterprising leader could also exploit this "zone of indifference"[2] and make them act in concert to their collectively best interest. As a possible, although largely hypothetical case, consider the importance of labour-saving inventions in keeping wages down (3.3.2). If the cost for the firm of giving a labour-saving bias to its search for innovations is negligible, there is scope for intelligent leadership and persuasion.

A more frequently discussed role of leadership is that of offering selective incentives for members, or – alternatively – punishment for recalcitrant individuals.[3] This is equivalent to a utility premium for cooperation, or a utility fine on defection. Like the informal sanctions discussed above, these are more important in stabilizing collective action than in generating it. The proper explanatory sequence must be to begin with individual motivations and ask how they generate behavioural patterns. These patterns may then crystallize into organizations that are able to enforce the behaviour, even in the absence of the original motivations. To answer the fundamental question about collective action -- *how is it at all possible?* – we cannot begin by assuming a situation in which it has already taken place. Hence the role of leadership in coordinating action, disseminating information and exploiting indifference is conceptually more fundamental than the tasks of coercion and selective inducements.

Marx did not give much thought to the problem of providing microfoundations for collective action. In his discussions of trade unions he downplays the immediate economic benefits, and emphasizes instead the role of strikes etc. in the formation of political class consciousness. In the *Communist Manifesto* we read that "the real fruit of [the workers'] battle lies, not in the immediate result, but in the ever-expanding union of the workers".[4] In the manuscript on "Wages" Marx, having discussed the

---

[1] Concerning this game, see also my *Ulysses and the Sirens*, pp. 120–1.
[2] Stinchcombe, *Constructing Social Theories*, p. 157.
[3] Olson, *The Logic of Collective Action*, pp. 66ff.
[4] *The Communist Manifesto*, p. 493.

objection that trade unions will prove harmful to the interests of the workers, adds that

All these objections of the bourgeois economists are, as we have said, correct, but only correct from their point of view. If in the associations it really were a matter only of what it appears to be, namely the fixing of wages, if the relationship between labour and capital were eternal, these combinations would be wrecked on the necessity of things. But they are the means of uniting the working class, of preparing for the overthrow of the entire old society with its class contradictions. And from this standpoint the workers are right to laugh at the clever bourgeois schoolmasters who reckon up to them what this civil war is costing them in fallen, injured and financial sacrifices. He who wants to beat his adversary will not discuss with him the costs of war.[1]

Marx here appears to assert both that the working class stands in need of unification and that it is already united. On the one hand, the struggle for economic benefits will unite the workers and prepare them for the later, political struggles. On the other hand the workers are said to be sufficiently advanced to discount the financial sacrifices that will be required of them. But to ask the workers to engage in economic struggle for the sake of developing a political class consciousness is to assume that they are in possession of the very maturity that the struggle is supposed to develop. Marx here commits *the fallacy of by-products*, briefly referred to above, when he assumes that any desirable state that may emerge as the by-product of action can also be chosen as the motivating goal for that action. It is true and important that if workers engage in economic struggles, the conflicts with the employers may help them develop a class consciousness that at some point requires them to go beyond economic struggles. What is false is that this *ex post* truth can be transformed into an *ex ante* motivation, so that the transcending of economic struggles could be the very point of engaging in them.

Since this point is fundamental, I shall give some further textual evidence and argument. In 2.4.2 I cited a text from the *New York Daily Tribune* where Marx argues that "the conflicts between masters and men" are "the indispensable means of holding up the spirit of the labouring classes". The next statement, in chronological order, comes in a letter from 1865. Here Marx states that in Germany:

Combinations, together with the trades unions growing out of them, are of the utmost importance not only as a means of organization of the working class for struggle against the bourgeoisie – this importance being shown by the fact, *inter alia*, that even the workers in the United States cannot do without them, despite

[1] "Wages", p. 435.

voting rights and the republic – but in addition, in Prussia and Germany generally, the right to organize is a breach in police rule and bureaucratism; it tears to bits the Rules Governing Servants and the control of the nobility in the rural districts. In short it is a measure for the conversion of 'subjects' into full-fledged citizens (*eine Massregel zur Mündigmachung der 'Untertanen'*).[1]

This is an argument about the development of self-respect out of the class struggle, creating the necessary prerequisite for political action. As such it is quite unobjectionable, on the condition that one does not lose sight of the immediate economic goals that form the *object* of the struggles. The *ex ante* prospects of success in the struggle are indispensable, even if *ex post* it turns out to be a failure.[2]

In *Wages, Price and Profit* from the same year Marx writes that "by cowardly giving way in their every-day conflict with capital, [the workers] would certainly disqualify themselves for the initiating of any larger movement".[3] In this work Marx admits that trade unions can obtain some economic results, although mainly of a defensive character. Hence there would be a point to the economic struggle as such, yet it is certainly subordinate to the goal of political emancipation. This subordination is also stated in a document that Marx drafted in 1866 for the International:

Trades' Unions originally sprung up from the *spontaneous* attempts of workmen at removing or at least checking [the competition amongst themselves], in order to conquer such terms of contract as might raise them at least above the condition of mere slaves. The immediate object of Trades' Unions was therefore confined to everyday necessities, to expediencies for the obstruction of the incessant encroachment of capital, in one word, to questions of wages and time of labour. This activity of the Trades' Unions is not only legitimate, it is necessary. It cannot be dispensed with so long as the present system of production lasts. On the other hand, unconsciously to themselves, the Trades' Unions were forming *centres of organization* of the working class, as the medieval municipalities and communes did for the middle class. If the Trades' Unions are required for guerilla fights between capital and labour, they are still more important as *organised agencies for superseding the very system of wages labour and capital rule.*[4]

Finally, in a letter from 1871 Marx asserts that "Where the working class is not yet far enough advanced in its organization to undertake a decisive campaign against the collective power, i.e. the political power of the ruling

---

[1] Marx to Schweitzer 13.2.1865, as quoted in Marx to Engels 18.2.1865.

[2] Against this one may consider the following answer by E. P. Thompson, when asked whether he thought that a political rally in Trafalgar Square would actually *achieve* anything: "That's not really the point, is it? The point is, it shows that democracy's alive. People aren't just inclined to accept what politicians tell them. A rally like that gives us self-respect. Chartism was terribly good for the Chartists, although they never got the Charter" (*Sunday Times* 2.11.1980).

[3] *Wages, Price and Profit*, pp. 151–2.

[4] "Instructions for delegates to the Geneva Congress", pp. 196–7.

classes, it must at any rate be trained for this by continual agitation against this power and by a hostile attitude towards the policies of the ruling class."[1] Trained by whom? Marx does not say. A few years earlier he had written to Engels about the importance of the International: "In the next revolution, which is perhaps nearer than it appears, we (i.e. you and I) will have this powerful engine *in our hands.*"[2] These are not phrases that suggest the workers becoming active, autonomous subjects.

From these various passages, the following conclusions seem to emerge. (i) Marx plausibly asserts that the struggle for economic benefits may change the workers so that they go beyond the economic struggle and into politics. This is the "coincidence of the changing of circumstances and of human activity or self-change".[3] (ii) He suggests, notably in the earlier works, that the economic struggles may prove futile. This is quite consistent with asserting that they are useful or even indispensable for the formation of a political class consciousness, on the condition that the assertion is taken as an *ex post* statement about cause and effect. (iii) If on the contrary the assertion is taken in the *ex ante* sense as a statement about means and ends, it is an instance of the fallacy of by-products. (iv) There is one sense, however, in which it can be meaningfully understood as a means–end statement, namely as a recipe for manipulation. Far-sighted leaders of the working class might lead the workers into battles which they know will be lost, because the very experience of defeat will bring a gain in consciousness[4] or because struggle – whether successful or not – is a condition for political maturity. This, however, is contrary to Marx's stated view that nobody outside the working class can tell it what to do, because "the educator must himself be educated"[5] and "the emancipation of the working classes must be conquered by the working classes themselves".[6] (v) There are strong teleological overtones in many of Marx's statements about trade unions, suggesting that their activity can be explained by their ultimate role in promoting political revolution and hence justifying his neglect of micro-foundations. (vi) Finally one can also find in Marx the more reasonable view that trade unions can achieve a limited success in their economic struggles – the success enabling one to exhort the workers to such struggle, the limits to predict that they will feel a need to go beyond it. In

[1] Marx to Bolte 23.11.1871.   [2] Marx to Engels 11.9.1867.
[3] "Theses on Feuerbach", p. 4; cp. also *The German Ideology*, pp. 53, 214.
[4] In *The Class Struggles in France*, p. 47 Marx makes this argument with respect to political struggle. Revolutionary defeat is necessary to liberate the workers from their illusions.
[5] "Theses on Feuerbach", p. 4.   [6] "Provisional rules of the International", p. 14.

my opinion this view is too adulterated with the fallacy of by-products, the teleological fallacy and the temptation of manipulation to allow one to assert it unambiguously as *the* Marxist theory of class consciousness.

6.3. Class struggle

Class consciousness is inextricably bound up with class struggle. In this section I discuss how social conflict arises through confrontations and coalitions between classes as collective actors. In 6.3.1, I link "negative class consciousness", defined in 6.2.1, to "latent class struggle" – that is behaviour that is intended to prevent class struggle, although it is not in itself any kind of struggle. In 6.3.2 I discuss social conflict as a non-cooperative game between collective actors, while 6.3.3 introduces a co-operative framework that allows for coalition formation. In 6.3.4 I conclude with a discussion of the centrality of classes in social conflict.

The empirical frame of reference will largely be England and France around 1850. Marx's writings on the social and political struggles in France from 1848 to 1851 are well known for their analytical and rhetorical brilliance. His articles on British politics do not similarly form a sustained narrative of events, but from a theoretical perspective I believe them to be equally central. By considering the two bodies of work together it is possible to bring out what Marx took to be the central characteristics of the class struggle under capitalism. I do not in this chapter refer to the writings on Germany, which are much more exclusively concerned with political events at the expense of an attention to the social background. In the next chapter these writings have a central place.

6.3.1. Latent class struggle
Following Steven Lukes's typology of "three dimensions of power",[1] we may discern three possible forms of class conflict. First there is overt, mutually recognized struggle. This forms the object of 6.3.2 and 6.3.3. At the other extreme we have the mere objective divergence of class interest, with no class actively seeking to oppress any other. The differential satisfaction of class interest that is observed results from other, non-intentional mechanisms.[2] It is perhaps not very plausible to refer to this as class *struggle*, but one may well speak of class *conflict*. In between

---

[1] Lukes, *Power: A Radical View.*
[2] This is the central theme in Veyne, *Le Pain et le Cirque.* Such objective class conflict has a potential for class struggle, in the sense that if the subjects did not of themselves generate an ideology justifying their submission, the rulers could and would resort to force, yet it *is* not class struggle.

these two extremes there is what I refer to as latent class struggle. It is an intermediate case in that *one* class is assumed to be fully class consciousness, and as a collective actor takes steps to prevent the members of other classes from achieving class consciousness. In particular, a class may try to manipulate the conditions of class consciousness discussed in 6.2.2 with a view to preventing collective action that is opposed to its own interests. When discussing such action great care must be taken to distinguish measures designed to prevent ̇the opposed class from attaining class consciousness, and measures that have this only as an unintended (or at least non-explanatory) consequence.[1] Thus the bourgeoisie may weaken the working class by opening its ranks to those who would otherwise have provided leadership material for working-class struggles, but this effect of upwards social mobility does not by itself prove it to be a form of latent class struggle. Only if there is evidence of intentional design would this conclusion follow.

This warning is particularly relevant with regard to the cognitive and motivational conditions for class consciousness. There are many mechanisms endogenous to the oppressed classes that prevent them from understanding that collective action is a feasible solution to their problems.[2] The historical evidence no less than social theory goes against the attempt to understand these phenomena in terms of class domination. It may well be true, as Marx argued, that the existence in England of two distinct enemies of the working class – landowners and factory-owners – had the effect of weakening their class consciousness. It is far less plausible to argue that the capitalists deliberately kept the landowners artificially alive in order to foster illusions about the real nature of the enemy.

Remoter background conditions lend themselves more to manipulation by the opposed class. Although Marx never to my knowledge discussed isolation, turn-over, group size or group homogeneity as instruments of social control, such conceptions are fully consistent with his general approach. Also, these are quite important and widespread modes of domination. One may cite, for instance, the extreme sensitivity of many governments to the political implications of railway

---

[1] The point of the parenthetical qualification is that a class may anticipate that its behaviour will reduce the capacity for collective action of another class, yet that effect may be neither sufficient nor necessary to induce it to act. For instance, employers may support state policies towards greater mobility of labour because at a given level of unionization this is good for aggregate profits, while also expecting as a welcome side effect that it will reduce the level of unionization.

[2] For a survey, see chs. III and IV of my *Sour Grapes*.

construction,[1] or the Chinese practice of rotating officials so that they would never have the time to form alliances with the local gentry.[2] The deliberate mixing of heterogeneous elements in the work force to prevent collective action is also a widespread phenomenon.[3] Such measures may, of course, be bad for productive efficiency. The railway may have been politically dangerous, but economically it was extremely useful. To rotate officials before they have had time to learn the job is not very efficient. Large factories in which many workers are brought together may be hotbeds of discontent, but necessary to exploit economies of scale. Hence there is a trade-off between class consciousness and efficiency to be considered (3.3.2).

6.3.2. Class confrontation

In this section I consider the outcome of non-cooperative encounters between two or more classes. I shall first examine the two-class case, and then more briefly the three-class case.

In the two-class case we need to distinguish between two forms of class struggle. On the one hand there is the struggle between two exploiting classes over the division of the spoils, on the other hand there is the struggle between an exploiting and an exploited class over the size of the spoils. It might appear as if the former case could be represented as a game of pure conflict, that is a constant-sum game, since the dividendum is given prior to the struggle. It is, however, given only in the sense that it cannot be increased. It can certainly be reduced, since the struggle itself requires resources that must be financed out of the gains. Since the classes have an interest in their *net* income, the game – as most other social situations of any interest – is really variable-sum. Yet there nevertheless is an important difference between such struggle and, say, worker–capitalist conflict. In the latter case the gross product is itself influenced by the struggle. Consider, for instance, the cost to the workers of going on strike. This is not simply a question of the cost of building an organization, paying the staff, etc. The workers must also consider that the strike paralyses economic activity and hence reduces the size of the product of which they demand a larger share. In this case the struggle is variable-sum both in production and distribution, while the struggle between exploiting classes is variable-sum only on the distributive side.

---

[1] Gerschenkron, "Agrarian policies and industrialization: Russia 1861–1917", p. 710.
[2] Skinner, "Cities and the hierarchy of local systems", p. 341.
[3] Ste Croix, *The Class Struggle in the Ancient Greek World*, pp. 65, 93, 146; Finley, *Economy and Society in Ancient Greece*, pp. 109, 171.

Marx usually discusses the struggle between landowners and capitalists as one of pure conflict. The clearest statement is perhaps in the *Theories of Surplus-Value*:

The capitalist is the direct exploiter of the workers, not only the direct appropriator, but the direct creator of *surplus-labour*. But since (for the industrial capitalist) this can only take place through and in the process of production, he is himself a functionary of this production, its director. The landlord, on the other hand, has a claim – through landed property (to absolute rent) and because of the physical differences of the various types of land (differential rent) – which enables him to pocket a part of this surplus-labour or surplus-value, to whose direction and creation he contributes nothing. Where there is a conflict, therefore, the capitalist regards him as a mere superfetation, a Sybarite excrescence, a parasite on capitalist production, the louse that sits upon him.[1]

Elsewhere Marx works out some implications of this difference:

The abolition of landed property in the Ricardian sense, that is, its conversion into State property so that rent is paid to the State instead of to the landlord, is the ideal, the heart's desire, which springs from the deepest inmost essence of capital. Capital cannot abolish landed property. But by converting it into rent which is paid to the State the capitalists as a *class* appropriate it and use it to defray their State expenses, thus appropriating in a roundabout way what cannot be retained directly.[2]

The landlord robs the capitalist as the latter robs the worker, but unlike the capitalist he does not "help create what is to be deducted" (4.3.2). The landlord performs no productive function; he neither works nor performs any managerial tasks. Hence in addition to the purely economic conflict of interests, there arises an ideological opposition between the productive and the unproductive classes.

This opposition also arises between industrial and financial capitalists. One might ask whether these really constitute separate classes. Against that view one could cite the fact that Marx refers to them both as members of "the bourgeoisie".[3] This, however, is not really an objection. In *The Eighteenth Brumaire* the landowners are also seen as part of the bourgeoisie, on the grounds that they are no longer enthusiastic about "monarchy, the church and the beauties of the old English constitution",[4] but only about *rent* – that is the very category that defines them as a class. The embourgeoisement of the landowners here simply means

---

[1] *Theories of Surplus-Value*, vol. 2, p. 328; cp. *Capital III*, p. 638.
[2] *Theories of Surplus-Value*, vol. 3, p. 472; cp. *New York Daily Tribune* 11.7.1853.
[3] E.g. *Class Struggles in France*, p. 48.
[4] *The Eighteenth Brumaire*, p. 128; cp. also *New York Daily Tribune* 21.8.1852.

that economic categories have become uppermost in their consciousness, not that they have become capitalists. Also, Marx explicitly states
that financial and industrial capitalists do form distinct classes[1] – a
distinction that is also needed on the theoretical grounds set out in 6.1.
The two groups engage in different economic behaviour, the lending of
capital and the hiring of labour respectively.[2]

As in the case of the landlords, but with less justification, Marx con-
siders the struggle between industrial and financial capitalists as one of
pure conflict. He repeatedly states that profit is created *before* its division
between these two classes,[3] thus neglecting the gains from specialized
financial markets as well as the losses from speculation. On the other
hand he also argues that financial capital could never be abolished in the
way the Ricardians wanted to abolish landed property: "As long as
money (commodities) can serve as capital, it can be sold as capital."[4]

Like the landlord, the financial capitalist who lends money to a
"functioning" capitalist "does not exploit workers and does not come
into opposition to labour",[5] although, needless to say, he is an exploiter
in the sense of working less than the number of hours embodied in what
he can buy for his revenue. In addition to the conflict with the industrial
capitalist over the division of the surplus, there also appears, as with the
landlord, an ideological opposition:

In relation to [the functioning capitalist] interest appears therefore as the mere
fruit of owning capital, of capital as such abstracted from the reproduction process of capital, inasmuch as it does not "work", does not function; while profit of
enterprise appears to him as the exclusive fruit of the functions which he performs with the capital, as the fruit of the movement and performance of capital,
of a performance which appears to him as his own activity, as opposed to the
inactivity, the non-participation of the money capitalist in the production process.[6]

[To] represent functioning capital is not a sinecure, like representing interest-
bearing capital. On the basis of capitalist production, the capitalist directs the
process of production and circulation. Exploiting productive labour entails exertion, whether he exploits it himself or has it exploited by someone else on his
behalf. Therefore, his profit of enterprise appears to him as distinct of interest,

---

[1] *Theories of Surplus-Value*, vol. 2, p. 123; *Capital III*, p. 376.
[2] Following the definition of class in 6.1.1, we may ask what determines who ends up as
industrial capitalists and who ends up as financial capitalists. In a text from *Capital III* (pp.
337–8) cited in 8.2.3, Marx suggests that from the point of view of the individual asset-
holder these two careers are equivalent, which can be read as stating that the choice
situation is one of multiple optima.
[3] *Capital III*, pp. 378, 381.   [4] *Theories of Surplus-Value*, vol. 3, p. 472.
[5] *Capital III*, p. 379; cp. *Theories of Surplus-Value*, vol. 3, p. 477.
[6] *Capital III*, p. 374.

as independent of the ownership of capital, but rather as the result of his function as a non-proprietor – a *worker*.[1]

Financial capitalists and landlords thus live off the work of others – the work of the industrial capitalist and that of the workers whom he exploits. Of course, the industrial capitalist also lives off the work of others, but to be able to do this he must perform some work himself. Observe that he is not a manager, but a working owner who is to some extent mortgaged to the bank or the money-lender.

Marx has little to say about the actual confrontation between the various classes that live off the surplus extracted from the workers. The main exception concerns the introduction and the abolition of the Corn Laws. In *Capital III* the origin of these laws is described:

Since landlords everywhere exert considerable, and in England even overwhelming, influence on legislation, they are able to exploit [the adverse situation of their tenants] for the purpose of victimising the entire class of tenants. For instance, the Corn Laws of 1815 – a bread tax, admittedly imposed on the country to secure for the idle landlords a continuation of their abnormally increased rentals during the Anti-Jacobin war – had indeed the effect, excluding cases of a few extraordinarily rich harvests, of maintaining prices of agricultural products above the level to which they would have fallen had corn imports been unrestricted.[2]

The laws, however, had an adverse impact on all capitalists, not only on capitalist tenants, since they tended to raise the wages of labour. Hence the manufacturers organized the Anti-Corn Law League, leading to the repeal of the laws in 1846. In an article from 1852 Marx saw this as merely confirming the real change of power that had taken place in the meantime:

The repeal of the Corn Laws in 1846 merely recognized an already accomplished fact, a change long since enacted in the elements of British civil society, viz. the subordination of the landed interest under the moneyed interest, of property under commerce, of agriculture under manufacturing industry, of the country under the city ... The substantial foundation of the power of the Tories was the rent of land. The rent of land is regulated by the price of food. The price of food, then, was artificially maintained at a high rate by the Corn Laws. The repeal of the Corn Laws brought down the price of food, which in its turn brought down the rent of land, and with sinking rent broke down the real strength upon which the political power of the Tories reposed.[3]

Later these views were drastically revised. In *Theories of Surplus-Value* Marx ridicules "Wilhelm Thukydides" Roscher for stating the controversy over the Corn Laws in terms of the opposition between

[1] *Ibid.*, p. 380.   [2] *Ibid.*, p. 626.   [3] *New York Daily Tribune* 21.8.1852.

"monied and landed interest", and argues that these were on the contrary united against the industrial capitalists.[1] More importantly, in *Capital I* he makes it clear that the landlords did not lose from the abolition of the Corn Laws. Rather it led to all sorts of improvements in agriculture, through drainage and similar measures. "The landed aristocracy advanced themselves to this end, of course, per Parliament, funds from the State Treasury, at a very low rate of interest, which the farmers have to make good at a much higher rate."[2] Here Marx argues that the political power of the landowners was the cause of their prosperity, not simply the reflex of it as the earlier text suggests. If so, whence did they draw their power? An answer is suggested in 7.1 below.

The paradigmatic case of class struggle between exploiters and exploited, with elements of cooperation as well as of conflict, is that between industrial capitalists and workers. Now, the following argument could well be made. True, there is an element of cooperation, but only if the shared premise of the struggle is the continued existence of capitalism. The struggle over its existence or abolition is, however, one of pure conflict. For reasons indicated above, this view is not defensible. The cost to the workers of the abolition of capitalism can be smaller or greater, depending on the strategies chosen by the two classes. In any case, this point is not really relevant for an understanding of Marx's empirical analyses. Although he exhorted the workers to move from the struggle over the working day and the wage level to a political struggle against capitalism as a system, and firmly believed that this move was bound to take place, the class struggles which he could actually observe revolved around distribution within the system. The basic sense in which there is a need for cooperation between workers and capitalists is that the means they use to increase their share of the total product, such as strikes or lockouts, also disrupt production and hence reduce the total to be shared. Also, the capitalists have an interest in the survival and reproduction of the workers, and the latter an interest in high profits that will ensure economic growth and future wage gains (4.1.2).

In 4.1.4 I discussed the confrontations between workers and capitalists at some length. Let me recall here that "the struggle between collective labour and collective capital" is but one of several determinants of the rate of exploitation. In addition we must invoke individual bargaining, monopoly or monopsony power, coalitions with other classes, state intervention and technical progress. The struggle between

---

[1] *Theories of Surplus-Value*, vol. 2, pp. 122ff.   [2] *Capital I*, p. 677.

workers and capitalists is embedded in an extremely complex social and temporal context that allows for a wide range of strategies and counterstrategies and leaves much room for unpredictable manoeuvring. Yet even if it may be hard to predict the outcome of any given struggle, Marx clearly believed it possible to anticipate the long-term trend in the class struggle, corresponding to the changing balance of power. The capitalist class, on his view, was being progressively undermined by the falling rate of profit and the increasingly severe crises, whereas the workers were making steady gains in education and organization. The capitalist tactics of alliance formation (6.3.3) might postpone the final breakdown, but not indefinitely.

Marx's detailed analyses of mid-nineteenth-century European politics do not mainly rest on such studies of two-class confrontations. In almost all cases, three or more classes are involved. The non-cooperative framework is then not very well suited.[1] To see why, consider a case of three contestants, A, B and C. A and B are both quite strong, and C definitely weaker. They are to engage in a series of tactical moves that in the end will leave one of them the winner, in the sense of having improved his initial position. Each move involves the allocation of one's resources between the two struggles, that is the struggles against the two opponents. It is then intuitively plausible, and in some cases it may be shown rigorously,[2] that A and B will use most of their strength against one another, leaving C as the winner. If, on the other hand, A and B are able to agree at the outset to eliminate C before they begin to confront one another, each of them will have a greater chance of emerging as the winner. Non-cooperative struggle in such cases leads to "tertius gaudens",[3] that is a benefit to a third party brought about by the struggle between the strong. A special case arises when each of the two strong contenders tries to solicit the weak as an alliance partner, leading to a non-cooperative struggle about who is to cooperate with whom. The outcome may be that no cooperation occurs, but that the weak party gains from the conflict between the strong. Marx, for instance, cites the English proverb "when thieves fall out, honest men come into their own"[4] in his discussion of the fate of the English agricultural workers.

Such cases of "strength from weakness" or "weakness from strength"

---

[1] By "non-cooperative" I intend the absence of coalitions, not the absence of common interests.

[2] Shubik, *Game Theory and the Social Sciences*, pp. 22ff.

[3] Simmel, *Soziologie*, pp. 82ff, citing the debate over the Factory Acts as an important example.

[4] *Capital I*, p. 675.

are not uncommon. They do, however, go together with a tendency towards the formation of an alliance between the strong, at least for the time it takes to neutralize the weak. This pressure towards inter-class cooperation is partly analogous to the tendency to intra-class cooperation that formed the object of 6.2. Both parties gain from cooperation, but it is not a dominant strategy. Yet the differences are also striking. The number of actors is smaller in the class coalition case than in the class consciousness case,[1] and some of the obstacles to cooperation are correspondingly easier to overcome. In particular, the free-rider problem does not arise to the same extent, because it is less easy for an organization than for an individual to renege on an engagement of cooperation. With the exception of a Leninist type of party, most organizations are subject to an inertia that ensures that agreements will be adhered to at least for some time (and in the light of the historical experience parties of the Leninist type find it increasingly difficult to find willing partners of cooperation). Of course, such alliances may not be very stable and enduring, but then they do not have to be if their purpose is only a temporary one. Alliances of intermediate duration are the stuff of politics. They are made and unmade as they attain or fail to attain their objectives; as circumstances change so as to make other constellations more attractive; or as the original engagement is eroded and the free-rider temptation becomes overwhelming. Hence I believe, as did Marx, that the concept of alliance formation is indispensable for an understanding of social conflict. And like him I believe that exogenous changes, for example in the economic situation of the classes, may help explain the *shifting* pattern of alliances.

6.3.3. Class coalitions

In an article from 1861, concerning the emancipation of the Russian serfs and the conflict it created between the landowners and the tsarist government, Marx suggested a general principle of coalition formation in class societies:

In this mutual strife, where the Government, despite menaces and cajoling, split upon the opposition of the nobles and the peasants – the aristocracy upon the opposition of the Government and of their human chattels, the peasantry upon the combined opposition of their central lord and their local lords – an understanding, as is usual in such transactions, has been arrived at between the existing powers at the cost of the oppressed class.[2]

---

[1] At least this is so if we assume that the "class coalition game" takes place after the "class consciousness game". Although Marx explored situations in which these proceed *pari passu*, it seems a reasonable assumption to make as the class struggle gains momentum.

[2] *New York Daily Tribune* 10.10.1860.

Marx's analyses of French and English politics around 1850 point to a more nuanced view. The outcome was indeed a tendency towards explicit or implicit alliance formation between the exploiting classes against the exploited class, but only as the result of long struggles in which the alliances often formed between an exploiting and an exploited class, against another exploiting class. I shall first consider the English and then the French case. Both involve the same classes: wage labourers, industrial capitalists, financial capitalists and landowners. True, in France there also existed a large peasantry, but according to Marx it had no developed class consciousness and hence did·not enter into any alliances. The discussion below is incomplete in that the political prolongations of the class struggle are kept in the background. In 7.1 and 7.2.1 these come to the forefront.

In Marx's writings on the class struggles in England the main actors are the workers, the industrial capitalists and the landowners. The financial capitalists play a quite subordinate role. In *Theories of Surplus-Value* Marx says, discussing Roscher, that

If Wilhelm Thukydides knew the history of the corn laws of 1815 and the struggle over these, then he would already have known from Cobbett that the borough-mongers (landed interests) and the loan-mongers (monied interest) combined against the industrial interests ... Furthermore, Wilhelm Thukydides should know from the history of 1815 to 1847 that in the battle over the corn laws the majority of the monied interest and some even of the commercial interest (Liverpool for instance) were to be found amongst the *allies* of the landed interest against the manufacturing interest.[1]

Writing about France, he makes this alliance into a general fact. "In general, the combination of large landed property with high finance is *normal fact*. Proof: *England*; proof: even *Austria*."[2] Marx does not, however, suggest any reason why this alliance should tend to form. Landowners and financial capitalists have in common that they live off the national product without contributing to it, hence one might expect that they would be perceived as one block by the "manufacturing classes", but it is hard to see how this negative "coalition consciousness" could be transformed into a positive one. Hence I am not able to take account of the financial capitalists when discussing the class struggles in England.

In 4.1.4 we saw some instances of class coalitions in English politics: between workers and capitalists in the abolition of the Corn Laws, between workers and landowners in the passing of the Ten Hours Bill.

---

[1] *Theories of Surplus-Value*, vol. 2, p. 123.   [2] *The Class Struggles in France*, p. 115.

The third possibility is illustrated by an 1862 proposal for a new regulation of the mining industry. This is

an industry distinguished from others by the exceptional characteristic that the interests of landlord and capitalists there join hands. The antagonism of these two interests had been favourable to Factory legislation, while on the other hand the absence of the antagonism is sufficient to explain the delays and chicanery of the legislation on mines.[1]

These, however, are skirmishes in the class struggles. They are motivated by immediate economic interests or even by petty revenge.[2] They are embedded, on the other hand, in a long-term conflict that shows a more general pattern of coalition formation. This pattern results from the dilemmas faced by the workers and the capitalists. The working class must decide whether to take on their remote or their direct antagonists, the capitalists whether to concentrate their forces against their former or their future enemy. To the extent that the workers opt for an alliance with the capitalists against the landowners, the capitalists will tend to side with the landowners against the workers. This, at any rate, appears to be the pattern that emerges from most of the writings on England. In 7.1 I return to the political implications of this constellation, which clearly gives a crucial position to the landowning class.

In the *Communist Manifesto* Marx offers an explanation for the tendency of the workers to fight the landowners before they turn to the capitalists:

At this stage the labourers still form an incoherent mass scattered over the whole country, and broken up by their mutual competition. If anywhere they unite to form more compact bodies, this is not yet the consequence of their own active union, but of the union of the bourgeoisie, which class, in order to attain its own political ends, is compelled to set the whole proletariat in motion, and is moreover, yet, for a time, able to do so. At this stage, therefore, the proletarians do not fight their enemies, but the enemies of their enemies, the remnants of absolute monarchy, the landowners, the non-industrial bourgeois, the petty bourgeoisie.[3]

In this conception the working class is not a collective actor, but a mere dummy, to be manipulated by other classes further advanced on the path to class consciousness. The text does not specify for which countries the description is intended to be valid, but it can hardly include

---

[1] *Capital I*, p. 495.
[2] In Marx's "Speech on the question of free trade", p. 457, and in *New York Daily Tribune* 1.8.1854, the landowners are said to be motivated by spitefulness and revenge.
[3] *The Communist Manifesto*, p. 492.

England, since Marx in a contemporary text attributes a highly developed class consciousness to the English workers:

> The English workmen have shown the English Free Traders that they are not the dupes of their illusions or of their lies; and if, in spite of this, the workers have made common cause against the landlords, it is for the purpose of destroying the last remnants of feudalism, that henceforth they may have only one enemy to deal with.[1]

This theme – the need to deal with one enemy at a time – must not be confused with the motivation behind the apparently similar policy that Marx advocated for Germany. Here his reasons for postponing the confrontation with the capitalist class was rather that the workers need a period of capitalist rule to gain numerical strength – the indispensable condition of class consciousness.[2] In England, the working class was fully formed, with a fully formed class consciousness. Later texts, however, retreat somewhat from this position.

Why should the working class prefer to deal with one enemy rather than two? Would it not be more rational to let the two enemies fight one another? Could not the workers play the game of *tertius gaudens*? Towards the end of 6.3.2 I sketched an argument why this might not be feasible. Another, somewhat conflicting argument is that there is a need for a single enemy in order to achieve class consciousness. This emerges if we look at the texts in which Marx discussed the plight of the bourgeoisie, notably two important articles from 1852 and 1854:

> Having obtained, in 1846, a grand victory over the landed aristocracy by the repeal of the Corn Laws [the British Bourgeois] were satisfied with following up the material advantages of this victory, while they neglected to draw the necessary political and economical conclusions from it, and thus enabled the Whigs to reinstate themselves into their hereditary monopoly of government. During all the time, from 1846 to 1852, they exposed themselves to ridicule by their battle-cry: Broad principles and practical (read *small*) measures. And why all this? Because in every violent movement they are obliged to appeal to the *working class*. And if the aristocracy is their vanishing opponent the working class is their arising enemy. They prefer to compromise with the vanishing opponent rather than to strengthen the arising enemy, to whom the future belongs, by concessions of a more than apparent importance. Therefore they strive to avoid every forcible collision with the aristocracy; but historical necessity and the Tories press them onwards. They cannot avoid fulfilling their mission, battering to pieces old England, the England of the Past; and the very moment when they will have conquered exclusive political dominion, when political dominion and economic supremacy will be united in the same hands, when, therefore, the struggle against capital will no longer be distinct from the struggle against the

---

[1] "Speech on the question of free trade", p. 457.   [2] *Neue Rheinische Zeitung* 22.1.1849.

existing Government – from that very moment will date the *social revolution of England*.[1]

The same industrial wave which has borne the middle class up against the aristocracy, is now assisted as it is and will be by emigration bearing the working classes up against the middle classes. Just as the middle classes inflict blows upon the aristocracy, so they will receive them from the working classes. It is the instinctive perception of this fact that already fetters the action of that class against the aristocracy ... The consequence is that the feudalism of England will not perish beneath the scarcely perceptible dissolving processes of the middle class; the honor of such a victory is reserved for the working classes. When the time shall be ripe for their recognized entry upon the stage of political action, there will be within the lists three powerful classes confronting each other – the first representing the land; the second, money; the third, labor. And as the second is triumphing over the first, so, in its turn, it must yield before its successor in the field of political and social conflict.[2]

Both texts assert that the capitalists will hesitate to destroy the aristocracy. The first states that they will nevertheless be compelled to do so, the second that this task will be left to the working class. The reason for the hesitation is most clearly stated in the first text. As long as the working class is divided between two enemies, Capital and Government, it will be ineffective in the struggle against either.

This inverted "divide and conquer" argument is crucial in Marx's analysis of the class struggles in capitalism. It turns upon the cognitive conditions for class consciousness, in the sense that the existence of two enemies will make the workers uncertain about whom to blame for what. In an article from 1853 Marx refers to "the carefully propagated delusions that could be conjured up at the hour of danger, in order to deflect the indignation of the working classes from their real antagonist, and to direct it against the antagonists of the millocracy, against the landed aristocracy".[3] He adds that this is by now a thing of the past, and that "there is no more charging the aristocratic protectionists with all the anomalies of the industrial system". Although the reference is here to the landowners as an economic class and not as the class possessing "the monopoly of government",[4] the passages cited earlier make it plausible that the existence of one economic and one political opponent could lead to the same cognitive delusions as the existence of two

---

[1] *New York Daily Tribune* 25.8.1852.
[2] *Ibid.*, 1.8.1854. This article is printed as an appendix to the *Collected Works* (CW 13, pp. 663ff), on the grounds that part of it must be attributed to the editors of the *New York Daily Tribune* rather than to Marx. I believe, however, that the cited passage is uncorrupted.
[3] *Ibid.*, 15.11.1853.   [4] *Ibid.*, 21.8.1852.

distinct economic enemies. It is also worth while citing a somewhat earlier text, asserting that "nowhere . . . does *social* inequality obtrude itself more harshly than in the eastern states of North America, because nowhere is it less disguised by political inequality".[1]

We shall see that Marx applied a similar reasoning to France. First, however, note that this line of argument is incompatible with the view, expressed in a passage cited above, that the English workers deliberately wanted to get the landowners out of their way so as the better to focus on the main enemy. This presupposes a degree of class consciousness that according to the later texts was precisely blocked by the existence of two enemy classes. Either Marx changed his mind between 1848 and 1852, or the earlier text rests on a confused inference from the effects of getting rid of the aristocracy to the motives that could incite the workers to overthrow it. If the latter, we have the fallacy discussed towards the end of 6.2.3 – an explanation of working-class behaviour in terms of the impact on class consciousness.

Marx's analysis of the French case is more complex. For one thing, he divides the class struggle into periods that correspond to the rule of different "fractions of the bourgeoisie", that is different surplus-appropriating classes. In *The Class Struggles in France* the following periodization is suggested, with some ambiguities. Under the Restoration, the big landed proprietors held the "monopoly of power";[2] under the July Monarchy this fell to the financial aristocracy;[3] while under the Republic the industrial bourgeoisie and the landowners acceded to power alongside the financial capitalists.[4] The main ambiguity, not to say contradiction, concerns the role of the industrial bourgeoisie during the July Monarchy. In the opening pages of the work Marx describes it as being "part of the official opposition",[5] and contrasts it at length with the financial capitalists who want "to get rich not by production, but by pocketing the already available wealth of others".[6] Later, however, Marx asserts that under the July Monarchy the "monopoly of power" was held by the finance aristocracy *and* the industrial bourgeoisie.[7] This, moreover, is also the scheme that Marx adopted twenty years later, in *The Civil War in France*. In that work, he succinctly says that "the Revolution of 1830, resulting in the transfer of Government from the landlords to the capitalists, transferred it from the more remote to the more direct antagonists of the working men".[8] Here,

---

[1] *Deutsche–Brüsseler–Zeitung*, 11.11.1847.   [2] *The Class Struggles in France*, p. 95.
[3] *Ibid.*, pp. 48ff.   [4] *Ibid.*, p. 54.   [5] *Ibid.*, p. 48.   [6] *Ibid.*, p. 51.   [7] *Ibid.*, p. 95.
[8] *The Civil War in France*, p. 138.

however, I shall follow the first periodization, which makes better sense of the main arguments in *The Class Struggles in France*.

Before 1848 these struggles, as depicted by Marx, involved three actors: the workers, the financial capitalists and the industrial capitalists. The pattern is simple and classic: an initial alliance between the industrial bourgeoisie and the workers against the "finance aristocracy", and then a reversal of the industrial bourgeoisie to form an alliance with the financial capitalists against the workers.[1] The initial alliance was based on the common opposition of the "manufacturing" or productive classes to the parasitic class. "In the minds of the proletarians, who confused the finance aristocracy with the bourgeoisie in general . . . the *rule of the bourgeoisie* was abolished with the introduction of the Republic."[2] Or again: "the Paris proletariat sought to assert its own interests *side by side* with the interests of the bourgeoisie, instead of enforcing them as the revolutionary interests of society itself".[3] Similarly, the industrial bourgeoisie did not initially perceive the danger of entering into an alliance with a partner that might soon turn against themselves. The emergence of this awareness is described as follows:

Only one faction of the party of Order was directly concerned in the overthrow of the finance aristocracy – the *manufacturers*. We are not speaking of the middle, of the smaller industrialists; we are speaking of the reigning princes of the manufacturing interests, who had formed the broad basis of the dynastic opposition under Louis Philippe. Their interest is indubitably reduction of the costs of production and hence reduction of the taxes, which enter into production, and hence reduction of the state debts, the interest on which enters into the taxes, hence the overthrow of the finance aristocracy. In England – and the largest French manufacturers are petty bourgeois compared with their English rivals – we really find the manufacturers, a Cobden, a Bright, at the head of the crusade against the bank and the stock-exchange aristocracy. Why not in France? In England industry predominates; in France, agriculture. In England industry requires free trade; in France, protective tariffs, national monopoly alongside of the other monopolies. French industry does not dominate French production, the French industrialists, therefore, do not dominate the French bourgeoisie. In order to secure the advancement of their interests as against the remaining factions of the bourgeoisie, they cannot, like the English, take the lead of the movement and simultaneously push their class interests to the fore; they must follow in the train of the revolution, and serve interests which are opposed to the collective interests of their class. In February they had misunderstood their

---

[1] A similar pattern obtained in Germany after 1848, but with the absolutist regime in the place of finance capital, and with the difference that here the dismantling of the progressive coalition occurred so early that it was virtually not formed at all. Cp. also 7.2.

[2] *The Class Struggles in France*, p. 57; also *Neue Rheinische Zeitung* 29.6.1848.

[3] *The Class Struggles in France*, p. 57.

position; February sharpened their wits. And who is more directly threatened by the workers than the employer, the industrial capitalist? The manufacturer, therefore, of necessity became in France the most fanatical member of the party of Order. The reduction of his *profit* by finance, *what is that compared with the abolition of profit by the proletariat?*[1]

The passage is not exemplary for its lucidity, but the opening and the final sentences explain well why the industrial bourgeoisie first began a struggle against the financial bourgeoisie and then retracted. Their dilemma was broadly similar to their English counterparts, who also had to sacrifice part of their economic interest in order to ensure their political survival. The details are, however, somewhat different. The English manufacturers pulled their punches in the struggle with the landowners in order to distract the attention of their common enemy, the workers. The French industrialists went much further when they entered into active cooperation with the other fractions of the bourgeoisie in order to repress the workers. In England the summit of class cooperation within the bourgeoisie was the dismantling of the Anti Corn Law League; in France the climax occurred in June 1848, with the brutal repression of the Paris workers. Or again: the British ruling classes cooperated to prevent the formation of working-class consciousness, the French to repress class-conscious workers. Such at least was Marx's view. Its plausibility is further discussed in 7.1.

The parallel to the English class is closer when we turn to Marx's analysis of Bonapartism. *The Eighteenth Brumaire* and Marx's first newspaper articles on British politics are virtually contemporary, hence it is not surprising that they use the same conceptual scheme. This is the idea of a voluntary abdication from power by the bourgeoisie (in France) or the voluntary abstention from power by the industrial bourgeoisie (in England), in both cases motivated by a desire to split the attention of the subjugated classes. Consider first Marx's argument that the open rule of the bourgeoisie in the Republic was less suited to their interest than the July Monarchy had been:

Instinct taught them that the republic, true enough, makes their political rule complete, but at the same time undermines its social foundation, since they must now confront the subjugated classes and contend against them without mediation, without the concealment afforded by the crown, without being able to divert the national interest by their subordinate struggles among themselves and with the monarchy. It was a feeling of weakness that caused them to recoil from the pure conditions of their own class rule and to yearn for the former more

[1] *Ibid.*, pp. 116–17.

incomplete, more undeveloped and precisely on that account less dangerous forms of this rule.[1]

Or again:

As long as the rule of the bourgeois class had not been organised completely, as long as it had not acquired its pure political expression, the antagonism of the other classes, likewise, could not appear in its pure form, and where it did appear could not take the dangerous turn that transforms every struggle against the state power into a struggle against capital.[2]

Hence there was a need for a *new blurring of the class lines*, providentially ensured by Louis Napoleon. The advantage of his regime for capital was precisely that of the regime which had preceded the Republic – to deliver the bourgeoisie from the dangers of its own rule. Observe that this account of the July Monarchy, while totally different from that offered two years earlier in *The Class Struggles in France*, is not incompatible with it. The first work explains the actual motivations of the various classes, based on their perception of who lost and gained under the rule of the financial aristocracy. The latter work adds a theory of the unperceived benefits of having a political regime whose policy did not immediately and obviously coincide with the interest of the bourgeoisie. The same benefits were provided by the Second Empire. In this case Marx also believed that they help to *explain* the establishment and (at least) the viability of the regime. To show how Marx viewed these benefits, and their explanatory power, we must look mainly to *The Civil War in France* and the drafts of that work, where Marx in retrospect comments on the regime that in 1852 he observed *in statu nascendi*. Consider first some passages where Marx attempts to distinguish between the appearance of the Bonapartist state and its class essence:

The Empire, with the coup d'état for its certificate of birth, universal suffrage for its sanction, and the sword for its sceptre, professed to rest upon the peasantry, the large mass of producers not directly involved in the struggle of capital and labour. It professed to save the working class by breaking down Parliamentarism, and, with it, the undisguised subserviency of Government to the propertied classes. It professed to save the propertied classes by upholding their economic supremacy over the working class; and, finally, it professed to unite all classes by reviving for all the chimera of national glory. In reality, it was the only form of government possible at a time when the bourgeoisie had already lost, and the working class had not yet acquired, the faculty of ruling the nation.[3]

---

[1] *The Eighteenth Brumaire*, p. 129; see also *The Civil War in France*, p. 36.
[2] *The Eighteenth Brumaire*, p. 142.   [3] *The Civil War in France*, pp. 138–9.

Apparently the final victory of this governmental power over society, it was in fact the orgy of all the corrupt elements of that society. To the eye of the uniniti- ated it appeared only as the victory of the Executive over the legislative, of the final defeat of the form of class rule pretending to be the autocracy of society under its form pretending to be a superior power to society. But in fact it was only the last degraded and only possible form of that class rule, as humiliating to those classes themselves as to the working classes which they kept fettered by it.[1]

At first view apparently the usurpatory dictatorship of the governmental body over society itself, rising alike above and humbling alike all classes, it has in fact, on the European continent at least, become the only possible state form in which the appropriating class can continue to sway it over the producing class.[2]

Observe the difference between the first formulation (from the final version) and the others (from the drafts). In the former, Bonapartism is said to be the only possible government *tout court*, in the latter the only possible *bourgeois* government. The first formulation is hard to fathom, for if the workers were not ready to rule, then presumably the naked class rule of the bourgeoisie would not be a danger to that class. Be this as it may, the corresponding analysis from *The Eighteenth Brumaire* insists only on the incapacity of the bourgeoisie:

Thus, by now stigmatizing as "*socialistic*" what it had previously extolled as "*liberal*", the bourgeoisie confesses that its own interests dictate that it should be delivered from the dangers of its *own rule*, that, in order to restore tranquility in the country, its bourgeois parliament must, first of all, be laid to rest; that, in order to preserve its social power intact, its political power must be broken; that the individual bourgeois can continue to exploit the other classes and to enjoy undisturbed property, family, religion and order only on condition that their class be condemned along with the other classes to similar political nullity; that, in order to save its purse, it must forfeit the crown, and the sword that is to safeguard it must at the same time be hung over its own head as a sword of Damocles.[3]

The bourgeoisie must "forfeit the crown", that is abdicate from the power it had achieved in the Republic. I return to the theory of abdi- cation in 7.1.4. Here I want to ask about the nature of the explanation that Marx suggests of the rise of Louis Napoleon. Clearly it is an expla- nation in terms of the benefits that the bourgeoisie would derive from his rule, and it sounds very much like an intentional explanation. Yet Marx offers no evidence that the united bourgeoisie actually deliberated in this way, nor that they welcomed Louis Napoleon's rise to power. As in the corresponding English case, also explained in the next chapter, it

[1] *Ibid.*, 55.   [2] *Ibid.*, p. 100.   [3] *The Eighteenth Brumaire*, pp. 142–3.

is more plausible to see Marx as suggesting a functional explanation. The *coup d'état* fitted into a suitably subtle pattern, that of a class ruling through the appearance of the abolition of class rule. As was his wont in such cases, Marx immediately made an explanatory use of this pattern, without pausing to look for a mechanism.

Hence I submit that it is implausible to argue that the *coup d'état* is to be explained by the need of the bourgeoisie to be delivered from its own incapacity. Yet the incapacity can enter the explanation in a different way, as a condition enabling Louis Napoleon to take power without much resistance. This is how Marx considered the situation from the vantage point of 1871:

[If] the party of order is united in its war against the working class, in its capacity of the *party of order*, the play of intrigue of its different fractions the one against the other, each for the prevalence of its peculiar interest in the old order of society, each for the Restoration of its own pretender and personal ambitions, sets in in full force as soon as its rule seems secured (guaranteed) by the destruction of the material revolutionary forces. This combination of a common war against the people and a common conspiracy against the Republic, combined with the internal feuds of its rulers, and their play of intrigues, paralyses society, disgusts and bewilders the masses of the middleclass and "troubles" business, keeps them in a chronic state of disquietude. All the conditions of despotism are created ... under this regime, but despotism without quietude, despotism with parliamentary anarchy at its head. Then the hour has struck for a *Coup d'Etat*, and the incapable lot has to make room for any lucky pretender, making [an] end to the *anonymous* form of class rule.[1]

There is nothing in this account that excludes the possibility that the bourgeoisie might fare as badly after the *coup d'état* as before it. The explanatory role played by its weakness is that of an enabling condition, not that of something to be overcome. True, the 1871 texts also assert that the bourgeoisie did in fact benefit from the new regime, but this is not to say that the benefits enter into the explanation of the transition. Clearly, even in 1871 Marx believed that the Bonapartist regime persisted because of its hidden class character, but he did not argue, as he did in 1852, that this also explains why it was introduced. Again, I refer to 7.1 for further discussions.

For all their defects and exaggerations, Marx's analyses of class struggle and class alliances in England and France add up to an impressive achievement. They tend to sin by excessive optimism about the prospects of the working class, and also by imputing to the various

---

[1] *The Civil War in France*, p. 37.

classes an excessively clear-sighted view of their own interests. Moreover, they have serious methodological flaws due to Marx's reliance on unthinking functionalism. Too little room is left for the sheer muddle of social conflict, where most actors do not know what they want nor how to get it if they do. Yet in spite of the subservience of the analysis to his broader philosophy of history, the analytical tools he forged remain extremely valuable. He anticipated Simmel and Caplow in his study of the mechanisms of coalition formation (although his functionalism prevented him from distinguishing between *divide et impera* and *tertius gaudens*). He did not content himself with the analysis of the struggle between classes at a given moment of time, but also tried to explain how the anticipated effects of future struggles motivated the currently chosen strategies. Nor did he assume that class alliances took place between fully formed collective actors, but considered the interplay between alliance formation and the development of class consciousness. That he only succeeded partially in these tasks is due largely to his taking them on simultaneously, as well as to an inherent lack of intellectual discipline.

6.3.4. Class struggle and social conflict

Let us assume that someone accepts all the arguments presented, on Marx's behalf, so far in this chapter. He accepts, that is, that classes as defined in 6.1 tend to acquire class consciousness under the conditions set out in 6.2 and to engage in class struggles of the forms set out in 6.3 up to this point. Yet he might want to say that class struggle is by no means all of social conflict. He could point to the existence of non-class collective actors, whose struggles are by no means less violently fought and no less decisive for the shaping of history. Regional conflict in Spain, religious conflict in Ireland or the Middle East, ethnic conflict in the US or South Africa, linguistic conflict in Belgium or nationalism in Poland seem to be at least as potent as class in generating durable and consequential social conflict. True, he might admit, the *relevance* of class in these struggles is not in question. The presence of class oppositions shapes and modifies the non-class struggles in numerous ways. Yet Marx was committed to the *centrality* of class, which is increasingly seen as an implausible proposition.[1]

To facilitate the discussion of this powerful objection, let us note that any given society can be depicted according to two sociological maps.

---

[1] This objection has been forcefully made by Parkin, *Marxism and Class Theory*.

One is the map of classes, as defined in 6.1. The other is the map of collective actors that form part of social conflicts. Broadly speaking, Marx's central intuition seems to have been that these two maps converged towards one another. This view can be summed up in two propositions. (i) Objectively defined classes tend to acquire class consciousness, or else to disappear. (ii) Non-class collective actors become increasingly marginal over time.

The first proposition has to some extent been discussed in 6.2. Marx clearly believed that "the three great classes" that make up modern society either had or rapidly were acquiring class consciousness. The landowning aristocracy in most European countries was a major collective actor, with a well-developed class consciousness. The industrial bourgeoisie was somewhat less developed as a collective actor, and the working class even less, yet these classes were rapidly being crystallized into class consciousness by their mutual opposition and the conditions of modern industry. The peasantry and the petty bourgeoisie lived under conditions that were less favourable to the development of class consciousness, but the introduction of capitalism in agriculture and the concentration of capital in industry would in any case tend to eliminate them. According to Marx this had already taken place in England, the country that "shows, to the less developed, the image of its own future".

Now Marx was clearly wrong on several of these counts. Other classes have arrived on the scene, made up of those who manage corporate or state property. The peasantry has not disappeared, but taken advantage of modern means of communication to achieve a degree of class consciousness comparable to that of other classes. Yet he was right in the broader sense that the classes of modern society are all in possession of class consciousness, being well organized politically as well as economically. In the ancient world, *slaves* represent a clear counterexample to proposition (i). Although they sometimes tried to escape the slave condition, they rarely attempted to improve it or to abolish it. The freedom they sought included the right to possess other individuals as slaves.[1] In 1869 Marx took cognizance of this fact when observing that the slaves merely formed the "passive pedestal" of the class struggles between the free rich and the free poor.[2] I do not think that this retreat in the direction of realism from the view of the *Communist Manifesto* is massively damaging to Marx's theory. It is awkward, but no more than that.

---

[1] Finley, *Economy and Society in Ancient Greece*, p. 119.
[2] Preface to 2nd edition of *The Eighteenth Brumaire*, p. 359.

There took place a latent class struggle (6.3.1) between slaveowners and slaves, in the sense that the former were influenced in their behaviour, by the danger of slave revolts.

The real challenge comes from the counterexamples to proposition (ii). In 6.3.1 I observed that the struggles between *orders* in the Roman Republic is an example of social conflict along non-class lines. The various national, regional, religious, linguistic and ethnic conflicts cited above have if anything become more prominent over the last century, not less. These oppositions cut across class divisions, and may command greater loyalty and generate greater hostility than the clash of class interests.

Let me survey some answers that have been or could be offered by Marxists to cope with this objection. A first line of reply could be that these non-class divisions – "cultural divisions" for short – are never class-neutral. It is invariably the case that classes are distributed non-randomly over the cultural groups. Hence behind the war between Protestants or Catholics, French and Flemish or blacks and whites, there is the class conflict between the propertied and the unpropertied. True, the correlation is rarely perfect, but in general is sufficiently robust to justify the macro-sociological view that collective action tends to form around economically defined classes. There may be "relegation to an exploited class because of race",[1] but this does not show that the struggle is not one of class.

I deny both the premise and the reasoning of this reply. Consider first the cases where there is indeed a robust correlation, as that between being black and being exploited in the US. Even in this case, race may be more important than exploitation for those who are relegated to an exploited class because of race. They may, for instance, mobilize more on issues such as busing than on issues of exploitation. Consider next cases where the cross-cutting is more extensive, and the correlation weak or non-existent. An instance could be workers and capitalists in the periphery allying themselves against workers and capitalists in the centre. True, it will typically be the case that the capitalists in the centre are richer than those in the periphery, but wealth is not a criterion of class. To say otherwise is to fall victim to *ad hoc* thinking. The undiluted Marxist theory of class must be that the bond between rich and poor capitalists will turn out to be stronger than regional bonds between workers and capitalists.

[1] Cohen, review of Parkin's *Marxism and Class Theory*.

Another argument could be that cultural divisions are a form of "divide and conquer". Non-class differences, then, could be explained in terms of class benefits. This would reinstate the centrality of class, albeit in a more indirect way than in proposition (ii). As stated more than once above, this argument fails because of its unsupported functionalism. From the fact that employers benefit from cultural division between workers, one cannot conclude that these divisions are to be explained by the benefits.[1] Moreover, even were one to accept the validity of the explanation, we would still expect that in the long run the divisions would be overcome and class consciousness proper would emerge, since otherwise the capitalist domination would meet no resistance. "Pessimist Marxism" may adopt divide-and-conquer as an explanation, but the traditional progressivist Marxist must believe in proposition (ii).

Furthermore, one might try to explain the persistence of cultural divisions by the absence of some of the conditions for class consciousness discussed in 6.2.2. If, for instance, the turn-over rate of the work force is quite high, there may never be time to overcome the cultural prejudices and hostilities among the workers. This line of argument, while not implausible, forms a very weak reply to the objection. It says, essentially, that cultural divisions are not inherently stronger than class divisions. The former dominate the latter only under certain conditions, that may or may not obtain. Now there may be some who would argue that culture is invariably more important than class, but there is no need to accept this view in order to object to the Marxist view that the priority invariably is the other way around.

Finally, one might adopt a broader historical perspective and argue that for *epochal transformations* class struggle alone is decisive.[2] One might fully accept, that is, the pervasive presence throughout history of social conflicts that cannot be reduced to class struggle in any of the proposed ways, and yet argue that these play no role in the setting-up of new relations of production. From the point of view of historical materialism, cultural conflicts are so much turbulence or noise: sound and fury that signify nothing. They may be crucially important for the individuals living during these periods, yet in the end irrelevant for the development of the productive forces and the ultimate advent of the classless society.

This reply probably is the most Marxist in spirit. It insulates economic

---

[1] Nevertheless this seems to be the argument underlying Bowles and Gintis, "The Marxian theory of value and heterogeneous labour" and Roemer, "Divide and conquer: microfoundations of a Marxian theory of wage discrimination".

[2] I am indebted to Charles Larmore for this suggestion, which is closely related to an argument offered in Cohen, "Restricted and inclusive historical materialism".

development from the influence of non-economic forces, while conceding some ground on the secondary point that the non-economic forces may be more autonomous than classically conceived. The reply is vulnerable on two counts. First, it remains to be shown that cultural conflicts could not shape the struggles that lead to a change in the relations of production. Secondly, it also remains to be shown why class struggles should tend to bring about relations of production that are optimal for the development of the productive forces. Marx and Marxists have been satisfied with postulating that both of these conditions obtain, without offering argument or evidence. I conclude that the counterexamples to proposition (ii) cannot be explained away, and that the centrality of class in social conflict cannot be upheld.

Let me end by citing some discussion in Marx's writings of this problem. It arises mainly in connection with the "national question" that has plagued Marxism from its inception.[1] This was the question whether socialists should support movements for national independence in countries, such as Poland and Ireland, that were oppressed by foreign nations, or rather work on the assumption that an international proletarian inflagration would do away with class oppression and national oppression in one fell swoop. This question did not enter into the earlier discussion (5.2.3 and 5.3.2) of the various scenarios for the international proletarian revolution. That discussion concerned mainly the problem whether the conditions for revolution can ever be united in one country or whether there will have to be some revolutionary division of labour, not whether the countries in question must all be independent nation-states. Marx apparently was an internationalist on the former issue, a nationalist on the latter. He believed that the revolution would take place by the interaction between several, independent countries.

Yet his motivation for this nationalist stance is somewhat unorthodox. There are few if any signs in his works of a recognition of nationalistic sentiments as an overpowering motivation that must be satisfied before the class struggle can begin. Nor does he suggest that the workers in the oppressing countries live off the surplus extracted from workers in the oppressed countries, and hence are less motivated to revolution than they would otherwise have been. In his discussion of the Irish question – the main source for an understanding of his ideas about nationalism – we find a series of quite different arguments. The general view is that independence is a condition for revolution in the *oppressing* countries:

[1] The following draws heavily on Cummins, *Marx, Engels and National Movements*.

The only means of accelerating [the social revolution in England] is to bring about the independence of Ireland. It is therefore the task of the 'International' to bring the conflict between England and Ireland into the foreground and everywhere to side openly with Ireland. It is the special task of the General Council in London to arouse the consciousness in the English working class that *for them* the *national emancipation of Ireland* is not a question of abstract justice or humanitarian sentiment but the first condition of their own social emancipation.[1]

The argument is not that the English workers must lose the economic benefits from the oppression of the Irish before they can turn against their own oppressors. To the extent that there is an economic argument here, it is rather to the effect that English workers fear the Irish as competitors who depress their standard of living.[2] The problem, however, is mainly a psychological one, not one of material interest. The presence of Irish workers alongside the English turns the indignation of the latter away from their real enemy, the capitalist class, and instead towards the former. Marx comments that "a people which subjugates another people forges its own chains",[3] echoing Rousseau's "Quiconque est maître ne peut être libre."[4] The underlying psychological mechanism has been suggested in 1.3.1.[5] Marx also adduces a few additional arguments, less important than the one just cited.[6]

As observed in 1.3.1, Marx tends to transform the argument from endogenous preference formation into one of divide-and-conquer. The bourgeoisie "know well that this split is the real secret of preserving their own power",[7] and hence keeps it artificially alive. He held a similar view on the religious strife within Ireland. In a singularly ill-judged comment on Ulster he writes that "Once the Irish church is dead, the

---

[1] Marx to Meyer and Vogt 9.4.1870.   [2] "Confidential Communication", p. 416.
[3] *Ibid.*, p. 417.   [4] Rousseau, *Lettres de la Montagne*, pp. 841–2.
[5] Note the parallel with the argument (6.3.3) that the workers' attention is distracted from Capital towards the Government by the apparent independence of the latter. Just as Marx wanted to get rid of the aristocracy so that the workers could meet the capitalists head-on, he wanted to eliminate the Irish workers from the English class struggle. The former was a response to a two-front war strategy, the latter a reply to divide-and-conquer.
[6] In the "Confidential communication", p. 416, Marx notes that Ireland is "the bulwark of English landlordism. If it collapsed in Ireland, it would collapse in England." Moreover, an Irish revolution would deprive the English government of "the only excuse it has for keeping up a large regular army which can, as we have seen, in case of need attack the English workers after having done its basic training in Ireland" (*ibid.*), p. 417. Finally we may note the rather absurd suggestion that the preponderance of Irish workers in the United States might generate a national opposition between that country and England, thus preventing the social revolution in either country (*ibid.*).
[7] "Confidential communication", pp. 416–17; cp. also Marx to Meyer and Vogt 9.4.1870, cited in 1.3.1.

Protestant Irish tenants in the province of Ulster will unite with the Catholic tenants in the three other provinces of Ireland and join their movement; whereas up to the present landlordism has been able to exploit this religious hostility."[1] Once again we meet the divide-and-conquer argument, tempered by optimism concerning the emerging solidarity between tenants of different religious persuasion.

In the event of the communist revolution taking place by the means of revolutionary wars between independent nation-states, Marx did not expect nationalist sentiments to form a serious obstacle to class interest. "The working-men have no country."[2] A newspaper article from 1855 spells this out as follows:

The industrial working population has, in both countries, almost the same peculiar position with regard to [the Crimean] war. Both British and French proletarians are filled with an honorable national spirit, though they are more or less free from the antiquated national prejudices common, in either country, to the peasantry. They have little immediate interest in the war, save that if the victories of their countrymen flatter their national pride, the conduct of the war, foolhardy and presumptuous as regards France, timid and stupid as regards England, offers them a fair opportunity of agitating against the existing governments and governing classes.[3]

The reference to the "honorable national spirit" is somewhat quaint, as is the concluding sentence in which it is unclear whether Marx was fooling only his readers or himself as well. Be this as it may, there is no doubt that Marx relegates nationalist feelings to second place.

There is, however, one way in which the workers and their struggle are shaped by their national attachment. This does not operate via nationalistic goals, but via peculiarly national character traits. These are particularly striking – and, to Marx, exasperating – in the case of the English working class. In a letter to Engels he refers to "the Christian slave nature" of the English workers.[4] In a document from the International he states that the English have all the material preconditions for a social revolution, "they only lack *the spirit of generalization* and *the revolutionary passion*".[5] By contrast, he much admired the "universal character typical of the French"[6] and "the revolutionary fire of the Celtic worker".[7] In 2.1.3 I cited an instance of his Russiophobia that imputes certain lowly character traits to a whole nation. There may perhaps be a

---

[1] Marx to Kugelmann 6.4.1868.   [2] *The Communist Manifesto*, p. 502.
[3] *New York Daily Tribune* 27.4.1855.   [4] Marx to Engels 17.11.1862.
[5] "Confidential communication", p. 415.   [6] *The German Ideology*, p. 412.
[7] "Confidential communication", p. 415.

psychological affinity between the presence of national peculiarities of character and peculiarly nationalistic goals, but only the latter lead directly to the formation of non-class collective actors. (Both, however, are opposed to the ideal of proletarian internationalism.) To the extent that such traits of national character form a problem for Marxism, they do so as counterexamples to proposition (i) above, not as objections to proposition (ii). If the English workers stubbornly refuse to acquire the class consciousness for which all the material prerequisites are present, this certainly tells against Marx's theory of class as set out here.

Let me conclude on a more general observation. There are good philosophical, psychological and sociological grounds for thinking that individuals will always have a narrower focus of loyalty and solidarity than the international community of workers and capitalists. The informational conditions for class consciousness discussed in 6.2.2 require small, stable groups. The strength of altruism declines as the circle of individuals expands. More profoundly, indiscriminate solidarity with vast numbers of people is hardly compatible with the personal integrity and strength of character one would surely want to prevail in the post-revolutionary society.[1] If *per impossibile* the workers could be brainwashed into thinking of themselves as members of the international proletariat, the cause of international socialism would be lost in advance.

---

[1] See Williams, *Moral Luck*, notably ch. 1.

7. Politics and the state

In this study of Marx's theory of political institutions and political processes, the focus will largely be on the capitalist societies that Marx observed around 1850. The discussion will build upon and extend that of the previous chapter, to take fuller account of the specifically political dynamics of the class struggle. Also Marx's predictions for the communist revolution and his visions about the post-revolutionary society will be studied in some detail, supplementing discussions in earlier chapters.

In 7.1 the emphasis is on the relation between the state and the class structure. I argue that, without fully admitting it, Marx found himself compelled by events to accord to the capitalist state a large measure of autonomy, certainly larger than his theoretical preconceptions had prepared him for. In 7.2 I turn to his theory of political process, and notably his theory of revolution. This involves examining, first, his theory of the classical bourgeois revolutions in England and France; next, his practical and theoretical interest in the revolutionary wave that swept over Germany in 1848–9; and finally, his ideas about the impending communist revolution. In 7.3 I consider his theory of the outcome of that revolution, that is the successive political and economic stages of communist society. I do not discuss Marx's writings on international politics. Doing so would require an amount of space out of proportion to the interest they can command today.[1]

7.1. The nature and explanation of the state

The theory of the capitalist state or, less tendentiously, of the state in capitalist society, has been among the most influential of Marx's ideas. By and large, the influence has been harmful rather than benign. The theory is set out in a half-conspiratorial, half-functionalist language that invites lazy, frictionless thought.[2] The parts that can be salvaged from it are the ones in which Marx, almost in spite of himself, views politics as an autonomous phenomenon that is constrained by economics but not reducible to it.

Since the notion of *state autonomy* is central, I begin in 7.1.1 by explaining the concept of the state and go on in 7.1.2 to discuss the concept of autonomy. In 7.1.3 I set out the best-known Marxist theory of the state, according to which it (or its "executive") "is but a committee for managing the common affairs of the whole bourgeoisie".[3] In 7.1.4 I argue that in the aftermath of 1848 Marx worked out a more complex theory, according to which the bourgeoisie abdicates from political power (or abstains from taking it) because this best serves its interest. In 7.1.5 I discuss an alternative and more far-reaching way of stating the abdication theory, according to which the autonomy of the state emerges as a permanent feature of the modern epoch, due to the continued presence of several opposed classes.

7.1.1. An ambiguity in the notion

The state may be defined either by *what* it does or by *how* it does whatever it does. An example of a definition of the second type is Weber's, in terms of the monopoly on the legitimate use of violence. Marx clearly tends towards a definition of the state in terms of its functions. In this he follows the tradition, or one tradition, in political theory. The state was commonly seen as the provider of public goods, notably law and order, but also economic goods that could not be provided efficiently by individuals. Broadly speaking, the state embodies the cooperative solution to a Prisoner's Dilemma involving all individuals in the society of which it is the state.[4] According to Marx, the task of the state can indeed be formulated in

---

[1] On this topic, see Papaioannou, *De Marx et du Marxisme* and Molnar, *Marx, Engels et la Politique Internationale*.

[2] For discussion and references see my "Marxism, functionalism and game theory".

[3] *The Communist Manifesto*, p. 486.

[4] For modern discussions, see Olson, *The Logic of Collective Action*, ch. IV; Baumol, *Welfare Economics and the Theory of the State*; Taylor, *Anarchy and Cooperation*; Schotter, *The Economic Theory of Social Institutions*.

terms of this dilemma, but with different players. The task of the state is to provide a cooperative solution for the Prisoner's Dilemma faced by the members of the economically dominant class, and, as part of this task, to prevent the members of the dominated class from solving *their* dilemma. I shall return to this instrumentalist conception in 7.1.3.

We must ask, however, whether Marx totally neglected the tasks of the state that benefit *all* members of society (even though possibly to unequal extents). In the *Grundrisse* there is a lengthy discussion of the conditions under which public works, for example road construction, will be undertaken by private enterprise.[1] First, there must be a sufficiently large concentration of capital to carry out the work. Secondly, the enterprise must be profitable. Thirdly, as a condition for the profitability, there must exist a demand for the public good. As Marx knew, the demand may in part be created by the good itself: "A road itself may so increase the forces of production that it creates new traffic which then makes the road profitable."[2] According to Marx, in a fully developed capitalist mode of production all public goods would be provided privately:

All *general conditions of production*, such as roads, canals, etc. whether they facilitate circulation or even make it possible at all, or whether they increase the force of production (such as irrigation works etc. as in Asia and, incidentally, as still built by governments in Europe), presuppose, in order to be undertaken by capital instead of by the government which represents the community as such, the highest development of production founded in capital. The separation of *public works* from the state, and their migration into the domain of the works undertaken by capital itself, indicates the degree to which the real community has constituted itself in the form of capital.[3]

Marx does not seem to have been aware of the obstacles to such transfers of public goods to private industry. It may be impossible to internalize the benefits from the public good; and even if this obstacle is overcome, by means of a toll or a similar arrangement, private provision may lead to a wasteful duplication of efforts.[4] True, Marx does mention in passing that private industry, to get a profit from public works, requires "protective tariffs, monopoly, state coercion",[5] but the reasoning behind this statement is obscure, and the mention of the state is in any case at odds with the central idea being defended.

The tasks that will devolve on private industry apparently do not include the provision of health and education services. The question, however, is

---

[1] *Grundrisse*, pp. 524ff.   [2] *Ibid.*, p. 531.   [3] *Ibid.*, pp. 530–1.
[4] The patent system, for instance, typically leads to a great deal of duplication of innovative activities, as briefly explained in ch. 4 of my *Explaining Technical Change*.
[5] *Grundrisse*, p. 531.

whether these are undertaken on behalf of all members in society, or on behalf of the capitalist class only. In 4.1.4 I argued that Marx was inconsistent on this point, sometimes explaining the health and education clauses in the factory legislation by the interests of "society" and at other times by the interests of the capitalist. If we adopt the latter view, and add the idea that the general conditions of production will be provided by private industry, then it appears that all the tasks of the state will either be performed on behalf of capital or devolve on capital. No tasks will truly be performed because they are in the interest of all members of society. This is certainly one major strand in Marx's thinking about the state, expressed in the general statements to be quoted in 7.1.3.

On the other hand Marx often makes a distinction between the class-specific and class-neutral tasks of the state, for instance in *Capital III* when he discusses the similarly dual nature of supervision in the capitalist factory:

The labour of supervision and management is naturally required wherever the direct process of production assumes the form of a combined social process, and not of the isolated labour of independent producers. However, it has a double nature. On the one hand, all labour in which many individuals cooperate necessarily requires a commanding will to coordinate and unify the process, and functions which apply not to partial operations but to the total activity of the workshop, much as that of an orchestra conductor. This is a productive job, which must be performed in every combined mode of production. On the other hand – quite apart from any commercial department – this supervision work necessarily arises in all modes of production based on the antithesis between the labourer, as the direct producer, and the owner of the means of production. The greater this antagonism, the greater the role played by supervision. Hence it reaches its peak in the slave system. But it is indispensable also in the capitalist mode of production, since the production process in it is simultaneously a process by which the capitalist consumes labour-power. Just as in despotic states supervision and all-round interference by the government involves both the performance of common activities arising from the nature of all communities, and the specific functions arising from the antithesis between the government and the mass of the people.[1]

In several texts from 1871–5 Marx discusses these "common activities arising from the nature of all communities". They refer to the "state" that will remain under communism, in the sense that administrative as distinct from governmental functions will still exist. These passages are cited and discussed in 7.3.3. For the present purposes the important fact is that the need for coordination and public goods will persist in communism. There is no reason why we should not refer to the coordinating agency as a state,

[1] *Capital III*, pp. 383–4.

in conformity with a main strand in political theory. The substantial question is whether there will be a need for violence to back the decisions of this agency. Although Marx is silent on the issue, the general tenor of his references to communism makes it hard to believe that he thought violence would be required.

Should we, then, define the state as an agency that executes the common interests of the economically dominant class? Or as an agency that realizes the common interests of society? Or is there some third alternative? Neither of the proposals will work both for capitalism and communism. Under communism, the first is useless; under capitalism, the second is misleading, as can be seen from the following case. Imagine that some public project, for example the construction of a railway, will bring material benefits to all members of society, but that workers benefit more than capitalists. If the latter control the state apparatus, they might abstain from the project if they fear it will upset the balance of class power to their detriment. In other words, a class state will act to further the common interest only to the extent that it coincides with the particular interest of the class.

Actually the proposals fail because they preempt important substantive questions. We need a definition of the state that enables us to locate it independently of what interests it serves. We may then ask whether the state, thus defined, actually serves some particular or general interest. The definition must also be consonant with Marx's general views if it is to be of any help in understanding his political theory. Thus Weber's definition fails doubly: first because Marx would deny that the capitalist state has legitimacy, and also because he would deny that the communist state rests on violence. A satisfactory definition could be in terms of the capacity to impose decisions that as a matter of fact have binding force, leaving it an open question whether the compliance rests on violence, a belief in legitimacy, solidarity or some other source. Or one could simply define the state apparatus in terms of its core component, the maintenance of internal order and defence against external enemies. Since my task here is not to provide a theory of the state, I do not have to choose one or the other of these options, since for practical purposes they give the same result. Also, they do not in any way preempt the question as to the interests, if any, served by the state.

7.1.2. The autonomy of the state

The central question in the Marxist theory of the state is whether it is autonomous with respect to class interests, or entirely reducible to them. The main issue that will concern us here is the causal, or – more generally –

the *explanatory autonomy of the state*. Now, for this issue to be a meaningful one, the state and the economic structure must in some sense be distinct entities. As in the case of the relation between productive forces and relations of production (5.1.1), the conceptual separation must be established before the question of a causal or explanatory link can be raised. Hence I begin by discussing the *conceptual autonomy of the state*.

This conceptual autonomy can be denied on two grounds: either by an argument that in *all* societies political phenomena, broadly conceived, are part of the economic structure; or, more specifically, by arguing that this is the case at least in *some* societies. I shall discuss these arguments in that order.

The first issue can be phrased as a question: "Can the base be distinguished from the superstructure?"[1] Briefly stated, the argument against the distinction is that since ownership must be backed by the state and hence presupposes a political system, it cannot enter as an independent variable in the explanation of that system. G. A. Cohen has recently attempted to answer this objection, by his distinction (referred to in 5.1.1) between legal ownership and effective control. On his view the economic structure can be defined in terms of relations of effective control, which in turn enter into a functional explanation of the legal relations of ownership. The forms of *de jure* ownership exist because they stabilize *de facto* relations of effective control. Cohen cites several historical examples to show that many legal innovations did in fact arise in this way.[2] The question is whether the programme can be carried out in all cases. I doubt that it can, since in many cases there is no independently existing control that is stabilized by the legal relations. In some cases, such as patentable knowledge, the control can *only* be achieved through legal rights (5.1.1). In other cases the control as a matter of fact has never been achieved by non-legal means, hence there is nothing for the law to stabilize. True, even in these cases one can say that the control is more stable than it would otherwise have been – but this is not to say that there is something (namely the effective control) that is stabilized by the law.

How serious is this difficulty? Does it do away with the ambition of historical materialism to explain political phenomena in terms of the economic structure? I do not believe it does. Observe that the explanandum includes both the structure of the political system and the actual decisions made.

[1] Cp. Lukes's essay with this title. Actually this question is more general than the issue of state autonomy, since it also covers the problem of distinguishing the economic base from kinship, religion etc.
[2] Cohen, *Karl Marx's Theory of History*, pp. 226ff.

Among the latter, some take the form of enacting laws while others do not; of the laws enacted some concern the forms of ownership while others do not. It is perfectly consistent to try to explain all political phenomena that do not relate to matters of legal ownership in terms of those that do. Moreover, one may attempt to explain changes in the legal ownership structure in terms of the interest of an economically dominant class. These attempts may or may not succeed, but at least there is no ground for thinking that the base–superstructure problem prevents them from getting off the ground.

The second objection to the conceptual autonomy of the state is more specific and more damaging. It concerns the problem of distinguishing the economic from the political in societies where the state is the principal owner of the means of production, as in the Asiatic mode of production where rent and tax coincide.[1] The point is not that in such cases the theses of historical materialism are false: rather they cannot even be coherently stated. How can the state be explained by the economic structure if the state *is* the economic structure?

To bring the problem into focus, we may distinguish between three ways in which economic and political phenomena can be separated from one another. First, they may be sustained by entirely different groups of *people*. This was approximately the case in classical Greece, where production was largely carried out by slaves, and trade by free non-citizens. M. I. Finley quoted Xenophon on the measures that "should be taken by the state in order that every Athenian may be maintained at public expense", and adds that the scheme reveals "a mentality which pushed to the extreme the notion that what we call the economy was properly the business of outsiders".[2]

Next, the two domains may be seen as sets of *roles* rather than persons, with the possibility that any given person may occupy both economic and political roles. This according to Marx is what distinguishes the modern state from the ancient: "The contradiction between the *democratic representative state* and *civil society* is the completion of the *classic* contradiction between public *commonweal* and *slavery*. In the modern world each person is *at the same time* a member of slave society and of the public commonweal."[3] In this case it is perfectly possible to argue that how people behave in one domain enters into the explanation of how they behave in other spheres. It could be the case, for instance, that the political relation

[1] *Capital III*, p. 791.
[2] Finley, "Aristotle and economic analysis", pp. 51–2.
[3] *The Holy Family*, p. 116; see also *Contribution to the Critique of Hegel's Philosophy of Law*, p. 32.

of domination is explained by the economic relation of exploitation even if the same individuals participate in both.

Thirdly, we may not be able to distinguish between the domains otherwise than by the fact that a given action may have different *aspects*, some of which may be singled out as economic and others as political. This is the case for the Asiatic mode of production as described by Marx, or for contemporary communist societies. The action of the imperial tax collector or the regional secretary for planning has an economic aspect in the sense that it has consequences for production, distribution and consumption. Similarly it has a political aspect in the sense that it has consequences for law and order, rebellion and acquiescence. These consequences could of course enter into the explanation of the action – but could they also serve to explain one another? G. A. Cohen has shown, by an ingenious example, that the economic aspect or consequence of a policy can indeed serve to explain the political aspects of the same policy,[1] so there is no conceptual objection to this idea. The empirical issue is whether the historical tributary societies were relevantly similar to the society imagined in this example. In my opinion they were not, and so it appears that there are cases in which the base is indistinguishable from the political superstructure and in which, therefore, historical materialism is inapplicable. Since my concern below is exclusively with the capitalist state, however, this need not retain us.

I shall say that the state has explanatory autonomy when (and to the extent that) its structure and policies cannot be explained by the interest of an economically dominant class. The explanation may be found in some other set of interests, for example the interest of the ruling clique or the interests of society as a whole. Or the actions of the state may be explained as the outcome of the internal decision-making apparatus of bureaucracy, including routines and bargaining procedures that do not realize any well-defined interest.[2] Whatever the alternative is, the autonomy is defined negatively, as the absence of class-interest explanation. It might appear obvious that Marx denied the autonomy of the state in this sense, but matters are more complex. Rather he tended to affirm it in many cases – and then go on to assert, paradoxically, that the autonomy itself can be explained in terms of class interest or, alternatively, in terms of class structure. State autonomy, that is, may be explained by the fact

---

[1] Cohen, "Restricted and inclusive historical materialism", note 30. He imagines that the ruling class could issue instructions simultaneously to peasants and to the police that are to supervise the peasants, since one and the same set of phonemes could mean different things in the peasant language and in the language spoken by the policemen.
[2] See Allison, *The Essence of Decision*.

that it is useful for the economically dominant class – or it may be allowed by the fact that there is no single dominant class.

These ideas form the topic of 7.1.4 and 7.1.5 below. I shall anticipate somewhat on that discussion by offering an analysis of what it means to have political power. I believe that Marx held a narrow, *pre-strategic* conception of power that prevented him from recognizing that the state had autonomy in a real sense and not only as a fief from the capitalist class. Observe first that there are two ways in which group interest can shape political policies: by serving as a maximand for the policy choices or as a constraint on them. On first glance, it is tempting to say that if the choice between the feasible political alternatives is always made according to the interest of one group, then it has concentrated all power in its hands. On reflection, however, we see that power also must include the ability to define the set of alternatives, to set constraints on what is feasible. The following scenario is intended to bring out the relation between these two ways of wielding power. It is constructed so as to be applicable to nineteenth-century European politics, as a strategic game between Capital and Government, with the working class as an important background variable. In slightly modified form, however, it could also be applied to aspects of twentieth-century politics.

Imagine that there are two agents: A ("Capital") and B ("Government"), initially facing a given number of alternatives. B has the formal power of decision to choose among the feasible alternatives, A may have the power to exclude some of the alternatives from being considered. We assume that in A's judgment some alternatives are very bad, to be avoided at all costs. Among those remaining, some are judged better than others, but none is outstandingly superior. If the bad alternatives can somehow be excluded from the feasible set, it might not matter much if B within the restricted set chooses an alternative that is not highly ranked by A. It might not even be necessary for A to exclude the inferior alternatives. B – acting on "the law of anticipated reactions"[1] – might abstain from choosing any of these, knowing that if he does A has the power and the motive to dethrone him. Moreover, to the extent that what is bad for A is also bad for B, perhaps because B's affluence depends on that of A, B might not want to choose an inferior alternative even if he could get away with it. On the other hand, A might actually welcome the fact that B does not choose the alternative top-ranked by A, for example if A does not want to be seen as having power or if he deplores his own inability to

---

[1] Friedrich, *Man and his Government*, ch. 11.

defer satisfaction. Or, if he does not welcome it, he might at least tolerate it as the lesser evil, compared to the costs involved in *taking* the formal power of decision (as distinct from the costs involved in *having* it). In either case B would be invested with some autonomous power of decision, although its substance might be questioned, since ultimately it can be said to derive from A. B, one might say, has autonomy as a fief from A.

Consider, however, the same situation from B's perspective. He will correctly perceive his power as deriving from the cost to A of having or taking power. To be sure, B's power is limited by the fact that there are certain bounds that he cannot transgress without provoking A into taking power for himself, possibly also by the need to avoid killing the goose that lays the golden eggs. But conversely A's power is limited by his desire not to assume power unless provoked. Both actors, in fact, have power, of an equally substantial character. They need not, of course, have equal amounts of power. The exact distribution of their powers to shape the outcome depends on the strength of A's aversion to having or taking power, as well as on B's need to avoid harming A.

Anticipating on 7.1.4, we may speculate on the motive A could have for not wanting power. One reason might be the presence of a third actor C ("the working class"), who is already involved in a struggle with A and who also tends to oppose whoever has the formal power of decision. For A it might then be better that B have the formal power, so that some of C's attention and energy should be directed towards B and correspondingly diverted from A. Another reason might be that A knows that if in power he will take decisions motivated by short-term gains to himself, and that he wants to prevent this by letting the power remain safely outside his reach. From the point of view of A's long-term interest it may be better having the decisions taken in accordance with B's interest (although not as good as if B would take them to promote A's long-term interest). A third reason could simply be that if one has to devote some of one's time to political decision-making there is less time left for pursuing private interests. Again, those interests may be harmed by someone else's exercising the formal power, but perhaps less so than if one is distracted by having to assume it oneself. As to the reasons for not wanting to *take* power, assuming one would not mind having it, one explanation could be a short time horizon. To go into politics is like a costly investment, bearing fruit only after some time, while requiring outlays in the present. If one's interests are reasonably well respected in the present, the prospect of a future in which they might be even better respected need not be very attractive, considering the costs involved in the transition. This also creates an incentive for B to make these costs as large as possible, and to make sure that A's interests are just sufficiently respected to make the costs an effective deterrent.

If Marx believed that the government held power as a fief from capital, it was because he held a limited view of what constitutes a political resource. On this view, power grows out of the end of a gun – or, more generally, out of money and manpower. Yet the power base of a political actor can also be his place in a web of strategic relationships. The capitalists' fear of the working class, for instance, gives a lever to the aristocratic government that has little to do with the positive resources which it actually has at its disposal. From a quite different domain, one may cite the disproportionate power that can accrue to a political party that happens to be in a pivotal position between the two major political blocs. These are forms of power that arise out of the political system as such, not out of pre-political resources.

I conclude that in such cases the fact of state autonomy can be explained in terms of class interest, even if the autonomously made state decisions cannot. A class may have the ability to take the political power: that option is within its feasible set. Yet it may have some weakness that makes abstention a superior option. I have been arguing that the autonomy of the state is not made less substantial by the fact that the class keeps out of politics rather than being kept out of it. We are, in fact, dealing with an intermediate case between two "normal" situations. At one extreme is the situation in which no class would be able to dethrone the government, because the latter has superior means of coercion at its disposal. At the other extreme we have the situation in which the economically dominant class has nothing to fear from taking power, and consequently takes it. Marx was concerned with the paradoxical case in which a dominant class has the ability, but not the inclination, to concentrate the formal powers of decision in its own hands.

7.1.3. The instrumentalist theory of the state

I first set out Marx's best-known theory of the state, according to which it is a mere instrument for the economically dominant class, with no autonomy – derived or substantial – of its own. I shall argue that Marx held this view up to about 1850, and then abandoned it when he saw that the European bourgeoisies shied away from the power that was supposed to be theirs for the taking. The intellectual problem this created for him is well formulated by Eric Hobsbawm: "In short, the bourgeois revolution had failed in 1848 or led to unpredicted regimes whose nature probably preoccupied Marx more than any other problem concerning the bourgeois state: to states plainly serving the bourgeoisie's interest, but not directly representing it as a class."[1] In 7.1.4 I argue that Marx's solution to this dilemma was the abdication theory of the state.

The canonical formula is that "the executive of the modern State is but a committee for managing the common affairs of the whole bourgeoisie".[2] The "but" (*nur*) expresses the reductionist conception of the state that Marx held before 1850. What are these common affairs? Clearly, they include the defence of the bourgeoisie against the workers, through anti-combination acts to prevent trade unions, use of police and army to repress strikes, harsh laws against theft etc. In addition they include the defence of the interests of the bourgeoisie as a whole against its individual members. "The bourgeois state is nothing more than the mutual insurance of the bourgeois class against its individual members, as well as against the exploited class."[3] I shall discuss the second task in somewhat more detail.

In *The German Ideology* Marx makes it clear that the relation between individual capitalists is that of a Prisoner's Dilemma (6.2.3): "The attitude of the bourgeois to the institutions of his regime is like that of the Jew to the law; he evades them whenever it is possible to do so in each individual case, but he wants everybody else to observe them."[4] Elsewhere in the same volume he dwells at length on the opposition between the individual and the collective interest of the capitalist class. The discussion is embedded in a polemic against Max Stirner, who had argued that the state was the real owner of private property. Marx comments:

The fact that the ruling class establishes its joint domination as public power, as the state, [Stirner] interprets and distorts in the German petty-bourgeois manner as meaning that the "state" is established as a third force against this ruling class and absorbs all power in the face of it . . . Because the bourgeois do not allow the state to interfere in their private interests and give it only as much power as is necessary for their own safety and the maintenance of competition and because the bourgeois in general act as citizens only to the extent that their private interests demand it, [Stirner] believes that they are "nothing" in the face of the state . . . Further, since the bourgeois have organised the defence of their own property in the state . . . [Stirner] believes that "the state has the factory as property, the manufacturer holds it only in fee, as possession". In exactly the same way when a dog guards my house it "has" the house "as property", and I hold it only "in fee, as possession" from the dog. Since the concealed material conditions of private property are often bound to come into contradiction with the *juridical illusion*

---

[1] Hobsbawm, "Marx, Engels and politics", p. 245.
[2] *The Communist Manifesto*, p. 486. Similar expressions are found in *The German Ideology*, p. 90; *Deutsche-Brüsseler-Zeitung* 11.11.1847; *Neue Rheinische Zeitung* 27.2.1849.
[3] Marx, review of Girardin's *Le Socialisme et l'Impôt*.   [4] *The German Ideology*, p. 180.

about private property – as seen, for example in expropriations – [Stirner] concludes that "here the otherwise concealed principle, that only the state is the property-owner whereas the individual is a feudal tenant, strikes the eye" . . . [Stirner] here transforms the contradictions belonging to the *existence* of private property into the *negation* of private property . . . [The] bourgeois, and in general all the members of civil society, are forced to constitute themselves as "we", as a juridical person, as the state, in order to safeguard their common interests and – if only because of the division of labour – to delegate the collective power thus created to a few persons.[1]

In addition to the tasks cited here – the maintenance of competition and the laws of expropriation – we should mention the limitation of the working day discussed in 4.1.4. Observe that the reference to the maintenance of competition shows that Marx had in mind the *long-term* interest of the capitalist class (6.2.1). At any given moment, it may rather be in the collective interest of that class, or of capitalists in individual industries, to form a cartel to maximize their joint profits. This, however, might jeopardize the dynamic force of competition that underwrites the continued viability of capitalism.[2] We may recall that Marx was also aware of the need for intertemporal capitalist solidarity with respect to the limitation of the working day.[3] Hence the state at any given time is not simply the instrument of the current generation of capitalists, but a means to the survival of capitalism as a system. It is in principle ready to sacrifice not only individual capitalists, but even the short-term interests of the class as a whole.

If this is so, we must ask whether the state could not also counteract the tendency to economic crises that according to Marx would bring about the downfall of capitalism. If capitalism is in the danger of being destroyed by individual entrepreneurs acting out of self-interest, why could not the state curb their greed as it did in the case of the Ten Hours Bill? To answer the question, we must consider the nature of the crises that according to Marx would bring capitalism to a halt (3.4). Broadly speaking, these rest on the falling rate of profit due to labour-saving innovations and on difficulties in realizing profit due to low effective demand. Marx would probably have dismissed as absurd the idea that the process of technical change could be controlled by the state so as to prevent a fall in the rate of profit, and it is indeed hard to imagine how this could be done. By contrast, creation of effective demand by the state has been a main tool in the regulation of modern capitalism. Marx discusses this idea in connection with Malthus, who had argued that to create "an adequate demand", the income from

---

[1] *Ibid.*, pp. 355ff.   [2] Cp. my *Logic and Society*, pp. 129–30.
[3] *Zur Kritik* (1861–3), p. 162, cited in 4.1.4.

rent must be supplemented by other means: "These consist of heavy *taxation*, of a mass of sinecurists in State and Church, of large armies, pensions, tithes for the priests, an impressive national debt, and, from time to time, expensive wars."[1] There is no indication, however, that Marx believed these proto-Keynesian remedies would have any effect in delaying the downfall of capitalism or in making it less probable.

7.1.4. The abdication theory of the state

In Marx's political writings from the 1850s we repeatedly encounter the idea that the state serves the interest of the capitalist class, without being the direct extension of its will as the earlier writings had argued. More-over he strongly suggests that it is no accident that the state serves that interest. There is an explanatory connection: the bourgeoisie abdicate from power (France) or abstain from taking it (England, Germany) because they perceive that their interests are better served if they remain outside politics. I shall refer to this as "the abdication theory of the state", taking "abdication" in the extended sense in which it also includes delib-erate abstention from power. It will be clear from the context when I am referring to abdication in the narrow, literal sense of giving up something one has and when it covers the case of not taking something one could get.

In Marx's writings the notion of abdication arises in several contexts, not just with respect to the state in capitalist society. I shall say a few words about the other references towards the end of this subsection, in order to support some general propositions about the reasons an actor could have for abdicating power. First, however, I survey the abdication theory of the state in capitalist society. Before 1848 Marx explicitly rejected the idea that the capitalist class would ever be content with government by proxy:

[According to Stirner] "it makes no difference" to the bourgeoisie whether it rules unrestrictedly or whether its political and economic power is counterbalanced by other classes. [Stirner] believes that an absolute king, or someone else, *could* defend the bourgeoisie just as successfully as it defends itself. And even "its principles", which consist in subordinating state power to "*chacun pour soi, chacun chez soi*" and exploiting it for that purpose – an "absolute monarch" is supposed to be able to do that! Let [Stirner] name any country with developed trade and industry and strong competition where the bourgeoisie entrusts its defence to an "absolute monarch".[2]

---

[1] *Theories of Surplus-Value*, vol. 3, p. 51.   [2] *The German Ideology*, pp. 200–1.

The view was reiterated a few years later, in an article in *Neue Rheinische Zeitung* criticizing the constitution of December 1848:

[There] is not the slightest doubt that the imposed Constitution solves the "social question" in keeping with the views of the aristocracy and the bureaucracy, in other words, it presents these gentlemen with a form of government which ensures the exploitation of the people by these demigods. But has the imposed Constitution solved the "social question" from the standpoint of the *bourgeoisie*? In other words, does the bourgeoisie receive a political system enabling it freely to administer the affairs of its class as a whole, i.e. the interests of commerce, industry and agriculture, to make the most productive use of public funds, to manage the state budget as cheaply as possible, to protect national labour effectively from without, and within the country to open up all sources of national wealth silted by feudal mud? Does history provide a single example showing that under a king imposed by the grace of God, the bourgeoisie ever succeeded in achieving a political system in keeping with its material interests? . . . Bourgeois industry *must* burst the fetters of absolutism and feudalism. A revolution against both only demonstrates that bourgeois industry has reached a certain level when it must either win an appropriate political system or perish.[1]

The event of the 1850s disproved this dilemma. The bourgeoisie in the main European countries flourished under a political system not so directly geared to their interest. Hence Marx made a theoretical retreat in order to explain this anomaly in a way consistent with historical materialism. He had to face the fact that the bourgeoisie was "la première classe possédante à n'être pas gouvernante",[2] and yet retain the view that ultimately economics is the explanation of politics. The abdication theory was supposed to provide the solution. I shall discuss it with respect to England, France and Germany, with the main emphasis on the English case. The reason for singling out England is that a number of writers have been struck by the apparently anomalous relation between state and society in mid-nineteenth-century Britain, and offered widely different comments on this fact. Using these as reference points, the specific character of Marx's explanation is better brought into focus.

(1) An editorial in *The Economist* from 1862 – possibly by Walter Bagehot – was titled "The advantage to a commercial country of a non-commercial government". It argued that "not only for the interest of the country at large, but especially for the interest of its commerce, it is in the highest degree desirable that the Government should stand high above the influence of commercial interest".[3] This suggests that the aristocratic

---

[1] *Neue Rheinische Zeitung* 22.1.1849; cp. *ibid.* 10.12.1848.

[2] Veyne, *Le Pain et le Cirque*, p. 117.

[3] *The Economist* 4.1.1862. I owe this reference to Grindheim, "How could the aristocracy govern when the bourgeoisie ruled?"

government of England was a solution to the bourgeoisie's weakness of will. Like Ulysses binding himself to the mast, the bourgeoisie accepted the aristocratic government because they could not trust themselves not to succumb to the temptation of short-term greed.[1]

(2) A related argument was offered by Joseph Schumpeter, substituting lack of ability for weakness of will. In his words, "a genius in the business office may be, and often is, utterly unable outside it to say boo to a goose – both in the drawing room and on the platform. Knowing this he wants to be left alone and to leave politics alone." Hence, "without protection by some non-bourgeois group, the bourgeoisie is politically helpless and unable not only to lead its nation but even to take care of its particular class interest. Which amounts to saying that it needs a master."[2]

(3) A more sober explanation was offered by G. D. H. Cole. He argued that the industrial capitalists "were too occupied with their own affairs to wish to take the exercise of political authority directly into their own hands" – "provided that the government did not govern too much, and protected their property against levellers from below as well as against extortions in the interest of the old aristocratic class".[3] I read this as suggesting that to the bourgeoisie the opportunity cost of going into politics exceeded the expected gains, given the knowledge that the government would not go too far against their interest.

(4) Seymour Lipset, citing Engels, argues in a quite different way from all the preceding writers. Engels had written that "the English bourgeoisie are, up to the present day, so deeply penetrated by a sense of their social inferiority that they keep up, at their own expense and that of the nation, an ornamental caste of drones to represent the nation worthily at all state functions". According to Lipset, this "is a situation in which an old upper class, which had declined in economic power, continued to maintain its control over the governmental machinery because it remained the highest status group in society".[4]

Of these, the first three writers argue that it was somehow in the interest of the bourgeoisie to stay away from power, but it is doubtful whether any of them offers an *explanation* of the abstention in terms of these benefits. This is rather implausible in the case of *The Economist* and Schumpeter, probably also with regard to Cole. The last clause cited from

---

[1] See also my *Ulysses and the Sirens*, ch. II.8.
[2] Schumpeter, *Capitalism, Socialism and Democracy*, p. 138.
[3] Cole, *Studies in Class Structure*, pp. 84–5.   [4] Lipset, "Social stratification: social class".

Cole is best taken to say that the bourgeoisie would have taken power if provoked, not that they decided to keep away from power unless provoked. The last idea is quite implausible, since the very point of Cole's argument is that the bourgeoisie were not a "they" in the sense of being a collective actor. Lipset, by contrast, definitely does propose an explanation, in which, however, the interest of the bourgeoisie plays no role whatsoever. His explanation nevertheless is compatible with either (1) or (2). It may be the case, that is, that the weakness of the bourgeoisie which permitted the aristocracy to retain power was also a weakness that made it in the interest of the bourgeoisie that the aristocracy should have the power.[1]

Marx differs, then, from all the preceding in arguing that the explanation of bourgeois abstention from power is to be found in the benefits it provided. In 6.3.3 I have cited some of the texts in which he makes this argument, to which I now add a few other, more immediately political passages. The central idea is that in England the Whigs traditionally held the monopoly on government, but that from a certain point onward it had to be exercised in the interest of the capitalist class:

The Whigs are the *aristocratic representatives* of the Bourgeoisie, of the industrial and commercial middle class. Under the condition that the Bourgeoisie should abandon to them, to an oligarchy of aristocratic families, the monopoly of government and the exclusive possession of office, they make to the middle class, and assist it in conquering, all those concessions, which in the course of social and political development have shown themselves to have become *unavoidable* and *undelayable*. Neither more nor less . . . Ever since the "glorious revolution" of 1688 the Whigs, with short intervals, caused principally by the first French Revolution and the consequent reaction, have found themselves in the enjoyment of the public offices. Whoever recalls to his mind this period of British history, will find no other distinctive mark of Whigdom but the maintenance of their family oligarchy. The interests and principles which they represent besides, from time to time, do not belong to the Whigs; they are forced upon them by the development of the industrial and commercial class, the Bourgeoisie. After 1688 we find them united with the Bankocracy, just then rising into importance, as we find them in 1846, united with the Millocracy. The Whigs as little carried the Reform Bill of 1831, as they carried the Free Trade Bill of 1846. Both Reform movements, the political as well as the commercial, were movements of the Bourgeoisie. As soon as either of these movements had ripened into irresistibility; as soon as, at the same time, it had become the safest means of turning the Tories out of office, the Whigs stepped forward, took up the direction of the Government, and secured to themselves the governmental part of the victory. In 1831 they extended the political portion of

---

[1] Hence it might be possible to establish a lawlike generalization to the effect that "Whenever abstention would be in the interest of the bourgeoisie, the bourgeoisie abstains", yet this would not provide an explanation.

reform as far as was necessary in order not to leave the middle class entirely dissatisfied; after 1846 they confined their Free Trade measures so far as was necessary, in order to save the landed aristocracy the greatest possible amount of privileges.[1]

Another article extends this reasoning to all "three fractions of the Aristocracy, Tories, Peelites and Whigs":

the entire Aristocracy agree, that the Government has to be conducted for the benefit, and according to the interests of the middle-class, but they are determined that the bourgeoisie are not to be themselves the governors of this affair; and for this object all that the old Oligarchy possess of talent, influence and authority are combined, in a last effort, into one Administration, which has for its task [to keep] the bourgeoisie, as long as possible, from the direct enjoyment of governing the nation. The coalized Aristocracy of England intend, with regard to the bourgeoisie, to act on the same principle upon which Napoleon I progessed to act in reference to the people: *"Tout pour le peuple, rien par le peuple."*[2]

Read in itself this might suggest an enlightened paternalism by the aristocracy on behalf of the bourgeoisie, but the first passage shows that the aristocracy was also moved by self-interest: that of the Whigs *qua* governing clique and that of the landowning class to which they belonged. The interests of the bourgeoisie were *constraints* on the realization of the aristocratic interests, but within them some scope was left for manoeuvring, because the bourgeoisie had positive incentives to stay away from power (6.3.3). The abstract logic of this argument was set out in 7.1.2, and there is no need to repeat it here.

Note, however, a crucial premise of that argument: the bourgeoisie was a collective actor that as such *decided* to abstain from political power. In the absence of this premise it is difficult, I believe impossible, to make explanatory use of the benefits that the bourgeoisie derived from having the working class fight a two-front war against Capital and Government. This is a rather paradoxical idea, that a class should crystallize only to decide to return to its former, uncrystallized state. Yet we must distinguish, as did Marx, between different levels of class consciousness. As stated in 6.3.3, his argument was that after the victory of the Anti Corn Law League the next, logical step would have been to go forward and form a political party. The refusal to do this, and the dismantling of the League, may be seen as a collective decision to leave politics in the hands of the aristocracy. Yet I also believe that in Marx this intentional reasoning was inextricably combined with subterranean functionalism, to the point where they become indistinguishable.

[1] *New York Daily Tribune* 21.8.1852.   [2] *Ibid.*, 28.1.1853.

This is also true of his analysis of French politics. True, the English and the French case differ in many respects. Whereas in England the bourgeoisie confronted (and made use of) the traditional Whig monopoly on power, in France they had to come to grips with a long tradition of *étatisme*. Yet, as already indicated in 6.3.3, the same intentional-cum-conspiratorial-cum-functional analysis underlies both arguments.

Consider first a statement about the independence enjoyed by the Bonapartist state:

[Under] the absolute monarchy, during the first revolution, under Napoleon, bureaucracy was only the means of preparing the class rule of the bourgeoisie. Under the Restoration, under Louis Philippe, under the parliamentary republic, it was the instrument of the ruling class, however much it strove for power of its own. Only under the second Bonaparte does the state seem to have made itself completely independent. As against civil society, the state machine has consolidated its position so thoroughly that the chief of the Society of December 10 suffices for its head.[1]

In an article entitled "The rule of the Pretorians" Marx later made the same point with respect to the French *army*, which from being a tool for a "specific social interest" had itself become the predominant interest group.[2] Numerous statements to the same effect occur in the various versions of *The Civil War in France*.[3]

In all these passages Marx points to the independence of the state, and then adds that this is only an appearance. In essence the Bonapartist state was a class state. Yet the way in which he tries to anchor it in the class structure is ambiguous. In the first of the cited passages he goes on to say that the state power is not suspended in mid-air, but rests on the support of the small peasantry. This support did not spring from the real interest of the peasants, but from their imaginary interests – the *idées napoléoniennes* that had made sense fifty years earlier, but were by then obsolete. This power base was not economic but ideological, yet none the less solid for that. It was not, however, a sufficient condition for the Bonapartist regime. In addition, it needed the support or at least the acquiescence of the bourgeoisie.[4] Bonaparte stood for tradition; he embodied a historical continuity that as it were brought him over the threshold to a plausible candidacy. For that candidacy to be crowned with success, the offer had to meet a corresponding demand. The helplessness of the bourgeoisie – which Marx interpreted as a cry for help – gave him what he needed.

[1] *The Eighteenth Brumaire*, p. 186.   [2] *New York Daily Tribune* 12.3.1858.
[3] *The Civil War in France*, pp. 53ff, 100ff, 137ff.
[4] Cp. the analogous explanations of fascism in terms of the active support of the petty bourgeoisie and the tacit support of capital.

In 6.3.3 I cited a passage where Marx says that the bourgeoisie "must forfeit the crown" to save its purse, a clear statement of the abdication theory. A similar assertion occurs towards the end of the work:

Manifestly, the bourgeoisie had now no choice but to elect Bonaparte. When the puritans of the Council of Constance complained of the dissolute lives of the popes and wailed about the necessity of moral reform, Cardinal Pierre d'Ailly thundered at them: "Only the devil in person can still save the Catholic Church, and you ask for angels." In like manner, after the coup d'état, the French bourgeoisie cried: Only the chief of the Society of December 10 can still save bourgeois society! Only theft can still save property; only perjury, religion; bastardy, the family; disorder, order! As the executive authority which has made itself an independent power, Bonaparte feels it to be his mission to safeguard "bourgeois order". But the strength of this bourgeois order lies in the middle class. He looks on himself, therefore as the representative of the middle class and issues decrees in this sense. Nevertheless, he is somebody solely due to the fact that he has broken the political power of this middle class and daily breaks it anew. Consequently he looks on himself as the adversary of the political and literary power of the middle class. But by protecting its material power, he generates its political power anew.[1]

Now, it may be true that the bourgeoisie offered little resistance to the *coup d'état*, and that they did well for themselves under the regime that followed. These two facts do not, however, add up to an act of abdication, nor to a deliberate acquiescence. Once again, Marx was misled by his search for meaning in history.

There are no similarly clear statements about the abdication of the German bourgeoisie after 1850. After the defeat of the 1848 revolution in Germany Marx made no dissection of its causes and consequences even remotely comparable to *The Eighteenth Brumaire*. In his articles during the 1850s there is virtually no mention of internal German developments until his visit to Germany in December 1858 and January 1859. Here he first describes how the revolution, and the ensuing counterrevolution, "succeeded in driving the Government back, not behind 1848, not behind 1815, but even behind 1807",[2] by restoring the power of landed aristocracy and gentry, corporations and guilds. He then adds that what the bourgeoisie thus lost in political power, it gained in wealth:

But there is another side to the medal. The revolution had dispelled the ideological delusions of the *bourgeoisie*, and the counter-revolution had done away with their political pretensions. Thus they were thrown back upon their real resources – trade

---

[1] *The Eighteenth Brumaire*, pp. 193–4.
[2] This, in fact, is the normal pattern of a counterrevolutionary movement: it attempts to go beyond the pre-revolutionary situation, not back to it, for a reason well expressed by Giscard d'Estaing in an interview with *Le Monde* 8.1.1975: "Il n'est certainement pas question de revenir à la situation d'avant 1968, et d'abord parce que la situation avant 1968 comportait les conditions qui ont créé 1968."

and industry – and I do not think that any other people have relatively made so immense a start in this direction during the last centennial epoch as the Germans, and especially the Prussians ... The rage of getting rich, of going ahead, of opening new mines, of building new factories, of constructing new railways, and above all of investing in and gambling with joint-stock company shares, became the passion of the day, and infected all classes from the peasant even to the coroneted prince, who had once been a *reichsunmittelbarer Fürst*. So you see the days when the Bourgeoisie wept in Babylonian captivity and drooped their diminished heads, were the very days when they became the effective power of the land.[1]

The last phrase closely parallels the conclusion of the text from *The Eighteenth Brumaire*: by protecting the material power of the bourgeoisie, Bonaparte generates its political power anew. The vanquished, turning inward on themselves and the pursuit of their private interest, become rich and prosperous to the point where a new bid for power becomes tempting. (Cp. also the "Babylonian captivity" of Germany and Japan after 1945.) In the comment on Germany, however, there is not any suggestion that this prosperity could in retrospect be invoked to explain the defeat of the German bourgeoisie in 1849 as a voluntary abdication from power.

I have surveyed various texts in which Marx suggests that the capitalist class might abstain from entering the political arena. I now turn to a few other texts that discuss the problem of abdication or political abstention with regard to other groups. In a text from 1847 Marx first explains why the German bourgeoisie "seek as far as possible to make the change from *absolute* to *bourgeois* monarchy without a revolution", and then adds why the prospects for a constitutional monarchy are poor:

But the absolute monarchy in Prussia, as earlier in England and France, will not let itself be amicably changed into a bourgeois monarchy. It will not abdicate amicably. The princes' hands are tied both by their personal prejudices and by a whole bureaucracy of officials, soldiers and clerics – integral parts of absolute monarchy who are far from willing to exchange their ruling position for a subservient one in respect of the bourgeoisie. Then the feudal estates also hold back; for them it is a question of life and death, in other words of property or expropriation. It is clear that the absolute monarch, for all the servile homage of the bourgeoisie, sees his true interest on the side of these estates.[2]

The passage may be read in the light of Adam Przeworski's theory of the conditions for a negotiated transition from authoritarian to democratic regimes. On his view, the main condition is that one finds an institutional compromise which ensures "that the forces associated with the

---

[1] *New York Daily Tribune* 1.2.1859.   [2] *Deutsche-Brüsseler Zeitung* 18.11.1847.

authoritarian regime find a significant presence under democratic conditions".[1] The emphasis is on the *institutional* compromise, as opposed to a substantive one. Substantive compromises have no enduring stability under democratic conditions; they may change as majorities come and go. Only if the compromise is built into the democratic institutional structures is there a chance that the authoritarian regime will be prepared to abdicate peacefully, as an alternative to violent dethronement. According to Marx, this condition was not met in Germany. For the feudal estates the continued presence of the regime was "a question of life and death" over which no compromise was possible.

Towards the end of his life Marx also became concerned with a different form of political abstention as a possible strategy for the working class. In an article from 1873 on "Political indifferentism" he warns against adoption of this policy, arguing that it is an ultra-leftist deviation that on the pretext of awaiting the definitive "social liquidation" leads to quietism in the present. He cites his anonymous opponent as arguing that "to combat the state is to recognize the state", because any involvement – even hostile – with bourgeois institutions must lead to a betrayal of the true principles. Hence, presumably, the working class should beware of accepting universal suffrage, should the ruling classes offer to abdicate from their monopoly on political power. Against this view Marx offers two arguments: in the first place power must be achieved step by step, and in the second place one does not have the right to neglect the sufferings of those currently living, if they can be allayed by political action within the system. I return to this issue in 7.2.2.

On this background we may conclude by a brief typology of the reasons for abdication from power, including "active indifference" and other forms of deliberate abstention. With one exception they are all taken from the works cited and discussed earlier.

First, one may abdicate from power because one has no trust in one's ability to use it in one's best interest, fearing that one may be betrayed by weakness of will or sheer incompetence. I have indicated how such arguments were used on behalf of the capitalist class in the nineteenth century. Interestingly, exactly the same reasoning has been applied to the working class in the twentieth century. It has been argued, for instance, that the working class should beware of worker-owned firms, because of the short time horizon and the low rate of investment they would imply.[2] "If capitalism did not exist, the workers would have to invent it." Also

---

[1] Przeworski, "Democracy as a contingent outcome of conflict".
[2] Kydland and Prescott, "Rules rather than discretion", p. 486.

trade unions have argued against industrial democracy on the grounds that their members do not possess the necessary competence. "We are not ready for it yet."[1]

Secondly, abdication may be the preemption of dethronement, that is the lesser of evils. This may happen both in the negotiated transition from authoritarian to democratic regimes, and in the reverse transition from democracy to authoritarianism. In both cases the abdicating group will need a guarantee that its interests will in fact be better protected than they would have been in the case of a violent overthrow. Following Przeworski, I have indicated that in the transition to democracy this would be some institutional compromise. In the reverse case, the abdicating group would have a guarantee against being killed off if in some sense it is the goose that lays the golden eggs. Hence the bourgeoisie may give up democracy and abdicate to Bonapartism or fascism because they know that their presence and their prosperity are required to fill the coffers of the state.[2]

Thirdly, there is the theme of the poisoned gift. The holder of power may give it away to an adversary in the expectation that the latter will use it "responsibly" and, in fact, in the interest of the former. Thus intelligent capitalists may give away part of their decision-making power, expecting that the workers will be more restrained in their wage claims when they are co-responsible for the firm. Conversely trade unions have often resisted cooptation, on the ground that their role is in the opposition, not in the government.[3] The ultra-leftist form of political indifferentism clearly rests on a similar argument.

Fourthly, there is the sheer opportunity cost of taking power or having it. Again, this applies to workers no less than to capitalists. Resistance to industrial democracy is sometimes due to the workers' belief that they have better things to do in their free time than participate in meetings about how to run the firm. Or at least they may be averse to undertake the training process that would be needed to be able to do so. Similarly, the capitalists may prefer to use all their time to run the firm instead of taking some time off to run the country.

Fifthly, abdication can be a way of defusing opposition, or shifting it

---

[1] This attitude is amply demonstrated in unpublished work by Trond Bergh on the Norwegian debate on industrial democracy after 1945.

[2] Note, however, that the tax policy that maximizes tax income will not in general be the same as the one that maximizes before-tax profits, hence the interest of the rulers is not in the prosperity *per se* of the bourgeoisie.

[3] This view has notably been championed by H. A. Clegg, e.g. in his *Industrial Democracy and Nationalization*, pp. 19ff.

onto another agent or group. This, we have seen, was Marx's major argument. He believed that the capitalists kept away from power in order to deflect the indignation of the workers against the government or against the landowning classes. This differs from the poisoned-gift strategy in that power is not shifted onto the main enemy, but to a third agent who can absorb some of the attention of that enemy.

Lastly, abdication may be motivated by the desire to improve one's bargaining situation by making certain concessions to the adversary physically impossible. This is the method of "public side bets" discussed with great subtlety by Thomas Schelling.[1] In typical cases, of course, a reduction of the set of options available to one entails a loss of power, but in certain situations this may actually enhance the probability of getting one's way. Thus the government in some countries has abdicated power to the International Monetary Fund in order to be able to reject inflationary wage claims. This reason for abdication has not been discussed in any of the examples cited earlier. It is not surprising that it is absent in Marx, given what I have called his pre-strategic conception of power. There is no inherent reason, however, why it should not find application to the kind of cases that concerned him. Local branches of multinational firms often abdicate power to the central office, so as to be able to resist the claims made by the workers. "Our hands are tied." (But, like Ulysses, we asked for the tie.)

To conclude, Marx never succeeded in proving that the state in a capitalist society must be a capitalist state. It is obvious that the government in any society based on private enterprise must take account of the interests of the entrepreneurs, since the state depends on them both for its tax base and for providing employment and welfare for the workers – a task that could otherwise fall to the state. Moreover, there is sometimes a real danger that the bourgeoisie might dethrone the government if its interests are not sufficiently respected. I suspect that in modern capitalist societies the latter constraint usually is redundant or slack, and that the first reason for respecting private property will make the government adopt a policy that is "good enough" for the bourgeoisie, given its various reasons for not wanting to take power and assuming that it could do so if it wanted to. (In feudalism, by contrast, the political constraint may have been the binding one.)[2] Yet, even admitting these facts, there will be some scope for autonomous decision-making by the state officials according to other criteria than the interest of the capitalist class. How much scope is a

---

[1] Schelling, *The Strategy of Conflict*, ch. 5.
[2] See notably Brenner, "The agrarian roots of European capitalism", pp. 50ff.

strictly empirical issue. It could turn out that the political risks to the bourgeoisie of taking power were so large that it could be made to accept a policy that went quite strongly against its interest, and that at the same time the policy that maximizes state income is quite different from the one that would maximize capitalist profit. If these two conditions are met, the state could in a real sense be more powerful than the economically dominant class. Or it could turn out that the state out of *its* self-interest is constrained to track very closely the policies that are optimal from the point of view of capitalists. The argument must be made on such empirical grounds, not in terms of conceptual juggling.

7.1.5. The class-balance theory of the state

Marx also suggests a different explanation for the autonomy of the state, namely that the struggle betwen two opposed classes allows the state to assert itself by divide-and-conquer. This holds especially for absolute monarchy, but the theory also has some claim to be considered as Marx's *general* theory of the modern state.

According to Marx, absolute monarchy in its inception was not the tool or the representative of any class – be it the aristocracy or the bourgeoisie. Perry Anderson, for instance, argues that it was a "feudal monarchy", whose seeming "distance from the class from which it was recruited and whose interests it served" was in fact "the condition of its efficacy as a state".[1] This says that absolute monarchy was for the feudal aristocracy what in Marx's view the Bonapartist state was for the bourgeoisie – a tool, but at one remove. Marx, however, did not apply this theory to absolutism. Rather, he looked at absolute monarchy as a competitor to the main classes, not as a tool, however indirectly, of either. In *The German Ideology* formulations abound to this effect. He refers to the period as one in which "royal power, aristocracy and bourgeoisie are contending for domination and where, therefore, domination is shared".[2] Elsewhere we find this characterization of the state in Germany:

The impotence of each separate sphere of life (one can speak here neither of estates nor of classes, but at most of former estates and classes not yet born) did not allow any of them to gain exclusive domination. The inevitable consequence was that during the epoch of absolute monarchy, which assumed here its most stunted, semi-patriarchal form, the special sphere which, owing to division of labour, was responsible for the administration of public interests acquired an abnormal independence, which became still greater in the bureaucracy of modern times. Thus, the state built itself up into an apparently independent force, and

[1] Anderson, *Lineages of the Absolutist State*, pp. 18, 108.   [2] *The German Ideology*, p. 59.

this position, which in other countries was only transitory – a transition stage – it has maintained in Germany until the present day.[1]

In a characteristically teleological vein, Marx here conflates the *apparent* independence of the state with its *transitory* independence, as if future weakness proved the illusionary character of present strength. Elsewhere a more interesting argument is offered, to the effect that the autonomy of the state was *self-defeating*, in that it was harnessed to a purpose that in the long run favoured one of its competitors, namely the bourgeoisie. The "actual progressive function" of the absolute monarchy, Marx writes in 1847, was the encouragement of "trade and industry and thereby at the same time the rise of the bourgeois class as necessary conditions both for national strength and for its own glory".[2] Similarly, in the articles on "Revolutionary Spain", he contrasts the development in that country with that of the "other great states of Europe". In the latter,

absolute monarchy presents itself as a civilizing center, as the initiator of social unity. There it was the laboratory in which the various elements of society were so mixed and worked, as to allow the towns to change the local independence and sovereignty of the Middle Ages for the general rule of the middle classes, and the common sway of civil society.[3]

This corresponds to the relation between Bonapartism (or the German government after 1849) and the bourgeoisie: "by protecting its material power, he generates its political power anew". The absolute monarchies could not assert themselves without promoting the interest of their main competitor, the bourgeoisie. "Plenty" was a means to "Power", and soon a rival to power.[4] According to the pre-1850 writings the absolute monarchy paved the way for the naked class rule of the bourgeoisie, by strengthening it to the point where it "had to claim its share of political power, if only by reason of its material interest".[5] According to the later writings, the development of the bourgeoisie showed that with the strength went a new weakness, its vulnerability to working-class opposition. I return to this perspective below.

[1] *Ibid.*, p. 195; see also p. 90.
[2] *Deutsche-Brüsseler-Zeitung* 18.11.1847. The passage is quoted more fully below.
[3] *New York Daily Tribune* 9.9.1854; see also the "Urtext" to *A Contribution to the Critique of Political Economy*, pp. 19–20.
[4] For this contrast, see Viner, "Power versus plenty as objectives of foreign policy". In the present context the point is that the power struggle between the absolutist state and the bourgeoisie was not simply over the division of the surplus, but also over its creation. By contrast, the relation between the state and the feudal nobility was closer to zero-sum (with the qualifications mentioned in 6.3.2), since they fought over the division of the surplus extracted from the peasantry. See also Brenner, "The agrarian roots of European capitalism", pp. 78ff.
[5] *Neue Rheinische Zeitung* 10.12.1848.

The Spanish case turned out differently. Initially the rise of absolute monarchy took place according to the general scheme just set out:

Several circumstances conspired in favour of the rising power of absolutism. The want of union between the different provinces deprived their efforts of the necessary strength; but it was, above all, the bitter antagonism between the classes of the nobles and the citizens of the towns which Charles employed for the degradation of both.[1]

Yet unlike what happened elsewhere on the continent, this process did not lead to the rise of the bourgeoisie. Spanish absolutism vegetated for several centuries, showing that it really belonged to a different genus altogether:

[While] the absolute monarchy found in Spain material in its very nature repulsive to centralization, it did all in its power to prevent the growth of common interests arising out of a national division of labour and the multiplicity of internal exchanges – the very basis on which alone a uniform system of administration and the rule of general laws can be created. Thus the absolute monarchy in Spain, bearing but a superficial resemblance to the absolute monarchies of Europe in general, is rather to be ranged in a class with Asiatic forms of government. Spain, like Turkey, remained an agglomeration of mismanaged republics with a nominal sovereign at their head.[2]

This suggests a general principle. A monarchical dynasty, to retain its power, must take care not to strengthen it, since it can do so only by strengthening its main competitor, the bourgeoisie. Of course, it then runs the risk that if it does not strengthen its power, it will be annexed by rival nations less cautious in this respect. The autonomy of the state is threatened from within, by the bourgeoisie, and from outside, by other states. What is strength with respect to the external enemy is weakness with respect to the internal, and vice versa. A balance may be found, but not easily. It can be stabilized only by the emergence of an enemy of the internal enemy – by the rise of the working class that drives the bourgeoisie to ally itself with its former opponent against the new one.[3]

This, in fact, corresponds well to Marx's analyses before and after 1848. Let me quote more fully from the 1847 article partly excerpted above:

---

[1] *New York Daily Tribune* 9.9.1854.   [2] *Ibid.*

[3] I do not suggest that many, or any, absolutist rulers were so clearsighted. In most cases they no doubt believed it possible to have their cake and eat it too; to have industrialization without modernization; an economically strong bourgeoisie with no political ambitions. For discussions of this form of wishful thinking in Russia and China around the turn of the century, see Knei-Paz, *The Social and Political Thought of Leon Trotsky*, pp. 100ff and *passim*, and Levenson, *Confucian China and its Modern Fate*, vol. I, especially chaps. IV and VII.

Once society's material conditions of existence have developed so far that the transformation of its official political form has become a vital necessity for it, the whole physiognomy of the old political power is transformed. Thus absolute monarchy now attempts, not to *centralise,* which was its actual progressive function, but to *decentralise.* Born from the defeat of the feudal estates and having the most active share in their destruction itself, it now seeks to retain at least the *semblance* of feudal distinctions. Formerly encouraging trade and industry and thereby at the same time the rise of the bourgeois class, as necessary conditions both for national strength and for its own glory, absolute monarchy now everywhere hampers trade and industry, which have become increasingly dangerous weapons in the hands of an already powerful bourgeoisie.[1]

At this time Marx believed that the sorcerer's apprentice would not be able to call back the forces he had unleashed. German absolutism would not be able to turn the clock back. The early phase of the 1848 movement seemed to prove him right, yet the outcome was the very re-feudalization which the regime had in vain strived for before the revolution. Writing in 1859, Marx describes the strengthening of feudal institutions and concludes that "the boldest dreams of the King, which had remained dreams during the eight years of his absolute regime, had all become fulfilled by the Revolution, and shone as palpable realities in the light of day during the eight years from 1850 to 1857".[2] Although the presence of the working class is not mentioned in this context, it is clear from other writings (7.2.1) that the retreat in 1849 was in fact due to the increasing salience of this new enemy.

The Bonapartist state may be understood in the same light, if we recall the various texts from *The Civil War in France* cited in 6.3.3. In the published version Marx says that the empire "professed to save the working class by breaking down Parliamentarism, and, with it, the undisguised subservience of Government to the propertied class". At the same time, "it professed to save the propertied classes by upholding their economic supremacy over the working class". And Marx concludes that the empire "was the only form of government possible at a time when the bourgeoisie had already lost, and the working class had not yet acquired, the faculty of ruling the nation".[3] Clearly, this is a class-balance theory of the state. By promising to each of the major classes to protect it against the other, the government can rule autonomously. True, in the drafts Marx says that the Bonapartist state was the only possible *bourgeois* government, which rather suggests an explanation in terms of abdication. There is an apparent tension between these two

---

[1] *Deutsche-Brusseler-Zeitung* 18.11.1847.   [2] *New York Daily Tribune* 1.2.1859.
[3] *The Civil War in France,* pp. 138–9.

points of view on the Bonapartist state. Did it exploit the conflict between the classes to promote its own interest, or did it exist to promote, albeit indirectly, the interest of the bourgeoisie?

From the discussion in 7.1.4 it should be clear that this nuance is little more than a verbal one. The state can indeed exploit the conflict between the classes present on the social arena to further its own interests, whatever these might be – imperialist expansion, economic growth, modernization of the nation, more power to the bureaucracy etc. Yet its interests can to a large extent only be promoted by respecting the interests of these classes themselves. This holds with respect to the bourgeoisie (7.1.4), as well as the workers, whose continued well-being and reproduction is a condition for their productive capacity (4.1.4). In fact, one peculiarity of the capitalist mode of production is that the state must relate itself to two distinct productive classes, each of which is indispensable for production and hence for the tax basis of the state. There is a contrast here to the absolutist state, which had an incentive to encourage the growth of the bourgeoisie at the expense of the unproductive nobility. The modern state must face the fact that there is not a single goose that lays the golden eggs. Rather, two geese are needed, and the state must take care that neither kills off the other. As long as it does, it can plausibly represent itself as defending the interests of the one against the other, and hence be able to demand concessions in return.[1]

To conclude, it is hardly too much to say that Marx made the autonomy of the state into the cornerstone of his theory. True, his intention was no doubt to explain it in terms of the deliberate abstention or abdication from power by the bourgeoisie, implying that the autonomy was granted rather than achieved, illusory rather than substantial. Yet we have seen that it is difficult to uphold this view. From his writings there emerges a picture that corresponds better to the actual historical development than to the theoretical professions he formed early on. It is a view of the state as an active, autonomous agent from the sixteenth century onwards, pursuing its own interests by harnessing those of others to its purpose. The basic explanation is to be found in the presence of several opposed classes, allowing the government to play an active rule by mediation and divide-and-conquer.

Only during one period, perhaps, was the state in danger of being

---

[1] In modern capitalist societies matters are more complicated, not only because of universal suffrage, but also because the main classes have become strategic actors in the full sense instead of simply being dummies to be manipulated by the state. For an illuminating approach to the problem see Przeworski and Wallerstein, "The structure of class conflict in democratic capitalist societies".

reduced to a mere tool of the bourgeoisie – an organ whose actions could be explained functionally through the interests of that class. This is the period separating the two great bourgeois revolutions, that of 1640–88 and that of 1789. Broadly speaking, this was the time when the bourgeoisie was yet unaware that when rising they carried with them a class that would ultimately be a greater threat to their interests than monarchy, landowners and bureaucrats had ever been. It did not take long, however, before the first confrontations with the workers impressed on them the need to compromise with their former enemy – giving the state a new leverage and independence of action. This closing of the ranks is nowhere better described than in a passage from the *Theories of Surplus-Value*. Here Marx first comments on Adam Smith's "hatred" of the unproductive state and church officials, saying that his "is the language of the still revolutionary bourgeoisie, which has not yet subjected to itself the whole of society, the State etc.". He then goes on as follows:

When on the other hand the bourgeoisie has won the battle, and has partly itself taken over the State, partly made a compromise with its former posses-sors; and has likewise given recognition to the ideological professions as flesh of its flesh and everywhere transformed them into its functionaries, of like nature to itself; when it itself no longer confronts these as the representative of productive labour, but when the real productive labourers rise against it and moreover tells it that it lives on other people's industry; when it is enlightened enough not to be entirely absorbed in production, but to want also to consume "in an enlightened way"; when the spiritual labours themselves are more and more performed in its *service* and enter into the service of capitalist production – then things take a new turn, and the bourgeoisie tries to justify "economically", from its own standpoint, what at an earlier stage it had criticized and fought against.[1]

If we look closely at Marx's writings, it is difficult to escape the con-clusion that what in Marxist theory is supposed to be the "normal case"[2] – the subservience of the state to the interests of the bourgeoisie – is only exceptionally realized. Similarly, "the 'natural' alliance between an impatient radically-minded industrial bourgeoisie and a formative proletariat was broken as soon as it was formed".[3] An

---

[1] *Theories of Surplus-Value*, vol. 1, pp. 300–1. To be sure, this passage tries to present the bourgeoisie as the main actor in the process; but I think the substance of the analysis fits into the perspective I have proposed.

[2] Draper, *Karl Marx's Theory of Revolution*, vol. I, p. 497.

[3] Thompson, *The Making of theEnglish Working Class*, p. 195. I quote the phrase somewhat out of context, since Thompson does not use it as a general characterization of the modern period, but only with reference to England.

essence that makes such rare appearances on the historical scene cannot be that essential.

7.2. The theory of revolution

Marx's theory of modes of production (5.1) says that changes in the relations of production occur when and because they enter into contradiction with the productive forces. At that point, according to the 1859 Preface, "begins an epoch of social revolution" – new relations of production replace the old ones. According to the usual view, this social revolution is *stabilized by* the legal and institutional changes brought about by a political upheaval, or revolution in the narrower sense.[1] Pre-legal and illegal changes in the relations of production are necessarily more limited in their effect than a political revolution. The former occur only or mainly to the extent that they correspond to individual interests, and will not respond to the collective interests of a class as such. In order to realize these class interests, formal changes in the legal system of rights and compulsions are needed. Capitalism may have emerged piecemeal by the individual actions of entrepreneurs, but for its full development it needed the stable framework of law. As for communism, Marx apparently thought that incremental and local steps were out of the question, some remarks on cooperatives and joint-stock companies notwithstanding (7.2.2). The superiority of communist relations of production presupposes that communism is established on a nation-wide scale.[2]

Given the central role of political revolutions in the process of social change, it is obviously important to arrive at an understanding of their causes and consequences. Marx has little to offer by way of a systematic account. His theory of revolution must be reconstructed from scattered passages, most of which were written with an immediately political purpose. In 7.2.1 I consider his accounts of the bourgeois revolutions in the three European countries that were his constant points of reference: The

[1] I have suggested in 7.1.2 that in some cases the political change may be part and parcel of the social change, in that the process of *de facto* change may be inseparably bound up with the changes made *de jure*. See also the following note.

[2] Hence we have to ask whether the explanation of the relations of production suggested by Cohen (*Karl Marx's Theory of History*, ch. VI) refers to their stabilized or non-stabilized form. It could be the case that the pre-legal form of new relations of production were inferior (*qua* promoters of the productive forces) to the legal form of the old relations, yet that the new relations would be superior when stabilized by law. Indeed, I argue below that Marx believed this to be true of communist relations of production as compared to capitalist ones. If this is the case, there can be no autonomous economic development: either there is no development (because the pre-legal forms are not taken up) or the development is not autonomous (because the legal form is essentially involved).

English Revolution of 1640–88, the French Revolution of 1789 and the German Revolution of 1848. In 7.2.2 I consider his various suggestions about the communist revolution – what could trigger it off and how it could develop subsequently.

7.2.1. The bourgeois revolutions

With the exception of a few remarks in *The Holy Family*, Marx nowhere offers more than brief comments on the French Revolution.[1] He deals somewhat more extensively with the English Revolution, in a review from 1850 of Guizot's *Discours sur l'Histoire de la Révolution d'Angleterre*. This also offers some useful comparisons between the two bourgeois revolutions, pointing to similarities as well as differences. By contrast, the comments on the German Revolution are abundant in the extreme, but often too immersed in the details to be of analytical value. For England and France we have a bird's-eye view that does not allow us to identify the actual mechanisms and forces at work; for Germany we see the mechanism at such close quarters that the overall design is lost. These textual constraints must be kept in mind.

Marx perceived the classical bourgeois revolutions as the transition from absolute to constitutional monarchy, with a republican interregnum. "Everywhere the transition from absolute to constitutional monarchy is effected only after fierce struggles and after passage through a republican form."[2] Hence it would be wrong to focus on the transition from monarchy to republic as *the* revolution; this is only a stage in a process whose overall form is "two steps forward, one step backward". Some other similarities between the English and the French Revolutions are the following. First, in their origin they were conservative rather than innovative, especially in France:

[The] French revolution began just as conservatively as the English, indeed much more so. Absolutism, particularly as it manifested itself finally in France, was here, too, an innovation, and it was against this innovation that the parliaments rose and defended the old laws, the *us et coutumes* of the old monarchy based on estates.[3]

Furthermore, both events were characterized by a vain appeal by the king to the people. Quoting Hobbes, Marx refers to the people as "*puer robustus sed malitiosus*, a robust, but ill-natured youth, which permits no kings, be

---

[1] *The Holy Family*, pp. 118ff.
[2] Review of Guizot, p. 254. With respect to France, the constitutional monarchy is the one established in 1815, not the brief episode after 1789.
[3] Review of Guizot, p. 253.

they lean or fat, to get the better of him". Both Charles I and Louis XVI appealed to "their People" as an ally against parliament, but the people responded by beheading them.[1] This should be read in the light of the following analysis of the triangular power struggle in the classical revolutions:

As we know, it is much easier for the peoples to cope with *kings* than with *legislative assemblies*. History gives us a whole list of abortive revolts of the people against national assemblies. It knows only two important exceptions to this rule. The English people in the person of *Cromwell* dissolved the *Long Parliament*, and the French people in the person of *Bonaparte* dissolved the *Corps Législatif*. But the Long Parliament had long ago become a *Rump*, and the *Corps Législatif* a corpse. Are the kings more fortunate than the peoples in their *revolts against legislative assemblies*? *Charles I, James II, Louis XVI* and *Charles X* are hardly promising ancestral examples.[2]

The analysis is distinctly weak. The reference to "the French people in the person of Bonaparte" is ludicrous, coming from Marx. The passage says little more than that in a bourgeois revolution the bourgeoisie will come out on top. Moreover it neglects a well-known phenomenon from pre-industrial societies, the alliances between king and people against the intermediate powers.[3] Si le Roi savait! Unfortunately, many of Marx's writings on the bourgeois revolutions have this trite character.

A further common feature of the classical revolutions is that the republican phase is accompanied by the formation of communist movements. Marx refers to "the most consistent *republicans*, in England the Levellers, in France *Babeuf, Buonarroti* etc." as instances of this general proposition.[4] In *The Communist Manifesto* there is a brief comment on these "first, direct attempts of the proletariat to attain its own ends, made in times of universal excitement, when feudal society was being overthrown". In the undeveloped state of the proletariat, these attempts had to fail. They mainly produced a revolutionary literature which "inculcated universal asceticism and social levelling in its crudest form".[5] (See also 7.3.2. below.) Elsewhere the events of 1794 are also said to represent a premature bid for power by the proletariat.[6]

Marx, however, could not resist the temptation to find a *meaning* in

---

[1] *Deutsche-Brüsseler Zeitung* 12.9.1847.   [2] *Neue Rheinische Zeitung* 12.11.1848.
[3] For Germany in 1848 and the aftermath, see Hamerow, *Restoration, Revolution, Reaction*, pp. 175, 211ff. In England, such alliances came largely to an end with the eighteenth century, as explained in Thompson, *The Making of the English Working Class*, ch. 2, notably pp. 79ff. For the general tendency of the subjects to invest the ruler with far greater wisdom than his bureaucratic underlings, see Veyne, *Le Pain et le Cirque*, pp. 558ff.
[4] *Deutsche-Brüsseler-Zeitung* 11.11.1847.
[5] *The Communist Manifesto*, p. 514.   [6] *Deutsche-Brüsseler-Zeitung* 11.11.1847.

these aborted attempts. The temporary victory of the proletariat is "only an element in the service of the *bourgeois revolution* itself".[1] Elsewhere he makes the point even more explicitly: when the workers "opposed the bourgeoisie, as they did in France in 1793 and 1794, they fought only for the attainment of the aims of the bourgeoisie, even if not *in the manner* of the bourgeoisie. *All French terrorism* was nothing but a *plebeian way* of dealing with the *enemies of the bourgeoisie*."[2] Marx might well have used a phrase that he employs elsewhere, that the workers when opposing the bourgeoisie were "the unconscious tool of history",[3] the embodiment of the Ruse of Reason. As in Hegel's analysis in the *Phenomenology*,[4] there was a need to make a clean sweep of the past before the bourgeois order could be constructed. According to Marx, this task fell to the workers. No similar historical function, however, is attributed to the English Levellers.

In his review of Guizot, Marx cites the following as "immediate causes" of the English Revolution:

the fear of the new big landed proprietors created by the Reformation that Catholicism might be re-established, in which event they would naturally have to give back all the lands of which they had robbed the Church – a proceeding in which seven-tenths of the entire area of England would have changed hands; the commercial and industrial bourgeoisie's dread of Catholicism, which in no way suited their book; the nonchalance with which the Stuarts, to their own advantage and that of the court aristocracy, sold all English industry, as well as trade, to the Government of France, that is, to the only country which at that time dangerously, and in many respects successfully, competed with the English.[5]

Again the analysis is unconvincing. Of the three causes singled out, the first is commonplace; the second remains mysterious (*why* did Catholicism not "suit the book" of the bourgeoisie?); and the third has an uncomfortably simplistic sound. Moreover, these are only "immediate causes", or "precipitants" in Lawrence Stone's terminology.[6] Marx has little to say about the "preconditions" of the revolution, long-term trends that lent efficacy to the precipitant causes.

The main difference between the English and the French Revolutions concerns the structure of the alliances that carried them out:

[1] *Ibid.*   [2] *Neue Rheinische Zeitung* 15.12.1848.
[3] *New York Daily Tribune* 25.6.1853. The passage is cited more extensively in 2.4.2.
[4] Hegel, *Phenomenology of Spirit*, pp. 355ff.
[5] Review of Guizot, p. 254.
[6] Stone, *The Causes of the English Revolution*, p. 117. He distinguishes the precipitants (1629–39) from the triggers (1640–2), and cites among the latter the refusal to pay taxes, bringing about the financial bankruptcy that together with military defeat form the "two necessary preludes to a 'Great Revolution'" (*ibid.*, p. 135). Marx also mentions that the English Revolution, like the American one, "began with a refusal to pay taxes" (*Neue Rheinische Zeitung* 27.2.1849).

In 1648 the bourgeoisie was allied with the modern aristocracy against the monarchy, the feudal aristocracy and the established church. In 1789 the bourgeoisie was allied with the people against the monarchy, the aristocracy and the established church.[1]

The big riddle for M. Guizot . . . is the persisting alliance of the bourgeoisie with the majority of the big landowners, an alliance that distinguishes the English Revolution essentially from the French, which eliminated big landed property by parcellation. This class of big landowners allied with the bourgeoisie – which, incidentally, arose as early as under Henry VIII – found itself not in contradiction with the conditions of existence of the bourgeoisie as did French landed property in 1789, but, on the contrary, in perfect harmony with them. In actual fact their landed estates were not feudal but bourgeois property. On the one hand, the landed proprietors provided the industrial bourgeoisie with the labour force necessary to operate its manufactories and, on the other, were in a position to develop agriculture in accordance with the level of industry and trade. Hence their common interests with the bourgeoisie; hence their alliance with it.[2]

Stone comments on the theory of the "divided gentry", attributing it to Engels and Tawney, without noting its origin in Marx. He finds it "attractive", but adds that "there is at present not a shred of evidence to support it".[3] Moreover, the idea that the provision of labour by the landowners to the "industrial bourgeoisie" cemented their alliance is as patent a piece of anachronistic functionalism as one could imagine. Finally, the contrast between England and France is misleading, in that the "French landed property" was more integrated with "bourgeois property" than suggested by Marx.[4]

The point is not that Marx erred on this or that specific point; it would have been surprising if he had not. Rather I want to emphasize the a priori nature of his reasoning – the speculative, teleological strand in his thought. The summit in this respect is reached in the assertion that these classical revolutions "reflected the needs of the world at that time rather than the needs of those parts of the world where they occurred, that is England and France".[5] True, the statement leads up to a denunciation of the provincial character of the Prussian March revolution, and may to some extent be seen as a rhetorical device. Yet it fits in very well with Marx's general tendency to explain the classical revolutions in terms of final causes – by looking at their achievements rather than at the social forces that set them in motion.

[1] *Neue Rheinische Zeitung* 15.12.1848.   [2] Review of Guizot, p. 254.
[3] Stone, *The Causes of the English Revolution*, p. 56.
[4] Furet, *Penser la Révolution Française*, pp. 137ff. The objection concerns Albert Soboul, but applies equally to Marx.
[5] *Neue Rheinische Zeitung* 15.12.1848.

Their main achievement, according to Marx, was the abolition of feudal privilege and the creation of a regime of free competition. In *The German Ideology* Marx notes parenthetically that "Free competition inside the nation itself had everywhere to be won by a revolution – 1640 and 1688 in England, 1789 in France."[1] A slightly more elaborate statement is the following:

In the English as well as the French revolution, the question of property presented itself in such a way that it was a matter of asserting free competition and of abolishing all feudal property relations, such as landed estates, guilds, monopolies etc which had been transformed into fetters for the industry which had developed from the sixteenth to the eighteenth centuries.[2]

This, however, offers a puzzle. On the one hand we have seen in 7.1.5 that Marx perceived the "actual progressive function" of the absolute monarchy as the encouragement of trade and industry, "allowing the general rule of the middle classes". On the other hand we now see him explaining the bourgeois revolutions as directed against the absolute monarchy for the purpose of furthering that very goal. The two views are reconciled in various passages in the *Civil War in France* and the drafts of that work:

The centralized State power, with its ubiquitous organs of standing army, police, bureaucracy, clergy and judicature – organs wrought after the plan of a systematic and hierarchic division of labour – originates from the days of absolute monarchy, serving nascent middle-class society as a mighty weapon in its struggles against feudalism. Still, its development remained clogged by all manner of seignorial rights, local privileges, municipal and guild monopolies and provincial constitutions.[3]

The first French Revolution with its task to found national unity (to create a nation) had to break down all local, territorial, townish and provincial independences. It was, therefore, forced to develop what absolute monarchy had commenced, the centralisation and organization of state power.[4]

Observe that here absolute monarchy is not said to be on a par with, and a rival to, the class power of bourgeoisie and nobles. Rather it is a "weapon" of the former class against the latter. It might thus appear as if Marx had given up the idea that absolute monarchy is a form of *divide et impera*.[5] The discussion in 7.1.5 should have made it clear that matters are

[1] *The German Ideology*, pp. 72–3.   [2] *Deutsche-Brüsseler-Zeitung* 11.11.1847.
[3] *The Civil War in France*, p. 137.
[4] *Ibid.*, p. 53; see also *The Eighteenth Brumaire*, p. 185.
[5] This belies Furet, *Penser la Révolution Française*, p. 138, note 55. Furet manifestly errs when he says that "there is no trace of a reference to the State of the Ancien Regime in *The Civil War in France*". Yet I agree with the substance of his interpretation, which underlines the autonomy of the absolutist state as conceived by Marx.

more complex. It is not a question of denying the autonomy of the absolutist state, but of pointing to the self-defeating nature of these autonomously chosen policies. One would go too far if one said that this view is stated in *The Civil War in France*, but it is fully compatible with the cited texts and supported by textual evidence from other works.

Hence an interpretation of the passages cited here and in 7.1.5 could be the following. On the one hand the absolutist state finds that it is in its interest as an autonomous agent to strengthen industry and hence the bourgeoisie. On the other hand, the protection of the material power of the bourgeoisie also tends to generate its political power and hence to threaten the autonomy of the state. The state, therefore, will be somewhat halfhearted in its defence of the bourgeois interest, and at some point the bourgeoisie will feel the need to go further than the monarchy wants to do. The revolution occurs when and because the bourgeoisie has become so strong that the monarchy attempts to fetter its further development – and also strong enough to oppose that attempt. This fits in with a well-known view of revolution, according to which advance followed by retreat is the most potent cause of social change.[1] The advance generates expectations of further progress, compared to which the actual retreat is doubly disappointing.

I am not saying that these views are totally vitiated by their teleological tendency. If the bourgeoisie had been a fully class-conscious collective actor, they might well have behaved in this way. Since they certainly had some degree of organization and common resistance to absolutist encroachments, the theory may go some way towards explaining their behaviour. Yet the objection remains that Marx largely took for granted what needs to be proved, namely that the world-historical consequences of the revolutions enter into their explanation. The same holds for his analyses of the German revolutionary movement, to which I now turn.

The main difference, perhaps, between the German Revolution and the classical bourgeois revolutions concerns the role of the working people. In the English Revolution the people played no role. In the French they were an ally of the bourgeoisie, occasionally doing their dirty work for them. In the German Revolution of 1848 they could no longer be content with this role. They might still fight the battles of the bourgeoisie, but only as a stepping-stone to the proletarian revolution. Such at least is the message of the concluding page of *The Communist Manifesto*, written on the eve of the revolution:

[1] Davies, "Toward a theory of revolution".

In Germany [the Communists] fight with the bourgeoisie whenever it acts in a revolutionary way, against the absolute monarchy, the feudal squirearchy, and the petty bourgeoisie. But they never cease, for a single instant, to instil into the working class the clearest possible recognition of the hostile antagonism between bourgeoisie and proletariat, in order that the German workers may straightway use, as so many weapons against the bourgeoisie, the social and political conditions that the bourgeoisie must necessarily introduce along with its supremacy, and in order that, after the fall of the reactionary classes in Germany, the fight against the bourgeoisie itself may immediately begin. The Communists turn their attention chiefly to Germany, because that country is on the eve of a bourgeois revolution that is bound to be carried out under more advanced conditions of European civilisation, and with a much more developed proletariat, than that of England was in the seventeenth, and of France in the eighteenth century, and because the bourgeois revolution in Germany will be but the prelude to an immediately following proletarian revolution.[1]

It is difficult to know how seriously the twice asserted "immediately" is to be taken. Richard Hunt has argued, plausibly to my mind, that it represents a compromise between the real view of Marx and Engels, that the proletarian revolution would become possible only after a lengthy period of capitalist development, and those of their artisan supporters, who wanted communism on the agenda at once.[2] In any case, when the revolution was a fact, Marx initially devoted his energy to supporting the bourgeoisie, exhorting them to stand fast and not be restrained by constitutional niceties.[3] In June 1848 he ridicules Prime Minister Camphausen for saying that the "new constitution [must] evolve from the existing structure with the legal machinery offered by it, without the bond which ties the old to the new being severed".[4] In September he returns to the constitutional issue in the following terms:

"Constitutional principle!" But the very gentlemen who want to save the constitutional principle at all costs should realise first of all that at a provisional stage it can only be saved by energetic action . . . Every provisional political set-up following a revolution requires a dictatorship, and an energetic dictatorship at that. From the very beginning we blamed Camphausen for not having acted in a dictatorial manner, for not having immediately smashed up and removed the remains of old institutions . . . In any unconstituted state of affairs it is solely the *salut public*, the public welfare, and not this or that principle that is the decisive factor.[5]

This passage is important in several respects. It provides a clue to the "dictatorship of the proletariat", suggesting that it refers to a breach of constitutionalism, not of democracy (7.3.1). Also, the emphasis on the

---

[1] *The Communist Manifesto*, p. 519.
[2] Hunt, *The Political Ideas of Marx and Engels*, vol. I, ch. 6.
[3] The following owes much to Maguire, *Marx's Theory of Politics*, pp. 56ff.
[4] *Neue Rheinische Zeitung* 3.6.1848.   [5] *Ibid.*, 14.9.1848.

need to smash the old institutions foreshadows the writings on the Paris Commune.[1] The Hansemann government, following that of Camp-hausen, made the mistake of thinking that since "the old Prussian police force, the judiciary, the bureaucracy and the army ... receive their *pay* from the bourgeoisie, [they] also *serve* the bourgeoisie".[2] Finally, note that Marx rejects the idea of constitutional bootstrap-pulling, of rebuilding the political ship in the open sea. A revolution is an alternative source of legitimacy that overrides the existing constitution.

In addition to paying excessive respect to the existing constitution, the bourgeoisie betrayed their natural allies – peasants and workers. In an article on "The bill proposing the abolition of feudal obligations" from July 1848 Marx summarizes the proposals by saying that "the right to pluck the peasants' *geese* is out of date, but the right to pluck the *peasants themselves* is not ".[3] The contrast to the French revolution is clear:

The French bourgeoisie of 1789 never left its allies, the peasants, in the lurch. It knew that the abolition of feudalism in the countryside and the creation of a free, landowning peasant class was the basis of its rule. The German bourgeoisie of 1848 unhesitatingly betrays the peasants, who are its *natural allies*, flesh of its own flesh, and without whom it cannot stand up to the aristocracy.[4]

The reason for the betrayal is cited as fear that an attack on landed property might be perceived as an attack on property *tout court*. What Marx on 15 June saw as a promise of "another night of August 4" – the date in 1789 when the French Constituent Assembly abrogated the feudal obligations – never materialized.[5]

In his articles on "The bourgeoisie and the counter-revolution", Marx offers his main explanation of the hesitation of the German bourgeoisie: "The German bourgeoisie developed so sluggishly, timidly and slowly that at the moment when it menacingly confronted feudalism and absolutism, it saw menacingly confronting it the proletariat and all sections of the middle class whose interests and ideas were related to those of the proletariat."[6] Their dilemma has been well stated by John Maguire: "bourgeois power could not rest on the bourgeois class alone, and the bourgeoisie had to choose between realising their own political

---

[1] See *The Eighteenth Brumaire*, p. 139, for a similar idea, with the additional comment that the material interests of the bourgeoisie were too much tied up with the state apparatus for a dismantling to be easily carried out. As individuals, the bourgeoisie stood to gain from the state apparatus, even if as a class they did not.

[2] *Neue Rheinische Zeitung* 31.12.1848.   [3] *Ibid.*, 30.7.1848.   [4] *Ibid.*

[5] *Ibid.* 18.6.1848. Later he comments on the non-materialization of this event in issues dated 24.6.1848 and 30.7.1848.

[6] *Ibid.*, 15.12.1848.

ideals more fully than they cared to, on the foundation of a popular alliance, and reverting to the old political foundation".[1] They found themselves, in fact, in a predicament similar to that of the French industrial capitalist in 1848: "the reduction of his profit by finance, what is that compared with the abolition of profit by the proletariat?" The bourgeois retreat from power was the choice of the lesser evil.

After the defeat or the retreat of the bourgeoisie Marx urged the workers and other "democrats" to continue the revolution. His analysis and tactics are further discussed in 7.2.2. Here I only want to point out that the cited explanation of the retreat of the bourgeoisie rests on the sound methodological premise (5.2.3) that they were no less rational than himself. If *he* could foresee that, having helped the bourgeoisie to power, the workers would go on to take it away from them, presumably the bourgeoisie could also foresee what lay in store for them if they accepted that help.[2] Even if "the *Neue Rheinische Zeitung* was almost embarrassingly silent on specific proletarian demands",[3] for fear of provoking the bourgeoisie, the leading members of that class were perfectly capable of reading the signs for themselves. Marx may initially have held the belief – and acted upon it – that the bourgeoisie would behave as the marionnettes of their historical destiny, but later he came to see that they were moved by enlightened self-interest. Writing in 1847 he asserts that "the proletariat does not ask what the bourgeoisie merely *wishes* to do, but what it *must* do".[4] This may be seen as a statement that the constraints within which the bourgeoisie had to move were so strong that little scope was left for choice (1.2.1), but it can also be seen as a sign of Marx's constant tendency to fuse, or confuse, philosophy of history and historical analysis.

7.2.2. The communist revolution
In one sense this is the central theme of the present work. Earlier chapters have discussed in some detail the causes, the process and the outcome of the communist revolution as Marx expected it to occur. The *causes* include alienation (2.2), economic crises (3.4), exploitation (4.1) and the contradiction between the productive forces and the relations of production

---

[1] Maguire, *Marx's Theory of Politics*, p. 67.
[2] Similarly, Marx for some time hoped that Russia would intervene against Germany and thus ignite the revolutionary struggle (*Neue Rheinische Zeitung* 25.6.1848; see also Molnar, *Marx, Engels et la Politique Internationale*, pp. 122ff). Yet "Russia, fearing revolutionary energy, avoided confrontations" (Felix, *Marx as Politician*, p. 87).
[3] Hunt, *The Political Ideas of Marx and Engels*, p. 196.
[4] *Deutsche-Brüsseler-Zeitung* 12.9.1847.

(5.2). The *outcome* – the communist society – has been described as one permitting the full and equal self-realization of individuals (2.2 and 4.3). Some further comments on the post-revolutionary society are offered in 7.3 below. The *process* of revolution is closely connected to the formation of class consciousness (6.2) and the forms of class struggle (6.3). Yet there has not been any occasion to offer a synthetical exposition of these themes and their interrelation, nor is it easy to do so on a purely textual basis. On the one hand Marx was so persuaded of the necessary advent of communism that he neglected to explain how the various *reasons* for introducing it could also have *motivating* efficacy. On the other hand he tended to see all the defects of capitalism as so intimately connected with one another that he did not bother to sort them out from one another. I return to some of these difficulties in the concluding chapter. Here I survey some of the writings that bear more directly on the political process of revolution: its dynamics, methods and goals.

First there is a methodological point to be made, concerning the principles of textual interpretation. Many of the works in which Marx raises problems of revolutionary tactics and strategy mainly had a practical purpose. They were written during, or in the hope of, a revolution and must be understood as means to furthering that goal. This introduces two distinct biases, which I shall refer to as the *bias of compromise* and the *bias of exhortation*. They should be distinguished from the omnipresent *bias of wishful thinking* in Marx's work.[1] The last distorted his thinking, whereas the former distorted the way in which he expressed it. Yet in any given case the distinction may be hard to make – we cannot know for sure whether Marx expressed himself in an excessively optimistic vein because he fooled himself or because he was trying to encourage his readers.[2]

The bias of compromise stems from the fact that some of the works in question were written on behalf of organizations that did not always share Marx's views in every detail, hence some of the final formulations may reflect the ideas of other members as well as his own. Richard Hunt, notably, has drawn attention to the possible importance of this bias in

[1] Also I should mention *the bias of anticipated censorship*. It is known that the editors of the *New York Daily Tribune* sometimes altered the text of Marx's articles, to tone down their revolutionary fervour (see for instance *New York Daily Tribune* 1.8.1854), hence he may well have pulled his punches on some occasions. This is also argued with respect to the absence of *classes* from the 1859 Preface (Printz, "Background and ulterior motives of Marx's 'Preface' of 1859") and with respect to the anti-climactic final chapter of *Capital I* (Rubel, editorial comments in Marx: *Oeuvres: Economie*, vol. I, p. 541).

[2] Yet there are some privileged sources, such as his letters to Engels about the revolutionary prospects, that show his sanguinity to be quite genuine (assuming that he felt no need to exhort Engels to believe in the imminence of the revolution).

Marx's writings on the German Revolution. I have cited his view that *The Communist Manifesto*, written on behalf of the Communist League, reflected a compromise between the "economically determinist" position of Marx and the more "voluntarist" views of the artisan members. Hunt argues that a similar compromise is embodied in the notorious *Address of the Central Committee to the Communist League* of March 1850, often cited as evidence of a temporary Blanquist attitude (or as reflecting a permanent Blanquist attitude that Marx normally kept well hidden from the world).[1] I find Hunt's argument plausible in both cases, but I lack the historian's competence that would be needed to form a definite judgment.

The bias of exhortation is more complex. There are several reasons why a theorist of revolution, who was also engaged in preparing or fighting one, might use "the analysis of the situation" as a tool to change the situation. First, the analysis might be offered as a self-fulfilling prophecy, that is with the intent of creating a state of confidence among the workers so that they will accomplish the task defined for them. This, however, comes up against the difficulty that even if we assume a self-fulfilling prophecy, a "fixed point" of revolutionary prediction,[2] to exist, it might not be very favourable to the cause of the workers. Normally it will not be possible to emit predictions that are both self-fulfilling *and* optimal with respect to a given goal.[3] Secondly, then, the exhortation might be harnessed just to that goal, without any ambition of making true predictions. In that case, however, the workers might soon come to lose faith in the predictions, causing them to lose whatever efficacy they may have had initially.[4] Thirdly, the exhortation might be part of the process of *discovering* the nature of the situation, in the spirit of one of Blake's *Proverbs of Hell*: "You never know what is enough unless you know what is more than enough." This may be what is meant by Hal Draper when, writing about 1848, he asserts that "the revolution had to pass the bounds of practicality in order to reach them; it had to go too far in order to go as far as possible".[5] The context shows, however, that he may also have had in mind the second use of exhortation, that of demanding too much to make sure that one gets at least something. In what follows these various biases should be kept in mind, although their importance in any given case is always hard to assess.

To discuss Marx's strategy for the transition to communism, the

---

[1] Hunt, *The Political Ideas of Marx and Engels*, pp. 235ff.
[2] See my *Logic and Society*, p. 111.
[3] Haavelmo, "The role of expectations in economic theory" makes an analogous point.
[4] *Ibid.*
[5] Draper, *Karl Marx's Theory of Revolution*, vol. II, p. 274.

analysis offered by Stanley Moore provides a useful starting-point. He finds three different strands in Marx's writings: the minority revolution, the majority revolution and the reformist strategy of "competing systems".[1] He defines these strategies by the temporal order in which they propose to accomplish the following goals: the seizure of power, the winning of a majority and the transformation of society. According to the strategy of minority revolution, one should first seize power, then start transforming society and finally win a majority. We may think of this as a Leninist strategy, in which the power is used to transform the peasantry into industrial workers who will adhere to the communist goal. According to the strategy of majority revolution, one must first wait until the workers are in a majority, then (assuming that all the workers are for the revolution) seize power and use it to transform society. The strategy of competing systems starts with the transformation of capitalist society from within, uses this to win a majority in the population and then to seize power formally.

Moore is right that there are elements of all of these in Marx's work, and, I may add, of a few others as well. In my opinion, the strategy of competing systems is the least important. Although Marx refers to joint-stock companies and workers' cooperatives as "the abolition of the capitalist mode of production within the capitalist mode of production itself",[2] we should not infer that he thought this would be the main road to communism. This is pretty obvious with respect to joint-stock companies, but the case for workers' cooperatives might seem more plausible. The obstacle that will soon be found on this path, however, is that such communist enclaves within capitalism will function badly precisely because they operate within a hostile and foreign environment. Reforms that are viable in the large may work out disastrously when implemented in the small.[3] Marx says as much in his "Instructions" for the Geneva meeting of the International:

[The great merit of the co-operative movement] is to practically show that the present pauperising and despotic system of the *subordination of labour* to capital can be superseded by the republican and beneficent system of *the association of free and equal producers* ... Restricted, however, to the dwarfish forms into which individual wage slaves can elaborate it by their private efforts, the co-operative

---

[1] Moore, *Three Tactics*, pp. 60–1 and *passim*.
[2] *Capital III*, p. 438. Actually this phrase refers to joint-stock companies, but a similar expression is used for the cooperatives a few pages later.
[3] For an argument to this effect, see Miller, "Market neutrality and the failure of co-operatives". On the general idea that "a little socialism may be a dangerous thing", see Kolm, *La Transition Socialiste*.

system will never transform capitalistic society. To convert social production into one large and harmonious system of free and co-operative labour, *general social changes* are wanted, *changes of the general conditions of society*, never to be realized, save by the transfer of the organized forces of society, namely the state power, from capitalists and landlords to the producers themselves.[1]

The textual evidence for the minority revolution view comes mainly from the writings on the German Revolution, after the retreat of the bourgeoisie in December 1848. Having given up the hope of a bourgeois revolution by a broad alliance between the bourgeoisie and other progressive elements, Marx first opted for a democratic revolution without the bourgeoisie. Events had shown that "a purely *bourgeois revolution* and the establishment of *bourgeois rule* in the form of a *constitutional monarchy* is impossible in Germany, and that only a feudal–absolutist counterrevolution or a *social republican revolution* is possible".[2] After the (limited[3]) success of the democratic candidates in the elections of 22 January 1849, Marx wrote that "the petty bourgeoisie, peasants and proletarians emancipated themselves from the big bourgeoisie, the upper nobility and the higher bureaucracy".[4] The former bloc of classes constituted the democratic republican alliance. If the bourgeoisie would not itself uphold their interest, this popular alliance would have to do it on their behalf. Immediately before the elections Marx had made the following appeal to these groups:

We are certainly the last people to desire the rule of the bourgeoisie. We were the first in Germany to raise our voice against the bourgeoisie when today's "men of action" were spending their time complacently in petty squabbles. But we say to the workers and the petty bourgeois: it is better to suffer in modern bourgeois society, which by its industry creates the material means for the foundation of a new society that will liberate you all, than to revert to a bygone form of society, which, on the pretext of saving your classes, thrusts the entire nation back into medieval barbarism.[5]

As a political appeal this exhortation to self-denial is somewhat defective. Had it been successful, it would have involved skipping the stage of a bourgeois regime such as a constitutional monarchy, and moving directly to a democratic republic governing on behalf of the bourgeoisie.[6] It would

---

[1] "Instructions to the delegates of the Geneva Congress", p. 195.
[2] *Neue Rheinische Zeitung* 31.12.1848.
[3] Hamerow, *Restoration, Revolution, Reaction*, p. 189, refers to the election as "a limited but distinct victory" for the *royalist* cause!
[4] *Neue Rheinische Zeitung* 1.2.1849.   [5] *Ibid.*, 22.1.1849.
[6] It would, in fact, have involved the abdication of the bourgeoisie to political forces *left* of itself. Draper, *Karl Marx's Theory of Revolution*, vol. II, pp. 238–9 notes the partial analogy to Bonapartism.

not, however, have involved minority rule. It has been argued that this further step was taken in April, practically as well as theoretically.[1] Marx withdrew from the local Committee of Democrats, asserting that it was too heterogeneous in composition and that there was a need to devote the energies to "a closer union of the workers' societies".[2] Around the same date, the articles on "Wage labour and capital" opened by opposing the feudal–absolutistic counterrevolution to the *proletarian* and no longer to the democratic revolution.[3] To these indirect pieces of evidence one may add the explicit statement from the 1850 Address that the democratic party is "far more dangerous to the workers than the previous liberal one".[4]

Others have argued that the April withdrawal did not really mean that Marx gave up the idea of a broad democratic alliance.[5] Also, recall Hunt's argument that the 1850 Address may reflect the bias of compromise, and hence itself be compromised as evidence for Marx's views. It is not clear to me that the weight of the evidence falls neatly on one or the other side of the discussion. Let me add, however, a couple of considerations to show that Moore's trichotomy does not exhaust all the possibilities.

For one thing, at least up until April 1849 Marx believed that the revolution would occur in two stages. The first would be made by a majority coalition, that might include the bourgeoisie and the "democratic bloc", or only the latter. The second would be made by the workers that initially were a minority in the majority coalition. One crucial question is whether the second revolution would be made while the workers remained a minority, or be postponed until they had gained a majority. Another crucial question, not to be confused with the first one, is whether Marx gave up the two-stage theory and instead opted for an immediate proletarian revolution. Hence there are not two but three views confronting one another, that may be labelled (i) majority + majority, (ii) majority + minority and (iii) minority.

For another, the sequence of stages in Moore's minority scenario might be different from the one he proposes. In the early 1870s we find Marx replying to Bakunin's charge that under Marxist rule the peasants would be dominated by the urban proletariat. Marx comments that "the proletariat must, as the government, take measures whereby the peasant sees his situation immediately improved and which therefore win him over to the revolution".[6] This reverses the order of the last two steps: having taken

---

[1] Draper, *ibid.*, p. 247.   [2] *Neue Rheinische Zeitung* 15.4.1849.   [3] *Ibid.*, 5.4.1849.
[4] "Address of the Central Authority to the League", p. 279.
[5] Hammen, *The Red 48'ers*, p. 380; Hunt, *The Political Ideas of Marx and Engels*, p. 222.
[6] "On Bakunin's *Statism and Anarchy*", p. 633.

power as a minority, the proletariat creates a majority for the revolution *before* setting out to transform society. More than the other scenarios, this suffers from lack of realism, as do also the two remaining logical possibilities.[1]

Whether or not Marx believed it made sense to work for a minority revolution in Germany, he did not think that by itself it could ensure the victory for communism. The revolution would have to move westwards, to France and notably to England (5.2.3). In England there was a well-developed working class and hence no reason to work for a minority proletarian revolution. Marx certainly never entertained the idea of making a revolution against the majority of the working class, nor against a majority that would include a substantial minority of the working class. In the second politically active period of Marx's life, from 1865 to 1875, he took it for granted that the revolution in an advanced industrial country such as England would be carried out by a majority.

Concerning the goal and the methods of these struggles, Marx had to face three, interrelated problems. First, was the working class to organize itself secretly or openly? Secondly, how should it relate itself to the existing political institutions? Thirdly, would it be possible to introduce communism by peaceful measures, or would a violent revolution be necessary? The combinations of possible answers to these questions include two extreme cases: a secret conspiracy plotting the violent overthrow of the existing system, and a peaceful transition using the capitalist state to transform the system from within. Marx definitely did not hold the former view and probably not the latter, but it is not clear which of the intermediate positions can most plausibly be ascribed to him. The texts are ambiguous, and possibly distorted by the biases mentioned above.[2]

Even during the earlier period there is no evidence that Marx ever advocated the conspiratorial method. On the contrary, he strongly argued against it even at the time of the March 1850 Address – the alleged summit of his ultra-leftist deviation (or the alleged revelation of his deeply held but usually well-hidden ultra-leftist views). In his review of A. Chenu's *Les Conspirateurs* we find the following characterization of these agitators:

It is precisely their business to anticipate the process of revolutionary development, to bring it artificially to crisis-point, to launch a revolution on the spur of the moment, without the conditions for a revolution. For them the only condition for

---

[1] Logically there are two other ways of ordering Moore's stages, in both of which the transformation of society immediately precedes the seizure of power. Both are implausible: if the majority exists it need not wait to take power, and if it does not there will be no transformation.

[2] See Collins and Abramsky, *Karl Marx and the British Labour Movement*, pp. 296ff.

revolution is the adequate preparation of their conspiracy. They are the alchemists of the revolution and are characterised by exactly the same chaotic thinking and blinkered obsessions as the alchemists of old. They leap at inventions which are supposed to work revolutionary miracles: incendiary bombs, destructive devices of magic effects, revolts which are expected to be all the more miraculous and astonishing in effect as their basis is less rational. Occupied with such scheming, they have no other purpose than the most immediate one of overthrowing the existing government and have the profoundest contempt for the more theoretical enlightenment of the proletariat about their class interests.[1]

Twenty years later the point is reiterated, following an accusation against members of the Parisian federation of the International for having prepared the assassination of Napoleon III:

If our statutes were not formal on that point, the organisation of an Association which identifies itself with the working classes, would exclude from it every form of secret society. If the working classes, who form the great bulk of all nations, who produce all their wealth and in the name of whom even the usurping powers pretend to rule, conspire, they conspire publicly, as the sun conspires against darkness, in the full consciousness that without their pale there exists no legitimate power.[2]

Marx's attitude towards the use of the existing political institutions was more complex. Broadly speaking, he warned against it in the authoritarian German and French regimes, but accepted it in the more democratic English system. In *The Civil War in France* he insists that "the working class cannot simply lay hold on the ready made state-machinery and wield it for its own purpose. The political instrument of their enslavement cannot serve as the political instrument of their emancipation."[3] Similarly the *Critique of the Gotha Program* comes out against the Lassallean attempt to enlist state aid for the building of socialism. Any such aid, in fact, would be a poisoned gift: "in so far as the present co-operatives are concerned, they are of value *only* in so far as they are the independent creatures of the workers and not protégés either of the government or of the bourgeois".[4]

But if Marx had to mark his distance from the Lassalleans on his right, he also had to demarcate himself from the anarchists on his left, to steer a middle course between state socialism and the anarchist opposition to all state activities. In 7.1.4 I cited from his article on "Political indifferentism" in which he warns against the idea that any involvement with the state is contrary to the interests of the workers. To prove the falsity of this view,

[1] Review of Chenu, p. 318.   [2] "Proclamation of the General Council".
[3] *The Civil War in France*, p. 100; cp. pp. 114, 137.
[4] *Critique of the Gotha Program*, p. 27.

he cites the English Factory Acts as instances of what can be achieved by political means. In his "Instructions" to the Geneva Congress Marx also insists on this idea. In the section dealing with the need for education of working-class children, he first states that under the given circumstances it can only be realized by "*general* laws, enforced by the power of the state". He then answers the obvious objection from the left by asserting that "in enforcing such laws, the working class do not fortify governmental power. On the contrary, they transform that power, now used against them, into their own agency."[1]

In Germany, Marx was afraid that octroyed measures would involve the cooptation of the workers. In France he feared that the state machinery was so strong that, if left in existence, it would end up asserting its own interests and not those of the workers. In England and other democratic countries the state apparatus, while largely reflecting the interest of the bourgeoisie, was yet sufficiently open to make political opposition a worthwhile task. In the 1850s he had been more sceptical in this respect. He twice referred to the political opposition as a mere "safety-valve" of the system: it "does not stop the motion of the engine, but preserves it by letting off in *vapour* the power which might otherwise blow up the whole concern".[2] In the 1860s his attitude, or at least his expressed attitude, had changed. In addition to the published writings, one may consult the *procès-verbaux* of the London meeting of the International in September 1871, where he constantly criticizes the tendency to political abstention.[3]

With respect to a possible peaceful transition to socialism, the following texts may be cited.[4] In 1852, Marx suggests that the "inevitable result" of the introduction of universal suffrage in England will be "the political supremacy of the working class".[5] In an interview with an American journal in May 1871 he makes a distinction between the countries where the transition to socialism may proceed peacefully and those in which this does not seem possible. "In England, for instance, the way to show political power lies open to the working class. Insurrection would be madness where peaceful agitation would more swiftly and surely do the work. In France a hundred laws of repression and a mortal antagonism between classes seem to necessitate the violent solution of social war."[6] In his

---

[1] "Instructions for delegates of the Geneva congress", p. 194.
[2] *New York Daily Tribune* 6.5.1853; cp. also *Neue Oder Zeitung* 28.2.1855. Another sarcastic comment on parliamentarism as mere play-acting occurs in *ibid.* 26.5.1855.
[3] "Procès-verbaux", pp. 698–9, 703, 710.
[4] The following draws on Avineri, *The Social and Political Thought of Karl Marx*, pp. 214ff.
[5] *New York Daily Tribune* 25.8.1852.
[6] "Account of an interview with Karl Marx", p. 454.

speech in Amsterdam in 1872 he told the audience that "We know that heed must be paid to the institutions, customs and traditions of the various countries, and we do not deny that there are countries, such as America and England, and if I was familiar with its institutions, I might include Holland, where the workers may attain their goal by peaceful means."[1]

The language of ends and means would have seemed inappropriate to the early Marx. In *The German Ideology* we find him holding the proto-Sorelian view that "the revolution is necessary . . . not only because the *ruling* class cannot be overthrown in any other way, but also because the class *overthrowing* it can only in a revolution succeed in ridding itself of all the muck of ages and become fitted to found society anew".[2] As Bernstein and others after him, but on diametrically opposed grounds, he held that the means were not neutral with respect to the ends. In his opinion, the revolutionary means would transform the class wielding them so as to make it capable of attaining its end – while the later revisionists argued that they would have the result of incapacitating the class using them. It is hard to tell whether Marx really came to give up his earlier view, or whether he merely affected to have done so. My conjecture, for what it is worth, is that after a lifetime of revolutionary fervour Marx could hardly bring himself to start thinking in a wholly new, instrumentalist framework. The context of the International made it expedient to use this language, but it may not have corresponded to his inner beliefs.

7.3. Communism

Communism for Marx was the unity of self-realization and community – self-realization of the individual for the sake of the community. The exact institutional implementation of that ideal remains elusive, both as concerns the system of production and distribution and as concerns the apparatus for political decision-making. In 7.3.3 I offer a tentative reconstruction of Marx's Utopia, but I can hardly stress too much the difficulty of steering a middle course between vagueness and implausibility. By contrast, it is easier to make sense of his writings about the paths to Utopia. Between capitalism and the final form of communism we find both a political transition stage ("the dictatorship of the proletariat") and an economic transition stage ("the first stage of communism"). Of these, the first transition occurs before the second, if we are to take literally

---

[1] "Speech on the Hague Congress", p. 160.   [2] *The German Ideology*, p. 53.

Marx's statements in the *Critique of the Gotha Program*. The revolutionary dictatorship of the proletariat is here said to lie "between capitalist and communist society",[1] hence it must occur before the advent of "the first stage of communism" to which corresponds the principle "To each according to his contribution."[2] The political transition to communism is the topic of 7.3.1. In 7.3.2 I consider the economic transition within communism, with main emphasis on the "state capitalism" described in the *Critique of the Gotha Program*, but also with a brief reference to the "market socialism" that Marx considered and rejected as an alternative transitional form.

7.3.1. The dictatorship of the proletariat

After the exhaustive researches of Hal Draper and Richard Hunt[3] we have a fairly clear idea of what Marx meant by that phrase – and what he did not mean by it. As these authors point out, and as is clear from Marx's own writings, dictatorship at his time and in his work did not necessarily mean anything incompatible with democracy. Rather it involved a form of extralegality, a political rule in breach of the existing constitution. That violation of a constitution need not involve a violation of democracy is easily shown by using as an example the extreme case in which the existing constitution requires unanimity for constitutional change. If a majority of 95 per cent of the population take matters in their own hands and set up a new constitution requiring only a two-thirds majority, they act unconstitutionally but hardly undemocratically. Rather the latter term would apply to the 5 per cent who oppose the change. I am not suggesting that constitutional guarantees should never be respected in a democracy,[4] although we shall see in a moment that Marx did not see the need for any such guarantee. My point is simply that there must be some correspondence between how difficult it is to change the constitution and the proportion of citizens who want it to be that difficult to change it.[5] If this correspondence does not obtain, there is a need for a political revolution and a new constituent assembly.

Could one consider the dictatorship of the proletariat as a constituent assembly, in which the working-class majority of the nation democratically but inconstitutionally imposes a new constitution? In 1848 Marx refers to "the right of the democratic popular masses, by their presence, to exert a

---

[1] *Critique of the Gotha Program*, p. 28.   [2] *Ibid.*, p. 21.
[3] Draper, "Marx and the dictatorship of the proletariat"; Hunt, *The Political Ideas of Marx and Engels*, ch. 9.
[4] The need for a constitutional foundation of democracy is well argued in Holmes, "Precommitment and self-rule".
[5] Cp. my *Ulysses and the Sirens*, pp. 95–6 and, especially, my "Constitutional choice and the transition to socialism".

moral influence on the attitude of constituent assemblies"[1] – and one might consider the dictatorship of the proletariat as a more direct means for achieving the same end. This, however, would be misleading. I have quoted in 2.2.6 the passage from *The German Ideology* where Marx discusses and rejects the idea that individuals might want to "bind themselves" politically, through a constitution.[2] In *The Civil War in France* Marx emphasizes that in the political transition stage all representatives should be immediately revocable at all times. The Commune – the prime historical instance of the dictatorship of the proletariat[3] – involved "doing away with the state hierarchy altogether and replacing the haughteous masters of the people into [*sic*] its always removable servants, a mock responsibility by a real responsibility, as they act continuously under public supervision".[4] Nowhere does he show any awareness of the problems involved in such direct democracy.[5]

The dictatorship of the proletariat, then, is characterized by majority rule, extra-legality, dismantling of the state apparatus and revocability of the representatives. With one exception Marx is silent about the fate of the bourgeois minority. The exception is in the article on "Political indifferentism", where Marx offers the following caricature of the views of his anarchist opponents:

If the political struggle of the working class assumes violent forms, if the workers substitute their revolutionary dictatorship for the dictatorship of the bourgeois class, they are committing the terrible crime of lese-principle, for to satisfy their own base everyday needs and crush the resistance of the bourgeoisie, instead of laying down arms and abolishing the State they are giving it a revolutionary and transient form.[6]

Embedded in the caricature is a statement of Marx's own views, with the notable reference to the "crushing" of bourgeois resistance – a phrase that in retrospect assumes a sinister meaning that may or may not have been there from the beginning. Note that when Marx speaks of replacing the bourgeois dictatorship with a proletarian one, the term probably does not have the same meaning in both cases. The reason for calling the rule of the bourgeoisie a dictatorship presumably is that it is the rule of the minority

[1] *Neue Rheinische Zeitung* 17.9.1848.   [2] *The German Ideology*, p. 334.
[3] For evidence that Marx considered the Commune to be an instance of the dictatorship of the proletariat, see Hunt, *The Political Ideas of Marx and Engels*, pp. 308–9, 330–2.
[4] *The Civil War in France*, p. 57; see also pp. 105, 140.
[5] To my knowledge Marx never discusses the Athenian democracy that in many respects was the closest historical realization of his political ideals. For the safeguards against excessive spontaneity that developed in this system, see Jones, *Athenian Democracy*, pp. 4, 52–3, 123 and Finley, *Politics in the Ancient World*, pp. 53ff.
[6] "Political indifferentism", p. 300.

over the majority, not that it is unconstitutional. (Or, alternatively, the passage could be invoked as an argument against the Draper–Hunt reading of the "dictatorship of the proletariat".)

7.3.2. Market socialism vs. state capitalism

In the *Critique of the Gotha Program* Marx describes a first or transitional state of communism that could be characterized as a form of state capitalism. Before considering this system, I want to point to Marx's discussion of an alternative system, that in similarly anachronistic terms could be called market socialism – a system of workers' cooperatives engaging in market transactions with one another. Both systems might be said to be based on *exchange* – exchange of labour against goods in state capitalism, exchange of products for money in market socialism. To that extent they retain some of the features of capitalism, while abolishing others. Market socialism abolishes classes, while conceivably retaining exploitation and certainly alienation. To the extent that the cooperatives are unequally endowed with natural or human resources, exploitation can indeed take place by market exchange even though there is no labour market.[1] State capitalism gets rid of both classes and exploitation, while also retaining alienation.[2] Hence the choice between the two forms might appear to be simple, were it not for the possible advantages of market socialism in terms of efficiency and workers' autonomy. Be this as it may, Marx certainly preferred state capitalism as the transitional stage to full communism.

In *The Poverty of Philosophy* Marx cites at length the views of John Bray, who proposed, in the spirit of Proudhon, a system of *equal exchange* that would do away with the inequalities and inequities of the capitalist system. Marx's refutation of his views is obscure, and does not require a lengthy discussion. Essentially Marx argues that the system of equal exchange (i) is incompatible with large-scale industry and (ii) in any case would lead to the reemergence of class relations.[3] Both objections rest on the premise that the exchange would take place between individual producers, not between workers' cooperatives. They do not bear at all on a system of market socialism based on cooperatives trading with one another in the market.

---

[1] Cp. Roemer, *A General Theory*, ch. 1, summarized in 4.1.3.
[2] This is a central theme in Moore, *Marx on the Choice between Socialism and Communism*. This valuable work is slightly marred by the failure to distinguish between the two forms of exchange – between individuals, or between the individual and the society – and the corresponding two forms of the transitional stage.
[3] *The Poverty of Philosophy*, pp. 143–4.

In *The Civil War in France* Marx produces a more powerful argument against "unplanned market socialism":

[Those] members of the ruling classes who are intelligent enough to perceive the impossibility of continuing the present system – and they are many – have become the obtrusive and full-mouthed apostles of co-operative production. If co-operative production is not to remain a sham and a snare; if it is to supersede the Capitalist system; if united co-operative societies are to regulate national production upon a common plan, thus taking it under their own control, and putting an end to the constant anarchy and periodical convulsions which are the fatality of Capitalist production – what else, gentlemen, would it be but Communism, "possible" Communism?[1]

I read this passage as being critical of the idea of pure market socialism, while not being hostile to some form of decentralized decision-making, supplemented by a "common plan". Observe that this is an argument against pure market socialism on a nation-wide scale, and hence different from the argument against "dwarfish" experiments with cooperatives cited in 7.2.2. Workers' cooperatives, to present a feasible alternative to capitalism, must both exist on a large scale and be supplemented by central planning. In the absence of planning, market socialism will inevitably lead to market failures – to periodical economic crises, with the concomitant phenomena of unemployment and wastefulness. Note that Marx mentions neither the possible reemergence of classes nor exploitation as arguments against the system.

In the *Critique of the Gotha Program* Marx sets out his distinction between the first and the final stages of communism. The first is described in some detail, the second only in the vaguest outline. The first stage involves a combination of the welfare state and state capitalism. Consumption is according to contribution, with social security providing for those who are unable to contribute. Since there is "common ownership of the means of production, the producers do not exchange their products".[2] In a sense the individual sells his labour-power, but to "society" rather than to any individual capitalist, hence there is no class formation. Nor is there exploitation, since there can be no consumption without a corresponding contribution (or some inability that prevents the individual from contributing).

As observed in 4.3.3, this is not a coherent picture of any society, since the heterogeneity of labour makes nonsense of the principle "To each according to his labour contribution." Moreover, if power relations in the

---

[1] *The Civil War in France*, p. 143.   [2] *The Critique of the Gotha Program*, p. 19.

management of corporate property is a basis for class formation in capitalism and pre-capitalist society (6.1.1), it is hard to see why this would not also be true of the first stage of communism. Nevertheless, in a very stylized way the first stage of communism bears some relation to present Soviet-type economies, just as the system of market socialism has some affinities to the Yugoslav regime. Marx would have said that both systems are based on alienation, since neither fulfils the need for self-realization through creative work.

The *Critique of the Gotha Program* is not the only work in which Marx distinguishes between several forms of communism. As stressed notably by Shlomo Avineri, a somewhat similar distinction is found in the *Economic and Philosophical Manuscripts*:

> In its first form, [communism is] only a *generalisation* and *consummation* of [the relation of private property]. As such it appears in a twofold form: on the one hand, the domination of *material* property bulks so large that it wants to destroy *everything* which is not capable of being possessed by all as *private property*. It wants to disregard talent etc. in an *arbitrary* manner. For it the sole purpose of life is direct, physical *possession*. The category of the *worker* is not done away with, but extended to all men ... This type of communism – since it negates the *personality* of man in every sphere – is but the logical expression of private property, which is this negation. General *envy* constituting itself as a power is the disguise in which *greed* re-establishes itself and satisfies itself, only in *another* way. The thought of every piece of private property as such is *at least* turned against *wealthier* private property in the form of envy and the urge to reduce things to a common level, so that this envy and urge even constitute the essence of competition. Crude communism is only the culmination of this envy and of this levelling-down proceeding from the *preconceived* minimum ... The community is only a community of *labour*, and equality of *wages* paid out by communal capital – by the *community* as the universal capitalist.[1]

Unlike Avineri, I do not think Marx here describes a *stage* through which the evolution from capitalism to higher communism must necessarily pass.[2] Rather he is characterizing one of the many *proposals* of communism that have been made throughout history.[3] Far from being a necessary stage of communism, it would, if realized, be a premature form, in which "*want* is merely made general".[4]

---

[1] *Economic and Philosophical Manuscripts*, pp. 294–5.
[2] Avineri, *The Social and Political Thought of Karl Marx*, pp. 220ff.
[3] See notably the reference in *The Communist Manifesto*, p. 514 to "the revolutionary literature that accompanied these first movements of the proletariat" and that "inculcated universal asceticism and social levelling in its crudest form". For discussion, see Moore, *Marx on the Choice between Socialism and Communism*, p. 12.
[4] *The German Ideology*, p. 49.

This being said, one cannot help reading the *Critique of the Gotha Program* in the light of this much more vivid early text. In the later work Marx merely refers to the first stage in abstract terms, as communist society "just as it *emerges* from capitalist society, which is thus in every respect, economically, morally, and intellectually, still stamped with the birthmarks of the old society from whose womb it emerges".[1] We must assume that one of these "hysteresis traces"[2] is the need for material incentives, corresponding to the contribution principle (4.3.3). The early work is more specific, with the references to greed, envy and the thirst for private property. In the later work Marx asserts that the individual producer "receives a certificate from society that he has furnished such and such an amount of labour", entitling him to draw from the "social stock of means of consumption".[3] In the earlier manuscripts it is said outright that the community becomes "the universal capitalist". To the early view that "the category of worker is not done away with, but extended to all men" there corresponds the later observation that the individuals "are regarded *only as workers*, and nothing more is seen in them".[4] What Marx in his youth saw as a blind alley, he later came to see as a necessary, if transitional, stage. In between, he had come to see the importance of the degree of development of the productive forces for determining whether the establishment of state capitalism will in fact be premature, or a framework within which the communist relations can develop.

There is no hint anywhere in Marx's writings about the dynamics of the transition from the first to the second stage of communism. In particular, we cannot tell whether the general theory of productive forces and relations of production (5.1) is still supposed to apply. One might, of course, form some kind of speculative conjecture. For instance, the transition to the first stage could occur when and because the "state capitalist" relations of production permit a better *use* of the productive forces by eliminating capitalist waste and irrationality. The further transition to the higher stage could occur when and because these relations become fetters on the optimal *development* of the forces. This two-stage model would, in fact, eliminate some of the contradictions in the theory set out in 5.2.3. Yet, to repeat, there is no textual basis for the model, nor is it in any way inherently plausible. It is cited only to give an example of the

---

[1] *Critique of the Gotha Program*, p. 20.
[2] "Can socialist man be created so as not to show any hysteresis trace of his bourgeois or peasant past?" (Georgescu-Roegen, *The Entropy Law and the Economic Process*, p. 126).
[3] *Critique of the Gotha Program*, p. 20.   [4] *Ibid.*, p. 21.

kind of theory that would have to be provided to supplement the static periodization of the *Critique of the Gotha Program*.[1]

7.3.3. The society of the associated producers

We must assume that the final stage of communism has some kind of *structure*; that it is not simply a land of milk and honey in which the springs of wealth flow so abundantly that no problems of allocation of resources, coordination of activities and distribution of goods ever arise. No one could deny the Utopian strand in Marx's thinking, but I for one am loath to attribute to him a view that could only be described as a pure expression of the pleasure principle. Marx did know that the reality principle, in the form of gravitation, would drag us to the ground if we simply stepped out of the window and tried to fly. Hence I proceed on the assumption that he would not be averse in principle to a discussion of how to build aeroplanes.

Although the two may, in the final analysis, be almost indistinguishable from one another, I shall discuss separately the economic and the political organization of the higher stage (henceforward referred to simply as "communism"). With respect to the organization of production and consumption, we may employ the useful framework proposed by Karl Polanyi and further developed by Serge Kolm.[2] Polanyi argued that the circulation of goods which is indispensable in any society not based on autarkic subsistence, can be organized in three distinct ways: by market exchange; by redistribution (i.e. a flow from the periphery to the centre and then back again to the periphery after some retention at the centre); or by reciprocity (i.e. institutionalized give-and-take of goods, without pricing and without records). In modern terms, redistribution can be referred to as planning, hence we get the trichotomy of market, planning and reciprocity.

Kolm observes that any actual society will contain elements of all three systems, in varying combinations. This can be expressed visually by placing some contemporary societies within a triangle (Fig. 4) whose corners represent the extreme, or pure types.

Where in the triangle could we locate Marx's communist society? First, let us note that, according to the early manuscripts, reciprocity is a central feature of communism. In order to produce "as human beings", each

---

[1] For some reflections on this problem, see Roemer, *A General Theory*, ch. 9.
[2] Polanyi, *The Great Transformation*, ch. 4; Kolm, "Introduction à la réciprocité générale".

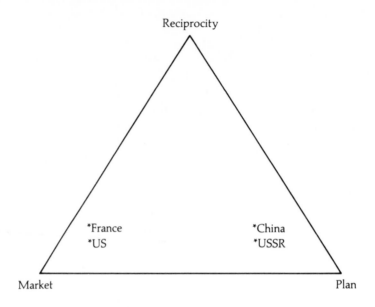

Fig. 4

individual must produce for the sake of another: "In your enjoyment or use of my product I would have the direct enjoyment both of being conscious of having satisfied a *human* need by my work, that is, of having objectified *man's* essential nature, and of having thus created an object corresponding to another *man's* essential nature."[1] It remains totally unclear, however, how this artisanal ideal can be carried out under conditions of large-scale industry. Since individual contributions to the final product cannot in general be identified, one could never know who produces what for whom. Kolm's solution is to advocate the practice of *general reciprocity*, in which each finds his pleasure in giving to, as well as taking from, "society". Besides the fact that such free-floating benevolence is not an obviously attractive notion (see the remarks at the end of 6.3.4), it is not a good approximation to what Marx had in mind. For him, the communist society was rather like the community of scholars, in which each member finds his satisfaction by offering *his* product to others, for criticism and appreciation. Identifiability then is of the essence.

[1] *Comments on James Mill*, pp. 227–8.

Next, the frequent references in Marx's work to production according to a "common plan"[1] show that there will have to a be a central agency for planning. It will at least have the task of providing public goods and of preventing cyclical fluctuations and other wasteful phenomena. Would the planning agency also have the task of regulating production in detail, that is of deciding how much shall be produced of the various goods and in what manner? I do not think it would. His various references to socially planned allocation of natural resources[2] or of labour-power[3] can be read in several ways, and do not have to imply detail regulation. They are also compatible with an agency that acts on certain key parameters of the economy, and then leaves it to the producers to choose what and how much to produce. In fact, given Marx's massive emphasis on self-realiz-ation and autonomy, it is impossible to attribute to him the view that com-munism would be a society in which all productive decisions were taken from the centre.

Clearly, the model of a community of scholars will have to go. Although today we live in a society in which technological advance makes small, decentralized and highly productive units more feasible than a hundred years ago, I cannot imagine that we will ever be able to forego large-scale activities. The productive units must be groups of individuals – call them *firms* – not single individuals. Communism, if it ever comes about, will neither be a single giant factory, nor the artisanal paradise imagined by William Morris. Given this premise, market socialism seems to follow unavoidably. The firms will have to exchange goods with one another. They can hardly do so according to face-to-face reciprocal relations, since firms are faceless. Nor can they do so according to a plan, since this has been eliminated by assumption. If we accept the trichotomy, only market exchange remains. And yet Marx was vehement in his rejection of the "commodity form". He would certainly have located communism on the right-hand line of the triangle, as far as possible from the market corner. On the other hand, autonomous workers' cooperatives would permit at least some degree of self-realization through work, while they would also be compatible with the need for large productive units. Hence one might argue that according to Marx's central values, market socialism would be the best compromise, since not all of them can be realized simultaneously and maximally. Yet, as observed earlier, Marx tended to assume that all good things go together, and that it is possible to enjoy the maximum of

[1] *Capital I*, pp. 78–9, 356; *Capital III*, pp. 120–1, 820; *Grundrisse*, p. 173; *The Civil War in France*, p. 143; *The German Ideology*, p. 83.
[2] *Capital III*, p. 120.   [3] *Capital I*, pp. 78–9; *Capital III*, p. 187.

individual self-realization *and* the maximum of productivity *and* the maximum of coordination. True, the "post-industrial society" may to some extent bring these goals closer to one another, but the gap is and will remain substantial.

I now turn to the political institutions under communism – the tasks to be performed and the way in which they will be performed. In the *Critique of the Gotha Program* Marx asks: "What transformation will the state undergo in communist society? In other words, what social functions will remain in existence there that are analogous to the present functions of the state?"[1] (The reason why these functions are analogous, not identical, is that "the governmental functions are transformed into simple administrative ones",[2] whatever this may mean.) It is possible to infer what some of these functions might be. When discussing the first stage of communism, Marx refers to three deductions that must be made from the net social product before it can be allocated to private consumption: for the "general costs of administration not belonging to production", for the "common satisfaction of needs, such as schools, health services etc." and for "funds to those unable to work".[3] He states that of these, the first will diminish and the second increase in proportion as the higher stage emerges, while nothing is said about the third, probably because they will obviously remain important. Hence the tasks of the state in the final stage of communism will include the provision of health, education and welfare services. In addition the central agency for planning will also be part of the state machinery. On the other hand, the task of maintaining law and order falls in the first category and hence will tend to disappear.

The Utopian side of Marx's thought comes out in two ways. Most obviously, there is the idea of the "withering-away" of the judicial machinery, as if communism would have neither criminals nor civil cases to be adjudicated. More importantly, there is the idea that the tasks to be performed by the state are non-conflictual. To bring out this view I shall reproduce his comments on Bakunin's *Statism and Anarchy* in the form of a dialogue. Marx's comments are somewhat ambiguous, in that it is not clear whether he refers to the dictatorship of the proletariat, the first stage of communism or the final stage. With the exception of the first comment, the text would mainly seem to concern the final, higher stage.

[1] *Critique of the Gotha Program*, p. 28.
[2] "The alleged divisions in the International", p. 50.
[3] *Critique of the Gotha Program*, p. 19.

Bakunin: What does it mean to say that the proletariat is organized as a ruling class?

Marx: It means that the proletariat, instead of fighting piecemeal against the economically privileged classes, has obtained enough strength and organisation to use general means of forcibly expressing itself in this struggle; but it can only use economic means which abolish its own character as wage-labourers, that is as a class; with its complete victory, therefore, its domination is at an end because its character as a class has disappeared.

Bakunin: Will, perhaps, the whole of the proletariat be at the head of government?

Marx: In a trade union, for example, is the executive committee composed of the whole of the union? Will all division of labour and the different functions that it entails disappear? And in Bakunin's construction from the bottom to the top will everyone be at the top? Then there will be no bottom. Will all members of the Commune manage the common interests of the enterprise at the same time? Then there is no distinction between enterprise and commune.

Bakunin: There are about forty million Germans. Will, for example, all the forty millions be members of the government?

Marx: Certainly! For the thing begins with the self-government of the Commune.

Bakunin: The whole people will govern and there will be no one to be governed.

Marx: According to this principle, when a man rules himself, he does not rule himself; since he is only himself and no one else.

Bakunin: Then there will be no government, no State, but if there is a State in existence there will also be governors and slaves.

Marx: This merely means: when class rule has disappeared, there will no longer be any state in the present political sense of the word.

Bakunin: The dilemma in the theory of the Marxists is easily resolved. By government of the people they mean government of the people through a small number of leaders, elected by the people.

Marx: Asinine! This is democratic verbiage, political drivel! An election is a political form, both in the smallest Russian commune and in the Artel. The character of the election does not depend on this description, but on the economic basis, the economic interrelations of the electors, and as soon as these functions have ceased to be political, then there exists (1) no governmental function; (2) the distribution of general functions has become a business matter which does not afford any room for domination; (3) the election has none of its present political character.[1]

This is Marx talking to himself, free from any bias of compromise or exhortation, hence we must assume that this massively Utopian construction really reflects his view. We may note the following components of the construction. (i) Marx apparently believes that in a "business matter" there is no "room for domination". This, presumably, reflects his distinction between the purely technical division of labour and that which is due to class domination (5.1.1). Yet the very fact that the two coexist

[1] "On Bakunin's *Statism and Anarchy*", pp. 634–5.

under capitalism shows that the organization of production is not determined by purely technical considerations, so that room is left for other determinants to operate.[1] (ii) Marx apparently thinks that "the distribution of general functions" shall take place by an election, not by rotation or by lot as in the Athenian democracy. Yet it is hard to see what the point would be of having an election unless there is or could be *disagreement* over whom to elect. This might or might not reflect disagreements over policy, but in any case the election would surely have a "political" character. (iii) Marx eschews a crucial question when he says that all forty million Germans will participate in the government of their Commune, without telling us how the activities of different Communes will be coordinated. The "common plan" cannot be settled as a pure business matter. (iv) Most importantly, Marx reveals a fundamental premise of his communism when he assimilates the self-rule of society to that of an individual. This is a *scale error* of monumental size and importance. Even assuming that the individual can rule over himself without any need to deposit his will in external constraints, not revocable at any given moment, the analogous assumption with respect to society is absurd.

The underlying question is to what extent there will be divergent preferences under communism. Even assuming people to be moved by altruism or a concern for the common good, they might not have a common conception of what that good is. It is a shallow conception of politics which assumes that all political disagreement must derive from the clash of individual, egoistical wills. Issues such as abortion, future generations, environmental values or regional independence command strong loyalties and generate violent conflict. Such issues are sometimes amenable to solution, in the sense of unanimous agreement rationally arrived at, but it would be absurd to set up a political system on the assumption that this happy outcome will always be produced. For one thing, *time* is a scarce resource even under communism. Sometimes decisions must be taken before unanimity has been reached, in which case the need for a procedure for aggregating conflicting preferences will make itself felt.[2]

---

[1] The point is not that technically suboptimal relations may be imposed to ensure class domination (3.3.2), but that class domination can be superimposed on the technical division of labour.

[2] For a more elaborate argument, see my "The market and the forum".

8. Ideologies

From his first writings, Marx was never content with stating his own views and criticizing those of others. In addition, he wanted to *explain* how others came to hold their erroneous views. The theories of others were not treated mainly as alternative views of the same social reality that he also studied – as legitimate if possibly incorrect explanations of society. Rather he considered them to be *part of the reality to be explained*. In 2.3.2 and 3.1.2 I have already discussed his attempt to endogenize social theories, by arguing that they are both effect and cause of the economic reality which they purport to explain. The difficulty and the interest of the theory of ideologies derives from this complex, threefold relation it posits between social thought and social reality. (i) The beliefs have society as their object – they are explanations or justifications of facts about men and their relations to one another. (ii) The emergence or persistence of such beliefs may itself be caused or, more generally, explained by social facts. (iii) The beliefs are themselves social facts and may as such have consequences for the social structure – to stabilize it or to undermine it.

Ideologies are elusive entities. Beliefs, like electrons, are unobservable: they must be identified indirectly. To ask people about their beliefs is already to interfere with them, since what we seek generally is the spontaneous, unreflective belief rather than the self-conscious answer to a question. Moreover, to believe in something is not one single, simple modality. Children may believe in Santa Claus, and yet ask their parents how much the Christmas gifts cost. Subjects may believe in the divinity of their rulers, and yet on important occasions turn to the traditional gods.[1] People may believe that they have certain beliefs, only to find out that they are not willing to act upon them. Yet beliefs cannot simply be inferred from actions. Beliefs are underdetermined by action and, in any case, people may act on the beliefs they want to be believed to hold, not on those they actually hold. For these and other reasons the study of ideologies is fraught with dangers and difficulties, provoking resignation in some, foolhardiness in others.

The Marxist theory of ideologies has had its full share of obscurantist and pretentious expositions. In addition to the usual pervasiveness of ill-founded functional explanations, this domain also offers great scope for arbitrary explanations in terms of "similarities" or "homologies" between thought and society. With some notable exceptions,[2] the practitioners in this area have engaged in frictionless speculations that have brought it into deserved ill-repute. Even more, perhaps, than other parts of Marxism the theory of ideologies is in acute need of micro-foundations. To this assertion some will respond by saying that the web of social beliefs is in principle irreducible to individually acquired and individually held beliefs.[3] As one reader of an earlier draft of this chapter wrote: "Try to *explain* English grammar this way, and you will see how misconceived this definition of methodological individualism is." I cannot attempt to reply in full here,[4] but broadly speaking my response would go as follows. True, the full set of conceptual or linguistic practices at any given moment may appear as a supra-individual entity that dominates and constrains the individual members of society. Yet, in the study of linguistic and conceptual *change* we find that the cracks in the structure appear when individuals find some of these constraints intolerable, or mutually incompatible with one another. *Pace* Saussure, I find it unacceptable that the study of structure and the study of change should be governed by different methodological principles. For some purposes it may be useful to study physiology in a different framework from that used in

---

[1] Veyne, *Le Pain et le Cirque*, pp. 248, 561, 589, 669; cp. also his *Les Grecs ont-ils cru à leurs Mythes?*

[2] Two outstanding attempts to clarify the Marxist notion of ideology are Cohen, *Karl Marx's Theory of History*, ch. V and Geuss, *The Idea of a Critical Theory*.

[3] Taylor, "Interpretation and the sciences of man".

[4] For some (comparatively brief) remarks see my replies to Charles Taylor (in "Reply to comments" in *Inquiry*, pp. 218–19) and to Anthony Giddens (in "Reply to comments" in *Theory and Society*, pp. 112–13).

embryology or pathology,[1] but ultimately they must rest on the same foundation.

Others may respond to the call for micro-foundations by viewing it as a case of premature reductionism (1.1). They might accept, that is, the argument of the preceding paragraph, and yet argue that in the present state of knowledge individual-level explanation of belief formation and belief change is unfeasible. Analogously to the procedure in 6.2.2, they might argue that the more urgent task is to establish some robust macro-correlations between social variables and belief systems. I am not unsympathetic to this reaction, but I would like to record an objection. The sheer task of establishing what *are* the prevailing systems of belief is very difficult, as just explained. To have some confidence in our beliefs about these beliefs, some knowledge about causal mechanisms seems, if not indispensable, at least extremely useful. Hence in this case establishing the data and explaining them go together, to a larger extent than is normally true.[2]

In 8.1 I set out the nature of the problem: what are the explananda of the theory of ideologies, and what are the available explanations? I also discuss the problem of the autonomy of thought, paralleling the discussion in 7.1.2 of state autonomy. In 8.2 I survey some specific mechanisms for ideological belief formation: the process of inversion whereby subject and predicate, creator and created change places with one another; the tendency to generalize from the particular to the general or from the local to the global; and the application of capitalist categories to contexts where they are out of place. In 8.3 I consider two main applications of the theory – the history of economic thought and the process of belief formation in religion.

8.1. Stating the problem

In 8.1.1 I consider the scope of the theory of ideology: what are the entities which it sets out to explain? I construe the theory so that the explananda are belief systems, including normative beliefs, but some other possible answers are also mentioned. In 8.1.2 I draw upon cognitive psychology to suggest a typology of the various explanations that could be used – "hot" or "cold" mechanisms, causal or functional explanation. In 8.1.3 I discuss

---

[1] An instructive example is again (cp. 1.1) that of Descartes, who used an atomistic methodology in his embryology and (what we would call) a cybernetic one in his physiology. Cp. my *Leibniz et la Formation de l'Esprit Capitaliste*, pp. 54ff.

[2] Cp. also Davidson, *Essays on Actions and Events*, chs. 11 and 12.

the passages, notably in *The German Ideology*, where Marx appears to deny the autonomy of thought.

8.1.1. The nature of the explanandum

I shall define the ideological in structural, not functional terms – as an entity, not a certain type of effect that one entity may have upon another. Broadly speaking (I speak less broadly below), these entities are beliefs and values consciously entertained by some individual or individuals. They are entities, that is, which (i) exist, (ii) exist in the minds of individuals and (iii) exist consciously for these individuals.

One alternative definition is to consider the ideological as a function, more specifically the function of providing legitimacy for the existing state of affairs or for the rule of a given class. On this view, as I said, we cannot speak of ideological *entities* at all, only of entities that serve ideological functions. The ideological, then, would be the non-coercive equivalent of the political, if the latter is similarly functionally defined in terms of repression. This would enable one to speak, for instance, of the "ideological functions" of the representative political system, which, by creating an "appearance of independence" or a "safety-valve"[1] to let out steam, disguises the fact that it is basically a tool for the ruling class. Or again, one might point to the ideological functions of the formal freedom of the worker under capitalism (4.2.2). My objection to this view is the same as to the analogous proposal for the state (7.1.1), namely that it preempts important substantive questions or unduly restricts the scope of the theory. A belief may be explicable in terms of class, and yet in no way serve the interest of the ruling class, as we shall see. It would go against the mainstream of the Marxist tradition were one to say that such beliefs are not ideological. This, however, is largely a terminological issue, which may be resolved in several ways (see also the comments in 1.4.4 and 1.4.5).

Some other definitions may be briefly noted. My focus will be on ideologies as mental entities. An alternative would be to understand them as institutional entities, as beliefs or values *qua* embodied in the legal system, the educational system, the church etc. Now these institutions form an important domain of inquiry, but one that was less central in Marx than it came to be in later Marxism. For instance, the question why people hold the scientific beliefs they have differs from the question why the scientific community is organized in the way it is. An answer to the

---

[1] See note 2, p. 445 for references.

latter may go a long way towards providing an answer to the former, but not the whole way. Similarly, the question why people have the religious beliefs they have differs from the question why the church is organized the way it is. Here, according to Marx, an answer to the former question is useful in suggesting an answer to the latter: if religion is explained by its useful function for the ruling class, the organization of the church is explained by its efficacy in promoting those beliefs. Yet whatever may be the relation between the mental and the institutional, I believe I follow Marx in concentrating on the former.

Also, one could define ideologies such that condition (i) or condition (iii) is not satisfied.[1] One might hold, for instance, that the *absence* of certain beliefs or values is an ideological phenomenon in need of an explanation. One of the definitions of alienation proposed earlier (2.2.5) – alienation as an objective, spiritual phenomenon – corresponds to this notion of ideology. I, for one, do not think that, once we have explained why people have the beliefs they have, there is any room left for explaining why they do not have the beliefs they do not have. One might argue, of course, that these absent beliefs are such that, if present, they would undermine the structures of domination and exploitation – and that this provides the reason why they are absent. Yet, as should be clear by now, I do not believe in the notion of society as a gigantic homeostat for repression which underlies this argument. Some of the beliefs that evolve spontaneously in class society are such that they reinforce the class structure – while others tend to undercut or transform it. The absence of certain beliefs may be condemned on normative grounds, especially if one can hold up the possibility of a society in which they would emerge spontaneously, but I do not think there is any scope here for *explanation*. By contrast, could one not include in the explanandum beliefs which are *unconsciously* present in the minds of individuals, so that we retain conditions (i) and (ii) but not condition (iii) above? I feel that this proposal is unappealing both on conceptual and methodological grounds. Conceptually, it does not seem to me that we have any clear notion of what it means to have an unconscious belief. Methodologically, the difficulties of finding out what beliefs people hold explicitly are so large that it would be ill-advised to take on the further task of identifying their unconscious beliefs, assuming that we knew what that meant.

The explanandum, then, is a set of individually and consciously held beliefs and values. It cannot, however, be any value or belief; nor the

---

[1] These suggestions are discussed in Geuss, *The Idea of a Critical Theory*, ch. 3.

values or beliefs of any single individual. In the first place, we must impose a restriction on the kinds of beliefs that constitute ideologies. I shall confine myself to beliefs and values *that have society as their object as well as their explanation.* This excludes, for instance, most of the natural sciences. (Biological theories also apply to human beings and hence, indirectly, to societies. They are therefore, in principle, open to ideological construal.[1]) Clearly, this restriction is merely one of convenience. It corresponds to Marx's intention and practice, but should not represent an obstacle to an inquiry into, say, the social origins of seventeenth-century physics. A second restriction is more substantial, and is intended to block certain lines of inquiry as likely to be infertile. It says that we should consider only belief systems that are *widely held*, in a certain society or among the members of a certain social group. Social science cannot be biography. It cannot look into the recesses of the individual mind, to find the reasons and causes that have led to the adoption of a certain belief or value. An individual may have a belief that apparently corresponds to his class position or class interest, and yet have arrived at that belief in a way entirely unrelated to this fact. Since intellectuals often go against what would appear to be the interest of their class, we should credit them with some independence of mind even when they conform to it.[2] Yet on the larger, sociological scale this possibility need not disturb us.

Marx often appears to violate the second restriction, as when he sees Malthus as the direct expression or emanation of the class interest of the aristocracy, or – more absurdly – Kant as the "whitewashing spokesman"[3] of the German bourgeoisie. He may well have been guilty here of some intellectual confusion, but I propose to understand him more charitably as explaining not the actual emergence of the views of Malthus or Kant, but their subsequent diffusion and acceptance. The study of ideologies purports to explain why many similarly situated individuals come to accept the same views, or to produce them independently of one another. It need not go into the actual mechanism of belief formation which is at work when one thinker comes up with an idea that is subsequently taken over by others. Of course, the sociological study of

---

[1] On the ideological aspect of Darwin, see Marx to Engels 18.6.1862. His letter to Paul and Laura Lafargue of 15.2.1869 shows that he was more critical towards "Darwinism" than towards Darwin. Whereas Darwin only argued from the *actual* war of all against all in English society to a similar situation in the organic realm, his later followers used his theory to argue that human society was *necessarily* subject to such struggles.

[2] Veyne, *Le Pain et le Cirque* (apropos of Cicero), pp. 468–9.

[3] *The German Ideology,* p. 195.

ideologies must appeal to mechanisms (8.2), but they can have a coarser grain than when we want to be sure that the beliefs of an *individual* are actually explained by the class interest or the class position to which they correspond.[1]

I have been referring sometimes to "beliefs", sometimes to "beliefs and values" as the object of the theory of ideologies. We may in fact talk about two kinds of beliefs – about the world as it is and about the world as it ought to be. These two kinds of attitudes are related and intertwined in many ways. In some cases they shade over into one another, as in the belief that a certain knife is a good knife. In other cases they may be functional equivalents of one another, in the sense that both may have the effect of reducing cognitive dissonance. Also, it is an important fact that beliefs about how the world ought to be sometimes shape our beliefs about how the world is – as in wishful thinking. I shall return to these matters in 8.1.2 and then again in 8.2.2.

Finally let me give notice that I am concerned here mainly with beliefs and values that enter into the determinants of action – that are in some sense and to some degree sincerely held, not just professed for the sake of appearance. Although Marx occasionally denounces an opponent for his conscious hypocrisy,[2] this belongs to a different domain altogether. To profess a belief for the sake of outward appearance *is* an action, not a mental attitude that enters into the determinants of action.

8.1.2. The nature of the explanation
There are two ways of classifying Marx's explanations of ideologies. On the one hand we may distinguish between the explanations that refer to the *interests* of the believer (or some other agent) and those that refer to his economic or social *position*. I shall refer to these as interest-explanation and position-explanation respectively. On the other hand we may distinguish, as in chapter 1, between causal and functional explanations. The two distinctions are partly overlapping. All position-explanations are causal, but interest-explanations may be causal as well as functional. A belief, that is, may be explained by the fact that it is *shaped* by interests as well as by the fact that it *serves* certain interests.

---

[1] We may have a general law stating that whenever conditions C are present, phenomenon X is produced. If in a given case C are present and X occurs, appeal to the law may be unsuccessful as an explanation, if the mechanism underlying the law has been preempted by some other mechanism also generating X (under appropriate conditions). Unless the latter is nomologically related to the mechanism underlying the law, such accidents of preemption will be rare and their possibility can be safely neglected on a larger scale.

[2] See for instance *The German Ideology*, p. 293; *Theories of Surplus-Value*, vol. 3, p. 501.

To look for micro-foundations for the theory of ideologies we have to go to cognitive psychology. Over the last decades there have developed two main types of explanation of distorted belief formation, associated with Leon Festinger and Amos Tversky respectively.[1] Festinger has proposed a "hot" theory of attitude formation and attitude change, that is a theory that explains attitudes by some motivational or affective drive. In his theory, this drive is the tendency to reduce cognitive dissonance. Tversky and his co-workers offer a "cold" theory that explains the distorted attitudes by various failures in the cognitive processing system.

The distinction between cognition and motivation enters twice into this classification. First, the explanandum may be either a cognitive or a motivational state, that is a belief about some matter of fact or a value. Secondly, the explanation may refer either to cognitive or to motivational mechanisms. Illustrative examples of the four ensuing combinations are the following. (i) A motivational explanation of motivational change is shown in the fable of the fox and the sour grapes. The unpleasant state of wanting something out of reach induces a motivation to cease wanting it. Here, of course, the "motivation" generating the change is of a different kind from the motivation that is changed. The former is a non-conscious drive, corresponding to some psychic mechanism for pleasure-seeking, the latter is a conscious desire.[2] (ii) A cognitive explanation of motivational change is offered by cases of "preference change by framing", in which our values are shown to depend on our systems for mental book-keeping.[3] (iii) The best-known motivational mechanism for cognitive change is wishful thinking, a phenomenon of overwhelming importance in human life. If is often, wrongly, considered equivalent to self-deception. The latter, unlike the former, presupposes some kind of duality within the mind – the simultaneous presence of a repressed belief and a professed belief.[4] (iv) A cognitive explanation for cognitive failures might refer to the "availability heuristic", that is the tendency to believe that the world at large is similar to the part of the world one knows.[5]

In any given case, motivational mechanisms may lead either to a change in beliefs (by wishful thinking) or to a change in values (adaptive preferences). Different persons or groups may react to the same situation

---

[1] See notably Festinger, *A Theory of Cognitive Dissonance* and Kahneman, Slovic and Tversky (eds.), *Judgment under Uncertainty*.

[2] For this distinction see my *Sour Grapes*, pp. 23ff, 111ff.

[3] Tversky and Kahneman, "The framing of decisions and the rationality of choice". See also Ainslie, "Specious reward".

[4] See *Sour Grapes*, ch. IV. 3 for further discussion.

[5] See Kahneman, Slovic and Tversky (eds.), *Judgment under Uncertainty*, part IV.

of cognitive dissonance in one or the other way.[1] Wishful thinking has obvious shortcomings, in that sooner or later the reality principle will assert itself. Acting on beliefs that are shaped by wishful thinking is not very conducive to successful goal attainment, which usually requires a correct perception of the world. Or again: acting on beliefs shaped by interest does not usually serve one's interest.[2] True, there are exceptions: sometimes one must believe oneself capable of achieving a great deal in order to get the energy or motivation to achieve anything at all.

The theme of the "benefits of bias"[3] is illustrated in Marx's explanation of the use of "Roman costume and Roman phrase" in the French Revolution. In "the classically austere traditions of the Roman Republic [the gladiators of bourgeois society] found the ideals and the art forms, the self-deceptions that they needed in order to conceal from themselves the bourgeois limitations of the content of their struggles". It is hard not to see him as citing the benefits of self-deception (he may only have meant wishful thinking) as somehow *explaining* these illusions. In fact, "the resurrection of the dead in those revolutions served the purpose of glorifying the new struggles, not of parodying the old".[4] The parody refers to Louis Bonaparte's attempt to exploit the glories of his great uncle. Marx, believing that he would fall, could hardly cite any explanatory benefits of his illusion, as he did in the case of the earlier revolutionaries. True to his functionalism, Marx seized upon the benefits of bias as the explanation of bias. In the teleological perspective the emergence of necessary conditions can be explained by that for which they are necessary conditions.

Hot and cold explanations correspond to *causal interest-explanations* and to *position-explanations* respectively. The central example in Marx involves the "material interest and social position"[5] of *classes*, further discussed in 8.2.2 and 8.2.3. A somewhat more broadly based type of position-explanation is discussed in 8.2.4. The mechanisms cited in 8.2.1 – the inversion of subject and predicate, of creator and created – are partly cognitive, partly motivational in character. The cases surveyed in 8.3 offer position-explanations as well as *functional interest-explanations*, the best-known and least well-founded of Marx's theories of ideology. Typically, they amount to explanations of the beliefs and values obtaining in a society in terms of their beneficial consequences for the ruling class. Sometimes they work in

---

[1] An instructive example is given by Levenson, *Confucian China and its Modern Fate*, vol. I, ch. iv. See also *Sour Grapes*, pp. 123ff, 154ff.
[2] Veyne, *Le Pain et le Cirque*, p. 667.
[3] For a discussion of such benefits, see *Sour Grapes*, ch. IV. 4.
[4] *The Eighteenth Brumaire*, pp. 104–5.
[5] *Ibid.*, p. 131.

tandem with position-explanations, as when the "harmony theory" of the vulgar economists is characterized both as an endogenous economic illusion and as an apology serving the interest of the bourgeoisie. Similarly, Marx's account of Christianity sometimes refers to its cognitive affinity with capitalism and sometimes to its useful consequences for the capitalist class. Also, Marx suggests that nationalist sentiments among the workers are due both to endogenous psychic mechanisms and to the benefits in terms of divide-and-conquer that they bring to the capitalist class (1.3.1). Generally, he seems to have proceeded on the assumption that there is no such thing as an accidental, non-explanatory benefit.

8.1.3. The autonomy of thought

The theory of ideologies, especially in some of its more extreme forms, raises several epistemological problems. Does the theory commit us to a denial of the autonomy and continuity of the history of ideas? Is the demonstration of social causation of an idea sufficient to refute it? Must the theory fall victim to its own thrust, as in the Liar paradox? Or does Marxism somehow have a privileged position, because of its historical mission? I shall discuss these questions mainly with reference to *The German Ideology*, since only here do they receive a more systematic treatment. I should give notice that the following remarks apply mainly to ideologies as world-views or comprehensive socio-economic theories, not to the everyday illusions of economic life.

In *The German Ideology* Marx repeatedly denies that man's mental creations can have a history of their own:

Morality, religion, metaphysics and all the rest of ideology as well as the forms of consciousness corresponding to these, thus no longer retain the semblance of independence. They have no history, no development; but men, developing their material production and their material intercourse, alter along with this their actual world, also their thinking and the products of their thinking.[1]

It must not be forgotten that law has just as little an independent history as religion.[2]

There is no history of politics, law, science, etc., of art, religion etc.[3]

The last statement is the most general, denying the autonomy not only of thought but also of politics. This comparison is pursued below. The last sentence is remarkable also in that science – presumably natural science – is included among these non-autonomous domains. The first statement, unlike the others, offers a sketch of an *argument* for the view that ideas

---

[1] *The German Ideology*, pp. 36–7.   [2] *Ibid.*, p. 91.   [3] *Ibid.*, p. 92.

have no history. It is further elaborated in Marx's comments on "the trick of proving the hegemony of the spirit in history":

1. One must separate the ideas of those ruling for empirical reasons, under empirical conditions, and as corporeal individuals, from these rulers, and thus recognise the rule of ideas or illusions in history.
2. One must bring an order into this rule of ideas, prove a mystical connection among the successive ruling ideas, which is managed by regarding them as "forms of self-determination of the concept" (this is possible because by virtue of their empirical basis these ideas are really connected with one another and because, conceived as *mere* ideas, they become self-distinctions, distinctions made by thought).[1]

Let us write A, B, C . . . for the successive modes of production, and *a,b,c* . . . for the corresponding ideas. Marx appears to argue that given the mode of production A, the corresponding set of ideas *a* is fully determined; and similarly for the other pairs. He is also committed to the view that the rise of the new mode B can be explained fully in terms of the preceding mode A, with no appeal to the preceding ideology *a*. Finally he states that the sequence *a-b-c* has a *semblance* of continuity that derives from the real continuity of the underlying sequence A-B-C. A and B, being cause and effect, have something in common. To the extent that this common element is causally involved in the production of *a* and *b*, the latter will also have some commonality that may be mistaken for real continuity. (This, at least, is one way of reconstructing Marx's argument. It rests on some rather dubious premises, but I have not been able to come up with a better rendering.)

These are highly implausible views. They are vulnerable above all to the objection that men, when constructing an image of the world, never start from scratch. They begin with an earlier image and work on it, to modify it in some direction. If the successive stages A,B,C . . . had instead been parallel stages at different planets, we would not expect to find the corresponding ideologies *a,b* and *c* internally related to one another, but we are not dealing with this case. Given the earlier ideology there are constraints on the possible ideologies that can arise with the new mode of production. A post-Cartesian philosophy had to relate itself to Descartes (if only to refute him), whatever were the economic changes that had taken place in the meantime. A Marxist response would be that a dominant philosophy in the era of industrial capitalism had to correspond to that mode of production, whoever were the dominant philosophers of the mercantilist era. A possible reconciliation would be to say that the

---

[1] *Ibid.*, p. 62.

new ideology *b* has to conform to the earlier ideology *a* as well as to the current mode of production B, that is that it will be found in the intersection defined by these two constraints. This would not have satisfied Marx in his more militant mood, since it lends to the history of ideas a continuity that goes beyond that of the underlying modes of production. Yet a theory of this kind is quite sufficient if one's main concern is to show that forms of thought have a social foundation. In the following I shall mainly consider such moderate forms of the theory – compromises between out-and-out reductionism and out-and-out internalism.

The compromise might take other forms than the one just mentioned. Instead of considering internal coherence and external correspondence as two constraints, one of them may be chosen as a constraint and the other as a maximand. I shall refer to this as *filter models* of ideologies, based on search and subsequent selection. In one filter model we assume that the thinkers of an epoch come up with various theories that satisfy the criterion of internal consistency, the further choice between which is made according to tightness of fit with the economic and social structure.[1] In another version we assume that in order to be accepted a theory must have a minimum of correspondence with the outlook of the ruling class, but that the further choice between theories satisfying this constraint is then made on internal grounds. Marx apparently held the latter view. This, at least, is a possible way of reading a famous passage from *The German Ideology*:

The ideas of the ruling class are in every epoch the ruling ideas, i.e. the class which is the ruling *material* force of society is at the same time its ruling *intellectual* force. The class which has the means of material production at its disposal, consequently also controls the means of mental production, so that the ideas of those who lack the means of mental production are on the whole subject to it. The ruling ideas are nothing more than the ideal expression of the dominant material relations, the dominant material relations grasped as ideas; hence of the relations which make the one class the ruling one, therefore, the ideas of its dominance. The individuals composing the ruling class possess among other things consciousness, and therefore think. . . . The division of labour, which we already saw above as one of the chief forces of history up till now, manifests itself also in the ruling class as the division of mental and material labour, so that inside this class one part appears as the thinkers of the class (its active, conceptive ideologists, who make the formation of the illusions of the class about itself their chief source of livelihood), while the others' attitude to these ideas and illusions is more passive and receptive, because they are in reality the active members of this class and have less time to make up illusions and ideas about themselves.[2]

---

[1] Dahl, *Child Welfare and Social Defence*, suggests that this is why the French school of criminology gained ascendancy over the Italian one in the nineteenth century.

[2] *The German Ideology*, pp. 59–60.

The first part of this passage appears to reiterate the view that ideas are totally subordinate to material production, whereas the second part asserts on the contrary that they possess some degree of independence. The latter idea is also expressed in other passages, as when Marx refers to "the struggle of the ideologists of a class against the class itself"[1] or to "the seeming contradiction between the form in which [German] theoreticians express the interests of the middle class and these interests themselves".[2] The tension between these two views closely parallels that found in 7.1 between Marx's two conceptions of the state, as instrumental and as possessing some measure of autonomy. In both cases the same solution helps to resolve the tension, namely by letting class interests appear as a constraint rather than as a maximand.

This also suggests a possible reading of another famous passage. In *The Eighteenth Brumaire* Marx warns that one must not imagine

that the democratic representatives are indeed all shopkeepers or enthusiastic supporters of shopkeepers. In their education and individual position they may be as far apart from them as heaven from earth. What makes them representatives of the petty bourgeoisie is the fact that their minds do not get beyond the limits which the latter do not get beyond in life, that they are consequently driven, theoretically, to the same problems and solutions to which material interest and social position drive the latter in practice. This is, in general, the relationship between the *political* and *literary representatives* of a class and the class they represent.[3]

If we are not to understand the correspondence between representatives and class as a mystical form of emanation, I believe the filter model proposed here is the most plausible reading. Metaphorically speaking, the class shops around for ideological spokesmen until they find someone who has both sufficient prestige among other men of ideas and views sufficiently close to the interest of the class. The filter model is one way of reconciling these two desiderata. Although they could also be reconciled in other ways, the notion that the class interest is a constraint rather than a maximand appears more plausible exegetically, and no less plausible substantively, than the alternatives.

The autonomy of the ideologists, like that of the state, is real but limited. The limits appear in times of divergence between the ideologists and the class they represent. Immediately after one of the above-quoted passages from *The German Ideology*, Marx goes on to say:

[1] *Ibid.*, p. 176.　　[2] *Ibid.*, p. 195.　　[3] *The Eighteenth Brumaire*, pp. 130–1.

Within this class this cleavage can even develop into a certain opposition and hostility between the two parts, but whenever a practical collision occurs in which the class itself is endangered they automatically vanish, in which case there also vanishes the appearance of the ruling ideas being not the ideas of the ruling class and having a power distinct from the power of this class.[1]

There is, however, an important difference between politics and ideology. The aristocratic or bureaucratic government in a capitalist society is conscious of the need not to overstep certain limits in its relations to the capitalist class. As explained in 7.1, the policies are consciously influenced by this constraint, and are liable to be changed if for some reason it becomes more imperative. Ideologists, on the other hand, must believe in what they are doing in order to have any efficacy. They may welcome the assistance of the ruling class, but typically they cannot change their views at a moment's notice if that class expresses dissatisfaction with them. In the case of a collision, either the class must find a new set of representatives, or the existing ideologists must be given time to adapt their views in a way not too incompatible with their image as truth-seekers. Hence the filter model of ideology differs importantly from the abdication model of politics. They have in common the idea that the economically dominant class can find it useful to have their political and ideological interests handled by someone other than themselves, but they differ in that the ideologists do not stand in a strategic relationship to the class, as do the political representatives.

The two cases also differ in the reasons that make the economically dominant class shy away from assuming power directly. When Marx says that the ruling class delegates ideological power because they do not have the "time to make up illusions and ideas about themselves", he offers an explanation that parallels the argument made by G. D. H. Cole with respect to the bourgeoisie's abstention from politics (7.1.4). The opportunity cost of taking time off from making money is such that they may have to satisfy themselves with less than optimal representation in other domains. This, however, was not Marx's own explanation of the political abdication. Rather, he argued in terms of the need to split the attention of the working class between two enemies, by engaging it in a two-front war against Capital and Government. Analogously, one might conjecture that the ruling class might find it useful not to be seen to have the ideological power in society, so that the suboptimal representation would actually – in a wider perspective – be optimal. Although this argument has an

---

[1] *The German Ideology*, p. 60.

unmistakably "Marxist" sound, it was not, to my knowledge, suggested by Marx.

If we accept the filter model, and reject the "emanation model" as sheer fantasy,[1] we are left with the question of the *mechanism* whereby a ruling class is able to selectively favour certain theoretical views at the expense of others. The question is most acutely seen in the model that has class interest as the maximand of the choice of ideology, but it is equally important in the model that has class interest as a side constraint. How does a ruling class make sure that the theoretically dominant ideas correspond, at least minimally, to its own "material interest and social position"? The question is not how a class selects its ideologists, but how the chosen ideologists come to acquire intellectual hegemony by virtue of the economic power of the class. Why should the ruling ideas be the ideas of the ruling class?

The lack of an answer to this question is the basic flaw in the Marxist theory of ideologies. No micro-foundations are provided to explain why the ideas that correspond to the outlook of the ruling class should gain disproportionate acceptance among intellectuals. In the case of the state, the answer to the corresponding question was given by the material interest of the government, which depends on the capitalist class for its tax base. The analogous explanation holds little promise in the case of ideologies. First, ideologists need little by way of material support. The dissemination of ideas is relatively inexpensive, because of the peculiar nature of information as a commodity. Hence on a priori grounds one may expect more pluralism in the domain of ideas than in the distribution of economic power. Secondly, privately supported ideologists are often ineffective. To act as "spokesmen", they should not be seen to be mere "mouthpieces".[2] Thirdly, state support of ideologists might well represent the autonomous interests of the state rather than those of the economically dominant class. No doubt one may think of exceptions to these statements, but they hold sufficiently generally to show that the argument from material support cannot be decisive. Nor do I know of any other way of defending the correlation.

I now turn to some epistemological questions that beset the theory of

[1] A well-known instance of this phantasmagoric mode of thinking is Borkenau, *Der Übergang vom feudalen zum bürgerlichen Weltbild*. He asserts, for instance (pp. 272, 277, 291, 353), that the philosophical and scientific theories of the seventeenth century are socially determined "in every detail", in fact "in every single line". For further comments on Borkenau see my *Leibniz et la Formation de l'Esprit Capitaliste*, pp. 18ff.

[2] The spokesmen, that is, should be independent – which is not to say that they must hold independent views. The latter requirement would only follow if the ruling class found it useful to have a less-than-optimal ideological representation, as discussed in the text.

ideologies. These concern the relation between the social causation of ideas, their well-groundedness and their truth. Broadly speaking, there is a presumption that socially caused ideas are not well grounded in the available evidence and hence a further presumption that they are false. Yet matters turn out to be more complex when we look at different sorts of ideologies and distinguish between the widely held beliefs that arise by diffusion and those that arise spontaneously and independently in the minds of many individuals.

Generally speaking, a belief is rationally caused if (i) the causes of the belief are reasons for holding it and (ii) the reasons cause the beliefs *qua* reasons, not in some accidental manner.[1] Conversely, they are shaped in the wrong way if irrelevant causes enter into their formation or they are irrelevantly shaped by relevant causes. Among such irrelevant causes we may cite the interest or the position of the believer; hence socially caused beliefs are not rationally caused. This does not, however, exclude their being rationally grounded, in the sense of being the beliefs that would have been arrived at had the believer considered the evidence rationally. It is perfectly possible to arrive through wishful thinking at the very same belief that one would have formed by rational assessment. Wishful thinking, unlike self-deception, need not imply any duality in the mind. This coincidence, however, could only arise by accident. The presumption is that the beliefs must be rationally caused to be rationally grounded.

Next, even if a belief is rationally grounded it need not be true. Rationally grounded reliefs are beliefs that have the right kind of relation to the *evidence*, not beliefs that stand in the right kind of relation to the *world*. Now of course the criteria for rational belief formation are defined by the goal of this process, which is to arrive at true beliefs. Yet even if the criteria are in general conducive to truth, they need not be so in any given case. If one is the victim of a conspiracy of coincidences that would lead every sane man to a false conclusion, the belief is not by that fact made any less rational. Conversely, even if by wishful thinking and the like one is led to disregard the evidence, one may yet by fluke arrive at a true belief. Once again, however, there is a presumption that true beliefs are rationally grounded.

Summing up, the presumptions that a socially caused belief will not be rationally grounded, and that a belief which is not rationally grounded will be false, creates a case for the falsity of socially caused beliefs. To repeat, such beliefs may well be true, like the broken watch that tells the

[1] The second clause is needed to exclude such phenomena as compensating errors. For examples, see Nisbett and Ross, *Human Influence*, pp. 267ff.

correct time once every twelve hours. The point is only that we cannot *expect* them to be true.

At this point we need to distinguish between the two cases cited earlier. Consider first a belief that arises in the mind of some individual thinker, and later by diffusion takes hold of the minds of many others because it corresponds to their material interest or social position. In that case the belief will be socially caused with respect to the great majority of the individuals holding it, and yet that does not create a presumption against its truth. To see this it is sufficient to observe that almost any belief, true or false, will correspond to the interest or position of some group or other. Human nature being what it is, the chances are good that the members of the group will adopt the belief because of that correspondence. According to the filter model of ideologies, there is no reason to think that the ideologists who first formulate the beliefs which later end up as the ideas of the ruling class are themselves in the sway of similarly irrational forces. They may be, but then again they may not.[1] True, Marx tended to suggest that Malthus and others were no less in bad faith than the class they represented, but I think we should dismiss this as a mere aberration.

Consider on the other hand the spontaneously arising illusion of every-day life, and the theories that are barely disguised expressions of these illusions. In this case the presumption for the falsity of socially caused beliefs acquires full force. Here the socially shared beliefs are only individual beliefs writ large, and there is no room for a distinction between non-socially caused origin and socially caused diffusion. It is when the theory of ideologies is directly concerned with the production of beliefs, rather than with their acceptance, that the problem of truth value becomes an urgent one.

We can thus avoid, or solve, a problem that has plagued the sociology of knowledge at least from Karl Mannheim onwards, the problem of internal inconsistency. The objection is that a theory which says that all theories are socially grounded, and hence false, must itself be socially grounded and condemned by itself to falsity. Georg Lukacs and others have tried to rebut this objection by referring to the privileged character of

---

[1] For a contemporary example we may cite the libertarian theory of justice proposed by Robert Nozick in *Anarchy, State and Utopia*. Clearly, many of those who most eagerly embrace his theory do so on non-cognitive grounds, but there is little justification for suspecting Nozick himself of having been the victim of bias. For example, his insistence on the need for a principle of rectification of past injustice would presumably horrify many of his followers, since it allows for the possibility of massive state intervention. This example also shows that a belief system does not always fully retain its identity when diffused. A class does not only select a theory; it also selects within the chosen theory which elements to emphasize.

Marxism.[1] Marxism is the theory of the proletariat, a class acting in the interest of humanity and not in its own narrow class interest. This defence seems to me completely worthless. Social causation is social causation; rational causation is rational causation; and a socially caused belief is not made any more rational by the fact that the interest generating it is that of humanity at large, not of any specific group. If Marxism is to escape the charge of self-referential inconsistency, another way out must be found. On the filter theory, it is immediately seen that the premise of the objection founders. Even if all widely accepted theories are socially grounded, this does not create any presumption against their truth if the social grounding operates via their diffusion and acceptance.

8.2. Mechanisms

The central task of the theory of ideologies must be to explain how ideas arise or take root in the minds of the persons holding them. I do not believe Marx took this problem as seriously as he ought to have done, wrongly believing that it could be sidestepped by considering the social consequences of ideologies. This is not to say that he has nothing to offer on the subject. In this section I survey several mechanisms that underlie his account of economic, philosophical, religious or political ideologies. In 8.2.1. I consider the "inversion theory" that in one form or another is to be found in all his writings on ideology. It is sometimes stated as the view that in ideologies the real subject appears as the mystical predicate and vice versa, sometimes as the (non-equivalent) view that the created appears as the creator and vice versa. In 8.2.2 and 8.2.3 I consider what in my view is the valuable core of Marx's theory of ideology. Their common theme is that *an ideology involves an understanding of the whole from the point of view of the part*, in two different senses that correspond, respectively, to the French terms "partial" and "partiel". In 8.2.2 I discuss the "hot" mechanisms which leads the members of a class to confuse their specific interests with those of society in general. In 8.2.3 the topic is the cognitive fallacy involved in generalizing locally valid relations, or believing that what may be true in *any* case can be true of *all*. In 8.2.4 I consider the "conceptual imperialism" that results from the imposition of specifically capitalist categories to pre-capitalist or non-capitalist social structures.

[1] Lukacs, "Die Verdinglichung und das Bewusstsein des Proletariats", pp. 331ff. For a devastating criticism see the chapter on Lukacs in Kolakowski, *Main Currents of Marxism*, vol. 3.

8.2.1. Inversion

Marx took over from Feuerbach the idea that religion and philosophy should be stood on their head, by systematically turning the speculative subjects – God or the Spirit – into predicates of their alleged predicates – empirical human beings. The idea is most explicitly present in the early *Contribution to the Critique of Hegel's Philosophy of Law*, but remains important in the later writings as well. The turning upside-down of the speculative propositions undoes an earlier speculative inversion – that whereby the real subjects are turned into the predicates of their predicates. This initial inversion is a mechanism for the formation of ideologies. Although Marx is not fully clear on this point, it appears to have two main subcategories: *abstraction* and *projection*. The latter is perhaps more appropriately described as the inversion of subject and object, or of creator and created. Abstraction rests on a cognitive fallacy, whereas projection appears to have a motivational basis.

The archetypal model of abstraction is Hegel's philosophy. At the most general level it rests upon the inversion of being and consciousness, the dissociation of thought from the act of thinking, of consciousness (*Bewusstsein*) from conscious being (*das bewusste Sein*).[1] In *The Holy Family* Marx entertains the reader with a heavily ironic recipe for doing philosophy in this way.[2] One starts with different fruits such as apples, pears, strawberries or almonds; distills their common essence "Fruit"; posits this abstraction as the substance of the particular fruits; and then finally deduces the latter as the "self-instantiation of the concept". Only the last step, of course, is presented to the dazzled reader – who may or may not be persuaded that the empirical fruits are only the accidents of the substance "Fruit".[3] At a more specific level, Marx argues that Hegel's political philosophy embodies a systematic inversion of subject and predicate.[4] This is asserted with respect to Hegel's discussion of the monarch,[5] of the estates[6] and especially of the institution of primogeniture that makes the owner of the land into "the property of the property".[7]

Now one may criticize the method of abstraction while unwittingly continuing to use it. Turning Hegel back on his feet was a favourite pastime of the young Hegelians, but Marx came to see that their liberation from his ways was far from complete. In *The German Ideology* Marx gives vent to his exasperation over this facile way of solving the problems of the

---

[1] *The German Ideology*, p. 36.   [2] *The Holy Family*, pp. 57ff.
[3] See also *The Poverty of Philosophy*, pp. 163ff for a similar exposition.
[4] *Contribution to a Critique of Hegel's Philosophy of Law*, pp. 11, 23.
[5] *Ibid.*, pp. 33ff.   [6] *Ibid.*, pp. 60ff.
[7] *Ibid.*, p. 106; cp. the *Economic and Philosophical Manuscripts*, p. 266.

age.[1] When Feuerbach, Bauer or Stirner demolish the Hegelian abstractions, they do so only to substitute new abstractions of their own – the Species, Man or the Unique. When "Man" is transformed from a predicate of the Spirit into a subject, he remains abstract man, a predicate of real men.[2] In *The German Ideology* concrete, individual human beings are made into the subject of history, and the abstractions are finally banished. As no other work by Marx, this book is characterized by a robust methodological individualism and a refusal to engage in speculative teleology (2.4.2).

In the *Grundrisse*, and to a lesser extent in the other mature economic writings, Marx reverted to the style of the young Hegelians. True, he is at pains to distinguish the speculative method from his own, according to which "the concrete totality is a totality of thoughts, concrete in thought, in fact a product of thinking and comprehending; but not in any way a product of the concept which thinks and generates itself outside or above observation or conception".[3] Yet the method of dialectical deduction (1.5.1) has "Capital" in the role of the self-differentiating concept, producing the many individual capitals as if by spontaneous generation.[4] The method of abstraction never lost its grip on Marx.

In what sense does the method of abstraction lead to ideologies – that is to socially grounded ideas? The answer is found in the theory of reification (2.2.6). Because of the fixation of the fluid activity of the individual into compartmentalized specialities, thinkers are separated from doers and, in the next step, thought is separated from the thinkers:

> Once the ruling ideas have been separated from the ruling individuals and, above all, from the relations which result from a given stage of the mode of production, and in this way the conclusion has been reached that history is always under the sway of ideas, it is very easy to abstract from these various ideas "the Idea", the thought etc. as the dominant force in history, and thus to consider all these separate ideas and concepts as "forms of self-determination" of the Concept developing in history. It follows then naturally, too, that all the relations of man can be derived from the concept of man, man as conceived, the essence of man, Man.[5]

In rough notes for *The German Ideology* the division of labour, itself a product of class society, is explicitly cited as the basic cause of ideological abstraction:

> *Why the ideologists turn everything upside-down.*
> Clerics, jurists, politicians.
> Jurists, politicians (statesmen in general), moralists, clerics. For this ideological subdivision within a class: (1) *The occupation assumes an independent existence owing to*

[1] *The German Ideology*, pp. 234ff, 394–5.   [2] *Ibid.*, pp. 29, 293.   [3] *Grundrisse*, p. 101.
[4] See also the self-critical remarks in *Grundrisse*, p. 151, cited in 1.5.1.
[5] *The German Ideology*, p. 61.

division of labour. Everyone believes his craft to be the true one. Illusions regarding the connection between their craft and reality are the more likely to be cherished by them because of the very nature of the craft. In consciousness – in juris-prudence, politics etc. – relations become concepts; since they do not go beyond these relations, the concepts of the relations also become fixed concepts in their mind. The judge, for example, applies the code; he therefore regards legislation as the real, active driving force.[1]

The idea of projection derives from Feuerbach. He saw religious thought, in particular, as the projection of the essence of man onto a supernatural being. In religion, man's "own nature appears to him first as that of another being".[2] The cause of this projection is basically a form of wish fulfilment: "it is not human misery *in itself* that creates the Gods, but the *satisfaction* this misery finds in the imagination, as the instrument of wish fulfilment, which creates and appropriates the *objects* of these wishes and desires; which, in effect, objectifies them, so that they *can* be appro-priated".[3] As in the psychoanalytical theory of projection, the relation of the projector and the projected is inverted. According to Freud, "I hate him" appears as "He hates me."[4] In religion, man's creation of God appears as God's creation of man. The underlying reasons are, however, quite different. According to Freud, my belief that he hates me justifies my hate of him. According to Feuerbach, God is invested with creativity because man projects his own desire to be creative onto him.[5]

The importance of this Feuerbachian analysis for the formation of Marx's thought can hardly be exaggerated. It provides the matrix not only for his theory of religion, but for his theory of politics and his theory of capital as well. The common theme in all three cases is that *man becomes the slave to his own product.* I shall pursue below the specifically ideological theme, but first adduce some passages that show how Marx came to generalize it to other domains.

In *Capital I* Marx notes that "as, in religion, man is governed by the products of his own brain, so in capitalist production he is governed by the products of his own hand".[6] Among the numerous other passages that affirm a similar view, the most striking occurs in the *Results of the Immediate Process of Production:*

[The] rule of the capitalist over the worker is the rule of things over man, of dead labour over the living, of the product over the producer. For the commodities that become the instruments of rule over the workers (merely as the instruments of the

[1] *Ibid.*, p. 92.   [2] Feuerbach, cited by Wartofsky, *Feuerbach*, p. 276.
[3] Wartofsky, *Feuerbach*, p. 216.
[4] Freud, "Über einen autobiographisch beschriebenen fall von Paranoia", p. 299.
[5] Wartofsky, *Feuerbach*, p. 322.   [6] *Capital I*, p. 621.

rule of *capital* itself) are mere consequences of the process of production; they are its products. Thus at the level of material production, of the life-process in the realm of the social – for that is what the process of production is – we find the *same* situation that we find in religion at the *ideological* level, namely the inversion of subject into object and *vice versa*. Viewed *historically* this inversion is the indispensable transition without which wealth as such, i.e. the relentless productive forces of social labour, which alone can form the material base of a free human society, could not possibly be created by force at the expense of the majority. This antagonistic stage cannot be avoided, any more than it is possible for man to avoid the stage in which his spiritual energies are given a religious definition as powers independent of himself.[1]

Observe that if ideologies are non-autonomous, the unavoidability of religion cannot be taken in the same sense as that of capital. Using the scheme of 8.1.3, the religious form *a* may be an inevitable effect of A, but cannot be an indispensable stepping-stone to *b* (or to B). We shall have to return to the sense in which religion is unavoidable, noting for future reference the strongly Feuerbachian overtones of the last sentence.

Consider next the analogy between religion and politics. In an early work, Marx notes that "just as it is not religion which creates man but man who creates religion, so it is not the constitution which creates the people but the people which creates the constitution".[2] The related idea that the representatives might come to dominate the people who elected them is affirmed in the following passage, which is buried in a footnote of *Capital I* on the importance of the capitalist farmer as a middleman:

Already it is evident here how in all spheres of social life the lion's share falls to the middleman. In the economic domain, e.g., financiers, stock-exchange speculators, merchants, shopkeepers skim the cream; in civil matters, the lawyer fleeces his clients; in politics the representative is of more importance than the voters, the minister than the sovereign; in religion God is pushed into the background by the "Mediator", and the latter again is shoved back by the priests, the inevitable middlemen between the good shepherd and his sheep.[3]

This may be read as a general argument about the delegation of political power, to the effect that the agents to whom it is delegated – whether from below or from above – soon come to wield it for their own purpose. This is consistent with Marx's insistence that in the dictatorship of the proletariat all representatives must be revocable at all times, lest they usurp the power delegated to them (7.3.1). Somewhat more tentatively, the bourgeoisie's

---

[1] *Results of the Immediate Process of Production*, p. 990; see also *Theories of Surplus-Value*, vol. 3, pp. 276, 496 and *Economic and Philosophical Manuscripts*, p. 280.

[2] *Contribution to the Critique of Hegel's Philosophy of Law*, p. 29.

[3] *Capital I*, p. 744; see also *Grundrisse*, pp. 331–2.

abdication from power to the aristocracy or the bureaucracy (7.1.4) may be seen in the same light.

Religion, capital, political institutions – these are *human objectivations that turn into alienation*, creations by men that come to dominate their makers. Marx believed that they would cease to be possible under communism (2.2.7). Against this I tend to agree with Jean Hyppolite, when he argues that alienation is, inevitably, embedded in the human condition.[1] The argument, of course, must be carried out separately for each form of alienation. The mechanisms that give rise to religious, economic and political alienation are so different that there can be no master argument that they are all avoidable or all inevitable. The similarity obtains in the end results, not in the processes that generate them.[2] For further discussion of these forms of alienation I refer to earlier chapters, notably to 2.2.5, 4.3.2 and 7.3.3.

Marx offers a large variety of explanations of the existence of religion. I postpone discussion to 8.3.2, except for the mechanism of projection that concerns us here. The following *tour de force* contains the clearest statement of this idea in Marx's writings:

For Germany the *criticism of religion* is in the main complete, and criticism of religion is the premise of all criticism. The *profane* existence of error is discredited after its heavenly *oratio pro aris et focis* has been disproved. Man, who looked for a superhuman being in the fantastic reality of heaven and found nothing there but the *reflection* of himself, will no longer be disposed to find but the *semblance* of himself, only an inhuman being, where he seeks and must seek his true reality. The basis of irreligious criticism is: *Man makes religion*, religion does not make man. Religion is the self-consciousness and self-esteem of man who has either not yet found himself or has already lost himself again. But *man* is no abstract being encamped outside the world. Man is *the world of man*, the state, society. This state, this society, produce religion, an *inverted world-consciousness*, because they are an *inverted world*. Religion is the general theory of that world, its encyclopaedic compendium, its logic in popular form, its spiritualistic *point d'honneur*, its enthusiasm, its moral sanction, its solemn complement, its universal source of consolation and justification. It is the *fantastic realisation* of the human essence because the *human essence* has no true reality. The struggle against religion is

---

[1] "Dans l'amour, dans les relations humaines, dans la reconnaissance de l'homme par l'homme, dans la technique au moyen de laquelle l'homme édifie son monde, dans l'administration politique de la cité, fût-elle socialiste, n'y a-t-il pas une représentation de soi hors de soi, une reconnaissance de soi dans l'autre qui implique une sorte de séparation, d'aliénation qu'on peut toujours tenter de déplacer, mais qui subsiste toujours?" (Hyppolite, *Etudes sur Marx et Hegel*, p. 101.)

[2] Cohen, *Karl Marx's Theory of History*, p. 125, suggests that the common mechanism at work in fetishism and in religion is that "when elements which need to be united are not united directly they are joined *ab extra* through a duplicate world of illusion". Yet this in my view is only a description of the outcome, not an indication of how it is brought about.

therefore indirectly a fight against *the world* of which religion is the spiritual *aroma*. *Religious* distress is at the same time the *expression* of real distress and also the *protest* against real distress. Religion is the sigh of the oppressed creature, the heart of a heartless world, just as it is the spirit of spiritless conditions. It is the *opium* of the people.[1]

We may note these features of this description-explanation. First, religion is a spontaneous invention of the oppressed, not an ideology imposed by their oppressors.[2] Next, the basis of religion clearly is motivational, and related to Feuerbach's notion of wish fulfilment. Unlike Feuerbach, however, Marx does not offer an explanation of the religious myth of creation. Inversion, for Marx, is the fact that man "is governed by the products of his own brain", not that he believes himself to be created by the creation of his own brain. Finally, there is a hint of an idea more fully elaborated in *The Jewish Question*, that to do away with religion one must do away with the social and political conditions that led men to invent it to compensate for their earthly misery.

The intrinsic interest of the ideas of abstraction and projection is, in my opinion, limited. They were not original with Marx, nor does he use them for explanations with much analytical cutting-edge. Yet they deserve mention because of their importance in moulding Marx's thought. Among the ideas to which he was exposed in his youth, these were perhaps the most decisive. Taken together, they amount to a theory of the alienated society in which some men, because of their exclusive pre-occupation with ideas, come to believe that ideas rule the world, while others, because of their miserable condition, are led to invent and ultimately be governed by the notion of a transcendental being. Both classes live in a world turned upside-down. Although the ultimate cause is the same, namely the division of society into classes, the proximate causes differ. The ideologists are the victims of a cognitive illusion, whereas the popular masses are the victim of their need for consolation or dissonance reduction.

8.2.2. Particular and general interest
Of the interest-explanations of belief proposed by Marx, the most penetrating is the idea that the bearers of a particular class interest tend to represent it as the general interest of society. This tendency does not necessarily lead to false beliefs. At certain times in history the specific interest of one class may indeed coincide with the interests of society at

[1] "Contribution to the critique of Hegel's Philosophy of Law – Introduction", p. 175.
[2] See Veyne, *Le Pain et le Cirque, passim*, as well as 8.3.2 below.

large, in the sense that the realization of that particular interest will also bring benefits to all but the small ruling minority. In such cases, that class obtains an irresistible momentum. In other cases, the belief in the coincidence of the particular and the general interest will be erroneous and the class will not make much headway. As noted in 8.1.3, a belief generated by a disreputable causal mechanism may well be true, even if only exceptionally. Any class tends to believe that its specific interests and those of society coincide, and it gains power in the periods when this belief is in fact true. The analogy with the broken watch that tells the correct time once every twelve hours has some heuristic value here. A social class and the corresponding political party represent a *standing offer* to the other classes.[1]

Consider first two characterizations of the petty bourgeoisie, that sincerely but wrongly believes itself to be the spokesman for interests wider than its own:

Yet, manifold as the *Socialism* of the different large sections of the party of Anarchy was, according to the economic conditions and the total revolutionary requirements of their class or fraction of a class arising out of these, in *one* point it is in harmony: in proclaiming itself the *means of emancipating the proletariat* and the emancipation of the latter as its *object*. Deliberate deception on the part of some; self-deception on the part of others, who give out the world transformed according to their own needs as the best world for all, as the realisation of all revolutionary claims and the elimination of all revolutionary collisions.[2]

The peculiar character of Social-Democracy is epitomised in the fact that democratic–republican institutions are demanded as a means, not of superseding two extremes, wage labour and capital, but of weakening their antagonism and transforming it into harmony. However different the means proposed for the attainment of this end may be, however much it may be embellished with more or less revolutionary notions, the content remains the same. This content is the reformation of society in a democratic way, but a reformation within the bounds of the petty bourgeoisie. Only one must not form the narrow-minded notion that the petty bourgeoisie, on principle, wishes to enforce an egoistic class interest. Rather, it believes that the *special* conditions of its emancipation are the *general* conditions within which alone modern society can be saved and the class struggle be avoided.[3]

The first passage affirms the presence of self-deception, the second the absence of narrow egoism on the part of the ideologues. As noted earlier, it is more appropriate to talk about wishful thinking than self-deception,

---

[1] I am indebted to Francis Sejersted for this formulation. Needless to say, I do not mean that the circumstances in which the offer is taken up by the other classes always recur cyclically.
[2] *The Class Struggles in France*, p. 126.   [3] *The Eighteenth Brumaire*, p. 130.

since the belief arrived at in this manner may be well grounded and even true, even though in the case of the petty bourgeoisie Marx believed it was not. The transformation of narrowly conceived self-interest into a vision of the general interest, by the intermediary of wishful thinking, is a necessary condition for success in politics. Only by the belief that one is acting on behalf of society will the enthusiasm be generated that is necessary for great achievements. This is the rational core of Marx's argument about the benefits of bias (8.1.2). To repeat, it is not a sufficient condition, since in addition there must exist other classes willing to rally themselves to the class as representatives of the general interest. Nor should we fall into the trap of believing that the presence of the condition is explained by the benefit it brings. The bias is necessary, not sufficient for success; and the success does not retroactively explain the bias.[1]

In a number of rather obscure passages in *The German Ideology* Marx asserts the tendency for special interests to transform themselves into an alleged general interest. Sometimes he seems to assert a two-stage process whereby private interests are first transformed into class interests, and the latter then represented as the general interest:

How is it that personal interests always develop, against the will of individuals, into class interests, into common interests which acquire independent existence in relation to the individual persons, and in their independence assume the form of *general* interests? How is that as such they come into contradiction with the actual individuals and in this contradiction, by which they are defined as *general* interests, they can be conceived by consciousness as *ideal* and even as religious, holy interests?[2]

The representative of personal interests is merely an "egoist in the ordinary sense" because of his necessary contradiction to common interests which, in the existing mode of production and intercourse, are given an independent existence as general interests and are conceived and vindicated in the form of ideal interests.[3]

---

[1] It is probably widely believed that the views discussed in this paragraph originated with Marx. If this is so (and even if it is not), it may be of some interest to note that identically the same analysis occurs in Tocqueville's notebooks for his American journey in 1831–2: "Ce que j'appelle les grands partis politiques, ceux qui s'attachent aux principes et non à leurs conséquences, aux généralités et non aux cas particuliers, aux idées et non aux hommes, ces partis ont, en général, des traits plus nobles, des passions plus généreuses, des convictions plus réelles, une allure plus franche et plus hardie que les autres. L'intérêt particulier qui joue toujours un grand rôle dans les passions politiques, se cache ici plus habilement sous le voile de l'intérêt public; il parvient même souvent à se dérober aux regards de ceux qu'il anime et fait agir. Les petits partis, au contraire, sont en général sans foi politique; leurs caractères sont entiers et empreints d'un égoïsme qui se produit ostensiblement à chacun de leurs actes; ils s'échauffent toujours à froid." (Tocqueville, *Voyages en Sicile et aux Etats-Unis*, p. 260.)

[2] *The German Ideology*, p. 245.   [3] *Ibid.*, p. 247.

Elsewhere Marx refers to it as a sign of contradiction between the forces and relations of production[1] when "the old traditional ideas of these relations of intercourse, in which actual private interests etc., etc. are expressed as universal interests, descend to the level of mere idealizing phrases, conscious illusion, deliberate hypocrisy".[2] A general expression of this idea is this:

[Every] class which is aiming at domination, even when its domination, as is the case with the proletariat, leads to the abolition of the old form of society in its entirety and of domination in general, must first conquer political power in order to represent its interest in turn as the general interest, which in the first moment it is forced to do.[3]

The last phrase seems to put the cart before the horse, when suggesting that the conquest of power is a means to the representation of a particular interest as the general interest. In his most general statement on the topic, the order of priority is reversed:

[Each] new class which puts itself in the place of the one ruling before it is compelled, merely in order to carry through its aim, to present its interest as the common interest of all the members of society, that is, expressed in ideal form: it has to give its ideas the form of universality, and present them as the only rational, universally valid ones. The class making a revolution comes forward from the very start, if only because it is opposed to a *class*, not as a class but as the representative of the whole of society, as the whole mass of society confronting the one ruling class. It can do this because initially its interest really is as yet mostly connected with the common interest of all other non-ruling classes, because under the pressure of hitherto existing conditions its interest has not yet been able to develop as the particular interest of a particular class. Its victory, therefore, benefits also many individuals of other classes which are not winning a dominant position, but only insofar as it now enables these individuals to raise themselves into the ruling class.[4]

To win power, a class must speak the language of universality and rationality, not the language of petty interests, as did the "German burghers".[5] The bourgeoisie attacked the feudal privileges in the name of all the classes that would benefit from their abolition. Marx suggests that in the process of transforming the "common interest" of the bourgeoisie into the "general interest", the latter takes a form in which the individual bourgeois can no longer fully identify with it. This, presumably, is the cause of the split between a class and its ideological representatives (8.1.3). We must assume, furthermore, that the rational and universal

---

[1] In *The German Ideology* the relations of production are referred to as "relations of intercourse" (5.1.2).
[2] *The German Ideology*, p. 293.   [3] *Ibid.*, p. 47.   [4] *Ibid.*, pp. 60–1.
[5] *Ibid*, p. 194; cp. the quote from Tocqueville in note 1, p. 484 above.

form of the ideologies is due to the tendency of the ideologists to carry ideas to their logical limits, instead of limiting them to what is useful to a particular class. To demand the abolition of some but not all privileges would have been impossible for any self-respecting intellectual. Hence it turns out that the autonomy of the ideologists – leading to more general and radical demands than the class interest in itself would suggest – actually is beneficial for the class, at least initially. In the radical phase of the French Revolution, for instance, the universality of the demands was a necessary condition for success. Later on, however, they appeared as an encumbrance and increasingly as a danger.[1] In later bourgeois revolutions (7.2.1) these dangers were anticipated from the beginning, so that the radical phase was never allowed to emerge. Hence the petty-minded – or soberly rational – attitude of the German bourgeoisie.

I should make clear the sense in which the members of a class engage in wishful thinking. Such thinking does not consist in the belief that special class interests coincide totally with the general interest. They know well enough that measures tailor-made to their interests would be more limited. Yet they engage in wishful thinking on two other counts. First, in the belief that other classes will have an interest in a generalized form of their own special interest. The petty bourgeoisie believe that the other classes have an interest in softening the opposition between capital and labour, that is in a generalized form of their own demands for debt moratorium, cheap credit and the like. The bourgeoisie believe that the other classes have an interest in the abolition of all privileges, that is in a generalized form of their own demand for the abolition of the privileges that directly concern them. Unlike the petty bourgeoisie, the bourgeoisie was proved right – not because of their superior insight, but because their clock happened to show the right time. Secondly, there is an element of wishful thinking in the belief that the other classes, joining them in the struggle for the generalized demand will not exploit the victory for their own purposes. In a single formula: wishful thinking consists in the belief that the specific interest of the class can be generalized into claims that go far enough to attract other classes and yet not so far as to render them dangerous when the claims are fulfilled.

[1] For the current state of the discussion see Higonnet, *Class, Ideology and the Rights of Nobles during the French Revolution*, especially ch. 5. On p. 180 he summarizes the Marxists' view to the effect that "the egalitarian excesses of the Jacobins were, so to speak oversights, brought into being by their need to go a bit further than they really wanted in order to secure the utter destruction of their arch-enemy, feudalism". He objects that the view is too narrowly instrumental and neglects the importance of a "moral restructuring" in Jacobin thought.

8.2.3. Local and global vision

I now turn to the "cold" or cognitive analogies of these motivational pro-cesses.[1] This is the tendency to believe that causal relations that are valid locally, or *ceteris paribus*, retain their validity when generalized to a wider context. More specifically, there is a natural cognitive tendency to believe that statements which are true from the point of view of *any* individual agent remain true when applied to the totality of *all* agents. In earlier chapters the topic has been broached several times. In 1.3.2 and in 1.4.3 the general logic of the fallacy of composition was set out. In 3.1.2 Marx's distinction between essence and appearance was understood in terms of the local–global opposition. In 4.2.2 the illusion of freedom under capi-talism was traced back to the same opposition. Hence the present exposi-tion will be relatively brief, the more so since I return to the topic in 8.3.1.

I shall cite arguments – from Marx and others – that there is a natural tendency for the exploited to believe in the inevitability of exploitation, because of this cognitive illusion. I also believe, however, that the exploiting classes can be victims of similar illusions. Cognitively based ideologies do not always operate to the benefit of the ruling classes. We may expect them to do so when the victim is an exploited class, but not when the exploiters themselves are subject to the same mechanism. Hence it is not true as a general proposition that ideologies – in the sense of beliefs derived from the interest or the position of the believer – always work to the benefit of the economically dominant class and the existing relations of production in society.

Within the framework of modern economic thought the fallacy appears in the idea that workers are not exploited if paid a wage that corresponds to their marginal product, that is if each worker is paid as if he were the last to be hired or, more to the point, the first to be fired.[2] If there are indi-vidual wage negotiations each worker can in fact be made to see himself in this light, since the employer can threaten him with dismissal and plau-sibly say that he cannot pay more than the value he creates at the margin. But not everybody can be at the margin. Since the infra-marginal product generally is larger than the marginal product, the argument is seen to break down when there is collective rather than individual bargaining. There is, of course, nothing like this in Marx, since he did not admit mar-ginalism in this form (3.2.1). He did, however, admit economies of scale that can give rise to an analogous phenomenon:

---

[1] This subsection draws heavily on my *Sour Grapes*, ch. IV. 2.
[2] For this neoclassical theory of exploitation see Bronfenbrenner, *Income Distribution Theory*, ch. 8 and my "Exploring exploitation".

The labourer is the owner of his labour-power until he has done bargaining for its sale with the capitalist; and he can sell no more than what he has – i.e. his individual, isolated labour-power. This state of things is in no way altered by the fact that the capitalist, instead of buying the labour-power of one man, buys that of 100, and enters into separate contracts with 100 unconnected men instead of with one. He is at liberty to set the 100 men to work without letting them co-operate. He pays them the value of 100 independent labour-powers, but he does not pay for the combined labour-power of the hundred. Being independent of each other, the labourers are isolated persons, who enter into relations with the capitalist, but not with one another.[1]

Here each worker is paid as if he were the *first* to be hired, that is according to what he could produce on his own without the cooperation of the other workers. Since a multiple of workers can produce more than the same multiple of what an individual worker can produce, the surplus "appears as a power with which capital is endowed by Nature – a productive power that is immanent in capital".[2] The worker, that is, is led to generalize his individual productivity to all workers, and to impute the remaining product to "capital". This provides an apparent justification for the right of capital to earn a profit, and leads the worker to accept the exploitation to which he is subject.

Following the discussion in 6.2.3, we may point to a clear political analogy of this mechanism. Since each worker is often dissuaded from protest by the loss from unilateralism, social change may never get off the ground. Paul Veyne has argued, similarly, that in classical antiquity any dependent man had to believe that he owed his security and his living to his master: "I owe my living and my existence to this master by the grace of God, for what would become of me without him, and that great domain which he owns and on which I live?"[3] The most despised of all was the Roman *plebs*, "parce que, n'étant à personne, elle n'est rien".[4] Since I would be worse off without a master, it follows on this logic that a society without masters would be intolerable, for who would then provide employment and protection? A similar optical illusion accounts for the view that feudalism was a voluntary and mutually beneficial arrangement between the lord and the serfs, the former providing protection in exchange for goods and labour services.[5] The impression of a voluntary and rational arrangement disappears when one observes that the lord provided protection mainly against other lords, much as a gangster can

---

[1] *Capital I*, pp. 332–3.   [2] *Ibid.*   [3] Veyne, *Le Pain et le Cirque*, p. 554.
[4] *Ibid.*, p. 696.
[5] This idea is argued in North and Thomas, "The rise and fall of the manorial system" (but retracted in North, *Structure and Change in Economic History*, p. 130).

justify his protection racket by pointing to the threat from rival gangsters. Feudalism, that is, may well have been a Nash equilibrium, in the sense that for each community subordination to the lord was optimal given that everyone else behaved similarly. Yet insubordination would also have been an equilibrium, for if all communities refused to sustain their lords there would be no predators to fear and no need for protection.[1]

Marx argues that the capitalists were victims of similar illusions. As noted in 2.3.2, money fetishism derives from an erroneous belief that the choice which is open to *any* individual capitalist – between investing his capital productively and using it as interest-bearing capital – is also open to *all* of them taken simultaneously:

> [The individual capitalist] has the choice of making use of his capital by lending it out as interest-bearing capital, or of expanding its value on his own by using it as productive capital, regardless of whether it exists as money-capital from the very first, or whether it still has to be converted into money-capital. But to apply it to the total capital of society, as some vulgar economists do, and to go so far as to define it as the cause of profit, is, of course, preposterous. The idea of converting all the capital into money-capital, without there being people who buy and put to use means of production, which make up the total capital outside of a relatively small portion of it existing in money, is, of course, sheer nonsense. It would be still more absurd to presume that capital would yield interest on the basis of capitalist production without performing any productive function, i.e. without creating surplus-value, of which interest is just a part; that the capitalist mode of production would run its course without capitalist production. If an untowardly large section of capitalists were to convert their capital into money-capital, the result would be a frightful depreciation of money-capital and a frightful fall in the rate of interest; many would at once face the impossibility of living on their interest, and would hence be compelled to reconvert into industrial capitalists. But we repeat that it is a fact for the individual capitalist.[2]

Although the view that money might generate profit independently of production is indeed preposterous, it was the foundation of mercantilist reasoning for a long time. We find the seventeenth-century cameralists arguing that wars would never run an economy down so long as the money remained in the country, as if soldiers could be fed on gold and silver.[3] According to Eli Heckscher, this mode of thinking even survived among German economists during World War I.[4] In 8.3.1 I discuss the related mercantilist fallacy that profit arises by the buying and selling of

---

[1] Although there would be no free-rider problem in a society without feudal lords, it would arise in the process of getting rid of them.

[2] *Capital III*, pp. 377–8.

[3] See for instance the texts by Leibniz quoted in my *Leibniz et la Formation de l'Esprit Capitaliste*, p. 115.

[4] Heckscher, *Mercantilism*, vol. II, p. 202.

commodities, based on the same inference that what is possible in any individual case could be true in all cases simultaneously. Clearly, these are illusions that, while arising spontaneously in the mind of the individual capitalist, are in no way beneficial for the class of capitalists. To the extent that they are made the basis of policy, they could well be extremely harmful, as in the mercantilist case.

8.2.4. Conceptual imperialism

Like the preceding, this mechanism also corresponds to a position-explanation of social thought. The position in this case is not class, but a somewhat broader standpoint. By "conceptual imperialism" I shall mean the tendency of people who live in one society to use categories that correspond to the main structures of that society, to understand the social structure of other societies or secondary structures within the same society. The phenomenon is related to ethnocentrism and anachronism, but also covers the case of "internal colonialism" on the cognitive level. Although most of the cases to be discussed refer to capitalism, the tendency is of course quite universal. Marx himself refers to feudalism, and today we may observe that Marx's analysis of Western history has become a conceptual strait-jacket for the study of much of non-Western history.[1] For convenience I shall distinguish between four subvarieties, depending on whether the imperialism is outward or inward in space, backward or forward in time.

Sometimes conceptual imperialism is accompanied by imperialism proper, as in the ethnocentric approach of the British to their colonies. The best-known example is perhaps the difficulties they met when having to decide whether the Indian cultivators of the land paid a tax to the state or rent to private landowners. In an article from 1858 Marx states the problem thus: "The great point in this controversy is, what is the exact position which the zemindars, talukdars or sirdars, so called, hold in the economical system of India? Are they properly to be considered as landed proprietors, or as mere tax-gatherers?"[2] He goes on to argue that the village corporation was the real owner, and that the "zemindars and talukdars were in their origin nothing but officers of the Government, appointed to look after, to collect, and to pay over to the prince the assessment due from the village". This progressive view was also defended by Lord Canning, then Governor-General of India and author of a

---

[1] See notably Black (ed.), *Rewriting Russian History* and Feuerwerker (ed.), *History in Communist China*.
[2] *New York Daily Tribune* 7.6.1858.

proclamation that was the object of Marx's article. It was opposed by the Derby ministry, which insisted "on the sacredness of vested rights and the importance of upholding an aristocratic landed interest". Marx comments that here "is one of the greatest inconveniences and difficulties of the government of India from England, that views of Indian questions are liable to be influenced by purely English prejudices or sentiments, applied to a state of society and a condition of things to which they have in fact very little real pertinency". As later noted by Max Weber, the Indian "landed proprietors" only emerged when the British made them responsible for the payment of taxes, that is treated them as landed proprietors.[1]

Instances of "internal colonialism" occur when capitalist categories are applied to non-capitalist economic sectors in a predominantly capitalist society. A passage from the *Theories of Surplus-Value* states the tendency with exemplary precision:

[Here] we come up against a peculiarity that is characteristic of a society in which one definite mode of production predominates, even though not all productive relations have been subordinated to it. In feudal society, for example (as we can best observe in England because the system of feudalism was introduced here from Normandy ready made and its form was impressed on what was in many respects a different social foundation), relations which were far removed from the nature of feudalism was given a feudal form; for example, simple money relations in which there was no trace of mutual personal service as between lord and vassal. It is for instance a fiction that the small peasant held his land in fief. It is exactly the same in the capitalist mode of production. The independent peasant or handicraftsman is cut up into two persons. As owner of the means of production he is capitalist; as labourer he is his own wage-labourer. As capitalist he therefore pays himself his wages and draws his profit on his capital; that is to say, he exploits himself as wage-labourer, and pays himself, in the surplus-value, the tribute that labour owes to capital. Perhaps he also pays himself a third portion as landowner (rent), in exactly the same way, as we shall see later, that the industrial capitalist, when he works with his own capital, pays himself interest, regarding this as something which he owes himself not as industrial capitalist, but *qua* capitalist pure and simple.

The *determinate social character* of the means of production in capitalist production – expressing a particular *production relation* – has so grown together with, and in the mode of thought of bourgeois society is so inseparable from, the material existence of these means of production, as means of production, that the same determinateness (categorical determinateness) is assumed even where the relation is in direct contradiction to it. The means of production become capital only in so far as they have become separated from the labourer and confront labour as an independent power. But in the case referred to the producer – the labourer – is the possessor, the owner, of his means of production. They are therefore not capital,

---

[1] Weber, "Hinduismus und Buddhismus", p. 70.

any more than in relation to them he is a wage-labourer. Nevertheless they are looked on as capital, and he himself is split in two, so that *he*, as capitalist, employs himself as wage-labourer ... *Separation* appears as the normal relation in this society.[1]

Marx here argues that the application of capitalist categories to the independent artisan or peasant is an ideological imposition of an already ideological view. The notion that the means of production are inherently capital is an ideological illusion that arises out of the capitalist mode of production itself.[2] It is an illusion, and hence cognitively inadequate; but an endogenous illusion, and hence in some other sense adequate to the mode of production. Applied to non-capitalist enclaves in the capitalist economy, it does not even have the latter kind of adequacy.

The understanding of the past in terms of the present can lead to a Whig interpretation of history, according to which past events are interpreted exclusively as stepping-stones to the present. It can also, however, lead to an over-assimilation of the past to the present – to anachronism rather than teleology. Marx deplores, for instance, the tendency of historians such as Mommsen to find capitalism in classical antiquity.[3] (From Weber to Finley the dangers of anachronism have been stressed even more strongly than Marx did, so that he himself has been included among the proponents of "modernism".[4]) Also, many of his strictures on Henry Maine refer to his tendency to look at ancient society through modern English categories.[5]

Hobbes observed that "No man can have in his mind a conception of the future, for the future is not yet. But of our conceptions of the past, we make a future."[6] Whence the apparently conservative character of many revolutions, a fact noted by Marx in his review of Guizot's book on the English Revolution.[7] In *The Eighteenth Brumaire* he notes that "Cromwell and the English people had borrowed speech, passions and illusions from the Old Testament for their bourgeois revolution".[8] In this work he also makes the general point that men have to do with the conceptual luggage they carry with them, even at the very moment they grope around for a way to jettison it:

[1] *Theories of Surplus-Value*, vol. 1, pp. 407ff.   [2] *Capital III*, ch. 48, e.g. p. 824.
[3] *Capital I*, p. 168; *Capital III*, p. 787. Marx suggests, however, that they erred as much by an incorrect understanding of capitalism as by an excessively capitalist understanding of antiquity.
[4] Finley, *The Ancient Economy*, pp. 49–50; see also 6.1.2 above.
[5] *Ethnological Notebooks*, pp. 308–9.
[6] Cited by Stone, *The Causes of the English Revolution*, p. 51.
[7] Review of Guizot, pp. 252–3.   [8] *The Eighteenth Brumaire*, p. 105.

Men make their own history, but they do not make it just as they please; they do not make it under circumstances chosen by themselves, but under circumstances directly encountered, given and transmitted from the past. The tradition of all the dead generations weighs like a nightmare on the brain of the living. And just when they seem engaged in revolutionising themselves and things, in creating something that has never yet existed, precisely in such periods of revolutionary crises they anxiously conjure up the spirits of the past to their service and borrow from them names, battle-cries and costumes in order to present the new scene of world history in this time-honoured disguise and this borrowed language. Thus Luther donned the mask of the Apostle Paul, the revolution of 1789 to 1814 draped itself alternately as the Roman Republic and the Roman Empire, and the revolution of 1848 knew nothing better than to parody, now 1789, now the revolutionary tradition of 1793 to 1795.[1]

This is not quite analogous to the other forms of conceptual imperialism. It offers an explanation of men's conception of the future in terms of the historical tradition, not their present position. Or, more precisely, the current position is defined so as to include memories of the past.[2] Clearly, this is a very different outlook from the view that ideas have no continuous history. It corresponds to the compromise suggested in 8.1.3, that men's ideas are constrained by the ideas bequeathed to them by the past, not only by the current economic and social structure. It is not a question of the "inertia" of the superstructure, important as this phenomenon may be. Rather the point is that ideas of the past can lie dormant for a long time and then be revived if they provide a useful language for analysis and action in the face of the future.

8.3. Applications

Marx considered many domains of thought from the perspective of the theory of ideology: political theory, economic theory, religion, philosophy, jurisprudence, art, natural science, as well as the economic illusions of everyday life. In most cases his analysis amounts to no more than fragmentary *dicta* that do not lend themselves well to an analytical reconstruction. I have singled out for more detailed discussion the two domains that in my view are the most important. In 8.3.1 I offer a rather selective discussion of Marx's sociology of economic knowledge, as it is found in the *Theories of Surplus-Value*. In 8.3.2 I survey his theory of the economic roots of religion. The latter can in many respects serve as an example of how a theory of ideology should *not* be constructed. Marx's

[1] *Ibid.*, pp. 103–4.
[2] See Assoun, *Marx et la Répétition Historique* and my "Note on hysteresis in the social sciences".

discussion of religion is arbitrary and largely incoherent. He seizes on any "similarity", real or imagined, between a religious doctrine and an economic system, and invests it with explanatory significance far beyond what is warranted. Later Marxists have followed the same procedure, with disastrous results. By contrast, I believe that Marx's treatment of the history of economic thought, while not flawless, is certainly worth taking seriously.

8.3.1. Economic theory as ideology

Schumpeter remarks somewhere that Marx was the most erudite economist of his time, and any reader of the *Theories of Surplus-Value* can attest to the enormous energy he devoted to the study of his predecessors. As noted several times, this was not only or even mainly out of a scholarly interest for their views, as explanations to be compared with his own. He saw their views as integral *parts* of the development of capitalism, not merely as *theories* of capitalism. Hence he systematically tried to link the successive economic doctrines to changes in economic and social structure. More precisely, each doctrine corresponds to a specific class at a specific stage in the development of capitalism. The correspondence pertains partly to the interest and partly to the position of the class in question. There is no general mechanism that operates in all cases.

I do not attempt to survey or summarize Marx's history of economic thought, only to focus on the parts that seem especially relevant from the viewpoint of the theory of ideologies. Hence I limit myself to his discussion of the mercantilists, the physiocrats, Malthus and the vulgar economists. His extensive analyses of Adam Smith and Ricardo contain more internal criticism, and less sociology of knowledge, which is why I neglect them here.

The mercantilists

Marx distinguished between less and more sophisticated versions of mercantilism. First, there is the form summarized in M . . . M', or money generating more money without any intermediary. Marx refers to this as "the isolatedly and rigidly retained form of the mercantile system".[1] I argued in 8.2.3 that the basic fallacy of mercantilism in this form is that of *pars pro toto*, of believing that the option of living on interest which is open to any capitalist could be open to all. The mercantilists erect this point of view of the "practical capitalist" into an economic theory with pretentions

---

[1] *Capital II*, p. 99.

to be valid for the economy as a whole. True, in the relevant passage from *Capital III* Marx refers to the "vulgar economists" rather than the mercantilists as proponents of the view he is opposing.[1] In a later chapter, however, he refers to "the mercantile system, which, with its crude realism, constitutes the actual vulgar economy of that period".[2] The mercantilists and the later vulgar economists are similar in that they confuse the essence and the appearance in the capitalist economy (3.1.2). They differ in that the appearance presents itself differently in the seventeenth and the nineteenth centuries. The mercantilists generalize from the point of view of the financial or commercial capitalist, the vulgar economists from that of the industrial capitalist.

Marx did not, however, think that the emphasis on interest-bearing capital (M . . . M') was typical of mercantilism. On the contrary:

The first theoretical treatment of the modern mode of production – the mercantile system – proceeded necessarily from the superficial phenomena of the circulation process as individualised in the movements of merchant's capital, and therefore grasped only the appearance of matters. Partly because merchant's capital is the first free state of existence of capital in general. And partly because of the overwhelming influence which it exerted during the first revolutionising period of feudal production – the genesis of modern production. The real science of modern economy only begins when the theoretical analysis passes from the process of circulation to the process of production. Interest-bearing capital is, indeed, likewise a very old form of capital. But we shall see later why mercantilism does not take it as a point of departure, but rather carries on a polemic against it.[3]

The second, more sophisticated version of mercantilism derives profit from circulation, not from the mere possession of money. "The so-called monetary system is merely an expression of the irrational form M-C-M', a movement which takes place exclusively in circulation."[4] In *Capital I* Marx explains that this version no less than the first rests on the fallacy of composition, which in this case is the erroneous inference from the fact that any commodity-owner can enrich himself, at the expense of others, by selling the product over the value, to the conclusion that all can do so simultaneously. "The capitalist class as whole, in any country, cannot overreach themselves." And Marx adds in a footnote: "Destutt de Tracy . . . held the opposite view. He says, industrial capitalists make profits because 'they all sell for more than it has cost to produce. And to whom do they sell? In the first instance to one another.'"[5]

---

[1] *Capital III*, pp. 377–8, quoted in 8.2.3.   [2] *Ibid.*, p 784.   [3] *Ibid.*, p. 337.
[4] *Capital II*, p. 60.   [5] *Capital I*, p. 163.

One may nevertheless believe that profit arises in circulation without falling into this fallacy. From the premise that profit is created in circulation, the more consistent mercantilists concluded that no net creation of wealth can take place, that is, that the economy is a constant-sum game. James Steuart, for one, was well aware that "gain on the one side therefore always involves loss on the other".[1] From the shared false premise some mercantilists argued incorrectly to the true conclusion that a net creation of wealth was possible, while others logically arrived at the false conclusion that it was not. Both sides were caught in the appearance of circulation, and unable to see that production is the real source of wealth.

Yet according to Marx one may recognize the importance of production and still remain mystified by mercantilist illusions:

M-C . . . P . . . C′-M′, fixed as the exclusive form, constitutes the basis of the more highly developed mercantile system, in which not only the circulation of commodities, but also their production appears as a necessary element. The illusory character of M-C . . . P . . . .C′-M′ and the corresponding illusory interpretation exists whenever this form is fixed as occurring once, not as fluent and ever renewed; hence whenever this form is considered not as one of the forms of the circuit but as its exclusive form.[2]

As far as I can tell, Marx does not say whether this mercantilism is a mere logical possibility or a doctrine actually found in the history of economic thought. Be this as it may, we should note that one of the reasons why it is illusory involves, once again, the local–global fallacy:

[If] we consider some newly invested capital describing for the first time the circuit M-C . . . P . . . C′-M′, then M-C is the preparatory phase, the forerunner of the first process of production gone through by this individual capital. This phase M-C is consequently not presupposed but rather called for or necessitated by the process of production. *But this applies only to this individual capital.* The general form of the circuit of industrial capital is the circuit of money-capital, whenever the capitalist mode of production is taken for granted, hence in social conditions determined by capitalist production. Therefore the capitalist process of production is assumed as a pre-condition, if not in the first circuit of the money-capital of a newly invested industrial capital, then outside of it.[3]

The point is that money capital, in order to create surplus-value in the process of production, must find in existence a class of wage labourers and hence the fully developed capitalist mode of production. From the point of view of a newly formed money capital, it may look as if money is the first stage in the process, but a consideration of the system as a whole

---

[1] *Theories of Surplus-Value*, vol. 1, p. 42.   [2] *Capital II*, pp. 60–1.   [3] *Ibid.*, pp. 61–2. My italics.

shows that there is no first stage, only an unending sequence of reproduction. In itself the argument is not very interesting. It deserves attention only as a further proof, if one was needed, that for Marx mercantilism was characterized by the systematic confusion of local and global viewpoints.

The physiocrats

According to Marx, the physiocrat school represented "the *bourgeois* view within the pre-bourgeois *way of looking at things*".[1] He suggests a twofold explanation of their doctrine: both in terms of the class position of the landed aristocracy and in terms of the class interest of the nascent bourgeoisie. In addition, he suggests elements of a purely intellectual explanation of the physiocrat views, as arising out of and partly in reaction to the mercantilist system – thus deviating from his adage that ideas have *no* autonomous history.

On the one hand the physiocrats shared with the enlightened mercantilists the view that industrial profits arise in circulation, and hence make no net contribution to the national wealth. "*The Physiocrats explain the profit of industry as prôfit upon alienation* (that is, in the Mercantilist way)."[2] On the other hand, they were convinced that net wealth *was* being created, namely in agriculture. They made a basic distinction between the productive classes engaged in agriculture and the sterile classes working in industry, and no further distinction between capitalists and workers within the latter category. "Profit is seen by them only as a kind of higher wages paid by the landowners, which the capitalists consume as revenue."[3] Although Marx praises them for having undertaken for the first time the analysis of capital,[4] he is also critical of their tendency to perceive it as a natural rather than a social category. In their work, "the surplus-value appears . . . as a *gift of nature*",[5] as the natural product of the soil, whereas in reality it is a social category. As argued in 3.2.3, here the physiocrats were right and Marx was wrong. They erred, of course, in thinking that industry could not produce a net surplus, yet their basic intuition was correct.

To explain the physiocrats' theory of surplus-value, Marx cites the fact that in agriculture "the creation of surplus-value appears in material and tangible form".[6] In his view, they failed to go beyond the manifest appearance of economic relations, being in that respect similar to the mercantilists. On the other hand, he also explains their aberration as an overreaction to the mercantilist doctrine:

---

[1] *Theories of Surplus-Value*, vol. 1, p. 385.   [2] *Ibid.*, p. 383; see also p. 380.
[3] *Ibid.*, p. 47.   [4] *Ibid.*, p. 44.   [5] *Ibid.*, p. 51.   [6] *Ibid.*, p. 48.

Since it is the great and specific contribution of the Physiocrats that they derive value and surplus-value not from circulation but from production, they necessarily begin, in contrast to the Monetary and Mercantilist system, with that branch of production which can be thought of in complete separation from and independently of circulation, of exchange; and which presupposes exchange not between man and man but only between man and nature.[1]

In their reaction against the mercantilists, the physiocrats went to the other extreme and neglected circulation altogether. Their formula is P . . . P' rather than M . . . M'.[2] The social significance of this view is ambiguous:

On the one hand it stripped rent – that is, the true economic form of landed property – of its feudal wrapping, and reduced it to mere surplus-value in excess of the labourer's wage. On the other hand, this surplus-value is explained again in a feudal way, as derived from nature and not from society; from man's relation to the soil and not from his social relations.[3]

The latter feature makes it "understandable how the feudal semblance of this system, in the same way as the aristocratic tone of the Enlightenment, was bound to win a number of feudal lords as enthusiastic supporters and propagandists".[4] These supporters did not understand the real historical significance of the system, nor did the physiocrats themselves:

The label of a system differs from that of other articles, among other things, by the fact that it cheats not only the buyer but often also the seller. Quesnay himself and his immediate disciples believed in their feudal shop-sign. . . . But as a matter of fact the system of the physiocrats is the first systematic conception of capitalist production.[5]

This refers to their discovery of the nature of surplus-value, a discovery that led Marx to find in their doctrine the "contradictions of capitalist production as it works its way out of feudal society".[6] This is a teleological interpretation of the physiocrat doctrine, in terms of the further clarifications it would undergo. This aspect of Marx's analysis is even more prominent when he goes on to point out that the policy consequence of the doctrine – to put all taxes on agricultural production and exempt industry which, being sterile, has no taxable surplus – actually favours the industrial capitalists rather than the landowners:

---

[1] *Ibid.*, p. 49.
[2] True, in *Capital II*, p. 99, Marx praises Quesnay for having chosen the form C . . . C' rather than P . . . P' in opposition to the mercantilist M . . . M', but he mentions this as a sign of his "great and true discretion" and it cannot be representative of the physiocrats.
[3] *Theories of Surplus-Value*, vol. 1, p. 52.   [4] *Ibid.*, p. 53.   [5] *Capital II*, p. 360.
[6] *Theories of Surplus-Value*, vol. 1, p. 52.

Hence also, in the conclusions which the Physiocrats themselves draw, the ostensible veneration of landed property becomes transformed into the economic negation of it and the affirmation of capitalist production. On the one hand, all taxes are put on rent, or in other words, landed property is in part confiscated, which is what the legislation of the French Revolution sought to carry through and which is the final conclusion of the fully developed Ricardian modern political economy. By placing the burden of tax entirely on rent, because it alone is surplus-value – and consequently any taxation of other forms of income ultimately falls on landed property, but in a roundabout way and therefore in an economically harmful way, that hinders production – taxation and along with it all forms of State intervention, are removed from industry itself, and the latter is thus freed from all intervention by the State. This is ostensibly done for the benefit of landed property, not in the interests of industry, but in the interests of landed property.[1]

The glorification of landed property in practice turns into the demand that taxes should be put exclusively on ground-rent, the virtual confiscation of landed property by the state, just as with the radical section of the Ricardians. The French Revolution, in spite of the protests of Roederer and others, accepted this taxation theory. Turgot himself [was] the radical bourgeois minister who prepared the way for the French Revolution. For all their sham feudal pretences the Physiocrats were working hand in hand with the Encyclopaedists.[2]

These statements, taken together with those cited earlier, are extraordinarily elusive. The terms "scheinbar", "angeblich" and "falsch" which are used characterize the feudal nature of the physiocrat doctrine, suggest more than a mere mistake by these writers about what their views implied. Still they do not imply deliberate deception, which in any case is ruled out by the statement that the physiocrats believed in their own shop-sign. I suggest that we are dealing with a functional explanation of the purest water. Marx is arguing that the physiocrat doctrine owed its existence to its progressive historical function, in paving the way for the bourgeoisie. The illusions of the landowners served the interest of the industrial capitalist – an *explanatory* interest. Not content with observing the irony of the situation, he turned it into a Ruse of Reason.

Malthus

For Marx, the distinctive feature of Malthus's doctrines was his insistence on maintaining effective demand, and his proposal to achieve this by creating a class of buyers who are not at the same time sellers of anything. This made him the ideal representative of the landed aristocracy and the state officials:

[1] *Ibid.*   [2] *Ibid.*, p. 66.

[Malthus] was a professional sycophant of the landed aristocracy, whose rents, sinecures, squandering, heartlessness etc. he justified *economically*. Malthus defends the interest of the industrial bourgeoisie only in so far as these are identical with the interests of landed property, of the aristocracy, i.e. *against* the mass of the people, the proletariat. But where these interests diverge and are antagonistic to each other, he sides with the aristocracy against the bourgeoisie. Hence his defence of the *"unproductive* worker", of over-consumption etc.[1]

It should be recalled, however, that at some point it becomes in the interest of the bourgeoisie to assuage the interests of the aristocracy (7.1). Initially the views of Malthus were contrary to "the still revolutionary bourgeoisie, which has not yet subjected to itself the whole of society, the State etc."[2] At this stage the bourgeoisie holds that "the State, church etc. are only justified in so far as they are committees to superintend or administer the common interests of the productive bourgeoisie; and their costs . . . must be reduced to the unavoidable minimum".[3] Later, however, the rise of the working class makes these unproductive expenditures appear in a new light, as stated in the passage cited at the end of 7.1.5. At this stage, the bourgeoisie "prefer[s] to compromise with the vanishing opponent rather than to strengthen the arising enemy".[4] Although Malthus in 1820 could not yet represent the interest of the bourgeoisie, which was still in its revolutionary stage, this had changed a few decades later. The "standing offer" (8.2.2) represented by Malthus could then be taken up by the industrial bourgeoisie.[5]

The vulgar economists

This group of economists are characterized by a shared outlook rather than by membership of any school. Among their numbers Marx cites Say, Garnier, Senior, Bastiat, Carey and others. Like the mercantilists they remain at the surface of the phenomena, unable to see through the appearance of economic relations. Unlike the mercantilists, they act as apologists for the existing system, which they present as the best of all possible worlds. Their central error is that of perceiving land, capital and labour as being somehow on a par, as independent factors of production

---

[1] *Ibid.*, vol. 2, p. 115.   [2] *Ibid.*, vol. 1, p. 300; see also *ibid.*, p. 175.   [3] *Ibid.*
[4] *New York Daily Tribune* 25.8.1852, more fully cited in 6.3.3.
[5] Actually the defence of the unproductive classes was later conducted in a different vein from what Malthus had done. The vulgar economists went to great lengths to show that these classes – themselves included! – were actually quite productive, whereas Malthus more classically defined a productive labourer as someone who directly "increases his master's wealth" (*Theories of Surplus-Value*, vol. 3, p. 35; cp. vol. 1, p. 176). He cynically defended them as useful idlers, whereas they made them out to be useful because productive. Yet broadly speaking I think it makes sense to say that they continued in the tradition he had initiated.

each of which earns and deserves a specific type of revenue. On the one hand this illusion springs directly from the nature of capitalist production, while on the other hand it serves to justify the perpetuation of the system. Hence Marx in this case offers both a position-explanation and a functional interest-explanation, as he makes clear in two programmatic statements:

In capital-profit, or still better capital-interest, land-rent, labour-wages, in this economic trinity represented as the connection between the component parts of value and wealth in general and its sources, we have the complete mystification of the capitalist mode of production, the conversion of social relations into things, the direct coalescence of the material production relations with their historical and social determination. It is an enchanted, perverted, topsy-turvy world, in which Monsieur le Capital and Madame la Terre do their ghost-walking as social characters and at the same time directly as mere things . . .[It] is . . . natural for the actual agents of production to feel completely at home in these estranged and irrational forms of capital-interest, land-rent, labour-wages, since these are precisely the forms of illusion in which they move about and find their daily occupation. It is therefore just as natural that vulgar economy, which is no more than a didactic, more or less dogmatic, translation of everyday conceptions of the actual agents of production, and which arranges them in a certain rational order, should see precisely in this trinity, which is devoid of all inner connection, the natural and indubitably lofty basis for its shallow pompousness. This formula simultaneously corresponds to the interests of the ruling classes by proclaiming the physical necessity and eternal justification of their sources of revenue and elevating them to a dogma.[1]

The form of revenue and the sources of revenue are the *most fetishistic* expressions of the relations of capitalist production. It is their form of existence as it appears on the surface, divorced from the hidden connections and the intermediate connecting links. Thus the *land* becomes the source of *rent*, *capital* the source of *profit*, and *labour* the source of *wages*. The distorted form in which the real inversion is expressed is naturally reproduced in the views of the agents of this mode of production. It is a kind of fiction without fantasy, a religion of the vulgar. In fact, the vulgar economists . . . translate the concepts, motives etc. of the representatives of the capitalist mode of production who are held in thrall to this system of production and in whose consciousness only its superficial appearance is reflected. They translate them into a doctrinaire language, but they do so from the standpoint of the ruling section, i.e. the capitalists, and their treatment is therefore not naive and objective, but apologetic.[2]

For Marx the source of all revenue is labour. Rent and profit are part of the surplus-value, while wages correspond to the value of labour-power. The illusion of three distinct sources arises naturally out of the existence of three distinct forms of revenue, and the fact that to the reception of a

---

[1] *Capital III*, p. 830.   [2] *Theories of Surplus-Value*, vol. 3, p. 453.

given form of revenue there corresponds the control of a certain factor of production. It is then easy to believe that the factor itself, not control over it, is the source or cause of the revenue.

The trinitary formula is not the only product of vulgar economy. I have already cited the mercantilist tendency to confuse interest-bearing capital with productive capital. Marx asserts several times that M . . . M' is the fundamental form of vulgar economy.[1] In *Capital III* he comments on the tendency of the capitalist to believe that his total profit is determined by the profit realized on each commodity multiplied by the number of commodities. In his view, the process is rather one of division, since in the essence of things the total surplus-value is given prior to its repartition among individual commodities. "The vulgar economist does practically no more than translate the singular concepts of the capitalists, who are in the thrall of competition, into a seemingly more theoretical and generalised language."[2] Here, as in his discussion of capital fetishism (2.3.2), Marx is misled by his reliance on the labour theory of value. More interesting is the argument advanced about the tendency of the vulgar economists to confuse the value of labour and the value of labour-power (3.1.2). These instances have in common the belief that the nature of economic phenomena can be immediately grasped from the point of view of the economic agents. "But all science would be superfluous if the outward appearance and the essence of things directly coincided."[3] The vulgar economists are like the astronomers who believed that the sun turns around the earth because this is how it appears to observers on earth.[4]

The vulgar conception of the sources of revenue

renders a substantial service to apologetics. For [in the formula] land-rent, capital-interest, labour-wages, for example, the different forms of surplus-value and configurations of capitalist production do not confront one another as alienated forms, but as heterogeneous and independent forms, merely different from one another but not *antagonistic*. The different revenues are derived from quite different sources, one from land, the second from capital and the third from labour. Thus they do not stand in any hostile connection to one another because they have no inner connection whatsoever. If they nevertheless work together in production, then it is a harmonious action, an expression of harmony, as, for example, the peasant, the ox, the plough and the land in agriculture, in the real labour process, work together *harmoniously* despite their dissimilarities. Insofar as

[1] *Ibid.*, p. 467; see also *Capital III*, pp. 405–6.
[2] *Capital III*, p. 231; *Theories of Surplus-Value*, vol. 2, p. 267.
[3] *Capital III*, p. 817.
[4] This Copernican analogy occurs in *Zur Kritik (1861–63)*, p. 2117.

there is any contradiction between them, it arises merely from competition as to which of the agents shall get more of the value which they have jointly created.[1]

This analysis is extremely suggestive. The last sentence, in particular, is a good expression of the view that capitalism is a bargaining game over how to divide the benefits from cooperation. This view, which is institutionalized in collective bargaining, is the dominant economic ideology in contemporary capitalist societies. I agree with Marx that it is a misleading conception, but for reasons that differ from his. He argued that the view rests on false *factual* premises with respect to the creation of value. The vulgar economists do not see that net revenue derives from labour only. I have argued in 3.2.3 that Marx's view on this point is incorrect. My objections to the vulgar conception are squarely *normative* (4.3.2).

Generally speaking, the views of the vulgar economists *arise* as cognitive illusions. They are the theoretical translation of the immediate conceptions of the "practical capitalist". Once arisen, however, it turns out that they also admirably serve certain interests of the capitalist class by making capital appear as productive in its own right. In this they differ from the views of the mercantilists, that did not serve any apologetic functions. They also differ, say, from the theories of Malthus that according to Marx had an apologetic character without any origin in cognitive confusion. The distinguishing character of the vulgar economists is that their views had a double footing: in the illusions of everyday economic life and in the interests of the bourgeoisie. Whence the immense appeal of their ideas. This case does not conform to the filter model (8.1.3), since the views are, as it were, tainted at the origin before being diffused in larger circles. True, at times Marx discusses the "harmonious" conceptions of the vulgar economists independently of any such cognitive origin, notably when referring to their tendency to find bourgeois society "the best of all possible worlds".[2] In such contexts he appears to define vulgar economics by its apologetic character rather than by its tendency to confuse essence and appearance. In some typical cases, such as the so-called "compensation theory",[3] there is no reason to believe that the vulgar views have an origin in cognitive illusions. Yet the main thrust of Marx's analysis is to suggest that the two aspects of vulgar economics are inseparably linked to one another.

---

[1] *Theories of Surplus-Value*, vol. 3, p. 503.

[2] For references and discussion, see my "Marx et Leibniz".

[3] *Capital I*, pp. 438ff. This is the view that "all machinery that displaces workmen, simultaneously and necessarily sets free an amount of capital adequate to employ the same identical workmen".

In summary I believe that Marx's sociology of economic knowledge was quite an impressive achievement, in spite of being flawed by its reliance on functional explanation and the labour theory of value. He pioneered in what came to be called "psychological economics", although his main emphasis was on the formation of beliefs rather than, as in most later studies, of preferences. The recent "capital controversy" shows that these are not dead issues. Surely some cognitive confusion lay at the origin of the idea that "capital" can be treated as a homogeneous "factor of production", for instance an inference from the fact that *capitalists* form a fairly homogeneous class. And conceivably the tenacity with which the neoclassical economists stuck to the notion of aggregate capital has something to do with non-cognitive interests. This, admittedly, is sheer speculation, and I may be quite wrong. Vested intellectual interests may suffice to explain the resistance. Be this as it may, the sociology of economic conceptions and economic theory is a field worth cultivating, if proper attention is paid to the many methodological pitfalls in this domain.

8.3.2. Religion as ideology

In numerous brief passages, scattered over some twenty-five years, Marx discussed the nature, the causes and the consequences of religious belief. These remarks frustrate any attempt to make sense of them as a coherent whole, and even when read in the piecemeal fashion in which they were written they have a rather limited interest. When discussing religion Marx gave free rein to his speculative tendencies, finding "functions" and "similarities" that lack foundations in individual psychology.

To my knowledge, Marx nowhere discusses religion in general. With the exception of a few remarks on natural religion and some rhetorical effusions on Judaism,[1] all his comments concern Christianity. He was more concerned to distinguish and compare various forms of that creed than to consider it in a truly comparative perspective, as one world religion among many. In this respect he was much more parochial than Max Weber. I shall also argue that his analysis of the relation between capitalism and Protestantism was more primitive than Weber's.

In his discussions of religion, Marx employs all the varieties of explanation distinguished in 8.1.2. I have mentioned in 8.2.1 the causal interest-explanation in terms of what today we call cognitive dissonance. As will be shown below, he also occasionally uses a functional interest-explanation, in terms of the benefits popular religion brings to the ruling class.

---

[1] For a survey see Carlebach, *Karl Marx and the Radical Critique of Judaism*. I confess my inability to make any interesting sense of Marx's article "On the Jewish Question".

And finally I shall show that he employs several forms of causal position-explanation, in terms of the economic and social structure. Religion is explained, that is, as *consolation*, as *social control* and as a *reflection* of the economic structure. Below I mainly survey the second and the third varieties, but some preliminary comments on the relation between the first and the second may be useful.

To bring out this relation, I rely on Paul Veyne's outstanding work *Le Pain et le Cirque*. A central theme of this book is that many beliefs held by the subjects in a given society are systematically useful to the rulers, yet cannot be explained in terms of these benefits. The Romans, for instance, tended to believe in the divinity of their rulers (with the nuances mentioned in 8.1), but the explanation of this belief is not to be found in the indubitable benefits it brought to the ruling class. Rather it must be sought in the benefits it offered the subjects themselves, by giving them a modicum of peace of mind. Veyne, referring to Festinger, argues that the belief in the divinity of the rulers reduced dissonance by placing power out of reach for ordinary mortals.[1] A similarly endogenous theory of religion was offered by Marx, in the passage which culminates in the statement that religion is the opium of the people (8.2.1). As is made clear by the rest of the passage, this statement does not mean that the rulers administer religion to the people in order to keep them in an illusory state of contentment. Rather, as is constantly emphasized by Veyne, if left to themselves the people will spontaneously invent the opium they need. We may add, however, that this does not provide an explanation of why the *ruling* classes in a society should also entertain religious beliefs.

According to a popular conception (rejected by Veyne) the Roman rulers offered their subjects "panem et circences", bread and circuses, to keep them from revolting. Marx, inspired by that conception, refers to "panem et religionem" in an article from 1847 that contains the clearest statement of his functional interest-explanation of religion. The incantatory and exhortatory aspects of the passage should not mislead us. When Marx says that the proletariat will not let itself be deluded by "the social principles of Christianity", he certainly means that this temptation is a real danger.

The social principles of Christianity justified the slavery of antiquity, glorified the serfdom of the Middle Ages and are capable, in case of need, of defending the oppression of the proletariat, even with somewhat doleful grimaces. The social principles of Christianity preach the necessity of a ruling and an oppressed class, and for the latter all they have to offer is the pious wish that the former may be

---

[1] Veyne, *Le Pain et le Cirque*, pp. 310ff and *passim*.

charitable. The social principles of Christianity place the Consistorial Counsellor's compensation for all infamies in heaven, and thereby justify the continuation of these infamies on earth. The social principles of Christianity declare all the vile acts of the oppressors against the oppressed to be either a just punishment for original sin, and other sins, or trials which the Lord, in his infinite wisdom, ordains for the redeemed. The social principles of Christianity preach cowardice, self-contempt, abasement, submissiveness and humbleness, in short, all the qualities of the rabble, and the proletariat, which will not permit itself to be treated as rabble, needs its courage, its self-confidence, its pride and its sense of independence even more than its bread. The social principles of Christianity are sneaking and hypocritical, and the proletariat is revolutionary.[1]

The same language is found in another article from 1847, directed against the "true socialist" Kriege and his call for a "religion of love":

> With this shameful and nauseating grovelling before a "mankind" that is separate and distinct from the "self" and which is therefore a metaphysical and in his case even a religious fiction, with what is indeed the most utterly "miserable" slavish self-abasement, this religion ends up like any other. Such a doctrine, preaching the voluptuous pleasure of cringing and self-contempt, is entirely suited to valiant – *monks*, but never to men of action, least of all in a time of struggle.[2]

True, these proto-Nietzschean passages do not have to be read as a functional explanation of religious beliefs. They could be read only as statements about the consequences which as a matter of fact follow from religion, leaving open the question of explanation. In his polemic against Kriege, in fact, Marx repeats the earlier idea that the "obsessions of Christianity are only the fantastic expression of the existing world", suggesting a causal interest-explanation of religion as consolation. The functionalist reading is nevertheless strongly suggested by the language of these texts, with their emphasis on the precise and multiple ways in which the Christian religion is useful for the ruling class. It is, moreover, supported by Marx's general tendency to lapse into functional explanation.

In the mature economic writings Marx almost never returns to the interest-explanation of religious belief. Rather we find several, mutually inconsistent position-explanations of the various forms of Christianity. To facilitate the discussion I shall first cite the relevant passages, enumerated for ease of reference:

> (I) In so far as the hoarder of money combines asceticism with assiduous diligence he is intrinsically a Protestant by religion and still more a Puritan.[3]

---

[1] *Deutsche-Brüsseler-Zeitung* 12.9.1847.   [2] "Circular against Kriege", p. 49.
[3] *Contribution to the Critique of Political Economy*, p. 108.

(II) The catholic fact that gold and silver as the direct embodiment of social labour, and therefore as the expression of abstract wealth, confront other profane commodities, has of course violated the protestant code of honour of bourgeois economists, and from fear of the prejudices of the Monetary system, they lost for some time any sense of discrimination towards the phenomena of money circulation.[1]

(III) The religious world is but the reflex of the real world. And for a society based upon the production of commodities, in which the producers in general enter into social relations with one another by treating their products as commodities and values, whereby they reduce their individual private labour to the standard of homogeneous human labour – for such a society, Christianity with its cultus of abstract man, more especially in its bourgeois developments, Protestantism, Deism etc., is the most fitting form of religion.[2]

(IV) One sees how the piling-up of gold and silver gained its true stimulus with the conception of it as the material representative and general form of wealth. The cult of money has its asceticism, its self-denial, its self-sacrifice – economy and frugality, contempt for mundane, temporal and fleeting pleasures; the chase after the *eternal* treasure. Hence the connection between English Puritanism, or also Dutch Protestantism, and money-making.[3]

(V) The monetary system is essentially a Catholic institution, the credit system essentially Protestant. "The Scotch hate gold." In the form of paper the monetary existence of commodities is only a social one. It is *faith* that brings salvation. Faith in money-value as the immanent spirit of commodities, faith in the mode of production and its predestined order, faith in the individual agents of production as mere personifications of self-expanding capital.[4]

(VI) The development of capitalist production creates an average level of bourgeois society and therefore an average level of temperament and disposition amongst the most varied peoples. It is as truly cosmopolitan as Christianity. This is why Christianity is likewise the special religion of capital. In both it is only men who count. One man in the abstract is worth just as much or as little as the next man. In the one case, all depends on whether or not he has faith, in the other on whether or not he has credit. In addition, however, in the one case, predestination has to be added, and in the other case, the accident of whether or not a man is born with a silver spoon in his mouth.[5]

To these late texts we may add a passage from the *Economic and Philosophical Manuscripts:*

(VII) To this enlightened political economy, which has discovered – within private property – the *subjective essence* of wealth, the adherents of the monetary and mercantile system, who look upon private property *only as an*

---

[1] *Ibid.*, p. 134.   [2] *Capital I*, p. 79.   [3] *Grundrisse*, p. 232.   [4] *Capital III*, p. 592.
[5] *Theories of Surplus-Value*, vol. 3, pp. 448–9; cp. *Grundrisse*, p. 839.

objective substance confronting men, seem therefore to be *fetishists, Catholics. Engels* was therefore right to call *Adam Smith* the *Luther of Political Economy.*[1]

The contradictions in these passages are fairly striking. Passages (I) and (IV) assert that the hoarding of gold and silver were especially associated with Protestantism. Against this, passages (II), (V) and (VII) state that the monetarist system is essentially Catholic. Marx, apparently, was confused by the fact that money has two distinct features which suggest different religious modes. On the one hand, metals unlike credit can be hoarded. Hoarding easily turns into an obsession (2.2.5), related to the fanatical self-denying practices of extreme Protestantism. On the other hand, money can be seen as the "incarnation" (this is the original German term used in passage (II)) of social wealth, and in that sense is related to the specifically Catholic practice of investing relics etc., with supernatural significance. When Marx compares fetishism with transsubstantiation,[2] it is also in connection with the specifically mercantilist fallacy of monetary fetishism (M ... M'). If evidence was needed of Marx's lack of intellectual discipline, even when dealing with matters that one would assume to be central, this contradictory attitude would be a major item, comparable to the inconsistencies in his explanation of the English factory laws (4.1.4). It is difficult to avoid the impression that he often wrote whatever came into his mind, and then forgot about it as he moved on to other matters.

Of the cited passages, some are more important theoretically than others. Passages (III), (V) and (VI) touch briefly upon doctrinal matters, suggesting an explanatory analogy between Protestantist theology and various aspects of capitalism. First, to abstract human labour corresponds the Protestant emphasis on the abstract individual, alone with his God; next, to the capitalist emphasis on credit-worthiness corresponds the Protestant emphasis on faith as a means to salvation; finally to the accident of who is born with money corresponds the analogy of who is elected to grace. In my opinion these analogies are totally arbitrary. Any writer with a modicum of ingenuity and eloquence can invent similar analogies or "structural homologies" between a set of mental attitudes and a socioeconomic structure. Later Marxist doctrines have provided many instances, worthy of prominent place in the chamber of horrors of science.[3] By his remarks on religion, Marx set an unhappy precedent for such speculations.

---

[1] *Economic and Philosophical Manuscripts*, p. 290.

[2] *Theories of Surplus-Value*, vol. 3, p. 494.

[3] See for instance the work by Borkenau cited in note 1, p. 473 above; Hessen, "The social and economic roots of Newton's *Principia*"; Goldmann, *Le Dieu Caché*.

It is instructive to compare Marx's suggestion with what one may call the Weber–Thompson view on the relation between religion and capitalism.[1] A schematic summary would include the following theses. (i) Given Calvinism or Methodism, inner-worldly asceticism was a way of reducing the cognitive dissonance between the belief in predestination and the personal concern for salvation.[2] There is an affinity here with Marx, who also suggested a connection between Puritanism and saving. The differences, however, are also striking. While Marx saw Protestantism connected with unproductive hoarding, Weber linked it to productive investment. Although there is a gap in Weber's reasoning here,[3] Marx's view is equally unsupported. It relies on mere analogy, with no attempt to provide a causal story. We should also note that in Weber the explanatory link goes from religion to capitalism, whereas in Marx it is the other way around.[4] (ii) The various forms of Protestantism, when adopted by the workers, were eminently useful to the capitalist class by reinforcing the work-discipline and contributing to the process whereby the worker "learns to control himself, in contrast to the slave who needs a master".[5] (iii) One would err, however, in concluding that this explains the adoption of these beliefs by the workers. Although indoctrination may have been a factor in their propagation, it was effective only in so far as the indoctrinators themselves believed in the doctrine – that is in so far as they did *not* preach it because of its instrumental efficacy.[6] Moreover, the adoption could not have taken place had the belief not also corresponded to a vital need for consolation among the workers. This account of the workers' religion is in a way the converse of the account of the religion of capitalists summarized in (i). Whereas Weber took the religion of the capitalists as given and explained their economic behaviour as a form of dissonance reduction, Thompson takes the economic situation of the workers as given and then explains their religious beliefs in terms of dissonance reduction, among other things. The two explanations are, of course, perfectly compatible. Yet even if they both turn out to

---

[1] Weber, *The Protestant Ethic*; Thompson, *The Making of the English Working Class*, ch. 11.
[2] For the underlying mechanism, see Quattrone and Tversky, "Self-deception and the voters' illusion".
[3] The step from *saving* to *investment* is not justified by Weber. He neglects not only the possibility of unproductive hoarding, but also that of charity. As pointed out to me by G. A. Cohen, a life of alms-giving would also count as worldly asceticism.
[4] A possible exception is the passage from the 1861–3 *Critique* cited towards the end of 5.2.2. Here Marx cites Protestantism and science among the spiritual preconditions of bourgeois society.
[5] *Results of the Immediate Process of Production*, p. 1033, more fully cited in 4.2.1. The passage does not refer to religion, but anticipates the argument in Fromm, *Fear of Freedom*, p. 80.
[6] *Sour Grapes*, ch. II; Veyne, *Le Pain et le Cirque*, p. 679 and *passim*.

be true – a question on which I am unable to pronounce myself – we still need an explanation of why capitalists embraced Protestantism in the first place.[1]

I conclude that of Marx's many attempts to come to grips with the formation of religious beliefs, the only one that retains some value is the early Feuerbachian idea – restated as late as in 1865[2] – that religion is "the sigh of the oppressed creature". This corresponds to part (iii) of the Weber–Thompson view. His functionalist explanation is based on an idea related to the view stated in (ii), but must be dismissed for reasons that by now will be familiar. The idea vaguely resembling (i), that there is an elective affinity between capitalism and Protestantism, turns out to be based on superficial and inconsistent analogies. His failure should be a lesson to all would-be practitioners of the science of debunking.

---

[1] Thompson, *The Making of the English Working Class*, pp. 391–2 suggests an implausible functional explanation in terms of the contribution of Puritanism to "the psychic energy and social coherence of middle-class groups which felt themselves to be 'called' or 'elected' and which were engaged (with some success) in acquisitive pursuits". If I understand him, Thompson is here turning Weber upside-down, suggesting that religion stabilized the economic behaviour of these groups rather than behaviour providing an outlet for a tension created by religion.

[2] See the passage cited on pp. 479–80 above.

Conclusion

9. Capitalism, communism and revolution

The revolutionary transition from capitalism to communism was the core of Marx's life and work. The study of pre-capitalist societies, and what came to be known as "historical materialism", were little more than a foil to that overriding concern. The whence, whither and how of that transition form the topic of this chapter. Summarizing and bringing together elements from earlier chapters, I first discuss his views on capitalism – its development, physiology and pathology. The last in particular claimed his attention. He believed capitalism to be an inhumane, unjust, wasteful system – and in all these respects at the opposite pole of the communist society that he believed to be imminent and inevitable. I next turn to his ethical, economic and political conceptions of communism. These are largely Utopian, but not all to the same extent. Shorn of their wishful thinking and exaggerations, they remain valuable guides to political theory and political action. I conclude by considering his views on how the ills of capitalism and the possibility of communism motivate the workers to revolutionary action. If his theory fails to persuade us, it is no doubt because he himself was so persuaded of the necessity of communism that he did not feel an argument was needed.

Capitalism

According to Wassily Leontief, Marx was the great character reader of the capitalist system. He did indeed have a powerful intuition for what motivates the capitalist entrepreneur and for how these motives appear, transformed, at the collective and political level. Despite many flaws, the historical chapters in *Capital I* brilliantly unite observation and synthesis. Marx set the agenda of problems and went a long way towards showing what would count as a solution. Yet the implicit critical side of Leontief's judgment should also be taken to heart. A character reader is not a psychologist; and a powerful economic and social historian need not be a good economic theorist. Although I remember being upset by Paul Samuelson's statement on the centenary of the publication of *Capital I* that Marx was basically "a minor post-Ricardian", I now largely subscribe to that view, if taken exclusively as an evaluation of the economic theories found in *Capital II* and *III*.

The most important achievement of *Capital I* was the analysis of the capitalist factory and the capitalist entrepreneur. Marx's portrait of the latter remains more multi-faceted and insightful than anything offered by Weber, Schumpeter or others. The interplay of property relations, power, technology and rational decision-making has never been captured so strikingly. No doubt some of his more manichean statements should be dismissed, but the writings of Andrew Ure are there to remind us that they were not without some foundation. Less focussed, but also masterful, are the analyses of capitalism as a *system* of firms – of competition, of the transition from manufacture to machinofacture, of accumulation, growth and technical change. At a further level we still gain much insight from his analysis of how these economic developments were shaping and being shaped by the class struggle, and its continuation into politics by other means. Finally, a neglected pioneering achievement was his demonstration that the beliefs entertained by the economic agents about the workings of the economic system also stand in a double causal relation to that system – being both endogenous products of it and a factor in its reproduction. Marx went all the way – from the individual level to the aggregate, from the static analysis to the dynamical, from the economic to the social, political and ideological levels. In earlier chapters I have been concerned to discuss each aspect separately, often in a very critical way. Even taken one by one, however, they are impressive – and taken together they are overwhelmingly so.

It is, however, necessary to extract this construction from the often misleading framework in which it is embedded. For one thing, there are numerous remnants of the Hegelian method. "Capital" at times appears, mysteriously, as an agent with a will of its own. The factory laws appear as if by magic to satisfy its needs; social mobility occurs to fortify its rule; the doctrine of the physiocrats emerged to represent it within the feudal system. I have characterized this procedure as an amalgam of methodological collectivism, functional explanation and dialectical deduction. These can all be subsumed, perhaps, under the more general heading of *teleology*. The invisible hand upholding capital is one of the two main forms of teleology in Marx, the other being the necessity of the process that will ultimately destroy it.

For another thing, the analyses of *Capital* are flawed by Marx's adherence to the labour theory of value. His own version of that theory was quite ingenuous in some respects, while marred by technical errors in others. More fundamentally, it comes up against the fact that when heterogeneous labour and different disutilities of work are admitted, the basic concepts of the theory are not well defined. And – the most basic objection – even if we disregard that problem, there is no analytical purpose to which the theory may be harnessed. It explains nothing that other theories do not explain more simply. For the purpose of explaining the equilibrium prices and rate of profit the labour theory of value is merely cumbersome. It does allow the correct deductions, but in a needlessly complex way. For the study of technical change and balanced economic growth it is positively harmful, for reasons that Marx as a Hegelian should have been able to discern. He was attached to the labour theory of value because the value accounting provided the inner essence of the capitalist system, compared to which the price system was a mere superficial appearance. Yet that also means that individual behaviour can never be explained by reference to values, which, being invisible, have no place in the purposive explanation of action. Hence when Marx and his later followers have tried to explain the choice of technique in terms of the maximization of surplus-value, or argued that the capital sector and the consumption sector should have the same rate of savings out of surplus-value, they have committed an error which is the converse of that of vulgar economy – they have put the essence where the appearance ought to be.

Marx's charges against capitalism can be summarized on three counts. First, it is *inhuman*, by leading to the alienation of men from their species-powers. By these powers Marx meant the creative activities that men are uniquely able to engage in, by virtue of their intelligence, language and tool-making ability. Marx believed that the deployment of these powers was the ultimate goal and the ultimate good both for mankind and for individual men. His arguments for this view have partly a utilitarian flavour: the development and use of one's abilities is the most deeply satisfactory activity one can engage in. Partly they are of an Aristotelian kind: men should realize their essence or inherent purpose, which is to be creative. Capitalism, on the one hand, is an immense step forward for mankind, permitting, as it does, an unprecedented expansion of the species-powers. On the other hand, it has disastrous effects for the all-sided development of the powers of the individual human being. This is alienation: the frustration of the most profound need of men, the need to use one's talents and abilities. It is unclear whether Marx also believed it to be the most deeply felt need of men. Sometimes alienation means not only lack of self-realization, but lack of consciousness of this lack. At other times it means a subjectively experienced state of frustration. It is not simply frustration at being unable to do what one wants to do. It is, more centrally, frustration of wants that could feasibly be realized in the actual state of society. Also, it is a collective phenomenon. In earlier societies men have also been frustrated individually, in the sense that each of them may have had wants that could feasibly have been realized at the expense of others. Capitalist alienation is the fact that need satisfaction on a large scale is possible, yet is not carried out. To the extent that this gap is perceived by the members of society – for which they must know both their need and the objective possibility of fulfilling it – it is an immense lever for action.

Next, Marx believed capitalism to be a profoundly *unjust* system. This is a controversial interpretation, since in the Marxist tradition justice has been a bourgeois category, to be debunked rather than employed. Yet I believe that Marx's theory of exploitation, and notably the frequent characterization of profit as theft, only make sense if we impute to him a theory of distributive justice. The central principle is that each should receive proportionally to his contribution, assuming his ability to contribute. Unfortunately this labour theory of exploitation is ill-defined, for a reason that also invalidates the labour theory of value. When labour is heterogeneous, the contributions cannot be measured on a common scale. Moreover, if one attempts to reformulate the principle in terms of hours of labour time, irrespective of the nature of the labour, one comes up against the problem that different forms of work have different degrees of disutility and hence ought to be rewarded accordingly. And if, as with the labour theory of value, one disregards these problems of aggregating and comparing different forms of labour, it can still be shown that the contribution principle is not an ethically attractive one. It is possible to generate counterintuitive situations in which the poor exploit the rich, if the former prefer leisure so much that they do not need even what little capital they have. This shows that in the standard cases when exploitation *is* morally condemnable, it is so by virtue of something else than the contribution principle. Also one can imagine cases in which exploitation is due to different endowments rather than to different supply curves of labour, but yet not obviously morally wrong. The endowment structure could have resulted from different time preferences. Some people could save and accumulate more capital than they could work themselves. If they offer others, who have preferred immediate consumption, to work for them and earn more than they would otherwise have done, how could anyone object? Freely undertaken and mutually beneficial arrangements

that arise in a situation with initially equal endowments cannot be condemned on grounds of the contribution principle.

I do not think this objection is very relevant in present-day capitalism,
since one would have to be in bad faith to argue that the differences in
endowments are largely due to voluntary choices to save rather than to
consume. Nor does it constitute a telling objection to Marx's views. He
would certainly have dismissed it, on the grounds that in a society that
had overcome alienation no one would freely undertake to work for
others, since this would undermine the fundamental value of self-realization. The objection gains full force, however, against any proposal to
create a feasible, non-Utopian communist society. Consider the following
passage from a novel by Wassily Grossman, quoted by Alec Nove in *The
Economics of Feasible Socialism*:

I wanted since childhood to open a shop, so that any folk could come in and buy.
Along with it would have to be a snack-bar, so that the customers could have a bit
of roast meat, if they like, or a drink. I would serve them cheap, too. I'd let them
have real village food. Baked potato! Bacon-fat with garlic! Sauerkraut! I'd give
them bone-marrow as a starter . . . A measure of vodka, a marrow-bone, and
black bread of course, and salt. Leather chairs, so that lice don't breed. The
customer could sit and rest and be served. If I were to say all this loud, I'd have
been sent straight to Siberia. And yet, say I, what harm would I have done to
people?

What harm indeed? And who would have been harmed if he had hired a
few waiters and a cook, who would rather work for a wage in a restaurant
than in a workers' cooperative? Would the Socialist Police have to step in
and forbid such contracting – to force the workers to be free?

Thirdly, Marx condemned capitalism because it was inherently, and
needlessly, irrational and wasteful. On his view it was inherently
wasteful for a number of reasons. The market mechanism in his opinion
was a very inefficient way of coordinating economic decisions. It involves
the permanent possibility and the frequent occurrence of economic crises,
in which capital goods lay idle, workers go without jobs and goods are
produced that meet no effective demand. Also, from the dynamic point of
view, the capitalist incentive system is such that less technical change is
forthcoming than if the socially desirable criterion – minimization of
labour time – had been used. The capitalist wants to minimize paid labour
time, not to minimize labour time *tout court*. If a given innovation leads to
a reduction of labour time, but also leads to more paid labour being used,
or to labour being paid more (because of the impact of the innovation on
the wage struggle), the capitalist may not adopt it. Marx was right in

pointing out these possible sources of inefficiency, although he exaggerated their importance. In any case, of course, it needs to be shown that another system is possible that lacks these defects and yet has all the other advantages of capitalism, notably the relentless incentive to search for new techniques. As long as this is not the case, the inherent wastefulness of capitalism must be put up with. Marx argued that the time was imminent when other relations of production would be superior in all these respects – as regards the search for new techniques, the criteria for selecting them and the efficiency with which they are used. Finally the capitalist system is irrational in the sense that it tends to destroy itself. It can remain economically viable only by means that undermine long-term viability. Specifically, in the face of the tendency of the rate of profit to fall, the capitalists react by measures that, when adopted by all, reinforce that tendency. Although the theory of the falling rate of profit has a certain superficial plausibility, it turns out, on closer inspection, to leak like a sieve. It starts from incorrect premises – the secular preponderance of labour-saving inventions – and then goes on to make invalid inferences from them to a declining trend in the rate of profit.

By and large, Marx did not condemn capitalism on the grounds that it led to increased misery in the sense of lower levels of consumption or, somewhat more generally, a lower standard of living. True, he wrote in terms of glowing indignation about the conditions of the English working class, but not to suggest that they were getting worse. His standard of comparison was counterfactual, not actual. He compared the fate of the workers in actually existing capitalism with what it would be under more rationally organized relations of production. Lack of need satisfaction has been an inescapable fact for most people throughout history. It becomes scandalous only when the objective possibility emerges of a society in which the full and free use of one's powers is within the reach of all. Similarly, the suboptimality of capitalism with respect to technical change did not mean that innovations were coming to a stop. On the contrary: the fall in the rate of profit made the capitalists innovate at an ever more frenetic pace. Rather, the point is that capitalism itself creates the conditions under which another system can perform even better. Alienation and "the contradiction between the productive forces and the relations of production" are defined as gaps between what is actual and what is possible. Alienation, broadly speaking, is predicated on the basis of a possible better *use* of the productive forces, and the contradiction on the basis of a possible faster *development*. Actually, the two phenomena are closely related. By suppressing alienation, free rein will be given to the

creative abilities of the members of society. Some of them will spontaneously choose scientific and technical work as vehicles for self-realization, with unprecedented productivity growth as the outcome. But, to
repeat, this is only possible on the technical basis created by capitalism
itself. It is the ladder that humankind kicks out from under itself when it is
no longer needed.

The economic analysis and indictment of capitalism is set out in a
narrow two-class framework. Capitalists and workers – individually and
collectively – are the only agents of any importance in *Capital*. The agricultural classes – peasants and the large landowners – make a brief appearance at the end of Book III. Artisans and the petty bourgeoisie generally
are virtually absent, as are the classes of managers and officials. In other
writings Marx provides the richer social setting in which this theory must
be embedded. The well-known writings on French politics are not sufficient for this purpose, since they do not deal with the most advanced
capitalist country. They must be supplemented by the numerous, briefer
articles on England. Together they amount to a theory of the nature of the
state in capitalist societies. In France and England power was wielded by
the classes that had come to acquire a kind of monopoly on it – the
centralized bureaucracy in France and the landed aristocracy in England.
Before and during the 1848 German Revolution Marx believed and hoped
that the capitalist class would take power for itself – to allow for a naked
class confrontation between workers and bourgeoisie. When his expectations were frustrated, he had to come up with an explanation why the
economically dominant class was content to take second place in the
political arena. He found it precisely in the fact that the bourgeoisie
wanted to avoid the confrontation with the workers that he had hoped
for. By splitting the energy and fighting spirit of the workers between two
enemies, Capital and Government, the bourgeoisie calculated that they
would gain more in the long run than they would have to sacrifice in the
short run. The main paradigm for the domination over the working class
is not divide-and-conquer, although Marx occasionally refers to that
mechanism. Rather it is that of the *two-front war* that, by confusing the
workers as to the identity of the main enemy, blurs the lines of class
conflict.

Between economics and politics, class struggle is the mediating
element. Classes are defined by their economic behaviour and brought
together by their common economic interests, yet to promote these interests they sooner or later must turn to politics. Analytically one may distinguish between two stages of this process. First, there is the formation of

class consciousness – the creation of class solidarity and its embodiment in class organizations. The crystallization of objectively defined classes into collective actors is influenced by various structural factors, such as the density of communication networks between class members, the rate of turn-over in the class and its degree of cultural homogeneity. Marx argued in particular that the peasantry, in the countries where it remained in existence, was structurally prevented from acquiring class consciousness. Peasants had a role to play as supporters of a Louis Bonaparte, but could not create an organization to promote their own interests. Secondly, there is the formation of class coalitions – alliances between classes that have developed into collective actors. It follows from the two-front theory that there should be a trend towards an alliance between the property-owning classes against the dispossessed, although initially the two industrial classes may have tended to ally themselves against the pre-industrial one. Yet, Marx believed, this anti-worker alliance could only delay the final confrontation and breakdown. As capitalism became increasingly vulnerable and crisis-ridden, no amount of political juggling could save it. He did not consider the possibility that the state could intervene to counteract crises, for example by bolstering demand or offering other forms of regulation.

A final dimension of Marx's analysis of capitalism is the international one. He was acutely aware of the relentlessly expanding and proselytizing character of capitalism, spreading from one country to another by the diffusion of goods, manpower, capital and ideas. Moreover, he turned the difference between pioneers and latecomers in capitalist development to analytical purposes. It would be wrong to say that he made the theory of combined and uneven development into the cornerstone of his analysis, as Trotsky was later to do. There are, nevertheless, non-negligible elements of this view in his writings. It took different forms in different phases of his life. Around 1850 he toyed with the idea of a communist revolution first occurring in the backward capitalist nations on the European continent, and then spreading to England – the only country in which a viable communist regime, capable of outpacing capitalism, was possible. This development rests on the diffusion of revolution from East to West. Thirty years later Marx put his hope in the propagation of technology from the advanced West to the revolutionary East. Both conceptions share the premise that the conditions for a successful communist *revolution* differ from those of a viable communist *regime*, so that some learning, borrowing or contagion must take place if the latter is to be a realistic possibility. In the early version the theory has some appeal, but the later conception is inherently implausible. For intrinsic reasons, the speed of diffusion of political ideas is much greater than that of technology.

Communism

Capital I is a work written for the happy few, by one of them. It makes no concessions whatsoever to the uneducated reader. Marx assumes that *his* readers know Latin, Greek and the main European languages. They should be as well versed in philosophy as in political economy, with a firm grasp of world history and current political affairs. Moreover, they should be able to recognize literary allusions even in fairly disguised forms. It is a book that stretches the reader's mind to the limits, as it had no doubt stretched its author's capacities. It is, in other words, an extreme feat of creativity. In the future communist society, everyone will be capable of understanding works of this stature. Indeed, everyone will be capable of writing comparable works, and devote most of their time to doing so.

This may sound like an exaggeration, and on some interpretations of Marx it certainly is. Yet in one sense it contains an undeniable truth. Marx was appalled by the miserable, passive, vegetative existence led by mid-nineteenth-century workers. At work they were mere appendages of the machines they operated; at home they were too exhausted to lead any sort of active life. At best they could enjoy the passive pleasures of consumption. Marx, bursting with energy, constantly creative and innovative, even despite himself when he had a work to finish, was at the extreme opposite pole. He knew the profound pleasures of creation, of difficulties overcome, of tensions set up and then resolved. He *knew* that this was the good life for man. And he strived for a society in which it would no longer be reserved for a small, privileged minority. Self-realization through creative work is the essence of Marx's communism.

I believe this is the most valuable and enduring element of Marx's thought. Although he himself only referred to intellectual achievements, this is not a necessary limitation. To be a good cook or carpenter or, for that matter, to make good embroideries are goals the striving for which can bring the same kind of pleasure. Indeed, to *do* pushpin may be as rewarding as to *read* poetry. Mill's distinction between the cruder and the finer pleasures is, to that extent, beside the point. If we supplement Marx and the creations of the mind with William Morris and the creations of the hand, a more balanced view emerges, and one to which Marx himself would probably have had no objections. To implement it, as far as possible, is a supremely worthwhile political task.

Yet how far is "as far as possible"? Are there inherent limits on the extent to which the ideal of self-realization can be satisfied? Could the ideal come into conflict with other values to which Marx also subscribed – or with unalterable facts about human nature and societies? The following series of objections are not intended to demolish the ideal, but to provoke needed reflections on the forms in which and the limits within which it can be carried out. Otherwise the best could quite easily become the enemy of the good – to use a phrase that provides a charitable explanation of the failure of actually existing socialism to realize Marx's vision.

(1) Marx, apparently, believed that communism would be characterized by the full and free self-realization of the individual. On one, strong reading this implies that the individual – each individual – (a) has all the capacities that any other has and (b) will develop and use them all. The first part of this conception is extremely Utopian, by its denial of any genetically determined differences in ability. Even if that view were to be modified, the second part of the conception is also quite implausible. There is a trade-off between depth and breadth of achievement that prevents the individual from doing as well in *all* the fields within his competence as he can do in *any* of them. A weaker reading could emphasize the freedom rather than the fullness of self-realization, by demanding that in communist society nothing should block the desire of the individual to realize himself in one particular line of activity. While more plausible, this view also leads to difficulties of social coordination, as explained later.

(2) The ideal of self-realization is a strenuous one. Is it too demanding? Would communist society exclude or stigmatize those who prefer the passive pleasures of consumption, be it in the contemplation of pushpin or of poetry? Would an allocation of resources to facilitate the process of creation do an injustice to those who would rather enjoy the fruits of creation? I confess to some doubt here. While I feel confident that the passive attitudes of many persons in contemporary societies are largely the result of remediable social causation, I am not at all sure that they could never be the object of an autonomous choice. I am not sure, that is, that if freed from such constraints as lack of time, energy, money or self-esteem, everyone would spontaneously choose creation over consumption. And since I do not think this can be decided in other ways than by the individuals concerned, the uncertainty should lead to some caution in the implementation of the ideal.

(3) The ideal of self-realization is one that easily can degenerate into narcissism or self-indulgence. In a society geared towards self-realization no one should be concerned with self-realization. They should be concerned with the tasks at hand – writing books, making embroideries or playing chess. It is only if they take those tasks with the seriousness and concentration needed to succeed in them that the pleasures of self-realization will be forthcoming, as supervenient on the performance. (In addition, of course, they must sometimes actually succeed.) This raises the problem that planning for self-realization may be self-defeating. Raising the ideal of self-realization to the central value in society could have the effect that there would be less of it. To some extent this is in danger of happening in reform movements for participation at the work-place. It is sometimes forgotten that participation, to be valuable, must have a goal outside itself – the making of good decisions or of good products.

(4) Work, in modern industrial societies, offers limited scope for the kind of self-realization Marx had in mind. It may or may not be repetitive, monotonous or boring, but it almost always has to be carried out under conditions of coordination and supervision that severely restrict free, creative activity. Alternative technologies will probably make this statement less true in the future than it has been over the last century, but not to the extent of making it irrelevant. On the other hand, the work situation is in many respects a suitable context, since it offers the external discipline that is often a condition for self-realization. Knowing that the customer might not want the product tends to concentrate the mind wonderfully. Conversely, the activities carried out privately, at home, with no such external spurs, may be diluted into dilettantism, with the concomitant danger of self-indulgence referred to above.

(5) Marx conceived communism as a synthesis of capitalist and precapitalist societies, reconciling the individualism of the former and the communitarian character of the latter. Individual self-realization should take place in creative work for the sake of the community. Yet an extreme emphasis on creative self-realization comes into conflict with the value of community. If production is to be for the sake of the community, at least some of the members, at least some of the time, must indulge in the passive pleasures of consumption – of consuming the products that are the outcome of self-realization through work. The only form of community which is fully compatible with extreme emphasis on creation is the community of creators. A novelist might know that there is no reaction to expect from the public, but he might eagerly wait for the reaction of his

fellow novelists. *Science* is one domain in which there are no customers, only colleagues. It is also a domain in which altruism takes second place to emulation, competition and self-assertion. In Hegel's phrase, it is "das geistige Tierreich". To some extent, this is unavoidable. Self-realization is closely linked to recognition by competent others. Customers, audiences and publics rarely have the kind of competence one looks for – it is found in the community of creators.

(6) The emphasis on community in Marx's vision of capitalism was intended as a contrast to the rampant self-seeking individualism that permeates capitalism. In particular, he wanted to show that there would be no incentive problems under communism, that is no need to link individual (material) reward to individual contributions. People would work because of the pleasure they derived from work, including the pleasure of watching others taking pleasure in their products. Yet self-interested attitudes could emerge even in communism, at a higher level. Different forms of self-realization are unequally demanding by way of material support. Torch sculptors need more than cooks, film directors more than chess players. If the overriding value is the *free* self-realization of all, this must at least mean that society should make available material support proportionately to what is needed, otherwise some individuals who went in for very expensive activities might be blocked in their self-realization. Yet if many choose the more expensive activities, as they might well do, the outcome would be that the general level of self-realization became quite low. This conclusion is derived from three premises, that should be made explicit. (i) There will not be abundance in communist society. There will still be scarce goods with alternative uses. (ii) The principle of distributive justice implied in Marx's theory of communism is that of equality of self-realization. (iii) The free choice of the form of self-realization could and probably would lead to some excessively expensive activities being chosen. If the first (and therefore the second) premise is denied, we are in a Cloud-cuckoo-land, and there is nothing more to be said. If the third premise is denied, it must be because one expects that the individuals will sacrifice some of their self-realization for the sake of the community, that is for the sake of the self-realization of others. This would require a more developed form of altruism than the one which is needed for incentive problems to disappear. And it would go against Marx's vision of communism as a society in which *full* self-realization will go together with *full* community.

(7) In capitalism, and more generally in class societies throughout history, we have observed the self-realization of Man at the expense of

that of most individual men. Marx asserted that in communism the supreme value would be the self-realization of individuals. Yet I believe he also took it for granted that the maximization of this value would go together with maximal flowering of mankind. The rate at which wonderful works of art, new scientific theories and ingenious inventions would be forthcoming under communism would be far in excess of what had been observed at any earlier stage. Yet here, as in general, we should be suspicious of any theory that claims the possibility of the simultaneous maximization of two different objective functions. Crudely put, the number of successful artists, scientists etc. is a function of two variables. On the one hand it depends on the number of individuals who engage in such activities, on the other hand on the proportion of them who turn out to be successful. Similarly, the number of frustrated and disappointed individuals is a function of the same variables: the number of those that try multiplied by the proportion that do not succeed. A society that maximizes the first function, will not be one that also minimizes the second. Under communism it may be possible to increase somewhat the proportion of those who succeed (at least with respect to a given number of attempts), because of the liberation from various material and psychological constraints. Yet the constraints of ability and uncertainty cannot be done away with. Since it is in general impossible to tell in advance who has and who lacks the ability to succeed, the only way in which to maximize the number of successful artists is to increase the material on which the selection process can operate – but this also means to increase the number of rejects.

(8) It is not obvious, finally, that self-realization will also produce the technical efficiency that is its precondition. The desire to produce things as cheaply as possible is not one that will obviously emerge as a vehicle for self-realization. Economy, unlike beauty and truth, is not a goal in itself. It is a purely instrumental value, in which compromises are of the essence and perfectionism is to be avoided. The goal is one that would have to be chosen for the sake of the community, that is out of the more developed form of altruism mentioned earlier. Yet one cannot go far in that direction without compromising the vision of communism. For one thing – who should thus sacrifice their personal self-realization? By what process should they be selected? For another, the outcome would curiously resemble a class society, with some who toil and some who are allowed to develop themselves. But, on the other hand, if all are allowed to choose self-realization in art and pure science, no one will be able to, since the material basis will be lacking.

To evaluate these difficulties we need to distinguish what is ir-redeemably Utopian in Marx's thought from what is not, or at least is not known to be. The following elements seem to me the most hopelessly unrealistic ones. First, the idea that communism would allow for material abundance, in the strict sense that when everyone had taken what they wanted, something would be left over of each and every good. Secondly, the idea that all individuals have the same inborn capacities – both quan-titatively and qualitatively. Strictly speaking, this means no inborn gen-etic defects, no acquired handicaps and no special talents like the gifts for mathematics or music that are often said to go in families. Taken together these assumptions imply a vision of communism as constrained only by time – which would probably be a scarce resource even then, unless men become immortal, which does not seem a less plausible expectation than the others.

Somewhat less Utopian, but still almost certainly false, is the following set of ideas. First, the idea that men could develop the superior form of altruism in which they would be willing to sacrifice not only their material welfare, but their personal development to "society". Secondly, the notion that an individual can *fully* develop and use *all* his potential abili-ties, so as not to become identified or obsessed with any one of them (this would be reification). Thirdly, the notion that social decision-making can occur without conflict, by unanimous approval or election. Lastly, the view that it is possible to achieve full coordination of economic activities by means of a central master-plan. All of these assumptions seem to me to go so strongly in the face of theory and experience that it would be foolhardy to start up a process of change on the assumption that they are true. Of course, one or more of them might turn out to be valid. The theories and experiences that appear to invalidate them come from the soft sciences – psychology, economics, political science – whereas the first set of assumptions came up against harder facts from physics and biology. Yet I submit that it would be a form of excessive scepticism on behalf of the social sciences were one on this basis to accept the assump-tions as working hypotheses. Men and societies are indeed malleable, but not infinitely so.

Lastly, there is a set of proposals that certainly appear as unfeasible today, but with respect to which there is little reason to believe that they will remain so indefinitely. For instance, the incentive problems that underlie Marx's proposal to use the contribution principle in the first stage of communism need not persist indefinitely. There seems to be so much truth in Marx's view that the use of one's capacities is inherently enjoyable, that the use of material rewards to solicit them could be made much less prominent. Today the bearers of rare skills are able to extract a huge reward by blackmail, that is by threatening to withhold them, but if that option was blocked they would choose to use them out of self-interest. Also, some inherently insatiable needs, such as the demand for positional goods, could become less prominent by a process of change that would essentially have no losers. This would not create abundance, but might liberate large amounts of resources for more constructive use. Finally, alternative technologies permitting decentralized, small-scale production processes could be far more systematically developed – and would be, were the incentives offered.

Very broadly speaking, the most Utopian proposals have relatively little textual basis in Marx; the moderately Utopian somewhat more; and the more reasonable proposals somewhat less again. This is, and must be, a rough intuitive appraisal, since the relevant texts are both few and extraordinarily ambiguous and elusive. In any case, it does not matter too much. We need not take our cue from specific textual evidence, but should rather consider the more general considerations underlying it. One can then support the general ideal of equal self-realization, at least if the equality is that of the material prerequisites for self-realization rather than of the extent to which it actually is assured. Autonomy in the work-place is one form of self-realization that would be open to everybody. Corresponding to the large-scale character of modern industry, it would have to be autonomy mainly at the collective level, in workers' cooperatives. This, certainly, is less than what Marx hoped for; equally certainly far more than what we have today. Central planning is out, being incompatible both with autonomy and with efficiency. Instead there would have to be a conflictual political process to decide on the specific forms of political intervention and regulation. This is a very far cry from Marx's vision, ultimately of organic character. He conceived of communism as a society of individual producers in spontaneous coordination, much as the cells in a body work together for the common good, each of them reflecting the whole from its point of view. No such society will ever exist; to believe it will is to court disaster. Although Marx stood for an *ethical* individualism in his approach to communism, he did not see that the actual organization must also take into account the possibilities and limitations of individuals. Had he done so – as we today must do – he might have set his goals lower, and made it possible to approximate even his undiluted goals to a greater degree.

Revolution

The advent of communism requires two conditions. First, the productive forces must be developed to a level at which communism is viable, in the sense that it will immediately or ultimately overtake capitalism. Secondly, the workers (and possibly their allies) must take the political power and set up communist relations of production. The second condition in turn subdivides into two. The workers must have an opportunity to take the power, that is the ruling class must not be able to repress them by force. Also, they must be motivated to the bid for power. The last, finally, can be further split into two conditions. The workers must be frustrated or unhappy with their life under capitalism; and they must believe that communism is a viable, superior alternative.

Marx never produced a theory of revolution to explain how all these conditions come together in the course of capitalist development. Concerning some of them, it is fairly easy to reconstruct his argument, while others remain elusive. The first issue, concerning the objective preconditions of communism, is the most clearcut. Marx believed that at some stage in the development of capitalism it would create the conditions under which further growth of the productive forces is best promoted by communist relations of production. Although that view is not particularly plausible, it might still have revolutionary efficacy if adopted by the workers, an issue that I postpone for the moment. Here we should only note that this argument underlies the problem of premature revolution – a bid for power before the productive forces were sufficiently developed.

It is not clear how Marx conceived the opportunity for revolution. According to one well-known view, revolution becomes feasible when a military defeat is conjoined with severe financial difficulties, leading to a general breakdown of the will and ability to resist among the ruling classes. There is no corresponding theory in Marx. The closest analogy is perhaps the theory of the falling rate of profit. Although Marx never says so explicitly, we must assume that this fall eventually would bring investments to a halt and undermine the belief of the ruling class that the system is worth defending. In some of his scenarios from c. 1850, he also seems to have envisaged a role for revolutionary wars, as during the French Revolution, which constantly formed his reference point. In any case, some objective difficulties of this kind form one necessary condition for revolution. The possibility of a superior arrangement is not in itself sufficient: it will not lead to the demoralization of the ruling class nor, as I shall explain shortly, to the rise of revolutionary motivations among the workers.

The question of revolutionary motivation is the central issue. I shall consider the three main charges against capitalism, in order to discuss whether they can provide the requisite will to change. In doing so we will also have to consider the communist alternative, since the "push" from capitalism and the "pull" from communism may be expected to interact in producing the motivation.

Consider, first, alienation as a motivation for revolution. Here, it is crucial whether we opt for the subjective or the objective notion of alienation – whether it is seen as the sense of a lack of meaning or the lack of a sense of meaning. Independently of the somewhat unclear exegetical issue, we may note that there are good *a priori* reasons for holding the theory in its objective version. Communism in Marx's vision represents a way of life totally different from capitalism. It is not a question of higher consumption levels, but of a shift away from (passive) consumption altogether. To appreciate the joys of active creation one must already have experienced them, which is something few have had a chance to do in capitalism. To feel the attraction of communism one must be there already. Or again: to make a rational choice one must know both sides of the question, but workers living in capitalist society know only one side. True, if they accept the promise of communism to be technically more efficient, they might desire it as a means to increased consumption – but why should they believe this when the technical efficiency is supposed to follow from the shift away from consumption and towards active creation? To the statement, "You don't know what you are missing" the workers might well reply: "If so, how can you expect us to miss it?"

Next, consider the motivational force of justice. Whether or not Marx held a theory of justice, he might have believed that it could provide a lever for action; and even if he did not, it is a question of some interest in its own right. The textual evidence is ambiguous, but some of it strongly supports the idea that the recognition of a state as unjust provides (as Marx says) the knell to its doom. In my view, the political, social and economic history of the last few centuries makes good sense when understood in this perspective. This history has been a somewhat uneven, but basically continuous process of increased democracy, pointing towards, but not reaching, communism as understood by Marx. The driving force has been the almost irresistible legitimacy of the notion of self-government. Once formulated and advocated, it acquires a compelling force that makes all attempts to resist it appear as retrograde and hopeless, even in the eyes of the resisters. Tactics and strategy then concern the timing and form of the changes, not their ultimate necessity. Hence justice could provide not only a motivation for the workers, but also a cause of demoralization among the rulers. Some will object that this argument goes far beyond what can reasonably be attributed to Marx. I agree, but at this point in my exposition that is not a major concern. Others will object to the view itself, on the grounds that it gives excessive importance to normative conceptions and pays insufficient attention to immediate interests in the shaping of motivations. I agree that people are unlikely to make a revolution on grounds of justice, unless it coincides with more urgent concerns. Revolution is a costly and painful process, that will be initiated only if the situation is experienced as desperate. Yet not all changes are revolutionary ones, and more gradual changes could be – and have been – upheld by such normative motivations.

Consider finally the inefficiency of capitalism as a motive to abolish it. Inefficiency by its very nature is predicated on the basis of counterfactual comparisons. It obtains if things could have been organized better than they actually are. This is compatible with the actual situation being "satisfactory", that is being felt by most people to provide them with a decent living. In the choice between a satisfactory actual situation and the prospect of a hypothetically superior alternative, almost everybody will take the former, for two reasons. First, the situation will always be clouded in some uncertainty. The communist theoreticians may tell the workers that communism will be statically and dynamically more efficient than capitalism, but in the absence of demonstrated superiority the arguments will be tenuous and meet with scepticism. Secondly, even assuming that such arguments are accepted, the revolution involves transition costs that may make the workers shy away from it. It does not seem justified to ask them to sacrifice themselves and their children for the sake of their grandchildren, when they could all live a reasonably good life under capitalist conditions. Hence the inefficiency of capitalism will provide motivating power only when accompanied by absolute hardship and misery, so that the workers have nothing to lose but their chains. If the cause of this misery also has the effect of destroying the morale of the ruling class, it will provide the opportunity as well as the motivation for revolution. The cause might well not have that second effect, in which case an attempted revolution will prove unsuccessful. Also, even if it has that effect and the revolution succeeds, the objective conditions for communism might not be present. Indeed, there are good reasons for thinking that they will not be present, since the development of the productive forces to the requisite level will rarely go together with hardships at the requisite level. The various diffusion scenarios mentioned above do not provide plausible solutions to this dilemma.

Two spectres haunt the communist revolution. One is the danger of premature revolution, in a combination of advanced revolutionary ideas and miserable conditions in a country not yet ripe for communism. The other is the risk of preempted revolutions, of reforms introduced from above to defuse a dangerous situation. The last century has seen many examples of what appear to be premature revolutions, although it could be that this judgment is itself premature. It is also likely that in the absence of the many reforms designed to prevent revolution, some revolutions would have occurred – prematurely or not. There has not been a single unambiguous instance of the kind of revolution that Marx advocated. True, it is not impossible that some existing communist countries at some later date will overtake capitalism, and hence retroactively justify the revolution, but there are no rational grounds for believing that this will happen. In one sense, therefore – the sense that to him was the most important – Marx's life and work were in vain.

Yet the influence of Marx has not run dry, by any means. It is not possible today, morally or intellectually, to be a Marxist in the traditional sense. This would be someone who accepted all or most of the views that Marx held to be true and important – scientific socialism, the labour theory of value or the theory of falling rate of profit, together with other and more defensible views. But, speaking now for myself only, I believe it is still possible to be a Marxist in a rather different sense of the term. I find that most of the views that *I* hold to be true and important, I can trace back to Marx. This includes methodology, substantive theories and, above all, values. The critique of exploitation and alienation remains central. A better society would be one that allowed all human beings to do what only human beings can do – to create, to invent, to imagine other worlds.

References

A. Works by Marx

With a few exceptions, page references to Marx are to one of three collected editions of his and Engels's writings. The main exceptions are the mature economic writings: the three volumes of *Capital, Theories of Surplus-Value, Grundrisse* and *Results of the Immediate Process of Production*. Here I refer to standard English translations, indicated below. Other exceptions are the *Ethnological Notebooks*, the *Mathematische Manuskripte* and *The Secret Diplomatic History of the Eighteenth Century*, none of which is available in a collected edition.

Wherever possible I refer to Karl Marx and Friedrich Engels: *Collected Works*, London: Lawrence and Wishart (abbreviated CW). For works not available in this edition I refer to one of the German editions of the collected works. In most cases this is *Marx-Engels Werke*, Berlin: Dietz (abbreviated MEW). In some cases I refer to the new *Marx-Engels Gesamtausgabe*, Berlin: Dietz (abbreviated MEGA), not to be confused with the MEGA edited by Rjazanov and Adoratskij before World War II. With one exception it is indicated from which English translations the citations are taken. The exception is the recently published *Zur Kritik der politischen Ökonomie (Manuskript 1861–3)*. This manuscript consists of twenty-one notebooks, of which notebooks VI to XV were published by Kautsky as *Theories of Surplus-Value* (with some material from the other notebooks as well). The remaining notebooks were published quite recently, and have not yet been translated into English. The passages cited in the present work have been translated by Mr Rodney Livingstone.

I refer to newspaper articles by giving the date and the name of the newspaper in question. Similarly, I refer to letters by giving the date and the name of the addressee. Most of the passages cited from letters are taken from the translations in Saul K. Padover (ed.), *The Letters of Karl Marx*, Englewood Cliffs, N.J.: Prentice Hall 1979. Works co-authored with Engels are prefaced by an asterisk (*).

"Account of an interview with Karl Marx published in the 'World'", MEGA I.22, 451–8.

*"The alleged divisions in the international", MEW 18, 7–51. Cited after the English translation (from the French original) in D. Fernbach (ed.), *Karl Marx: The First International and after*, New York: Vintage Books 1974.

"Aus der 'kritischen Geschichte'", MEW 20, 210–38. (This is a part of Engels's *Anti-Dühring* that was written by Marx.)

"Briefwechsel mit Vera Sasulich", MEW 19, 386–403.

Capital I, New York: International Publishers 1967.

Capital II, New York: International Publishers 1967.

Capital III, New York: International Publishers 1967.

"Circular against Kriege", CW 6, 35–51.

The Civil War in France, MEGA I.22, 15–159. This includes the first draft (15–81), the second draft (85–117) and the final version (123–159).

The Class Struggles in France, CW 10, 45–145.

"Commentary on Friedrich List's book *Das nationale System der politischen Ökonomie*", CW 4, 265–93.

Comments on James Mill, Elémens d'Economie Politique, CW 3, 211–28.

"Comments on Adolph Wagner's *Lehrbuch der politischen Ökonomie*", MEW 19, 355–83. Cited after the (incomplete) English translation in D. McLellan (ed.), *Karl Marx: Selected Writings*, Oxford University Press 1977, and after the translations in Allen Wood, "Marx on right and justice: A reply to Husami", *Philosophy and Public Affairs* 8 (1979).

*The Communist Manifesto, CW 6, 477–519.

"Confidential communication", MEW 16, 409–20. Cited after the English translation in D. Fernbach (ed.), *Karl Marx: The First International and after*, New York: Vintage Books 1974.

Contribution to the Critique of Hegel's Philosophy of Law, CW 3, 3–129.

"Contribution to the critique of Hegel's Philosophy of Law – Introduction", CW 3, 175–87.

A Contribution to the Critique of Political Economy, MEW 13, 7–160. Cited after the English translation published in Moscow: Progress Publishers 1979.

Critique of the Gotha Program, MEW 19, 15–32. Cited after the (incomplete) English translation in D. McLellan (ed.), *Karl Marx: Selected Writings*, Oxford University Press 1977.

Economic and Philosophical Manuscripts, CW 3, 229–346.

The Eighteenth Brumaire of Louis Napoleon, CW 11, 99–197.

The Ethnological Notebooks of Karl Marx, L. Krader (ed.), Assen: Van Gorcum 1974.

*The German Ideology, CW 5, 19–539.

Grundrisse, Harmondsworth: Penguin Books 1973.

Herr Vogt, CW 17, 21–329.

*The Holy Family, CW 4, 6–211. In this work written jointly with Engels their responsibility for the various parts is indicated. I only refer to those written by Marx.

"Instructions for delegates to the Geneva Congress", MEW 16, 190–9. Cited after the English original in D. Fernbach (ed.), *Karl Marx: The First International and after*, New York: Vintage Press 1974.

"Letters from the *Deutsch-Französische Jahrbücher*", CW 3, 133–45.

Mathematische Manuskripte, W. Endemann (ed.), Kronberg: Scriptor 1974.

"On Bakunin's *Statism and Anarchy*", MEW 18, 597–642. Cited after the (incomplete) English translation in D. McLellan (ed.), *Karl Marx: Selected Writings*, Oxford University Press 1977.

"Political indifferentism", MEW 18, 299–304. Cited after the English translation in D. Fernbach (ed.), *Karl Marx: The First International and after*, New York: Vintage Books 1974.

The Poverty of Philosophy, CW 6, 105–212.

"Preface" to the second edition of *The Eighteenth Brumaire of* Louis Bonaparte, MEW 16, 358–60.

"Procès-verbaux de la Conférence des délégués de l'Association Internationale des Travailleurs réunie à Londres du 17 au 23 septembre 1871", MEGA I.22, 641–748.

"Proclamation of the General Council", MEW 16, 422–3.

"Provisional rules of the International", MEW 16, 14–16. Cited after the English original in D. Fernbach (ed.), *Karl Marx: The First International and after*, New York: Vintage Books 1974.

"Reflections", CW 10, 584–94.

Results of the Immediate Process of Production. Appendix to Karl Marx, *Capital. Volume One*, translated by Ben Fowkes, New York: Vintage Books 1977.

Revelations concerning the Communist Trial in Cologne, CW 11, 395–457.

Review of A. Chenu, *Les Conspirateurs*, CW 10, 311–25.

Review of E. Girardin, *Le Socialisme et l'Impôt*, CW 10, 326–37.

Review of Guizot, *Pourquoi la Révolution d'Angleterre a-t-elle Réussi?*, CW 10, 251–6.

The Secret Diplomatic History of the Eighteenth Century, in T. Payne (ed.), *The Unknown Karl Marx*, London: University of London Press 1972.

"Speech on the Hague Congress", MEW 18, 159–61. Cited after the English translation (from a German translation from the French original) in D. Fernbach (ed.), *Karl Marx: The First International and after*, New York: Vintage Books 1974.

"Speech on the question of free trade", CW 5, 450–65.

Theories of Surplus-Value, vols. 1–3, London: Lawrence and Wishart 1972.

"Theses on Feuerbach", CW 5, 3–5.

Urtext to *A Contribution to the Critique of Political Economy*, in MEGA II.2, 17–93.

"Wages", CW 6, 415–37.

Wages, Price and Profit, MEW 16, 101–52. Cited here after the English original as published in Peking: Foreign Languages Press 1975.

Zur Kritik der politischen Ökonomie (Manuskript 1861–3), MEGA II.3, vols. 1–6. Of these vol. II.3.1 includes pp. 1–328, vol. II.3.5, pp. 1543–888 and vol. II.3.6, pp. 1891–2384. The other volumes correspond roughly to the three volumes of *Theories of Surplus-Value*.

B. Works by other writers

Acton, H. B. Dialectical materialism, in Paul Edwards (ed.), *The Encyclopedia of Philosophy*, vol. 2, 389–97. New York: Macmillan.

Ainslie, G. Specious reward. *Psychological Bulletin* 82 (1975), 463–96.

A behavioral economic approach to the defence mechanism. *Social Science Information* 21 (1982), 735–80.

Beyond microeconomics. In J. Elster (ed.), *The Multiple Self*, to be published by Cambridge University Press.

Alexander, L. A. Zimmerman on coercive wage offers. *Philosophy and Public Affairs* 12 (1983), 160–4.

Allison, G. *The Essence of Decision*. Boston: Little, Brown 1971.

Anderson, P. *The Lineages of the Absolutist State*. London: New Left Books 1974.

Arneson, R. What's wrong with exploitation? *Ethics* 91 (1981), 202–27.

Aron, R. *Les Etapes de la Pensée Sociologique*. Paris: Gallimard 1967.

Arrow, K. *Essays in the Theory of Risk-bearing*. Amsterdam: North -Holland 1971.

Assoun, J.-L. *Marx et la Répétition Historique*. Paris: Presses Universitaires de France 1978.

Avineri, S. *The Social and Political Thought of Karl Marx*. Cambridge University Press 1969.

Axelrod, R. and Hamilton, W. The evolution of cooperation. *Science* 211 (1981), 1390–6.

Balibar, E. Les concepts fondamentaux du matérialisme historique, in L. Althusser *et al.*, *Lire le Capital*, vol. 2, Paris: Maspero 1966.

Bardhan, P. Class formation in India, *Journal of Peasant Studies* 10 (1982), 73–94.

Barrow, J. H. *Slavery in the Roman Empire*, London: Methuen 1925.

Baumol, W. *Welfare Economics and the Theory of the State*, 2nd edn, London: Bell 1965.

Beauchamp, T. and Rosenberg, A. *Hume and the Problem of Causation*. Oxford University Press 1981.

Beck, B. *Animal Tool Behavior*. New York: Garland.

Black, C. (ed.) *Rewriting Russian History*. New York: Praeger 1956.

Blau, P. and Duncan, O. D. *The American Occupational Structure*. New York: Wiley 1967.

Blaug, M. Technical change and Marxian economics, in D. Horowitz (ed.), *Marx and Modern Economic Theory*, 227–43. London: MacGibbon and Kee 1968.

Economic Theory in Retrospect, 3rd edn, Cambridge University Press 1978.

A Methodological Appraisal of Marxian Economics. Amsterdam: North-Holland 1980.

The Methodology of Economics. Cambridge University Press 1980.

Another look at the reduction problem in Marx, in I. Bradley and M. Howard (eds.), *Classical and Marxian Political Economy*, 188–202. London: Macmillan 1982.

Bleaney, M. *Underconsumption Theories*. New York: International Publishers 1977.

Bliss, C. *Capital Theory and the Distribution of Income*. Amsterdam: North-Holland 1975.

Bloch, M. The rise of dependent cultivation and seignorial institutions, in M. Bloch, *Mélanges Historiques*, vol. I, Paris: S.E.V.P.E.N. 1963.

Bodemann, E. *Die Leibniz-Handschriften*. Hanover 1889.

Bois, G. *La Crise du Féodalisme*. Paris: Presses de la Fondation Nationale des Sciences Politiques 1976.

Borkenau, F. *Der Übergang vom feudalen zum bürgerlichen Weltbild*, Paris: Alcan 1934.

Boserup, E. *Population and Technological Change*, University of Chicago Press 1981.

Boudon, R. *Education, Opportunity and Social Inequality*. New York: Wiley 1974.

Effets Pervers et Ordre Social. Paris: Presses Universitaires de France 1977.

Bourdieu, P. Condition de classe et position de classe. *Archives Européennes de Sociologie* VII (1966), 201–29.

La Distinction. Paris: Editions de Minuit 1979.

Bowles, S. and Gintis, H. The Marxian theory of value and heterogeneous labour, *Cambridge Journal of Economics* 1 (1977), 173–92.

The power of capital: on the inadequacy of the conception of the capitalist economy as "private". *The Philosophical Forum* XIV (1983), 225–45.

Bowman, J. The logic of capitalist collective action. *Social Science Information* 21 (1982), 571–604.

Braverman, H. *Labor and Monopoly Capital*. New York: Monthly Review Press 1974.

Brenkert, G. Freedom and private property in Marx. *Philosophy and Public Affairs* 8 (1879), 122–47.

Brenner, R. The origins of capitalist development: a critique of neo-Smithian Marxism. *New Left Review* no. 104 (1977), 25–82.

The agrarian roots of European capitalism. *Past and Present* no. 97 (1982), 16–113.

Bronfenbrenner, M. *Das Kapital* for modern man, in D. Horowitz (ed.), *Karl Marx and Modern Economic Theory*, 205–26. London: MacGibbon and Kee 1968.

Income Distribution Theory. London: Macmillan 1971.

Brunt, P. A. *Social Conflicts in the Roman Republic*. London: Chatto and Windus 1971.

Buchanan, A. *Marx and Justice*. London: Methuen 1982.

Buckland, W. W. *The Roman Law of Slavery*. Cambridge 1908.

Carlebach, J. *Karl Marx and the Radical Critique of Judaism*. London: Routledge and Kegan Paul 1978.

Chambers, J. D. and Mingay, G. E. *The Agricultural Revolution 1750–1880*. London: Batsford 1966.

Chambliss, The political economy of crime. A comparative study of Nigeria and the USA, in I. Taylor *et al.* (eds.), *Critical Criminology*, 167–80. London: Routledge and Kegan Paul 1975.

Clegg, H. A. *Industrial Democracy and Nationalization*. Oxford: Blackwell 1951.

Cohen, G. A. Karl Marx and the withering away of social science. *Philosophy and Public Affairs* 1 (1972), 182–203. Reprinted as an appendix to *Karl Marx's Theory of History* (see below).

Bourgeois and proletarians, in S. Avineri (ed.), *Marxist Socialism*, 101–25. New York: Lieber-Atherton 1973.

Karl Marx's dialectic of labour. *Philosophy and Public Affairs* 3 (1974), 235–61.

Karl Marx's Theory of History: A Defence. Oxford University Press 1978.

Robert Nozick and Wilt Chamberlain, in J. Arthur and W. Shaw (eds.), *Justice and Economic Distribution*, 246–62. Englewood Cliffs, N.J.: Prentice Hall 1978.

Capitalism, freedom and the proletariat, in A. Ryan (ed.), *The Idea of Freedom*, 9–26. Oxford University Press 1979.

Review of F. Parkin: *Marxism and Class Theory. The London Review of Books* 15 May 1980.

Freedom, justice and capitalism. *New Left Review* no. 126 (1981), 3–16.

Illusions about private property and freedom, in J. Mepham and D.-H. Ruben, *Issues in Marxist Philosophy*, vol. 4, 223–42. Brighton: Harvester Press 1981.

Functional explanation, consequence explanation and Marxism. *Inquiry* 25 (1982), 27–56.

Reply to Elster, "Marxism, functionalism and game theory", *Theory and Society* 11 (1982), 483–96.

Reconsidering historical materialism. *Nomos* XXVI (1983), 226–51.

Reply to four critics. *Analyse und Kritik* 5 (1983), 195–222.

Restricted and inclusive historical materialism. In B. Chavance (ed.), *Marx en Perspective*, pp. 53–76. Paris: Editions de l'Ecole des Hautes Etudes en Sciences Sociales, 1985.

Review of Wood: *Karl Marx. Mind* XCII (1983), 440–5.

The structure of proletarian unfreedom. *Philosophy and Public affairs* 12 (1983), 3–33.

Cohen, J. Review of G. A. Cohen: *Karl Marx's Theory of History. Journal of Philosophy* 79 (1982), 253–73.

Cole, G. D. H. *Studies in Class Structure*. London: Routledge and Kegan Paul 1955.

Coleman, J. *The Mathematics of Collective Action*. London: Heinemann 1973.

Power and the Structure of Society. New York: Norton 1974.

Collins, H. and Abramsky, C. *Karl Marx and the British Labour Movement*. London: Macmillan 1965.

Collins, K. Marx on the English agricultural revolution. *History and Theory* 6 (1967), 351–81.

Collins, S. *Selfless Persons*. Cambridge University Press 1982.

Conry, Y. *L'Introduction du Darwinisme en France au XIXe Siècle*. Paris: Vrin 1974.

Constant, B. De la liberté des anciens comparée à celle des modernes, in B. Constant, *De la liberté chez les Modernes*, ed. M. Gauchet, 491–517. Paris: Le Livre de Poche 1980.

Crouzet, F. Capital formation in Great Britain during the Industrial Revolution, in F. Crouzet (ed.), *Capital Formation in the Industrial Revolution*, 162–222. London: Methuen 1972.

Cummins, I. *Marx, Engels and National Movements*. London: Croom Helm 1980.

Dahl, T. S. *Child Welfare and Social Defence*. Oslo: Universitetsforlaget 1985.

Dahrendorf, R. *Class and Class Conflict in Industrial Society*. London: Routledge and Kegan Paul 1957.

Davidson, D. *Essays on Actions and Events*. Oxford University Press 1980.

Davies, J. Toward a theory of revolution. *American Sociological Review* 27 (1962), 1–19.

Dennett, D. *Brainstorms*. Hassocks, Sussex: Harvester 1979.

Dobb, M. *Political Economy and Capitalism*. London: Routledge and Kegan Paul 1937.

Domar, E. The causes of slavery and serfdom. *Journal of Economic History* 30 (1971), 137–56.

Draper, H. Marx and the dictatorship of the proletariat. *Etudes de Marxologie* 6 (1962) (= *Cahiers de l'ISEA* no. 129), 5–74.

  Karl Marx's Theory of Revolution. Volume I: State and Bureaucracy. New York: Monthly Review Press 1977.

  Karl Marx's Theory of Revolution. Volume II: The Politics of Social Classes. New York: Monthly Review Press 1978.

Dumont, L. *From Mandeville to Marx.* University of Chicago Press 1977.

Dunn, J. The success and failure of modern revolutions, in J. Dunn, *Political Obligation in its Historical Context*, 217–39. Cambridge University Press 1980.

Dworkin, R. What is equality? Part 1: Equality of welfare. *Philosophy and Public Affairs* 10 (1981), 185–246. Part 2: Equality of resources. *Philosophy and Public Affairs* 10 (1981), 283–345.

Elster, J. *Leibniz et la Formation de l'Esprit Capitaliste.* Paris: Aubier-Montaigne 1975.

  A note on hysteresis in the social sciences. *Synthese* 33 (1976), 371–91.

  Some conceptual problems in political theory, in B. Barry (ed.), *Power and Political Theory*, 245–70. Chichester: Wiley 1976.

  Exploring exploitation. *Journal of Peace Research* 15 (1978), 3–18.

  Logic and Society. Chichester: Wiley 1978.

  Ulysses and the Sirens. Cambridge University Press 1979.

  Négation active et négation passive. *Archives Européennes de Sociologie* 21 (1980), 329–49.

  Reply to comments, *Inquiry* 23 (1980), 213–32.

  Review of G. A. Cohen: *Karl Marx's Theory of History. Political Studies* 28 (1980), 121–8.

  Marxism, functionalism and game theory. *Theory and Society* 11 (1982), 453–82.

  A paradigm for the social sciences? (Review of van Parijs: *Evolutionary Explanation in the Social Sciences.*) *Inquiry* 25 (1982), 378–86.

  Roemer vs. Roemer. *Politics and Society* 11 (1982), 363–74.

  Explaining Technical Change. Cambridge University Press 1983.

  Sour Grapes. Cambridge University Press 1983.

  Further thoughts on Marxism, functionalism and game theory. In B. Chavance (ed.), *Marx en Perspective*, pp. 627–48. Paris: Editions de l'Ecole des Hautes Etudes en Sciences Sociales, 1985.

  Marx et Leibniz. *Revue Philosophique* 108 (1983), 167–77.

  Exploitation, freedom and justice. *Nomos* xxvi (1983), 277–304.

  Reply to comments. *Theory and Society* 12 (1983), 111–20.

  The market and the forum, in A. Hylland and J. Elster (eds.), *Foundations of Social Choice Theory.* Cambridge University Press 1985.

  Constitutional choice and the transition to socialism. To be published in R. Slagstad (ed.), *Constitutionalism and Democracy.*

Engels, F. *Anti-Dühring.* MEW 20.

  Preface to the 1891 edition of *Wage Labour and Capital.* MEW 22, 202–9.

Erckenbrecht, U. *Marx's materialistische Sprachtheorie.* Kronberg: Scriptor 1973.

Evans-Pritchard, E. *The Nuer.* Oxford University Press 1940.

Fagen, R. *Animal Play Behavior.* Oxford University Press 1981.

Fararo, T. S. *Mathematical Sociology.* New York: Wiley 1973.

Felix, D. *Marx as Politician.* Carbondale and Edwardsville: Southern Illinois University Press 1983.

Fellner, W. Two propositions in the theory of induced innovations. *Economic Journal* 71 (1961), 305–8.

Festinger, L. *A Theory of Cognitive Dissonance*. Stanford University Press 1957.

Feuerwerker, A. "China's modern economic history in communist Chinese historiography", pp. 216–46 in the following work.

(ed.) *History in Communist China*. Cambridge, Mass.: MIT Press 1968.

Field, A. The problem with institutional neoclassical economics. *Explorations in Economic History* 18 (1981), 174–98.

Finley, M. I. *The Ancient Economy*. London: Chatto and Windus 1973.

Aristotle and economic analysis, in M. I. Finley (ed.), *Studies in Ancient Society*, 26–52. London: Routledge and Kegan Paul 1974.

Ancient Slavery and Modern Ideology. London: Chatto and Windus 1980.

"Politics", in M. I. Finley (ed.), *The Legacy of Greece*, 22–36. Oxford University Press 1981.

Technical innovation and economic progress in the ancient world, in M. I. Finley, *Economy and Society in Ancient Greece*, 176–98. London: Chatto and Windus 1981.

Politics in the Ancient World. Cambridge University Press 1983.

Foster, J. *Class Struggle and the Industrial Revolution*. London: Methuen 1974.

Frankfurt, H. G. Coercion and moral responsibility, in T. Honderich (ed.), *Essays on Freedom of Action*, 63–86. London: Routledge and Kegan Paul.

Freud, S. Psychoanalytische Bemerkungen über einen autobiographisch beschriebenen fall von Paranoia, in Freud, *Gesammelte Werke*, vol. VIII, 240–320. Frankfurt a.M.: Fischer Verlag 1945.

Friedrich, C. J. *Man and his Government*. New York: McGraw-Hill 1963.

Fromm, E. *Fear of Freedom*. London: Routledge and Kegan Paul 1960.

Furet, F. *Penser la Révolution Française*. Paris: Gallimard 1978.

Garnsey, P., Hopkins, G. and Whittaker, C. R. (eds.) *Trade in the Ancient Economy*. London: Chatto and Windus 1983.

Gellner, E. "A Russian Marxist philosophy of history", in E. Gellner (ed.), *Soviet and Western Anthropology*, 59–82. New York: Columbia University Press 1980.

Genovese, E. *Roll, Jordan, Roll*. New York: Pantheon 1974.

Georgescu-Roegen, N. *The Entropy Law and the Economic Process*. Cambridge, Mass.: Harvard University Press 1971.

Gerschenkron, A. Agrarian policies and industrialization: Russia 1861–1917, in H. J. Habakkuk and M. Postan (eds.), *Cambridge Economic History of Europe*, vol. VI, 706–800. Cambridge University Press 1965.

Geuss, R. *The Idea of a Critical Theory*. Cambridge University Press 1981.

Goldmann, L. *Le Dieu Caché*. Paris: Gallimard 1954.

Gould, C. G. *Marx's Social Ontology*. Cambridge, Mass.: MIT Press 1978.

Grégoire, F. *Etudes Hégéliennes*. Louvain: Publications Universitaires de Louvain 1958.

Grindheim, S. How could the aristocracy govern when the bourgeoisie ruled? (in Norwegian). Master's Thesis in History at the University of Oslo, 1975.

Haavelmo, T. Some observations on welfare and economic growth, in W. A. Eltis, M. Scott and N. Wolfe (eds.), *Induction, Growth and Trade: Essays in Honour of Sir Roy Harrod*, 65–75. Oxford University Press 1970.

Haavelmo, T. The role of expectations in economic theory (in Norwegian). Memorandum from the Department of Economics at the University of Oslo 1971.

Hamerow, T. S. *Restoration, Revolution, Reaction: Economics and Politics in Germany 1815–1871*. Princeton University Press 1966.

Hammen, O. *The Red 48'ers. Karl Marx and Friedrich Engels*. New York: Scribner 1969.

Hanagan, M. P. *The Logic of Solidarity*. Urbana, Ill.: University of Illinois Press.

Harcourt, G. C. *Some Cambridge Controversies in the Theory of Capital*. Cambridge University Press 1973.

Hardin, R. *Collective Action*. Baltimore: Johns Hopkins University Press 1982.

Harsanyi, J. Cardinal welfare, individualistic ethics and interpersonal comparisons of utility. *Journal of Political Economy* 63 (1955), 309–21.

Rational Behavior and Bargaining Equilibrium in Games and Social Situations. Cambridge University Press 1977.

Hayek, F. A. The results of human action but not of human design, in F. A. Hayek, *Studies in Philosophy, Politics and Economics*, 96–105. London: Routledge and Kegan Paul 1967.

Hechter, M. (ed.) *The Microfoundations of Macrosociology*. Philadelphia: Temple University Press 1983.

Heckscher, E. *Mercantilism*, vols. I–II. London: Allen and Unwin 1955.

Hegel, G. W. F. *The Philosophy of Right*. Oxford University Press 1945.

The Science of Logic, vols. I–II. London: Allen and Unwin 1961.

The Phenomenology of Spirit. Oxford University Press 1977.

Heller, A. *The Theory of Needs in Marx*. London: Allison and Busby 1976.

Hessen, B. The social and economic roots of Newton's *Principia*, in N. Bukharin *et al* (eds.), *Science at the Cross Roads* (1931), reprint. London: Cass 1971.

Hernes, G. Structural change in social processes. *American Journal of Sociology* 83 (1976), 513–37.

Hicks, J. *A Theory of Economic History*. Oxford University Press 1969.

Higonnet, P. *Class, Ideology and the Rights of Nobles during the French Revolution*. Oxford University Press 1981.

Hilton, R. *Bond Men Made Free*. London: Methuen 1973.

Hirsch, F. *Social Limits to Growth*. Cambridge, Mass.: Harvard University Press 1976.

Hirschman, A. The changing tolerance for inequality in the course of economic development, in A. Hirschman, *Essays in Trespassing*, 39–58. Cambridge University Press 1982.

Exit, voice and the state, *ibid.*, 246–65.

Shifting Involvements. Princeton University Press 1982.

Hobsbawm, E. "Marx, Engels and politics", in E. Hobsbawm (ed.), *The History of Marxism*, vol. 1, 227–64. Brighton: Harvester Press 1982.

Holmes, S. Precommitment and self-rule. Reflections on the paradox of democracy, to be published in R. Slagstad (ed.), *Constitutionalism and Democracy*.

Hume, D. *A Treatise on Human Nature*, ed., Selby-Bigge. Oxford University Press 1960.

Hunt, R. *The Political Ideas of Marx and Engels*. Vol. I: *Marxism and Totalitarian Democracy 1818–1850*. University of Pittsburgh Press.

Husami, Z. Marx on distributive justice. *Philosophy and Public Affairs* 8 (1978), 27–64.

Hyppolite, J. *Etudes sur Marx et Hegel*, Paris: Marcel Rivière 1955.

Johansen, L. The labour theory of value and marginal utilities. *Economics of Planning* 3 (1963), 89–103.

Johansson, I. Der Minimalkül. *Compositio Mathematica* 4 (1936), 119–36.

Jones, A. H. M. *Athenian Democracy*. Oxford: Blackwell 1977.

Kahneman, D. Slovic, P. and Tversky, A. (eds.) *Judgment under Uncertainty.* Cambridge University Press 1982.

Kalleberg, A. L. and Griffin, L. J. Class, occupation and inequality in job rewards. *American Journal of Sociology* 85 (1980), 731–68.

Kemeny, J. G., Snell, J. L. and Thompson, G. L. *Introduction to Finite Mathematics* 2nd edn. Englewood Cliffs, N.J.: Prentice Hall 1966.

Kennedy, C. Induced bias in innovation and the theory of distribution. *Economic Journal* 74 (1964), 541–47.

Kenway, P. Marx, Keynes and the possibility of crisis. *Cambridge Journal of Economics* 4 (1980), 23–36.

Keynes, J. M. *A Treatise on Money*, in *The Collected Works of John Maynard Keynes*, vol. V, London: Macmillan 1971.

Knei-Paz, B. *The Social and Political Thought of Leon Trotsky*. Oxford University Press 1977.

Kolakowski, L. *Main Currents of Marxism*, vols. 1–3. Oxford University Press 1978.

Kolm, S.-C. *Justice et Equité*. Paris: Editions du CNRS 1971.

La Transition Socialiste. Paris: Editions du Cerf 1977.

Le Bonheur-liberté. Paris: Presses Universitaires de France 1982.

Introduction à la réciprocité générale. *Information sur les Sciences Sociales* 22 (1983), 569–622.

Kydland, F. and Prescott, W. Rules rather than discretion: The inconsistency of optimal plans. *Journal of Political Economy* 85 (1977), 473–92.

Lancaster, K. A new approach to consumer theory. *Journal of Political Economy* 74 (1966) 132–57.

The dynamic inefficiency of capitalism. *Journal of Political Economy* 81 (1973), 1092–1109.

Leibniz, G. W. Considérations sur les principes de vie, in G. W. Leibniz, *Die philosophischen Schriften*, ed. Gerhardt, vol. 6, 539–46. Reprint Hildesheim: Olms 1965.

Nouveaux Essais sur l'Entendenement Humain, ibid., vol. 6.

Opuscules et Fragments Inédits, ed. Couturat. Reprint Hildesheim: Olms 1966.

Levenson, J. *Confucian China and its Modern Fate*, vols. I–III. Berkeley: University of California Press 1968.

Liebermann, Y. and Syrquin, M. On the use and abuse of rights. *Journal of Economic Behavior and Organization* 4 (1983), 25–40.

Lipietz, A. The so-called "transformation problem" revisited. *Journal of Economic Theory* 26 (1982), 59–88.

Lipset, S. Social stratification: social class, in E. Shils (ed.), *International Encyclopedia of the Social Sciences*, vol. 15, 296–316. New York: Macmillan 1968.

Lucas, E. Marx und Engels' Auseinandersetzung mit Darwin. *International Review of Social History* 9 (1964), 433–69.

Lukacs, G. Die Verdinglichung und das Bewusstsein des Proletariats, in G. Lukacs, *Geschichte und Klassenbewusstsein*, 257–397. Neuwied und Berlin: Luchterhand 1968.

Der Funktionswechsel des historischen Materialismus, *ibid.*, 398–431.

Lukes, S. *Power: A Radical View*. London: Macmillan 1974.

Can the base be distinguished from the superstructure? in D. Miller and L. Siedentorp (eds.), *The Nature of Political Theory*, 103–20. Oxford University Press 1983.

Marxism and Morality. Oxford University Press 1985.

Maarek, G. *An Introduction to Marx's* Das Kapital. London: Martin Robertson 1979.

Macfarlane, A. *The Origins of English Individualism*. Oxford: Blackwell 1978.

Maguire, J. *Marx's Theory of Politics*. Cambridge University Press 1978.

March, J. G. and Lave, C. A. *An Introduction to Models in the Social Sciences*. New York: Harper and Row 1975.

Margalit, A. Ideals and second-best, in S. Fox (ed.), *Philosophy for Education*, 77–90. Jerusalem: The van Leer Jerusalem Foundation 1983.

Marglin, S. What do bosses do? in A. Gorz (ed.), *The Division of Labour*, 13–54. London: Longman 1976.

Marvel, H. Factory regulation: an interpretation of the early English experience. *Journal of Law and Economics* 20 (1977), 379–402.

Marwell, G., Oliver, P. and Teixeira, R. Group heterogeneity, interdependence and the production of collective goods: a theory of the critical mass, I. To be published in *American Journal of Sociology*.

Meisner, M. *Li Ta-chao and the Origins of Chinese Communism*. Cambridge, Mass.: Harvard University Press 1967.

Melotti, I. *Marx and the Third World*. London: Macmillan 1977.

Miller, D. Market neutrality and the failure of co-operatives. *British Journal of Political Science* 11 (1981), 302–29.

Moene, K. Strike threats and the choice of production technique. Working Paper, Department of Economics, University of Oslo, 1983.

Molnar, M. *Marx, Engels et la Politique Internationale*. Paris: Gallimard 1975.

Moore, S. *Three Tactics*. New York: Monthly Review Press 1963.

Marx on the Choice between Socialism and Communism. Cambridge, Mass.: Harvard University Press 1980.

Morishima, M. *Theory of Economic Growth*. Oxford University Press 1970.

Marx's Economics. Cambridge University Press 1973.

Marx in the light of modern economic theory. *Econometrica* 42 (1974), 611–32.

Needham, J. *Science and Civilisation in China*, vol. II: Cambridge University Press 1956. Vol. IV. 3. Cambridge University Press 1971.

Nelson, R. and Winter, S. *An Evolutionary Theory of Economic Change*. Cambridge, Mass.: Harvard University Press 1982.

Nisbett, R. and Ross, L. *Human Inference: Strategies and Shortcomings of Social Judgment*. Englewood Cliffs, N.J.: Prentice Hall 1980.

North, D. *Structure and Change in Economic History*. New York: Norton 1981.

North, D. and Thomas, R. P. The rise and fall of the manorial system: a theoretical model. *Journal of Economic History* 31 (1971), 777–803.

The Rise of the Western World. Cambridge University Press 1973.

Nove, A. *The Economics of Feasible Socialism*. London: Allen and Unwin 1983.

Nozick, R. Coercion, in S. Morgenbesser *et al.* (eds.), *Philosophy, Science and Method: Essays in Honor of Ernest Nagel*, 440–72. New York: St Martin's Press 1969.

Newcomb's problem and two principles of choice, in N. Rescher (ed.), *Essays in Honor of Carl G. Hempel*, 114–46. Dordrecht: Hempel 1969.

Anarchy, State and Utopia. Oxford: Blackwell 1974.

Nuti, M. Capitalism, socialism and steady growth. *Economic Journal* 80 (1970), 32–57.

O'Connor, J. *The Fiscal Crisis of the State*. New York: St Martin's Press 1973.

Okishio, N. Technical change and the rate of profit. *Kobe University Economic Review* 7 (1961), 85–99.

Ollmann, B. *Alienation*, 2nd edn. Cambridge University Press 1976.

Olson, M. *The Logic of Collective Action*. Cambridge, Mass.: Harvard University Press 1965.

The Rise and Decline of Nations. New Haven, N.J. Yale University Press 1982.

Ossowski, S. *Class Structure in the Social Consciousness*. London: Routledge and Kegan Paul 1963.

Pagano, U. *Work and Welfare in Economic Theory*. Oxford: Blackwell 1985.

Panico, C. Marx's analysis of the relationship between the rate of interest and the rate of profit. *Cambridge Journal of Economics* 4 (1980), 63–78.

Papaioannou, K. *De Marx et du Marxisme*. Paris: Gallimard 1983.

Parfit, D. Prudence, morality and the Prisoner's Dilemma. *Proceedings of the British Academy*. Oxford University Press 1981.

Reasons and Persons. Oxford University Press 1984.

Parkin, F. *Marxism and Class Theory*. London: Tavistock 1979

Parijs, P. van. The falling-rate-of-profit theory of crisis: a rational reconstruction by way of obituary. *Review of Radical Political Economics* 12 (1980), 1–16.

Evolutionary Explanation in the Social Sciences. Totowa, N.J.: Rowman and Littlefield 1981.

Marxism's central puzzle, in T. Ball and J. Farr (eds.), *After Marx*, 88–104. Cambridge: Cambridge University Press 1984.

Pasinetti, L. (ed.) *Essays on the Theory of Joint Production*. New York: Columbia University Press 1980.

Pearson, H. The economy has no surplus, in K. Polanyi, C. M. Arensberg and H. Pearson (eds.), *Trade and Market in the Early Empires*, 320–41. Glencoe, Ill.: The Free Press 1957.

Pen, A. *The Wage Rate under Collective Bargaining*. Cambridge, Mass.: Harvard University Press 1959.

Perkin, H. *The Origins of Modern English Society 1780–1880*. London: Routledge and Kegan Paul 1969.

Plamenatz, J. *German Marxism and Russian Communism*. London: Longman 1954.

Karl Marx's Philosophy of Man. Oxford University Press 1975.

Polanyi, K. *The Great Transformation*. Boston: Beacon Press 1957.

The Livelihood of Man. New York: Academic Press 1977.

Popkin, S. *The Rational Peasant*. Berkeley: University of California Press 1979.

Popper, K. What is dialectic? *Mind* 49 (1940), 403–26.

Posner, R. *Economic Analysis of Law*, 2nd edn. Boston: Little, Brown 1977.

Printz, A. Background and ulterior motives of Marx's "Preface" of 1859. *Journal of the History of Ideas* 30 (1969), 437–50.

Przeworski, A. Democracy as a contingent outcome of conflict, to be published in R. Slagstad (ed.), *Democracy and Constitutionalism*.

Przeworski, A. and Wallerstein, M. The structure of class conflict in democratic capitalist societies. *American Political Science Review* 76 (1982), 215–38.

Quattrone, G. and Tversky, A. Self-deception and the voters' illusion, to be published in J. Elster (ed.), *The Multiple Self*, Cambridge University Press.

Quine, W. V. O. *Methods of Logic*, 2nd edn. New York: Holt-Dryden 1959.

Rapoport, A. and Chammah, A. *Prisoner's Dilemma*. Ann Arbor: University of Michigan Press 1965.

Robinson, J. *The Accumulation of Capital*. London: Macmillan 1956.

Robinson, R. V. and Kelley, J. Class as conceived by Marx and Dahrendorf. *American Sociological Review* 44 (1979), 38–58.

Roemer, J. Divide and conquer: microfoundations of a Marxian theory of wage discrimination. *Bell Journal of Economics* 10 (1979), 695–705.

Analytical Foundations of Marxian Economic Theory. Cambridge University Press 1981.

A General Theory of Exploitation and Class. Cambridge, Mass.: Harvard University Press 1982.

Methodological individualism and deductive Marxism. *Theory and Society* 11 (1982), 513–20.

Property relations vs. surplus value in Marxian exploitation. *Philosophy and Public Affairs* 11 (1982), 281–313.

Are socialist ethics consistent with efficiency? *The Philosophical Forum* 14 (1983), 369–88.

"Unequal exchange, labor migration and international capital flows: a theoretical synthesis", in P. Desai (ed.), *Marxism, the Soviet Economy and Central Planning: Essays in Honor of Alexander Erlich*, 34–60. Cambridge, Mass.: MIT Press 1983.

Why labor classes? Working Paper no. 195 from the Department of Economics, University of California at Davis.

Choice of technique under capitalism, socialism and "Nirvana": reply to Samuelson. Working Paper no. 213 from the Department of Economics, University of California at Davis.

Should Marxists be interested in exploitation? *Philosophy and Public Affairs* 14 (1985), 30–65.

Rorty, A. Akrasia and self-deception, to be published in J. Elster (ed.), *The Multiple Self*. Cambridge University Press.

Rosdolsky, R. *Zur Entstehungsgeschichte des Marxschen "Kapital"*. Frankfurt a.M.: Europäische Verlagsanstalt 1968.

Rousseau, J.-J. *Lettres de la Montagne*, in Rousseau, *Oeuvres Complètes* (edn Pléiade), vol. III, 685–897. Paris: Gallimard 1964.

Routley, R. and Meyer, R. K. Dialectical logic, classical logic and the consistency of the world. *Studies in Soviet Thought* 16 (1976) 1–25.

Rowthorn, B. Skilled labour in the Marxist system, in B. Rowthorn, *Capitalism, Conflict and Inflation*, 231–49. London: Lawrence and Wishart 1980.
Marx's theory of wages, *ibid.* 182–230.
Rubel, M. Editorial comments in Marx, *Oeuvres* (edn Pléiade), *Economie I*. Paris: Gallimard 1965.
Rubel, M. Plan et méthode de l' "Economie", in M. Rubel, *Marx Critique du Marxisme*, 369–401. Paris: Payot 1974.
Ruben, D.-H. *Marxism and Materialism*, 2nd edn. Brighton: Harvester Press 1979.
Review of G. A. Cohen: *Karl Marx's Theory of History*, *British Journal of Political Science* 11 (1981), 227–34.
Runciman, W. G. and Sen, A. Games, justice and the general will. *Mind* 74 (1965), 554–62.
Salter, W. G. *Productivity and Technical Change*. Cambridge University Press 1960.
Samuelson, P. The normative and positivistic inferiority of Marx's *values* paradigm. *Southern Economic Journal* 49 (1982), 11–18.
Sartre, J.-P. *Critique de la Raison Dialectique*. Paris 1960.
Questions de méthode, *ibid.*, 15–111.
Schelling, T. C. *The Strategy of Conflict*. Cambridge, Mass.: Harvard University Press 1963.
Micromotives and Macrobehavior. New York: Norton 1978.
Schotter, A. *The Economic Theory of Social Institutions*. Cambridge University Press 1981.
Schumpeter, J. A. *Imperialism and Social Classes*. New York: Kelley 1951.
A History of Economic Analysis. London: Allen and Unwin 1954.
Capitalism, Socialism and Democracy. London: Allen and Unwin 1961.
Sen, A. *Poverty and Famines*. Oxford University Press 1981.
Seton, F. and Morishima, M. Aggregation in Leontief matrices and the labour theory of value. *Econometrica* 29 (1961), 203–20.
Shaikh, A. Political economy and capitalism: notes on Dobb's theory of crisis. *Cambridge Journal of Economics* 2 (1978), 233–51.
Shapley, L. and Shubik, M. Ownership and the production function. *Quarterly Journal of Economics* 80 (1967), 88–111.
Shubik, M. *Game Theory and the Social Sciences*. Cambridge, Mass.: MIT Press 1982.
Simmel, G. *Soziologie*. Berlin: Duncker und Humblot 1908.
The Philosophy of Money. London: Routledge and Kegan Paul 1978.
Skinner, G. W. Cities and the hierarchy of local systems, in G. W. Skinner (ed.), *The City in Late Imperial China*, 275–352. Stanford University Press 1977.
Smolinski, L. Karl Marx and mathematical economics. *Journal of Political Economy* 81 (1973), 1189–204.
Sombart, W. *Der moderne Kapitalismus*, 2nd edn, vols. I–III. München and Leipzig: Duncker und Humblot 1924–7.
Sraffa, P. *Production of Commodities by Means of Commodities*. Cambridge University Press 1963.
Ste Croix, G. E. M. de. *The Class Struggle in the Ancient Greek World*. London: Duckworth 1981.
Steedman, I. *Marx after Sraffa*. London: New Left Books 1977.

A note on the "choice of technique" under capitalism. *Cambridge Journal of Economics* 4 (1980), 61–4.

Heterogeneous labour, money wages and Marx's theory. In B. Chavance (ed.), *Marx en Perspective*, pp. 475–94. Paris: Editions de l'Ecole des Hautes Etudes en Sciences Sociales, 1985.

Stigler, G. and Becker, G. De gustibus non est disputandum. *American Economic Review* 67 (1977), 76–90.

Stinchcombe, A. *Constructing Social Theories*. New York: Harcourt, Brace and World 1968.

Merton's theory of social structure, in L. Coser (ed.), *The Idea of Social Structure: Papers in Honor of Robert Merton*, 11–33. New York: Harcourt, Brace, Jovanovich 1974.

Stone, L. *The Causes of the English Revolution 1529–1642*. London: Routledge and Kegan Paul 1972.

Stroebe, W. and Frey, B. Self-interest and collective action: the economics and psychology of public goods. *British Journal of Social Psychology* 21 (1982), 121–37.

Sweezy, P. *The Theory of Capitalist Development*. London: Dennis Dobson 1962.

Tartarin, R. Gratuité, fin du salariat et calcul économique dans le communisme, in M. Lavigne (ed.), *Travail et Monnaie en Système Socialiste*, 233–55. Paris: Economica 1981.

Taylor, C. Interpretation and the sciences of man. *Review of Metaphysics* 25 (1971), 3–51.

Taylor, M. *Anarchy and Cooperation*. Chichester: Wiley 1976.

Thernstrom, S. Working class social mobility in industrial America, in M. H. Richter (ed.), *Essays in Theory and History*, 221–40. Cambridge, Mass.: Harvard University Press 1970.

Thompson, E. P. *The Making of the English Working Class*. Harmondsworth: Penguin Books 1968.

The moral economy of the English crowd in the eighteenth century. *Past and Present* no. 50 (1971), 76–136.

William Morris. London: Merlin Press 1977.

Tilly, C. *From Mobilization to Revolution*. Reading, Mass.: Addison-Wesley 1978.

Tocqueville, A. de. *The Old Régime and the French Revolution*. New York: Anchor Books 1955.

Voyages en Sicile et aux Etats-Unis, in *Oeuvres Complètes*, vol. V. Paris: Gallimard 1957.

Democracy in America. New York: Anchor Books 1969.

Trivers, R. The evolution of reciprocal altruism. *Quarterly Review of Biology* 46 (1971), 35–57.

Trotsky, L. *The History of the Russian Revolution*. London: Pluto Press 1977.

Tsou, T. Back from the brink of revolutionary-"feudal" totalitarianism, in V. Nee and D. Mozingo (eds.), *State and Society in Contemporary China*, 53–88 and 268–75. Ithaca, N.Y.: Cornell University Press 1983.

Tsuru, S. Keynes vs. Marx: the methodology of aggregates, in D. Horowitz (ed.), *Marx and Modern Economic Theory*, 176–202. London: MacGibbon and Kee 1968.

548   References

Tversky, A. and Kahneman, D. The framing of decisions and the rationality of choice. *Science* 211 (1981), 543–58.
Veblen, T. *The Theory of the Leisure Class*. London: Allen and Unwin 1970.
Veyne, P. *Le Pain et le Cirque*. Paris: Le Seuil 1976.
Les Grecs ont-ils cru à leurs Mythes? Paris: Le Seuil 1983.
Viner, J. Power versus plenty as objectives of foreign policy in the seventeenth and eighteenth centuries. *World Politics* 1 (1948), 1–29.
Von Weizsäcker, C. C. *Steady-State Capital Theory*. New York: Springer 1971.
Modern capital theory and the concept of exploitation. *Kyklos* 26 (1973), 245–81.
Wartofsky, M. *Feuerbach*. Cambridge University Press 1977.
Weber, M. *The Protestant Ethic and the Spirit of Capitalism*. New York: Scribner 1958.
Hinduismus und Buddhismus, in Weber, *Gesammelte Aufsätze zur Religionssoziologie*, vol. II, 1–378. Tübingen: Mohr 1966.
Economy and Society, vols. 1–3. New York: Bedminster Press 1968.
Weintraub, S. *Microfoundations*. Cambridge University Press 1979.
Williams, B. A. O. A critique of utilitarianism, in J. J. C. Smart and B. A. O. Williams, *Utilitarianism: For and Against*, 77–150. Cambridge University Press 1973.
Moral Luck. Cambridge University Press 1982.
Wilson, E. *Sociobiology*. Cambridge, Mass.: Harvard University Press 1975.
Wittfogel, K. Die natürlichen Ursachen der Wirtschaftsgeschichte. *Archiv für Sozialwissenschaft und Sozialpolitik* 67 (1932), 466–92, 579–609, 711–31.
Oriental Despotism. New Haven, N.J.: Yale University Press 1957.
Wolfstetter, E. Surplus labour, synchronized labour costs and Marx's labour theory of value. *Economic Journal* 83 (1973), 787–909.
Wood, A. *Karl Marx*. London: Routledge and Kegan Paul 1981.
Wright, E. O. *Class Structure and Income Determination*. New York: Academic Press 1979.
Wright, E. O. and Perrone, L. Marxist class categories and income inequality. *American Sociological Review* 42 (1977), 32–55.
Zimmerman, D. Coercive wage offers. *Philosophy and Public Affairs* 10 (1981), 121–45.
More on coercive wage offers: reply to Alexander. *Philosophy and Public Affairs* 12 (1983), 165–71.

Index of names

Index of subjects